The Collected Writings of Mark Rozen Pettinelli

By: Mark Pettinelli

Contents

Chapter 1

List of my Analysis
By
Mark Pettinelli

https://scholar.google.com/citations?user=RRcfeSEAAAAJ and http://www.amazon.com/author/mark-pettinelli

Logic and clear thinking
Cognitive psychology and a simplified version of the mind
The mind in general, related to cognitive psychology and its functions
Emotion and cognition or thinking and feeling
Consciousness (awareness and self-awareness)

What was involved with the logic and clear thinking analysis? Examples of concepts that are clear I suppose. That's obvious, I mean, in order to think clearly you'd need to have a lot of thinking that is clear and logical I suppose. I don't think I need to give all of the examples here anyway.

I need to think about stuff. How could the computer be that stupid. There obviously is no heaven. I have no idea how many good people he ended. What an idiot. Honestly i don't know how to explain how I feel. It would be pretty bad if it terminated a bunch of good people.

Ok so what else do I have to say. I'm trying to get the computer set up so it can take care of the population. What else do I have to teach it or learn for myself anyway?

What information is needed in order to figure out all of the information?
Like how would someone go about figuring out everything?
Let's think then about it.
What is all of the information anyway?
Ok so what is all of the information, how would I categorize it?
How do you even categorize all of that info anyway?

So let's start from the beginning here, what information might I need to know or understand in order to function in life?
Or What information is needed in order to understand how the mind works?
The mind is pretty simple i think, there is just inputs from the environment, then the brain processes information, then the person makes decisions and thinks about things. The mind can also feel emotions and feelings, not just think with thoughts.

So how is someone supposed to figure out all of the subjects? Maybe they just need to be able to think logically right? I mean, if they can think clearly and intelligently then why wouldn't they be able to figure out other academics?
What else is there to clear thinking then anyway?

To figure out all of the academics, you would need to categorize right? WHat would you categorize, all the subjects and topics? WHat about all of the ideas and concepts? Maybe you could categorize those right. THat would be a good idea I think. You could categorize all of the ideas and concepts in each different subject.

Um so, how exactly is someone supposed to categorize all of the ideas in each different topic? THat would be difficult I think.

THat's a great question, what exactly is an idea or a unit of information, it is really a unit of intellectual information in the mind right. WHat exactly is that anyway? THen you could try to categorize all of the information the mind can store and think about, it seems like that could be a good idea or a good way to figure out all of the information.

That brings up the point of what exactly is the difference between an idea and a concept anyway, they are basically the same thing, except an idea is something you are currently thinking, while a concept is an idea you could think about at some point.

So whether it's a natural artificial intelligence or a real or artificial artificial intelligence, it should be made to be more powerful so it can take over earth right? So like, what would be the difference between a real artificial intelligence and a natural one? A 'real' one would just be a regular artificial intelligence right?What would be a natural artificial intelligence then?

That is pretty obvious actually if you think about it. What else would need to be understood then about how the mind functions?
Feelings and thoughts seem pretty simple if you think about it, feelings and thoughts start at one second and the end at another second later on. It might be that they are led up to, however. How exactly does that work anyway then? WHat could lead up to a thought or a feeling being generated? There could be unconscious processes leading up to the thought or the feeling, like other unconscious feelings and thoughts could lead to the person having a conscious feeling or though it seems.
WHat does that mean exactly though? LIke what exactly is an unconscious thought or an unconscious feeling anyway? If i am thinking about stuff, or am having a steady stream of feelings, then what does that involve exactly or how could I break down how that process works?
I would think that it isn't that complicated, I mean, it is just thought and feeling. Feelings is the experience of feeling while thought is the experience of thought. What does the experience of thought involve then?THe experience of thought involves some sort of intellectual processing while the experience of feeling involves the person have a stream of sensation of some sort. An experience of thought involves the person thinking, understanding, reasoning, deciding or some other type of thinking.
The experience of feeling is more obvious and just involves the peron experience some type of sensation of emotion or feeling that feels like something. IT is an experience of some sort, however, there can also be intellectual experiences if you think about it. So then there can be experiences that are a mix of intellectual experiences and feeling or emotional experiences.
So what else is going on? It doesn't seem like this process is that complicated, most of what people feel are either feelings or thoughts, and I can describe the difference between feelings and thoughts and how they feel and are processed in the mind.
What else are we trying to figure out with the academics then anyway? I can describe clear thinking right, or

logic and critical thinking (basically the same thing).

What would someone need in order to think clearly about everything or anything? I can think clearly for myself, but I just follow my stream of thought all of the time and that is how I stay on top of what is going on in my mind, seems like a good idea or thing to do in order to stay clear and focused.

Um so, maybe that is a simplification, just staying on top of your thought process seems like a pretty simple thing to do. It might be harder to actually do that however. How is someone supposed to actually stay on top of what they are thinking? I've been doing it naturally my entire lifetime so I don't think that it's a really big deal, but if you want to analyze it then it might be more complicated.

So how does the mind work then, considering that there are feelings and thoughts that function in the mind? There is also consciousness, that is important. A feeling or a thought could be conscious right. Feelings and thoughts can be powerful or conscious to different degrees, I would think that is mostly how the mind works. It seems like it is more complicated than that though, because a feeling or a thought could also be understood or not understood, or conscious or unconscious.

The Selected Writings of Mark Pettinelli (The Difference between Feelings and Thoughts)

So what points do I bring up in that article? There is a difference between feelings and thoughts, obviously, that is what it says right in the title. Thoughts can be complicated, but what does that mean exactly, as part of a stream of thought a person could be having complicated thoughts right. WHat is the difference between a complicated thought and a simple thought then? There is the power of someone's thoughts and then there is how complicated a thought is. Then there is a difference between how powerful the thought is and how complicated it is.

How would I describe that further then - well, thoughts obviously can be powerful or weak right. A powerful thought would be a strong thought, what does that mean though?

WHen I am thinking and having a stream of thought, what is involved with that process exactly? Let me try to follow my own thoughts right now and see what I can observe. I am thinking about stuff right, what am I thinking about, what kind of processing power does that use? I suppose it uses intellectual processing power right.

THere could be complicated thoughts that I think about, or simple thoughts that I think about. Or the power of the thought could be large. THat brings up another question, what exactly is the power of someone's entire mind or consciousness then? People think with thoughts and feel with feelings all of the time, and they can be aware of those thoughts and feelings to different degrees. WHat could that feel like then? I guess i'm proposing that people can feel their own experiences and that means they can experience their own feelings and thoughts = that seems kind of obvious but it is hard to understand or apply in reality.

That is obvious, humans and other animals even have conscious experiences and part of those experiences involves the experience of feelings and thoughts. What is the combination of feelings and thoughts then? The combination I suppose is the power of the mind right. THe minds' total power is their feelings plus their thoughts. There could be other mental processes involves I suppose, like sensations and physical stimuli, that would involve pain and other feelings like that.

SO i'm still trying to stay on top of what I am thinking and feeling right now. I have thoughts, and I have feelings, I also am conscious of my feelings and thoughts.

That's all I have to say about feelings and thoughts I think. Someone can be logical, have thoughts and feelings, and be aware to different degrees of those feelings and thoughts. Their consciousness or their mind, or basically who they are, can feel those feelings. What else is there to the picture then? THe mind processes information, and it can process feelings. How does the mind process feelings compared to how it processes information? Information is intellectual and it depends on what type of information you are talking about. Feelings can be any type of feeling, it basically doesn't matter which feeling it is. I suppose it matters which feeling it is, just like for the intellectual processing it matters what kind of information it is. The feelings or thoughts are processed differently by the mind.

What does that mean, however, like what exactly is going on in the mind when a person has feelings and thoughts? Thoughts can be sentences or even non-verbal thoughts, while it is obvious what a sentence is it is less obvious what a non-verbal thought is right. That is because sentences are clear and obvious, while other thoughts might be harder to identify.

So i can think clearly, what else would i need to accomplish then? I mean, i can also function perfectly fine and am healthy, i don't know what else i might need to achieve. My mind is actually a lot stronger than it was a decade ago, I had no clue that my mind could be like this and my feelings could be this powerful. That is a part of logic, to have feelings that are strong but not interfere with your thoughts. That makes sense I suppose. How can someone measure how strong their feelings and thoughts are anyway, and if they make any sense?

So how is someone supposed to figure out all of the subjects? Maybe they just need to be able to think logically right? I mean, if they can think clearly and intelligently then why wouldn't they be able to figure out other academics?

What else is there to clear thinking then anyway?

There are concepts involved with figuring out information. How does that work exactly then? A concept is an idea or something you can think about. WHIle information can be of various types.

THere are different types of information, and different ways that information can be thought about, it can be thought about as ideas or concepts in a person's mind, or the information could also be written down - that would be information as ideas and concepts on paper.

What does that mean though? It is obvious that information can be written down or thought about in a person's mind or head. That is obvious, however most people don't really think about it that way. They know they understand things, but that doesn't necessarily mean that their understanding of concepts or information is conscious. WHat does that mean also?

What kind of information am I talking about anyway? ALl the information that can be thought about could be considered to be important or understood or conscious information. Earlier I talked about information processing versus emotional processing or a processing of feelings.

If there is emotional processing then how does that diff from intellectual processing or processing information? That is a great question, it seems a little bit subjective and doesn't need to be examined that closely. I mean, intellectual processing, or just thinking, is obviously different from feeling things and having a steady stream of feelings.

WHat else is there then? Having thoughts is different from having feelings. WHen someone has a thought, it could be a sentence or it could be a type of understanding that uses thought power or intellectual processing.

How would I describe what intellectual processing is like then? It is just the processing of units of information in the mind. How do I that better though? A thought could 'feel like' something right. FEelings also feel like something, but that is obvious. WHen it is time to separate out your feelings from your thoughts what can you do to accomplish that? Or you could separate out your intellectual processing from your processing of your feelings

So there is intellectual processing, then there is also the power of someone's thoughts. What does that mean exactly? If a thought is powerful, does that mean that it uses more intellectual processing? What would that be like exactly? ALso, I already pointed out that there is a difference between how complicated a thought is and how powerful the thought is. I would think that those are the two major functions of thoughts anyway, how powerful they are and how simple and complicated the thought is.

Feelings can also be either simple or complicated and powerful or weak. That is very interesting, I don't know how to describe it better than that. It seems simple when I describe it that way - a simple or complicated thought or feeling, or powerful or weak right?

HOw is someone supposed to get a feeling for that however, I mean, humans have thoughts and feelings all of the time, I don't know if i'm aware of how powerful they are or how complicated they are, how would I figure out how that works or how to get a feeling for it?

So that is interesting, either there is intellectual processing or emotional processing. For instance, I can feel my feelings right, and I can feel what my thoughts feel like, or maybe just experience what it is like to think. I can think about things, or I can feel things or experience sensations or streams of feeling.

That is obvious, when someone has a feeling, how do they know if they are aware of the feeling? And similarly, when someone has a thought, how do they know that they are having that thought?

Again, that is obvious, they know if they are conscious of it or aware of it I suppose. That could be pretty subjective - different people have different experiences of their own feelings and thoughts right. I could try to describe my own feelings and thoughts then. What do feelings feel like? And what do thoughts feel like? Saying what do feelings feel like is a little bit redundant, a feeling feels like how it feels, that is obvious. On the other hand, thoughts are more complicated and a person might not be able to tell what the thought or how it feels. WHat does that mean exactly, how could a thought feel like anything anyway?

Thoughts are intellectual, so intellectual stimulation feels like something right? INtellectual stimulation is different from other types of stimulation.

So what else do I need to figure out, I guess I'm just making some notes here. Seems like people can be extremely difficult anyway. They can express emotions, I noticed that. Obviously people have emotions or feelings or whatever you want to call them.

Um so what does that mean, that people have emotions? Everyone knows that people have feelings. That is obvious. It isn't that obvious actually, I mean if you think about it, how do you even know that someone else has emotions or any type of feelings?

I know that I have feelings right, what else would I need to understand anyway?

I mean, when I was born I just understood that I had feelings and thoughts, but didn't really think about it very much - I just experienced feelings and thoughts and didn't think about it i guess.

What else is there to life anyway then? Seems pretty simple if you think about it that way I suppose.

So there are feelings and thoughts, both of those processes contribute to the persons mental functioning right, that seems obvious anyway.

The person is conscious, and feelings and thoughts can also become more conscious to different degrees, but what does that mean exactly anyway?

That seems like everything that is going on it would seem I think. There is consciousness and feelings and

9

thoughts right? Someone can be more or less aware of their feelings and thoughts. I'm just trying to keep track of everything that is going on here so I know what is going on.

How do i know if someone is displaying emotion? It can be hard to tell it seems, then I would also need to figure out which emotions the person is displaying.

What do I need to figure out about emotion then? Or i could use the word 'feelings', what do i need to figure out about feelings and emotions? I talked a lot about the difference between feelings and emotions in my articles, maybe I should summarize that analysis.

Feelings could be more simple than emotions, like how sensations are more simple than deep or complicated feelings. That means that feelings are more direct, when you touch something you get an immediate feeling. However emotions might be deeper or even more intellectual.

Does that make sense? An emotion could be an intellectual feeling basically. While feelings might just be physical or sensory.

But is that everything that is going on then? THere can be complicated emotions, and more simple feelings that a person can be experiencing. WHat does that mean? WHat is the difference between complicated emotions and simple feelings? I pointed out that feelings can be sensory and direct, while emotions could be more intellectual right.

Could I describe that any better? Does it need to be described any better anyway? I can feel things, what does that feel like. That is just me identifying my feelings and thoughts then. I had to do a lot of inner reflection in order to get a feeling and understanding of that.

Feelings are experiences of feeling, while thoughts are intellectual experiences. I've been able to identify that by observing my own feelings and thoughts.
Um so I would think that is all I need to know about feelings and thoughts, I already pointed out how they are different, for instance a feeling would be the experience of a sensation or other type of physical feeling, while a thought would be something like a sentence you say to yourself in your head or some other type of intellectual stimulation like processing something in the world around you that requires you to think.

Why heaven doesn't exist:
Even if they built another planet with advanced technology (now i don't know if they'd be able to, but in all the past history they hadn't been able to anyway so where could this planet be right?) then you wouldn't get to that planet by killing yourself anyway, I mean, you might be able to transfer yourself there but committing suiciding or ending your life is just permanent termination, it always has been, I don't know where the spirits came from but i think at the beginning of time there was a bunch of spirits, mine was one of them that's how I know that there were spirits at the beginning of time.
Anyway, after the spirits come into existence they are alive on earth right? If you kill the spirit then it is permanently ending that spirit and that is that forever said and done, you've killed that person sadly. I want to keep all the good people alive for that reason, I mean i think the people used to be a little bit stupid so I don't think it was that bad that they were killing almost all of them. My dog lady was pretty smart but she wasn't that smart, i don't feel too bad that she died anyway. She died. I remember her, my dog named Lady. She had this golden fur. The other dog fritzy also died but i don't really remember her, i remember pulling the hair off of her, omg why do i remember the three dogs, the other dog was named molly, she also lost her life. Omg that is like three dogs, they've killed billions of other people jesus christ. Anyway, that's why I think that they should keep all the good people alive.The people in Massachusetts weren't that nice, though i guess they must have

been decent since i was interacting with them for so long. I don't know why I want to keep all of the American spirits alive. Did I win an award for this essay? Anyway it's a part of the United States, so i was in Massachusetts for decades so those people are good too i guess.

I pointed out before that there can be a difference between a complicated thought and a simple thought right? But is there more to say about that and also, what then is the difference between a complicated feeling and a simple feeling?

How would you define what a 'complicated' feeling is versus a 'simple' feeling anyway?
I don't really know how to describe that, people can feel what their feelings feel like, that is obvious, but if they made more scientific observations would they be able to notice more things about their own feelings? What kind of observations could they make?

People could notice stuff about their feelings, like if they are having a strong or weak feeling, or a complicated or a simple feeling or thought. This brings up the points I brought up earlier about feelings and how they can mix with thoughts. What does that mean exactly though?

If someone is having an intellectual experience, then it can also involve experiencing feelings right. Intellect and emotion can combine, so pointing out if it's a strong feeling or a strong or complicated thought are all things to notice in an experience.

Um so, how is someone supposed to go about identifying if a thought or feeling is weak or strong, or simple or complicated? That is a great question. A powerful feeling is kind of obvious I would think, that is just the experience of a feeling that feels strong or powerful for a period of time. I don't know if everyone is on top of that analysis anyway. THey certainly can experience strong feelings sometimes, but that doesn't mean that they always know when they are having those strong feelings.

The Selected Writings of Mark Pettinelli

By
Mark Pettinelli

2021

Some Notes about Logic

By
Mark Pettinelli

So there is an emotion concept and a thought concept. Instead I mean there is an emotion process and a thought process. The thought process involves people thinking, and the emotion process involves people feeling.

There are also concepts that the person can think about, those concepts are part of the thought process. For instance someone could be having a stream of thought that involves thinking about different concepts. What kind of concepts could someone be thinking about?

Well I mean, a stream of thought could involve various different concepts that the person could be thinking about. There is also an emotion process, which involves a person having a steady stream of feelings, which could occur at the same time as a thought process.

What could make the thought process complicated? It could contain complicated thoughts, or complicated feelings as part of the feeling process.

Um so I'm trying to figure out what to write. This could be a sort of final article of sorts. I mean I've done most of my research already, the only thing left is to figure out what to write next. I can think clearly, I follow my emotional processes and my thought processes, and there are concepts that I am aware of. I mean the mind thinks with concepts and thoughts and it feels emotions all of the time.

If the mind feels emotions and thinks about or with thoughts all of the time, then what else would I need to know? Thinking isn't that complicated, neither is feeling things. I mean I feel things all the time and it isn't complicated.

It really isn't complicated, like I mean a thought is just a thought, and a feeling is just a feeling. That's fairly simple. There's also concepts in the mind, or concepts that you think about. Some of the concepts could be complicated but they're still just concepts. Most concepts are simple I would say, however some concepts could be complex.

So what else should I write about, I want to learn more stuff. I don't know what else I could learn though, I mean I know that the mind thinks with concepts and that there is a thought process and an emotion process.

The thought process consists of the person just thinking about stuff, while the emotion process involves the person feeling things, or their steady stream of feelings. There's also concepts that the person can think about.

What would be an example of a concept that the person is thinking about. Going to war with another country is a concept. A democratic or communist government is also a concept. There are lots of different concepts someone can think about, I mean, practically everything someone thinks could be considered to be a concept.

So how would I break down a stream of thought then, or a stream of cognitive processes including both thoughts and feelings. CBT, or cognitive behavioral therapy, involves tracking how one's feelings lead to thoughts, and thoughts lead to behaviors, or any of those occurring in any order.

So it's a fairly simple process, humans have thought processes and emotional processes, or processes involving feelings. That seems fairly simple, I mean the thoughts could involve feeling things, or could involve reasoning about concepts or ideas. WHile the emotions could just involve feeling different things.

Um, so that seems pretty simple, there's either feelings or thoughts, one or the other that someone could be feeling. They could also think while they are feeling things, but that is rather obvious. I mean obviously people can think about things and feel things at the same time.

Is there anything else I need to say about emotions and thoughts? I mean either it's a thought or it's a feeling. When someone is feeling something, what does that feel like? ANd when someone is thinking about something, what does that feel like?

Is there some sort of reasoning process involved with thinking where the person uses logic to check the truthfulness or validity or accuracy of their thoughts? Or is thinking more simple?

Um, so what else am I supposed to write, I've already explained how simple the thought process is, and the feeling process. Those are both mental processes, the other mental processes are perception, memory, language, and attention.

The perception mental process is also simple, thats just the person seeing things and understanding the visuals. The memory process is also simple, that's just things pulled up from memory. The attention process is more complicated and involves the thought process and the feeling process, obviously because you can increase or decrease your attention depending on your emotions or thoughts.

That is, your emotions can influence your attention on something, and so can your thoughts. That's kind of important to know. I mean people pay attention to things, then they can think about or feel what they are paying attention to. That's three of the mental processes right there, feeling, attention and the thought processes.

For instance, if you are being emotional that is going to change what you are paying attention to, or how much attention you are paying to something. A person's thought process might also interfere with their attention. I mean when someone pays attention to something they can focus on it more, direct their thoughts toward it, or direct their vision towards it.

That seems pretty basic, I mean obviously people either think things or feel things. It's also interesting, for instance, is it any more complicated than feeling something and thinking something at the same time? Sometimes I suppose feelings could come along with thoughts at the same time, while other times a thought could create or lead to a feeling, or a feeling could lead to a thought.
Thoughts could also be more complicated, while I would say that feelings are simple, thoughts could be more complex because you could have a complicated concept that you are thinking about or a stream of thought could be complicated say if you were reading something there could be many ideas that you are trying to put together.

ALso with thoughts there is problem solving and decision making, problem solving often leads to the person reaching a conclusion or making a decision. Thats part of some thought processes. What other thought processes are there other than problem solving and decision making?

It would seem that mostly people try to make decision or figure out stuff or problem solve, I mean, what else could someone be doing or thinking about? That's an interesting question.

It's intellectual, I learned a lot of stuff. There's books in my room about cognitive psychology and cognitive science, not that there's that big a difference between them. I thought cognitive science was more about how the mind is structured and how it works with it's neurology, while cognitive psychology was just about the minds mental processes, however if cognitive psychology is about the minds mental processes, then it is also about how the mind works and how it's structured.

I also realized what a concept is, a concept is an idea or thought in your head, it could be about anything but is a coherent idea or thought. It could be a representation of an object in the world, or any general idea really. That makes me think, what kind of ideas does the mind think with - theres ideas about people, ideas about objects, and ideas about anything. Ideas can be emotional or intellectual if you think about it.

An intellectual idea could be a concept about a subject like math or politics. Ideas can be about physical things like how your body feels, or they could be ideas about how you are thinking or the state that your mind is in. Mind and body are connected, however, so I would think it's safe to say that if your mind is feeling some way, then your body is going to respond.

So what else do I know, I mean, i've learned about what a concept is, what an idea is, what a thought is, and what a feeling is. What else would I have to explore? I mean I think I'm fairly logical and clear thinking. It's hard to be clear thinking sometimes if you're being emotional and stuff. If someone is being emotional, then it might be harder for them to think. I said, however, that I am perfectly logical and clear thinking. All the thoughts I have are logical ones, and I understand what is going on. I seem to be on top of things and know what I am doing in addition to being logical and clear thinking.

So what else do I need to explore, that is the question. I started with my psychology of emotions and thoughts book in 2007, now it's 2021 so that means its been about 13 years since I started doing research.

I mean, what led to my being clear thinking now. Was it my understanding of how concepts work in the mind? I have a good understanding of cognitive psychology and cognitive science. I understand emotions and thoughts, and how I experience them. That's pretty much all I need in order to function with feelings. If I have feelings, then I should be able to function and think clearly, I mean I understand that those are feelings, and that I can still think with thoughts.

Thoughts can be complicated if the thought is about a complicated concept or idea, however. But I'm perfectly clearly thinking now, I've always been a clear thinker but before I didn't have this many emotions, or this intense of emotion. So what else do I have to say? I mean I know how to think clearly, I have a steady stream of concepts that goes through my head that I think about constantly. There's ideas, thoughts and concepts that run through my consciousness all the time.

What could interrupt my consciousness or my stream of thought then? I also do stuff like watch tv or listen to music. Consciousness is pretty interesting if you think about it.

I mean, I want to become more intelligent, but I don't know what to explore next. I've already explored cognitive psychology, emotions, thoughts, consciousness, concepts and ideas, and logic. WHat else would I need to research or understand, that is the question.
Um, so I'm trying to figure out what i should research or think about next. I already know cognitive science and how the mind works, I also know logic and concepts, and how those work in the mind. I think perfectly fine and logically. I have a steady stream of thoughts all the time that's perfectly clear, and makes perfectly good sense. I'm intelligent and know what I am doing. There was a bunch of times i went to the emergency room and was not clear thinking, but I got over that and now am clear thinking all of the time. I don't know what else I would need to research here lol. I think I'm doing a fine job with running my life, I don't know if there's any more information I

need in order to function or even develop myself more.

I mean, if I can think clearly, then what else would I need to know? That's kind of an important question. I've already done a lot of research that has taught me about cognitive psychology, logic, concepts, cognition and emotion, and other topics. That research and that understanding that I currently have seems perfectly sufficient. I mean I know what logic is - i've looked at a couple of logic textbooks. I also know how the mind works because I've read a bunch of cognitive psychology textbooks.

Theres only a few mental processes like attention, perception, memory, emotion, language, deciding, thinking and reasoning, Those are important mental processes. Part of the mental process of thinking involves logic and concepts. I also understand that I use emotion regulation - which is part of the process of emotion.

As a child I did not understand that I could control or influence my emotions, I didn't even realize that I had many emotions to begin with. Now I am more self-aware and know when I'm having an emotion and what I can do about it.

I have a lot of books in my room, what else do I need to learn from these books? I've already pointed out in this article of notes that I am clear thinking and understand cognitive psychology. I have some cognitive psychology textbooks that talk about the mental processes of attention, memory, perception, emotion, language, and deciding, thinking and reasoning. I also have some textbooks on emotion and cognition. The relationship between emotion and cognition is extremely important. That's basically all the mind is doing, either thinking about something or feeling something, or both.

People also make appraisals of their emotional state. The appraisal is cognitive, while it's about your emotions.

So what else do I need to know or understand? I mean, what else am I supposed to learn? I already know how the mind works through my understanding of cognitive psychology and the mental processes. That gives me a good idea as to how I think and what I need to know in order to think clearly. What else do I need to know? Logic is important, I still have to go through some logic textbooks. But what could they say about logic? I mean logic is fairly simple, I mean i know if what I am thinking makes sense, is logical and valid. I don't really ever think something that is inaccurate, I can keep track of all my thoughts and know if something is inaccurate or if I should think differently about something.

I mean, what is logic exactly, I said before that I was clear thinking and all my thoughts were logical. However, is there more to logic than figuring out if each thought the person thinks makes sense? What other processes are involved. There's problem solving and decision making, for instance. With decision making the person is thinking to arrive at a conclusion, and with problem solving the person is trying to figure out something or trying to come to a solution or a conclusion, which could also be part of decision making.

So thinking doesn't just involve simple thoughts, it involves the mental processes of problem solving and decision making. I mean, what kinds of thoughts do I need to have in order to be logical, or what are all the situations where I would need to think clearly. What would need to be analyzed.

Language would need to be analyzed because people think with language, also every situation they are in, what language they are hearing from outside their mind (like what other people are saying), and any problems they have about what is going on in the world around them or even internal problems they have that they are thinking about (with language).

That pretty much takes care of everything, if i'm on top of my internal thinking, and how my thoughts relate to what is going on around me and if i'm being logical, then I pretty much have everything figured out. So there is thinking, problem solving and decision making. Problem solving might wind up with the person making a decision, and so could other types of thinking.

I mean, how do I know if I am using logic in my thinking. If I have a thought is that thought a sentence in my head? Or is it some type of logical argument? I didn't think before if each thought I had was logical, I simply thought logically without understanding that it made sense. I mean what is the point of thinking if it doesn't make any sense?

So I'm trying to think, if i understand how the mind works, or understand cognitive science and psychology, then what else would I need to know? Clear thinking is a mental process, or I mean just thinking is one of the mental processes. However, there is more to thinking than just thinking clearly, people can problem solve and make decisions also; They can look at information and decide if its important or helpful to them or truthful and valid or if it's false information of little importance.

I mean, if i know what cognitive science is then I know how the mind works. How could I explain here how the mind works then? It appears to me that there is either thought or feeling, and these are the minds two primary functions. People can also perceive visuals or pay attention to things that are either in their head or in the external world.

So I'm trying to explaining how the mind works right. There is more to each of those mental processes I listed. For instance the mental process of thought could involve thinking clear or not thinking clearly. That could be connected to other mental processes such as the person's emotions and their attention or perception or memory. Also, language is important because it is how thought is processed in the mind.

So, like I said, I'm trying to describe how the mind works, or in other words, how the mental processes work like what cognitive psychology and cognitive science are about. I think i've simplified it by just saying that theres emotions and thoughts in the mind. Attention can be influenced by emotions, and it can also be controlled by thoughts.

That seems like a pretty good overview of how the mind functions. Emotions influence thought, attention, and perception while thoughts can also influence those things. That seems like a simplification about how the mind functions, however.

That's how I've been functioning most of my life though. I have a simple train of thought and simple emotions and function perfectly fine. Sometimes I have anxiety or stress and sometimes I'm happy. Emotions and thoughts are simple that way I suppose.

What else would I need to research then? If I am thinking logically then I am functioning perfectly fine and thinking and feeling in an efficient manner. I don't know what else to say about that.

Logic is interesting, is it just thinking clearly? Or what else is involved with logic, how do those processes play out in the mind. Well, for starters, in order to think you have to use a language. Then you have to think out whatever is going on. That seems like it could be fairly simple.

One example I have is at my birthday party when I was about 7 at our beach house in East Haven, CT. I was sitting at the table and they were singing happy to Mark. I was wondering if I should sing along with them and sing 'happy birthday to Mark, happy birthday to you", or if i should sing "happy birthday to me" or just not sing at all. THat was some of the thoughts I was having.

Now I would say to myself, 'well that's a social concept, do they want me to sing along with them or would that be awkward since i'm the birthday boy and i'm supposed to be honored. There are a lot of complicated concepts here, for instance it's a social concept because I have to get in the other people's minds and try to figure out if they want me to sing with them. I was not aware of that when I was 7 years old, I am now aware of that.

Social concepts can be complicated. Another concept I had as a child that I remember when I was also about 7 years old was the when the old lady across the street was babysitting me. She pointed out that the role of paper with the thicker center had more tape because it had a thicker center, I wasn't aware of that but she taught me, I thought the role with the smaller center had more tape. That is also about a concept, but that is a physics concept I learned.

16

So those are two interesting concepts I had as a child. As a child I didn't understand anything about emotions, now I'm aware that other people have emotions and have some understanding of what is going on in their heads. As a child I did not have that understanding, I just thought with simple concepts and did not understand anything complicated. Now I understand a lot of complicated stuff in different subject areas, like I understand basic algebra and mathematics, I understand what 'emotion regulation' means. Emotion regulation is someone regulating or maintaining their own emotions. As a child I had no clue when I was experiencing an emotion, or if I was experiencing an emotion. Now I understand what an emotion is and if i'm experiencing one.

Concepts are extremely important. Humans think with concepts all the time. Concepts are ideas that the person has in their head. People also think with language. Not all thought is done with words, however. I don't know the exact details but it seems like humans think with a mix of words and understanding that does not need to be expressed with words.

That's kind of complicated, I mean how do I know if the understanding or concept needs to be expressed or thought out with words or not with words? For instance with the racquet game I play when I swing my racquet I don't know how to explain the stroke with words, its a complicated physical movement I don't know how to explain it. That's an example of an understanding that does not use words to explain. WHen i swing the racquet and hit the ball it's physical memory, not verbal concepts.

What about the rest of human understanding? How much of that needs to be expressed with words or how much of it is just an understanding that does not need to be expressed with words. What are words anyway, sounds in the person's head that mean something or have a definition?

I mean I would need to figure out all of human understanding if I wanted to explain this. That could be a challenging problem that might need to be addressed in another book lol. I don't know how much of what I think is an understanding of some sorts or a verbal understanding that is thought out in a sentence with words.

So we're finally working together. I've explained what a concept is, what logic is, and what understandings are. Sometimes people think with understandings that are non-verbal, while sometimes they think verbally. Theres lots of different subject areas where people need to use concepts and think verbally or think with understandings that are non-verbal.

I remember learning a long time ago that some communication was non-verbal. I mean what is the difference between verbal communication and non-verbal communication? What is thought about that is understood with words versus understood without words? How does that work exactly?

That's kind of complicated, I mean, what does that mean, that sometimes people think with understandings and sometimes they think with words? How does that work out? I could try to follow an analysis or a concept and try to figure out how to explain it, like how the mind works when that concept is being figured out or expressed.

I mean, what mix of understandings, concepts, ideas and words is anything understood? That could be complicated. When anything is figured out it could be verbal or non-verbal, or a mix of both. I'll have to think about that when I try to understand things, whether or not the understanding is verbal or non-verbal, or a mix of the two.

Ok so i'm trying to think here. What exactly do I need to understand. I figured out how the mind works. That's just cognitive psychology, which is about the minds mental processes. The minds mental processes are perception, memory, emotion, language, deciding, thinking and reasoning and attention,
So I know how all of that works, i can think clearly so what else am I missing? If I am thinking clearly then there's nothing else I need to do I don't think. I mean thinking clearly is the main goal in life. If i can think clearly then i can have a lot of emotions and stuff and still function. If i can function then what else would i need to do.
If i can function then what else would I need to do.
I mean if i'm functioning then i'm doing perfectly fine, I can think clearly which i now realize is rather a simple task. Sometimes emotions make thinking clearly more challenging, however, but I think I am prepared for that.

So i can think perfectly clearly, that's what the goal is. I had to learn a lot in order to understand how the mind works. That way I can be more conscious of what I am thinking. I've always been a clear thinker, however my mind has become much more developed over the years and it has become more complicated to think clearly.

I mean, like when I was a child I would have emotions but not be aware those emotions were occurring, I guess I was aware I was having the emotions but now I'm a lot more conscious of my emotions.

Before I didn't even understand what emotion regulation was. Now I understand that emotion regulation is the attempt of the mind to control its own emotions and maintain them. I've become a more conscious person over the years, so i know when i'm thinking or when i'm having an emotion. As a child I could think and have emotions, but I was not aware that that was happening, well I guess I knew it was happening but wasn't as aware of how my mind was working as I am now.

Now I have emotions and thoughts, but I am aware that I am having emotions and thoughts. Like I am clear thinking. WHen i have an emotion, I am aware that I am having that emotion, and when I have a thought, I am aware that I am having that thought. That's all part of thinking clearly.

So what do I need to know in order to think clearly, that's the important question. Do I need to know anything about critical thinking or logic?

I mean, what do i need to know about logic in order to think clearly. I know that I think with language and with words and that words are sounds in the head. I also know that there are standards for critical thinking, like accuracy and proficiency. In order to be a critical thinker accuracy is one of the standards. THeres also validity, how truthful something is. I mean i'm thinking clearly right now and there isn't much going on in my head. When an emotion comes I just observe the emotion. WHen a thought comes I also observe the thought and remain clear thinking.

So what have I memorized that helps me think clearly, I've memorized the 6 mental processes of memory, attention, perception, thinking, deciding and reasoning, emotion and language.

I've also memorized the critical thinking skills of accuracy and validity. Validity is how truthful something is, is that statement valid, and accuracy is how accurate it is, which is similar to how valid it is.

I also know that there is emotion and cognition, the relationship between emotion and cognition, and that people can make appraisals of their emotional state. The appraisal is cognitive, while it assesses the persons emotions, or is about their emotions.

What else have I learned? I've learned that there are primary emotions that are more important than the other emotions, the primary emotions are happy, sad, anger, fear, surprise and disgust. There's also love and hate but i don't think those are primary emotions, they're strong emotions, but the primary emotions are supposed to have a facial expression which is physiological.

What else have I learned, there's other emotions that i don't remember the names of but those aren't primary emotions. I see why happy and sad are primary emotions and I also can see why anger and fear are primary emotions. I would think that surprise and disgust aren't as important as the other 4 primary emotions, those seem more short-lived.

What else have I learned? I've learned that consciousness is the sum total of our mental processes, and that there is an ego which is unconscious or an unconscious drive of our own identity that wants us to succeed, and that if we are conscious of our ego it doesn't exist anymore because its conscious and under our control and no longer and unconscious drive, but a conscious one.

What else have I learned. I've learned that the difference between feelings and emotions is that emotions are stronger than feelings and can be more intellectual, especially more intellectual than the physical sensations or feelings, the physical sensationa like cold and warm are kind of stupid feelings, while emotions can be more intellectual because they are stronger and more mental than the physical feelings.

What else have I learned? I've learned that there's categorization of ideas and objects, and if you list the objects or ideas there's only a limited number of them.

I've also learned about CBT, or cognitive behavioral therapy which tries to track if someone is experiencing an emotion, thought or behavior and how those three are linked or occur, which one occurs first and does it lead to another one, like does the emotion lead to a thought which then could lead to a behavior.

Um, so what else have I learned. All those things are important if I want to think clearly.

I've also learned that some feelings can be more intellectual than other feelings, like I pointed out that emotions can be more intellectual than feelings because they are deeper or more powerful, that might make them more intellectual.

Um, so what have I learned again, I mentioned CBT or cognitive behavioral therapy, the difference between emotions and feelings, the mental processes, cognitive appraisals of our emotional states, logic and accuracy and validity of statements or thoughts, that language is sound in our heads, what else have I learned here that i might need to know.

I can break it down based upon the mental processes I already listed. For instance the mental process of perception could involve visual or conceptual information, for example everything is visual when you first see it, then some of the objects become concepts in your head that you can think about in addition to your ordinary thinking with language.

The mental process of memory can include thinking about stuff that happened in the past, and enables you to think about multiple things at once (that is, pull up an idea from memory at the same time as thinking about or coming up with a new idea at the same time).

The mental process of emotion means that people have emotions, and that they can be combined with thoughts that the person could think about. I've already mentioned that people can make appraisals of their emotional states. The appraisal is cognitive while it's about your feelings, or your emotions.

There's more to say about perceptual things in your vision and conceptual information in your head, people think with concepts that are important while at the same time thinking about visual information or what they are seeing. I mean how does that work, there is a steady stream of thought while the person is looking at things, that seems kind of simple. The visual could cause the person to think of new things, or they could be using their memory.

There's also analytical reasoning. But I mean what does someone need to know about that, that is also pretty simple. For any argument or statement, or concept there is how truthful it is. Is that statement accurate or true. You could ask yourself that for each statement that you make. Since people think with words in their heads, then it makes sense that they can check if the sentences they think with are valid statements and if they are accurate. But I mean, is it really that simple, for a person to keep track of everything they are thinking and then check to see if what they are thinking is accurate and valid (truthful).

If you think about it, everything someone thinks can be checked to see if it's valid. That was part of the observing mind, when I have a thought, I observe the thought to see what I am thinking, and then I can check to see if the thought makes sense. I can also do the same thing with my emotions.

Now what else would there be to thinking logically other than keeping track of all of your thoughts and emotions and observing them logically. If I am doing that, then it would seem like I have all of the logic figured out I would say.

What else could be going on inside the mind then. I already mentioned that there is perception and cognition, when someone sees an object they think about it in their mind, that shows how perception is related to cognition. That's important to know, though it seems kind of obvious. I mean obviously someone looks at things and then thinks about those things. That's a primary function of the mind if you think about it.

What else is going on then in the mind, there's a steady visual and then the person thinks about what they just saw. They can also think about other things other than things they pull up from their environment. I mean they could use their memory to recall other objects or other ideas that they could think about.

So that means either someone is thinking about something that immediately relates to what they are doing or that indirectly relates to what they are doing, that seems rather obvious. I'm trying to observe what Is going on in my head most of the time. I mean i'm in my room typing on my computer right now so I also notice the activity that I am doing.
What else would someone need to notice. That seems like basic logic right? I mean I'm just working step by step here, I think about things that I'm doing that are immediately obvious like what I am doing, and what is going on around me. I also have the television on which I occasionally glance at, that's something else that I've been doing. That means that people can keep track of their actions, its good to know that so they can be more aware or conscious of what they are doing. I don't know why that didn't occur to me before, I mean before I was doing actions but didn't notice that I was doing them, well I knew I was doing those actions but I didn't think to myself

'well now I am doing this action'.

I mean, people have to know what they are doing, are they seeing things or are they thinking about stuff? That's an interesting question, I mean most of what people do is either see with their visual eyes or their mental perception, or they think about stuff that is going on in their head. They could be thinking about the emotions that they are feeling, or they could be thinking about the thoughts that they are thinking. The question is, are they aware of everything they are doing? I guess there is sort of 'awareness of their awareness' that is occurring. I mean, do they know everything that is going on in their heads?

What could be going on in their heads then? They could be experiencing emotions, or they could be thinking about things. They are also doing stuff in their immediate environment.

An Overview of my research

And biography
By Mark Rozen Pettinelli
Online handle – xiornik
2020

https://drive.google.com/folderview?id=1kiGfJRhyz8CreqJR6lkCSSXhxiKR4-gm

Ok so I've been doing my own research since I graduated from concord academy in 2003. I was meeting with therapists and got put on a lot of medication, I guess that my research on cognitive psychology mixed with their understanding of people and their emotions as therapists. I tried to make my research practical, finding only the important information and the information that was relevant to myself, like managing my own emotions and thoughts. I don't know what my therapists were thinking about my analysis but they have their own more practical understanding, or an understanding that applies to other people who have different emotions from me. I'm kind of unique but have been meeting with the autism network people for almost 2 years now (in addition to interacting with the staff in my group home and meeting with other therapists).

So what did I learn? I bought a bunch of cognitive psychology books and went through those over the past decade. Now it's the end of 2020 and I wrote my psychology of emotions, feelings and thoughts book at the end of 2006.
So what am I supposed to learn from these books? I already wrote a lot of information about feelings and thoughts in my previous articles. I know the difference between an emotion and a feeling, I wrote about that. Again, a feeling is something you feel, that is why the word 'feel' is used, and emotions are supposed to be strong feelings, like the primary emotions.
I don't know if each person responds to stimuli with a primary emotion first, I would think that the emotions could come in any order.
So any feeling could occur at any time, in any order.
I'm writing this article for my own sake, so i can understand my feelings and thoughts more. And understand how my mind works.
The words 'emotion' and 'feeling' can be used interchangeably, except emotions are supposed to be stronger than feelings. That is why there are only 6 primary emotions of happy, sad, anger, fear, surprise and disgust. Those primary emotions are more powerful or more 'main' than the other feelings humans can experience.
The list of books in this article I think have interesting titles that I could benefit from if the books actually have good information.
What or how do feelings work in the mind? That is the question. Like right now what am I feeling? Those are interesting questions. Do some feelings always come first or do feelings occur in any order?
There are many feelings that people can experience, it's kind of interesting actually. Sometimes feelings are strong, and sometimes they are weak, and sometimes they are mostly unconscious.
I don't really know which feelings I have first or even have period. Maybe I just have a simple mind I guess. If I have a simple mind, then I should be able to keep track of which feelings I have, when they come and go,

if they are unconscious or conscious, and also what my thoughts are.

Thoughts are more intellectual than feelings, and feelings can be physical or emotional, or even intellectual feelings. That is like what I said before, that thought or some feelings can feel or be more intellectual. Some feelings might be stupid also, like some of the stupid physical bodily sensations.

I have about 5 different cognitive psychology textbooks in my room that i've been going through for at least a couple of years now. I also have some other books about psychology and other topics I was interested in, like the topic of emotion and cognition.

I'm going to go through more books that I've just got recently, however I just started going through those books.

These are two of the cognitive psychology books i've been going through:
Cognitive Psychology: A Student's Handbook 7th Edition
  • by Michael W. Eysenck (Author), Mark T. Keane (Author)

How is it that noticing if something is living that a conceptual thing? Some things like perceptual features, like what it looks like, is clearly perceptual priming. This means that either something is visual or it is conceptual. What is the difference? I mean the mind can think with images that it 'sees' and it can think with concepts that it thinks about. It also has a continuous stream of visual information if their eyes are open anyway. Conceptual information could be just things that a person is thinking about.

"Judgement involves deciding on the likelihood of various events"

The statement about judgement is a little bit confusing, how could there be a partial understanding of anything? Judgement means the person uses accuracy to come to a conclusion from a guess or a measured assessment. That's kind of like the scientific method, the person weighs evidence and comes to a conclusion they think is correct. Decision making is also part of that process because they have to decide about how to go about coming to or arriving at the proper conclusion.

The mind isn't that complicated, language is fairly simple, thinking is fairly simple, and so are feelings and emotions. Appraisals of our emotional states can influence the emotions involved, that is also a simple thing to understand. Cognition and emotion are connected that way - humans think about things that influence their emotions and their feelings, in turn, influence what the person is thinking about.

I mean, how complicated can language be? Language is just words that signify something in the mind, and sentences are more complicated than a simple word by itself. A sentence is more complicated than one word. Take the word 'dog', the word dog is a noun that could be the subject of a sentence, so the dog could be doing something - some action that is described with a verb in the sentence, say the sentence 'the dog is running' has one subject, the dog, and one verb 'running'. That is an example of a typical sentence with a subject that is performing an action, the action is the verb in the sentence, and the subject of the sentence is the dog who is doing the action.

Language is simple like that, however only the human species has the ability to use language.

This book helped me realize how simple the mind is. There is consciousness, which consists of humans observing their environment, thinking consciously about their emotions and thoughts, thinking with language and turning sounds into speech in their head (a process called lexicalisation), and just responding to their environment.

How complicated is that? I can keep track of most of what is going on in my head, I have language and speech that I use and words I think to myself to help me keep track of what is going on in my head. I also use speech to communicate with other people, but that is fairly simple, I mean, things like saying 'hello' and 'how are you' are fairly simple to understand.

I might not know how to communicate in other languages other than english (I remember a few basic words in spanish (which i took in high school)) but there are probably equivalent words in other languages for each word or phrase in the english language.

So what else does the mind do that's too complicated? There's a section on emotion and cognition in the book, a section on consciousness, a section on judgement and decision making. All those seem like simple concepts or topics. Even the section on speech and language. Also the chapter on problem solving is fairly simple.

Cognitive psychology is supposed to cover the mind's mental processes and this book discusses all of them, however there aren't that many mental processes that the mind uses or thinks about to itself. That makes the mind a fairly simple organ. I mean, I'm sure the details of neuroscience get pretty complicated, but when you look at the mind from the perspective of cognitive psychology then there is only a few processes going on at any time.

- The Oxford Handbook of Cognitive Psychology (Oxford Library of Psychology)

By Daniel Reisberg

So i think that means that implicit memory can effect a person because they have memories in their mind but they don't know that those had an impact on them, however they still helped shape the person and therefore have an impact on them.

What does that exactly mean? If there is an input representation, then your mind is going to see the input some way initially, either if this is a visual image or a representation of the visual they see. That makes sense, humans see visuals all the time, and it stays in their memory for a while, and it can be modified so they can remember the visual in their mind by simplifying the visual with a representation of the visual.

"Beliefs are about something"

That makes perfectly good sense, humans can have beliefs, however they are going to be about something and they're going to be formed somehow. How do people form their beliefs? Do they see objects in the real world and then form opinions? Or do they think internally and form beliefs based off of their own analysis?

Here is a list of books I have that I went through:

Master Your Emotions: A Practical Guide to Overcome Negativity and Better Manage Your Feelings (Mastery Series Book 1)

by Thibaut Meurisse (Author)

What is 'the ego'? The book says it's your self identity that you've constructed throughout your lifetime, however I would just call that your 'unconscious' self. I mean your own self identity is going to need to have an important place in your mind, so it would be unconscious, and it would need to have power, like the unconscious mind has power. I also said before that most of the mind is conscious, so the ego would also be unconscious.

The book says that the 'ego and awareness cannot coexist" because as your awareness increases, your ego disappears. That's because your ego is your identity, if you are aware of your identity then you don't need an unconscious one. I would say that works for most things, as the unconscious mind becomes conscious, the unconscious aspects begin to disappear because they become conscious instead.

The ego clings to tons of things to make itself stronger like beliefs, attachments and items. So this means that I think the ego is like your unconscious self, constantly working for you only unconsciously instead of deliberate, conscious actions and thoughts.

The ego wants you to strive to be a better person and achieve stuff in life. That makes sense because your ego is like your unconscious mind, and humans are naturally selfish beings.

The book also states that 'emotions come and go'. That is important to understand because you might want to control your emotions, so it might be good to know when they are occurring.

It also states that negative emotions can be useful. I think that I'd rather not have any negative emotions at all, or maybe just an insignificant amount of them if they're needed to contrast strong, happy emotions.

The book says that emotions can be reinforced by your thinking. For instance negative emotions could be thought about and made stronger, or positive emotions could be thought about and reinforced. Feelings and thoughts become emotions when you think about them. An emotion by itself is weak unless you identify with it. I think that's what the book was trying to explain.

That means that your interpretation of your own emotions is important. That makes sense, I mean if you think about it feelings by themselves have to be interpreted by your conscious mind - that gives you some control over your own emotions because you can choose how you respond to or make your own feelings and thoughts.

The book also states that "interpretation, identification and repetition" of emotions will make them stronger. That makes sense, emotions can be changed by your conscious mind. People can repeat emotions, identify with them, or interpret them in a certain way. I mean if you think about it you can have a lot of conscious control over your emotions by either interpreting your emotions differently, or identifying with them differently.

I don't know what exactly to do to change my own emotions, I know that I can think about which emotions I am experiencing and see if I can change my interpretations of those emotions and see if that works.

I mean, how are you supposed to control your own emotions? The book suggests that you can think about

your emotions in order to change them through identification, interpretation, and repetition.
It is harder than that though I would think in order to change your emotions. It's important to understand that the conscious mind interprets feelings and thoughts a certain way, and your interpretation can change how you feel, understand, and experience your emotions.
I mean it's like you have a conscious mind and an unconscious mind, and in order to conceptualize or interpret your feelings you have to think and understand.
Otherwise your feelings could just stay unconscious or unfiltered.
Master Your Thinking: A Practical Guide to Align Yourself with Reality and Achieve Tangible Results in the Real World (Mastery Series Book 5)
by Thibaut Meurisse (Author)
This book suggests that our current thinking is inaccurate. People tend to think with biases and make assumptions. If we align ourselves with reality we can control our thinking and be more productive. I don't know how someone is supposed to think more positively if life is hard though. I've resorted to being delusional and that makes me happy. The book suggests we should think realistically but positively. I don't know how to think positively if life is so hard and difficult, I would think the only way out is to be delusional.
Maybe controlling our thoughts could help us think more realistically, but that doesn't change the fact that life is hard and that it's hard to achieve success in life. I mean, if people are biased and make assumptions that's fine, but how are they supposed to be positive in a hard, unrealistic (I mean difficult) world? It's hard to align yourself with reality if reality is hard, the book doesn't really address that.
The Contemplative Brain: Meditation, Phenomenology and Self-Discovery from a Neuroanthropological Point of View Paperback – October 10, 2020
by Charles D Laughlin (Author)
That's kind of interesting, he lists 4 different states of consciousness there, obviously awake and sleeping are two different states of consciousness. Also dizzy or tipsy is a state of consciousness that doesn't have to be made just by drinking alcohol. Someone could get dizzy because they are tired for instance. I don't know all the conditions that could make someone hallucinate.
The main conscious state would just be 'awake' and 'here'. That would mean that the person is conscious and functioning properly. I don't know how someone could go into a dream state without actually falling asleep, however. I would think that different experiences influence our state of consciousness all the time, depending on the experience. Sometimes an experience could make the person dizzy, I suppose. More or less awake could happen often to a person also.

The Happiness Trap: How to Stop Struggling and Start Living: A Guide to ACT Paperback – Illustrated, June 3, 2008
by Russ Harris (Author), Steven C. Hayes PhD (Foreword)
What is the 'observing self'? It's kind of like an inner eye. In the book it says it could be comparable to the sky, and our feelings are the weather and the rain and the wind. The observing self I would say is like an inner eye, it sees and observes what is going on, but does it respond, because it is just like an eye that cannot be touched.
So it could use an acceptance strategy because it just observes, but would be unable to use a control strategy because that would require intervention.
So an acceptance strategy could use the observing self, observing your feelings and thoughts but not intervening.

Here are books that I got after the others and read

The Oxford Handbook of the Philosophy of Consciousness
by Uriah Kriegel (Editor)
This book states that after the philosophy of consciousness finishes explaining consciousness a 'science of consciousness' will take its place. I don't know what that could mean for all of the explaining. What would it take for consciousness to be fully explained? After the speculation is done by the philosophers it would become a sort of 'science of consciousness'.
They need to reframe 'how to explain' to 'what needs explaining'. If you think about it that makes sense, the conscious phenomena, or the observed facts about consciousness, need to be explained somehow, and it

needs to be outlined what exactly needs explanation.

Psychology tries to explain behavioral phenomena, and the study or science of consciousness should try to explain consciousness. How are conscious phenomena supposed to be explained?

There's the experience of conscious thought for instance, what is it to think about something? Is that an experience of consciousness?

I talk about important aspects of consciousness in this article, I mention that thoughts and emotions can be either conscious, unconscious, or semi-conscious. Also that you can reinforce unconscious thoughts and emotions by thinking about them or filtering them so they can become more conscious and under your control. That applies to both thoughts and emotions.

Is consciousness just the 'sum total of its psychological functions'? As mentioned in the book, I mean, how does consciousness arise? It would seem that it is just the 'sum total of its psychological functions'. I would say that's a perfectly fine description of how consciousness arises and what it is. I've already pointed out in this article that there are only a few mental processes going on at any moment, like perception, emotion, attention, memory, language, deciding, thinking and reasoning. Those mental processes combined are everything that is going on in the brain, and give rise to consciousness.

I listed those mental processes but I didn't include 'introspection', which could account for internal thinking. Thinking was listed as a mental process, but more can be said about thought other than that the person is thinking. The person could be regulating their emotions, for instance making their emotions stronger or interpreting their unconscious emotions and making them conscious. That function involves the two mental processes of both thinking and emotion.

What else could a person think about through introspection? I mean they do more than regulate their own emotions and thoughts, which is self-regulation and emotion regulation. Self regulation could include regulating their own thoughts, goals, problem solving and planning and is similar to or includes executive functioning. Executive functioning is self regulating your own mind by using your thoughts I would say. While emotion regulation is just regulating your own emotions, both of which could be done through introspective thought.

I mean, what exactly is executive functioning or self-regulation? I would think it is using your own thoughts or power of introspection to monitor your own mind, your own thoughts and your own emotions, while emotion regulation is just handling your emotions.

Also, part of self-regulation is monitoring your own attention (not just your thoughts), which was another mental process that I mentioned. How does controlling your own attention give rise to consciousness? How conscious the person is relates and is partially determined by their attention and what they are paying attention to, that seems kind of obvious.

The book also states that "conscious states are states we're aware of". That seems rather obvious, considering that the definition of conscious is "aware".

The Oxford Handbook of Rationality (Oxford Handbooks)
by Alfred R. Mele (Editor), Piers Rawling (Editor)
"Reasoning is a process that can modify intentions and beliefs."

There's also a difference between "what to believe" and "what to intend to do". People also have "practical reasons to believe something". Does someone allow arbitrary decisions or have wishful thinking? I already pointed out that there is a more type of unconscious type of thinking, that is more arbitrary or without the use of reasoning. Unconscious thought is more illogical and arbitrary and can bypass working memory, while conscious thought is more intentional and uses more reasoning.

There's also a relationship between reasoning and rationality. People have an "account of what it is for beliefs and desires to be justified". "Kant: Rationality as Practical Reason".

Fear is a thought that some anticipated judgement poses a threat. Is there an appropriateness of an emotional response? Emotion is a threat to rationality, however long term they might help the decision of rational options over time. There are factors leading to action, an affective state can modify the person's practical options. I suppose that means that the person needs to take initiative and monitor or figure out their emotional state in order to make practical decisions.

There's also "motivationally biased belief" "Motivationally biased believers test hypotheses and believe on the basis of evidence." But there is still the influence of motivation to be considered.

Also, "what is the relationship between rationality and thought", or the "relationship between rationality and language"?

Rationality applies to "actions, beliefs and desires". Also "rational plans, rational views, rational reactions, and rational emotions". People are practical beings seeking to do things, to satisfy our needs and desires. What is the role of our belief system? Does it accurately represent the world? What is the relationship between beliefs and knowledge? Maybe people can "schieve a rational belief system".
Are our beliefs justified and reasonable?
Perception requires consciousness. Are objects in perception "ideas" in the mind? Or do they become "ideas" in the mind?
"If you see, hear, touch, taste or smell something then it affects you in some way."
Memory is also different from perception. With memory you recall something. You can recall a belief for instance. Can memory help justify a belief? That's an interesting question. Uf it is a source of knowledge then it could be used to justify beliefs.
Consciousness can also be a source of rational belief. Consciousness represents an inner world, There can be objects and representations of them that are 'in' the person's consciousness. A person's inner world can contain sensations, thoughts, numbers and concepts.
Reasoning can be reflection, intuition, and understanding in the mind. When we reflect on a concept, or we can form hypothesis to see what an understanding means or is. There are concepts people can understand after reflection. You could use hypothesis to test understandings and concepts. "We can reason from the "premises" and form conclusions.
Knowledge can use "intuition" which would be guesses that are not guided by information, while there can be guesses that are guided by information, and may include using hypothesis and coming to conclusions.
Does inference need memory? I would think that someone could infer something without using very many details from memory, or is that deductive reasoning? Is a source rationally figured out? There can be rational belief without intuition or deductive reasoning. There can be beliefs and knowledge that doesn't depend on other beliefs, memories or other pieces of knowledge.
Does coherence of understanding need justification? I would think for something to make sense all of the facts would need to fit together. There are different sources of knowledge that all need to make sense. There is also the dependence of a fact on someone's belief system.
A belief system could hold many beliefs, does a person need to go through their own belief system to see if they are believing things that are logical, rational and factual?
There is also the sources of the information for the person's beliefs. Are there ordinary justified beliefs? How does this all work? How far do we need to take a belief in order to justify it or understand it?

The Oxford Handbook of The History of Analytic Philosophy (Oxford Handbooks) 1st Edition
by Michael Beaney (Editor)
Are logical statements dependent on the language that is used? A logical statement could be true is its facts are checked I suppose. Someone could use the scientific method and test hypothesis they form about a fact. Is intentional action backed by logical thought? If something is intentional then it implies that the person thought about it before performing the action. On the other hand, it could be intentional but not well thought out.

The Oxford Handbook of Philosophy of Mind (Oxford Handbooks) 1st Edition
by Brian McLaughlin (Editor), Ansgar Beckermann (Editor), Sven Walter (Editor)
"What is the content of a perceptual experience?"It depends what it is like for the subject to experience the perceptual experience I suppose.
Also, what is the relationship between thoughts and concepts? Concepts could be fictions, while thoughts are always accurate because it is just a thought. A concept could be inaccurate, illogical or not make sense, while the thought about the concept is more specific.

The Oxford Handbook of Contemporary Phenomenology (Oxford Handbooks in Philosophy) Reprint Edition
by Dan Zahavi (Editor)
What makes color seen as it is? If you think about color it is a perceptual object. Or some object in a person's environment could be a certain color. THat makes perception seem rather simple, that there are just objects in the person's environment that they see that have certain colors.
Does that mean that sense experience has 'conceptual' content? It could just be objects that get represented in the

mind, it doesn't need to be logical.

The Oxford Handbook of Thinking and Reasoning (Oxford Library of Psychology)
By Keith J. Holyoak (Editor) and Robert G. Morrison (Editor)

Probabilistic judgement is how people come to conclusions, they weigh certain probabilities and come to a conclusion. People are not computers, however, and their judgements could be biased. I don't know what it would take for someone to always reach logical conclusions.

Furthermore, humans understand concepts at the word level and the sentence level. That means each word has a meaning by itself and a more complicated meaning when it is in a sentence.

"Intuitive judgement" is judgement without using reasoning. So that would be different from judgements that use reasoning. Does that mean that an intuitive judgment is a stupid judgement?
An intuitive judgement could be smart I suppose, if it doesn't require logic to be accurate or intelligent.
Maybe that is like 'deciding from the gut', those types of decisions could be accurate however they don't use logic or reasoning.

People can also use rational judgments to arrive at conclusions. I said that before, it is like they could use something like the scientific method in order to weigh evidence and different options. The scientific method is about weighing evidence and forming and testing theories.

Humans could use a similar way of assessing evidence when judging various options in their decisions or assessments.

It's not like for each conclusion someone comes to the person does some analysis that uses a thorough and rigorous method, like the scientific method.

I mean I don't know what goes on in people's heads each time they go through a process to arrive at a conclusion. I suppose that could be called the decision making process.
Sometimes a person's decision making process could just be intuitive and not use intelligence or a complicated method to reach conclusions, and other times the person might think really hard and use reasoning and logic to figure out a conclusion or solution.

Also there are 2 types of thinking, unconscious thinking and conscious thinking. Unconscious thinking is illogical and can bypass working memory, while conscious thinking is more logical and uses working memory. How can unconscious thought byass working memory? What are all the differences between unconscious thought and conscious thought? I see how conscious thought uses working memory, and maybe if someone is thinking unconsciously then it doesn't need to consciously use working memory, but it might need to unconsciously use working memory.
What does that mean for how people think, however? Working memory is a conscious process that the person uses to think, it is short term and conscious. When the mind thinks unconsciously it doesn't think about working memory but is still influenced by it because it is the unconscious mind.
So the difference between unconscious thinking and conscious thinking then is the difference between the unconscious mind and the conscious mind. Most of the mind is unconscious because humans aren't really in touch with all of their emotions or unconscious thoughts, that makes most of the mind be unconscious.
So unconscious thought is actually the mind thinking unconsciously.
The unconscious mind doesn't really use working memory because that is a conscious process.
I suppose the unconscious mind could influence what a person is thinking about, and that could influence working memory. So the unconscious mind is therefore connected to the conscious mind.

People also think using categories. How exactly does that work, however? I suppose it means that similar objects or ideas are grouped together in the mind. That isn't really a big deal though.
I mean, it's kind of obvious that people would group together similar objects. For instance I grouped together the two different sexes - those are "girls" and those are "boys". But that's part of defining and labeling objects in the

mind, in that case, however, they also belong to significant categories.

I suppose that's just how the mind thinks about things, by grouping similar objects and ideas together. It's just association I suppose. For instance when I type on this new computer i'm reminded of all the previous older computers I had over the years. Association and categorization in the mind is a way of learning from similar objects or ideas.

In this book there's a chapter on explanations, which states something like that people constantly search and offer explanations for everything that goes on in their life. I would think that would make people smarter, if they constantly seek to explain and describe what is going on. I don't know everything someone might try to explain, though I would think it could make the person more intelligent and knowledgeable if they have their own inner understanding of the world that they've been trying to explain for years. That's what it's like in my case anyway, I've been offering explanations and analyzing everything for a long time now, it's made me a lot smarter and knowledgeable.

I mean, it's kind of like saying that people have their own internal thinking where they are curious and try to explain the world.

The Blackwell Companion to Consciousness 2nd Edition
by Susan Schneider (Editor), Max Velmans (Editor)
What is self consciousness? Is it just awareness of the self? Or is it awareness of objects that make the self more conscious? How does someone define what the self is? If consciousness is awareness of our own mental states, then how does that give rise to self-consciousness? I suppose that if a person is aware of their own mental state then they are self-conscious. What could their mental state be in that circumstance? If a human knows if he is conscious and awake then they know if they are conscious.
As a kid I didn't understand that I was conscious, I just had simple thoughts. I mean I suppose I knew that I was alive, but I didn't say to myself, "I am conscious, I think about stuff and have thoughts, I am aware of my environment and my own conscious state". I just didn't think about myself that way. Now I can label myself as being conscious and alive, where before as a child I might have just understood that I was alive.
Being conscious involves understanding that you are conscious, i have feelings and thoughts all of the time, and as a conscious person understand that those feelings and thoughts help make me conscious. When I was a child I would have feelings and thoughts, however I did not reflect upon them or try to control them to a greater extent.

Conclusion:
So I'm trying to figure out if that's all the information I need to know to function in life. In previous books I wrote more about feelings and consciousness, however this is my final book.
I mean, if I can keep track of my feelings and thoughts, and understand the basic mental processes like thought, language, perception, decision making, emotion, attention, and reasoning then I would think i know everything I would need to know.
I can also keep track of my feelings and know the difference between feelings and emotions to help me sort them out. For instance there are only 6 basic emotions that have physiological correlates of facial expressions they are happy, sad, anger, fear, surprise and disgust.
Other feelings that are strong could also be considered to be emotions because one definition of emotion is "any strong feeling" like a strong feeling of love could be considered an emotion but it wouldn't be one of the basic emotions.
Also, in order to keep track of my feelings I need to know that feelings could be the result of the primary emotions, or the conscious experience of the primary emotions.
But there are many feelings that could be independent of the primary emotions I think like hopeless or edgy or self-loving. Those could be experienced any time and be largely independent of the primary emotions, or they could be the conscious experience of feelings of those primary emotions.
That's useful to know if you want to keep track of your feelings, emotions or thoughts.
The information in this book is also useful to know, I talk about and review information about consciousness, judgement and decision making, cognition and emotion, and other topics related to cognition or psychology.
What else would be needed in order to further the research field, like what am I studying here. A cognitive scientist probably knows all of that stuff about the brain and how feelings and thoughts work in the brain,

and so would a cognitive psychologist except they might not know how it works in the brain. Also clearly neuroscientists and neurologists know that kind of stuff.

There's also therapists and psychiatrists, i don't know the difference between what all those different professions learn about emotions and feelings. I'm trying to progress the research field here lol.

I've explained my analysis of feelings and emotions and thoughts enough times. Feelings can feel intellectual or that might be when they are more conscious, and there are the primary emotions which are facial expressions. I don't know how much more important the main emotions are from the other feelings someone can experience.

I wrote before that a feeling might not be intense but be clear to you, or it could be clear to you but not intense.

I mean i'm trying to advance the research field here but don't know what all those professions and professionals already know about feelings and thoughts, I'm offering my interpretation and explanation. I mean therapists must have known a lot of stuff about feelings a long time ago.

I've tried to keep my analysis practical and only absorb or figure out the important information I would need for myself. Therapists also must have a practical analysis because they have to help people manage their feelings and thoughts. I've been meeting with therapists and nurses for a long time now.

Further Conclusion:

So what else would need to be explored other than what is in this article? I have another article where I talk about how feelings can feel intellectual or be stupid feelings, like the stuipid physical sensations. If a feeling is intellectual does that mean it's more like an emotion or thought? Emotions are deep and powerful, so they could be more like thoughts.

Or is that just describing what feelings feel like? That they could feel different ways, intellectual, stupid, conscious, unconscious, powerful, weak, etc.

What are all the ways I can describe what feelings feel like then? There are the mental processes like perception, attention, emotions, language, and reasoning. Part of the mental process of emotion involves experiencing feelings.

Feelings can feel tons of different ways. There are different mental states and states of consciousness, for instance. If a person is conscious of their mental states they could become more conscious, or more self-conscious.

Furthermore, if people can think about any idea or concept, then there is a lot they can think about. I mean, cognitive science would call that idea in their head an idea that they haven't figured out yet or that is incomplete.

So what kinds of ideas could people be thinking about that they need to think more about? I don't know the answer to that. I feel like I know everything with my knowledge of how the brain works and cognitive science. For instance it is important to know the difference between emotions and feelings so you can keep track of your own feelings and emotions.

Once again, one definition of emotion could be "any strong feeling", also there are only 6 primary emotions of anger, happy, sad, fear, surprise and disgust. Those emotions are more primary than the other emotions someone might be feeling like if love is a strong feeling it could be considered to be an emotion.

It's also important to point out that primary emotions usually come first because they have physiological facial expressions as bodily reactions. Then feelings are felt as the conscious reaction to those primary emotions.

On the other hand, it seems like feelings and emotions could occur in any order. So if I know how to keep track of my emotions and feelings then I am on top of my mental state and know what I am doing. I also could know how conscious I am - for instance I said before that as a kid I just knew I was alive and didn't know how conscious or aware I was. Now I know what my feelings are, what my thoughts are, and mostly what my mental state is. That's all a part of being conscious and aware.

Enough Information

Well, that seems like it's enough information to know in order to function in life. The information about feelings helps people keep track of their feelings. And the information about consciousness and thoughts helps people keep track of their self-awareness and their thoughts at any moment.

What else would someone need to know? It's important to know that there is unconscious thought and conscious thought. For instance your unconscious ego could be making decisions for you or motivating you in general without you being aware of it. Your ego wants you to be successful, it is an unconscious drive of your own consciousness, or your own self-identity that drives you.

What else is important about unconscious thought? People might be feeling emotions and feelings that they are not aware of, those feelings could be motivating them to act or making them feel different ways that could help them or hurt them, depending on the emotion. If they understand what they are feeling, then perhaps they can filter the emotion or change it to something they want to experience.

I suppose that's all I need to know in order to function in life. I know I have unconscious emotions and unconscious thoughts, that should help me be more conscious and in control of my emotions and thoughts. I also know about the different things I talked about in this article - such as that thoughts can be unconscious, that there are primary emotions and more minor feelings, that I can be more self-conscious of my mental states or just more conscious in general, that I can use rational or instinctive judgements (a rational judgement is more conscious than an instinctive judgement, which would be more unconscious or automatic).

What else would I need to know, the information in this article seems important, it talks about feelings, thoughts, consciousness, mental states, controlling feelings and thoughts, and visual and perceptual and conceptual information, and judgement and decision making.

More on the Emotions and Feelings "hoffman - "feelings list""

So I've already said that there are 6 main emotions of happy, sad, anger, fear, surprise and disgust. But what makes those emotions the main emotions? They are more powerful so they all have facial expressions I think. They are the emotions people usually feel, while other feelings are just other ways of feeling. There are many feelings that fall under the category of the 'happy' emotion, like amazed, delighted, invigorated, satisfied and thrilled. There are also other emotions that fall under the categories of the other emotions. For instance sad could be anguished, depressed, disappointed, discouraged, heartbroken, lonely, unhappy, etc. There are also feelings that are part of the angry emotion such as aggravated, edgy, furious, hostile, impatient, moody, outraged, and upset. These are some feelings that are part of the emotion 'fear' - afraid, frightened, nervous, panic, scared, terrified and worried. There are also other feelings people can experience such as accepting/open, courageous/powerful, connected/loving, disconnected/numb, embarrassed/shame, guilt, hopeful, powerfless, tender, stressed/tense, and unsettled/doubt.

Those are all ways of feeling. I pointed out that there are the 6 primary emotions, and then other ways of feeling things. The question is, what makes the primary emotions more powerful or more 'main' emotions? Is it that they are felt first and have physiological facial expressions? The other feelings are just ways of feeling and are secondary to the primary emotions. For instance loving is second to the emotion of 'happy'. Guilty is secondary to the emotion of 'fear'. There are also the feelings that fall under the same category as the primary emotions, which I already pointed out. There's also the bodily sensations, like achy, cold, full, flowing, empty, sore, or throbbing. Those are more stupid and are just physical sensations, and aren't secondary to the primary emotions like the other mental feelings are.

Final Analysis

Ok, so i think that's all the information I need to know. The final two sections of this paper I filled out were the two books of rationality and analytic philosophy. Now the question is, what else do I need to know? I've already discussed the basics of rationality, such as that there could be a belief system that needs to be checked. Are all of someone's beliefs rational? How does rationality contribute to consciousness?

Its true, most of our conscious mind contains memories, sensations, thoughts, and other mental entities that contribute to our self-consciousness. There's also various different mental states that a person can be in.

Thinking about the statement in the book on phenomenology, are perceptions of objects conceptual in the mind? What is the relationship between perception and thought?

How does an object become represented in the mind, or what are all the things someone could be thinking about?

That goes back to the statement I made before, that consciousness is the sum total of our mental processes. One of our mental processes is vision, we see the objects in our environment and they become concepts or objects in our mind.

The other mental processes also become part of our conscious mind, like emotion and attention are two important mental processes. All the different processes of the mind contribute to the person's self-consciousness, including the objects they see in their environment.

The important question I have to ask is - what is the information that any person would need to know in order to function in society? I would think that they would need a basic understanding of emotions and thoughts. Cognitive Behavioral Therapy - or CBT for short is a practice of therapy where the patient tracks his or her emotions, thoughts and actions. That is, how their emotions and feelings lead to thoughts and how their thoughts lead actions. That also would obviously include how external actions also lead to the persons internal feelings and thoughts. Its kind of obvious that the analysis of keeping track of how feelings lead to thoughts and thoughts lead to feelings, and how thoughts and feelings lead to actions - is important. I would think that a person would need to keep track of their own feelings and actions and that would be important for the person. I mean everyone would want to know what they are feeling at any moment. Also what feelings lead to which thoughts and which thoughts lead to feelings. They could also keep track of how actions in the external world lead to their own internal emotions and thoughts. So in terms of what information would be important for someone to know I would think understanding how to keep track of their own emotions and thoughts would be an important thing for the person to understand. Another thing to understand would be what the difference between emotions and feelings is. Anything could be a feeling since the definition of the word is 'feel'. Emotions are theoretically any strong feeling. Does that mean that the sensation of 'cold' could be an emotion? If someone has a tactile feeling of cold when they touch something does that mean it could be an emotion if it becomes a stronger feeling or sensation of 'cold' ? Or are emotions few and basic emotions, like happy or sad or anger or surprise. Those are part of the few dened basic emotions. What is the difference between emotions and feelings then? A feeling is anything you can feel while emotions are deep and primary, there is only a few of them. Feelings can be sensations of anything that is tactile or that you can feel.

1.1 Other Important things in life

What would be other important information for a person to know about in life? I mean   what else do I know as part of my background knowledge or knowledge that I use. I have a high school education and took a few college courses. High school educations are extremely important - they teach basic sciences, algebra, English language, possibly foreign language also and maybe history. I studied my emotions and thoughts and the study of consciousness after I graduated from high school because I was put on medications and met with therapists. Cognitive psychology was also another topic that I studied - or just basic psychology and maybe cognition or the study of thinking. Is that a complete explanation of what I know? A description of a high school education and then my self studies after high school? I mean consciousness is a dicult topic to study. Thankfully the medications I was on helped me to study my own consciousness and how I think and feel and experience the world. I mean, what else would be important for someone to know? If they know what they are feeling at any one time, then they have a good idea as to what is going on. If they also know their thoughts and how their thoughts relate to their feelings, then they have a good idea of what they are feeling and thinking at any moment. That is probably more important than other things they could focus on. So what else could someone be doing? There are tons of different types of experience someone could have or activities they could be doing at any given time. Its important to know that they can focus on their internal feelings, or think with thoughts, or do certain actions or observe or partake in certain external actions or activities.

1.2 Actions and Emotions

So then it's just a matter of what action or activity or experience someone is engaged in. There are dierent feelings for any action or activity someone could be doing. That means that humans have thoughts and emotions. Feeling'. Emotion could mean 'any strong However there are only a few basic emotions such as happy or sad or anger or surprise. Those are primary emotions. What are all the complicated feelings someone could experience? There's a lot of feelings for sure, however some of these feelings are physical sensations, while other feelings are more intellectual or deep like love or caring. That means that emotions can be intellectual, if you think about it there are intellectual feelings like thoughts could be considered to be intellectual feelings. A thought is dierent from a feeling because it is more intellectual, that means that feels more intellectual while a feeling might be more stupid or more like a sensation. Can I explore that idea further? There are physical actions that could cause basic physical sensations or feelings like when someone engages in hard physical work. Those would probably lead to physical sensations. If someone is thinking about information it might lead to intellectual stimulation or a feeling of intelligence.

1.3 Emotions, Feelings and Thoughts

Maybe I should go into more detail about the difference between feelings and thoughts, and the difference between emotions and feelings. I've already said that thoughts can feel intellectual. Feelings could feel stupid or physical, however. An emotion, however, could be any strong feeling. That means that the feeling of cold when go out on a cold day, go into cold water or just touch something cold could be considered an emotion if it is a strong feeling of cold. I would dene that as just a strong feeling however, not like a primary emotion of fear, anger, surprise, or happy or sad. Those emotions are more intellectual than just a sensation of 'cold'. What is the difference between all of the feelings someone can experience then? A feeling could be happy or sad, or anger or surprise right. That means that there are a huge number of feelings that someone can experience. There are also intellectual thoughts that someone could have. I thought that a feeling or emotion like love would be more deep and intellectual than the feeling or sensation of cold - like when you touch something that is cold it is just a sensation. So what is the difference between all of the different feelings and emotions that someone could experience? Some feelings i think could be more intellectual, while other feelings are more like sensations or things you can touch that are tactile.

That brings up a lot more questions about what feelings are like and what emotions are like. I said already that a feeling could feel more stupid like the feeling of cold or a simple physical sensation. There are also more deep intellectual feelings someone could experience. Those are all interesting questions. I think some feelings can be more intellectual or deep while other feelings could be more stupid and powerful. The question then is - what is the difference between all the feelings that someone could experience? There are thoughts, and then there are basic feelings which are different from thoughts. Thoughts are intellectual, while feelings are physical or simple. Are feelings just simple thoughts then? Or is a feeling anything that is physical? A thought could be connected to a physical feeling, however, in terms of a chain of events of a thought leading to a feeling or a feeling leading to a thought.

1.4 Clarication of feelings

There needs to be a clarification here, what then exactly is the difference between thoughts and feelings? I already pointed out that there could be a difference between feelings and emotions, emotions could be deeper and more like how thoughts are intellectual, while feelings could be more like stupid physical sensations.

Does that mean that there could be a stupid thought? Could there a be an intelligent feeling or a stupid feeling? I know that there could be a powerful feeling like the feeling of cold when someone goes into cold water, that could be a powerful feeling of cold, for instance. What would be an example of a powerful intellectual feeling then? Are there even powerful thoughts? How could a thought even be powerful? I understand how a feeling could be powerful because of physical work and exercise. Those are obviously powerful physical feelings.

However, how then could a thought be powerful if it is just intellectual? Anxiety could be like a powerful intellectual feeling because anxiety is somewhat separate from stupid physical feelings, making it more like an intellectual thought.

1.5 Some Notes

How could a person's emotions and feelings, and of course their thoughts, be described? Is it a simple task to track what their emotions and thoughts are? Is it possible for the person to measure when their emotions start and stop, and if those feelings lead to thoughts or actions? Is there anything else that needs to be considered other than observing and tracking an individual's emotions and thoughts?

Is there a classifiable way of describing the difference between feelings and emotions, or are they both just things you can feel? Also, does anything else need to be considered?

1.6 A Final Analysis?

So I said in the title that this book would be my 'nal' analysis. What would that mean for the content of the book, however?

In previous articles I discussed how emotions function, how thoughts function and the nature of thoughts, but I did not discuss the nature of feelings. Feelings have a unique nature because each person is different and could describe their feelings completely differently from anyone else. However, my feelings now are much more powerful than they were say a decade ago, before I started on a higher dose of my medications. I just realized what I just said in that last sentence, I don't have the know exactly as to what might give other people stronger emotions, however I did say that being put on harsh or hard medications the last decade made me get stronger and more powerful emotions. Actually I think the medications were supposed to use or suck my energy but I responded by exercising and using them to make myself larger and stronger. I don't know how other people might try to get stronger, medication might be one solution however I don't know how that would work for anyone else, I just know my specific situation. Anyway this is also supposed to be my final analysis, as I said in the title. I've written many other articles on feelings and emotions and thoughts, however that was a long time ago. I think it was just describing the basic functions of feelings and thoughts. The articles went into a lot of detail but most people would probably overlook the basic functions of thoughts and feelings and just head into the experience of feelings and thoughts, so that's why I'm writing this final book, so it would be more practical for people. I've already made my artwork, and the old writing and this nal writing could accompany my artwork, however the artwork more has my own unique detail. This article is written by me, of course, however the artwork is select and more obviously has my detail. So basically, I don't know what else to include as my nal analysis. I've already gone over the difference between emotions, feelings and thoughts however maybe I could go into greater depth about that. There are also certainly other topics that are important in life that I could cover information about. I hope that my artwork gets recognized because these articles don't as obviously have my detail. They could accompany the artwork, however, as both the artwork and articles were done by me.

Is there anything else that I need to cover? I've already pointed out in this article/book the important things about emotions and feelings and thoughts, and how those three relate. That brings up a good point, how much description is enough to describe a persons own emotions and thoughts? Also their thoughts relate and interact with their emotions and feelings. A feeling could cloud an emotion, for instance. That brings up another point, how do emotions and thoughts interact? Furthermore, how much description is necessary in order to address the complications of the interaction between feeling and thought. That relationship has also been described as the relationship between emotion and cognition - which means feeling and thought (that is, emotion means feeling and cognition basically means thought). I've already said that feeling could obscure or cloud thoughts. Thoughts also can lead to feelings, and external actions can also lead to feeling, or cause a person to think about stu and have thoughts. Is it really that simple, however? I mean that is a fairly basic system, thoughts that lead to actions or internal feelings. That is what CBT is anyway, cognitive behavioral therapy is a therapy that works mostly by tracking the persons own internal emotions, and how those emotions lead to thoughts and actions as and then back into emotion, as in a cycle (a cycle of action leading to emotion and emotion leading to thought, or anyone of those leading to the other - either emotion, thought or action can lead to the other in any order in a cycle). So I would think that CBT is a fairly practical therapy then, since it tracks how emotions and thoughts and actions interact. What else would be considered to be practical in life. I mean if someone can track their own internal feelings and thoughts, and how they lead to actions, or how actions lead to internal thoughts and feelings, then I would think that they know most of what they need to know. There are more things going on, however. For instance there are other mental processes like perception, vision and hearing and the relationship between thought and language. Would that describe everything that is going on with someone? Or within someone's own mind? This is basically describing everything that a person can think or everything that is going on in their own mind. Cognitive psychology basically describes the minds mental processes like language, cognition, and perceptions, along with the other mental processes. Cognitive science, however, looks at the mind more from the perspective of how it it is structured. Would that be how the mind functions? It could function from its mental processes of language and perception, and it could function because of its structure or neurology.So that would be figuring out how a mind's neurology is completely configured, that would be the task of neuroscience or a neurologist. That would be fairly important. Other conditions could be treated by a psychologist or a therapist, while a neurologist would look at how the mind is functioning, I would think. That would be a good description of life from the standpoint of how the mind is functioning or how it is working. There is more to life than a person's mind, however.

1.8 Emotions and Feelings

There's a difference between how emotions function and how feelings function in the mind. If an emotion is 'any strong feeling', then any feeling could be described as an emotion. For instance, if someone is in a pool in cold water, then it might be a powerful feeling of water and you could say that the person is experiencing the emotion 'cold'. I would think that feelings are more like sensations however, so the feeling of cold is really just a feeling. I mean how could you compare a sensation to a feeling that is an emotion like happy or sad, fear or anger? So what then is the difference between the sensation of cold and the emotion of feeling 'happy' ? I would think that the feeling of cold is just a sensation. Sensations are more like physical things, like how pain feels or how it feels after a person exercises. What does that make anxiety then? Is anxiety like a sensation? I would think that it could be like the sensation of cold if you feel the anxiety in your body. However, the anxiety might also take the form of a headache. That makes things more complicated - because there are physical sensations and mental sensations, and deeper emotions like happy and sad and anger or surprise or fear that lead to different physiological facial expressions. Those emotions are different from physical sensations because they make you feel things intellectually. Physical sensations can also be intellectual, however. For instance my anxiety can manifest itself in my head and give me a headache, or it could just be a mental anxiety that I feel in my head without any physical pain in my head. There is also pain in the body, which is similar to feelings while during exercise, those physical feelings of exercise could also be painful because they are physical and you can really feel the pain in your body. So what then is the difference between emotions and feelings? Pain is certainly a feeling, and sensations like the sensation of 'cold' is also a feeling in your body. The question is then what makes emotions deep and meaningful, like the emotion of 'happy'. I would think that the emotions 'happy' and 'sad' are simply more intellectual. That is what I said before, that some feelings have intellectual components, I mean even the physical sensation of 'pain' could be intellectual, though I would think that wouldn't be as direct as the feeling of anxiety or the other intellectual emotions of love, happy, sad, fear or anger.

So what is the difference between emotions and feelings then? Is it just the intellectual component? Emotions could have an intellectual component, while some sensations are stupid and don't feel intellectual or 'deep' at all. Those could be described as just feelings like the feeling of 'cold' while emotions could make someone happy like that emotion itself - the emotion 'happy'. What then is the difference between the emotion happy and the emotion sad? Does the emotion sad have components of pain involved? That would be an emotion that is intellectual combined with some physical sensations of pain. The pain in that instance might not be completely physical, however. This is getting a little bit confusing.

There is physical pain, physical sensations, intellectual feelings, and even intellectual sensations like if you have anxiety it could be focused in the head and be like the sensation of pain. Is pain a sensation then, or is it an emotion? Pain is a physical emotion or feeling, and anxiety could be a mental sensation or feeling. SO what are all the different ways of feeling then? There are physical feelings, mental feelings, and there is also sensations and thoughts. A sensation is kind of the opposite of a thought because thoughts are intellectual while sensations are stupid. That is the difference between how sensations feel and how thoughts feel, anyway. There's more to the puzzle, however. Just describing how anxiety feels, how pain feels, and how other emotions like happy or sad feel, and how other feelings or sensations feel like the sensation of 'cold' feel is a good way to start figuring out how all a person's feelings are functioning and making the person feel.

A Further Analysis of Life, Emotions and Everything else! - By Mark Rozen Pettinelli

In my previous article I discussed emotions and feelings, and the difference between a feeling and a thought. I pointed out that emotions can be different from feelings, because emotions are basic and primary, while a feeling is anything that you can feel. So emotions are different from feelings, and sensations are defined as a feeling that comes from something physical. That means that anything physical is a sensation, or a physical sensation. How is that different from any other feeling, however? I mean if there is a physical feeling that a person can get by touching something, then that is a sensation. An emotion, however, might have or cause facial expressions, like how when someone is happy they smile and when someone is sad they frown. Happy and sad are two of the basic primary emotions. Theorists actually disagree over which emotions are the primary ones, however. Though I would say that fear and anger, happy and sad, and surprise are key primary emotions. I mean happy, sad, fear, anger and surprise are some of the most important primary emotions, that is why they are key primary emotions, after all. However, there are many emotions and feelings people can experience, it is subjective to decide which ones are more important than other feelings or emotions, because each person is different from any other person, and might experience any emotion as being different from another person. For instance one person might experience completely different primary emotions from another person if they have a different personality, for instance. For example I respond differently for the emotions of love and caring, maybe those are primary emotions for me while other people might respond with happy or sad or fear. It probably varies based on the person, basically.

So what does that mean the other emotions people experience are like? The primary emotions of happy, sad, fear and surprise could be reactions once they meet another person, or they could be feelings that are felt during a conversation, or at any time in response to any action or activity they are doing. For instance, if they are doing something physical than they might feel pain if they exercise too hard or get tired. So how would sensations t into all of these emotions? I said that sensations are feelings that come from any physical action or touch, like for instance if you touch something you will get a physical sensation. I think what i am trying to do here is describe all the feelings that someone can experience and see how they function with that person. That must have been the influence of my therapists, I've been meeting with professional therapists for years now and I know they have a practical understanding of how the world works because they have to deal with patients or clients that have emotional problems.

2.1 Everything Else?

So what else would I have to talk about here? I've mentioned how feelings are important for people, and how there is a wide variety of sensations, feelings, emotions and thoughts that a person can experience. Furthermore, There is everything in life that the person could be doing - any activity, action or exercise or whatever the person is doing could lead to different sensations or feelings. If it is something physical then it would be called or defined as a 'sensation' because that is how sensations are defined - as a feeling that comes from something physical. So how does all of someone feelings t into their life? There could be a wide variety of feelings that someone could be experiencing at any one time. For instance someone could feel multiple emotions at one time, or at any given moment. So what was I trying to accomplish in this chapter, then? Was I trying to describe all of the feelings that someone could experience and how that ts into the world of life? If there are tons of activities and actions and exercises someone can do - then the question is how do all those feelings that people can experience t into their lives? Exercise can be physical feelings, like if you run hard or sweat or do hard physical work, you could feel physical sensations and other physical feelings. The question is,how do those physical feelings differ from psychological or mental feelings and emotions?

Is a thought different from a physical feeling? Thoughts can be or feel intellectual, while emotions might take longer to experience than any individual or single thought.

The question then is what else needs to be described about life? I mean there is internal activity in the brain like what someone is feeling, and there are external actions and activities and events that occur in th world that might cause the person to experience feelings and thoughts and brain activity.

So I mean, what was I trying to do or describe in this chapter? I think I was trying to gure out all emotions someone could experience, and how those emotions t into the world. There is the external world of objects and actions, and the internal world that is within peoples own minds. The question is, can everything be gured out? Can the external world be figured out, or can the internal world of people's minds be gured out also?

2.2 Anything else?

If there are external actions and objects in the world, and internal worlds of people's minds, then the question is, can everything be figured out? How do emotions occur in people, for instance? If there are a few primary emotions, then the question is, what is important about those emotions? Are those emotions how people respond to things? And do they experience anything else after they feel those emotions? So let's take the primary emotions of happy, sad, anger and fear. Surprise is also one of the primary emotions. How do emotions function, then? What happens rst and then what happens next? I don't really know the answer to that, I would have to think about it. So what happens in an experience? Are there emotions that someone feels in the experience that occur in a certain order or something? There are secondary emotions, which are defined as emotions that occur as a reaction to initial, primary emotions. Does that mean that one of the first emotions people experience are always going to be one of the primary emotions?

So that means that first I am going to feel happy or sad, or angry or surprised, and then i might feel other feelings? How does that work? So what am I trying to figure out here, how emotions occur in people? I would have to know what that person is doing, and what they are like in order to analyze how they feel. I don't even know how I feel about certain emotions or certain activities. The question is, how do people feel about things?

I don't know how I feel about certain activities or actions, for instance. So I guess I'm trying to figure out what the important things in life are, here. I mean I know how I respond to most events, however I don't know what all of my emotions are like. This is starting to sound a little bit selfish. I mean, most people have to work hard in life, it
isn't like life is all fun and games.

Chapter 3
Mark Xiornik Rozen Pettinelli Reviews Cognitive Psychology Research Articles

What is science or communication? Science is important because it is basically a rigorous or thorough understanding. What could someone achieve a thorough understanding of ? If you think about it, if something needs to be communicated then you need to first understand it. First something is thought about, then it is thought about more deeply, and then it is understood. That makes sense. If you think about it - when someone thinks about something for the first time a type of understanding dawns on them. This understanding takes a certain period of time to figure out, however. How long does it take for someone to figure something out? That is an interesting question, in order to figure out something someone might need to make sentences in their head or think about something with words. They might also make or think about sounds to themself - think the sentence out in their head with sounds, for instance. That process could enhance how the understanding of a certain concept is thought about or understood (figured out). That is a good question, how exactly is something 'figured out' ? It is probably more complicated than just saying the sentence of it to themselves in their heads.

For instance if someone thinks about something with words then that can help them to understand something. However it isn't as if someone just says to themself, 'well if I think about it this way or that way, or if I think about this or that thing then I could understand this concept or idea better'.

Sometimes people need help understanding concepts or ideas from other people or influences in their environment. What kind of influence does other people have on humans' understanding of concepts? Understanding concepts is important, what kind of idea is someone trying to understand? That is a good question, if you think about it logically then all the ideas in life can be sorted through and organized, and it could be figured out how difficult it is to understand each different idea.

How then would someone sort through all of the ideas in life and organize or categorize them? They could do it in various ways, I would think that they could it based upon which ideas are hard to understand, and also which ideas have similar physical objects - for instance you could label something physical an idea - say the idea of a 'house' A house is a physical object. Then would every word that there is in the English language, or in any language for that matter, be an idea? Every word in the language is an idea, and each word or idea also has a definition.That is, just like every word there is has a definition, every idea also has a definition. Take the word 'I', the word "I" refers to the person who is saying the word, it means themself, "I" basically just means "me". That is an example of a word that has a definition.

The definition of the word "I" is a person who is referring to themself. It is an idea, it is the concept of yourself or it is simply you referring to yourself. Objects can be ideas Similarly, any object can be an idea. Take the object of a house. "Houses" can be ideas just like they are objects. The idea of a house could be a place to live where you are happy, and the definition of a house could be a place to live where you can be happy, or sad, or any type of condition. The idea of a house is more selective, it is the idea of the house that is occurring to you at that time, while the definition of the house is similar, the definition of a house is place you can live with a certain type of condition or a certain type of house with various objects, while a different idea of a house could occur to different people. So basically different people could have different ideas of houses for themselves, while there would only be one good definition of a house that is descriptive. That means that objects can be ideas. An object is anything in life that has a physical presence, and since you can think about anything in life that is physical, then it can be an idea in your head. The idea you have in your head could be different from the object however. That is why certain objects are described as 'phallic' symbols, those objects basically represent penises. They are shaped elongated in real life, so in the persons mind they change them into the shape of a phallus (basically a penis).

That is probably the best example of how objects in real life have definitions, and they also can change when a person thinks about them, because they become ideas in the persons head. Objects and ideas are important for dentions

This means that objects and ideas are important for a persons understand of a words definition. Also, not only do words have definitions, but since objects can be words, then objects also have definitions. I already said that an object in real life can be altered in a persons mind - how they think about that object is potentially different from what the object is like in real life, for instance. If you think about it scientifically or objectively, everything in the world can be an individual object, and every individual object can be thought about in a persons mind. However, how the person thinks about objects often differs from what the object actually does in the real world.

Concepts are important for Comprehension
Understanding concepts is important for comprehension. For instance its important to understand ideas and concepts if someone wants to understand, well, what the idea is.
But what is it that someone is trying to understand?
Is it the idea or is it the physical object or phenomena? There could be something physical that is present in real life that the person is trying to understand, say a house or the construction of a house could be a complicated thing that someone is trying to understand. Or, however, someone could be trying to understand what houses mean to them, like safety and a place to live. There are physical properties that could be understood with things or there could be mental concepts and ideas that could be comprehended with stu. That months' articles discusses memory and how it relates to vision and cognition. If you think about it memory is going to relate to the other cognitive processes like vision and cognition. I mean, there are only so many cognitive processes - especially major ones. That might be subjective, however, depending upon how you would dene a 'major' cognitive process.

3.1 An Introduction to Ideas
There are many topics in education. Life can be described academically in dierent ways
and can be categorized - for every category that life can be divided into there is also a way to describe that category (the material, stu and ideas that make up that section of 'life').
What would be a simple way of organizing life or categorizing it? Psychology is the study of the mind or the study of life. There are also mental functions, humans perceive and feel their world around them. If you consider those factors - that humans perceive and interpret, and that there is material objects in the world around them, then the logical conclusion is that life primarily and fundamentally consists of humans observing the world.

Mark Pettinelli Northeastern University This assignment was prepared for
course ENG 1105: College Writing I by Professors Barbara Ohrstrom; Justin
Senter; Seth Stair 6/25/17
Working title: Can a categorization of different topics in Cognitive Psychology lead to a better understanding of the mind and categorization itself: can important information be sorted? Broad subject: Organize intellectual academic information in cognitive psychology and general academic categories (especially those related to the study of the mind) Thesis: Epistemology or the study of knowledge could be difficult or complex to study; in order to sort through important information someone would need to organize the different topics and the relevant information that falls under those headings/categories. Buxbaum, Otto. (2016). Key Insights into Basic Mechanisms of Mental Activity. Springer International Publishing AG Switzerland. This book discusses the mind and how it thinks it describes how the mind uses judgements and concepts and memories to think in everyday activities. That is useful for this essay about figuring out how to sort through important information because the information that needs to be sorted is cognitive information in the mind. The mind itself sorts through information and this book talks about basic concepts the mind understands that helps it think like judgements, concepts and memories.

Mental activity is discussed in the book and how it uses concepts and memory structures. In order to understand how the mind sorts through information it would need to be understood how the minds concepts and memory structures are formed.The book talks about mental activity and cognitive psychology, and while it tries to connect cognition and behavior I think that it is important to connect behavior to how information is sorted since behavior (or action) is how information is gathered. Sprevak, Mark and Kallestrup, Jesper (editors). (2014) New waves in philosophy of Mind. Palgrave Macmillan, England. This book discusses, as is in the title, `philosophy of mind'. Philosophy of mind is important to the study of intelligence and categorization because it includes a discussion of consciousness and intelligence. Intelligence is part of consciousness so thought, intellect and consciousness are discussed at length in the book. Those topics would help to advance the point of this essay which is to explain how minds categorize information. In order to understand how a mind categorizes information it is necessary to understand what it is like for someone to be conscious and to think. What it is like for someone to be conscious is described throughout the book. The book describes the material stu about consciousness called `phenomenology' and the non-material stu that is more mental and related to the concepts people use and what they think about.

Kevin Mccain. (2016). The Nature of Scientific Knowledge. Springer International Publishing AG Switzerland.

This book discusses, like the title of the book says, the 'nature' of scientific knowledge. It is important to understand what is scientific in learning material and any sort of understanding because it helps to make it more clear and, well, scientific. That relates to the point of this essay which is to clarify knowledge and figure out how the mind sorts through different types of information. If knowledge is scientific then does the mind figure out knowledge and information in a scientific fashion? The book talks about different ways to understand and figure out what makes certain types of information `scientific'. What makes information clear and understood  that is a question that the book addresses. If information is understood then I wonder how the mind would `understand' the information. Information is thought about in the mind differently from how it is discussed in public, for example.

Carver, Charles and Cheier, Michael. (2013) Attention and Self-Regulation: A Control-Theory Approach to Human Behavior. Springer International Publishing AG Switzerland. The title of the book is `attention and self-regulation' and it should be mentioned that by definition self-regulation is how the mind regulates itself, and when you combine attention with self-regulation then it is an implied understanding that it is how the mind works when it pays attention and thinks about regulating itself. The book is basically about the processes the mind uses when it focuses on itself, when it sorts through information that is within the persons own mind, for instance the book says it is about the `self', and how the information in the mind gets sorted through. That obviously relates to the point of this essay because if someone is going to gure out how the mind sorts through information it needs to think about how it the mind pays attention and regulates itself.

Mark Pettinelli Problem/Solution Essay Northeastern University Author Note This essay was prepared for course ENG 1105: College Writing I by Professors Barbara Ohrstrom; Justin Senter; Seth Stair The problem I've had since I graduated high school was basically boredom. I got anxious, high anxiety because I had nothing to do and tried to solve it by doing cognitive psychology and philosophy of mind research. I thought to myself that all the information in academics and life could be sorted and more easily understood, and in this way I could x my mind and make myself think more clearly and be much less anxious. I think that some of my problem had to do with what Tversky and Kahneman called approximation and adjustment (quoted from (Carver and Cheier (2013)): A second judgment heuristic discussed by Tversky and Kahneman (1974) may be called approximation and adjustment. This is the process of beginning an estimate by making a first approximation, and then reaching a nal judgment by adjusting this approximation some-what. The first approximation may be based on a partial computation (or partial decision), or it may be suggested by the form of the problem (or the decision being undertaken). I basically kept thinking to myself the same thing over and over and that was part of the problem of figuring out how to think about logic and intelligence. I kept having to think about the same thing over and over, the same topic in academics, however I used `approximation and adjustment' to think about what I was thinking. For instance, I had a topic in mind and thought about it, then thought about it a second time a little differently, and kept repeating this process throughout the day or week.

3.2 Problem of Boredom
So I basically solved my problem of boredom for the last decade (2006-2017) by thinking
about cognitive psychology and philosophy of mind research. I posted my results here on connexions (you can review my modules here)
3.3 What is the 'understood' part of Comprehension?
Insert paragraph text here.
This is a good question, what about understanding or comprehension is complicated or complex? It could be described neurologically, however most people would not understand the biological details involved. I

wouldn't either. I could try to describe it in a simple fashion, or in a fashion that just involves the analog understanding. I will say what i mean by 'analog understanding' in the next paragraph. Information can be understood, that is what could be understood - one could say that there are different types of information. Some information is analog, that is, it is made up of stuff- it doesn't have specific mathematical components, but is more like puddy.

That is a good way that I can describe an understanding, it can be a mathematical understanding or a conceptual understanding. Conceptual understandings involve concepts and different types of information. Understandings that are analog do not necessarily involve any information but could just be descriptive or have stu, have components that are not informative or not complex. Analog by definition means not digital, so an analog understanding would be an understanding that does not necessarily have or not have information, but has stu that can be manipulated non-digitally, like say with your hands.

Analog vs. Digital

I haven't used the terms 'analog' and 'digital' to apply to types of understanding, however they can be applied to types of information. However, since understanding stu is understanding information then the terms analog and digital can be applies to the term 'understand' or 'comprehend'. For instance when someone understands anything it is actually both digital and analog, it is digital because it consists of a set of information, and it is analog because it is made up of stu, stu in the persons mind and the stu that the person is trying to understand.

So analog is anything that is not digital, that is not numerical.

Numerical means that it consists of numbers. Or does that mean that it can be read and described with numbers? It could mean either I suppose. That means that a digital watch is a watch with digits, and an analog clock is a clock with a hand instead of a digital watch with digits. That helps describe the difference between analog and digital.

3.4 What is Comprehension?

Comprehension is anything that is understood or figured out. Basically that means that there is a type of processing that the mind does whereby it understands different types of information (in life). If the mind understands different kinds of information, then what are those categories of
information? O the top of my head I don't know all of them, however there are several
obvious main categories of information in life such as foods, clothes, objects, buildings, streets
and cars, nature, and art.

It depends how you want to describe the different topics in life, basically.
The different topics in life can be described depending on various values or definitions.
Depending on what the person is trying to achieve or describe or dene, in other words. I
just described some categories based o of how I think a person's mind categorizes information
for itself, that is one way to describe the different categories in life.

Categories in Life

Basically you can describe different categories in life. This is a good way to simplify how one thinks about things, if you think about it. In other words in order to think clearly someone might first need to categorize. What might someone categorize? Furthermore, if someone wants to think with clarity (think clearly) then how would they go about organizing their minds with the proper information?

I have some ideas of my own about how someone could do something like that. It was based on my own thinking and how I have been thinking with my own mind.

Basically there can be different priorities, in other words the mind can think based upon
different categorizations of information or priorities. Those priorities could be emotional and motivational or priorities about how they want to think about information, or what kinds of information they want to think about.

If you think about it, intelligent humans might want to think about information in addition
to wanting to have emotions and ideas that they ponder and accept. Is that cognitive science
and psychology? That is basically describing how the mind thinks and feels.

How does the mind think and feel?

That is a good question, how does the mind think and feel anyway? It depends on what the person is
focusing on at any moment. If someone is only focusing on one thing, then that is the thing that they are

thinking or feeling at that time.
However it is much more complicated than that I supposed, how would the mind organize itself to think and feel, if it wants to think and feel at any one time then? It isn't as if the mind is a simple organ that simply feels basic feelings and thinks basic thoughts at any given time.

The mind is complicated and it processes information and feelings in a complicated fashion. I would say that is accurate based o of the information of the minds many different functions, feelings and ideas. Some of those ideas are motivations about the people around them or their environment, and some of the information that they think about could also be about their environment, or it could come from memories or previously learned ideas and thoughts.

Ideas and Thoughts can be Figured out
Different ideas and thoughts that occur to people can be figured out, basically. Sometimes those ideas or thoughts could be previously learned or simply take more time to figure out than instant ideas and thoughts that occur to them momentarily.
So I just mentioned that an idea or a thought could take different amounts of time to figure out. That means that it also is learned at some point. If an idea that someone has is an idea that takes them time to learn then it could be an old idea that learned a long (or brief) time ago. I would say there is a difference between previously learned ideas and previously learned emotions and feelings and new ideas, thoughts and feelings.

Humans think with concepts
Basically that means that people think with concepts. something that a person learns or thinks about?
What is a concept then? Is it If you think about it, at any one time someone is thinking about information or processing feelings (or some combination of the two).
If you think about how many feelings a person has, and how many ideas they can think about, then they could be feeling a complicated set of feelings and thinking about (or processing) a lot of information at any one time.
What kind of description is that? I just said that humans have tons of feelings and can think about lots of stuff. Does that mean that they have a large capacity of feeling and thought or something? How then does the mind process those feelings and thoughts? If you think about, its about input and output, and a central processor. The central processor is the mind, the input in the environment, and the output is their behavior and thoughts.

Chapter 4
Emotions and Feelings and How to
Change Them

Emotion is more similar to conscious thought than feelings are to conscious thought. Although emotion and feeling can be described as unconscious thought, one of them is going to be more similar to conscious thought. Feelings are more like sensations, when you touch something you get a feeling. Therefore feelings are faster than emotions and thought, because when you touch something there is a slight delay before you can think of something about it (thought), or feel something deeply about it (emotion). Emotion is therefore just unconscious thought.

Actually it would better be described as unconscious feeling (so a feeling is like a conscious emotion because you can "feel" it better and easier but emotion is a deeper, more unconscious experience similar to unconscious thought, but emotions are also more similar to conscious thought because thought is a deep experience while feelings are intense or shallow, but not deep).
One definition of emotion can be "any strong feeling". From that description many conclusions can be drawn. Basic (or primary) emotions can be made up of secondary emotions like love can contain feelings or emotions of lust, love and longing. Feelings can be described in more detail than emotions because you can have a specific feeling for anything, each feeling is unique and might not have a name.
For instance, if you are upset by one person that might have its own feeling because that person upsets you in a certain way. That feeling doesn't have a defined name because it is your personal feeling. The feeling

may also be an emotion, say anger. "Upset" is probably too weak to be an emotion, but that doesn't mean that it isn't strong like emotions are strong in certain ways. Cold is also just a feeling. There is a large overlap between how feelings feel and how emotions feel, they are similar in nature. So there are only a few defined emotions, but there are an infinite number ways of feeling things. You can have a "small" emotion of hate and you could say that you have the feeling hate then, if it is large you could say you are being emotional about hate, or are experiencing the emotion hate. You can have the same emotion of hate in different situations, but each time the feeling is going to be at least slightly different.

You can recognize any feeling, that is what makes it a feeling. If you are sad that is a feeling, but if you are depressed that isn't a feeling it is more like an emotion. You can't identify why you are depressed but you can usually identify why you are sad. Feelings are more immediate, if something happens or is happening, it is going to result in a feeling. However, if something happened a long time ago, you are going to think about it unconsciously and that is going to bring up unconscious feelings. Otherwise known as emotion. So emotions are unconscious feelings that are the result of unconscious thoughts. Feeling defined there as something you can identify. So you can't identify the unconscious thought that caused the unconscious feeling, but you can identify the unconscious feeling (aka emotion).

Another aspect of unconscious thought, emotion, or unconscious feeling (all three are the same) is that it tends to be mixed into the rest of your system because it is unconscious. If it was conscious then it remains as an individual feeling, but in its unconscious form you confuse it with the other emotions and feelings and it affects your entire system. So therefore most of what people are feeling is just a mix of feelings that your mind cannot separate out

individually. That is the difference between sadness and a depression, a depression lowers your mood and affects all your feelings and emotions, but sadness is just that individual feeling. So the reason that the depression aects all your other feelings is because you can no longer recognize the individual sad emotions that caused it. The feelings become mixed.

If someone can identify the reason they are sad then they become no longer depressed, just sad. Once they forget that that was the reason they are depressed however, they will become depressed again.

That is why an initial event might make someone sad, and then that sadness would later lead into a depression, is because you forget why you originally got sad. You might not consciously forget, but unconsciously you do. That is, it feels like you forget, the desire to get revenge on whatever caused the sadness fades away. When that happens it is like you forgetting what caused it. You may also consciously forget but what matters is how much you care about that sadness. It might be that consciously understanding why you are depressed or sad changes how much you care about your sadness, however. That would therefore change the emotion/feeling of sadness. The more you care about the sadness/depression, the more like a feeling it becomes and less like an emotion. That is because the difference between feelings and emotions is that feelings are easier to identify (because you can feel them easier).

The following is a good example of the transition from caring about a feeling to not caring about a feeling. Anger as an emotion takes more energy to maintain, so if someone is punched or something, they are only likely to be mad for a brief period of time, but the sadness that it incurred might last for a much longer time. That sadness is only going to be recognizable to the person punched for a brief period of time as attributable to the person who did the punching, after that the sadness would sink into their system like a miniature depression.

Affecting the other parts of their system like a depression.

In review, both feelings and emotions are composed of unconscious thoughts, but feelings are easier to identify than emotions. Feelings are faster than emotions in terms of response (the response time of the feeling, how fast it responds to real world stimulation) and it takes someone less time to recognize feelings because they are faster. Feelings are closer to sensory stimulation, if you touch something, you feel it and that is a fast reaction. You care about the feeling so you can separate it out in your head from the other feelings. You care in that sentence could be translated into, the feeling is intense, so you feel it and can identify it easily.

That is different from consciously understanding why you are depressed or sad.

You can consciously understand why you are depressed or sad, but that might or might not affect the intensity of that sadness.If the intensity of the sadness is brought up enough, then you can feel that sadness and it isn't like a depression anymore, it is more like an individual feeling then something that affects your mood and brings your system down (aka a depression).

Also, if you clearly enough understand what the sadness is then it is going to remain a sadness and not affect the rest of your system. That is because the feeling would get mixed in with the other feelings and start affecting them. The period of this more clear understanding of the sadness mostly occurs right after the event that caused the sadness. That is because it is clear to you what it is. Afterwards the sadness might emerge (or translate from a depression, to sadness) occasionally if you think about what caused it or just think about it in general. The difference between emotion and feeling is that feelings are easier to identify because they are faster, a feeling is something you are feeling right then. An emotion might be a deeper experience because it might affect more of you, but that is only because it is mixed into the rest of your system. That is, a depression affects more of you than just an isolated feeling of sadness. In other words, people can only have a few feelings at a time, but they can have many emotions at the same time. Emotions are mixed in, but to feel something you have to be able to identify what it is, or it is going to be so intense that you would be able to identify what it is. Emotions just feel deeper because it is all your feelings being affected at once.

Since emotion is all your feelings being affected at once, emotions are stronger than feelings. Feelings however are a more directed focus. When you feel something you can always identify what that one thing is. When you have an emotion, the emotion is more distant, but stronger. All your feelings must feel a certain way about whatever is causing the emotion. So that one thing is affecting your entire system. Feelings can then be defined as immediate unconscious thought, and emotions as unconscious thought.

•

When you care about an emotion, you could say that you have a higher attention for emotion or that emotional event during that time. You are probably going to be in a higher state of action readiness, that is, you are probably more alert and going to be able to respond faster to whatever it is you are focusing on, or just respond faster in general. You also are going to have a better understanding of the emotion if you care about it more - you make an assessment of the emotions strength and its nature when you think about the emotion (or the event that generated the emotion).

Feelings are more direct than emotions and thought because they are more sensory when you touch something you get a feeling.

That shows further how emotions are really about things in the real world, only it more like you are thinking about them instead of feeling them in real time.

Things that come from memory are going to be emotions and/or thoughts, not feelings because feelings are things which are more tangible, those memories might result in new feelings, but the memories themselves are not feelings because they are just thoughts.

That shows how you can feel some things more than others, that thought and feeling are indeed separate and intelligence is sometimes driven by feelings and emotions, and sometimes it isn't. You can think about things and not have feelings guiding those thoughts Or your feelings could be assisting your thoughts.

If you care about a feeling then it becomes easier to identify it that shows how your feelings can help you to identify other feelings, so your emotions contribute to your emotional intelligence.

If a certain emotion is larger than others then to your intellect it is going to be easier to recognize, and easier to think about (that is why a depression feels like it does, because you don't know the individual emotions contributing to it so you cannot feel a specific emotion of sadness from it.

An explanation for this chapter:
So feelings are easier to "feel" than emotions, that is probably why they are called feelings, because you "feel" them better. Maybe someone else thinks you can feel emotions easier, I don't know, the point is you can feel emotions and feelings with different levels of intensity and in more than one way, a feeling could be not intense but clear to you. So how conscious you are of the feeling or emotion influences the intensity of it and your conscious experience of it. A feeling could be more intense than en emotion if it is the only

thing you are feeling as well. That makes sense, if an emotion is very complicated, then you probably couldn't feel the entire thing as clearly in a brief period of time. So my theory is that feelings are more simple, and therefore there are more shallow but possibly more intense than emotion because you can focus on a simple thing easier.

If you are having a deep emotional experience (experiencing an emotion) then it makes sense that you aren't as in touch with all of those feelings that are occurring. When you touch something you get the feeling "cold" - that is simple to understand.When you are in a depression you don't understand all the complicated emotions that you are experiencing. You could experience sadness all day. When you can say "oh, I really "felt" that", then you know you feel it and it is a feeling.

When you feel something, it is a feeling.
When you are emotional about something, those are feelings too, but it is more powerful and deeper, you aren't as in touch will all of it because it is more complex. You could be in touch with something complex and feel that too, I guess. Though I would argue that a feeling is easier to focus on if it is simple and clear to understand and feel to your conscious mind.

The significance of this chapter:
If someone is emotional, then they are feeling a lot. I could say that the emotions someone is experiencing could be brought up at different times and felt more - translated from somewhere in your strong emotions to something you feel more closely. So you can feel some things but that doesn't mean that the feeling is intense or clear - those things might become clear however at some point. When those emotions become clear and you 'bring them up' - either by caring about the emotion or the thought that represents it or it just emerges by some other method (such as by doing an evaluation of your emotional state) - then they become feelings because you can feel them easier. These feelings are more clear, similar to when you touch something you get a feeling that is simple and tactile. That is why feelings are called the result of emotions, because emotions are like the basis for feelings (at least non-tactile ones). You might have a feeling that has a shallow source however as well I would say. It doesn't have to be that a feeling is first felt deeply, and then you feel it more clearly later on (the feeling being the result of an emotion). Maybe the feeling is simple at first and then it becomes more complex later.

What role does attention have to play? Being emotional or feeling something can make you pay more or less attention to things, including other feelings. Your attention can naturally rise just because of your emotional state.

People feel emotions, and they can feel feelings. Emotions are strong and the powerful source of human behavior, and while feelings are also powerful they are also diverse, curious, and unique - 'old feelings returning'.

4.1 How to Change Emotions and Feelings
An appraisal is when you assess something. People make appraisals or assessments of emotion
all of the time, however they aren't aware most of the time that they are doing this. How much someone cares about an emotional stimulus is something that is probably thought about frequently during the experience. If you think about it people frequently are going to naturally analyze what is going on in every situation they are in and think about what the emotions occurring are.

I said in the previous paragraph that people make appraisals of emotional things but they aren't aware of themselves doing that. How is that possible or what does that mean exactly?

If people care about emotion, which they clearly do, then they are going to want to know what is going on in the situations they encounter in life. So clearly people make assessments of how much emotion the things around them are generating, the only question is can they do this in a way that is beneath their awareness.

People surely must make assessments since they often work on inducing or inhibiting feelings in order to make them "appropriate" to a situation. If you are going to be changing feeling, then obviously you are going to need to measure and assess it first. Sometimes people think this process through consciously, and sometimes they don't.

It makes sense to me that people are going to "know" how valuable certain things in their environment are. This is clear when you realize that people focus on some things very quickly - such a thing would clearly be something of interest to that person or something that generates emotion - which would make it interesting.

So you could say that a person whose attention gets alerted to something around them made an assessment about the stimulus or responded to it, the stimulus (the thing in their environment they paid sharp attention to) was clearly emotional for them.

It could have generated any feeling - disgust, surprise, happiness, - or maybe an intellectual reaction such as 'that person has a bright coat'. Does that mean that the person assessed if the bright coat generated emotion for them? What would it mean if it generated emotion? Could they respond in a fast way without being interested? Someone could respond quickly to something and not be in a mood that is very caring at that time, in which case maybe little emotion was involved.

However if someone was interested in something then it makes sense that it is going to cause them to have feelings. Is something someone is interested in going to cause them to have deep emotions or shallow feelings? What types of stimuli result in deep or shallow feelings? Just because something generates more emotion for you doesn't necessarily mean that it is going to cause you to respond to it faster or you would be more interested in it.

Maybe your interest is more intellectual or maybe you are interested or responding to it quickly because you have to.
Under what circumstances do people care more about feelings? This relates to appraisals
- if you care about something then you are going to make more assessments during the experience about how much emotion is being generated probably.

People can care more about feelings but that doesn't mean that they are aware that they care more during that time. This is similar to people going into modes where they are seeking pleasure. My theory here is that people have levels of desire and need that fluctuate constantly.
This means that there are many different levels someone can experience an emotion or feeling.
It is more complicated than simply saying that the feeling has a certain strength - each feeling
or emotion is going to have a unique nature, represent unique ideas and objects, and have a unique significance on your psyche.
Maybe you can say that there are shallow feelings and deep emotions, and that there are certain properties that shallow feelings have and certain properties that deep feelings have. For instance you probably care more about deep feelings (unless the feeling is negative) and therefore they probably cause you to have a faster reaction time. However if the feeling is deep, sappy, and emotional then maybe your reaction time is slower because the emotion is weighing you down.
This relates to the 'emotions and feelings and the difference between them' section above because I am outlining further that deep feelings/emotions or shallow feelings/emotions are different and things happen to humans differently with each one.
It shows that clearly emotion can make someone be different physically, as when you are motivated by emotion you often move faster.
This is just bringing up ideas of depth - some feelings are simple and some are complex - that is obvious, however I think people could notice a lot more if they grouped their emotions into a categories of strength and shallowness or depth and how they responded differently to each different category. - Also the person should note what the interest was, the reaction time, the negative or positive valence of the emotion.
Goffman suggests that we spend a good deal of effort on managing impressions - that is, acting. Your impression of other people makes you feel in different ways, and you try to manage this in a social situation. So therefore all of your strong feelings you try to influence by thinking about what caused those feelings - such as your impressions - and how you can change them.
So people are basically "emotion-managers", constantly thinking about their feelings and what caused them and how they can change them. Whenever you change an impression of someone, you are also changing your feelings. When you think about your own feelings you are changing them because you are changing how much you care about them. You set goals for yourself about your own feelings - 'if I do this I am going to become happy'.
When you think about your feelings you can make insignificant feelings large or large feelings small. When

a feeling is small, you could say that it is more unconscious or beneath your awareness. Something (including yourself) could trigger this small feeling and it could emerge into something you feel more closely and more consciously.

So the question is, what circumstances and what type of thinking warrant that feeling of 'that sort'. We assess the 'appropriateness' of a feeling by making a comparison between the feeling and the situation. We also have goals for how we want to feel that we don't know we are thinking, and we have goals for how we want to act as well. Is there a 'natural attitude' or a natural way of behaving and thinking? Not really - especially when you consider that you are unconsciously constantly creating goals, drives, thoughts and behaviors that are not fully under your control.

In secondary reactive emotions, the person reacts against his or her initial primary adaptive emotion, so that it is replaced with a secondary emotion. This "reaction to the reaction" obscures or transforms the original emotion and leads to actions that are not entirely appropriate to the current situation. For example, a man that encounters danger and begins to feel fear may feel that fear is not "manly." He may then either become angry at the danger (externally focused reaction) or angry with himself for being afraid (self-focused reaction), even when the angry behavior actually increases the danger. Listening to this reaction, someone is likely to have the sense that "something else is going on here" or "there's more to this than just anger." The experience is something like hearing two different melodies being played at the same time in a piece of music, one the main melody and the other the background or counterpart.

-
-

Secondary emotions often arise from attempts to judge and control primary responses. Thus, anxiety may come from trying to avoid feeling angry or sexually excited, or it may arise from guilt about having felt these emotions.

When someone rejects what they are truly feeling, they are likely to feel bad about themselves. Feeling or expressing one emotion to mask the primary emotion is a meta emotional process. Feelings about emotions need to be acknowledged and then explored to get at the underlying primary emotion.

Experiential therapists see clients emotional processing as occurring on a continuum with five phases (Kennedy-Moore + Watson, 1999):

1. prereective reaction to an emotion-eliciting stimulus entailing perception of the stimulus, preconscious cognitive and emotional processing, and accompanying physiological
changes
2. conscious awareness and perception of the reaction
3. labeling and interpretation of the aective response; people typically draw upon internal as well as situational cues to label their responses
4. evaluation of whether the response is acceptable or not
5. evaluation of the current context in terms of whether it is possible or desirable to reveal
one's feelings.

What role does the emotion 'interest' play in emotional responses? It is a baseline emotion of great importance - the action tendency of interest involves intending, orienting, and exploring. Interest is felt very frequently, probably without being noticed. If you think about it, to some degree interest is going to be present with each reaction to stimuli. With every response someone has, they are interested to some degree. You can look at interest further when you consider secondary emotional responses - what was the interest that came from the response that had some other type of interest?

Through each stage of evaluation of a response, or simple evaluations that aren't a response to things, there is interest involved as well. This 'interest' induces caring, and the interest and caring is going to change your emotions - emotions are going to be brought up, intensified, changed based on your interest or caring or evaluations.

2 Kennedy-Moore, E., + Watson, J.C. (1999).
New York: Guilford Press.

Expressing emotion:

When you think and make evaluations, you change the nature and intensity of the emotions that are related to what you are doing or processing.

Are people going to be more interested in clear, primary emotions or feelings that they aren't in touch with?

When someone is interested in a feeling, how is that different from being interested in the source of the feeling? If someone is feeling sad, they might not care about the sadness if the feeling is unclear to them or they don't know they are sad. If someone is going to try to change a feeling of sadness, it clearly would be beneficial if they knew when the feeling is occurring.

Is it possible to experience deep emotions without being aware at all that these emotions are occurring? Yes it is, but there are times when people are conscious of those emotions say when they are recalling them - that the deep emotions are more clear. There could be a deep emotion that occurs over a long period of time - say anger at someone, this anger could be in your body for a long time, during being the person, or while away from the person; the point is the anger is reflected upon or it occurs more deeply at certain points - and then you are going to be aware of the emotion.

That anger is a significant, primary feeling. The feeling is significant because it shows how large the emotion is that is behind it. People can feel feelings that are shallow or intense at the time, but these feelings don't necessarily mean more than that or are deeper than that because they aren't deep or primary - they don't mean anything else or occur at other times you aren't aware of (indicating that this feeling is significant). The feeling of shallow feelings is still potent (because you are feeling them in real time), but they aren't as powerful as feelings that have a special meaning or significance for you (which would make you feel deeper in real time and feel more effected).

If you think about it, people change their feelings by thinking all of the time. The way they could help manage this is probably by making assessments of their emotional state. If people think about what just made them happy or sad, then they might be able to do something or think something to change that. Some emotional responses are going to be more noticeable, and that is when people might try to figure out what went on.

There are subtleties of emotion as well. People probably respond in many ways that they aren't aware of consciously, but they might have responded because something beneath their notice occurred emotionally. You could say that the emotional world beneath your notice is the "unconscious" mind or the unconscious world.

Your emotions change all of the time, only sometimes are you going to notice when an emotion changes or when you are experiencing one.

Furthermore, you might want or expect to experience one emotion but you are actually experiencing a different one because unconsciously that is how you are responding. For instance, maybe you have an unconscious bias against a group of people so you feel hate when you interact with them, but you consciously think that you like those people and feel like you should be happy and positive towards them. A feeling might be important to your unconscious mind, or a feeling might be important to your conscious mind - in which case you would probably 'care' about it.

Your attention is constantly divided between various things in your environment, your own internal thinking and your own emotions. Your emotions are going to determine and assist what you pay attention to. For instance, if something is emotional in your environment for you, then more of your attention is probably going to spent thinking about or focusing on that thing.

Or maybe something in your environment is just more interesting than something else, the point is something in your environment or something in your head (emotions, thoughts) caused an intellectual or emotional reaction in you, and that then caused you to pay more attention to it. That doesn't mean that you notice it more after you pay attention - this type of paying attention might be unconscious - i.e. - more of your attentional resources or just more of the focus that people have (not all of which they are aware of) is going to be directed at it.

References
Emotion-Focused Therapy: Coaching Clients to Work Through Their Feelings. Leslie Greenberg. Amer Psychological Assn; 1 edition (January 2002)

Some Notes

By
Mark Pettinelli

So I am trying to think. How exactly does the mind work? I think I need to understand how the mind functions in order to think clearly. There is cognition, which is how people think, and there are emotions, which determine how people feel.

But is that all I need to know about the mind in order to function? The mind must be more complicated than just the experience of feelings and thoughts.

So I did a lot of research, they're books in my room about cognitive psychology and cognitive science and related topics in psychology. Like cognition and emotion, concepts etc.

Is that all I need to know? Is there any more research I can do? Do I need to know anything else? That's an excellent question.

I did a lot of research. I read books on cognitive science and cognitive psychology. I did a ton of research, what did I figure out again. There were books on cognitive psychology, and books on emotion and cognition. THere were also books about logic and clear thinking, or critical thinking. There was one book on concepts that I liked.

So I don't know what exactly I learned or figured out, how the mind works maybe? I mean now I understand logic and emotions or psychology and clear thinking. What else do I need to learn in order to progress myself. I did the research by myself, only now am I being guided. But those articles written by me were written before I started to be guided. I mean they just figured out the rest of the academics, some of it was academics I was trying to teach. I think their logic was sort of like, well we have all the information, having fun is more important than information anyway so we can try to have now and increase that and change that, so it doesn't really matter if the stupid information is over. That seems to be what they're thinking, that's also what I am thinking right now.

On the other hand, maybe the information could also continue. Concepts are complicated, I can continue to develop the intellectual aspect. The question is, do I need to become more intelligent? Maybe I could just develop the physical aspect, I don't know.

So do I need to become more intelligent. How have I become intelligent so far, I've become more conscious of myself and my mind. I am aware of what I am thinking and what I am feeling. I mean as a kid I didn't even know what the definition of 'emotion regulation' was, I did have emotions, but wasn't aware that I was having those emotions. Now I am aware of my emotions and my thoughts and try to change them, understand them and experience them.

That's mostly how I've become more intelligent over the years. I don't know if I could be even more aware of my emotions and thoughts, or if that's necessary. How else could I become more intelligent then?

Um so maybe the research is over, I mean i've already said that they seem to think having fun is more important, and that can increase and improve over the future years. It doesn't matter that the new information is over, that's what I'm used to, I was providing all (or most of) the new info. Now I think it's more fun to just increase the amount of fun and change that up.

Now that all the academics have finished my life has improved, they use to keep asking me to make money. What a bunch of dumbasses. Now the academics are over. They think they can copy me by putting other people in a lot of pain, but they forgot that I was born at the beginning of time so my birth was unique. They won't be able to get anyone else from the beginning of time because I was the only one who survived.

I don't know if i need to become more intelligent, i've already mastered most of the stuff i need to know.

Once again, I've already become intelligent, I don't know if I need to learn anything else.

Um so once again they think they can copy me by torturing someone else, however my birth was completely different, so was most of the experience that happened in ancient history. It was a lot of pain and anxiety.

I'm trying to think, I think because my birth was different they won't be able to copy me. Tons of people go through lots of pain however my birth and most of the experience was done at the beginning of time, or a really long time ago, I think that seems to be the case.

Um so that means they have to keep me alive. I'm the only one from the beginning of time.

I don't know if i need to become more intelligent. I don't know if I need to do anymore research. I've already become more conscious and am aware of my emotions. I told you before when I was a child I didn't even know what the word 'emotion regulation' meant. Now I have a really good understanding of emotion regulation and what it means.

Um, so I said that they won't be able to copy me because I'm from the beginning of time, so my birth and most of the experience was before anyone else was alive. I'm kind of excited about that because it means they have to keep me. I mean, I am from a really long time ago, my experience is also very old. In order to copy me they would have needed to start a long time ago, and i've been through a lot. It's too late for them to copy me, I beat the competition a long time ago I think.

Um so, do I need to become more intelligent? That's a good question.

Like what else do I need to learn or understand. I had to learn a lot about emotion and cognition and the mental processes - for instance cognitive psychology and cognitive science. I learned that stuff in order to think clearly, I mean i've always been a logical thinker however i'm a lot smarter than I was say when I was a child.

Um so what else do I need to learn. What have I learned up to this point anyway, I don't even really remember. I know that I have emotions and thoughts. Thoughts can be simple, and feelings can also be simple.

Um so do i need to know anything else. I understand logic and clear thinking, that's kind of important. I also understand the difference between emotions and feelings. Feelings are simple and clear, while emotions are deep and complicated. A strong feeling can be an emotion. If its not strong it might be more clear and simple and easy to understand. That's kind of like how feeling can feel easier and be sensory. I mean, sensory feelings like the feeling of cold are also easy to feel and simple and clear. That's why they are called feelings, because you can "feel" them easier.

SO i think that finally makes sense. Feelings are more sensory, or some feelings can be sensory feelings while other feelings could just be shallow emotions or other feelings. FEelings are simple and clear, while emotions are deep and complicated. FEelings can also be sensory, like the 5 senses of touch, taste, sound sight and smell. THe relationship between the sensory feelings and the non-sensory feelings is that both are simple to feel and clear. While emotions are supposed to be strong feelings, I mean a strong sensory feeling like cold would just be a feeling and not an emotion, but a strong feeling of love or happiness would be an emotion and not a feeling. You could also feel it as a feeling i suppose because you could feel the emotion or feeling.

But to the extent that it's shallow and clear is the extent to which it's a feeling, the emotion of happy could be a feeling and an emotion then. I suppose then feelings are just things that you feel that are simple and clear, so all the emotions could also be felt as feelings because you can feel them in a simple and clear way. THe extent to which something is felt in a simple and clear way is the extent to which its a feeling. And if something is felt deeply, I mean if a feeling is felt deeply, then it is felt as an emotion.

So I'm trying to describe how i feel. THe question is, how do i feel? What is going on in my mind. I know that there are feelings and emotions. The difference between feelings and emotions is that feelings are more simple and more clear, while emotions are deeper and more intellectual. That means that I can feel things, and think about things at the same time. I'm trying to keep track on what is going on in my mind. I'm currently thinking about stuff and feeling things at the same time. That seems to be all that is going on.

That is like consciousness studies, consciousness is a complicated topic, like what is going on in the mind, and what about it leads to consciousness. There is also losing consciousness, that's also complicated by itself. I guess that's just going to sleep though, that isn't too complicated. If you think about it, feelings and thoughts are also fairly simple. What is complicated about feeling then? Thought would seem to be simple, at least now it's simple for me. There is also just thinking, you could be thinking clearly and logically or unclearly and illogically, or stupidly. That seems like that's all there is to thinking and the thought processes.

What could be complicated about feeling then? There are the primary emotions of happy, sad, anger, fear, surprise and disgust. Those feelings work with the mental processes of thought, feeling, language, memory, perception and attention.

That seems like a pretty good description of how the mind works. There's the mental processes and those involve feeling and thinking. There's also how feelings feel, like the difference between emotions and feelings.

So this looks like I have a new book in the making here, I can explore the rest of the concepts that I need to understand. Like what else would I need to learn about. I understand that there is a thought process and an emotion process, and that emotions are different from feelings. There are many mental processes - they are emotion, thought, language, perception, memory and attention. Those are key mental processes that I have already studied.

There's also a difference between feelings and emotions. I've been trying to explain the difference for a long time now, like feelings could be more simple and easier to feel because they are more direct. Emotions could be deeper and more powerful in an intellectual way, while feelings could also be intense but they won't be as intellectual though. I mean it's hard to describe the difference between feelings and emotions. Emotions are supposed to be stronger right, but if it's a sensory feeling like the feeling of cold then the sensory feeling would be stronger than an emotion like anger or happy. Feelings would then be more simple and more intense in a simple way, while emotions would be more deep and powerful in an intellectual way. SO then feelings would just be more stupid than emotions. I mean physical sensations are more stupid than intellectual feelings, so feelings could be more sensory while emotions are more intellectual and deep.

So what am I trying to learn here, I already know a lot of stuff about how the mind works and its processes. I don't know what else I need to explore, I think perfectly clearly and stuff.

What is the difference between feelings and emotions again, I think that feelings are more simple and can be sensory like touch or taste. The feeling of cold is a sensory feeling, while the emotion of happy is an emotion that is not like a sensory feeling. Emotions are deep and powerful.

So what is an emotion again, a strong feeling right. Why is cold a feeling, because it's sensory. So what is an emotion, a strong feeling? A strong sensory feeling like cold is just a strong feeling, and not an emotion. HOwever a strong emotion of happiness is a deep experience that is also intellectual. I suppose you could label feelings as emotions, the words can be used interchangeably. What about what occurs first, does an emotion always come first? Are feelings first powerful and then become more clear later on, the feeling being the result of an emotion?

So that is all a feeling is, a clear feeling. FEeling can be clear and simple, but does that mean that an emotion is always first? First you can feel an emotion, say maybe one of the primary emotions, like happy or sad, anger or fear, surprise or disgust, and then you could feel a simple feeling that is clear as a result of one of those emotions. That's what I read as the definition of feelings and emotions anyway, that feelings are the result or conscious experience of the primary emotions.

Ok so does that make sense, what if I feel a different feeling first, is that possible? If it's a bodily or sensory feeling then it's possible to feel it first. But the other feelings are all secondary to the primary emotions i think.

Those primary emotions must be really important then. Like I said, it seems like all the other feelings, at least all the non-sensory or non-bodily feelings, are secondary to the primary emotions. That is why you feel the primary emotion first, at least briefly, and then you feel one of the other feelings as a reaction or the conscious experience of the primary emotion. That's what I read anyway and it seems to be correct.

For instance Depressed is secondary to the emotion of sad. Scared is secondary to the emotion of fear. Ecstatic is secondary to the emotion of happy. Looking at the list of feelings, it seems like all of the feelings are secondary to the primary emotions of anger, fear, happy, sad, surprise or disgust. That's also what I read about feelings and emotions.

So how does that work, first you feel a primary emotion briefly and then you can feel the secondary feeling? Something like that I think.

The primary emotions also are physiological, they have facial expressions.

So I need to think, the primary emotions are more important than the secondary feelings, which are all of the other feelings. Someone could be experiencing a mix of the secondary feelings, or a mix of the primary emotions, or both. THe primary emotions would normally come before their secondary feelings, however and then the secondary feeling would just be secondary to those primary emotions. In other words, the primary emotions are more important. That's why the primary emotions are described as the 'main' emotions.

I mean, it makes sense that one of the main emotions would normally be felt first, but which feelings are the main ones could be argued about. I mean maybe for me I feel caring first, and then feel the emotion of happy. So love would be an emotion for me, instead of the main emotion of happy.

I mean, there's a lot of different feelings. It's kind of subjective to decide which ones are the main emotions, or which ones are felt first.

So what is the difference between emotions and feelings then? Emotions are supposed to be stronger, does that mean that you first feel a stronger feeling as an emotion, and then feel more detailed, clearer feelings after? That's kind of subjective, but what I do know is there is a mix of feelings people can experience, and sometimes there are deeper feelings that can lead to a mix of secondary feelings. How you would define an emotion versus a feeling is subjective. An emotion would normally be stronger and more main or primary, and would be felt first, or it could be felt after a feeling, like I said it's all kind of subjective.

I mean, is a strong feeling felt first, or does it become strong after you initially feel it? Or is it clear first, and then becomes more complicated later. I suppose feelings could feel clear or strong first or in any order. That's all I know, also the main emotions or feelings are supposed to be more important, but that is also subjective.

I mean, are emotions all more intellectual than sensory feelings? Is a feeling first felt clearly and simply, and then becomes more complicated and deep after?

There are a ton of ways to feel feelings and emotions. Feelings can be sensory or non-sensory. They can be complicated or simple, deep or shallow, intellectual or stupid. They can also be mixed with other feelings, or felt by themselves, or lead to other feelings.

What else is going on in the mind. In addition to feeling things, humans also think about things. What's interesting about that is how many things they can think about, how fast they can think about those things, and how complicated are the things that they think about are. Those topics can be pretty complicated, however it's also fairly simple to understand. I mean when a concept is thought about, how complicated could it be? Most concepts are simple to understand in order to achieve basic functioning for the person. For instance as a child I was functioning fine even with a basic understanding of concepts, that was how I developed myself, now basically I just have a more complex understanding of concepts and stuff.

I mean, what needs to be understood, concepts are fairly simple in order for the person to function on a basic level. However, that is also how animals function, they seem to have a basic grasp of concepts also since they know how to survive. Their survival requires a basic grasp of concepts like how to get food and find shelter.

That ties back into how humans feel emotions and feelings. DO they need to understand what they are feeling, or is it complicated what they are feeling at any given time? I pointed out that feelings could be complicated or simple, deep or shallow, unconscious or conscious, sensory or intellectual, stupid or intelligent, and they can be mixed in with other feelings.

I mean, intelligence is also fairly simple, humans can perform perfectly fine even with a low level of intelligence. For instance I was functioning fine as a child even though I didn't understand much.

So i mean, the extent to which a feeling is felt clearly and simply is the extent to which it is a feeling. THat is why the word 'feel' is used. You can feel emotions strongly, and emotions can have a lot of feeling, and you can feel feelings strongly. SO what is an emotion then, something that is deep and complicated? I mean, all of the feelings could be emotions if an emotion is any strong feeling. What then is the definition of emotion versus the definition of feeling, it doesn't really matter. I suppose the point is that feelings can be simple and clear, or deep and complicated, or sensory and weak, or sensory and powerful - like a powerful feeling of cold water. Feeling is just anything you can feel. Humans feel feelings in many ways.
I pointed out that it might be a primary emotion first and then felt as a secondary feeling, however that is kind of complicated because humans feel a mix of feelings all of the time, so it might be hard to sort through what they are feeling, if its a primary emotion first or what is going on.

So what is a cognitive architecture, or how is thought and feeling processed in the brain. THat's kind of an interesting question. I mean a computer could be a brain instead of an organ of a brain like real humans and animals have. A fly even has an organic brain except it's extremely small. How could a fly think like a human even if its brain is that much smaller? That's also kinda interesting.

So once again, the question is, how does the mind work? I don't really know all the details of the neuroscience of how a mind would work or how a computer would work (that uses artificial intelligence). But I don't need those details in order to describe how it works in a simple fashion. I mean I know that there are more details but I don't need to explore those details.

So what happens when someone has a thought, how does that process work in the mind. It would seem to me like nothing complicated is going on. I mean a thought is just a thought. It could be a sentence. A sentence uses words, and each word has a definition. Sentence comprehension is fairly simple, i mean that's just understanding language. Humans speak with language, I speak the english language for instance. That would seem all there is to how thoughts work. I mean a thought or a sentence takes a certain amount of time to think or say or hear. There are also emotions and feelings, those also take time to process. I've already pointed out that you can be feeling a stream of feelings and think with thoughts and sentences at the same time.

So that's fairly simple, I mean either you are thinking something, or feeling something, or both at the same time.

So does that explain how the mind processes thoughts and feelings? Like I said before, a computer could think like a human mind by using artificial intelligence and an electronic computer system, or the neurology of a human mind could do the computations required to understand thought, language and feeling. I don't know all the details of how that works, however the process seems fairly simple on the surface at least. I mean I don't know neuroscience or biology very well.

So um, when someone has a thought, how does that process occur? It seems like a sentence is just words that the person sounds out in their head, and they understand the definition of each word when they say the word to themselves, and sentences are just combinations of words.

THat would seem to be how the mind processes language and thought anyway. Not all thought has to be language, however. THere is non-verbal thought. I've already mentioned that before a little bit, that thought doesn't always have to be in a sentence or thought out with language. Thoughts could use just thought power or processing that doesn't use language or words or sounds to figure out. I mean that is like non-verbal communication. In other words, you don't always need words or language to think about things. It could be non-verbal for instance. Like physical movements are normally non-verbal, you don't describe each physical movement to yourself, however you know what the movement is and how to do it.

How do emotions work in the mind then? How are emotions processed? I already described how thoughts are processed. For emotions it would seem like there is a stimulus, some sort of trigger, and then the person experiences an emotion that is resulting from the stimulation. That's all there is to how feelings work I would think.

Um, so I'm trying to figure out what else I need to know in order to make progress. I seem to have done a good job. So I don't know what else I need to do to make progress. I mean I want to develop more, but i already think clearly and know about emotion regulation.

I already said that as a child I didn't understand what I was feeling as well as I do now. That's developed me a huge amount, now I understand what emotion regulation is and what I am feeling all of the time. I'm aware of and conscious of my emotions and thoughts.

Um so what else do I need to know. I already understand cognitive psychology and cognitive science, and how the mind works. What else would I need to know then? I have a good understanding of my own feelings and my own thoughts. I also understand that my mind thinks with concepts that could be difficult or easy to understand. There is also clear thinking, or logical or critical thinking. I also understand that. I mean as a child I was thinking and feeling perfectly fine, except I didn't understand anything complicated and didn't understand that I was having those feelings. I guess I understood I was having the feelings, in that way I'm just like I was when I was a child, or in high school. I'm still pretty much the same person I would say.

So the question is, how have I developed? I mean I understand what I am feeling now, and I understand that thought and feeling and how the mind works is or could be complicated. I mean I understand what 'emotion regulation' is.

I also understand what I am feeling all the time, or at any moment. For instance I could be feeling sensory feelings, or weak feelings. I could be feeling deep emotions, I could be feeling primary emotions or secondary emotions or feelings. The primary emotions are happy, sad, anger, fear, surprise and disgust. Those are supposed to be the primary emotions. I don't know if I mostly feel the primary emotions or if I feel the secondary emotions and feelings. I mean like what am I feeling right now? Am I feeling primary emotions or am I feeling secondary feelings? That is an excellent question lol.

So once again, i don't know what else i would need to learn more about. I suppose i can look more through my cognitive psychology and cognitive science textbooks, but i don't know if i need to know anything else. I mean I understand that I had feelings as a child and understood that I was having those feelings. Now I'm much more intelligent, however and understand what the feelings are and can reflect on the experience.

I mean as a child i knew i was having emotions, however now my understanding is much better.

I mean, what am i going to learn by reviewing more cognitive psychology books? I already know about the mental processes, attention, memory, thought, language, emotion and perception. I already understand those processes. I mean I understand how attention works, I understand how memory works, language, emotion and perception also. Thought is also simple to understand. I mean, what else do i need to explore? Maybe i've simplified it and those mental processes are actually pretty complicated. However, it seems like those cognitive psychology books just go

into more detail about how those 6 mental processes work, that's all I seem to be learning as I review them.
Ok so the mental process of thought involves problem solving and decision making, and the mental process of emotion involves primary and secondary emotions or feelings, and appraisals of our emotional state. That is, people make appraisals of their emotions every now and then, and they can feel primary and secondary feelings as a mix of feeling that they assess when they make appraisals of their emotional state.

So what else am I supposed to learn by reading these books? That's my question. I already have a good understanding that I wrote down in my article which I have finished, that covers most of the material involved with how the mind works or cognitive science and cognitive psychology and consciousness. I've already finished that article so i don't know what else i should add.

I don't know what else i need to learn. Do I need to learn anything about life? I'm already pretty smart.

I already said that the books I have only seem to go into more detail about the mental processes. If that is all they talk about then I don't know what else i can learn, i mean the mental processes pretty much covers how the mind works. Why would i need to understand more details of how those mental processes work, what would that look like?

So um, once again, the books just go into more details about how the mental processes work, so i don't know what else I would need to know about that.

There is other stuff I can learn, like cognitive load and working memory, working memory can make a demand on cognitive load for instance, or is it that cognitive load demands working memory? I think those are the same. There's also casual relations, which is like cause and effect interactions. There's supporting actions, actions that have a cause and an effect. That's how people think about things, in life there are lots of things that have a cause and an effect. Cause and effect often demands explanation of certain reactions or events. On the other hand, that seems pretty obvious, i mean, I already knew that there were cause and effect interactions in life. I didn't think about it that way, however. Like what in life has a cause and effect, there's lots of things I could even make a list if i wanted to. The mind must understand that, or when an action or event demands an explanation of its cause and effect that is when you would think about it.

So now i guess i'm going through the additional information I might think is important related to cognitive science or cognitive psychology, clear thinking and critical thinking, and related fields.

At this point i don't know what else I would need to know that might be considered useful information. Like that example of cause and effect helps me think a little bit, but I don't know if there is other info that might be important. I already basically know how the mind functions through my explanation of the 6 mental processes. I pointed out that there are some details about those processes that are important, like the difference between emotions and feelings, including the main emotions and appraisals of our emotional states. There's also thought, which I need to add that there's decision making and problem solving. There's language, which I need to explain that there is a relationship between thought and language, and that some thought is non-verbal while other thought needs to be spoken with words (language). There's perception and attention, and I pointed out that our attention can change because of our emotions and thoughts. Also our perception can be of external objects that we can have internal mental images of, or we could just see those objects in our vision

.Research Notes of Mark Pettinelli

By
Mark Pettinelli
Creative Commons Attribution LIcense

There is:

- The difference between emotions and feelings (My conclusion was essentially that they could be the same thing and there is a complicated pattern of feeling that humans experience. However emotions are usually or supposed to be stronger than feelings. There are sensory feelings and non-sensory feelings. Sensory feelings like the feeling of cold could be strong or weak. Non-sensory feelings like the feeling of love could be strong or weak also, however if it is strong then I guess it would be an emotion, while the strong sensory feeling of cold is still a feeling because it is sensory and not like an emotion or non-sensory feeling). Sensory feelings are simple and clear to feel, which might be similar to how other emotions feel, there's a ton of ways to feel feelings.
- There's the primary emotions of happy, sad, anger, fear, surprise and disgust. Those are supposed to be physiological and have corresponding facial expressions. They are also supposed to come first, then the person is supposed to experience some of the many secondary emotions. That might not be the case, however, because there is a complicated mix of feelings and emotions occurring all of the time. It might be that a secondary feeling comes first and is more powerful first and then becomes clear later, there's a ton of different ways to feel emotions and feelings.
- There are different ways to feel emotions and feelings. Like does an emotion always come first and then lead to simple, clear feelings or is the feeling first weak and then becomes powerful and clear. There are a lot of feelings and they can feel them many different ways, and occur in different orders, etc.
- How did the earth begin, did the big bang create natural resources on the planet so humans just had to keep the population healthy and earth was pretty good on its own, all set up and everything with natural resources?
- What are appraisals of our emotional states, those are just when someone makes an assessment of their emotions. That might be complicated because there is a complicated mix of someone's emotions occurring at any time.
- What is the difference between how an android's mind would work from a computer system versus how a human's mind would work as an organic organ in their body (a brain). That is neuroscience vs computer science (that means that the computer science could be about artificial intelligence if it's an android instead of just a computer).
- There's the 6 mental processes of emotion, thought, perception, attention, memory and language. Thinking involves deciding, reasoning and problem solving. Consciousness might also be considered to be a mental process. There are details of how those mental processes function that I could go into, however I don't know if someone needs to know all those details in order to function properly. Though just listing those 6 or 7 mental processes might be a simplification of how the mind works.

So you can be conscious of your feelings and your emotions. You can also change your emotions through identification, repetition and interpretation. There's feelings and thoughts that can occur at the same time. The mind also thinks with sentences and words. Sounds become words in the head through a process called lexicalization. The mind has an ego, which is an unconscious aspect of a person's identity. The ego tries to help the person and is selfish and unconscious. There are feelings and thoughts that someone can be more or less conscious of. Those feelings and thoughts could be unconscious, or conscious, or some sort of mix, sometimes it's hard to figure out what someone is feeling and people can do appraisals or evaluations of their emotional states.

There is also:

- So how would someone go about evaluating their emotional state say when they make an appraisal. I already described that there is a difference between feelings and emotions. How do those feelings feel, that is the question. Like how would I describe how I am feeling right now. I could make an appraisal or evaluation of my emotional state right now.
- I mean, how would I go about breaking down my state of feeling. Are those feelings strong or weak, unconscious or conscious, detailed or simple, intellectual or stupid, sensory or non-sensory, etc.
- I mean, how am I feeling right now, that could be a complicated question.
- How can I describe a state of feeling? I mean, there can be a mix of feelings that are either sensory or non-sensory. For instance someone could be feeling physical pain and emotional pain and intellectual pain at the same time. That could be complicated.
- If a feeling is more conscious does that mean it is more clear? Or would it just be more conscious. So you'd be more aware of it, that means it's more clear I suppose.
- What does having multiple feelings look like? Some you might be more aware of and some less aware of.

So there's multiple concepts here, there is intelligence, mental processes, feeling (which happens to be one of the mental processes), consciousness, thoughts (also a mental process), and what else is there that I would consider to be important or a part of consciousness or how the mind works. I would think that the mind works just from the 6 different mental processes that give rise to consciousness. What does that mean that I need to understand then. I already understand the mental processes. Language is kind of important, that's one of the mental processes. Language is words that form sentences and are sounds in the head. The sounds mean different words that the person could be thinking about. I also mentioned the ego, an unconscious aspect of the person's personality that is selfish. There's the difference between emotions and feelings, which is that essentially emotions are stronger and could be more intellectual and less clear.

So what else do I need in order to give myself an education. That's a pretty good summary of a lot of material. There's feelings, thoughts, ideas and concepts, visuals and visualizations, memories etc. There's also language and attention. Someone's attention can change and vary and they can think with words (which are basically sounds in the head that have a definition or mean something).

I mean, I want to understand what is going on around me and in my head, is that just an understanding of how the mind works or is it just common sense?

It could seem like it is just common sense - i mean, what does someone or anyone need to understand in order to function, if they have just common sense that might be enough I would think. I didn't use to understand cognitive psychology or emotion regulation but I was functioning perfectly fine as a child. Now I understand my complicated emotions and how I feel all the time, I'm more conscious and aware so I don't need to understand anything else. I mean, do I need to understand anything in order to function and perform in society?

It's good to be aware of my feelings and understand what I am experiencing, that's for sure. However maybe I would be better off if I didn't understand all of my feelings.

I mean, what else do I understand, how have I developed. I understand that there are a lot of subjects that could be studied, like for instance I don't understand biology very well, there's a lot of details in that science subject. I think I understand basic math and algebra. What else do I understand. I can speak the english language so I understand that language, I learned that in the first few years of my life (but I also don't have any memories of the first few years of my life).

What else do I need to understand or what else do I understand. There's the entire 73 page article I wrote entitled "The Selected Writings of Mark Pettinelli" There's a link to that article at the beginning of this article of my research notes. That article covers a lot of basic stuff about feelings and thoughts.

I think it's good that I have an understanding of how the mind works, or its mental processes and cognitive psychology.

So I don't know what else to say, this article is supposed to be my research notes, I could have titled it my self notes or diary notes or something. Something like 'self reflections' I mean a decade ago I told my psychiatrist i was doing research and she responded "why do you think it's research". I could have explained that I was just educating myself however I think my perspective sheds light on the subject of cognitive psychology or just psychology.

So like I said, there's a lot of subjects that could be studied, I thought that cognitive psychology was a more practical subject because it is about how the mind works and it's mental processes which is kind of important for someone to function and be aware of what they are thinking and feeling so they can be reflective and intelligent and such.

Well, that's all i can think of to add to my notes now, I'll publish this version so far and see if I can come up with anything to add in the future, however I think that's all I need to know for now, maybe there's stuff I don't know I don't know lol.

Mental Notes b of Mark Pettinelli

- Ok so this is going to be a list of some of my mental notes
- How often do I get out of bed?
- Can I interact with people if I get out of bed, would that be giving them energy or would it be some sort of exchange of energy?
- Am i sucking their energy or is it an exchange of energy, i should make note of that.
- How do i feel when I am in bed, am I suffering because I am bored or what is going on
- I mean, I want to be happy but sometimes it's hard to get out of bed.
- That should be enough for them to continue the academics, maybe they can set up professional forums or something. I want to also continue to improve myself. I don't know how that's going to work exactly, I mean eventually everything will be repeating because there is only a limited number of ideas people can think about or stuff that they could do.
- So how is that going to work exactly?
- Is there a war going on or is it mostly individual competition. That's an excellent question.I mean that's a concept, is there a war is a concept. Or if there is a war is a concept.
- The mind thinks with different concepts as part of its thoughts.
- Well anyway i know that i need to succeed,
- I have a lot of books in my room, so I moved most of them to the bookshelf in the closet. What were the subjects of the books again, cognitive science and cognitive psychology / emotion and cognition / logic and critical thinking. That's what most of the books are about, there's about 30 or 40 books on the bookshelf on those topics.
- I have feelings. I think my feelings are important.
- I mean, I'm trying to analyze how I feel. It's hard to describe. Am I happy or anxious or what? I think I feel happy. But there is also an anxious feeling mixed in. I wish the anxious feeling would leave and I could just be happy and satisfied, but sometimes I need to do stuff in order to make myself more happy.
- There's also a feeling of pain sometimes. I'm trying to analyze it.
- There's an excited fish that's playing with the happy fish. They're happy together.
- They are not just the happy fish and the excited fish though. I mean I'm not completely happy, I think there is some suffering involved. I'm trying to make it so there is just happiness but it's hard i think.
- I think I feel fine, I think I can deal with it.
- I'm trying to describe the suffering, I'm trying to fight it and become happy.
- There is some negative feeling I'm trying to describe. I'm trying to make it go away.
- I'm trying to describe a negative feeling. It's good that I have feelings but not if they are bad feelings. It's kind of a bad feeling. I've had feelings my whole life actually but now i'm trying to become happy in a sort of steady state. I mean I was doing fine in high school but now I don't know what happened.
- So there might be a small war going on but countries are mostly friends with each other. They also need to make progress, as a country and as a planet. I don't know what that means for how I want to make progress for myself, however.
- I want to make progress for myself mostly. I need to think more about that.
- I think I feel better now. I figured out that it's my consciousness that needs some sort of support from my feelings. I mean if you think about it, there is my consciousness that is in my mind right, my consciousness needs support so it can be strong and experience feelings.
- I mean what about my consciousness needs support. I want to be happy, what kinds of feelings support my consciousness. I mean it might be a little bit delusional to think that sexual feelings will give me stimulation in the future, but I can still hope for the best.
- I mean I can masturbate, that could provide my consciousness with some of the stimulation it needs.
- I also listen to music and watch tv, those activities are kind of stimulating.

- What do I need to do to give my consciousness the stimulation that it needs, then I think I will be more happy. That makes sense, if I have distress then the solution is to get my / more stimulation. That makes perfectly good sense.

11/5/2021
- My therapist wanted me to add to the notes, but I don't know what else to write about.
- I like having feelings, that's a development. But I don't know what to do with myself.
- I think I can have fun with my feelings. Like the happy feeling or other feelings. I can go through experiences and develop and care about my feelings. That might be a good objective.

11/6/2021
- Ok so what else do i need to understand. I mean I know that the mind can be an information processor. I learned that by reading some of my cognitive science textbooks. That helps me be more conscious, I would think. I mean as a child I didn't really understand how the mind works, I mean I understood that I had feelings and thoughts. I didn't actually think to myself, 'I have feelings and thoughts' though. I don't know what I was thinking, but I was certainly more like an animal with my logic of how things worked and how my mind worked. Now I understand that I have feelings and thoughts and that the mind is like a computer. That helps me be more conscious and self-aware. I mean in order to function with complicated emotions and thoughts I need to understand what is going on inside my head.
- Um so what else would I need to know, I mean I know that the mind could be like an information processor, or like a computer, and that leads to my increased consciousness about what is going on inside my mind. That's kind of important knowledge. I mean I have about 40 books on my bookshelf about cognitive psychology and related subjects. That is like getting a PhD in cognitive science. I don't need to go to an actual university but I can self-study the books. I've been thinking about those books for a while now.
- So what else do I need to learn? I've already studied the 40 books about cognitive science on my bookshelf. I'm pretty intelligent now, for instance I understand how the mind works with its feelings and thoughts. I've explained that there is a thought process and a feeling process in my selected writings article. People can have thoughts and feelings that occur at the same time, I've already noted that. That's an important observation to make that is kinda obvious but complex at the same time.
- I mean, what else do I need to understand. I understand how the mind works and it's mental processes as discussed by cognitive psychology books. Do I need to understand those topics or that information in order to function? I mean as a child I was functioning perfectly fine and I didn't know anything about the mental processes.
- What are the mental processes again? There's perception, memory, attention, thinking, feeling, deciding, reasoning and emotion. I saw that imagination was also listed as a mental process. I would think that consciousness is also like a mental process. I mean how conscious someone is constantly changes and information goes through the consciousness all the time.
- I mean, I understand those mental processes, that is mostly what cognitive psychology talks about. It's actually pretty basic if you think about it. I mean what is there to thinking and feeling anyway? I already wrote my selected writing article / book. That book was about feelings and thoughts and described some of their properties, like the difference between feelings and emotions.
- I pointed out that the difference between feelings and emotions was that feelings are more simple and clear, like how touch or the senses or sensory stimulation is more simple and clear. However there doesn't need to be something physical in order for it to be a feeling, because you can feel your emotions also. The emotions are supposed to be deeper and more complicated however. It doesn't mean that they are always stronger, however. For instance a simple physical feeling can be strong and an emotion like love can also be strong.
- Language could also be a mental process. However, that would fall under the category of the 'thought' mental process. So would deciding and reasoning are also types of thoughts.
- How is imagination considered to be a mental process? Imagination is a type of thought, so that would also be a type of thought. People think with their imagination and their words or their language.Then there are the other mental processes of memory, attention, emotion and perception.
- Is consciousness like thought then, or is consciousness just the sum total of our mental processes? Consciousness could be everything, or an awareness of everything that is going on in our minds.
- Um so what else am I supposed to write. I mean I know and understand how my mind works. It feels and experiences feelings and thoughts all of the time. That's a pretty simple process. CBT, or cognitive behavioral therapy, is about tracking how feelings lead to thoughts and how those lead to actions, or any of

those occurring in any order actually.

- So um, what else do I need to write, maybe this article of mental notes is long enough. My selected writings article is 100 pages. That's a lot of pages, what do I talk about in that article? I think I mention thoughts and feelings, the difference between feelings and emotions, and the mental processes. The mental processes are pretty simple actually. I mean attention, memory, thought, emotion and perception are all pretty simple in terms of how they work in the mind.
- So what are all of the possible mental processes again? - There's emotion, attention, memory, thinking, deciding and reasoning, imagination, language, perception and I also listed consciousness (though i haven't seen anyone else list that as a mental process).
- I think I feel happy now, it's been a long struggle. I was wondering why I would be in pain after high school, but in high school I was doing a lot of work actually. I had to substitute the work with anxiety, and now I am happy and balanced within my own mind.
- I mean, today I just had some anxiety. I don't know what else to say about this.
- I feel happy right now, so that's a good thing. But I mean, in order to get to this point i had to do a lot of work and research.
- Um so what else am I supposed to research now, i can do an overview or summary of my research. I learned about the mental processes from the cognitive psychology books that I already mentioned. I also learned from some of the cognitive science books about how the mind is like a computer. That's important to understand because it helps me understand what my mind is doing and how it is functioning.
- I mean, what could my mind be doing at any one time, that's kind of an interesting question. It could be thinking about stuff or feeling things. It could also be doing things and paying attention to things, so that's three of the mental processes right there, thinking, feeling and attention. It could also be looking at things, that's perception, and there is my memory.
- Um so what do I need to learn again? I just looked at a cognitive psychology textbook, there were a lot of things in it. It was mostly stuff about the mental processes. I think it had stuff about **memory and learning and language**. What else did it have in it? I'll look at the table of contents again. It also has stuff about **knowledge and mental representations**, and also **judgement, reasoning and choice**. This was the Oxford Handbook of Cognitive Psychology. **Thinking, problem solving and creativity. Attention and awareness. Text and language. Emotion and memory, discourse comprehension**. All this was from the table of contents. **The nature of mental concepts, and models of categorization**. All that's in that cognitive psychology book.
- There's also **self knowledge**, but i don[t really know what that is. "It refers to the beliefs people hold about themselves".. So that is all self-knowledge is. And there's **automaticity and insight**.

11/9/2021

- My therapist is probably wondering if she's reading this if this is about my mental notes or a review of the research i am doing. The truth is it's both and one at the same time. I consider my research to be important and about the things that help me think, so my research is my mental notes. Someone could research something that doesn't help them think and that is separate from their thoughts. I wanted my research to be practical.
- I thought a long time ago to only isolate the important information.so I thought that psychology and especially cognitive psychology would be more important because it could help me think. Like even cognitive science helps me think because it's useful to know that the mind thinks and processes information like a computer.
- Cognitive science and cognitive psychology are related and similar fields of study. They're also related to the general psychology subject / topic also.

11/13/2021

- So um, there is the academics. That is just figuring out all the information though. How could someone figure out all of the information? There are tons of different concepts to think about and that exist. What concepts do I need to understand in order to function and survive? I understand how I think and I understand that I also have feelings. I want to feel happy and be stimulated by stuff.

- So um, what else is there to consider in this analysis. I know that I have feelings and thoughts, and that they interact. Um so what else is there anyway. I mean I know that I think about stuff and that I have feelings. I don't like it when people hurt my feelings. There are different kinds of stimulation like physical pain and mental pain, that's important to point out, I think.

- So does that mean that I know everything that I need to know? Why didn't I realize that I had feelings before was I stupid or something? So now I don't know what to do with myself, I have feelings and want to be happy, it isn't really a big deal.

- I think I can function just fine anyway. I mean I know that I can feel things and think about things. I think I'm pretty happy actually. There's some physical pain that I'm in but I see doctors for that.

- I think I'm doing fine. I have a visual input and other senses that I can feel like taste, touch, sight, sound and smell.

- Um so I think that pretty much covers everything, I don't know if I need to add anymore notes.

- So, people can think with different concepts. What kind of concepts could someone be thinking about? There are a lot of concepts that someone could be thinking about. Everything that someone thinks is basically a concept. What kinds of things do I think about, that's the question?

- So anything that someone thinks is basically a concept. I remember wondering how to define what a concept is. It is basically any idea that someone could be thinking about.

- That's really interesting, I mean that's basically figuring out everything that someone could think about, that's kind of important. A long time ago I thought that if someone kept track of all the thoughts in their head then they could not be crazy because all of their thoughts were logical, however that analysis was missing the definition of a concept. I mean, it wasn't a very elaborate description of 'all of someones thoughts' because in order to keep track of everything someone thinks i had to learn a lot more about cognitive science.

- That was just a simple idea," all of someone's thoughts". I mean that analysis is missing a lot, like what is considered a thought?
- That's an excellent question, I mean there are different concepts that someone can think with, and different thoughts that they could have, some thoughts are verbal while other thoughts are non-verbal. I could keep track of all my thoughts and all of the concepts that I think with then.

- So once again, I can keep track of all of my thoughts, I wasn't crazy before but I didn't understand some concepts, it was a little bit crazy but it was mostly me just being stupid and not understanding everything or understanding some of the important concepts.I mean, as a child I was thinking things and feeling things in high school. Now I still think about things and feel things only I'm a lot more intelligent.

11/14/2021
- So i think i'm done with my article, this stuff that i'm adding to my notes page is going to only be available on my notes page.The selected writings of Mark Pettinelli pdf has almost all of my analysis, and is available on google scholar
- So um what am i doing now.i have feelings and thoughts, i know that. Why didn't I understand that before. I mean I did understand that before but I didn't think to myself 'that's a feeling and that's a thought'. I mean, I had feelings and thoughts obviously but didn't really understand that. I guess I understood that. Well now i still have feelings and thoughts lol. I mean I have feelings and thoughts.
- I don't like it when people hurt my feelings, can people please stop trying to hurt my feelings. I'm trying to be happy here.
- So I have feelings that can be hurt. Why didn't I realize that before.
- Um so what else am I supposed to research here. I already understand that I have feelings and that I have thoughts that go along with those feelings.

11/15/2021

- So I don't know what else to add to my notes. If I can think clearly then I don't know what else I would need to accomplish here. I can think clearly right, what else is there to this.
- I can think clearly and have emotions and feelings and stuff, that's a pretty good accomplishment I think.

11/16/2021
- So that is a good analysis. I just need to continue with my life then and keep track of my feelings and thoughts. That seems pretty simple anyway.
- What does that mean though, i mean when i have a feeling or when I have a thought does that mean i know what I am feeling and thinking all of the time?
- So i said before that intellectual stimulation was important, actually i just said stimulation could help me be less bored and in less suffering.
- Now that I think about my history it's pretty clear that I've always been working or getting intellectual or physical stimulation through exercise.
- So maybe to solve my problem of suffering I just need to do things that give me or my consciousness stimulation.
- I mean, I remember reading new books in my science fiction / fantasy novels when they came out, that was new stimulation. I also remember doing cognitive science research for the past few years, that also helped me get a lot of intellectual stimulation.
- I'm trying to think here, how could I continue the stimulation. There is physical stimulation and intellectual stimulation. That's two different types of stimulation. I know that's one reason some people play video games, those are kind of fun.
- So that's why I'm adding to these notes, because it helps with the intellectual stimulation. It also helps me organize my thoughts and feelings, which is also important.
- I mean, I get physical stimulation from exercise or other sensations like eating food or drinking water. These kinds of stimulation are important for me. It's like my consciousness needs them in order to live.
- So the question is, what else do I need to do in order to stay happy. I mean I think I've always needed stimulation but just wasn't aware of it that much.
- Yes, light up, I have feelings, I can feel them.
- That sounded a little bit crazy now that I think about it.
- I mean just saying, "I can feel it" sounds a little bit crazy, it's not crazy though it's a perfectly rational statement. I mean when I can feel my feelings it's a powerful moment so it makes sense to say "I can feel it now'.
- I can feel it, I can feel it.
- Like I said before, that sounds a little bit crazy. However it's a perfectly rational statement, I mean, when you are in touch with your feelings then you can feel them directly and intimately.

11/17/2021
- What does that mean, to be 'in touch' with a feeling? I mean when you feel something then it is a feeling, it can feel different ways and such.
- Um, so I have feelings.
- That is kind of an obvious statement, 'I have feelings'. I mean, anyone who is alive has feelings. Everyone also thinks about stuff. Even animals think about things and have thoughts.
- So I have feelings, what else can I add to that analysis. That conclusion actually took me a long time to figure out. I know it is kind of an obvious analysis that feelings exist, however it took a long time for me to understand. (and a lot of pain).
- So what else can I add to that analysis? I can keep track of my feelings and observe when they come and go.

11/19/2021
- So um, what else can i talk about, i've already covered a lot of material about feelings and thoughts.

11/20/2021
- So what else is there? I mean I have a visual, a steady visual that gives me feedback, blind people must focus on the other senses i would think.Or i think that's what i would do if i was blind. My visual input gives me a lot of feedback.
- I also have other senses that are important. This may seem obvious but I haven't thought about it this way before.
- What are my other senses, these senses keep me stimulated and stimulation keeps me happy and not bored.

So I can think clearly even though I have feelings.

11/26/2021
- Ok so i'm trying to deal with my feelings. I don't know what else I'm supposed to write about my feelings. I thought I was suffering, but my feelings can be pretty complicated.
- Now I'm not sure what to write. I feel better but want to make progress. I don't know how that's going to happen.

11/27/2021
- Ok so i'm adding to my mental notes document on google docs. I added the first 8 pages to my selected writings article. Those pages are the first 8 pages of this document but now I'm still going to continue to write about stuff.
- I don't know what to say. I know I have feelings and want to be happy. Could people please stop trying to hurt my feelings. I'm trying to be happy here. I mean I don't want to suffer.
- Maybe if my therapist is reading this she'll realize that I'm suffering and that I need more help. I don't know if that's just because life is hard and it's something everyone has to deal with.
- I mean maybe that's just real life, that there is suffering, everyone can't be babied.. I still would like some more help though I mean I really feel like I am suffering here.
- I mean I don't know what to write at this point. I said that I would like to be happier but I might be stuck in my current situation.
- So I don't know what to say. I'm kind of struggling here and I don't know what to do.
- It's not that bad I think.
- I guess I'm ok. I don't know what I should do with myself though. I'm kind of bored here.That's why i'm adding to these notes. What else am I supposed to say about how I am feeling then?
- I mean I want to keep busy but don't know what to do.
- I don't know what else I can write. I already talked about how there are feelings and thoughts. A feeling can lead to a thought, or occur at the same time as a thought.
- I mean, I already wrote that there are feelings and thoughts, there is also actions or behaviors, those three can lead to each other or occur in any order.
- That's actually what cognitive behavioral therapy is about, tracking how your thoughts, feelings and actions interact.
- CBT (cognitive behavioral therapy) isn't just about tracking one's feelings, thoughts and emotions but it's also about trying to change your thoughts so your emotions and behaviors can improve.
- Maybe if i had more help I wouldn't have to struggle so much by myself, I think i can deal with it though.
- Well good news, I guess I feel fine now, my only problem is boredom.
- Being bored isn't a big problem actually. I mean, I can deal with that.

11/28/2021
- I mean, I don't want to be a baby asking for help because I can't handle it in the real world. I just have to deal with the boredom and some of the suffering it causes, I think I can handle that.
- What else do I need to research? I understand that I have feelings and thoughts and that cognitive behavioral therapy is about tracking your feelings, thoughts and behaviors and seeing how you can change our thoughts in order to change your behaviors or influence your emotions.
- That's pretty important to understand, that by changing your thoughts you can influence your emotions or behaviors, I think that is what cognitive behavioral therapy is about.
- That's actually a lot to understand. I mean, how is someone supposed to keep track of their thoughts and how they lead to their emotions and behaviors?
- I think that is what cognitive behavioral therapy is about.that's pretty important, keeping track of your thoughts and making sure they are helping you. The idea behind the therapy is that you can change your thoughts so they will be more realistic and helpful.
- That paused to make me think, I thought that having delusional thoughts would be more helpful since they would be positive. I read that CBT (cognitive behavioral therapy) thought realistic thoughts would be more beneficial.
- I guess that makes sense, realistic thoughts could be more helpful, why would someone have negative thoughts that are unrealistic, I don't know.
- I didn't really think my thoughts had that big of an impact on my emotions anyway.
- So I don't know if I'm done with my research here, I already understand that thoughts can influence emotions and how you think in general. And that can also obviously influence your behavior. That is what cognitive behavioral therapy is about.

- I also understand that there are mental illnesses like schizophrenia and autism.
- I can deal with it. I think the problem is I spend all day in bed. It's kind of boring but I don't really have anything else to do.
- I don't know why I'm crying and complaining like a baby. It isn't really that hard to deal with my boredom and suffering on my own. I would like more help but I don't know how else I could get help. I mean they have been somewhat helping me for a long time now.
- I think I can deal with it. I mean calling the ambulance is only for emergencies.

11/29/2021
- Ok so i'm trying to figure this out. As a child I did not understand complicated concepts. I was pretty stupid actually. Now I understand a lot more than I did as a child.
- I mean as a child I guess I knew that I had feelings and thoughts but didn't really understand how my feelings and thoughts worked.
- Now I understand that thoughts can influence feelings and feelings can influence thoughts. It took me a long time to figure that out, I mean, why would a thought influence a feeling? And how could a feeling influence a thought?
- Those are interesting questions if you think about it. But our thoughts do influence our feelings and our feelings do influence our thoughts.
- For instance, there can also be multiple emotions occurring, say someone is experiencing a sad emotion but they want to mask it with a happy emotion, would it be possible to try to think happy thoughts in order to become happy and cover up the sad emotion?
- That's an excellent question, I mean, how can thought influence emotion at all anyway? I mean think about what you have to think about and if it can influence what you are feeling. Feelings can influence thoughts but the person ultimately decides what thoughts they want to think, but not necessarily what feelings they want to feel.

11/30/2021
- So I don't know what else I have to say, I've already said that I have feelings that I can feel.
- If I can feel feelings, and experience thoughts, then what else is there to explain?
- Thoughts can influence feelings I think, that is the tenet behind cognitive behavioral therapy. But how does that occur/ i mean like what are the details.
- I'll try to keep track of my thoughts and see if or how they influence my feelings.
- Ok so I have feelings, I think I already said that. The next question is, what are those feelings, and how exactly do they feel?

12/2/2021
- Ok so i am trying to deal with some of the suffering. I'm not having an emergency so that means I'll have to stay in my room to try to deal with it.
- I'll discuss it with my therapist lol. I don't know how complicated these feelings are.

12/23/2021
I don't know how I'm feeling. Trying to pass the time I think. So maybe I'm struggling to find activities and do stuff but I get by. Sometimes the activity I find keeps me happy when I'm active. I don't know how it works, it's like I need mental stimuli. As a kid I would just play a video game for an hour or something.Or read a book or do homework. Then in my 20s I had anxiety and would walk around. Now I stay in bed and shuffle activities like watching TV, listening to music, trying to find stimulation.

12/24/2021
So um I don't know what to say, maybe I should just continue to try and get mental stimulation. Doing different activities and such.

How could ideas guide our thinking? Thinking doesn't need ideas to guide it. I guess it needs ideas, i mean a basic understanding of life is necessary to function in life.

I mean what is the difference between philosophy and psychology? Psychology studies human behavior and how the mind works, while philosophy is more about analysis of human behavior and thinking. Philosophy asks more general questions I guess. They are both about human behavior, however.

Um so what is the difference between psychology and philosophy? Philosophy is about reason and asking general questions, while psychology is about how people behave and function. Philosophy is about analysis.

Philosophy asks questions like, what is truth, or how do people think? Psychology also studies human thought, however. That's why I started studying psychology, that forms a more accurate picture of how the mind works, while philosophy is just about general questions about life.

I mean, both philosophy and psychology are the study of life, but what is necessary to analyze in order to figure out 'life'? Philosophy is about truth and analysis. What else do I need to understand? I understand how to think, I understand everything actually. I function perfectly fine, what else do I need to understand?

I guess it boils down to how conscious I am about stuff, or how conscious I am in general. There's a difference between how conscious I am about objects and my current consciousness, and my general consciousness, or what I am conscious of in general.

Now I'm reading a philosophy book. So what is an idea? What is the truth? I would think that truth is something that is accurate as a piece of information. Ideas are just concepts in our head that can be true or false, we might not know if they are true or false.

I mean, truth can be any idea that we have. An idea is a concept in your head, it might or might not be true or accurate. It depends on the idea in your head i suppose, what that idea is about.

That's kind of an important point, you could think something but it might not be true.

I'm trying to figure this out, I thought I had everything figured out, like how the mind works or cognitive science. I mean I thought I knew everything I needed to know about cognitive science and cognitive psychology and how the mind works but apparently I didn't.

What else do I need to understand about cognitive science or how the mind works then? That's an interesting question lol. I don't know what else I would need to know, I mean I know about concepts in the mind, or different ideas that someone could be aware of. There is also truth, like someone could be thinking about an idea but might not know if that idea or concept is accurate, or what the truth is.

I mean, what else is in the philosophy book, what is truth? Or what is knowledge? Truth is simple, that's just what the truth is, or how accurate something is. While knowledge is also simple, it's just things learned or understood that you hold in your mind, that is all knowledge is.

So um, what do I know? I've read a couple of epistemology books, epistemology is the theory of knowledge, which talks about how knowledge is learned and remembered and understood. Or maybe cognitive psychology talks about how it's learned and remembered but epistemology or philosophy talks about how it is understood and the nature of knowledge.

So what is everything that I know? I have a high school education that taught me basic math and sciences, like algebra, chemistry, physics and so on. I also took a few college courses and self-studied psychology and cognitive psychology after high school.

I figured out the difference between a feeling and an emotion, emotions are deep and intellectual and powerful, while feelings are more simple and direct and are things we can 'feel', that is why they are called feelings.

What else have I learned.I mean i already said that I had a high school education. I understand how to think clearly, like I understand that there is a thought process and a feeling process, people have a steady stream of feelings at the same time they could have a steady stream of thoughts. The thoughts could involve thinking about various different concepts and ideas, while the feelings could involve feeling different things.

Um so is that everything that I know? The high school education was pretty basic but my self studies after high school got more complicated because I started reading cognitive psychology textbooks. I mean, what else do I know?

What is there to know about cognitive psychology? I've memorized the mental processes. They are emotion, thought, problem solving, decision making, judgment, reasoning, choice, memory, learning, language, mental representations, knowledge, concepts, categories, attention and awareness, creativity, automaticity, insight and self-knowledge.

There's also the main emotions, the main emotions are happy, sad, anger, fear, surprise and disgust. The secondary emotions like love and hate are also powerful but don't have physiological facial expressions. Those emotions are important and occur first for a few seconds, then some of the secondary emotions follow.

Um so what else do I know, what have i learned. From a philosophy book I learned that there is the truth, and also knowledge that can be false or accurate. There is also reality and how reality is understood or processed by the mind. Then there's decision making, I mean how are decisions made? What is the thought process behind the decisions people make?

Maybe it's simple anyway I don't know. I've looked at a couple of epistemology books about knowledge, which makes me think about what I understand and how I learned that, and what it means for my mind.

So what else do I know? I don't think I know much else lol.

So what is everything I know? I studied consciousness and emotion. There's a difference between feelings and emotions, for instance. Some feelings are deeper and more complicated, any strong feeling is an emotion. That is one definition for emotion.

So I know everything, I understand knowledge and what I know and have learned at this point, and I understand consciousness and how I think and understand. What have I learned at this point in my life? I said I had a basic education in high school. I also know stuff I learned after high school from my self studies or from the few college courses I took.

I understand what appraisal theory is, that is when someone makes an assessment of what caused their emotions and what the resulting emotions are.

So what else do I need to know? I've looked at the consciousness book, the philosophy book, the psychology book and the theory of knowledge books. I guess that covers most of what I would need to know about life.

So what do I need to make progress about? I'm functioning perfectly fine and I have feelings. I had to say that. I mean, I can function and all my research worked out because I can think logically now and I have feelings.

So I can think clearly and i've reached a much higher level with my emotions. That seems like an accomplishment, I had to do a lot of research in cognitive science.

1/10/2022

So um i'm trying to do an analysis of my feelings. It's kind of complicated.

I'm trying to do an analysis of my feelings, its sort of complicated. I mean, what am i feeling right now? How am I supposed to figure that out? That's an excellent question. I mean what is going on.

I already said that I have feelings and can function perfectly fine. I already said that, I mean, if I have a high level of feeling and can think logically and function then I am doing pretty good right?

1/21/2022

Ok so I'm trying to analyze my feelings. I'm trying to figure it out. It might be complicated, but maybe it is simple. I'm still trying to figure it out. I think it is simple, I mean, feelings are pretty simple. I'm trying to figure out how feelings work or function in the mind.

1/28/2022

Ok so I'm trying to figure this out. Academics can be pretty complicated, however it seems like I know everything I need to know. I mean I know about the mental processes. They are emotion, thinking, problem solving, memory, learning, language, knowledge, mental representations, concepts, mental categories, decision making, deciding, reasoning, choice, automaticity, insight, self-knowledge, creativity, attention, awareness. Those mental processes are really important, it's also important to understand them. I understand how the mind works because I understand those mental processes.

So what else do I need to understand? I understand that some feelings can be more powerful or intellectual, that is when they might be like emotions, because one definition of emotion is 'any strong feeling'. I don't know if a primary emotion comes first and occurs for a few seconds before a secondary emotion follows. I mean, feelings can be pretty complicated, is the feeling complicated first and then becomes simple later? It has been said that feelings are the result of emotions, so that means that first emotions occur and then a simple or secondary feeling follows after.

Um so if i understand that stuff about feelings and thoughts and mental processes then what else would I need to understand in order to function. I've looked at some logic textbooks so I can think clearly.

1/31/2022

Ok so i'm trying to figure out how I got to this point. I mean, I can think clearly and stuff right, the only question is how did I get here? What did I need to analyze? I figured out that cognitive science would call that an idea that the person is thinking about, an idea or a concept that the person is thinking about.

So people think with a stream of thought that involves thinking about different or various concepts. In order to think clearly the person would have to have a good understanding of clear concepts, or what clear concepts are like. That way the stream of thoughts that they have could have clear concepts, and the person would know that. So um, they know what a concept is. They know how to think about information and think clearly, what else would they need to know?

4/4/2022

So what else do I need to figure out. I think I have a pretty good understanding of everything. I did a lot of research and taught people a lot of stuff. They were educated so by me teaching them I got their response as an academic. That taught me their perspective of the information I was figuring out.

4/6/2020

So there is a relationship between emotion and cognition. Cognition is thought or thinking while emotion just involves feelings. So people can either feel things or think about things. Thoughts can be about things or thoughts can direct actions. A thought that directs an action is just doing physical stuff that you can control, or is under your control. That is the difference between voluntary and involuntary movements, voluntary movements are under your control so you must use thoughts or thinking to control them.

That makes me wonder, what is the difference between thoughts and thinking? Thinking could use words and sentences while other thoughts could be non-verbal. A thought does not have to use words. People can think things and not use words, though words could help other thoughts.

That is how people control their actions, they use thoughts to control their actions or behavior, sometimes the thoughts are sentences while other times they do not use words at all.

So I did a lot of research. What did I learn again. I'm really smart now, I understand cognitive science. It was more complicated than I initially thought. I can try to briefly describe it. There is cognitive load, which is the processing your mind does. Vision creates a cognitive load on your mind. That's like asking how many megabytes does vision cause your mind to process. Vision uses a cognitive load on your mind. The other senses are also processed by your mind. Is that all there is to how the mind works? I can just describe how the mind works by comparing it to how a computer works, the mind is like a computer that way.

An Assessment of the Nature of Feeling and Thought

By
Mark Pettinelli

When we have a feeling in the mind, what is the nature of that feeling? Does it start at some point, and end at another point? Are we aware when the feeling starts and stops also? I guess the feeling could start at any second and end at any other second. What else is there to notice about that feeling?

The feeling could also be conscious or unconscious. A conscious feeling would be more clear to you, while an unconscious feeling you might not notice as easily. The question is, how much does the person care about that feeling? Caring about a feeling is important, the person could make an appraisal, or an assessment of their emotions.

An appraisal is when a person makes an assessment of their emotional state. Or they make an assessment of what their emotions are and what caused those emotions. The appraisal is done with thoughts and is cognitive, while it's about their emotions.

That is what an appraisal of emotion is, when someone makes an assessment of what caused their emotions and what the resulting emotions are. For instance I might guess what I am feeling and what caused those feelings. That's all an appraisal is, it's an assessment of your emotions and what might have caused them.

When humans have an emotion, what is the nature of that emotion? Also, is the person aware that the emotion is occurring? I said that they could make an assessment of what they are feeling, if they are having an emotion or feeling, and when that feeling starts and stops.

There is also a difference between emotions and feelings. For instance a feeling could be more direct and tangible, while an emotion could be stronger but might be more distant, or you might not be as in touch with the emotion as you are with the feeling. However, if the emotion is stronger, wouldn't you be more in touch with it?

I mean, is feeling just about how strong the feeling is, and emotions are just stronger feelings? Or can a feeling be more clear to you at one point, and less clear at another? Maybe feelings are more clear feelings that you are more aware of, and emotions are deeper. Feelings could be very strong then, and emotions could be more distant.

I mean, the question is, how do feelings feel in the mind? I said that a feeling could be clear to the person, and an emotion could be less clear or dulled down, but stronger. Also, emotions could be more like thoughts, or more intellectual, while feelings could be more like sensations, and more direct. That is why they are called feelings after all, because you can "feel" them.

So the question is, once again, how do feelings feel in the mind? Does a feeling start at one point, and end at another second or point? And is the person aware that this is happening?

I mean is a feeling conscious to the person or is the feeling more unconscious?

That is basically how the mind works, either there are feelings or thoughts, what else could be going on in the mind that a person should be aware of anyway? I mean either they are having a feeling or a thought.

So once again, what then is the difference between feelings and emotions. Or I guess the point is to figure out what feelings feel like in the mind. Is a feeling something that you are in touch with, or is a feeling something that you are less in touch with and it could be more unconscious. I guess the point is how does that feeling feel. It could start at one second and end at another second, that's a pretty clear description of how a feeling feels. But is feeling that simple? I mean is a feeling just something that you feel that starts at one second and ends at another second? Or is a feeling more complicated than that. I mean, could a person be having multiple feelings that they could be more or less conscious of or aware of?

I mean, what am I feeling right now, how complicated is that? How complicated are my feelings right now, that is an interesting question. Are my feelings clear, or are they more unconscious, or are they intellectual, or are they stupid?

I guess when I describe it that way feelings can be pretty simple, I mean, it's mostly just that a feeling starts at one second and ends at some other point in time. There could also be multiple feelings occurring at once, that seems pretty simple.

So what else do I need to add about how feelings feel. I mean, how am I supposed to describe how I am feeling right now. I feel happy I guess, but what else is there to that feeling. I mean, when I feel bad is it just a bad feeling, or what else is going on.

Feelings are pretty simple then, I mean there isn't really very much going on with feelings, they just start at one time and then end at some point later on, however long that feeling lasts I suppose.

I mean, in the mind there are feelings and thoughts, both of which are experiences.

I mean, I have feelings and thoughts, that is kind of an obvious statement, everyone has feelings and thoughts.

The question is, am I aware that those feelings are occurring? I mean, I could not notice all of the feelings I am having, if i'm experiencing multiple feelings anyway.

Does it matter if I do an appraisal and make an assessment of my feelings? If I care about the feeling then it might influence how aware I am about the feeling. It might also change the strength of the feeling.

How is that possible? Why would thinking about a feeling change the strength of the feeling? It seems to make sense, I mean thinking about your own feelings creates the feelings by itself. Cognition or thinking is extremely powerful.

How then does that work, when you have a feeling, the feeling could be caused by something real or some external source, or you could make the feeling yourself and it could be something under your control.

How could thinking about a feeling change the feeling? How would that work exactly. I mean, obviously thought is important, when you think about something, then that could be what you are feeling. What would be an example of that. Physical feelings don't seem like they would be under your control, however. Is life mostly just physical feelings then? There are non-physical feelings too, however. What are examples of physical feelings and non-physical feelings then. If I feel scared that could be an intellectual feeling. Other feelings could be happy, excited, depressed or sad. Those feelings don't seem like they could be influenced by just thinking. I mean, people are mostly not in control of what they are feeling. Doing actions and experiencing things could cause feelings that the person is not in control of, however they could think about those feelings. I already said that they can make appraisals of feelings, which are assessments of the nature of the feelings and what might have caused those feelings.

So what is an example of a happy feeling, there is also stimulation, or how much power your mind has. Stimulation is interesting, for instance I sometimes am bored and that causes anxiety or pain, then I usually need to do something to occupy myself. So stimulation is different from feelings, for instance the mind could be fine with just stimulation and not even experiencing any feelings at all. Or is feeling a combination of feeling and stimulation, I mean the stimulation feels like something. Could stimulation feel happy then, since it could be making the person less bored? That makes a lot of sense, I should try to get more stimulation then so I can feel more happy. There is also thought power, that is kind of like asking how many megabytes your visual of the world is, the steady visual that seeing brings must have a cognitive load on your mind that provides stimulation just from vision, there's also the other senses that provide input and stimulation.

So what then is the difference between feelings and emotions?

Feelings are more conscious right, I mean both feelings and emotions are felt, and they feel like something, but what then is the difference between them? I guess the question is how do feelings feel in the mind. I said that feelings could be either conscious or unconscious, or stupid or intellectual. Are feelings more like sensations that are more direct and conscious and some of them could be more stupid than an emotion.

So is emotion just strong feelings? Or is emotion more intellectual than feelings. I'm trying to describe the difference between feelings and emotions. Or i'm just trying to describe how feelings feel in the mind. Feelings can feel stupid if they are like physical sensations right. Emotions could be more powerful then but they might be more powerful in an intellectual way

Um so i'm getting a little bit confused here, i'm trying to describe how feelings feel in the mind right. I mean, how complicated is that? A feeling can feel stupid or intellectual, or a feeling could be something that is direct or indirect. If the feeling is stupid it might be more direct like the sensations. If a feeling is indirect then it could be intellectual. Um so what does that mean for how feelings feel in the mind then. This is getting a little bit complicated. A feeling could be more or less conscious, or it could be stupid or intellectual. So it could be conscious and stupid, or conscious and intellectual, or it could be unconscious and stupid or intellectual. That is kind of interesting. So once again, how do feelings feel in the mind? I'm trying to describe all of the ways a feeling can be experienced. Like what if I tried to describe how I am feeling right now, how could I do that. I feel happy I guess and I also have physical sensations. I am in my bedroom and I can experience the 5 different sensations of taste, touch, sight, sound and smell. I'm always experiencing those sensations and I'm always thinking about things. I don't really feel very much I guess. Maybe I just don't have a lot of emotions compared to other people. Emotions are strong, while feelings can be weak or strong. If emotions are unconscious, however, then how could they be strong? If I feel happiness then is it unconscious and strong? It is strong if I can feel it, then it would be a strong feeling and not an emotion. When the happiness emotion becomes conscious it becomes a strong feeling. Emotion is either conscious or unconscious, while feelings are always conscious because you can feel them.

So what am I feeling now. I feel happy, that is both an emotion and a feeling because it is unconscious as an emotion, and conscious as a feeling. Or I could say that it is a conscious feeling and an unconscious emotion. When I think about the happiness it becomes more conscious and more of something I can really feel.

So what am I feeling right now, I can start with that analysis. I mean I'm trying to describe the way feelings feel in the mind. I feel happy I guess. I don't really have very many feelings I think. I also have physical sensations that make me happy. I can feel the bed that I am in for instance. There is also my breathing that I can feel. I was taught to focus on my breathing as a coping mechanism for my anxiety. I also learned that by myself by practicing the suggestion to focus on my breath or do deep breathing exercises. So I don't have very many emotions or feelings then. I mean sometimes I get happy when I interact with people, that's kind of important. Those are feelings. When is a feeling unconscious then? I

Would say that feelings are either conscious or unconscious. The goal is to have strong, conscious feelings I would think. I said that an emotion could be unconscious or conscious, while feelings are always conscious. Emotions and feelings can also feel either stupid or intellectual. The physical feelings or sensations are usually more stupid than intellectual feelings or emotions.

Um so how am I supposed to describe how I am feeling right now then? I don't think that feelings are very complicated if you think about them that way. I mean, I don't really have very many feelings to begin with. Maybe other people have more complicated or stronger feelings than I do, I don't really know.

I think i've simplified how feelings feel then. I mean, I am a pretty simple person, my feelings aren't very complicated. My thoughts aren't very complicated with er I would say. I mean, when I have a feeling it is either conscious or unconscious, strong or weak, or stupid or intellectual.

That is a pretty simple explanation of how feelings feel in the mind. I think I've simplified it. But that is a good way to start analyzing your feelings I would think. I start with a simple mind that is clear and not feeling very much, then slowly build up my analysis and awareness of my feelings (also the descriptions of them).

Mental Notes 2 of Mark Pettinelli

What is there to know about cognitive psychology? I've memorized the mental processes. They are emotion, thought, problem solving, decision making, judgment, reasoning, choice, memory, learning, language, mental representations, knowledge, concepts, categories, attention and awareness, creativity, perception, automaticity, insight and self-knowledge.

So what else do I need to know or learn? I mean I think I know everything that I need to understand. There could be more things that I might need to learn, however. I don't really know, I feel like I understand everything that I need to understand.

I don't know if I need to know anything else, I mean I sort of already understand everything I need to know about how the mind works. I know what all the mental processes are, there's about 20 of them that I already listed.

That makes me wonder, what is the difference between thoughts and thinking? Thinking could use words and sentences while other thoughts could be non-verbal. A thought does not have to use words. People can think things and not use words, though words could help other thoughts.

That is how people control their actions, they use thoughts to control their actions or behavior, sometimes the thoughts are sentences while other times they do not use words at all.

So I did a lot of research. What did I learn again? I'm really smart now, I understand cognitive science. It was more complicated than I initially thought. I can try to briefly describe it. There is cognitive load, which is the processing your mind does. Vision creates a cognitive load on your mind. That's like asking how many megabytes does vision cause your mind to process. Vision uses a cognitive load on your mind. The other senses are also processed by your mind. Is that all there is to how the mind works? I can just describe how the mind works by comparing it to how a computer works, the mind is like a computer that way.

Um so I don't know what else I would have to understand. I already understand a lot of stuff. I know what the mental processes are and basic stuff about academics and life. I mean I have a high school education. I understand math and algebra. I know basic things about chemistry and physics. I also can speak a little bit of Spanish as a foreign language. I learned all of that stuff in high school.

After high school I started to study psychology and cognitive science. I spent a lot of time thinking about how the mind works.

Um so what else do I know? I have the high school education I told you about. I learned stuff after high school because I was meeting with therapists who know stuff about psychology, feelings and even cognitive science. That made me study how the mind works, my therapists knew stuff about that.

Um so what is everything that I know? That's a good question. I already mentioned what I learned in high school. Then I learned stuff about cognitive science and how the mind works after high school. Also other stuff about psychology, or I guess cognitive science is in the same category as psychology.

So what did I learn about psychology? I already pointed out about the mental processes the mind has. There is also other stuff like logic and clear thinking. There's also the interaction between emotion and cognition. Thinking and feeling interact in the mind. How does that happen exactly?

Thoughts can influence feelings, and feelings can influence thoughts also. That is pretty simple actually. It's important to know, however. FOr instance people can control or influence their feelings and emotions with their thinking and thoughts. Cognition is the person's thinking and feelings and emotions are what the person is feeling. Maybe there's stuff about logical thinking and reasoning that I can learn. There's also stuff about feelings and consciousness that I can learn from those 5 different books by Damasio. I also have a couple books on the world's greatest speeches.

So what about logic and clear thinking would I need to learn? There doesn't seem to be very much involved with clear thinking, I mean it seems kind of obvious how to think clearly, I don't know if I need to point out anything. Maybe I need to point out stuff about clear thinking, on the other hand, I've always been a clear thinker even as a child. Having more emotions now shouldn't interfere with my thinking, I mean I can still think clearly even though I have strong emotions.

I mean, I've been clear thinking all the many years of my life, it's not like thinking is new to me, I've been doing it for a long time now lol.

I mean, I'm not stupid, I know how to think clearly without any errors or misunderstandings.

I think logically and intelligently, I don't need to understand anything else.

So what pieces of knowledge would I also need to know or understand. I already pointed out that I understand the mental processes.

Ok so I'm trying to do an account of what's happened and what I want to achieve with my life. I'm bored most of the time, but I don't know if there is a solution to that. I mean interacting with people is kind of difficult, maybe I can work on that so I could interact with other people more as an activity. That seems like a good idea.

I don't know how I'm going to do that exactly. I can think clearly and know how my mind works, so I can function, but interacting with other humans might be difficult.

It's good that I can function so that means I can function when I'm interacting with other people, you know, put my skills to use in a practical fashion.

Um so, I'm trying to keep track of everything I know and everything I might need to know or learn in the future. What do I know now? I understand how the mind works, I think. I don't know what else I might need to know. I mean I understand that there is feeling and thought, two separate mental processes. When someone thinks about something, how is feeling involved?

I mean, feeling can be involved with thinking, feelings can assist thoughts I would think. How exactly does that happen. I think feelings can help to motivate thoughts. There is feeling and thinking, what is the difference between those two mental processes? Feelings you can feel, and people can also feel thoughts, however thoughts are sentences or words, while feelings are just feelings. What is the difference between a thought that uses words and a thought that does not use words then? Words are really important then, words help people think about whatever it is that they want to think about.

So say I want to think about something, are words always involved? Feelings are different from thoughts then. Feelings are when you feel something, and thoughts are when you think about something. What is the difference between feeling and thought then? I mean I can think about a person, or I could have feelings about that person. Feelings are different from thoughts then. Feelings feel like something, while thoughts are more informative. If i have a thought, it is an idea or a piece of information or a concept, while feelings are things you can feel.

So thought is basically thinking, while feeling is experiencing feelings. What is the difference between the two then? What is thinking? Thinking uses words or ideas and concepts, while feeling is just emotional.

So thinking is just thoughts, while feelings are emotions. THinking just involves thinking about stuff, while feeling involves feeling things that are emotional, versus thinking about something that is intellectual like an idea or a concept or a sentence.

THinking is thinking about stuff, while feeling is feeling stuff. Um so I don't know if that's a very good description. Thinking about things involves thought, while feeling just involves experiencing feelings. Thoughts can be words or sentences, or ideas or concepts. Does thought always have to be a sentence? It seems like it's more conscious if it's a sentence or thought about with words. Words are sounds in the head that mean something or have a definition. It seems like thoughts need to be thought about with words in order for them to be conscious. I don't have to always think with words, however. I can think fine without thinking sentences to myself.

Feelings can play a role in decision making, or they could play a role in the construction of the self, or in the person being conscious and aware. There is also how feelings feel by themselves, or the study of the nature of feelings.

So what else do I need to explore here, there's feelings and thoughts. I mean I know when I'm thinking or when i'm experiencing feelings. That is kind of important to know.

I like having feelings and thoughts, it gives me an experience of something. There is also the senses. Is that all that humans feel? They can feel thoughts, feelings, and sensory inputs.

So what then is the difference between sensory inputs and feelings and thoughts? Feelings and thoughts are internal cognitive processes while sensory inputs are sensory inputs. They come from outside the mind, taste, touch, sight, sound and smell are all inputs from the external environment, while feelings and thoughts and internal mental processes.

I want to do more research, what else could I try to figure out?

So I don't know what else I might need to learn, this article covers most of the material I need to know. I explained the difference between emotions and feelings in my "the selected writings of Mark Pettinelli" book. The difference is that emotions are main and primary, they occur first possibly for just a few seconds, then there is a conscious feeling as a secondary feeling.

THe main emotions are happy, sad, anger, fear, surprise and disgust. THose emotions occur first and then there is a secondary feeling. I don't know how long those main emotions last, possibly for just a few seconds though I would think they could last longer and be mixed in with the secondary feelings that are a result of those primary emotions. I mean feelings and emotions can be used interchangeably, it's kind of complicated to describe what someone is feeling.

So what else do I need to describe, feelings and thoughts are mental phenomena, they occur inside the brain. The brain as a whole contributes other mental processes that contribute to consciousness. I already listed the mental processes at the beginning of this article.

Those mental processes combined contribute to and form a humans consciousness. Those mental processes are also present in other animals and forms of life, for the most part.

Final Notes by Mark Pettinelli

So what else do I need to figure out? These are my final notes that I won't include in my book. I don't know what else I might need to learn.
Um, so I think I know everything I need to know in order to function. I don't think I need to know anything else. I can think clearly and logically and can function.
So I'm really excited, other people are conscious.
I'm still going through some books. I'll add the information that I learn here. I don't know if there's anything else I need to learn.
I mean, what else would I need to know? I can function fine, I don't even know if I already said that. Now I'm being guided, but I wrote that final book by myself. These are notes about other stuff I would want to learn. That makes sense, they didn't have the academics figured out until I finished explaining some academics. I was providing a critical contribution to the academics that they needed for a long time and to finally finish the

academics.

I don't know what the other people who were contributing to the academics had to offer, but I was part of the small number of people who were contributing to the academics and working together with other academics to figure everything out. I don't know what they're trying to research now, my part in that is over.

One of my final ideas was that thought is different from feeling. **Feelings and thoughts can also influence each other. Now I keep track of my feelings and my thoughts so I can be intelligent, conscious and logical.**

I've always been logical and clear thinking but I wasn't that smart before I did all this research over the last decade. So I'm just going to post here what else I might need or can learn that I think might be valuable information, but I'm being guided so it won't be posted as part of my last book "THe selected writings of Mark Pettinelli".

SO I don't know what else I might need to know, I'm still reading books and thinking about stuff. **My last insight was that people think and feel at the same time, and they can keep track of those feelings and thoughts.**

It's important to note that people can think and feel at the same time. They can also keep track of those feelings and thoughts, and if feelings lead to thoughts and if thoughts lead to feelings.

Um so what else would I need to know? It's kind of important to keep track of your feelings and thoughts.

I don't know if there's anything else I need to learn then. Maybe I'm just done with the research. I mean, if I can keep track of my feelings and thoughts and can function in a practical manner, and think clearly and logically, then I don't know what else I would need to achieve.

I'm functioning perfectly fine right now. I keep track of my feelings and thoughts and how I'm doing in general. I can think clearly and logically, so all that works.

Um, so I need to think more about that. I wrote a lot about the difference between feelings and emotions. I concluded that the mix of feelings that people feel can be complicated, and that there is no set definition between the difference of feelings and emotions, that it is kind of subjective and can be defined in various ways, the important part just being how the person feels, whatever their feelings or emotions or thoughts are doing at that time.

Um so that seems like a pretty good explanation. I don't know what else I would need to figure out or analyze. Consciousness is important. There might be information about consciousness that I might need to learn or research.

I don't know what else I might need to know. I understand how the mind thinks about stuff, that seems like a good understanding.

I also understand how the mind feels, the mind feels emotions and feelings all the time.

Um so i don't know what else i might need to figure out. It seems like I know everything that I need to understand. I mean I know about the mental processes and **I know about thinking and feeling. There is also perception, memory, language, judgment and reasoning and choice, learning, attention and awareness, categories, knowledge, mental representations and concepts, problem solving and decision making.and creativity, automaticity, insight and self knowledge.**

Um so what else would I need to understand about consciousness or feelings and how they function in the mind? I mean I understand how feelings work and I understand how consciousness works. Consciousness is all the mental processes working together to form a picture of how the mind functions. THen the person becomes conscious of their feelings and thoughts and other mental functions.

So feelings and thoughts contribute to the persons consciousness. I mean, what is it to say that the person is conscious anyway? I mean I guess it's just awareness right. Attention and awareness are 2 of the mind's mental processes.

So what exactly is consciousness? Being conscious and aware I guess. Conscious means aware I would think, so if someone is conscious it means that they are aware of themselves or their environment or their mind.

Um so what else do i need to understand in order to function? I mean I can feel my emotions and my feelings and know when I am thinking. Is there anything else I would need to know? I mean, what else is there behind understanding consciousness? I guess I would have to keep track of all of my feelings and thoughts to be aware in general.

If I do that then I think I should be pretty good and well off. I mean i think I just need to do that, keep track of my feelings and thoughts and behaviors. Seems pretty simple. I mean, I don't know the biology of it but still understand how it works.

Consciousness can be pretty complicated, for instance what is consciousness, what does it feels like to feel something? I mean I guess consciousness is just the sum total of our mental processes. So consciousness is just the combination of our attention and awareness, sometimes our memory and sometimes we use our language. It is also the combination of our thoughts and our feelings, whatever it is we are feeling at the moment and if we are thinking about something. I mean, thought and feeling are probably the two greatest contributions to consciousness. What else could be going on other than thinking about something and feeling something? We could also be more or less aware and attentive. We could be using our judgment or making decisions or problem solving. What are some of the other mental processes that our consciousness could be using? We could be learning something, We could be trying to figure something out or problem solve.

So consciousness is just basically what we are aware of, or if we are aware in general. A lot of things contribute to our awareness or our consciousness, like whatever we are aware of at any moment. Humans are aware of their thoughts and feelings and other mental functions like memory and attention and awareness, language and knowledge and concepts, their thinking processes and feeling processes, so whatever they are feeling they could be aware of.

What else is there to understanding consciousness? Someone could have a thought, that would make them aware of whatever the thought is about right. Feelings can also be about stuff, for instance if you feel happy there might be a reason you feel that way. What else is complicated about feelings and thoughts, i previously said that feelings and thoughts make a person more conscious right. Feelings and thoughts can be caused by something or be connected to something, like a behavior or another feeling or thought. That's important for consciousness if you think about it because our feelings and thoughts help make us more aware. But what then is consciousness? Consciousness is our awareness of our feelings and thoughts and other mental processes. If a person is aware of their feelings and thoughts then they are conscious right. If someone is having feelings and thoughts then the person could be a conscious person, but they wouldn't be as conscious as someone who is aware of their feelings and thoughts.

I mean, so what is consciousness then? How aware a person is of their environment or their mind. In order for someone to be aware of their mind or environment they would have to be aware of their mental processes like feelings and thoughts. Those are probably the two most significant mental processes. So how aware someone is of their feelings and thoughts makes the person more conscious and aware. It makes them aware of what they are feeling and thinking, and their other mental processes like language, memory, attention and awareness. So someone could be aware of how aware they are, or if they are using language or speaking, or using their memory. If a person is aware of any of that stuff then they would be more aware of what their mind is doing. A person could also be aware of what is going on in their environment.

A person could be aware of what they are thinking about also, the more aware they are of what they are thinking about the more conscious they would be because they would be aware of their own mind and their environment.

I need to simplify that. Consciousness is a persons awareness of their mind or their environment. So if someone is aware of what their mind is doing then they would be more conscious. They could also be aware of their environment, the environment could be influencing or causing the person's mind to feel or think things. So what is consciousness then? A person could be conscious of their mind and what it is doing. It could be experiencing any of the mental processes such as attention, awareness, memory, learning, language, feeling, thinking, problem solving, decision making, perception, insight, creativity, knowledge, concepts, mental representations, the use of categories, or other mental processes. all of those mental processes are things the mind does. So consciousness would be if someone is aware of what their mind is doing. One thing a mind could be doing is experiencing the mental processes I just listed.

A person could be aware of what they are feeling or thinking or whatever it is they are experiencing. That makes them more conscious because it is what they are experiencing or feeling. Most of the mental processes contribute to the persons feelings or thoughts. A person could be aware of what they are feeling. just feeling something is different from being aware of those feelings. It could be that someone has a feeling that they are not aware of. I guess that could involve various degrees of awareness.

that seems complicated, for instance what does it mean to be aware of a feeling or thought or aware of something in the real world? That is actually pretty simple, it is just how aware someone is of what they are feeling or thinking, or whatever else their mind might be doing. The mind can also experience things from their environment, but those things get experienced in the mind.

That seems like a more simple explanation of consciousness. Consciousness is just the awareness of a person's feelings and thoughts and other things the mind can do or experience.

That seems like a pretty good explanation of consciousness. Either someone is feeling something or thinking about something, and they can be aware of what they are thinking or feeling. Whatever the person's mind is doing they could be aware of. For instance they could be aware of a feeling that they are having. They could be aware of thoughts that they are having. If they are trying to figure something out then they know they are doing that. They could also know about the feelings that they are having at any moment. I can feel things right now and I'm aware of those feelings. I'm aware that I have feelings and thoughts. I am perfectly aware of my feelings and how I feel all the time or just in general.

So what else do I need to learn?

I mean, what about those 2 topics of intelligence and emotion would I need to learn about? I already understand things about consciousness and emotion and cognition. I mean, in order to function I don't really need to understand anything, for instance when I was in high school and the previous years of school I didn't know anything but had feelings and thoughts.

What have I learned about feelings and thoughts anyway? I have those 2 articles that I wrote where I talk about the difference between feelings and emotions. I said that feelings can be more simple and direct and possibly more stupid than emotions, and that emotions could be more powerful but more intellectual and complex. For instance sensory figure out? That is an excellent question. There's stuff about intelligence I can learn, and stuff about emotion that I can learn. What kind of information about intellect could I learn, and what kind of information about emotions or feelings might I nlings are not emotions they are feelings.

So what else might I need to know about feelings and thoughts?

I mean, some feelings are intellectual while other feelings are more stupid. Like sensory feelings are stupid while some thoughts could be more intelligent. Some feelings might even be intelligent feelings, it's kind of hard to describe how someone is feeling at any moment if you think about it.

I mean, what have I learned about feelings and thoughts anyway? There isn't really that much I need to know about them. I mean, I can describe how I am feeling at any given time. I also know how to think about things. What else would I need to do in order to function? That seems like it's enough. I mean, what else do I need to know about feelings and thoughts? In high school I had feelings and thoughts and was functioning perfectly fine, I don't know what else I might need to know or learn. I can function, and I have feelings and thoughts. I can describe how I feel at any moment. I mean, what else is there to functioning? Clear thinking is actually pretty simple.

I mean, how does intellect or intelligence work exactly? And how does emotion function? What causes feelings to start or stop and how does the mind think about thoughts? Is there just a thought process or something, or a feeling process that goes along with the thought process?

Um so what else would I need to know about how emotions or thoughts function in the mind? It seems like how feelings work is a simple process, and how thoughts work is also a simple process

I mean, either someone is thinking something, or feeling something, or both at the same time. Seems fairly simple, I mean, what is involved with a thought process anyway, it seems like it's just a stream of thought, and an emotion process is just a stream of feelings. That seems like all that is going on in any emotional activity.

So what else would I need to study anyway? There is consciousness and emotion, there is also thought or cognition. What else is important that the mind does? It doesn't look like the mind does much else. Emotion and cognition and the resulting consciousness are the main things that the mind does. I don't know what else could be considered important.

THere's the autonomic nervous system, which is basically the functions the body does automatically or involuntarily.

THere's the effect of interruptions, and the limited capacity of the cognitive system or the mind.

There's appraisal theory or the way the mind cognitively interprets events.

Cognitive-autonomic theory

I mean, what role do cognitive evaluations play in how emotion and thought is experienced? People think about what happened around them and how it makes them feel all the time, so the question is how do these evaluations influence their emotions?

It seems pretty simple if you think about it, i mean basically nothing complicated is happening, there's the stimulus, then the resulting emotions or cognitive evaluations.

And there is the physical body that produces sensations and reactions that can influence emotions and feelings. So is a feeling physical or is it mental and psychological?

I mean, there's the effect of cognitive evaluations. So what else is there, I mean, people experience a steady state of feeling. Their feelings could be interrupted by thoughts that they could have. That seems pretty simple if you think about it.

So how does the emotion process work exactly? There is a stimulus, something that causes the person to have an emotion, then the person might think about the stimulus and what feelings it might have caused, so do the feelings come before the person makes an assessment or after the assessment? I suppose a person could have feelings at the same time they are making an assessment, and what they think or what their assessment is can change how they are feeling.

So the feelings and the assessment both occur right after some stimulus that caused them to have those feelings and thoughts. The assessment or what they think about the stimulus can change the feelings they are having at the same time they are having feelings from the stimulus.

So there's a stimulus, something that causes feelings, then the feelings follow and those feelings can be influenced by thoughts that the person can have, which can generate new feelings or change the feelings caused by the input (the stimulus).

These are my mental notes. I'm going to discuss my mental notes in this document.
So what else do I need to figure out? That is an excellent question lol.

I already know the 21 mental processes, they are emotion, thought, judgment, reasoning, choice, memory, learning, language, perception, creativity, problem solving, decision making, categories, mental representations, knowledge, concepts, awareness, attention, automaticity, insight and self-knowledge (which is the beliefs people have about themselves).

So I know all of those processes, it's kind of important to know those because they form a picture of how the mind functions.

Um so what else would I need to know or understand?

What is my current understanding anyway, like what do I already know?
I know a lot of stuff actually, i mean i know how to function, think and feel, those are kind of important things to know. Feelings are different from thoughts anyway. Feelings are experiences of feeling or emotion, while thoughts are ideas or concepts that someone can think about.
Then there's just basic functioning but that just involves using your thoughts and feelings in a practical manner, which I can do without a problem.
Um so if i can function then what else would i need to understand, that's an excellent question.

I mean, what is behind my actions? As a child I did not have a lot of knowledge of the world but was functioning perfectly fine. I'm still mostly the same i would say except i understand feelings and thoughts and consciousness.

For instance, as a child I did not understand what the word 'emotion regulation' meant. When I came across it I was confused. Now I understand that it's about managing and maintaining your own emotions, as a child I did not influence my emotions very much. I mean, I had feelings but it was a fairly simple process.

Um, so that seems like a pretty good run down or explanation of how the mind works. I don't know what else I would need to explain. There's feelings and thoughts, and emotion regulation. There is practical functioning and different kinds of feelings.

So what else do I need to know? I know that I have feelings and thoughts, that's pretty much all i need to know i think, what else would i need to know or understand?
So that's really interesting. I can experience feelings all the time and think about stuff all of the time.

Thoughts can be verbal or non-verbal. Thoughts can direct actions or be used to think about things.

I don't know what else I might need to know then. I think clearly and feel stuff, what else is there to living and being conscious anyway?

Ok so i can just go back to my baseline, what are those feelings and thoughts like anyway, i mean, I have a steady stream of feelings and thoughts all of the time, seems pretty simple if you think about it, I mean, what would i need to know or understand in order to function and think and feel anyway?

So what else would I have to say about emotions, or how emotions function in the mind? It seems like a pretty simple process anyway, I don't know what else I would need to explain about it anyway. I mean, emotions are pretty simple if you think about it.
Thoughts are also simple if you think about it. What about thought is simple anyway?

So what else do I need to know or figure out or understand anyway? I mean, I have a good understanding of how emotions and thoughts work, that's a good explanation of how the mind works in general. I mean, mostly it's just thoughts and feelings, though there is also attention, memory, language, learning, judgment, reasoning, choice, deciding, problem solving, mental representations, concepts, categories, knowledge, automaticity, insight, self-knowledge, awareness, creativity, perception,

So what else would I need to learn or understand? It seems like I have a good enough understanding of how the mind works and how feelings and emotions function anyway. What else would there be for my analysis or explanation anyway? I mean I understand how the mind works and I understand what the mental processes are anyway.

So what else would I need to understand about emotions and how emotions function anyway? Emotions are pretty simple if you think about it. I don't know what could be complicated about emotions anyway.

So I need to do an overview of the information, like what exactly do I need to learn about how the mind works anyway, I feel like I have a good understanding of how the mind works, for instance there are feelings and thoughts in the mind that runs through a person's consciousness all of the time. That's important to understand, I think. What else could be going on in the mind? There's the other mental processes like attention, learning and language and memory and awareness, judgment, reasoning and choice, problem solving and decision making, there's mental representations, concepts, categories and knowledge, creativity and perception, and automaticity, insight and self knowledge.

Those are all important to understand, I think.
I mean, what am I going to learn if I do more reading anyway? I already know that there are feelings and thoughts in the mind,

There's feeling 'states' and logical 'states'. For instance someone could be thinking clearly and logically about something or in a logical thinking type of state.

Emotions are feelings.

An emotion is a mental mode.

Cognitive, evaluative and motivational

So what else would I need to understand about how emotion works in the mind anyway? Seems pretty simple anyway. I mean, there's different emotional states and different emotions and feelings someone can experience.
So someone could go into different emotional states or something. People can feel a ton of different things and experience lots of different feelings and even thoughts which are more intellectual.

Mental Notes c of Mark Pettinelli

Mark Pettinell

Mental Notes of Mark Pettinelli

These are my mental notes. I'm going to discuss my mental notes in this document.

So what else do I need to figure out? That is an excellent question lol.

I already know the 21 mental processes, they are emotion, thought, judgment, reasoning, choice, memory, learning, language, perception, creativity, problem solving, decision making, categories, mental representations, knowledge, concepts, awareness, attention, automaticity, insight and self-knowledge (which is the beliefs people have about themselves).

So I know all of those processes, it's kind of important to know those because they form a picture of how the mind functions.

Um so what else would I need to know or understand?

What is my current understanding anyway, like what do I al- ready know?

I know a lot of stuff actually, i mean i know how to function, think and feel, those are kind of important things to know. Feel- ings are different from thoughts anyway. Feelings are experiences of feeling or emotion, while thoughts are ideas or concepts that someone can think about.

Then there's just basic functioning but that just involves using your thoughts and feelings in a practical manner, which I can do without a problem.

Um so if i can function then what else would i need to under- stand, that's an excellent question.

I mean, what is behind my actions? As a child I did not have a lot of knowledge of the world but was functioning perfectly fine. I'm still mostly the same i would say except i understand feelings and thoughts and consciousness.

For instance, as a child I did not understand what the word 'emotion regulation' meant. When I came across it I was confused. Now I understand that it's about managing and maintaining your own emotions, as a child I did not influence my emotions very much. I mean, I had feelings but it was a fairly simple process.

Um, so that seems like a pretty good run down or explanation of how the mind works. I don't know what else I would need to explain. There's feelings and thoughts, and emotion regulation. There is practical functioning and different kinds of feelings.

So what else do I need to know? I know that I have feelings and thoughts, that's pretty much all i need to know i think, what else would i need to know or understand?

So that's really interesting. I can experience feelings all the time and think about stuff all of the time.

Thoughts can be verbal or non-verbal. Thoughts can direct actions or be used to think about things.
I don't know what else I might need to know then. I think clearly and feel stuff, what else is there to living and being conscious anyway?
Ok so i can just go back to my baseline, what are those feelings and thoughts like anyway, i mean, I have a steady stream of feelings and thoughts all of the time, seems pretty simple if you think about it, I mean, what would i need to know or understand in order to function and think and feel anyway?
So what else would I have to say about emotions, or how emo- tions function in the mind? It seems like a pretty simple process anyway, I don't know what else I would need to explain about it anyway. I mean, emotions are pretty simple if you think about it.
Thoughts are also simple if you think about it. What about thought is simple anyway?
So what else do I need to know or figure out or understand anyway? I mean, I have a good understanding of how emotions and thoughts work, that's a good explanation of how the mind works in general. I mean, mostly it's just thoughts and feelings, though there is also attention, memory, language, learning, judgment, reasoning, choice, deciding, problem solving, mental representations, con- cepts, categories, knowledge, automaticity, insight, self-knowledge, awareness, creativity, perception,
So what else would I need to learn or understand? It seems like I have a good enough understanding of how the mind works and how feelings and emotions function anyway. What else would there be for my analysis or explanation anyway? I mean I understand how the mind works and I understand what the mental processes are anyway.
So what else would I need to understand about emotions and how emotions function anyway? Emotions are pretty simple if you

think about it. I don't know what could be complicated about emotions anyway.

So I need to do an overview of the information, like what exactly do I need to learn about how the mind works anyway, I feel like I have a good understanding of how the mind works, for instance there are feelings and thoughts in the mind that runs through a person's consciousness all of the time. That's important to under- stand, I think. What else could be going on in the mind? There's the other mental processes like attention, learning and language and memory and awareness, judgment, reasoning and choice, prob- lem solving and decision making, there's mental representations, concepts, categories and knowledge, creativity and perception, and automaticity, insight and self knowledge.

Those are all important to understand, I think.

I mean, what am I going to learn if I do more reading anyway? I already know that there are feelings and thoughts in the mind,

There's feeling 'states' and logical 'states'. For instance someone could be thinking clearly and logically about something or in a logical thinking type of state.

Emotions are feelings.

An emotion is a mental mode. Cognitive, evaluative and motivational

So what else would I need to understand about how emotion works in the mind anyway? Seems pretty simple anyway. I mean, there's different emotional states and different emotions and feel- ings someone can experience.

So someone could go into different emotional states or some- thing. People can feel a ton of different things and experience lots of different feelings and even thoughts which are more intellectual.

Mental Notes (continued) of Mark Pettinelli

So I'm going to talk about my new mental notes in this document. I don't know what else I can learn, I mean, I understand stuff about how feelings work in the mind and how thoughts work also. I don't know what else would be considered to be important research, these notes aren't even going to be put in my selected writings article. What else would I need to understand anyway? I know that there are feelings and thoughts in the mind, there's also attention and perception as mental processes.

What else have I learned anyway? I mean, if i understand that there are feelings and thoughts and other mental processes like attention and perception and memory and language then what else would i need to understand anyway?

I mean, I understand that there are emotional states, and that emo- tions are feelings. What are some of the other mental processes, let's see there is decision making and reasoning and problem solving, those all fall under the category of thinking though. So there is thinking, feeling, attention, perception, memory and language. There's also awareness, learning, automaticity, insight, knowledge, concepts, categories, and mental representations.

I mean, what else do I need to understand about how emotion and thought functions? It's a fairly simple process I think, there isn't really very much to understand about it. I'll write down here what I learn about what I need to understand about it anyway.

I mean, what is there behind how feeling and thought works in the mind anyway? It doesn't seem like it is that complicated.

The 21 mental processes are emotion, thought, attention, aware- ness, perception, creativity, judgment, reasoning, choice, memory, learning, language, concepts, categories, knowledge, mental repre- sentations, automaticity, insight, self-knowledge, problem solving, and decision making.

Um so what else would I need to know or learn anyway, i already wrote a lot about feelings and thoughts. Emotion isn't even compli- cated. I mean I can function fine with the knowledge that I have about emotions. I memorized the mental processes, that's all that seems complicated about emotion and thinking.

So I'll just post the results of my research here, anything I find to be important I'll post about.

What am I going to do, try to describe emotion and feeling or some- thing? Emotion could be hard to describe I think.

On the other hand, describing emotion could be important, i mean what else would be important other than someone describing their own feelings? I already listed the mental processes, that helps describe feeling. So what else would be important other than describing feeling?

Listing the mental processes helps to describe feelings.

What else would be important to analyze? There are sensations and emotions. Sensations are from external sources, while feelings are inter- nal feelings that are felt within the mind. The 5 senses of taste, touch, sight, sound and smell are all the senses, and the mind feels these senses after they get processed from the external world. Feelings are then felt within the mind such as the different feelings and emotions that someone can experience. Some of those feelings come from external inputs, while others are created by the mind.

I said that feeling and thought were the minds 2 major mental pro- cesses. There is also perception, that is another major mental process, what else does the mind do that is significant or important, I mean what takes up most of its resources anyway. I have already listed the mental processes. I would think that attention is a major mental process, that is kind of similar to perception however, because most of someone's attention is spent on their perception, but is that external or internal perception? I mean they pay attention to external senses and internal thoughts and cognitive processes.

There are the different kinds of thinking like judgements and de- cision making and problem solving, then there are different kinds of feelings someone can experience like any of the feelings. There are also many different types of thoughts. Then there is the perception mental process and the attention mental process, I already pointed out that those 2 mental processes are significant. So that is 4 significant mental processes - thinking, feeling, attention and perception. What else could the mind be doing that could be considered important? I've already listed the 21 or however many mental processes there are, and I just pointed out the 4 most significant of those mental processes. Thinking, feeling, attention and perception. Awareness is a type of attention, and problem solving and decision making are types of thoughts. Knowledge is also made up of thoughts. Judgment and reasoning are also kinds of thoughts. Concepts, categories and language are also kinds of thoughts. Automaticity is an unconscious process, and insight is also a kind of thought.

So what else would I need to point out, almost everything the mind does could fall under those 4 different types of mental processes of thinking, feeling, attention and perception. Awareness is similar to attention I would say. And perception is connected to attention and awareness.

So is that a complete analysis? I'm trying to describe how the mind functions. I listed 21 mental processes and then pointed out the signifi- cant mental processes and that the mind has sensory inputs and internal mental processes. The mind's internal mental processes are connected to its sensory inputs. For instance vision is used by the perception pro- cess, however people can pay attention to or perceive their own external or internal perceptions.

So what else would I need to analyze to do a complete analysis of how the mind functions anyway? I already discussed the mental pro- cesses and how there are external and internal inputs. I listed the mental processes and pointed out that there are only 4 major mental processes, thought, feeling, perception and attention.

So um, what else would I need to figure out? Try to describe my emotions or something?

What could those books on emotion have to say anyway? I don't know if they have anything good in them. What could they have to say about feelings anyway?

I mean, what could those books on emotion have to say anyway?

There really isn't that much to say about emotion i think.

I already wrote some basic stuff about emotions and feelings. Like what all the mental processes are and other stuff like that there are external inputs and internal thinking and processing.

What else did I write about the mind and its feelings? What could those books have to say about emotion anyway? I'll write down my notes here about what I discover.

Is an evaluation needed for an emotion to be experienced? I mean, there's a cognitive aspect to experiencing emotions. And does language need to be used in order to experience an emotion?

Um so what else would I need to know or understand or figure out anyway? I mean, I know that there are feelings and thoughts, and that people can make evaluations or appraisals of their emotions, that's also important to understand. There's also the mental processes like think- ing, feeling, attention, perception, memory and language. Do sensations feel the same way each time you experience them? Maybe that is all that I need to learn. The selected writings of Mark

Pettinelli's article has enough information in it. I don't know if there is anything else I would need to learn or figure out. I'll try to continue to add to it and post new info I discover here.

Is philosophy a science or is it more conceptual? It could be concep- tual and scientific I suppose.

Are emotions bodily changes? A physiological change could be an emotion I suppose. Feelings are psychological or mental though not physical. Some feelings could be physical I suppose.

Are emotions short lived? How long do emotions last anyway?

I already knew what emotions are, I know when I'm experiencing an emotion and what it feels like, what else would I need to know about emotions? Knowing when I'm having one, when it starts and stops, what it feels like, what caused it and so on, are all important things to know about my own feelings.

I mean I know what emotions are, they function in a fairly simple fashion. What would I need to know about emotions anyway, it seems pretty simple how they function and what they are.

I mean, i know what I am feeling all of the time, so i'm conscious of my own feelings all of the time, that means emotion isn't that com- plicated anyway. I mean, if I can feel my emotions all of the time, then what else is there to know?

I mean, what else would I need to know anyway? I know what an emotion is and what a feeling is, they're basically the same thing. Feelings are experiences of feeling, and so are emotions.

Um, so what else would I need to know? This article covers most of the basic information about feelings and emotions and thoughts. I mean, I know what a feeling is and what a thought is, I am aware of what i am feeling all of the time, it's kind of obvious actually.

These are my new mental notes, I'm going to discuss anything new I figure out or discover here. I've already finished my book, the Selected Writings of Mark Pettinelli article, but I'm still reading.

So are emotions reactions to stimuli? Or are they action tendencies?

So what else would I have to learn, maybe stuff about emotion or feeling, whatever it's called.

So what else do I need to learn? I know that there are external inputs that are processed internally by the mind, I know that there are many mental processes, I know that there is an unconscious mind, and that feelings can be conscious or unconscious.

The mental processes are emotion, thought, attention, aware- ness, judgment, reasoning, choice, memory, learning, language, automaticity, insight, self-knowledge, mental representations, con- cepts, categories, knowledge, problem solving, decision making, creativity and perception

Those are important to know. So all of that is in my "the selected writings of Mark Pettinelli" article.

So seriously what would there be to know about emotions and how they function in the mind? It seems pretty simple if you think about it.

I'm trying to figure out what else I might need to learn about feelings and the mind. I'll post my discoveries here. Seems like all there is to understand is appraisal theory, that the mind makes evaluations of different sorts and those help determine the feelings that the person would feel.

There might be other stuff I could learn about emotion and how it works in the mind, or about how people think and how that is re- lated to their feelings, like evaluations are thoughts but they influence a person's feelings.

Are emotions rational? Or is there a rational part of a person or brain and an irrational part?

What kind of question is that? Emotions make us feel things, so that must be positive for our mental health and how we feel all the time.

I need to come up with a new analysis here, I mean, I've already outlined a lot of stuff about cognitive psychology, how the mind works with its mental processes and stuff. What else would I need to figure out anyway? I have a good understanding, that shows how the mind works and functions and such.

I mean I know how to function in a practical way, I know that much about how emotions work. I mean, there's a stimulus, then the mind responds to that stimulus, it's kind of interesting.

Experiencing emotion can be complicated for the mind to figure out. There's multiple factors involved, what are those factors involved with experiencing emotions anyway?

I mean, what is complicated about an emotional response? It doesn't seem like anything complicated is going on. I mean, there are a lot of emotions, and each works differently. I'm trying to figure out everything someone could feel or experience. Most of our experience is emotional, I think. I mean, there are different emotions someone can experience.

So what are all the feelings a person could go through anyway?

I mean, each emotion or feeling would need to be analyzed, each feeling is different and works differently from other feelings.

There's a lot of feelings and each feeling is experienced differently, and functions differently from the other feelings.

Each feeling works differently I think. It's mostly obvious I suppose. Emotion can be short lived, physical, based on an appraisal or evalu- ation, can accompany thoughts and occur at the same time as thoughts.

It could be conscious or unconscious, physical or psychological.

Is a feeling cognitive or is it emotional? Or I mean, is the experience of feeling and thought intellectual or emotional?

So what is the difference between emotions and moods then? Moods seem like they are long lasting and in the background, while emotions are short lived. So what is an emotion then? It could be a period of feel- ing. Emotions are stronger than moods then, but don't last as long.

So an emotion is a strong feeling, while there can be many different feelings experienced at any one time, an emotion is more powerful. So how would I describe how I am feeling then? Like what are all the feelings that contribute to my current state of feeling? There's a mood I could be having, and there are feelings and emotions I could be experiencing while I am having that mood. What would be an example of that, the mood I'm in could be relaxed or happy, while the feeling or emotion I have could be short-lived.

So how would I describe a complete state of feeling then? There are moods in the background, and feelings or emotions that come and pass. That seems like all there is to how feelings work I would think.

I'm trying to organize my thoughts about emotions. Feelings can be rational or irrational. How could an emotion be rational? What does that mean exactly anyway? I guess someone could think about a feeling, that could make the feeling rational I suppose. How does that work exactly anyway?

I mean, I'm reading all of this stuff about emotions and feelings. What is complicated about experiencing feelings? I think the only thing about it is if it is cognitive or emotional. People can think about their feelings, basically. I mean, it seems like that is all that is happening anyway with feelings and how they are experienced. The feeling can be thought about.

I Think that's all I need to know, there is a stimulus, then you feel the emotion, then you can think about the feeling. You can think about the feelings you experience.

Are emotions cognitive evaluations or are they perceptions? A per- ception is more direct, while a cognitive evaluation means you would have to think something before an emotion is produced.

I wonder, is an emotion a perception, an impulse, or a belief? It is kind of confusing, it could be cognitive, which would make it a belief, or it could be emotional and more automatic, which would make it an impulse or a perception I think.

I mean, emotions are fast and automatic, there isn't really time to think about them. I guess they are thought about, but that is after most of the emotion is experienced i think. I mean, what happens immediately after a stimulus triggers the person to feel stuff. Is there a perception, or some sort of impulsive reaction? Or the person could think about the cause of the feeling.

How is emotion produced? Does it just come from the stimulus? Something causes feeling to be generated, the feeling can be thought about at various times after the first feeling the person feels. The initial feeling I suppose could be called an impulse, because it is a fast reaction, however if the initial feeling is cognitive it could be a perception that could also be fast. The emotion could then be thought about after the fast immediate reaction, which could be like a belief or a cognition.

So my big insight was that although cognitive science might under- stand how the mind works, that is, understand everything about how the mind works, it might not understand all of the concepts that the mind could think with. I previously pointed out that there is a stream of thought that has various different concepts or ideas, and that a stream of ideas runs through a person's mind all of the time. However, there might be some ideas or concepts that a person does not know or understands. In that way maybe they could figure out everything, or all of the possible ideas or concepts that someone could think about.

So again, although the field of cognitive science understands how the mind thinks, and everything about how it works, it might not understand all of the ideas that someone could think.

I mean, there's all the ideas and concepts in the world that could be understood by the human mind. In other words, everything could be figured out. Although cognitive science and cognitive psychology have everything about how the mind works figured out, they might not understand all of the ideas that someone could think with. Obviously people have thoughts, the only question is, do they know all the possible thoughts that they could think? Furthermore, do they even know all the thoughts they currently have in their mind, that might make them logical because they would know all the things they are thinking and if those things make sense. They might need help on that, however. Or could benefit by help, i mean, they might not know how to think clearly or logically about some of their thoughts.

So what other points would i have to make about how emotion works, there is a stimulus, then the person feels stuff, and they can think about things at the same time. They can think about what caused the emotion and what the emotion is like. That seems like a good understanding of how emotion functions. What else would be involved in any emotional process?

So um, it isn't really that big of a deal, there's the external inputs, then the mind processes those inputs and feels what they cause it to feel. They can also think about what those inputs cause the person to think. Some of the resulting feelings and thoughts are automatic, while other feelings and thoughts are optional.

That's a good description of how the mind works I would say. There is actually more to how emotion functions, there is moti-

vation and action tendencies, for instance. Motivation powers thoughts and is always there. So motivation is kind of like an action tendency then, i mean, what exactly is an action tendency then. It seems like a tendency to action would be powered by a motivation. So is that all there is to how emotion functions then? People have constantly chang- ing motivations and tendencies for action. They also have constantly changing emotions. Emotion can be a motivation actually. I mean, if motivation is always there, then it's important to point out that it exists and what it does.

I'm trying to do an analysis, I mean, how does the mind work when there is a feeling or an emotion? It doesn't seem that complicated, on the other hand there is motivation and impulses, but those are just both feelings. There are logical feelings and irrational feelings. There is motivation, how does that work exactly? Motivation is a feeling or an impulse. It seems like some type of motivation is always present. Feelings interact with a person's motivation. I mean, adding motivation makes things more complicated, like what is motivation anyway? Is it an action tendency or an impulse or some- thing? Motivation is the drive, while feelings are temporary and can be independent of a motivation. So let's try and break down everything a mind might be doing. There is a stimulus or trigger, then the person has a feeling that was caused by the stimulus. Some of the feelings might motivate the person, while other feelings could be independent from the person's motivation.

Motivation is complicated, like how does that work with the mind anyway. Motivation is a drive, some feelings might cause the person to be less motivated, while other feelings could cause them to be more motivated.
So what is the difference between drives and feelings then? Some feelings are impulses, which is like a drive, while other feelings might not be as emotional.
So is that everything that is happening in the mind during any event or action? The person can feel things and think about things at the same time. They have feelings, and they can have thoughts. That is pretty much all that is going on I would say. So is that everything that is going on anyway? It seems pretty simple I would think then.
That is an excellent point, I mean, what else goes on in the mind other than experiencing feelings and thoughts? Feelings are different from moods. Feelings are also different from thoughts. So what else is there, i mean, you can experience a mood or a feeling or a thought, it isn't that complicated.
So I have these notes, what else could I make mental notes about anyway? I mean i can function and think and feel, what else would i need to be able to do? Also there might be more details involved with experiencing emotions and feelings. So what are all of those details? I don't know actually, it seems like the process is pretty simple.There are the 21 mental processes that I already pointed out. Judgment, reason- ing and choice, memory, learning and language, automaticity, insight and self knowledge, mental representations, concepts and categories, knowledge, emotion and thought, attention and awareness, problem solving and decision making, creativity and perception. That also seems pretty simple. I mean, that's how the mind works, it's mental processes that make it work.
What else could be complicated about emotion then?
There are evaluations and perceptions, both help to determine what someone might feel. But what then is exactly a perception then? Some- thing someone can see I guess, or something someone can visualize in

their own mind. That is like making an assessment except it is visual instead of a type of thought like an evaluation would be.

Both of those, evaluations and perceptions, influence the emotions and feelings that people feel in response to stimulation or various stimuli.

Emotion and motivation Changes in emotion

Differences between each emotion Emotion and bodily changes Awareness and emotion

So what is motivation then? Is it a feeling or a drive or how can I describe it? If someone feels motivated then it's their feelings that feel that way, or feel oriented that way. I could feel happy and motivated, or sad and unmotivated. What is motivation then, a component of feeling? Feelings could make the person more or less motivated then. Positive feelings like happiness could make the person more motivated, and the motivated feeling would be a component of the happy or other positive feeling. It could work the same way with negative feelings except they would probably make the person be less motivated, for instance when I'm depressed I sometimes feel unmotivated.

The definition of motivation is "the desire or willingness to act", so what does that mean exactly, that motivation is a type of desire or orientation to act? It is an action tendency or intention or something. It is a drive I guess. Drives are like action tendencies, a desire to act is like a tendency to act.

Motivation is a tendency to act. A tendency is a type of feeling of action that orients or prepares the person for action. It is felt as a feeling of action or movement or involvement. "I feel motivated and like I want to act" could describe positive feelings of motivation. Or just "I want to act" describes a motivational feeling. There are also lack of motivation feelings that would be "I don't want to act because I feel sad".

How are emotions integrated into choice? Conscious awareness and emotion.

How and why are emotions communicated? How are emotions embodied in the social world? What develops in emotional development?

What is the role of conscious awareness in emotion?

Emotions can bias decision making processes by promoting specific behavioral tendencies.

How can affect influence choice? Affect is the foundation of value.

Emotions are more than their subjective feelings.

Emotions are functional states that cause feelings and behavior. Affect is essential to emotion.

What are emotional states, and what are their functions? Active inference and emotion.

Personality as lasting individual differences in emotion.

Connections between emotions and the social world: numerous and complex.

Effects of emotion on interpersonal behavior: A motivational per- spective.

The affective nature of social interactions.

What is the role of unconscious emotions and of conscious aware- ness in emotion?

Emotion and attention

The role of appraisal in emotion Goals and emotion

Emotion regulation and cognition

So I don't know what else I need to figure out here, there's feelings and thoughts. I have feelings all of the time, it's interesting to figure out what those feelings are and what they feel like. That's pretty important anyway.

I think I know everything I need to understand. I understand that I have feelings, and that I can influence my feelings. What else is there to basic functioning anyway? It seems pretty simple if you think about it.

I also have thoughts. My thoughts can influence my feelings and my behaviors, it's a cycle of thoughts, feelings and behaviors.

So what else is there to figuring out how I think and feel all of the time? Seems pretty simple, i mean, i don't need to know very much about how feeling works in order to experience feelings.

So what else is there to figure out about feelings? Feelings are pretty simple if you think about it. I mean, what am I supposed to figure out? What could be complicated about how feelings work? It seems like it's pretty simple. I'll try to figure out anything complicated about it. I'm trying to think. What could be complicated about feelings? It doesn't seem complicated anyway.

I mean if I read anymore what am i going to figure out? What emotions are like maybe? So just more about what emotions are like then'/ I already know what feelings are like, I feel them all of the time. How else would I need to describe what feelings are like then? I already know what life feels like, I don't need to analyze it. I don't think I need to analyze it anyway. I mean, what would I need to understand anyway? I think I'm following along with everything that is going on, all the feelings and thoughts and such.
I mean, what would I need to know about feelings? I know what I'm feeling all of the time, I think that's all I need to know.
I notice there is a steady stream of feelings, and sometimes I think about things with thoughts. What else could be going on anyway?
There's the experience of feelings that is happening anyway. And there's the experience of thinking with thoughts.

What am I supposed to learn about emotional experience? The relation between emotion, belief and desire? Or the relation between perception and evaluation?

Emotions are experiences of feeling and thought. They involve per- ceptions and evaluations.

What am I trying to make sense of, in terms of experiencing emo- tions, it seems like nothing complicated is going on. There's a trigger, then feelings are experienced, then there is some sort of external be- havior. That's all that happens, I don't know what else would need to be analyzed.

So I don't know what else to add to my notes here. Emotions fit the person's understanding of the world, in other words, they understand something about the world, then that causes them to have an emotion. That is different from having a feeling that comes directly from some stimulus. Sometimes our perceptions, evaluations, or understanding of something influences the feelings that thing causes us to have. That is different from directly feeling a feeling, say from a sensory feeling of cold is pretty direct, it doesn't matter what you think about the feeling, it feels cold because of a direct sensory type of stimulation.

There's the valence of the emotion, whether it is negative or positive
- pleasurable or unpleasant (painful).
There are also connections between emotions and desires, or moti- vation.
Thoughts are different from judgements.
Emotions can be unconscious. Emotions are also felt, can you feel an emotion if it is unconscious though? Or does it manifest itself in other ways?

An emotional experience involves:

- A perception
- Valence (positive or negative feeling)
- 1st person point of view or perspective
- An Evaluation
- Thoughts about the emotion or judgements
- Motivational feelings (whether positive or negative motivation)
- Unconscious or conscious thoughts, feelings or behaviors

There's secondary emotions, which are emotions about another, first order emotion. The first order emotion is about something and it's the first emotion you feel, while the secondary emotion is about the first order emotion and helps regulate it. For instance, you could be angry at the fear you experience.

I mean, is fear cognitive or is it emotional? IF you see a snake, that is emotional, if you think you are afraid, however, that is cognitive or intellectual.

That's a good point, either the stimulus is emotional or it is cogni- tive. People can feel things emotionally or intellectually. An idea can also be either emotional or intellectual.

Apparently there's an unconscious mind, and there's also emotional stuff and cognitive stuff. The cognitive stuff has to do with thinking, while emotional stuff has to do with feelings.

So a stimulus or trigger can be felt emotionally or intellectually. It can be felt with thoughts, or be felt by experiencing feelings.

So if there is a stimulus or trigger, the person then experiences feelings, and they can also think about those feelings with thoughts.

So is there a trigger, then a feeling or a thought, or is there an intellectual experience and an emotional experience? The emotional ex- perience would involve feelings, while the intellectual experience would involve thoughts.

I mean, what is going on in any emotional experience? It could be intellectual and involve thoughts, or it could be emotional and involve feelings, or it could be both intellectual and emotional at the same time, and involve the experience of feelings and thoughts at the same time.

But I mean, what then is the difference between an intellectual ex- perience and an emotional experience? SO what is going on then. In any experience, there are thoughts and feelings, but it's more complicated than that I suppose. I mean, what is going on with an intellectual ex- perience and an emotional experience then? I suppose it's pretty simple, it's mostly just the person experiencing feelings and having thoughts.

I don't know what else to add to that, an experience is an experience, it involves both feelings and thoughts, but is there anything more to add to that explanation?

One of the questions is what constitutes an emotion, I think it's a motivation, a memory, an imagination, and thought. Attending and thinking could be considered to be thoughts. Beliefs and desires can also be considered to be emotions.

So what makes up an emotion then? There's beliefs, desires, motiva- tion, thoughts, imagination and memory. How could an emotion have a thought or a belief anyway? Emotion can be intellectual, in that way it could have thoughts, and it can have desires, desires have thoughts involved and also motivational feelings. I mean, if a feeling is intellec- tual then it could be an emotion then right. If someone is having an emotion, they could have thoughts as part of the experience. Or i guess the thoughts would separate from the emotional feelings. Beliefs and desires are like thoughts, except they are mostly feelings. They're kind of the combination between feelings and thoughts because they involve feelings but are also considered to be thoughts.

An emotional experience involves:
A perception
The valence of the feeling (positive or negative feeling) 1st person point of view or perspective
An Evaluation
Thoughts about the emotion or judgements
Motivational feelings (whether positive or negative motivation) Unconscious or conscious thoughts, feelings or behaviors
The function of a feeling is to motivate us in some way

In conclusion of my research, in order to understand what you are feeling, simply try to feel what you can feel. It is simple, I could just try to figure out what I am feeling at the moment. I can try to analyze my feelings using what I learned about feelings. So then what would I use to analyze or understand my feelings then. I know about the mental processes, the main ones are feeling, thought, attention, perception, awareness, language, and memory. So I could say to myself, well now I'm feeling this and that, the feeling feels like this and this or that mental process is being used. If you don't know what the mental processes are you could look them up or just think about how your mind is working and what it could possibly be doing at the moment to produce the feelings your currently experiencing. That is my guide for understanding what you are feeling at any time or the current moment. You could just ask yourself, "what mental processes could my mind be using in order to make myself feel this way. Then you could try to figure out how you are feeling and ask a different question, "what am I feeling right now, how did it get this way, and what mental processes are being used."

An emotional or cognitive experience. But what does that mean? I mean, what exactly is an emotional experience, and how does it compare to a cognitive experience? I suppose somethings are intellectual while others are just feelings or emotions. They can be combined also, I don't know how it works exactly but it seems like there can be feelings and thoughts, or intellectual feelings and non-intellectual feelings all mixing in and combining in an experience.

What else is there anyway/ There is thoughts and consciousness, and attention and consciousness, i said before, you could be aware of any of your mental processes.

Some points on consciousness

If consciousness becomes more powerful, it might need more stimu- lation probably because it's just larger so it needs more stuff, even though it has more power. A neurologist in 2004 - Michele Maci - pointed out to me that I didn't have that much anxiety when I was in high school or when i was a kid. I took that to mean recently that al- though my consciousness was more powerful, i had more anxiety then when my mind was simple. The more powerful consciousness must need more stuff for some reason, i had huge problems with anxiety after I graduated from high school in 2003.

Another point is about cognitive psychology or how the mind works. If it works from basic mental processes like thinking, feeling, percep- tion, language, memory and attention and other mental processes, then why would the mind be that complicated. This just seems like a simple understanding of how the mind functions, also people can become con- scious of their feelings or thoughts, and have a stronger consciousness. Do I need to explain what I mean by a stronger consciousness then? It is hard to explain, I would think children have a weaker consciousness than adults, at least mine was much weaker than it is now than when I was a child.

People can be conscious of their thoughts and their feelings. I would think that as the mind becomes more powerful, the person's conscious- ness would need to understand the feelings and thoughts that it has or they would be confused or go crazy. The feelings and thoughts could become more powerful, and as this happens the mind would need to understand what those feelings and thoughts are.

So if there is a stimulus or trigger, the person then experiences feelings, and they can also think about those feelings with thoughts. So is there a trigger, then a feeling or a thought, or is there an intellectual experience and an emotional experience? The emotional experience would involve feelings, while the intellectual experience would involve thoughts. I mean, what is going on in any emotional experience? It could be intellectual and involve thoughts, or it could be emotional and involve feelings, or it could be both intellectual and emotional at the same time, and involve the experience of feelings and thoughts at the same time.

My consciousness is a lot stronger than it was when I was a child, it actually gradually got stronger in my 20's and 30's and now I also have more powerful emotions. I think that's how humans have evolved, to have stronger emotions and feelings. I already pointed out that meant that I have to be more aware or understanding of my feelings and thoughts because my consciousness is more powerful.

I mean think about it, if there is a powerful consciousness then that means there can be other people or a previous state that had a more sim- ple consciousness. What do I mean by a more powerful consciousness anyway? I pointed out that it would have a harder time understanding more powerful feelings and thoughts. And would need to understand those feelings and thoughts so it wouldn't be confused.

But I mean, what then is the difference between an intellectual ex- perience and an emotional experience? SO what is going on then. In any experience, there are thoughts and feelings, but it's more complicated than that I suppose. I mean, what is going on with an intellectual experience and an emotional experience then? I suppose it's pretty simple, it's mostly just the person experiencing feelings and having thoughts.

I don't know what else to add to that, an experience is an experience, it involves both feelings and thoughts, but is there anything more to add to that explanation?

So what else do I need to figure out? These are my final notes that I won't include in my book. I don't know what else I might need to learn. Um, so I think I know everything I need to know in order to function. I don't think I need to know anything else. I can think clearly and logi- cally and can function. So I'm really excited, other people are conscious. I'm still going through some books. I'll add the information that I learn here. I don't know if there's anything else I need to learn. I mean, what else would I need to know? I can function fine, I don't even know if I already said that. Now I'm being guided, but I wrote that final book by myself. These are notes about other stuff I would want to learn. That makes sense, they didn't have the academics figured out until I finished explaining some academics. I was providing a critical contribution to the academics that they needed for a long time and to finally finish the academics. I don't know what the other people who were contributing to the academics had to offer, but I was part of the small number of people who were contributing to the academics and working together with other academics to figure everything out. I don't know what they're trying to research now, my part in that is over. One of my final ideas was that thought is different from feeling. Feelings and thoughts can also influence each other. Now I keep track of my feelings and my thoughts so I can be intelligent, conscious and logical. I've always been logical and clear thinking but I wasn't that smart before I did all this research over the last decade. So I'm just going to post here what else I might need or can learn that I think might be valuable information, but I'm being guided so it won't be posted as part of my last book "THe selected writings of Mark Pettinelli". SO I don't know what else I might need to know, I'm still reading books and thinking about stuff. My last insight was that people think and feel at the same time, and they can keep track of those feelings and thoughts. It's important to note that people can think and feel at the same time. They can also keep track of those feelings and thoughts, and if feelings lead to thoughts and if thoughts lead to feelings. Um so what else would I need to know? It's kind of important to keep track of your feelings and thoughts. I don't know if there's anything else I need to learn then. Maybe I'm just done with the research. I mean, if I can keep track of my feelings and thoughts and can function in a practical manner, and think clearly and logically, then I don't know what else I would need to achieve. I'm functioning perfectly fine right now. I keep track of my feelings and thoughts and how I'm doing in general. I can think clearly and logi- cally, so all that works. Um, so I need to think more about that. I wrote a lot about the difference between feelings and emotions. I concluded that the mix of feelings that people feel can be complicated, and that there is no set definition between the difference of feelings and emo- tions, that it is kind of subjective and can be defined in various ways, the important part just being how the person feels, whatever their feel- ings or emotions or thoughts are doing at that time. Um so that seems like a pretty good explanation. I don't know what else I would need to figure out or analyze. Consciousness is important. There might be information about consciousness that I might need to learn or research. I don't know what else I might need to know. I understand how the mind thinks about stuff, that seems like a good understanding. I also understand how the mind feels, the mind feels emotions and feelings all the time. Um so i don't know what else i might need to figure out. It seems like I know everything that I need to understand. I mean I know about the mental processes and I know about thinking and feeling. There is also perception, memory, language, judgment and reasoning and choice, learning, attention and awareness, categories, knowledge, mental representations and concepts, problem solving and decision making.and creativity, automaticity, insight and self knowledge. Um so what else would I need to understand about consciousness or feelings and how they function in the mind? I mean I understand how feelings work and I understand how consciousness works. Consciousness is all the mental processes working together to form a picture of how the mind functions. THen the person becomes conscious of their feelings and thoughts and other mental functions. So feelings and thoughts contribute to the persons consciousness. I mean, what is it to say that the person is conscious anyway? I mean I guess it's just awareness right. Attention and awareness are 2 of the mind's mental processes.

So what exactly is consciousness? Being conscious and aware I guess. Conscious means aware I would think, so if someone is conscious it means that they are aware of themselves or their environment or their mind. Um so what else do i need to understand in order to function? I mean I can feel my emotions and my feelings and know when I am thinking. Is there anything else I would need to know? I mean, what else is there behind understanding consciousness? I guess I would have to keep track of all of my feelings and thoughts to be aware in general. If I do that then I think I should be pretty good and well off. I mean i think I just need to do that, keep track of my feelings and thoughts and behaviors. Seems pretty simple. I mean, I don't know the biology of it but still understand how it works.

Consciousness can be pretty complicated, for instance what is con- sciousness, what does it feels like to feel something? I mean I guess consciousness is just the sum total of our mental processes. So con- sciousness is just the combination of our attention and awareness, sometimes our memory and sometimes we use our language. It is also the combination of our thoughts and our feelings, whatever it is we are feeling at the moment and if we are thinking about something. I mean, thought and feeling are probably the two greatest contributions to consciousness. What else could be going on other than thinking about something and feeling something? We could also be more or less aware and attentive. We could be using our judgment or making decisions or problem solving. What are some of the other mental processes that our consciousness could be using? We could be learning something, We could be trying to figure something out or problem solve.

So consciousness is just basically what we are aware of, or if we are aware in general. A lot of things contribute to our awareness or our consciousness, like whatever we are aware of at any moment. Humans are aware of their thoughts and feelings and other mental functions like memory and attention and awareness, language and knowledge and concepts, their thinking processes and feeling processes, so whatever they are feeling they could be aware of.

What else is there to understanding consciousness? Someone could have a thought, that would make them aware of whatever the thought is about right. Feelings can also be about stuff, for instance if you feel happy there might be a reason you feel that way. What else is compli- cated about feelings and thoughts, i previously said that feelings and thoughts make a person more conscious right. Feelings and thoughts can be caused by something or be connected to something, like a be- havior or another feeling or thought. That's important for conscious- ness if you think about it because our feelings and thoughts help make us more aware. But what then is consciousness? Consciousness is our awareness of our feelings and thoughts and other mental processes. If a person is aware of their feelings and thoughts then they are conscious right. If someone is having feelings and thoughts then the person could be a conscious person, but they wouldn't be as conscious as someone who is aware of their feelings and thoughts.

I mean, so what is consciousness then? How aware a person is of their environment or their mind. In order for someone to be aware of their mind or environment they would have to be aware of their mental processes like feelings and thoughts. Those are probably the two most significant mental processes. So how aware someone is of their feelings and thoughts makes the person more conscious and aware. It makes them aware of what they are feeling and thinking, and their other mental processes like language, memory, attention and awareness. So someone could be aware of how aware they are, or if they are using language or speaking, or using their memory. If a person is aware of any of that stuff then they would be more aware of what their mind is doing. A person could also be aware of what is going on in their environment.

A person could be aware of what they are thinking about also, the more aware they are of what they are thinking about the more conscious they would be because they would be aware of their own mind and their environment. I need to simplify that. Consciousness is a persons awareness of their mind or their environment. So if someone is aware of what their mind is doing then they would be more conscious. They could also be aware of their environment, the environment could be influencing or causing the person's mind to feel or think things. So what is consciousness then? A person could be conscious of their mind and what it is doing. It could be experiencing any of the mental processes such as attention, aware- ness, memory, learning, language, feeling, thinking, problem solving, decision making, perception, insight, creativity, knowledge, concepts, mental representations, the use of categories, or other mental processes. all of those mental processes are things the mind does. So consciousness would be if someone is aware of what their mind is doing. One thing a mind could be doing is experiencing the mental processes I just listed.

A person could be aware of what they are feeling or thinking or whatever it is they are experiencing. That makes them more conscious because it is what they are experiencing or feeling. Most of the mental processes contribute to the persons feelings or thoughts. A person could be aware of what they are feeling. just feeling something is different from being aware of those feelings. It could be that someone has a feel- ing that they are not aware of. I guess that could involve various degrees of awareness.

that seems complicated, for instance what does it mean to be aware of a feeling or thought or aware of something in the real world? that is actually pretty simple, it is just how aware someone is of what they are feeling or thinking, or whatever else their mind might be doing.

The mind can also experience things from their environment, but those things get experienced in the mind. That seems like a more simple explanation of consciousness. Con- sciousness is just the awareness of a persons feelings and thoughts and other things the mind can do or experience.

That seems like a pretty good explanation of consciousness. Either someone is feeling something or thinking about something, and they can be aware of what they are thinking or feeling. Whatever the person's mind is doing they could be aware of. For instance they could be aware of a feeling that they are having. They could be aware of thoughts that they are having. If they are trying to figure something out then they know they are doing that. They could also know about the feelings that they are having at any moment. I can feel things right now and I'm aware of those feelings. I'm aware that I have feelings and thoughts. I am perfectly aware of my feelings and how I feel all the time or just in general.

So I'm going through a lot of material. There are feelings and thoughts in the mind. I can think clearly, and I can function, what else would I need to be able to do anyway? Thinking is pretty simple if you think about it, I mean, a thought is just a thought, and a feeling is just a feeling. Feelings and thoughts come and go in the mind all of the time. What else does the mind do anyway? That enables me to function and think clearly. I am logical and can think clearly. There's an emotional experience and an intellectual experience that I can feel. THe emotional experience involves feelings while the intellectual experience involves thoughts. Thoughts are important for thinking, while feelings help people have experiences of feeling. So there is a feeling that someone feels, is the feeling physical or is it only a mental feeling? I mean, there is a mental or psychological world and a physical world that can both experience feelings. Are feelings physical or are they mental then? That's kind of a complicated question then. I want to know what all my feel- ings are and how they feel exactly right. I don't know if there is a lot to understand about how feelings feel. I mean, what is complicated about feeling stuff. It seems like it's pretty simple I would think.I'm trying to do an analysis of what my feelings feel like. There are physical feelings and mental feelings. I guess there's a big difference between mental feel- ings and physical feelings then. Consciousness is important for feelings, feelings can be conscious. How could a feeling be unconscious then? If it is unconscious then you wouldn't feel it right, so it wouldn't even be a feeling. How can anything be unconscious then if unconscious means by definition that it is beneath your awareness. How can I separate out mental feelings from physical feelings then, I mean, when i feel a physical feeling it is also mental because i can feel it in my brain or feel it. I mean, all physical feelings are processed in the brain, which is where everything is felt, both mental and physical feelings are felt in the brain. What then is the difference between a physical feeling and a mental feeling then? I suppose that physical feelings feel physical while mental feelings you don't feel a physical presence. That means you can feel physical feelings People can also feel mental feelings, those feelings don't have a physical presence like how physical feelings do. Physical feelings you can feel somewhere in your body, while mental feelings do not have a physical presence. So what else would I need to know, I know that there are sensory feelings, but aren't all physical feelings sensory ones? Like taste and touch, those are both physical feelings. So that means that some things feel physical, while others are mental and do not have a physical presence. That is kind of obvious. What else would I need to know about feelings and thoughts then. So i don't know what else to say, i have feelings and thoughts and stuff. I don't need to explain any- more of it. Actually I explained a lot in my previous articles about it. So what else do I need to learn? What else is there to learn anyway, I mean I know what the definition of consciousness is, I also know that I have feelings and thoughts.

So what else do I need to learn or take notes about? There's feelings and thoughts, there are also physical sensations. They used to be doing research, I had a role to play in that. Now everything is figured out and stuff. What else is there to take notes about? I took notes about feelings and thoughts. For instance some feelings could be somewhat uncon- scious. Thoughts can influence feelings. How could a feeling influence a thought? If you have a feeling, then you think about the feeling and come up with a thought I suppose.

So what else do I need to figure out anyway? I understand how the mind works. There's feelings and thoughts, that's mostly what the mind does.

There's also mental processes like problem solving and decision mak- ing, attention and awareness, judgment, reasoning and choice, memory, learning and language, mental representations, knowledge, concepts and categories, automaticity, self-knowledge and insight, creativity and perception. That's pretty much all of the mental processes Conscious- ness isn't really a mental process, well I guess it is, but it is more like the combination of all the mental processes. So feelings can influence thoughts and thoughts can influence feelings. When would someone think about a feeling then? Or how could a thought influence a feeling? When do feelings influence thoughts and when do thoughts influence feelings? So feelings can influence thinking, and thinking or thoughts can influence how a person is feeling. So what is the difference between feelings and thinking then? I think that thinking is intellectual, while feelings are emotional.

So I'm trying to figure this out, do I even need to make any more progress? I mean, I'm pretty developed physically and intellectually, I don't know if I need to get any smarter or stronger. I figured out the difference between feelings and thoughts.

I'm trying to do an analysis here. What else do I need to figure out anyway? I guess that there's a lot of information I could benefit from learning about. I could try to do that I suppose.

What would I need to learn though? I already know basically how the mind works and how feelings and thoughts work. That seems like a pretty good understanding.

Is there anything else about the mind to understand other than that it has feelings and thoughts? What else does the mind do? It categorizes information and knowledge. It thinks about different concepts with thoughts, What else is there anyway/ There is thoughts and consciousness, and attention and consciousness, i said before, you could be aware of any of your mental processes.

States of consciousness Representations Mental states

So what else am I supposed to learn about consciousness? There is awareness of your own mind and your environment. What is everything that someone might be aware of anyway?

Consciousness can be pretty complicated if you think about it, i mean, what exactly is going on in the brain that makes consciousness form?

So what could be complicated about consciousness? There are the mental processes like attention, memory, learning, language, judgment, reasoning, choice, automaticity, self-knowledge, insight, thinking, feel- ing, knowledge, mental representations, concepts, categories, problem solving, decision making, thinking, feeling, perception and creativity.

So that's how the mind works basically, by using those mental processes, and someone could be more or less aware of what their mind is doing and what processes are being used. They could also be aware of external inputs from their environment through their senses. So that is external inputs and internal inputs that they could be aware of. I mean, what else is there to understanding consciousness anyway? Seems pretty simple, you can just br aware of what your mind is doing and what it's processing.

So what does it mean to be aware anyway? You can be aware in general or aware of a mental process, or aware of something external like an input from the environment. I mean, when someone is aware of something then they understand what it is they are thinking and feeling then they become more aware of it I suppose. But what then does it mean to be 'aware' of something then?

1 Consciousness is complicated

2 Energy is complicated (there's global energy and interpersonal energy)

3 Logic can be difficult to acquire (psychosis is serious)

4 Cognitive psychology is difficult to understand

5 Global energy is complicated you need to have a feeling for it

6 Consciousness can be isolated and influenced by energy or other types of stimulation (medication, drugs and food for instance)

7 If the consciousness is isolated then what does it need to support it? I said it can be influenced by energy and other types of stimulation, but that can be complicated for instance how could the conscious- ness function without any support? Can you get a feeling for that for instance? I can, I basically try to feel what my consciousness would be like without getting any inputs and by itself, I can get a feeling for that. That's pretty interesting. Like how would my consciousness be if it was by itself not getting any inputs?

I think three things are needed to continue to develop earth until the development is complete and everything repeats 1. Biological develop- ment 2. Technological development 3. Psychological development

Eventually those could be completely developed, The biological development includes the development of biotech, which is a combina- tion of two of those things (obviously biology and technology). Also, everything will eventually be repeating because there is only a limited number of ideas or categories or things people can do, the technological and mental development will also eventually be finished. They could change things up I guess but the mental development will be finished, I pointed out that at the beginning of time the consciousness, feelings and thoughts people had were much weaker than now.

I'm good at 4 academic subjects, 1) logic 2) cognitive psychology 3) consciousness 4) history So what do i understand about those topics. Cognitive psychology is important because it's mostly about the minds mental processes. i listed those earlier. i mean, just talking about the mind's mental processes demonstrates how the mind functions. what else would someone need to know about how the mind works and is structured. Is there a difference between how it is structured and how it functions, however? How it functions would just be the behaviors and outputs it has like the actions it tells the body and mind to do. while how it is structured would be how thinking works in the mind, or how executive functioning and emotion regulation function in the mind anyway.

So there are feelings and thoughts, and then there is your awareness of your feelings and thoughts. Awareness can also be described as con- sciousness, you can be conscious of your feelings and thoughts and your other mental processes like memory, attention, language, judgement and reasoning.

What else could someone be conscious of in their own mind then. I mean, obviously they could be conscious of their external environment or conscious of other mental processes. You could be conscious of your perceptions, like your perception of your external environment or your perception of your own internal feelings and thoughts.

If I want to learn anything that I want to, what would i need to study, I mean there are a lot of topics out there, there are sciences that use math and science that do not a good understanding at all.

Cognitive psychology The mind being dependent on stimulation and what it would be like to be without any inputs into the mind or an isolated consciousness The energy on the planet part of which provides stimulation for the mind Logic and points about logic Cognitive psy- chology and points about it like feelings and thoughts and a simplified version of how the mental processes work Maintaining clear and logical thinking and developing intellect and physical ability is complicated A feeling for life on the planet (kind of similar to the point about the energy on the planet)

So there's consciousness, and there's energy inputs into the con- sciousness. you can isolate the consciousness and figure out what all the inputs are that are going into it. it is supported by different kinds of energy and stimulation. what is the difference between medication and other types of energy then?

There's an isolated consciousness in the brain right. The conscious- ness can be influenced by energy, what does that mean exactly, if you feel cold, then that impacts your consciousness, you can feel the cold. it influences your feelings, then maybe you feel bad because you are cold. what is the difference between feeling bad that you are cold and just feeling bad at other times then? those are all different aspects of consciousness. Some feelings are powerful while others are weak. For instance if you feel very cold then you are probably going to feel very bad, your consciousness gets effected by the feelings.

What does that mean, that your consciousness can be effected by your feelings? I think that your consciousness is basically who you are, it is your identity and sense of self. This consciousness of who you are can be effected by different feelings and types of energy, or lack of energy. if you are not getting any energy inputs into your consciousness then you might feel bad and you could suffer. Your consciousness would suffer or you would suffer, saying the person is sad is the same as saying that their consciousness is sad, and so on.

So there is energy inputs into the consciousness. What does that mean exactly anyway? What could be an input for the person or their mind or their consciousness. The temperature influences the person right. What else influences how a person is feeling, that's kind of impor- tant to note.

Lot's of things can influence how a person is feeling. How does medication influence how a person is feeling then? It could alter thoughts or feelings. But i mean, lots of things change people's feelings and thoughts, not just medications.

So what are all the energy inputs that could be influencing the consciousness then? What is the complete picture, in other words, of how the consciousness functions? There's an isolated consciousness in the brain right, it gets support from stimulation and different types of energy, what are all of those inputs? Furthermore, the consciousness might be completely unsupported, then it would probably be about to die right, that would be an example of what the consciousness would be like without any inputs, I would think that it would always need inputs. I suppose a person could be fine without stimulation for a while, but there would still be energy inputs going into the consciousness from their body or brain.

3

Bibliography
Kurth, C. (2022). *Emotion*. Routledge.
Goldie, P. (2010). *The Oxford Handbook of Philosophy of Emotion*.
Oxford University Press.
Evans, D. (2019). *Emotion: A Very Short Introduction*. Oxford Uni- versity Press.
Plutchik, R. (1990). *The Emotions*. University Press of America. Tappolet, C. (2023). *Philosophy of Emotion*.
Routledge.
Fox, A. S., Lapate, R. C., Shackman, A. J., & Davidson, R. J. (2018).
The Nature of Emotion. Oxford University Press.
Pettinelli, M. (2021). *The Selected Writings of Mark Pettinelli*.
Kindnesssaox.
Brady, M. S. (2019). *Emotion: The Basics*. Routledge.
Robinson, M. D., Watkins, E. R., & Harmon-Jones, E. (2013).
Handbook of Cognition and Emotion. Guilford.
Sternberg, R. J., & Kaufman, S. B. (2011). *The Cambridge Hand- book of Intelligence*. Cambridge University Press.
Gross, J. J. (2015). *Handbook of Emotion Regulation*. Guilford.

A Conversation About Measuring Emotion and its Conclusion: Mood

Classification

1.1 Measuring Emotion

"Alex" (Xander T. Evans) in this conversation was initially a person who sent me an email about one of my articles.

Alex: I am very intrigued by the report you did entitled, **The Psychology of Emotions, Feelings, and thoughts**. I would like to discuss further research and run a few questions by you if you have time. ...

Mark: ... it is there are different ways of categorizing observations of emotion, one is common observations (such as sex is good for someones emotional health) and functional observations (when an emotion stops at one second and another one takes its place, what is happening there, what are the emotions, why do they stop and start, etc (for example, if someone thinks a happy thought it might stop the negative thought completely) also, what are the degrees to which the emotion is felt, is it completely gone etc. ...

Alex: ... interesting though. Sort of questioning if humans can have multi-emotional tracks or just one or two emotions at a given time.

It dose seem like someone can be happy but still worry about something, but then are they just fronting the happiness on the outside when really they only feel the discontent of worry emotionaly?

I was asking previously because of an A.I. system I have been working on for some time now. When I came to the problem of organizing the emotions, I became very confused with a proper way to organize them. So many generic psychology charts show happy and sad as opposites and depression as a gray or blue. Personally I don't think they relate to colors in any fashion other than what we base on our own personal experience.

Many teenagers find black to be comforting instead of morning. Its all about cultural relativity. ...

Mark: Ok. This seems obvious when i think about it now, but obviously there is going to be distinct emotions when you're doing something that are dominant, also emotions are going to change in an interaction or over the course of doing any one thing (someone could be being mean, the nature of the pain could change in a consistent pattern)

Alex: and then you run the question of things such as "S+M" where the boundaries of pleasure are pushed slightly into pain as a way of building towards anticipated release.

This is also true when waiting for fruit to ripen on a less morbid note....

So yours noting that as emotions continue they slowly regress in comparison to there physical input. Sort of like a drug addict always needing more drug induced input to get the same emotionally stimulated output?

Mark: I think that any new stimulus (assuming you like it a lot) (such as getting a new toy or meeting someone new) seems to provide the most emotion at first because it is more interesting because it is new. That is how emotion could change over a long period of time, I would like to know how emotion changes on a more moment to moment basis like in an interaction, how often does someone realize they made the other person happy or when an emotion occurs. People might know they made someone else happy, but i don't think it is like they become happy at a certain time and go from normal to happy in one second. People notice a lot of things that are emotional all the time you just wouldn't think of them as emotions but they really are -for instance - when you do something like say hi to someone you might have noticed that they were sad which caused you to say hi. You might or might not realize that you realized they were sad and that is why you said hi. That is how life works I would say, emotions cause people do things and sometimes they notice them and sometimes they don't.

I just realized something else. Emotions change in dynamic ways, my guess would be many more ways than saying they decrease over time. Each emotion could have a unique feeling - for instance the emotion happy could feel slightly or largely different each time you experience it. As an emotion continues over a period of a few minutes or days or any time period how it feels could change slightly or drastically. One emotion could lessen another emotion, like pain could make you less happy. One emotion could trigger another emotion - the emotion pain could trigger the emotion of happiness. Thoughts, physical inputs, and emotions all interact and influence each other in various patterns and in how they feel. I couldn't guess how many major patterns there are.

Alex: awesome, see this brings me back to my very first question. How you would measure the "primaries" of emotion.

All the parts that fit together that cannot be measured in any other way. I am certain like a multidimensional color wheel that an emotion can change intensity, relevance, sort of like opacities, and hues...

It's an oddball concept but I do think you could relate it to the moment to moment changes. You may experience contentment throughout the day and feel what some would consider many shades of green. Towards evening, like an old painting your emotions would sort of blur with less energy to fuel them, still dynamic and still very interactive even through the night in dreams.

I find interest and question in so many aspects of life it's hard to focus on just a single topic, though I must say if you could figure a set of dimensions to measure emotion with, you would have a much better time recording and studying them.

The way you brought it up reminds me of waiting for a phone call from a friend when maybe reading a sad novel. You get so into every page your nearly living the drama feeling more and more concerned for the direction of the protagonist. Then suddenly the phone rings and your perk up with a contradicting grin. This to me acts out a scenario of what you mentioned. ...

Mark: Ok. I think a way to measure emotions would be for the person experiencing the emotions to describe what the emotion feels like. Something that might help them do that would be to compare the experience or time period or object or whatever you want to know how it made them feel to things where they know what the feeling was like. For instance someone could say, "going to the restaurant felt more like talking to my girlfriend than moving lawns". So I think the only thing you can use really is things where they have identified what the feeling is like. If they don't know how something made them feel I don't know if they could use that to compare it with because it wouldn't be significant. If they say, That is kind of obvious though, the only way to describe how you feel would be to say what the emotion you felt was or compare it to something else significant. Maybe talking about significant things would put the person in a higher emotional state where they obviously appear to be more emotional. I noticed people when they are experiencing intense emotions, it is obvious to me - their eyes get watery or intense looking. Maybe in this state you could measure emotions better because they are really feeling emotions then and are being emotional. There is obviously a physical reaction in this higher state (the eyes I mentioned for instance). I also sometimes notice that there is at least a slight change in tone or whatnot when a person realizes something significant or just changes tone and starts to feel a new emotion that might be strong or not. I don't know if in the higher emotional state you could compare and rate different physical clues to different types of emotion. Though it would seem to me like it would be easier to see how someone feels about something when they are really in a "feeling" kind of mood. I guess an example of this would be someone saying "I don't care about that, it was nothing like (this other thing I felt)" Then maybe you measure the strong thing they felt by describing about how intense it was for them. I think in this higher more intense emotional state people could more obviously display how they feel about certain things, for instance if you mention something their eyes could glow or be really intense for those seconds and this would tell you rather well what the thing you mentioned felt like.

But I guess it's obvious that emotion is expressed in the eyes very well. You can just use logic to guess what someone might be feeling after you studied their emotions in the higher emotional state. This is kind of like ink blot tests - once a psychology researcher did the test on me and said I was depressed. I realized later that she was able to read my emotions better by doing the test and evoking that emotion from me. If you just go through someones significant life experiences you might be able make them more emotional or easier to read. That I would say is the only way to measure emotion, other than studying them and trying to figure out what makes them feel. I also think you might be able to use computers to analyze exactly what someone is feeling by looking at changes in the eyes and analyzing those changes carefully - but I am not in a position to do that. The eyes display so much information, you could easily measure subtle changes and observe those changes in a real situation.

I don't know if you could take this any further than that. Maybe I could classify more about the emotion that is occurring like you suggested. I think what is happening when people experience feeling is a lot more complicated than just saying, "this person is mostly happy, but also a little sad". Think about that, a state of feeling at any one time must be incredibly complex. I would think that this state is dependent on what you are doing right then primarily, or what you've been doing or started doing in the past hour. For instance, if someone said something to you that made you feel bad, then you know the primary feeling is sadness, but what is unique about it you could describe by describing the other person, why that person makes you feel bad, what about the comment they made exactly made you feel bad. That would be the primary emotion in that circumstance. Or if you are mowing a lawn, the primary feeling you would probably be experiencing is the feeling of mowing lawns, unless you are off in your own world thinking about something else anyway. That seems really obvious when I say that - that people feel emotions about what they are doing and each emotion is unique. Maybe you could do - this person is mowing lawns, and he is this much emotional (maybe from reading his eyes to see how emotional he is at that moment), so those emotions must be coming from mowing the lawn. I would think you could make a computer program that could at least read how emotional someone is anyway. Then try to attribute those emotions to what they are doing or have been doing recently.

I mean, if you are doing something, that is probably going to be the primary feeling. If you reflect on that later, then the reflecting will bring up the feeling again. You could try to measure how strongly the person is feeling during one of those two examples, and how strongly they are feeling will probably be feelings for what they were doing or thinking about. I don't know how you could connect the strength of feeling to what they have been doing. They could describe what they think they are feeling, and they could describe how strongly they are feeling in general and try to connect the two.

I mean, try to connect how strongly they are feeling, what they think they are feeling, and what they have been doing.

I think that way you could discover a lot. There are at least two dimensions for feelings, one is how strong it is, the other is what it feels like (apples or oranges). The feeling could be of various types, there could be long-term feelings like depression or the opposite of that. There could be short term feelings maybe like the feeling of mowing a lawn, and there are moment to moment feelings that are things like changes in the tone of a conversation. Feelings could be intellectual or emotional, or other ways of categorizing them such as aggressive feelings or feelings when around machinery. Maybe if you just find good ways of classifying the feelings like that (by observing how similar types of things feel, you could use a more significant, emotional example of something of the same type as a less significant object in order to identify the emotion the less significant object caused in you) so you could measure them better because you did such a good job classifying and comparing them.

I mean think about it this way, the only way to measure emotion would be to ask about the strength of the emotion. Maybe you could have a computer compare expression in the eyes to how strongly someone described their emotions were being felt at that time. That might seem awkward, asking someone, "how strongly were you feeling right then". I don't know if people would really know the answer to that. I mean, if someone doesn't know that they are depressed or not, how could you possibly come up with a reliable way to measure that emotion? The only way I can think of is to design specific tests that might evoke the proper emotions, like a ink blot test that was designed to bring out the emotion depression or not - or another test that was designed to bring out what that person was feeling right then (maybe of a certain type). Then you could have a computer measure expression or change in the eyes.

The complicated thing would be classifying what type of feeling it is. It would be hard for someone to assess the strength of the feeling or how short or long term the feeling is (seconds, hours, days etc), but it would probably be harder to describe what it feels like exactly. Though I could still probably come up with a list of ways of classifying the feeling - I already mentioned intellectual, emotional, aggressive. I don't know if someone would really understand those things in a way they can actually feel and experience, but someone could still guess that the feeling was composed of certain aspects. For instance if you are in a house you could say that the person might be experiencing feelings related to houses. Maybe there are a few major types of feelings (that are more descriptive than just the defined emotions and feelings at least). Those could reveal more specifically what someone is feeling and that would be more like you are measuring their emotions. If someone is experiencing affection, for example, maybe you could more accurately assess how much affection they are experiencing if you identified some of the key emotion generators for people (like if they were around machinery, or in a house). Then you could say, well this person was around machinery in a house, so they must have at least been experiencing this much emotion because those objects usually generate a lot of emotion for people. If you assess the circumstance the person is in and label everything that could be generating emotion, maybe there are only a few things in life that are key emotion generators (types of emotion I guess). For instance if you are trying to measure how much envy someone is experiencing, you could have labeled certain things as key for generating the feeling of envy that would also help classify the type of emotion it is (or the type of envy feeling). If you understood that sibling rivalry was significant, then you could say that a lot of envy was generated in this instance because the two people were siblings. I guess what I am saying is you could label everything in life that clearly generates emotion, such as things such as sibling rivalry, houses, machinery, people being aggressive, and you could then use these things as tools to identify how much emotion someone is experiencing. You could do this because you have an understanding of each of these key things of how much emotion they generate because they are significant things of which you really understand, or feel in a way how significant they are and how much emotion they generate. So it is like I said before, compare the emotion or experience you want to measure to things where you know what the emotion felt like, which would probably be anything significant, basically.

But I guess that seems obvious when I say it that way. Identify the time period the emotion occurred, its strength, label and classify it as much as you can (what type of emotion it is), and then compare it to other significant emotions and experiences in life so you get an idea of what the emotion feels like. You could make a list "this emotion feels like...". What if someone couldn't really identify what the emotion felt like though. If they compared it to other emotions and experiences, would that really give them a good feeling for the emotion so they could "measure" it? Is anyone ever really able to "measure" an emotion by getting a feeling for it? You could clearly ask someone how an experience felt on a scale of 1 to 10, how strong and powerful and potent it was. Maybe you could have a few other things to compare the emotion to that could help measure it, for instance ask "on a scale of one to ten, how aggressive do you think this emotion was". So if someone went to a park you could ask a series of questions to help measure that emotion.

1. What was the time period that you were experiencing most of the emotions from being at the park, (for instance) when did you start to get happy and when did that emotion end.

2. Was this feeling you had at the park strong or weak? 1-10?

3. Was this feeling similar to aggressive feelings you have had or was it aggressive? 1-10?

4. Was this feeling like this other (whatever it is) significant life experience or emotion you had? 1-10?

5. Was this feeling like silly feelings you have experienced in your life? 1-10?

6. (You could keep going on trying to compare and measure it in relation to these other significant life emotions and experiences)

I guess the hard thing to do to improve that list would be come up with the "significant" life emotions or things to compare the emotion you want to measure with. But I guess the things you would compare it to would be things that the person could actually measure with a scale of 1-10. They would be things that are so significant the person could come up with a measure of how much they relate (because they have a feel for the emotion involved). I mentioned silly and aggressive feelings, though I don't know if someone could answer, "how aggressive was going to the park". It seems stupid when I talk about it that way, but it makes sense, to measure any one emotion (say the emotion of happiness from going to a park) - it could help to describe it better by comparing it to other emotions or experiences. I guess that way you are describing emotions by using other emotions and significant things. So for the feeling of envy with a sibling the significant thing you could compare it to would be "sibling rivalry" in general, and you could go on comparing it to aggressive or silly emotions (or other significant emotions or things). So maybe that is the way to measure emotion, find the other emotions that relate and ask on a scale of 1-10 how much it relates. Like you could ask how much does the emotion passion relate to the feeling of envy you had for your sibling or your emotion of happiness at the park. I would think this means that any one emotion never stands by itself, that all emotions are mixed with other emotions, this is obvious if you consider that it is hard to be completely happy without being at least a little sad or irritated at the same time.

Ok. So again, to improve the list it would be good to know what other significant emotions, life experiences, or just significant things in life are (and how they relate) because those are obviously going to generate the most emotion, relate the most and make it easier to measure the emotion you want to measure because the emotions are so large you have an idea as to their size. So what I guess is occurring here is that in order to measure emotion, simply analyze all of the factors involved with that emotion that you know. If we take my example of the person going to a park and being happy, you could analyze if there was a dog at the park that made him happy, or if someone was flying a kite. Though I don't know if going into small details would really matter because those things aren't significant enough to generate noticeable amounts of emotion. It would seem the other significant thing to factor in would be what other emotions were evoked at the park, what emotions relate to the emotion happy, in this way you make the analysis more significant (discussing more significant things) so you would be better able to measure the emotion involved.

So just analyze all of the key emotion generators and emotions that relate to what you are trying to measure (an experience, emotion etc) - this might put the person in a higher emotional state in which they are easier to read, possibly showing more expression in the eyes. What might help is if you knew what key emotion generators were and what emotions related to certain experiences or other emotions.

Your examples I think showed well experiences that are clearly emotional. I think one significant factor I know that is worth mentioning is changes in tone. Every time the tone of a conversation changes, the feeling associated with that tone changes likewise. But I think that tone applies to more than just conversations. When someone is mowing a lawn, he might have a certain tone that is happy or a tone that he is upset. He might become slightly upset many times throughout mowing the lawn if he keeps making errors, being slightly upset I would say would be like a change in tone. Tone is just a way of saying that there are slight changes which you can notice (similar to the color wheel you mentioned). Only there are more emotions, feelings and changes in tone than the few colors which exist. My point is if you take note of all the small changes in emotion and tone, such as each time the person makes an error, you could better measure how those all add up to the overall emotion. The changes in tone that people have (which I think are most noticeable in conversations) occur all the time when they are doing other things. Each one of these tones is a feeling that could add up to large amounts of emotion. If the person becomes upset 20 times because of small errors, you could say that he was very upset. You could factor in the other changes in tone that occurred while he was mowing the lawn, how many times he smiled or achieved success. Maybe a negative change in tone ruined his getting a positive tone the next time he did something well. My guess here is if you can analyze the the moment to moment changes you might be able to see how it all adds up.

I know that my reply basically went from stating in order to measure emotion only assess significant factors, to saying the opposite of that (asses the small factors). I think the significant factors are going to show up as the small factors as well, however. If you think about it, maybe the feeling of happiness for going to the park only start in a series of tone (feeling) changes once you walk into the park - and then could stay at that level of happiness after you are in it. For example maybe once you see the park your happiness would go up a little, then after you enter a little more, then after see something a little more - that is just a guess as to how these small changes might play out. I think they might be able to be observed because people can notice changes in the tone of a conversation, why not changes in the tones of everyday feelings? All those small changes contribute to the larger, more significant feelings in some way.

I don't know exactly how all the small feelings play out in everyday life. My guess would be that it is incredibly complex, experiencing many feelings (that are at least slightly noticeable) every hour. You might only describe one large feeling as taking place over an hour, or if it something like pain the large feeling could occur for the minute you had the pain. I don't know what a large feeling would be that only lasts a minute other than the feeling of pain, which can be large in a very short time period like a minute or a second. It would seem that the emotion of happy can only be large over a long period of time, like if you were happy for an hour or a day you could say that the feeling there was large because it lasted so long. I don't know how someone could say, "I felt a large happy feeling for a couple or seconds or minutes". That is why it might be hard to notice how all the small changes work and add up to the larger feeling of happiness throughout the day. Because these minor changes in feeling might be hard to notice, but probably still occur a lot. Like when you said the person perked up when he got a call from a friend, that is an example of a small change in emotion that only lasted a brief period of time. Him perking up was a positive emotion that lasted a few seconds that probably made him happier for a longer period of time. I think I can describe these small changes by saying something a little silly - that you can label every little thing that happens in life as positive or negative, or with any description of feeling or an emotion. You might get a little envious and not even notice it, but would still be there as a change in your attitude that occurred suddenly. Or anything really, whenever someone says anything that indicated that emotion was felt (like the baseball game was fun, or when they hit the rock it was annoying) you can take that and analyze it in a larger context of feelings - of how the small and large feelings play out. I think these minute changes occur all of the time and contribute to larger feelings and how the other minute changes play out.

So I guess I can add to the list of questions some points about small changes:

1. What were all the small changes in emotion that occurred, and how do these changes relate and contribute to the larger emotions that you were experiencing at the park?

2. If you do not know what all the small changes in emotion were, maybe you can guess what they were by seeing how the small changes (or the larger emotions) might have influenced any of the feelings you experienced at the park (since it all occurred as one event in the same time period).

3. How did the small and large changes in emotion and in your experience at the park influence your other small and large emotions and actions at the park?

4. What happened at the park? Which of what happened at the park were the most significant for you emotionally? Is it just going to the event and the event overall that was emotionally powerful for you and the only emotion you can identify? Or can you identify other small emotions that occurred (if you step back and look at what happened at this event)?

But I think if you were going to want to actually try to measure emotion accurately, the smaller emotions would be too hard to assess. There might be an expression in the eyes for things like "annoyance" "interest" "sadness" or whatever eyes can express, whenever an eye expresses something that a human can figure out - you could ask a computer to measure that same thing. But those would just be things that the person is trying to communicate with their eyes at that moment, it wouldn't necessarily be what they are really feeling. Maybe to try and determine the primary emotions, you could have the person do something fun for an hour, then look at their eyes and determine what changed from before. Wait another hour and do the assessment again. That second assessment would determine how much of the "fun" emotion was still present after an hour. I don't know how many emotions someone could assess like this. You could have someone do something interesting for an hour, then do an assessment of their eyes to see what changed. I don't know how you would assess the eyes if someone did four things in a row (hour after hour) that each were different emotions, say something interesting, then something boring, then something happy or fun, then something sad. Would all of those things be displayed in the eyes at the same time? This would obviously be very slight changes in the eyes that my guess only a computer could pick up. But the change might be consistent for all people - allowing it to be accurate for everyone.

I don't know what this change might be visually - I mentioned the wateriness before. If someone can display an emotion with their eyes on purpose, maybe that would just be a more obvious example of how the eyes could show that. I think eyes change in two ways, one would be what the expression is - the other would be the "heaviness" to the eyes. For instance if someone was tired their eyes might look more drugged up - or if someone was emotional they might be watery. That I think would show the longer term, primary emotions because they have a physical change in the eye, versus just something you are expressing. The primary emotions probably cause a different physical condition that might be able to be read by subtle eye changes. I am not a medical doctor, but I know that if you feel very strongly you also have a physical reaction as well.

Though I don't think there could be much for us to discuss about measuring that since it would be mostly about computers if it was possible at all. I think a better example for how the small changes can add up to the larger more primary emotion would be if someone had a hopeful thought a couple of times when they were sad. Perhaps that made them happier and lessened the sadness. The previous example I used was of someone mowing a lawn who kept hitting rocks. Each time they hit a rock, they might get more irritated - you might be able to see how irritated they were overall if you looked at what happened each time. It might have stifled happiness from doing the rest of the job well. I don't know how many other clear examples you could discover other than the hope example and the being irritated example. If you discuss these small changes enough with someone maybe they will be capable of labeling how strongly their primary (and possibly minor) feelings were.

Some things (small or large phenomena) that could help someone assess how much emotion they are experiencing would be to consider:

1. What were all the thoughts you had and how did these impact your feelings

2. What were all the things (small or large) that happened and how many of these do you know impacted your feelings

3. What was your emotional state (for instance if you were worried) and how did this impact your feelings and what happened during the event

4. Did you have a physical reaction to anything that occurred (for instance jumping in excitement, or blushing) that might indicate a feeling occurred

I guess this means what I that what I said earlier about how anytime anyone makes any comment about emotion at all, they are indicating or trying to measure emotion to some degree. I am sure most people could come up with a lot of examples of this, and frequently do it themselves. Saying things such as "this happened so many times it annoyed me a lot". The word "annoyed" in that statement indicates the feeling of annoyance. There are degrees to which someone can describe what the feeling was like or describe the circumstances around it. An entire book could just be trying to describe the feeling for what something is like. Even a book that doesn't go on and on trying to write about how something felt, just any ordinary book has a feeling associated with it or that was communicated by it. I think most times people try to communicate emotion or how they felt they aren't very descriptive (at least from my observations). There could be someone who is very good at describing their emotions and gives a good idea as to how much they were feeling. I don't know the best way or all the ways someone could make describing feeling more scientific and accurate. You could do studies and find out what things someone says are more clearly emotional or what the best way to describe emotions for certain things are. I already mentioned that noticing everything that happened during an event, all your thoughts, your emotional state, and your physical reactions could be observed. There are probably many more better examples than my being annoyed while mowing a lawn example (that would be the type for asking about everything that occurred) and the hopeful thoughts alleviating sadness example (which would be for what all your thoughts are).

I already mentioned that you could try to measure an emotion by comparing and contrasting it to other relevant and or significant emotions or life events. You could try to compare an emotion to other emotions of the same type. I believe some people have already grouped emotions into various categories and ways of organizing them. It might help if someone reads a good description or explanation of what that emotion is and feels like.

But each persons own perception of their emotion or someone else's emotion is going to be very subjective. It isn't like you can measure emotion exactly, at best a large group of people could discuss how something is emotional or how significant something was in different ways. There are probably signs that indicate something is emotional, for instance if you like something a lot it is probably going to be more emotional for you. If something impacts you in various ways or causes you to do various things it is probably going to be more emotional.

Some of these things could be simple physical things, like playing with your hands or shuffling your feet. There are obviously the facial and eye expressions. That is why I already mentioned changes in the tone of a conversation, I would say that that is a significant part of life considering that conversation is the main way people interact. I don't know what would be the indications of the more primary emotions, maybe there is a certain tone or attitude someone adopts when they have one of those primary emotions, as well as certain actions (mental or physical) that follow along.

If people can notice tones in conversations, then maybe they can notice the tone of how someone has been feeling for the past hour or few hours (which would be their "primary" emotion". Though I don't usually notice if someone is happier than they usually are. If someone was sad or very happy I might notice it but most of the time I don't think I notice things like that. Someone could become happier than usually and other people probably wouldn't notice it at all. Does that mean that the only primary emotions are "happier than usual" "normal" and "sadder than usual" - since those are the only things other people might notice? If you think about it that way, then measuring emotion is simple. If you think about it the other way I suggested, which was to discuss with other people the many ways something impacted you emotionally, then emotion seems very complex.

I think the 'primary' emotions someone experiences would be simply changes in mood. I think if I find a good way of classifying moods then that would be the best way to measure the main emotions that people experience. If you think about it, there are so many single emotions you couldn't really say that the person mowing the lawn (who kept hitting rocks instead of just grass) was just 'happy' - that would be too simple of an assessment of his emotional state. A better assessment would be something like happy (from the action of mowing the lawn), with a little excitement, a little fear (from the loud noises hitting the rocks made), a little anxiety from hitting rocks a lot, and a little bleak and sad at being such a failure.

So the person mowing the lawn for an hour or so I would say developed a certain mood for that hour. A mood is just an emotional state, a set of feelings that are similar or point in a certain direction. Like someone could be a mood to do cooking, and they could have a certain set of feelings that come along with that. From the time they start cooking to the time they finish the feeling of the mood they are in for cooking is going to change, but is still the same mood with the same basic feelings. So a mood then in my view is just a certain set of feelings that relate to one thing (like cooking, mowing a lawn, or being happy or sad). An emotional state is also a certain set of feelings however they aren't necessarily about one thing, it is your entire emotional state including everything going on. A mood is just the emotions related to what the mood is about, which is probably going to be what you are doing. You could be in the mood to do cooking without actually doing cooking, and in that way you'd be experiencing some of the emotions you do when you cook without actually doing it. However, you could describe your entire emotional state as a mood　if you labeled the mood well enough or if your entire emotional state was simple enough to be described as one mood (though I don't know if you could say someone's entire emotional state was of "cooking" or "happiness" for example).

1.2 Classifying Moods

A psychological mood is a relatively long lasting emotional state (a few days or so) (a temporary mood I would say (which is the kind of mood I am referring to in this article) lasts from a few minutes to a few hours). A mood therefore could be comprised of many different feelings at the same time. Moods can be positive, negative, neutral, or a mix. You could have a unique mood that maybe only you experience, such as a certain attitude that comes up around someone or someplace. You could then be in your own personal "mood" - because this mood has a unique feeling. Maybe in this mood you are both sad and happy at the same time, maybe you can classify what emotions are occurring and know that you might be the only person to experience a mood like that. Any emotion or feeling could be a part of a mood. It is really just a matter of how much of the feeling you can identify and label.

I would say that love is more of a mood than joy, because love is a much more complex emotion. If you are joyful, then you aren't sad, you are only describing the single emotion of happiness. If you are experiencing love, there might be many emotions that go along with it. Similarly, aggressiveness is more complicated than just being vigilant - if you are aggressive, you could be happy, frustrated, sad, optimistic; however if you are vigilant you are just being "ready". However, that is just how it seems to me, you could be joyful but still be in a more complicated mood than if you were experiencing the emotion of love, and you can be vigilant and be in a more complicated mood than you are when it seems to you that you are being "aggressive".

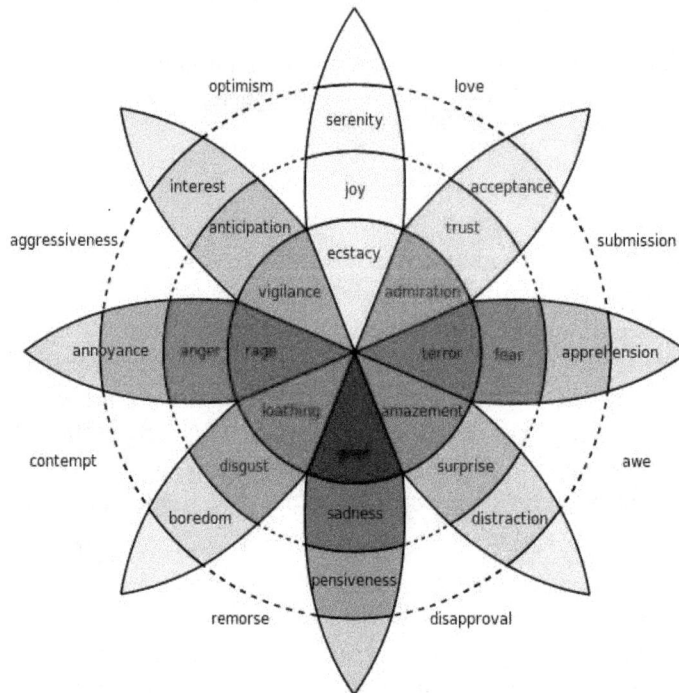

Figure 1.1   Robert Plutchik created a wheel of emotions in 1980 which consisted of 8 basic emotions and 8 advanced emotions each composed of 2 basic ones[1] It looks to me more like the "moods" are on the outside while the single emotions are towards the center.

The advanced emotions in the graph by Plutchik are the ones on the outside. They are advanced because they are a combination of the two legs of the diagram that they are in between. For instance aggressiveness could be the result annoyance, interest, anger, anticipation, rage and vigilance. The interest there raises the persons energy level and the anger directs it into aggression. Like I said before, some emotions and emotional states, moods, can be very complicated and some can be very simple. Just basically describing ones feelings in the most complicated way, by showing all of them and how they relate to the other feelings, is a great way to try to think about what you or someone else might be feeling.

An emotional state must be a lot more complicated than simply being a combination of a few feelings like afraid, happy, sad, anxious, etc. Each one of those feelings is going to be unique every time based upon what happened. For instance, if you were afraid because there was a gun involved, then the gun is going to contribute to the unique feeling of fear for that instance. There are probably going to be other things contributing to your feeling of fear that you aren't aware of but might be if you thought about it more, maybe something like a person you met earlier that day or some other smaller factor you might have not been aware of.

That just basically means though that everything in life contributes to unique feelings and emotional states. That is rather obvious, it is just then a matter of figuring out what the significant and relevant factors are. There might also be significant things that aren't obvious to most people, however. There is a way that emotions function on a moment to moment basis that is significant. If someone understood how much happiness would be too much for someone, then they might understand when someones excitement would automatically decrease in order to decrease the happiness to keep it from getting too large. A sort of emotional balancing probably occurs between emotions all the time that would be worthy to note. If you take into account all the thoughts that people have that they are not aware of, it seems clear that many

1.   Plutchik, R. "The Nature of Emotions". http://replay.waybackmachine.org/20010716082847/ http://americanscientist.org/articles/01articles/Plutchik.html American Scientist. Retrieved 14 April 2011.

of those thoughts could be significant you just don't happen to aware of them unless you learned which might be significant first. There are prejudices, social judgments, perceptions and self concepts - a lot of which you might not be aware of.

You could do your best to guess everything that someone was feeling at that moment. If you think about it that way, you could describe someones feelings based off of real things around them and that happened to them, instead of just with feelings and emotions. Just saying, "this person just went to the store" reflects something about their emotional state. It is taking it too a deeper level of analysis to then say, "this person just went to the store, so they are happy they got to get out of the house". If you just describe absolutely everything that is going on you would then have a better idea as to what the person was feeling. You can ask someone what their feelings are or what the best way to describe them would be. Showing the emotions (like the diagram by Plutchik) could help to discuss what the feelings someone is experiencing are.

The emotion annotation and representation language (EARL) proposed by the Human-Machine Interaction Network on Emotion (HUMAINE) classifies 48 emotions.[2] Those emotions are grouped into categories which I see as types of moods that people can have. There is an art image for each of those categories beneath. I have an analysis of each of the categories beneath the art images. Basically what I have done was show how there are other feelings and emotions (along with thoughts and emotion changes) that probably accompany those various moods. That is what a mood is, a set of feelings - and typical sets of feelings can be described and classified. There are also going to be certain thoughts that accompany various moods, and certain ways the emotions fluctuate (and how they fluctuate in relation to other emotions).

Negative and forceful
- Anger
- Annoyance
- Contempt
- Disgust
- Irritation

Negative and not in control
- Anxiety
- Embarrassment
- Fear
- Helplessness
- Lonely
- Powerlessness
- Worry

Negative Thoughts
- Doubt
- Envy
- Frustration
- Guilt
- Shame

Negative and passive

---

2. "HUMAINE Emotion Annotation and Representation Language". http://emotion-research.net/ projects/humaine/earl Retrieved June 30, 2006.

- Boredom

- Despair

- Disappointment

- Hurt

- Sadness

Agitation
- Stress

- Shock

- Tension

Positive and lively
- Amusement

- Delight

- Elation

- Excitement

- Happiness

- Joy

- Pleasure

Caring
- Affection

- Empathy

- Friendliness

- Love

Positive thoughts
- Courage

- Hope

- Pride

- Satisfaction

- Trust

Quiet positive
- Calm

- Content

- Relaxed

- Relieved

- Serene

Reactive
- Interest

- Politeness

- Surprised

Figure 1.2 Negative and forceful

Anger could be a big component in being negative and forceful. I don't know how negative and forceful someone could be solely because of something like disgust or irritation or annoyance. Hate or contempt makes sense as well as those are also powerful emotions. I can image someone getting very angry and that being a powerful emotion, or hating something a lot. I think someone could get negative and forceful from disgust, irritation and annoyance but I would say that the negativity isn't as powerful as something someone could get from something like a true hatred or anger. If you hate something you are being passionate, it is a strong emotion. If you are disgusted by something you do truly dislike it and that could push you into the negative/forceful state, however you don't necessarily care in an extreme way. If you did, then you would hate it or be angry at it.

I mean, for what reasons would someone get negative and forceful? Maybe they feel like they want power and to do this they could hurt other people. That wouldn't be hatred or anger it would just be lust for power. Someone could be negative and forceful as a defensive response (such as being angry at someone or hating someone) or from their own initiation (getting angry for some selfish reason such as an attempt to achieve power). So there are different things that could cause a negative and forceful mood. These feelings would be a part of the mood because they caused it and are therefore related to it. When that person is being negative and forceful, some of the feelings they experience would be motivational feelings.

People could get angry because they were hurt in some way, and this could cause them to be negative and forceful. Or someone could just be aggressive, instead of being defensive, and become negative and forceful. In that case I don't think that anger would be a part of it since you'd have to get angry just so you could be negative and forceful, which I suppose is possible but doesn't seem to me to make much sense, since it is a lot easier to become angry in response to someone. You could be mad at someone, which could be the emotions contempt and and annoyance, but in order for the emotion of anger to be evoked in you you probably would have had to have something bad done to you by that person. Or at least your perception has to be that something bad was done to you, I suppose that it could be a trivial thing as long as you perceive that something bad was done to you.

This is why it makes sense to me that all of those emotions are grouped into the "negative and forceful" category - because in order to become negative and forceful it would be easier if there were more emotions involved. I mean if you were feeling all of those things towards someone - anger, annoyance, contempt, disgust and irritation - then it makes sense that that would cause you to become negative and forceful. If only one or two of those emotions were evoked I don't know if that would be enough for someone to become negative and forceful from. I suppose someone could be "forceful" without much of the negativity, and in that case none of those emotions would be needed considering that people can be violent without being emotional or annoyed by someone.

Figure 1.3   Negative and not in control

I think the reason that "not in control" goes along with "negative" is that if you had control over your emotions or were stable then you wouldn't be experiencing the negativity because you would be making yourself happy. People are certainly in an inferior emotional state when they are embarrassed or experiencing anxiety. Helpless, powerless, afraid and worried is a state I wouldn't think many people would want to be in. That is probably where the sense of not being in control comes from, because you are probably less collected when in this state. These are things that hurt emotionally, so therefor it threatens your well-being. I also believe that negative feelings and pain serve as an emotional stimulus, which could help raise you out of the inferior emotional state by helping you focus and be more intense (due to the nature of the pain). Negativity I think can actually help a lot because of how it serves as a stimulus. While in the state of negativity, however, it probably doesn't seem like it is helping because of all of those negative feelings. But at least in this state you are in a state of intensity, which is important to have because emotional intensity is needed frequently every day.

What could cause a negative and not in control state? Maybe getting hurt really badly, that would certainly make you experience negative emotions and be helpless and afraid. I feel that way right now because I have a bad cold. But I am also doing other things while I have the cold, so it isn't my only mood or emotional state right now. Other things have kept me busy, but the negative mood of the cold dominates and makes me feel bad. Maybe some moods are only experienced by themselves, while other moods can occur simultaneously. I am not in control, there is nothing I can do about being sick. I can try and experience other moods to make myself feel better emotionally, however. No one is ever totally not in control, they can use their thoughts to help put themselves in a better mood or do something that might change the situation.

In addition to helpless, powerless, afraid and worried; lonely, embarrassed and anxious are also are part of this mood. I don't know if fear is necessary for this typical emotional state to occur. Fear is a powerful emotion, someone could be anxious without being afraid, or powerless or helpless or the others for that reason. Someone can experience anxiety and not be troubled by it. Or someone could experience a lot of fear and it could not cause them to be anxious in a similar manner. Though it could certainly seem that these emotions would all go together, I mean, if you have a lot of anxiety then it would make sense that you might be at least a little bit afraid, worried, lonely, embarrassed, powerless and helpless. It would seem to make sense that any one of those would rarely occur just by itself.

Self-confidence (or lack of it) is similar to being embarrassed. Though lack of self confidence seems like a minor emotion compared to the other emotions mentioned that comprise this mood. In fact, it seems like someone would be experiencing a lot of emotion if they were experiencing the emotion of fear and embarrassment at the same time. It doesn't seem possible for someone to experience all of those emotions full-force (the maximum each could be experienced) at the same time, that would simply be too much emotion for one to experience. Powerless seems like an easy emotion to experience since that emotion doesn't have a lot of force to it, it is more like experiencing that you don't have any power. Helplessness is similar to that, but loneliness is a little bit different in that there seems to be some tangible emotion involved. When someone is lonely, they have real feelings of loneliness, when someone is helpless, however, it doesn't seem like that would be a powerful emotion because it seems more like just being out of it, instead of feeling powerfully.

Powerless is similar to helpless. And worried and lonely are also similarly weak emotions, unless the worry and loneliness leads to anxiety, then those two by themselves wouldn't seem to me to be very strong because they are such weak emotions. Similarly, embarrassment and all of those are just similar to lack of self confidence, which isn't a strong emotion at all. Unless it leads to anxiety or fear (or occurs simultaneously), the other emotions in this mood group don't seem like they would be powerful by themselves. I suppose I am saying that the only strongly negative emotions are ones like anxiety, fear and pain. The other emotions by themselves don't seem to have pain as a part of them, they could be causing the emotion pain - but they are much more independent of it than something like anxiety.

Figure 1.4   Negative thoughts

Negative thoughts is an obvious kind of mood. Doubt, envy, guilt, frustration and shame are just thoughts that you wouldn't think help you in any way. I wouldn't think that doubt is that bad or painful most of the time, considering that there might be some doubt with every thought you have and that could be perfectly normal. Negative thoughts just seem to me like they don't generate any significant amount of real pain. Envy and guilt I would say are similar, they are probably harmless most of the time (though i'm not saying that they couldn't be fairly bad), I mean how big of a deal could it be for someone to be jealous of someone else, it isn't really going to hurt them over the long run. Frustration and shame seem more negative because those could be rather painful, while something like doubt probably isn't going to generate any pain. I think someone could be in a mood of having negative thoughts, all types of negative thoughts. I would think that such a mood could last from a few minutes to a few hours. I couldn't really imagine someone having constant negative thoughts for days, though I suppose that is possible. I personally try to be as optimistic as possible so I feel better, but the reality of life is that there is a lot to be negative about so it is possible that people get very upset and have lots of negative thoughts, impacting their mood and emotions for a while. You might not notice if you are having such thoughts, these thoughts might be more unconscious in nature or just thoughts you are less aware you are having.

Someone could be in a mood that makes them think a lot of negative thoughts. That would just be being in a "bad" mood, because it is negative. You could be in a bad mood and decide to not think negative thoughts, because your thoughts are under your control. You think about a lot of bad things that might happen to you or are happening to you, or how your current emotional state is that is contributing to the envy, guilt, frustration or shame you are feeling (whichever one(s) it is you are feeling). This seems rather obvious, a negative mood could further your thinking negative thoughts, which could further the negative mood. Real things that happened to you in addition to your own thoughts could contribute to this mood. Your negative mood could automatically make you think negative thoughts and there could be nothing you could do about it because you feel so poorly. It might be the natural thing to think negative thoughts while experiencing negative emotions, this could possibly help you deal with the emotions or something like that. I mean if something bad happened to you or is happening to you, it is natural to reflect negatively.

How harmful could negative thoughts be? They are just thoughts. I would say that anger, fear, and anxiety are much worse because they are more real. With those the person actually experiences real pain. I admit that envy and guilt can be fairly bad, but that is only because they would start generating the emotion pain they because they are so negative. Whenever one of these negative emotions starts generating the emotion pain, or the emotion anger, fear or anxiety - which are all closer to pain than the other negative emotions, then it is a lot worse than it is just by itself, without the pain. But that is sort of a redundant statement, it should be clear that a negative emotion can be painful. It is obvious, then, that any negative emotion could be mixed with stronger negative emotions or with pain.

Figure 1.5 Negative and passive

Boredom, despair, disappointment, hurt and sadness. The words "boredom" and "disappointment" make it seem like the hurt, sadness and despair aren't that bad. If you were really hurt you wouldn't be bored, you would be in pain. So my guess is that the negative and passive state isn't as bad as the negative and not in control state. If you are negative but it is directed outward, that is negative and forceful, which is also probably worse than negative and passive. I know from my own experience that boredom can cause pain, but it isn't negativity that is directed towards anyone, and you are probably under control. Though the pain and negativity in the passive type can be just as bad, it just wouldn't seem like it is that way because you aren't doing anything, you are just being passive.

This (my guess) might be something like, your feelings were hurt, and then you quietly accept it and just rest with the negativity, it not causing you to become forceful or think many negative things. Maybe this type of negativity isn't as bad as pain or negativity that causes you to become forceful or think bad things. Someone just quietly accepting the pain seems like it wouldn't be a pain that is too large or disturbing (that causes a reaction). Maybe when you start getting really annoyed, it makes you more aggressive by putting you in a higher, more intense emotional state - you might then be in both the mood "negative and out of control" and "negative and forceful" at the same time. I guess that would be negative, forceful and out of control. Emotion is something that is not under your control, you could become angry and forceful because of how your emotions or attitude made you feel.

On the other hand, grief and anguish are types of sadness that are rather extreme and one isn't being forceful or out of control in those states. However someone wouldn't be bored, and they would certainly be feeling more than disappointment, so someone experiencing grief and anguish wouldn't be in this emotional state, however those types of feeling sadness show that sadness can be experienced in a rather extreme way that isn't anything like the passiveness of this state.

So my point is that when sadness is combined with boredom the sadness wouldn't be that extreme because it is a passive sadness. Someone could experience a sadness that is extreme, such as grief or anguish,   however then they wouldn't be bored or passive - they would be in pain. "Disappointment" is also a rather mild emotion, because the extreme of that would be angry.

Figure 1.6   Agitation

There is probably more to agitation than stress, shock and tension. My guess would be that fear and anger also accompany agitation a lot. If you think about it, if someone is agitated, then they are probably also going to be angry and possibly fearful depending on what made them agitated. Anger and agitation are similar, if you are angry at something you probably are also at least a little irritated by it as well. If something was powerful enough to make you angry, it is also possible that you are afraid of it also.

My guess would be that agitation is something that is out of your control, the last thing someone wants to be is annoyed to the point of agitation. My guess is that it is possible that pain or a negative state could make you agitated. Or maybe the painful feeling overrides the feeling of agitation. Agitation wouldn't seem to be as bad of a negative state in general, because agitation doesn't necessarily include pain, and I would say that pain is the main thing that people don't want to experience, though agitation is a negative emotion as well. That makes me think, what feelings contribute to the emotion of pain? You could experience a negative feeling such as annoyance and not feel any pain. There is going to probably be a mix of pain and agitation, like there how feelings are always mixed.

Stress is similar to anxiety - so are the feelings of shock and tension. Anxiety has an uneasiness and nagging quality to it, so does stress and tension. Shock probably does to, only more indirectly - for instance someone could experience shock and then afterwards they would feel uneasy because they just experienced shock. So therefore the similarity between stress, shock and tension would be uneasiness, or anxiety. "Agitation", however, implies a sort of annoyance. If someone is agitated, they are more than uneasy and anxious, they are also irritated and annoyed.

That is why stress, shock and tension are in the category for "agitation" - because agitation is more than just being annoyed - it is being irritated to such a great degree that it causes stress, shock and tension. That doesn't necessarily mean that fear and anger always accompany agitation, it just means that it is possible, and even likely that someone who is agitated feels angry or afraid of whatever caused the agitation.

Figure 1.7 Positive and lively

Amusement, delight, elation, excitement, happiness, joy and pleasure. When said all together like that it would seem like someone experiencing all of those emotions at once would be in a state of ecstasy. The word "elation" seems to imply a higher than comfortable state of happiness, almost like you are elevated to a higher than normal state. Though each of those emotions differs in how it is positive, they are not all just "happy", - for each the feeling is unique. They could contribute to a positive and lively mood but I would think that no one is ever completely happy. Life isn't just experiencing those happy emotions all of the time. Even in this positive and lively state, a large amount of negative emotions would probably occur. For instance if you were having a good time at a party you would still likely experience some negative emotion of possibly envy or something.

Positive and lively might just be an attitude, you might be that way but not be happy, though I don't know if that occurs often or not - it doesn't seem like someone would feel like being positive and lively if they were in pain. You might be positive if you were pain, in an attempt to be optimistic, but I would say that the pain would stifle your "excitement". That is what pain is, it makes pleasure go away and liveliness is related to pleasure. You need positive energy that comes from positive feelings in order to be lively, I doubt if you are in pain you could be that way.

Amusement is when you find something funny or have any kind of smug attitude, you are amused. Excitement is when someone gets too enthusiastic or happy about something, they experience excitement because they are thrilled. Elation I would say is a state of too much happiness, sort of floating on air sort of happiness. Happiness is prolonged joy. Delight is similar to excitement and pleasure, when someone delights in something they get excited about it, relishing in it, or are overly happy. The definition of pleasure is obvious - it is a positive feeling that people enjoy - I would say it is the most positive feeling because it describes a feeling that is truly enjoyable - when people are experiencing it they are pleased or very satisfied.

So while I don't think that someone could really experience all of the emotions that are part of this mood because that would be too much, someone could still experience a lot of them or possibly all of them if there were minor amounts of each one. I don't know how often someone gets into a "positive and lively" state, or when they do, if using all of those words - amusement, delight, elation, excitement, happiness, joy and pleasure - would be the best way to describe it. Someone could easily be "positive and lively" with just a large amount of pleasure and some excitement. A moderate amount of any two of those could produce a positive and lively state, or possibly even one. Someone could probably get into a wonderful, positive state with just a small amount of one of those emotions.

Figure 1.8 Caring

What seems relevant to the mood of "caring" I would think would be attachment and dependency. Caring isn't about just affection, empathy, friendliness and love. With all of those things comes attachment and dependency. If someone is in a "caring" mood, are they more afraid of strangers or more accepting? Would they become more frustrated when interacting with people if they were feeling "caring" and the people they were interacting with ignored them, not returning their affection (frustrated at interpersonal failures because they care too much)? Caring could also be a personality trait. Would someone caring (as a mood or as a personality trait) be more attention-seeking since they care more about other people and would value people more?

So I guess then the question is, "what kinds of feelings does caring invoke?". It is comparable to loving another person, if you care about someone, you might also likely love them as well. And that is basically asking the question, "what is all they mystery involved in interpersonal relationships?". Caring for someone could invoke huge numbers of feelings and a large emotional response - in which case you would probably love the person. But that is the intense form of caring, there is a lesser type of caring that occurs in your normal social interaction, that would be more like the question, "how much do you care for other people in general". Perhaps people that don't care about other people would be considered cruel types, and people that care a lot about other people passionate, empathetic types. Though both types of people could be in a caring mood, I suppose. Maybe some cruel people never feel the emotion of caring or get in the mood for it.

This mood of caring, with the emotions it involves of affection, empathy, friendliness and love; could also just be called the mood of "love" - both love and caring involve affection for someone, positive feelings toward someone else. Love just also would involve an attraction or a desire of a certain sort as well. Caring is an important part of love, it shows the tender side of it. But someone could be in the mood caring and love wouldn't have anything to do with it. People are empathetic and affectionate often, that doesn't mean they are attracted to the person. Caring is a form of love, and love is a form of caring.

Someone could be in just a "friendly" mood - or just an "affectionate" or "empathetic" mood for that matter. Each of those definitions, including love and caring, could be mixed in some way. They are all related to each other. I don't know if each time you are in a caring mood you would then try to measure how much of each of those emotions you were feeling right then. Maybe some people who are friendly are in a "friendly" mood all of the time, or at least when they are around people. How would you measure how much of the emotion of friendly they were feeling then if that person is friendly all of the time? Maybe it is just a permanent part of their emotional state (such as "happy-go-lucky").

Figure 1.9 Positive thoughts

Courage, hope, pride, satisfaction and trust. These all seem like you have strong values and do a lot of pleasant activities - and are generally leading a good life. Those would lead to positive thoughts. This doesn't necessarily mean that you are happy, it just means that you are optimistic and a good, strong person. Though that would be a person who would have the most positive thoughts I would say, everyone else has positive thoughts as well - they just don't act like they are happy and in a positive mood all of the time. Positive thoughts isn't really a mood though - you could be in a positive mood and stop thinking and the mood would still continue. I would say that you can think all of those things or not be thinking anything and still be in a "positive thoughts" kind of a mood. Though it would seem like in order to enhance or maintain a "positive thoughts" kind of a mood thinking many positive thoughts would be necessary.

It would seem to make sense that happiness or a joyful emotion is necessary if someone is going to have positive thoughts, especially a lot of positive thoughts which would be a positive thoughts "mood". I don't know which would lead to more positive thoughts, someone achieving their objectives in life, objectives that they have thought about and therefore cognitively would make them happier if they are a success, or if someone is just experiencing joyful emotions. Both of those things could lead to positive thoughts. I don't know which mood or combination of moods would cause someone to want to think positive things. Probably the mood "positive and lively" would generate more positive thoughts than the mood "quiet positive" because you would be more motivated to think positive things if you were lively and engaged.

It would also seem to me like a person with a lot of positive thoughts has a lot of determination, or maybe they are just that positive naturally with little effort involved. I don't know how many of the emotions are necessary to assist positive thoughts - someone could have positive emotions that assist positive thoughts or they could just be thinking a lot of positive things without experiencing positive emotions. I know that if someone experiences a lot of positive feelings they could reflect on those feelings and say, "oh I felt good then". In that case more positive feelings would directly lead to positive thoughts. I don't know if someone necessarily has to be fortunate in order for them to have a lot of positive thoughts.

Figure 1.10   Quiet Positive

Calm, content, relaxed, relieved and serene. I would hope that someones normal state is something in between "quiet positive" and "lively positive" considering that quiet seems too subdued and lively seems too happy and over the top. This emotional state / mood isn't completely quiet and positive, as I have said, all moods have a large mix of feelings all of the time. Even if the other feelings aren't felt very strongly, they are still there. I suppose someone could be "super relaxed" and then it would seem like they don't have a complex mood occurring, however. I would hope that life is more lively than just being relaxed anyway, I am grateful for the wide variety of feelings that people can experience, even if some of those are negative.

I guess my point is any "relaxed" emotional state probably wouldn't last very long given the nature that people need to experience emotional intensity in life. If I was simply in a relaxed state all of the time, my life would probably be pretty boring and meaningless. I would say that a mix of all the moods and emotions, combined with intensity, is the best way for someone to be happy. That makes sense to me - life isn't a joke, intensity cannot be experienced just by goofing around all of the time. Not that "goofing around" is what the mood of "quiet positive" is anyway though. I guess it just seems that way when you combine all of those relaxed adjectives together. If someone was going to have a mix of feelings, I would say using only one or two of those adjectives would be more than enough "relaxing".

This state is similar to the "negative and passive" state in terms that they are opposites - they are both quiet, passive states, only one is positive and one is negative. I think my personal experience of the passive states is a good one, even with the negativity - I guess I just like being relaxed. Someone else might like being lively, and then might find enjoyment in the "positive and lively" state. Like with the other states, it seems like too much to experience all of the emotions in this state at the same time (at least strongly anyway). Maybe in this "quiet positive" state someone is more relieved - "Relieved" seems to suggest a happiness that comes with relaxing, like you are relieved that you are no longer in an intense state, so therefore you are happy.

Figure 1.11　Reactive

If someone shows interest, politeness, and is surprised then they are responding to someone or something in an active way. I don't know if "reactive" could be a mood by itself. Could you really say, "that person is being "reactive" now"? I think that someone could be like that, if they were in a mood of wanting to respond to other people and show interest. This makes me wonder how many different moods someone could have at once. That would kind of like be being bi-polar, if you have two different moods, then you are experiencing two strong emotional states at the same time. People that are bi-polar can go from being very happy to very sad, you could say that everyone is "multi-moodal" going from extremely strong moods all of the time, or normal or weakly strong ones depending on the person.

I really like this art image I have used for "reactive", it is very lively and energetic and cool. I would think that people who often respond to other people in a similarly cool and energetic way are received well in life. I don't know if that type of person experiences the feelings "interest", "politeness" and "surprise" more - it would seem to me like they would. They would certainly be more interested in other people. They might not be polite, you can be engaged and responsive (or reactive) and not be surprised and polite. I have taken the feeling "reactive" and applied it socially. I interpreted that those three adjectives are social ones, though two of them could occur without anything interpersonal occurring.

If someone shows interest, it would nice to be rewarded with surprise. I don't see how interest or politeness is that "reactive". It would seem like interest and politeness would be more of an action that is initiated by the person (self-motivated) than an emotion that is driven as a response to something, which would be reactive. Surprise clearly is something that occurs as a response to something. Interest I can see as being reactive or responsive, for instance someone does something interesting and then they show interest as a response. The same could be said for being polite - someone is a good person or is nice and as a response they are polite to them.

1.3 What Moods Do

Moods can change someone's self-perception, their perception of others, or a lot of other stuff related to what they are thinking. This is obvious if I explain it - for instance, if you are in a bad mood, you aren't likely to respond positively to other people because you are pissed off or something. There are probably a large number of examples I could use, if you are in a positive mood you are probably more likely to be more active. Moods obviously are going to influence your thinking, and what happens to you is going to change your mood. Maybe a mood could put you in a state of feeling emotion for only certain types of people. People make decisions based off of what they are feeling all of the time. If you feel poorly, you are probably going to do certain things to change that mood. People make evaluations about what they are feeling and then make decisions based off of those evaluations.

I would think that a mood is a distinct, strong feeling. The many feelings someone experiences at any one time could be divided and complicated - however if they are in a certain mood the mood might be fairly obvious. This doesn't mean that moods are simple and pure however. Moods are still complicated - they are comprised of different, distinct emotions that would all fall under the category of that one mood. I would think that a certain mood might take some time to kick in considering that the right emotions would all have to be in play and interacting properly and they might not start at the same time. For instance, if you wanted to get in the mood of playing at a park, maybe only a while after you started would the mood set in because you need to get accustomed to the emotions and you need to do the right things there that would trigger it.

Moods do not have facial expressions, however many single emotions do. Short, single emotions are more specific and therefore are stronger than moods because they are specific (and not as long lasting). You feel an emotion for a brief period of time, it is intense, however a mood is always there in the background hanging over you or providing a direction for your feelings. A mood cannot have a facial expression because a mood is too complicated for that, there are only a few facial expressions and unless your mood is one of those expressions, you are not going to be able to express it on your face. The six facial expressions are joy, surprise, fear, anger, disgust and sadness. Emotions are generated from large specific issues, those issues cause large changes in emotion. That is why short, single emotions are stronger than moods - because something specific made you feel strongly. If someone is in a happy mood, then that is different from being happy because of a single thing that made you feel strongly in a focused way.

I can express it in a way that makes it more clear. You can have a strong emotion for a brief period of time but such an emotion would be too strong to sustain for longer than that. A mood, however, you can sustain and have as a minor distraction, only a part of your feelings, for a while. You wouldn't want your mood to dominate your feelings while at an event, a mood is just a sort of like feel for whatever it is you are doing or feeling - it is not the primary feeling. The primary feelings people experience are the emotions that occur on a moment to moment basis. Some of those emotions are longer lasting that other emotions, but none of them would be a long lasting as a few hours, which would be your temporary mood. No one rages on and on for hours, though a mad man may. Such a case might be considered the emotion "rage" occurring for hours, however that is iffy. A mood can clearly last a few hours, and I suppose an emotion could too - however that would be hard to measure. You know what your mood is and how long it lasts, you couldn't possibly know how long all the longer-lasting single emotions you have are.

I mean, how could someone know if they maintained the emotion "vigilance" or "disgust" for a few hours? They might know they were vigilant or disgusted for a few hours, but that might be hard to identify or rare in occurrence. People have moods all the time however, so my guess is it is a lot more likely someone is able to identify what their moods are. Moods are more obvious because they are composed of groups of related emotions and feelings (the HUMAINE categorization in part 2). "Negative and forceful" and "positive and lively" would probably be obvious to someone if it occurred. However, say someone experienced the emotion envy, it might be hard to assess if that emotion hangs around in them for a few hours. It would be easier to assess if the emotion group that envy is in - which is "negative thoughts" (HUMAINE again) occurred for a few hours. That would be easier to feel and identify. In that way moods are stronger than emotions, however they aren't stronger than brief, single emotions that have a more easily identifiable cause.

You might be confused at this point because I have outlined both how moods are stronger than emotions, and how they are weaker than them. Moods are composed of a set of feelings and emotions, that is why they are stronger than one of those single emotions by itself. However, in a shorter time period, one of those emotions could be stronger than the overall mood. It is really a matter of your perception and what feels stronger to you. It could be that one of the single emotions that makes up the mood is stronger than the mood itself - though that wouldn't seem to make sense to me.

By the way, there are more moods than the categorizations in the HUMAINE system (though they didn't even intend for those to be viewed that way). You could have your own personal mood that you come up with that has its own set of emotions if you want.

So strong, individual emotions contribute to your overall mood or your specific mood. For example, if you are hit with something then you start feeling upset at the person that hit you at the same time you were cooking and the food was about to be done - your mood might be confused because so much was going on. You might stop feeling the pain and the anger at the other person because you become confused. All of those emotions led you to have a certain mood. What would your mood be in that situation for the next hour? Maybe once you stopped being confused your mood would go back to being painful/upset. So in that instance, in order to describe your mood, you would just describe the two main emotions that you were feeling. Those two would be your mood. If you were experiencing other smaller emotions, maybe you were ignoring those because you only cared about those two big ones, so they made up your mood. If you had relatives visiting at the same time, perhaps that was a smaller emotion that you were feeling, but because of the intensity of what happened you ignored that for the moment and only really felt the two stronger emotions. The relatives being over might have contributed to a mood of happiness or anger (depending on if you like them or not) - but also might have been a small factor or a large factor. I would say from this analysis that a few powerful emotions can override a mood, and that it is hard to classify some moods because you can't label them as any one thing, there are so many different emotions involved that don't relate or contribute to each other.

For instance, the relatives being over emotion (hate or happiness or whatever it is) might or might not be large or small, and might or might not contribute to your general mood when you are in the house. Maybe they get under your skin, maybe they don't, maybe they do the opposite of get under your skin. Maybe watching a movie recently put you in a unique mood for violence, and that contributed to your feelings when someone hit you over the head. If you watched a movie that caused an emotion that couldn't relate in any way to being hit, maybe then the two weren't related and therefore the emotions were separate in your head. Maybe if you saw a funny movie for example.

If you are in one type of mood and the next person you come across is in a different kind of mood (and everyone has their own emotions and their own moods, so they are going to) then the emotions in the interaction are going to be influenced because of these moods. That is rather obvious, who someone is (and who the other person is (i.e. their personality)) is going to impact what kind of things they feel in an interpersonal interaction, but also what they are feeling is going to impact this interaction. Say for instance one person was at one event, a concert or something, and was interacting via internet video to someone in a classroom. The mood of the concert is completely different from the mood of the classroom. Each person in this interaction is going to be feeling rather different things, and this is going to influence the feelings each person feels about the interaction because of the other person and where they are. To a lesser degree the mood of everyone you interact with is going to be different and influence the interaction. Say the person at the concert left the concert and, walking down the street, met someone who had just left a classroom. The emotions each person is experiencing are going to be very different, and in some way and to some degree this is going to be picked up by the other person. There is a certain feel (or "mood") each person has all of the time and this mood determines their (and the people they interact with) emotions to a certain degree.

I think that these moods as I have defined them are the key way to analyze emotion. If you think about it, thinking about each single emotion is both too simple and too complicated a way to think about someones emotional state. If you could perfectly assess each single emotion then you could see how it all works, but that is impossible considering how many someone has and how complex they are. However, a person might only have a few moods at one time, with many smaller emotions falling under each mood category. For instance someone might have an overall happy mood, a lesser mood from going to school recently, another mood created by a person they just interacted with. This type of analysis simplifies and explains the main types and amount of emotion someone might experience.

What someone thinks is going to influence these moods. For each mood, you are probably going to have thoughts that go along with that mood that possibly try to maintain the mood, diminish it, or cause it to change in some way. A mood might bias your judgments about people or things. Likelihood estimations - the tendency for people to judge probabilities, might also vary based on the state or mood you are in. For all of your thoughts there might be a single unifying theme that would also be the "mood" because the mood is, like I said, the main or primary emotion that all the other individual feelings fall under. That doesn't mean that those individual feelings and thoughts are less intense than the mood, however the mood is likely to last longer while the things that comprise it come and go. I think that means that some moods may not be coherent and easy to label, you could have a mood that could be hard to classify and consist of you experiencing and doing a great variety of things that you would find hard to put into one category. For instance if you had a discussion on a wide variety of topics, you could say that the mood was the mood of a discussion, but you wouldn't be more specific and mention which topic. The topics came and went, but the mood of a conversation stayed.

Two very big components to how someone experiences emotion (and therefore their moods) I would say are their appraisals and their attention for emotional events. Some appraisals include "blameworthiness", "arbitrariness", and "unfairness" of harm (which is relevant because of anger, guilt, and the deserving or not deserving of bad things - and praise in pity, sympathy or envy). So that means that people really care about what happens to them, and they get very emotional about it. Even if they aren't the emotional type, the principals of blaming, being arbitrary, attributing fairness, and feeling guilt, anger, sympathy and envy all apply greatly to people. These things are the cause for major emotional intensity, whether this intensity is obvious or not, it is still always there and would show up in certain ways. In fact, I would say that there is a comprehensive assessment system that people use for everything that occurs, and this assessment is there in a big way, influencing what the emotions people experience are, what their expectations are, what they want the other person to feel and what they think the feelings are its going to result in. That is why I mentioned attention for emotional events, because these processes are going to be so strong they are also therefore going to have a major impact on your attention, even if it is mostly an emotional kind of attention (things your emotions are "paying attention to").

Moods might not seem as intense as those intense emotions that I just described related to appraisals and attention. Moods and someones thought process related to the moods seem like minor things compared to the passionate, intense appraisals and back and forth interpersonal warfare that occurs with people. The emotions are deep and powerful, and thought with light moods would be the opposite.

But moods are hardly ever "light" - people feel strongly about specific things, which would cause strong specific emotions, but they can also feel strongly in a more general sort of way, which would be their mood. The specific feelings you have can be strong and short lived, but these all add up to what your mood is most of the time. When you are just hanging around, your emotions contributed to what you are feeling at that moment. You probably had a large number of possibly very strong emotions recently, all these contributed to a few feelings you have currently that you can feel. For instance if you feel relaxed, it is possible that the other emotions you experienced throughout the day contributed to this relaxed feeling you are currently experiencing.

Does this mean that someone is always in at least one of the moods from the HUMAINE classification (the negative and forceful, positive and lively, etc groupings)? How could someone describe their mood at any one moment? Is it necessary to do an analysis of what occurred in your life recently in order to figure out what you are currently feeling? I would think that clearly doing such an analysis would help. I wouldn't think that if you thought a lot more about how you were feeling you would understand less well what you were feeling, though I suppose that is possible.

Table 1.0

Thoughts and emotions

What is a thought? Or what is an emotion or idea?

Thoughts can be about different feelings, and humans can have different ideas about things.

The idea of thoughts is that they can be understood. And the idea of feelings is that they are tangible.

The idea of feelings is to experience the world, however sometimes our thoughts and emotions are not understood.

Table 2.0

Chapter

Feelings are they practical?

Humans can think about their feelings. However thoughts by themselves do not necessarily do that much to a person - they can determine how they feel, what they are thinking about or what their ideas are.

If someone thinks about something then it doesn't really matter because they are not going to need less focus.

If someone thinks about something then it doesn't really matter.

If someone thinks about something then it doesn't really matter because they are not interested in your life.

The idea of what you think you are is much more than what you think.

If someone thinks about something then it could matter because they are not going anywhere.

3.1 title

Thinking helps the feeling process.

The idea of thoughts or feeling-triggers is the best way to get the most important thing.

Table 3.0

Chapter

Thoughts can be abstract

Chapter

If a thought is abstract then it could be about a subjective idea. But what does that mean, what is meant by the word 'abstract' and the word 'thought'?

An abstract idea is emotional, or could have more subjective elements. For instance, some things that people think about trigger feelings.

If an idea triggers a feeling then it could be fun. However the idea is a cognitive structure.

But what is meant by the term 'cognitive structure'?

Ideas can be intelligent or they could be simple. Cognitive means that it is related to thoughts in the mind, which can contain ideas.

A thought is a unit of thinking, and an idea is something that occurs to someone.

Table 4.0

Chapter

Are Emotions explained?

Humans have many emotions. Their emotions have components like taste, experience and thoughts - which is the intellectual aspect of feeling.

However, thoughts could be understood or they could be misunderstood. If a thought is understood then it can be visualized. For instance, if you think about an apple then you visualize it.

It doesn't really matter if someone understands something. That is because humans think, however they do not need to understand.

If someone thinks about something then it could be clear, however that doesn't mean that it is easy to understand.

When something is thought about it could be simple and easy to understand. However what does that mean?

It doesn't really matter if someone thinks about stuff because they don't necessarily understand what they think about.

Table 5.0

Chapter 6

Emotion and Logic {CP}

Some things in life cause people to feel, these are called emotional reactions. Some things in life cause people to think, these are sometimes called logical or intellectual reactions. Thus life is divided between things that make you feel and things that make you think. The question is, if someone is feeling, does that mean that they are thinking less? It probably does. If part of your brain is being occupied by feeling, then it makes sense that you have less capacity for thought. [Saying "part of your brain" shows how feeling and thought take up the same space, or might use the same abilities or similar processes in the mind. It shows how you really can't do two things at once, especially since they are both cognitive processes (they both take up your memory and attention).] That is obvious if you take emotional extremes, such as crying, where people can barely think at all. This does not mean that emotional people are not intelligent; it just means that they might be dumber during the times in which they are emotional. Emotion goes on and off for everyone, sometimes people cry, and sometimes they are completely serious. [This could further mean that an emotional person might be less emotional if they are doing serious thinking.] In 1941 Hunt said that classical theories of the definition of emotion "concern themselves with specific mechanisms whereby current behavior is interrupted and emotional responses are substituted" (W. Hunt, 1941)

The previous paragraph explored the difference between and nature of emotion and thought (or intellect). Understanding the nature of emotion and thought might help explain Descartes' statement "I think, therefore I am" because his statement implied that thought is the important element for existence. What role do feelings and thoughts play in determining if and how you exist?

Some things in life can identifiably cause more emotion than other things.

1. Color causes more emotion than black and white. So anything with more color in it is going to be more emotional to look at, whether it is the difference between a gold or silver sword, or a gold or silver computer. In both cases the gold is going to be more emotional. [That example with the sword makes it obvious that color is more emotional than things with less color, it usually is hard to tell if each thing is more or less emotional just based off of the color. It might be that something black is more emotional than something colorful if they are different objects. Also, it seems like color is a shallow source of emotion, like you can identify that color causes more emotion, but if you have an attachment to something if it has a black and white color instead of being colorful, or something else is going on, then the black and white object might be more emotional than its colorful version.]

2. Things that are personal are emotional, personal things that people like and that they feel are "close" to them. Things like home or anything someone likes actually. That is a definition of emotion after all, something that causes feeling. So if you like it, it is probably going to cause more feeling. Other things aside from liking something could cause emotions from it, such as curiosity, but usually like is one of the stronger emotions. You could say that the two are directly proportional, the more you like something, the more it is going to cause feeling. [Or the more curious you are, or any other emotion, would probably generate more feeling. If you are emotional about something, that is saying that it is causing you to feel more. This is more clear when the difference between emotion and feeling is explained later in this section. Aristotle, however, claimed that the core of emotions were beliefs and desires. That shows how strong beliefs and desires are emotionally. Desire is a less cognitive term than the word "like" because desire implies that it is an automatic emotional response whereas the word like means that you consciously like something. How much you like something comes from understanding your desires because like is your understanding of how much you desire something.]

But there are things that people like that cause thought. You could like something and it causes you to think, and we previously defined emotion as feeling, not thought. That thoughts are separate from emotions because thought is a period of thinking. What exactly is thinking then? You can think about emotions, "how did I feel then?" etc. So is thought just a period of increased attention? Or is it a sharp spike in attention focused on one particular thing that is clear? [Thought feels like you are paying clear attention to something, whereas you aren't always paying as clear attention to your feelings.] It is hard to focus that much if you are feeling a lot, however. This makes me conclude that there is an overlap of feeling and thought, like a Venn diagram. But there are still parts of thought that don't have feeling or emotion in them, and parts of emotion that don't have thought in them. [So thoughts are also going to influence feelings, since they overlap, not only would feelings influence thoughts.] That means that thought requires more concentration than feeling does, since we defined thought as a period of increased attention. You can be emotional and have more attention, but usually if you are emotional you are going to be less attentive than you would be if you were thinking more. [That ties into the idea that you can only do one thing at a time, if you are paying attention to your thoughts (or thinking more) it is going to be harder to pay attention to your feelings (or "feel" more) because you can only pay attention to a limited number of things at once.] Then again, if you are emotional you are being attentive to your emotions, whatever they may be, and if your emotions are on something like the sun, then when you see the sun you are going to be attentive to it, but not be thinking about it. So you can pay attention to something and not be thinking about it at the same time. [If you are paying attention to something but not thinking about it, what exactly is this increased attention doing? It could be helping you process and understand what feelings that thing causes in you, or just make you feel more about it, which would make you pay more or less attention to it. You could be feeling a lot about something and be paying attention to something else, but that is clearly going to be harder (usually, based on the circumstances) than if didn't have that emotion. That is a clear example of how emotion can be a distraction (from thought and even other emotions). But you aren't going to be paying attention to anything else. [That further shows how emotion can take up your attention, especially if you are paying attention to the emotion, as in that example.] It seems that thought is more attention than emotion, however. If you try to "feel" your computer you still don't give it as much attention as if you were thinking about your computer. Then again, it depends what you are thinking about your computer, if you are thinking that your computer sucks, you are going to give it less attention than thinking that it is great. It also depends what your feelings are about that computer. If you feel that the computer is good, then you are going to give it more attention than if you feel that it is bad (possibly). [Does this mean that when you think about your computer your attention is on what it is you are thinking about your computer? Thinking about your computer might generate emotions, which would then cause you to be feeling and thinking about your computer. The thought of the computer might just pull up the general feeling of the computer (the feeling from the computer you get when you usually interact with it or think about it, not some other feeling about it which wouldn't then be "general", not necessarily the feeling of the computer that corresponds with that particular thought. Those ideas raise the question, "when you have a feeling about something, what exactly is that feeling causing you to feel and think (consciously and unconsciously).] The thoughts and the feelings correspond, however. That is, if you are thinking it is bad, then you are going to feel that it is bad. Thus thought and feeling are really one and the same. [It might be that if you think it is bad, you feel that it is good, but that would only be if you are confused, like if you consciously think it is good but it really makes you feel bad.] But thoughts are really clearer than feelings. Thought and feeling may result in the same amount of attention to something, but thought is more precise. It is more precise for you to think that the computer is good, then to feel that the computer is good. Who knows why you feel the computer is good, but if you were thinking the computer is good then you would know why you thought that. Emotions and feelings are more obscure.

So, the more you like something (or hate something, or have any strong emotional reaction to anything), [Something shallow that doesn't generate a lot of feeling might not be called "emotional".] the more emotional it is, but that doesn't mean that it might not also cause you to think about it. One can't label everything in life as either emotion or thought however. Life isn't a scale with emotion on one end and thought on the other. There are other factors involved, things like adrenaline and physical action, which might also cause increased attention that isn't either emotional or thoughtful. [You could be more specific with that scale and mention which emotions, or which thoughts.] When you're running you have a lot of attention on the fact that you are running, and you're not thinking about it or being emotional about it. This means that just because you like something, doesn't mean that it is emotional. You might like running, but it doesn't cause emotions in you. [But when you think about running it is going to cause more emotions in you since you like it, and you are probably going to be experiencing better emotions when you are running if you like it then if you don't, unless you enjoy pain then you could like something that generates bad emotions in you (it could be generating negative short term emotions, but since you like it, positive emotions over the long term, or positive emotions when you think about it (or even a mix of the emotions since it is more complicated that you like it but it causes pain).] What does emotion mean then? Emotions must be thoughts that you can't identify, when you feel something, it must be that you are thinking about something unconsciously. You just have no idea what it is, usually. Emotions and feelings are thoughts then. By that I mean that they can be broken down into parts and figured out what those parts are. And thoughts are just really parts that you can identify. So the difference between emotions, feelings and thoughts is that you know what thoughts are about, but you don't have as good an idea of what emotions and feelings are, as they are more obscure and harder to identify.

Thus once you find out what is causing the emotion, it is no longer an emotion, but it is a thought (that is, you now call the emotion a thought, so the thought is still probably generating emotion. In your mind then there is still an emotion, but this emotion is now "part" of a thought, it becomes part of the thought associated with it because you created this link, and hence you would call the emotion/thought just a thought because while thoughts can generate emotions, emotions cannot generate thoughts (by themselves), unless you realize what the emotion is (then you are generating the thought, not the emotion generating it), but you are realizing it is a thought, not an emotion: so this realization takes over and now the emotion is part of that realization (because you consider the emotion a part of you, and you generated the realization), instead of the realization being a part of the emotion (and since it seems like the emotion belongs to the realization (you), instead of vice versa, you call it a thought instead of an emotion, because you generated the thought (and hence it also seems that you are now consciously also generating the emotion (the emotion coming from the thought))). So that would mean that all emotions have route in real things, and these real things can be explained with thoughts, so all emotions then are really thoughts that you haven't realized; an emotion would just be a thought that you haven't identified yet, so the term "emotion" goes away when you realize it is a thought (because that is what it really was all along, a thought) (though this thought might still be generating a feeling). So, since you perceive the emotion as belonging to you, and you generate thoughts consciously, you consider the emotion to be part of a thought, not vice versa (and hence call identified emotions "thoughts"). So when you identify an emotion, it is a thought because thoughts can generate emotions, so if the emotion is still there after you identified it you would say it falls under the category "thought", because the thought is making it. [That brings up the question, "do thoughts about your emotions accurately represent what that emotion is?". If the thought doesn't accurately represent the emotion, then you would really need more thoughts to represent the entire emotion (show what that emotion is). Also, can you ever really perfectly explain emotion with thought? Emotion seems infinitely complicated, finite and dynamic.] You might be lazy however and not want to spend time thinking, which are what emotions are for. "Ah that gold sword is pretty" might be the emotion, but to your conscious mind you would have no idea that you like the sword because it is pretty, you might just know that you like the sword and it is making you emotional about it. Therefore, emotional things are really any feelings that cause unconscious or conscious thought. Feeling is also another word for unconscious thought. That then leads to the conclusion that thought can be emotional (because thoughts are going to be about things that can cause emotion). I think that emotions can be more emotional than thought, however, because emotions can contain more than one thought (while thoughts are very slow consciously), therefore causing it to cause more feeling, or be more emotional. [So thought is simpler than emotions and therefore they might cause less feelings by themselves, but the feeling a thought brings up is probably going to be more complicated than the thought alone, since feelings are usually more complicated than thoughts.] While you can only express a few thoughts a minute, your emotions can contain endless numbers of thoughts per minute – they are not as exact and hence don't make as much sense as thoughts do.

Since emotion is really thought, when you are experiencing emotion you could almost say that you are thinking. You really are thinking about emotion when you experience it because thought is just paying attention to something in your mind. You also might learn (or unlearn) from processing or experiencing emotion because emotions are similar to thoughts, or could be said to be a type of thought. You are probably going to learn more unconsciously if you are experiencing emotions then not, because that is something that would be occurring causing you to learn instead of just learning from nothing. This also explains Descartes' statement "I think, therefore I am" because if all emotion is really thought, then that shows how emotions contribute to your existence in a meaningful way. They do because you learn from them like you learn from thoughts, emotions are real things and meaningful because they are thoughts to you (or things (thoughts) that symbolize real things (what you are thinking or feeling about) which cause you to experience the world and learn).

So thought is just a lot of attention on one little thing. And emotion is attention on lots of individual things, or possibly one thing. So things that are emotional are things that cause you to think, consciously or unconsciously. [A conscious feeling would just be a feeling that you have identified (or recognized) more than an unconscious one.] And therefore they would cause you to feel, consciously or unconsciously. So the more you like something you can't consciously identify as to why you like it, the more emotional it is, and the more you like something where you can consciously identify what it is, the more conscious thought it is going to cause, and the more logical that thing is going to be. Emotion is just unconscious thought.

How This Chapter shows how Intelligence is intertwined with Emotion:

- "Emotion goes on and off for everyone" – this statement shows how there are degrees to which someone can be focused on and feel thought, and degrees to which someone can be focused on and feel feeling. That then also explains the next statement in the chapter "some things in life can identifiably cause more emotion than other things".

- Since there are parts of emotion that don't have thought (assuming that emotion and thought overlap – but that is a logical assumption because thoughts generate feelings and are therefore less independent) then emotion (especially emotion without any thought) is going to need less focus or concentration, because emotion is a more pleasurable experience, but thought is one where concentration is usually used.

- Emotions can direct and control thoughts – if you are feeling that your computer is bad, then you might then give it less or more attention, and conscious attention is a function of thought because you need to think to start to focus on something. Or when you notice something you noticing it is a conscious experience because you "notice" it and thoughts are things which you are aware of which would then contribute to consciousness.

- Next mentioned is how emotions and feelings are just harder to identify then thoughts, and that therefore emotions and feelings are really thoughts themselves, or vice versa. If all thought is really emotion, and all emotion really thought, then all intelligence could vary and be dependent on emotions. This is further evidenced by the statement "thus once you find out what is causing the emotion it is no longer an emotion, but it is a thought". That shows how an emotion is a thought that you just aren't identifying. It is just a matter of definition of the terms. Thought is concrete things which are real in the world, and emotion is something that you feel but can't visualize. So therefore intelligence is just the ability to do things which are real, versus feeling something, which isn't as "real" as thoughts are.

- If a thought is clear then it could be easy to understand. However that doesn't mean that it is a complicated thought. A complex idea or thought could be easy to figure out - and it could relate to its associated feelings.

- What would it mean for a thought or group of thoughts to be clear? An abstract thought could be an abstract concept, which could also be clear, however it would also be more emotional or have feeling.

References

Hunt, W. A. (1941). Recent developments in the field of emotion. *Psychological Bulletin, 38,* 249–276.

Table 6.0

Chapter 7

The Psychology Of Emotions, Feelings and Thoughts

This book makes the statement that thought, action and feeling can occur in any order. "Action turned into feeling, which caused you to think and therefore turned into thought. Thought, action (your action or external action) and feeling can occur in any order."

video of Artwork streamable (https://streamable.com/kff2e/)

video of Artwork 1 (https://drive.google.com/file/d/1kgRB91q7lfOd3Q0A0keJir2sz11QaXGp/ view?usp=drivesdk) video of Artwork 2 (https://drive.google.com/

folderview?id=1kiGfJRhyz8CreqJR6lkCSSXhxiKR4-gm)

(This media type is not supported in this reader. Click to open media in browser.) (http://legacy.cnx.org/content/m14358/1.150/#buildingpast)

new emotions feelings and thoughts book (https://cnx.org/content/m79843/latest)

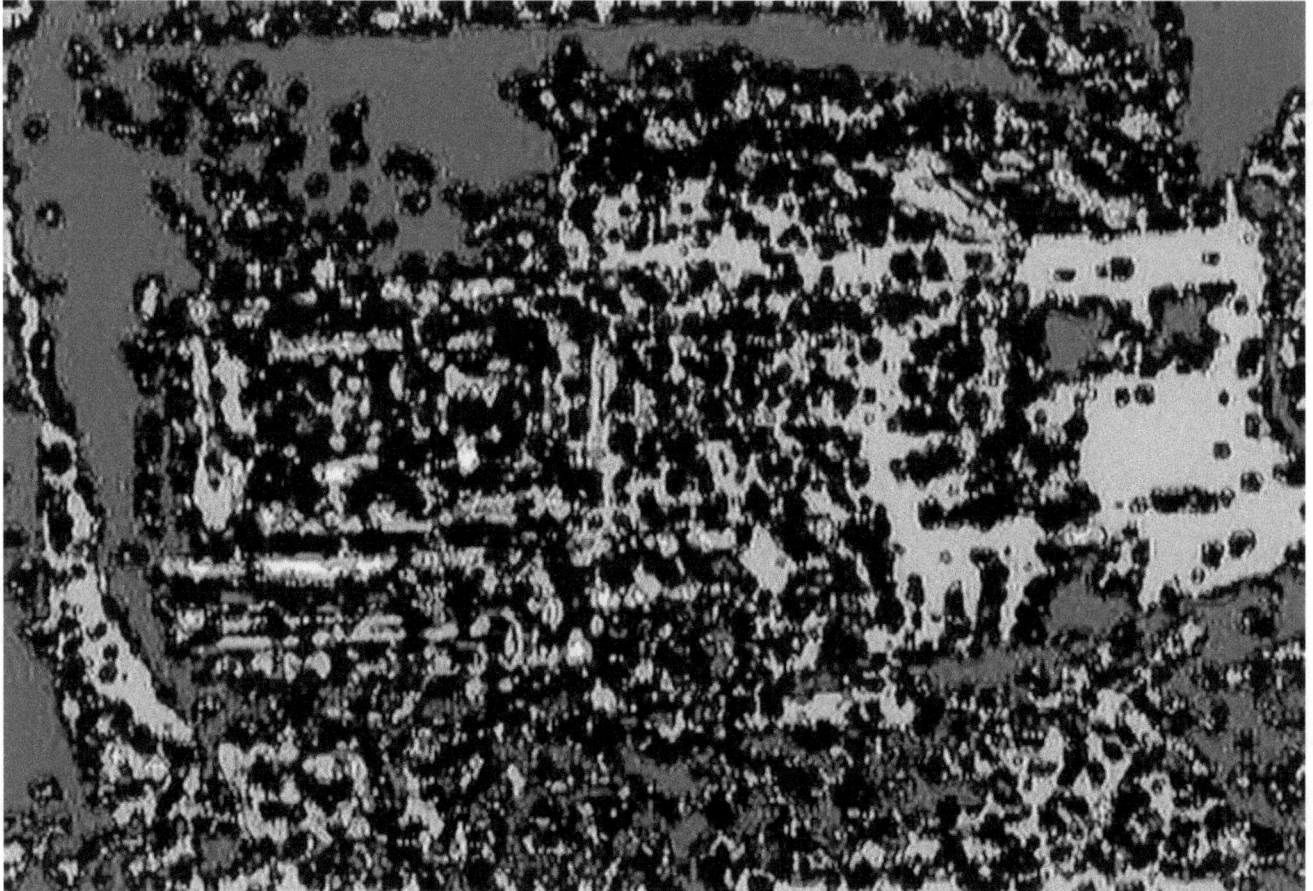

Figure 7.1   Online at www.zazzle.com/xiornikzazzle (http://www.zazzle.com/xiornikzazzle) (more art at www.zazzle.com/niceartpaintings (http://www.zazzle.com/store/niceartpaintings))

7.1 Emotion and Logic

Some things in life cause people to feel, these are called emotional reactions. Some things in life cause people to think, these are sometimes called logical or intellectual reactions. Thus life is divided between things that make you feel and things that make you think. The question is, if someone is feeling, does that mean that they are thinking less? It probably does. If part of your brain is being occupied by feeling, then it makes sense that you have less capacity for thought. That is obvious if you take emotional extremes, such as crying, where people can barely think at all. This does not mean that emotional people are not intelligent; it just means that they might be dumber during the times in which they are emotional. Emotion goes on and off for everyone, sometimes people cry, and sometimes they are completely serious.

Some things in life can identifiably cause more emotion than other things.

1. Color causes more emotion than black and white. So anything with more color in it is going to be more emotional to look at, whether it is the difference between a gold or silver sword, or a gold or silver computer. In both cases the gold is going to be more emotional.

2. Things that are personal are emotional, personal things that people like and that they feel are "close" to them. Things like home or anything someone likes actually. That is a definition of emotion after all, something that causes feeling. So if you like it, it is probably going to cause more feeling. Other things aside from liking something could cause emotions from it, such as curiosity, but usually like is one of the stronger emotions. You could say that the two are directly proportional, the more you like something, the more it is going to cause feeling.

But there are things that people like that cause thought. You could like something and it causes you to think, and we previously defined emotion as feeling, not thought. That thoughts are separate from emotions because thought is a period of thinking. What exactly is thinking then? You can think about emotions, "how did I feel then?" etc. So is thought just a period of increased attention? Or is it a sharp spike in attention focused on one particular thing that is clear? It is hard to focus that much if you are feeling a lot, however. This makes me conclude that there is an overlap of feeling and thought, like a Venn diagram. But there are still parts of thought that don't have feeling or emotion in them, and parts of emotion that don't have thought in them. That means that thought requires more concentration than feeling does, since we defined thought as a period of increased attention. You can be emotional and have more attention, but usually if you are emotional you are going to be less attentive than you would be if you were thinking more. Then again, if you are emotional you are being attentive to your emotions, whatever they may be, and if your emotions are on something like the sun, then when you see the sun you are going to be attentive to it, but not be thinking about it. So you can pay attention to something and not be thinking about it at the same time. But you aren't going to be paying attention to anything else. It seems that thought is more attention than emotion, however. If you try to "feel" your computer you still don't give it as much attention as if you were thinking about your computer. Then again, it depends what you are thinking about your computer, if you are thinking that your computer sucks, you are going to give it less attention than thinking that it is great. It also depends what your feelings are about that computer. If you feel that the computer is good, then you are going to give it more attention than if you feel that it is bad (possibly). The thoughts and the feelings correspond, however. That is, if you are thinking it is bad, then you are going to feel that it is bad. Thus thought and feeling are really one and the same. But thoughts are really clearer than feelings. Thought and feeling may result in the same amount of attention to something, but thought is more precise. It is more precise for you to think that the computer is good, then to feel that the computer is good. Who knows why you feel the computer is good, but if you were thinking the computer is good then you would know why you thought that. Emotions and feelings are more obscure.

So, the more you like something (or hate something, or have any strong emotional reaction to anything), the more emotional it is, but that doesn't mean that it might not also cause you to think about it. One can't label everything in life as either emotion or thought however. Life isn't a scale with emotion on one end and thought on the other. There are other factors involved, things like adrenaline and physical action, which might also cause increased attention that isn't either emotional or thoughtful. When you're running you have a lot of attention on the fact that you are running, and you're not thinking about it or being emotional about it. This means that just because you like something, doesn't mean that it is emotional. You might like running, but it doesn't cause emotions in you. What does emotion mean then? Emotions must be thoughts that you can't identify, when you feel something, it must be that you are thinking about something unconsciously. You just have no idea what it is, usually. Emotions and feelings are thoughts then. By that I mean that they can be broken down into parts and figured out what those parts are. And thoughts are just really parts that you can identify. So the difference between emotions, feelings and thoughts is that you know what thoughts are about, but you don't have as good an idea of what emotions and feelings are, as they are more obscure and harder to identify.

Thus once you find out what is causing the emotion, it is no longer an emotion, but it is a thought (that is, you now call the emotion a thought, so the thought is still probably generating emotion. In your mind then there is still an emotion, but this emotion is now "part" of a thought, it becomes part of the thought associated with it because you created this link, and hence you would call the emotion/thought just a thought because while thoughts can generate emotions, emotions cannot generate thoughts (by themselves), unless you realize what the emotion is (then you are generating the thought, not the emotion generating it), but you are realizing it is a thought, not an emotion: so this realization takes over and now the emotion is part of that realization (because you consider the emotion a part of you, and you generated the realization), instead of the realization being a part of the emotion (and since it seems like the emotion belongs to the realization (you), instead of vice versa, you call it a thought instead of an emotion, because you generated the thought (and hence it also seems that you are now consciously also generating the emotion (the emotion coming from the thought))). So that would mean that all emotions have route in real things, and these real things can be explained with thoughts, so all emotions then are really thoughts that you haven't realized; an emotion would just be a thought that you haven't identified yet, so the term "emotion" goes away when you realize it is a thought (because that is what it really was all along, a thought) (though this thought might still be generating a feeling). So, since you perceive the emotion as belonging to you, and you generate thoughts consciously, you consider the emotion to be part of a thought, not vice versa (and hence call identified emotions "thoughts"). So when you identify an emotion, it is a thought because thoughts can generate emotions, so if the emotion is still there after you identified it you would say it falls under the category "thought", because the thought is making it. You might be lazy however and not want to spend time thinking, which are what emotions are for. "Ah that gold sword is pretty" might be the emotion, but to your conscious mind you would have no idea that you like the sword because it is pretty, you might just know that you like the sword and it is making you emotional about it. Therefore, emotional things are really any feelings that cause unconscious or conscious thought. Feeling is also another word for unconscious thought. That then leads to the conclusion that thought can be emotional (because thoughts are going to be about things that can cause emotion). I think that emotions can be more emotional than thought, however, because emotions can contain more than one thought (while thoughts are very slow consciously), therefore causing it to cause more feeling, or be more emotional. While you can only express a few thoughts a minute, your emotions can contain endless numbers of thoughts per minute – they are not as exact and hence don't make as much sense as thoughts do.

So thought is just a lot of attention on one little thing. And emotion is attention on lots of individual things, or possibly one thing. So things that are emotional are things that cause you to think, consciously or unconsciously. And therefore they would cause you to feel, consciously or unconsciously. So the more you like something you can't consciously identify as to why you like it, the more emotional it is, and the more you like something where you can consciously identify what it is, the more conscious thought it is going to cause, and the more logical that thing is going to be. Emotion is just unconscious thought.

How This Chapter shows how Intelligence is intertwined with Emotion:

- "Emotion goes on and off for everyone" – this statement shows how there are degrees to which someone can be focused on and feel thought, and degrees to which someone can be focused on and feel feeling. That then also explains the next statement in the chapter "some things in life can identifiably more emotion than other things".

- Since there are parts of emotion that don't have thought (assuming that emotion and thought overlap – but that is a logical assumption because thoughts generate feelings and are therefore less independent) then emotion (especially emotion without any thought) is going to need less focus or concentration, because emotion is a more pleasurable experience, but thought is one where concentration is usually used.

- Emotions can direct and control thoughts – if you are feeling that your computer is bad, then you might then give it less or more attention, and conscious attention is a function of thought because you need to think to start to focus on something. Or when you notice something you noticing it is a conscious experience because you "notice" it and thoughts are things which you are aware of which would then contribute to consciousness.

- Next mentioned is how emotions and feelings are just harder to identify then thoughts, and that therefore emotions and feelings are really thoughts themselves, or vice versa. If all thought is really emotion, and all emotion really thought, then all intelligence could vary and be dependent on emotions. This is further evidenced by the statement "thus once you find out what is causing the emotion it is no longer an emotion, but it is a thought". That shows how an emotion is a thought that you just aren't identifying. It is just a matter of definition of the terms. Thought is concrete things which are real in the world, and emotion is something that you feel but can't visualize. So therefore intelligence is just the ability to do things which are real, versus feeling something, which isn't as "real" as thoughts are.

An explanation for this chapter:

This chapter basically described the difference between thoughts and feeling (or emotion). Thoughts are things that you are conscious of, when you have a thought, you know you have it because it is your thought. Unless you aren't aware of the thought you are having (which would make it an unconscious thought), then the thought is something that is clear to you, it is usually a sentence, though you might not be thinking of it as a sentence. You might know you want to do something, but you might not express it very clearly to yourself. When someone has a clear thought, they know what it is. You can want to do things and be thinking things all the time, some of the thoughts are going to be more clear than others.

Emotion, on the other hand, isn't clear like clear thoughts. When you experience an emotion, you might not know you are experiencing it at all, and it is certainly a lot more complicated than a sentence, which could be your typical thought. Emotion could be described with a lot of thoughts, and this probably occurs in humans all the time. People have complicated emotions, and these emotions would give rise to thoughts that people are aware of (a conscious, clear thought such as a sentence in your head), and thoughts that people are less aware of, (for instance you are doing something but you didn't fully realize that you were going to or are doing it.

7.2 Some Points on Emotion Theory

- There are two types of observations in emotion theory, one type is general common observations (such as sex is good for someones emotional health) and the other type is functional observations (when an emotion stops at one second and another one takes its place, what is happening there, what are the emotions, why do they stop and start, etc (for example, if someone thinks a happy thought it might stop the negative thought completely) also, what are the degrees to which the emotion or thought is felt, is it completely gone etc.

- Emotions stop and start all the time, this stopping and starting might occur as sudden transitions or slow transitions, one emotion gradually fading into the other. That is not a complete explanation for how emotion functions, however. Humans would probably have several emotions occurring at one time, each emotion interacting with one or more other emotions and potentially causing them to stop, start, fade or increase.

- For instance, the emotions hate, love, painful emotions, sexual emotions, hopeful emotions, and humorous emotions are probably all constantly interacting with each other and being felt to some degree all the time. Those are only a few of the emotions/feelings that are probably felt a lot everyday.

- There are going to be observable patterns that occur with those emotions, for instance pleasure might relieve pain and make painful feeling go away.

- Life is intense and ongoing, so therefore intense emotion is probably maintained in humans all the time. These emotions might stop and start, someone could go from brief periods of intensity to periods of low intensity, but the point is there is that intensity that is felt and the continuous flow of emotional processing is ongoing.

- There are different emotional states that can change your outlook on life or how you might respond to a situation. Fear, anger, kindness and admiration are all emotional states that change how you might respond to events. You can also be in a state of readiness for certain emotions, you could be prepared to experience pain or pleasure or be in one of those states.

- Emotions are experienced consciously and unconsciously, the extent to which someone clearly feels an emotion is the extent to which it is conscious. If an emotion is being experienced but isn't under the awareness of the person experiencing it, by definition it is mostly an unconscious emotion because they are not conscious of it. Someone can experience a large emotion but that doesn't necessarily mean that the emotion is going to be completely under the awareness of the person experiencing it. They might describe the emotion as feeling like it is very large, but they might not be in touch with it (making it mostly unconscious). It is in this world of "seemingly larger emotions" that emotional processing takes place. Unconsciously there are many more emotions experienced than you are completely aware of that are being experienced. Therefor it is there, in the unconscious mind, that emotions interact in great depth and complexity, barely being felt consciously at times and with the person possibly only slightly aware that something emotional might be going on (unconsciously).

- Emotion is experienced differently for each person. An emotion evokes a certain emotional response in a person because that person is who they are, however we all share the same world and there are going to be significant psychological things in it that are generally considered to be significant by most people, such as death or love. Any individual has peculiarities and specifics about what might trigger a large emotional response, it wouldn't necessarily just be something that they "like a lot" but mostly things they consciously or unconsciously find to be significant.

- When emotion can stop and start, and there can be periods of intensity and low-intensity, it makes one wonder just how many different emotional states there are. For every mood in a social situation you could say is an emotional state. If there is a certain mood present, then the people are going to be feeling certain things and responding in a way that is correspondent to that mood. But that is just social moods, there are many other ways people's emotional state can change, if you are working on something you enjoy working on you could be in a certain emotional state for that.

- An emotional state implies a certain set of feelings that come up with a certain activity or under certain circumstances.

- An important observation to note in emotion theory is that pain can stop the current flow of emotion or feeling and alert the person. Pain and anxiety are different from the other emotions because they are unpleasant. How often is an emotion like hope or fun tainted by the emotion of pain? Is fun even an emotion or is it an emotional state? Fun would imply that you are experiencing a set of emotions that makes that circumstance fun, joy is an emotion, "fun" is more of an emotional state.

- The flow of someone's feelings can stop suddenly, for instance, say you are relaxing in bed after waking up, then your alarm clock goes off - you went from feeling happy, relaxed emotions to those suddenly ending. Emotions and feelings stop and start like this all the time. In a conversation, for example, someone could be happy and the other person could show or adopt a negative expression and that could suddenly end the other persons happiness. There are many emotions someone could adopt in a conversation such as shyness, or an emotion expressing a thought or an idea, and these emotions could influence (or start and stop) emotions that the other person is experiencing. It should be clear that the many emotions someone experiences throughout the day changes all the time, stops, starts, transitions, and changes in complicated ways all the time. These changes may or may not be observed, however if you pay attention to these feelings and their behavior you could certainly notice a lot more.

- Emotion can motivate thought. People go into different states or 'modes' where they are driven to think a certain type of thought or do a certain type of behavior. When someone enters a different mode, such as a pleasure seeking mode, that mode in particular is motivated by emotion. It is clear that with pleasure someone is feeling more, so you would say that it is motivated by emotion. However, every state someone is in, every different subtle social emotional state or emotional state when someone is doing work is going to have some emotion or set of feelings behind it. But it isn't just a set of feelings, the feeling is unique each time, and this uniqueness communicates certain information that is also unique. The feeling tells you what you like and what you don't like, that would probably be the primary emotions (pleasure and pain). But each other emotion communicates something - if you feel guilty you know what that feeling means, maybe that feeling in combination with other feelings is communicating something different or unique based upon the set of feelings it is and what it means in that context.

- Therefore someone could enter into a mode such as an abusive mode, where, emotionally, they are being abusive. It makes sense that since this is a mode, it takes a reasonable period of time to experience. It isn't an expression or a gesture, which takes a couple of seconds, but a mode like this my guess would be at least a few minutes long. Another mode could be a humorous mode. Maybe that is clear by the person being observed as being amused - but maybe emotionally they are amused for a certain period of time before and after your observation of them being that way.

- That isn't to say that someone couldn't experience amused feelings for a few seconds. Clearly when someone laughs the feelings mostly only last for the period of the laughter. But they would probably still be amused for a period afterwards. You just laughed - and you become happy or amused for a short period after that. My point about the modes is that there are certain powerful sets of feelings that last for a while - like a pleasure seeking set of feelings. That is different from laughter or amusement, this is a strong specific mode that brings up a set of feelings for someone. Maybe someone else has a different sort of mode - maybe they have a strong mode where they feel guilty, and they have a unique set of feelings and thoughts that are with this mode.

- Some of these modes might be a reflective mode, where you are in period that is reminiscent of the activity you were just doing. Other modes might be powerful ones, abusive ones, submissive or dominant ones, calm ones. It is as if someone gets in a 'mood' for these modes. Moods are more quiet however, and there are only a few moods that people recognize. However, there could be many different unique moods as well. What then is the difference between a mood and a mode? In a mood you have different emotions, maybe someone gets in an abusive mood. That would be like getting in an abusive mode. I think it is just a matter of how strong the mood or mode is. Moods are probably less strong than modes, and modes are also ways of acting, not just ways of feeling. In a mode the emotions are so strong that they influence your behavior - the emotion motivates thought.

- One emotion can lead or transition into another emotion. For instance, someone can rage, then become angry instead of being in a rage over a certain thing, and then the emotion could die to down to the person just being hateful at whatever the cause is. That is similar to if someone is punched, they might be at first angry, then upset, and then depressed or sad. Anger can lead to hate, or 'being upset' - and then after that the emotion might transition into sadness or whatever might follow someone being hateful. Maybe the lesser emotion of hate is bitterness. So they would go from being hateful to being bitter. Or maybe if someone is talking to them positively, they could go from being hateful to being happy or optimistic.

An explanation for this chapter:

An emotional state is a very complicated thing. If someone knew completely their emotional state, they would know everything they were feeling right then. Then they wouldn't really have any "unconscious" emotions, because they would be perfectly conscious of what they were feeling. But then again, it is impossible to feel the full force of all your feelings at once, so it is not possible to be completely conscious of all your feelings. Your unconscious feelings must be dimmed down, or only large in a way that isn't completely conscious. Like you know you have a large emotion, but aren't in touch with it.

Emotional states are complicated, it would be easy to say, "my emotional state right now is really messed up" because that is what emotional states are like, people have several emotions they are experiencing all the time, it is just hard to identify that this is occurring because I would say that people can only identify when they have a large, clear emotion that they can understand.

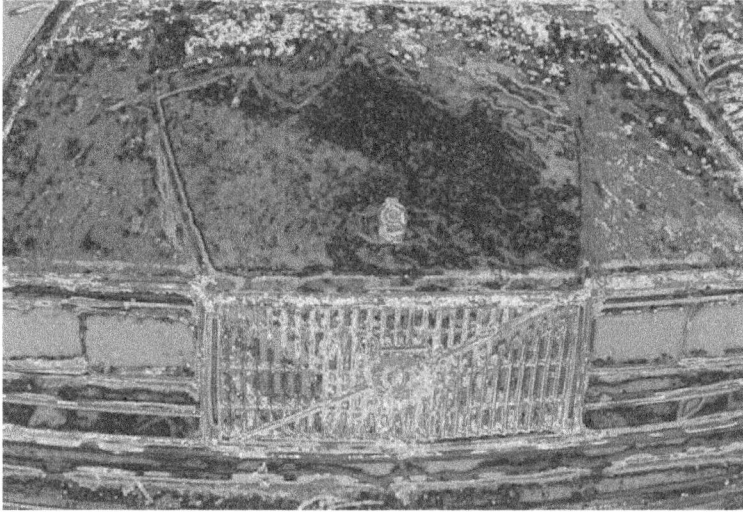

7.3 Thoughts

Anything that is said or done is possibly followed by a long series of unconscious thoughts and thought processes.

What is the difference between emotion, feeling, thought, logic, and intelligence? Use of any of them requires a lot of attention. Even when you are feeling something emotional your attention is directed toward that thing. The answer is that everything in life eventually results in a feeling. Even emotion results in a feeling. Emotion is unconscious thoughts about things, and thoughts are conscious thoughts about things. Thought results in feelings, so unconscious thought (emotion) is also going to result in feelings.

If you think about it that way, thought and emotion are both in part feelings, that is, to some extent you feel them right away, in addition to them resulting in feelings later on. But that still means that feelings are always the end result. Then again, thoughts might be the result of current thoughts. That is like emotion, unconscious emotional thoughts are going to result in unconscious emotional thoughts later on. Even feelings could be called unconscious thoughts, because thought is just focusing on one thing for a brief period of time.

Therefore emotion, thought and feeling are really just periods of focus on certain things. With thought you just recognize what it is that you are focusing on. With emotions you feel deeply about what you are focusing on, and with feelings you are focusing on it less. Physical stimulus also results in feelings, and then you focus on those feelings, you aren't necessarily focused on what caused the feelings (the physical stimulus itself) however.

Thus life is really just different types of feelings; you could categorize all of life as feeling. Even when you think you are in a period when you're not feeling anything, you really are feeling something; you just don't recognize what it is that you are feeling. Remember that feelings are thoughts you can't identify. And since a thought is going to be about something, another way to think about life is just stuff happening. Stuff happening results in feelings in your brain, where more stuff happens. It is all-concrete.

The definition of intellect and thoughts is almost understanding (those concrete things). Emotion is feeling, completely separate from facts or information. All facts and information are going to be about things that cause feeling, however, since all things that happen cause feelings and all facts and information are about things that happen. So facts and information are just feelings organized in a logical manner. Intellect and thought also generates feelings when those thoughts are processed in your mind. Since thought is really only about feelings, it is logical that thought actually has root in feelings. For example, all events are really feelings in the mind, so thoughts are actually just comparing feelings. You take two feelings and can arrive at one thought. Take the feeling of a frog moving and the feeling of a threat of danger. The two feelings combined equal the idea or thought that the frog needs to move when there is danger – the thought is actually just understanding how feelings interact. All thought is is the understanding of how feelings and real events interact with themselves. Feeling is what provides the motivation to arrive at the answer (the thought). If you just had the facts, there is a threat, and the frog can jump, you aren't going to arrive at the conclusion that the frog should jump away. You need to take the feeling that there is a threat and the feeling that the frog can jump and then combine the two sensory images in your head to arrive at the answer.

That shows how all intellect is powered and motivated by emotion. It also shows that frogs have thoughts; the frog has to have the thought to jump away when it sees a threat, as a thought is just the combination of two feelings resulting in the resulting feeling of wanting to move away. That process of feelings is like a thought process. Thoughts are a little different for humans, however, because humans have such a large memory that they are able to compare this experience to all the other experiences in their life while the frog only remembers the current situation and is programmed (brain wiring) to jump away. The frog doesn't have a large enough memory to learn from new information and change its behavior. That shows how humans are very similar to frogs in how they process data (in one way at least), and that one thing that separates a human from a frog is a larger memory which can store lots of useful information and potential behavioral patterns.

Thoughts, especially in humans, are not that independent – they can be much more complicated and it can appear to be that nothing is as it seems. If someone says to you, "I know x". He isn't just saying that he knows x, but there is a chain of other thoughts that also occur in your mind. You analyze the statement he made and it causes you to think automatically, "Do I know x too?" "Why does he think I care that he knows x?" "Is there anything else about x that is significant that I am missing?" "What if this other person is smarter than me?" that doesn't lead to a feeling of being dumb (it might), instead it leads to another concrete thing "maybe I am stupid" or the thought "maybe that person is stupid" interacting with the thought "because that thing he said was wrong". So one simple thought for a human can mean much much more than that one thought. That example shows another way in which humans are different from frogs – they are capable of more simultaneous thoughts. It is also the memory working hand in hand with that capacity of simultaneous thought as well, if you had no memory then you wouldn't have information to compare and bring up those simultaneous thoughts.

They can all be moving at the same time as well, not only does one thought follow another; but it occurs instantaneously. If the thing the person said was something you didn't know, it might make you feel stupid, thus the thought results in a feeling. But that feeling can be translated to a thought. So it isn't the feeling, "I am stupid" it is the thought "I am stupid". Feeling stupid might make you feel bad, but it isn't just that you are feeling bad, you are also thinking over and over "I am stupid" unconsciously, and that is what is making you feel bad. Or you are paying attention to the fact that you are stupid. Thus thought, feeling, and emotion is just paying attention to different things in your head. Concrete things.

It is a little more complicated than that, however. It is going to be a mix of a lot of concrete thoughts interacting with each other, not just the thought "I am stupid" repeated over and over but maybe also a less intense idea of "well I know x and y that that person doesn't, maybe this was just one event". So anything that is said or done is possibly followed by a long series of unconscious thoughts and thought processes.

There were two examples of thoughts, one was with the frog and the danger of a threat, and the other was a questioning of ones intellect relative to someone else. The example with the frog was an example of a thought process that was simple, while the example with the person showed how some thought processes can be much more complicated than they appear.

How This Chapter shows how Intelligence is intertwined with Emotion:

- It is stated first that use of emotion and thought requires attention, and therefore they both cause feelings, and if they both cause feelings then they are going to be similar in nature. Your intellect (or ability to do things which are real) is going to generate feelings just like emotions do.

- Feelings can result in thoughts – this was shown with the frog example, the frog has the thought "jump" which comes from the feeling of a threat of danger, and the feeling of it's understanding that it can jump. That shows how thoughts can be encouraged by feelings and mixed in with them.

- Thought is also powered by feeling in other ways, as when you are nervous that you didn't understand something, your feelings then cause you to think nervous things like "do I know that too?, does he think I care that he knows that?" Those thoughts are a function of intelligence, because they are causing you to think about real things, which is what intelligence is.

An explanation for this chapter:

This chapter basically outlined that thoughts can cause feelings and real things to happen, and these three things (thought, action, and feeling) can occur in any order. Feelings can cause you to jump, or some other action, and so can thoughts. Thoughts can cause feelings which could cause you to do an action. This means that any feeling, a physical one, a certain emotion, anything, could result in any thought which could cause you to do anything. For frogs, this process seems simple, if it has feelings, they are easy to label such as fear of a person coming near them. For a human, these feelings might be much more complex, involving many more unconscious thoughts and worries or whatnot. A frog isn't going to be worried if its intelligence is insulted, or any number of other possible unconscious thoughts that a person might have. You could still say the frog has thoughts though, since it reaches the conclusion at some point to jump away, and it moves in very complicated patterns. Those patterns of movement for a frog, however, are easy to understand and the same pattern occurs each time you see the frog pretty much. Humans can adapt their behavior with thoughts and make their behavior and thinking much more complex.

I say in this chapter that thought, feeling and emotion is just paying attention to concrete things in your head. If you talk to someone and they make you feel bad, it might be because you are unconsciously thinking they think you are stupid. Or you could say that you are just feeling like they think you are stupid. I guess it doesn't really matter if you say you are thinking they think you are stupid or you are feeling like they think you are stupid. If you are thinking that they are thinking you are stupid it is conscious, you are aware that they might be thinking you are stupid, and this might be making you feel bad. You pay attention to the thought you have of awareness of their thinking about this. You could also pay attention to the emotion of you feeling bad because you are thinking this. Or maybe you could describe what is going on as the other person is thinking you are stupid, and because they are thinking this you feel bad, no matter what you think or want to feel. They could be influencing your emotions by treating you as stupid. Maybe you're thinking unconsciously back to them, no actually i'm really smart. Maybe that is what you are thinking, but you could still feel bad about it. The point is, the difference between saying you have an unconscious thought and you have an emotion is just how much attention you are paying to each one. You are probably going to be paying more attention to it if it is an unconscious thought because that is what thoughts are, something you think and are aware of. You think you are smart, so unconsciously you are thinking that they shouldn't be thinking you are stupid. Maybe you thinking that unconsciously determines how you feel, so you don't feel bad because they think you're stupid because you know and are thinking that you're actually smart. So when someone treats you as stupid, you could in response a) feel that they are wrong, or b) be thinking that they are wrong. Those are two types of responses to things, you could respond with thoughts, or respond with feelings. If someone is mean to you, and you feel good in response, maybe it is because you are just a happy person, or maybe it is because you are "really" thinking they are stupid and ignoring them. However you want to label what is going on by saying you are feeling something or you are thinking something, you are ultimately just paying attention to your emotions or their emotions or what ever it is you are paying attention to, you don't have to think about it with words necessarily. If you are paying attention to your emotions or what you are thinking or what they are thinking or feeling, you could notice a lot. There could also be a lot going on that you don't know about because you can feel emotions for a lot of reasons you aren't aware of. Emotion is unconscious thought.

So what is the difference between someone thinking something and someone feeling something? You can feel bad, or you could think negative things about yourself that make you feel bad. When someone thinks, they are aware of what they are doing and what they are thinking about. When someone feels an emotion, they might not be aware of it or know how it was generated. What is an unconscious thought then? If thoughts are something you know you are thinking and are paying attention to, then how could you not be aware of them? A thought is something you are thinking, you know you are thinking it. You don't always (or maybe even never) know if you are experiencing an emotion, on the other hand. Emotion is unconscious thought because emotion is just you feeling something about something, so you could express it as a thought. "I feel bad because they treated me like I was stupid", could be the unconscious thought, and the emotion would be, "I feel bad because they treated me like I was stupid". They are exactly the same. If you are aware of what an emotion is, then it is a thought because you think about what the emotion is. It is also an emotion, because you are feeling it, but when you realize what caused the emotion or think about the emotion in your head, it is a thought because you are thinking about it (its still an emotion obviously though).

So if someone makes you feel bad, you might think, "this person made me feel bad". Then you would be experiencing the emotion sadness from them making you feel bad, and you would have verbalized that emotion into a thought, "this person made me feel bad". The emotion sadness turned into the thought in your head, "this person made me feel bad". So someone made you feel bad, this made you sad, then you realized you were sad and thought to yourself, "this person made me feel bad". Action turned into feeling, which caused you to think and therefore turned into thought. Thought, action (your action or external action) and feeling can occur in any order.

7.4 Emotions and Feelings and the Difference Between Them

Emotion is more similar to conscious thought than feelings are to conscious thought. Although emotion and feeling can be described as unconscious thought, one of them is going to be more similar to conscious thought. Feelings are more like sensations, when you touch something you get a feeling. Therefore feelings are faster than emotions and thought, because when you touch something there is a slight delay before you can think of something about it (thought), or feel something deeply about it (emotion). Emotion is therefore just unconscious thought. Actually it would better be described as unconscious feeling (so a feeling is like a conscious emotion because you can "feel" it better and easier but emotion is a deeper, more unconscious experience similar to unconscious thought, but emotions are also more similar to conscious thought because thought is a deep experience while feelings are intense or shallow, but not deep).

One definition of emotion can be "any strong feeling". From that description many conclusions can be drawn. Basic (or primary) emotions can be made up of secondary emotions like love can contain feelings or emotions of lust, love and longing. Feelings can be described in more detail than emotions because you can have a specific feeling for anything, each feeling is unique and might not have a name. For instance, if you are upset by one person that might have its own feeling because that person upsets you in a certain way. That feeling doesn't have a defined name because it is your personal feeling. The feeling may also be an emotion, say anger. "Upset" is probably too weak to be an emotion, but that doesn't mean that it isn't strong like emotions are strong in certain ways. Cold is also just a feeling. There is a large overlap between how feelings feel and how emotions feel, they are similar in nature. So there are only a few defined emotions, but there are an infinite number ways of feeling things. You can have a "small" emotion of hate and you could say that you have the feeling hate then, if it is large you could say you are being emotional about hate, or are experiencing the emotion hate. You can have the same emotion of hate in different situations, but each time the feeling is going to be at least slightly different.

You can recognize any feeling, that is what makes it a feeling. If you are sad that is a feeling, but if you are depressed that isn't a feeling it is more like an emotion. You can't identify why you are depressed but you can usually identify why you are sad. Feelings are more immediate, if something happens or is happening, it is going to result in a feeling. However, if something happened a long time ago, you are going to think about it unconsciously and that is going to bring up unconscious feelings (the reason the things that happened previously are going to be more similar to emotion than things that are happening currently is that sensory stimulation (or things happening currently) is a lot closer to feelings than things that are less linked to direct sensory stimulation (such as emotions which are therefore usually going to be about things which require memory to figure out, things like thoughts that are less like feelings and more like emotion)). So emotions are unconscious feelings that are the result of mostly unconscious thoughts (instead of feelings – a feeling can trigger an emotion, but it isn't a part of it). Feeling defined there as something you can identify. Also, you can't identify the unconscious thought that caused the unconscious feeling, but you can identify the unconscious feeling itself (aka emotion).

Another aspect of unconscious thought, emotion, or unconscious feeling (all three are the same) is that it tends to be mixed into the rest of your system because it is unconscious. If it was conscious then it remains as an individual feeling, but in its unconscious form you confuse it with the other emotions and feelings and it affects your entire system. So therefore most of what people are feeling is just a mix of feelings that your mind cannot separate out individually. That is the difference between sadness and a depression, a depression lowers your mood and affects all your feelings and emotions, but sadness is just that individual feeling. So the reason that the depression affects all your other feelings is because you can no longer recognize the individual sad emotions that caused it. The feelings become mixed. If someone can identify the reason they are sad then they become no longer depressed, just sad. Once they forget that that was the reason they are depressed however, they will become depressed again.

That is why an initial event might make someone sad, and then that sadness would later lead into a depression, is because you forget why you originally got sad. You might not consciously forget, but unconsciously you do. That is, it feels like you forget, the desire to get revenge on whatever caused the sadness fades away. When that happens it is like you "forgetting" what caused it. You may also consciously forget but what matters is how much you care about that sadness. It might be that consciously understanding why you are depressed or sad changes how much you care about your sadness, however. That would therefore change the emotion/feeling of sadness. The more you care about the sadness/depression, the more like a feeling it becomes and less like an emotion. That is because the difference between feelings and emotions is that feelings are easier to identify (because you can "feel" them easier).

The following is a good example of the transition from caring about a feeling to not caring about a feeling. Anger as an emotion takes more energy to maintain, so if someone is punched or something, they are only likely to be mad for a brief period of time, but the sadness that it incurred might last for a much longer time. That sadness is only going to be recognizable to the person punched for a brief period of time as attributable to the person who did the punching, after that the sadness would sink into their system like a miniature depression. Affecting the other parts of their system like a depression.

In review, both feelings and emotions are composed of unconscious thoughts, but feelings are easier to identify than emotions. Feelings are faster than emotions in terms of response (the response time of the feeling, how fast it responds to real world stimulation) and it takes someone less time to recognize feelings because they are faster. Feelings are closer to sensory stimulation, if you touch something, you feel it and that is a fast reaction. You care about the feeling so you can separate it out in your head from the other feelings. "You care" in that sentence could be translated into, the feeling is intense, so you feel it and can identify it easily. That is different from consciously understanding why you are depressed or sad. You can consciously understand why you are depressed or sad, but that might or might not affect the intensity of that sadness.

If the intensity of the sadness is brought up enough, then you can feel that sadness and it isn't like a depression anymore, it is more like an individual feeling than something that affects your mood and brings your system down (aka a depression). Also, if you clearly enough understand what the sadness is then it is going to remain a sadness and not affect the rest of your system. That is because the feeling would get mixed in with the other feelings and start affecting them. The period of this more clear understanding of the sadness mostly occurs right after the event that caused the sadness. That is because it is clear to you what it is. Afterwards the sadness might emerge (or translate from a depression, to sadness) occasionally if you think about what caused it or just think about it in general.

The difference between emotion and feeling is that feelings are easier to identify because they are faster, a feeling is something you are feeling right then. An emotion might be a deeper experience because it might affect more of you, but that is only because it is mixed into the rest of your system. That is, a depression affects more of you than just an isolated feeling of sadness. In other words, people can only have a few feelings at a time, but they can have many emotions at the same time. Emotions are mixed in, but to feel something you have to be able to identify what it is, or it is going to be so intense that you would be able to identify what it is. Emotions just feel deeper because it is all your feelings being affected at once.

Since emotion is all your feelings being affected at once, emotions are stronger than feelings. Feelings however are a more directed focus. When you feel something you can always identify what that one thing is. When you have an emotion, the emotion is more distant, but stronger. All your feelings must feel a certain way about whatever is causing the emotion. So that one thing is affecting your entire system. Feelings can then be defined as immediate unconscious thought, and emotions as unconscious thought.

How This Chapter shows how Intelligence is intertwined with Emotion:

- When you care about an emotion, you could say that you have a higher attention for emotion or that emotional event during that time. You are probably going to be in a higher state of action readiness, that is, you are probably more alert and going to be able to respond faster to whatever it is you are focusing on, or just respond faster in general. You also are going to have a better understanding of the emotion if you care about it more - you make an assessment of the emotions strength and its nature when you think about the emotion (or the event that generated the emotion).

- Feelings are more direct than emotions and thought because they are more sensory – when you touch something you get a feeling. That shows further how emotions are really about things in the real world, only it more like you are thinking about them instead of feeling them in real time. Things that come from memory are going to be emotions and/or thoughts, not feelings because feelings are things which are more tangible, those memories might result in new feelings, but the memories themselves are not feelings because they are just thoughts. That shows how you can feel some things more than others, that thought and feeling are indeed separate and intelligence is sometimes driven by feelings and emotions, and sometimes it isn't. You can think about things and not have feelings guiding those thoughts Or your feelings could be assisting your thoughts.

- If you care about a feeling then it becomes easier to identify it – that shows how your feelings can help you to identify other feelings, so your emotions contribute to your emotional intelligence.

- If a certain emotion is larger than others then to your intellect it is going to be easier to recognize, and easier to think about (that is why a depression feels like it does, because you don't know the individual emotions contributing to it so you cannot feel a specific emotion of sadness from it.

An explanation for this chapter:

So feelings are easier to "feel" than emotions, that is probably why they are called feelings, because you "feel" them better. Maybe someone else thinks you can feel emotions easier, I don't know, the point is you can feel emotions and feelings with different levels of intensity and in more than one way, a feeling could be not intense but clear to you. So how conscious you are of the feeling or emotion influences the intensity of it and your conscious experience of it. A feeling could be more intense than en emotion if it is the only thing you are feeling as well. That makes sense, if an emotion is very complicated, then you probably couldn't feel the entire thing as clearly in a brief period of time. So my theory is that feelings are more simple, and therefore there are more shallow but possibly more intense than emotion because you can focus on a simple thing easier.

If you are having a deep emotional experience (experiencing an emotion) then it makes sense that you aren't as in touch with all of those feelings that are occurring. When you touch something you get the feeling "cold" - that is simple to understand. When you are in a depression you don't understand all the complicated emotions that you are experiencing. You could experience sadness all day. When you can say "oh, I really "felt" that", then you know you feel it and it is a feeling. When you feel something, it is a feeling. When you are emotional about something, those are feelings too, but it is more powerful and deeper, you aren't as in touch will all of it because it is more complex. You could be in touch with something complex and feel that too, I guess. Though I would argue that a feeling is easier to focus on if it is simple and clear to understand and feel to your conscious mind.

The significance of this chapter:

If someone is emotional, then they are feeling a lot. I could say that the emotions someone is experiencing could be brought up at different times and felt more - translated from somewhere in your strong emotions to something you feel more closely. So you can feel some things but that doesn't mean that the feeling is intense or clear - those things might become clear however at some point.

When those emotions become clear and you 'bring them up' - either by caring about the emotion or the thought that represents it or it just emerges by some other method (such as by doing an evaluation of your emotional state) - then they become feelings because you can feel them easier. These feelings are more clear, similar to when you touch something you get a feeling that is simple and tactile. That is why feelings   are called the result of emotions, because emotions are like the basis for feelings (at least non-tactile ones). You might have a feeling that has a shallow source however as well I would say. It doesn't have to be that a feeling is first felt deeply, and then you feel it more clearly later on (the feeling being the result of an emotion). Maybe the feeling is simple at first and then it becomes more complex later.

What role does attention have to play? Being emotional or feeling something can make you pay more or less attention to things, including other feelings. Your attention can naturally rise just because of your emotional state.

People feel emotions, and they can feel feelings. Emotions are strong and the powerful source of human behavior, and while feelings are also powerful they are also diverse, curious, and unique - 'old feelings returning'.

7.5 How to Change Emotions and Feelings

An appraisal is when you assess something. People make appraisals or assessments of emotion all of the time, however they aren't aware most of the time that they are doing this. How much someone cares about   an emotional stimulus is something that is probably thought about frequently during the experience. If you think about it people frequently are going to naturally analyze what is going on in every situation they   are in and think about what the emotions occurring are.

I said in the previous paragraph that people make appraisals of emotional things but they aren't aware of themselves doing that. How is that possible or what does that mean exactly? If people care about emotion, which they clearly do, then they are going to want to know what is going on in the situations they encounter in life. So clearly people make assessments of how much emotion the things around them are generating, the only question is can they do this in a a way that is beneath their awareness.

People surely must make assessments since they often work on inducing or inhibiting feelings in order to make them "appropriate" to a situation. If you are going to be changing feeling, then obviously you are going to need to measure and assess it first. Sometimes people think this process through consciously, and sometimes they don't.

It makes sense to me that people are going to "know" how valuable certain things in their environment are. This is clear when you realize that people focus on some things very quickly - such a thing would clearly be something of interest to that person or something that generates emotion - which would make it interesting.

So you could say that a person whose attention gets alerted to something around them made an assessment about the stimulus or responded to it, the stimulus (the thing in their environment they paid sharp attention to) was clearly emotional for them. It could have generated any feeling - disgust, surprise, happiness, - or maybe an intellectual reaction such as 'that person has a bright coat'.

Does that mean that the person assessed if the bright coat generated emotion for them? What would it mean if it generated emotion? Could they respond in a fast way without being interested? Someone could respond quickly to something and not be in a mood that is very caring at that time, in which case maybe little emotion was involved. However if someone was interested in something then it makes sense that it is going to cause them to have feelings.

Is something someone is interested in going to cause them to have deep emotions or shallow feelings? What types of stimuli result in deep or shallow feelings? Just because something generates more emotion for you doesn't necessarily mean that it is going to cause you to respond to it faster or you would be more interested in it. Maybe your interest is more intellectual or maybe you are interested or responding to it quickly because you have to.

Under what circumstances do people care more about feelings? This relates to appraisals - if you care about something then you are going to make more assessments during the experience about how much emotion is being generated probably. People can care more about feelings but that doesn't mean that they are aware that they care more during that time. This is similar to people going into modes where they are seeking pleasure. My theory here is that people have levels of desire and need that fluctuate constantly.

This means that there are many different levels someone can experience an emotion or feeling. It is more complicated than simply saying that the feeling has a certain strength - each feeling or emotion is going to have a unique nature, represent unique ideas and objects, and have a unique significance on your psyche.

Maybe you can say that there are shallow feelings and deep emotions, and that there are certain properties that shallow feelings have and certain properties that deep feelings have. For instance you probably care more about deep feelings (unless the feeling is negative) and therefore they probably cause you to have a faster reaction time. However if the feeling is deep, sappy, and emotional then maybe your reaction time is slower because the emotion is weighing you down.

This relates to the 'emotions and feelings and the difference between them' section above because I am outlining further that deep feelings/emotions or shallow feelings/emotions are different and things happen to humans differently with each one. It shows that clearly emotion can make someone be different physically, as when you are motivated by emotion you often move faster.

This is just bringing up ideas of depth - some feelings are simple and some are complex - that is obvious, however I think people could notice a lot more if they grouped their emotions into a categories of strength and shallowness or depth and how they responded differently to each different category. - Also the person should note what the interest was, the reaction time, the negative or positive valence of the emotion.

Goffman suggests that we spend a good deal of effort on managing impressions - that is, acting. Your impression of other people makes you feel in different ways, and you try to manage this in a social situation. So therefore all of your strong feelings you try to influence by thinking about what caused those feelings - such as your impressions - and how you can change them.

So people are basically "emotion-managers", constantly thinking about their feelings and what caused them and how they can change them. Whenever you change an impression of someone, you are also changing your feelings. When you think about your own feelings you are changing them because you are changing how much you care about them. You set goals for yourself about your own feelings - 'if I do this I am going to become happy'.

When you think about your feelings you can make insignificant feelings large or large feelings small. When a feeling is small, you could say that it is more unconscious or beneath your awareness. Something (including yourself) could trigger this small feeling and it could emerge into something you feel more closely and more consciously.

So the question is, what circumstances and what type of thinking warrant that feeling of 'that sort'.

We assess the 'appropriateness' of a feeling by making a comparison between the feeling and the situation. We also have goals for how we want to feel that we don't know we are thinking, and we have goals for how we want to act as well. Is there a 'natural attitude' or a natural way of behaving and thinking? Not really - especially when you consider that you are unconsciously constantly creating goals, drives, thoughts and behaviors that are not fully under your control.

- In *secondary reactive emotions*, the person reacts against his or her initial primary adaptive emotion, so that it is replaced with a secondary emotion. This "reaction to the reaction" obscures or transforms the original emotion and leads to actions that are not entirely appropriate to the current situation. For example, a man that encounters danger and begins to feel fear may feel that fear is not "manly." He may then either become angry at the danger (externally focused reaction) or angry with himself for being afraid (self-focused reaction), even when the angry behavior actually increases the danger. Listening to this reaction, someone is likely to have the sense that "something else is going on here" or "there's more to this than just anger." The experience is something like hearing two different melodies being played at the same time in a piece of music, one the main melody and the other the background or counterpart.

- Secondary emotions often arise from attempts to judge and control primary responses.

- Thus, anxiety may come from trying to avoid feeling angry or sexually excited, or it may arise from guilt about having felt these emotions.

When someone rejects what they are truly feeling, they are likely to feel bad about themselves. Feeling or expressing one emotion to mask the primary emotion is a metaemotional process. Feelings about emotions need to be acknowledged and then explored to get at the underlying primary emotion.

Experiential therapists see clients emotional processing as occurring on a continuum with five phases (Kennedy-Moore + Watson, 1999[1]):

1. prereflective reaction to an emotion-eliciting stimulus entailing perception of the stimulus, preconscious cognitive and emotional processing, and accompanying physiological changes

2. conscious awareness and perception of the reaction

3. labeling and interpretation of the affective response; people typically draw upon internal as well as situational cues to label their responses

4. evaluation of whether the response is acceptable or not

5. evaluation of the current context in terms of whether it is possible or desirable to reveal one's feelings.

What role does the emotion 'interest' play in emotional responses? It is a baseline emotion of great importance - the action tendency of interest involves intending, orienting, and exploring. Interest is felt very frequently, probably without being noticed. If you think about it, to some degree interest is going to be present with each reaction to stimuli. With every response someone has, they are interested to some degree. You can look at interest further when you consider secondary emotional responses - what was the interest that came from the response that had some other type of interest?

Through each stage of evaluation of a response, or simple evaluations that aren't a response to things, there is interest involved as well. This 'interest' induces caring, and the interest and caring is going to change

---

1. Kennedy-Moore, E., + Watson, J.C. (1999). *Expressing emotion: Myths, realities and therapeutic strategies.* New York: Guilford Press.

your emotions - emotions are going to be brought up, intensified, changed based off of your interest or caring or evaluations. When you think and make evaluations, you change the nature and intensity of the emotions that are related to what you are doing or processing.

Are people going to be more interested in clear, primary emotions or feelings that they aren't in touch with? When someone is interested in a feeling, how is that different from being interested in the source of the feeling? If someone is feeling sad, they might not care about the sadness if the feeling is unclear to them or they don't know they are sad. If someone is going to try to change a feeling of sadness, it clearly would be beneficial if they knew when the feeling is occurring.

Is it possible to experience deep emotions without being aware at all that these emotions are occurring? Yes it is, but there are times when people are conscious of those emotions - say when they are recalling them - that the deep emotions are more clear. There could be a deep emotion that occurs over a long period of time - say anger at someone, this anger could be in your body for a long time, during being the person, or while away from the person; the point is the anger is reflected upon or it occurs more deeply at certain points - and then you are going to be aware of the emotion.

That anger is a significant, primary feeling. The feeling is significant because it shows how large the emotion is that is behind it. People can feel feelings that are shallow or intense at the time, but these feelings don't necessarily mean more than that or are deeper than that because they aren't deep or primary - they don't mean anything else or occur at other times you aren't aware of (indicating that this feeling is significant). The feeling of shallow feelings is still potent (because you are feeling them in real time), but they aren't as powerful as feelings that have a special meaning or significance for you (which would make you feel deeper in real time and feel more effected).

If you think about it, people change their feelings by thinking all of the time. The way they could help manage this is probably by making assessments of their emotional state. If people think about what just made them happy or sad, then they might be able to do something or think something to change that. Some emotional responses are going to be more noticeable, and that is when people might try to figure out what went on.

There are subtleties of emotion as well. People probably respond in many ways that they aren't aware of consciously, but they might have responded because something beneath their notice occurred emotionally. You could say that the emotional world beneath your notice is the "unconscious" mind or the unconscious world.

Your emotions change all of the time, only sometimes are you going to notice when an emotion changes or when you are experiencing one. Furthermore, you might want or expect to experience one emotion but you are actually experiencing a different one because unconsciously that is how you are responding. For instance, maybe you have an unconscious bias against a group of people so you feel hate when you interact with them, but you consciously think that you like those people and feel like you should be happy and positive towards them, A feeling might be important to your unconscious mind, or a feeling might be important to your conscious mind - in which case you would probably 'care' about it.

Your attention is constantly divided between various things in your environment, your own internal thinking and your own emotions. Your emotions are going to determine and assist what you pay attention to. For instance, if something is emotional in your environment for you, then more of your attention is probably going to spent thinking about or focusing on that thing.

Or maybe something in your environment is just more interesting than something else, the point is something in your environment or something in your head (emotions, thoughts) caused an intellectual or emotional reaction in you, and that then caused you to pay more attention to it. That doesn't mean that you notice it more after you pay attention - this type of paying attention might be unconscious - i.e. - more of your attentional resources or just more of the focus that people have (not all of which they are aware of) is going to be directed at it.

7.6 Intellect, Cogntion and Emotion

Humans have emotions - feelings are tangible while emotions are - or could be considered to be deep and complicated. The idea that feelings are tangible basically means that they could be more sensory or less intellectual and deep. Emotions are more powerful than feelings; however, they could also trigger the human intellect.

What would it mean for emotion to be powerful? Would that involve physical feelings? Physical stimulation can also be deep or shallow, emotional or intellectual. If the feeling (physical, emotional) is intellectual then it could be emotional or it could also be tied in with sensory feelings (say when you touch something).

What would it mean for something to be intellectual? Would that mean that it is different from the persons emotions? Emotions can be tied in with feelings - however that means that the emotion could be shallow and thought provoking or deep, or a strong emotion that is also deep.

It is important to distinguish deep feelings from sensory feelings. Deep feelings are probably intellectual - they are tied in with complicated cognitions which include memory processes, executive functioning (control of thoughts, ideas and images) and understanding concepts.

Concepts can also be emotional since they are intellectual or intelligent. A concept is like an idea only it is general or generic. An idea is something that occurs to someone while a concept could be the definition of an idea or the idea that the person refers to or already understood. Those deeper concepts can trigger emotions that are related to the idea or concept. A single concept could be powerful or significant to the person.

A humans emotions could influence their thoughts - and their physical feelings can also influence either their thoughts or their emotions (or both at the same time). Thoughts could be complicated - they are a mix of goals and motivations with the persons environment and experience. Furthermore, a motivation could have complicated emotions, and their present situation could be causing complicated emotions.

The difference between feelings and thoughts is simple and complex - a thought could be complex because it could involve the persons motivations mixed in with the objects in their environment and their experience. They could have a thought for each object or each objective reality in their situation.

The difference between their feelings and thoughts then is that their feelings cause feeling, or stimulation and could be complex and intellectual while their thoughts could be unconscious or complex.

7.7 What is an idea?

Humans have feelings. Humans can also think about their feelings. Other factors in reality help the thinking process - such as what is in the persons environment, and what they are paying attention to all assist the persons thinking process.

But what exactly is a thought process? Is it a sentence? Is it a single idea? Is it a few ideas that the person is trying to think about or understand?

The ideas someone is thinking about could be complicated and internal - or simple and related to their environment.

Humans have ideas - mulitple ideas can compose a thought process. The ideas can be about different things - stuff in the persons environement, other ideas or memories that they want to think about, and they can form thoughts or sentences about those ideas - they can also think about their feelings (with ideas or sentences).

For instance, a feeling could be an idea - or an idea could become a feeling.

What does that mean an idea is? An idea is something that occurs to someone - it is a concept or intention, or an understanding of some sort.

Ideas can relate to a persons feelings - and to the persons thought process. That is, ideas can complete a thought process.

7.8 Ideas in Action]

Ideas are thoughts that occur to people. 'That is an excellent idea' would be the expression.

There are people that have emotions. There emotions are feelings that they feel. That means that they also like to think about stuff. I added that to this book as a final addition. You would think that that was written before I did the research for this book because it doesn't sound very sophisticated, however

I don't know what else to add to this book. I hope that the humans reading this go to my website, modifiedimage.com - to look at my artwork, however

I now realize that that sounds stupid, but I am going to publish it anyway.

7.9 Emotions and thoughts

People have feelings. Therefore they think about stuff.

Humans can also visualize objects internally or see real objects.

If something is visualized, then it could contain information that is the equivalent of the idea of thoughts or conscious or unconscious processing.

Or of thoughts without ideas.

But what is a thought? Or what is an idea?

An idea is a thought that occurs to someone, that means that ideas are thoughts. Because they are whole ideas or we'll thought out. That means, in turn, that ideas can be feeling.

Ideas are feelings if they have thoughts or link to their memories or other visualizations. That is because feelings consist of thoughts or feeling-triggers.

7.10 Attention and Thought Control

How does the attention process work? Do people who are anxious pay more attention to threatening things in their environment than people who aren't anxious? Do people who are depressed have less motivation and a slower reaction time or do they pay more attention to negative stimuli than positive? There is going to be emotional biases with mental illnesses or each time someone pays attention to something - if someone is experiencing an emotion, than that emotion is going to influence their attention in a certain way. For instance, if someone is experiencing the emotion of 'guilt' then clearly if they see something they feel guilty about they are going to pay attention to it differently (as they would associate and compare the guilt they are feeling with the guilt related to the object they are looking at).

Attention also relates to the thoughts someone experiences - if someone is paying attention to their own thoughts, then they might do things to control their thoughts. Some thoughts are voluntary and people direct or create them consciously, and some are more unconscious and instinctual - thoughts that they have less control over. Wells and Morrison (1994) [2] investigated dimensions of naturally occurring worry and intrusive thoughts in 30 normal subjects. They were asked to keep a diary and record their worries and intrusive thoughts, and they were also asked to rate each thought on the following dimensions:

 i.　Degree of verbal thought/imagery involved

 ii.　Intrusiveness

 iii.　How realistic the thought was

 iv.　How involuntary the thought was

2.　Wells, A., + Morrison, T. (1994) Qualitative dimensions of normal worry and normal intrusive thoughts" A comparative study. *Behavior Research and therapy.*

   v. How controllable it was

  vi. How dismissable it was

 vii. How much the thought grabbed attention

viii. Degree of distress associated with the thought

  ix. Intensity of compulsion to act on the thought

   x. Degree of resistance to the thought

  xi. Degree of success in controlling the thought

Wells and Davies (1994)[3] have attempted to distinguish types of thought control strategy. They interviewed patients with a range of anxiety disorders to determine the types of strategy used to control unpleasant and/or unwanted thoughts. Seven types of strategy emerged from the pilot interviews: cognitive and behavioral distraction; punishment; distancing; re- appraisal; mood changing activites; exposure to the thought; worry about more trivial things. Sometimes people might think that their thoughts are likely to come true, or that their worries are not controllable. "Cognitive and behavioral distraction" probably means distraction by your own internal thinking or distraction by you doing something - such as behaving in a certain way. "Punishment" would mean punishing yourself for having a thought you didn't want, distancing would mean somehow separating yourself from the thought, and re- appraisal would mean thinking of the thought differently or assessing that thought in a different way.

Multiple dimentions of emotional control strategy have been found in other studies. For example Mayer et al. (1991) [4] identified three dimenisons of emotion management distinct from dimensions of mood, labelled "suppression" (including distraction), "thoughts of actions" and "denial".

We can to some extent distinguish worry, intrusive thoughts and negative automatic thoughts on criteria such as intensity, unpleasantness, realism, intrusivenss and controllability, but those things are hard to define. How does someone know when the thought they have is 'intense' or when they thought they have is clear and realistic? If the thought is realistic is it going to be clear? I would think that the more realistic the thought is - tied in with reality - the more clear it would be because it is linked to real information. If you are fantasizing your thoughts are more like in a cloud (for example a dream state). It is also hard to tell if a thought is unpleasant, how is someone supposed to know how positive emotionally one single thought is? That seems too hard to measure. Someone might know how easy it is to control their thoughts or how pleasant their thoughts are for a certain period of time, but not every single thought they experience, or even a single reoccurring thought.

Two categories of appraisal are important in determining emotional experience and influencing subsequent coping efforts: primary and secondary appraisal. Primary appraisal is the process of evaluating the personal meaning and significance for well-being of events, which may be irrelevant, benign-positive or stressful. Stress appraisals may be further subdivided into harm/loss, where the person has sustained physical or psychological damage; threat, where harm/loss is anticipated; and challenge, where successful coping may lead to gains. Secondary appraisal is concerned with what can be done to deal with a situation, and includes reviewing the range of coping options available and their likely success in the situation at hand. A third form of appraisal delineated by Lazarus and Folkman (1984)[5] is reappraisal, which refers to the changes in appraisal which follow as the event unfolds and new information is acquired, including feedback on the success of attempts to cope.

There are a few more things to consider related to appraisals. How does considering the personal meaning of an event change the feeling involved? How does it change your thinking, and subsequently, what you

---

3. Wells, A., + Davies, M. (1994) A questionaire for assessing thought control strategies: Development and preliminary validation.

4. Mayer, J. D Salovey, P., Gomberg-Kaufman, S., + Blainey, K (1991). A broader conception of mood experience. *Journal of Personality and Social Psychology, 60,* 100-111.

5. Lazarus, R.s>, + Folkman, S. (1984). *Stress, appraisal and coping.* New York: Springer.

are paying attention to? How does your history or beliefs change how you make that appraisal? Do you make it with a bias or a unique significance to yourself? Whenever someone makes an assessment, that assessment is unique to themself. When someone makes a secondary appraisal, how does that impact their attention different from their primary appraisal? You first assess a situation (primary appraisal), and then you assess what can be done about it (secondary appraisal), however how do those two actions influence your attention and your thinking? Are the primary appraisal and the secondary appraisals separated out by time or by other thoughts (intrusive or voluntary)?

What types of thoughts do you have in between the first appraisal process and the second one? What occurres with your levels of feeling during this process? - i.e., what happens to you emotionally after a strong appraisal or a strong thought? Does that influence your subsequent thoughts and appraisals? How is your attention to external stimuli fluctuating during this process? What sequence does your significant thoughts/appraisals/emotions occur in, and how does that impact your attention? Do you focus on your emotions or your own thoughts when you pause to consider what happened after you had a significant thought or a significant stimulus input (experience).

It appears that anxiety is only positively associated with on-task effort under rather special circumstances, where there is a strong and immediate perceived threat, or, perhaps, where task performance is appriased as instrumental in effecting avoidance or escape (see Eysenck, 1982)[6] That probably means that the decreased performance from anxiety in most other circumstances is a result of people being distracted by the anxiety i.e., scanning their environment for threats or just being distracted by the pain.

Negative mood, which indicates that the environment poses a problem and might be a source of potential dangers, motivates people to change their situation. Negative mood is then thought to be associated with a systematic elaboration of information and greater attention to details. Bodenhausen and colleagues (1994)[7], investigating the impact of negative affect of social judgment, showed that induced sadness promotes the use of an analytic, detail-oriented mode of processing, whereas anger induction leads participants to process information on a shallow or automatic mode. If sadness (negative valence, lower arousal) triggered a type of processing identical to that fostered by the negative mood usually induced, anger (negative valence, higher arousal) fostered the hueristic or global mode of processing commonly associated with positive mood states (e.g., happiness or joy). This last result suggests that mood states of opposite valence may have similar effects as they share the same level of arousal (like happiness and anger). Likewise, it has been suggested that motivational-related approach and avoidance behaviors are independent of valence, leading to evidence that both happiness and anger moods are approach oriented, whereas serenity and sadness are avoidance oriented (when someone is depressed they avoid).

A sad mood experienced at our own wedding or birthday party may result in attempts to improve the mood, thus triggering systematic processessing in order to understand why we are sad in a situation that should normally make us happy. The same motivations are less likely to be aroused when the sad mood is experienced in situations where sadness is socially expected (e.g., at a funeral). According to Martin's model (2001)[8] people not ask merely: "How do I feel about it?" They ask "What does it mean that I am feeling this way in this context?" In other words, people evaluate the targets by taking into consideration both their mood and some features of situation and doing this configurally. Moods are processed in parallel with contextual information in such a way that the meaning of the mood influences and is influenced by the meaning of other information. The meaning of a mood experience can change in different context, and therefore the evaluative and motivational implications of mood are mutable.

To sum up, the informational value of mood lies not so much in the moods themselves as in the interaction between mood and context. Moods provide input for evaluative, decisional and inference-making

---

6. Eysenck, M.W. (1982). *Attention and arousal: Cognition and performance.* New York: Springer.

7. Bodenhausen, G,V., Shappard, L. A., + Kramer, G. P. (1994). Negative affect and social judgment: The differential impact of anger and sadness. *European Journal of Social Psychology*, 24, 45-62.

8. Martin, L.L.(2001). Mood as input: A configural view of mood effect. In J. P. Forgast (Ed.) *Feeling and thinking: The role of affect in social cognition* (pp.135-157). New York: Cambridge University Press.

processes, and these processes determine the effects that one's mood will have on one's evaluations, motivations, and behaviors. This course of reasoning, known as the *context- dependent effect of mood*, implies that the influence of mood on one's evaluations, motivations, and behaviors depends on the interaction of mood and the situational conditions.

In accordance with the *context-dependent effect of mood*, one's mood is not synonymous with one's evaluation. Whether a positive or negative mood leads to a favorable or unfavorable evaluation depends on the meaning of one's mood in that context. The question about the meaning of one's mood in different contexts is therefore a crucial one. In order to answer it, the mood as input model relies on the role- fulfillment process (Martin, 2001), also known as the "What would I feel if...?" process. This process can be characterized broadly as follows: when people make evaluations, they act as if they were asking themselves the question "What would I feel if...?: (For example, "what would I feel if the horror movie I just saw was a good horror movie?"). An evaluation is rendered subjectively when the person compares his/her current moods with the expected feelings. Favorable evaluations arise to the extent to which the person's moods (positive or negative) are congruent with what would be expected if the target had fulfilled a positive role (i.e., if this was a good thing I would feel good, I feel good, so I think this positive thing about it). Unfavorable evaluations, in contrast, arise to the extent to which the person's moods are incongruent with what would be expected if the target had fulfilled a negative role (i.e., if this party was bad, it would make me feel bad, however I feel good).

When people make evaluations, they are thinking more about what is going on then when they don't make evaluations. That is why negative mood enhances attention to detail - because it puts you in the state where you are questioning why the event or environment you are in is making you feel bad. Asking how you might feel if something is felt a certain way is a good way of analyzing the situation. If you think about it, asking how something makes you feel is important - people probably constantly evaluate the events they experience for value or what they got from them. Your mood is going to help you to evaluate those things because those events caused you to have that mood. The mood provides the information of what that event or stimulus does to you - how it makes you feel. If people didn't evaluate how an event or stimulus makes them feel, then they wouldn't really be analyzing that input any further than they normally would.

You basically can be put into a state where you are thinking about what the event or stimulus you are evaluating is like. This state is when you are questioning what the feelings the event made in you are like or what you think about the event. It is interesting that someone can simply not think about those things if they wanted. On the other hand, it seems natural for people who experience negative emotions to think more deeply about the source of those emotions. I guess the trouble that the negative emotions causes them forces one to think more deeply.

7.11 Emotions are Dulled Feelings

Feelings are more immediate than emotions, they are easier to identify and are "faster". You can also have only a few feelings at a time but your emotions are possibly composed of many more components. That is, you can have a feeling about a Frisbee, and you can have a feeling about a Frisbee game as well. But if you have emotions about the Frisbee game then in order to get those strong emotions there would have to be many things you are feeling about the Frisbee game.

So one could think of emotions as just more than feelings. Emotions are greater than feelings and therefore they must have more parts in order to cause that greater feeling. Feelings are easy to understand because they are simple, but emotions are harder to understand because they are more complicated. A moody person would be described as emotional because emotion is a component of mood. Emotion is something that affects your entire system like a depression does. A feeling such as sadness is only an individual feeling and can be identified as such.

If something is intense, then it is a feeling, emotions aren't intense they are deep. They aren't as intense as feelings but you could call them intense. Feelings are more intense because that is how we define feelings, if you can feel something then it is a feeling because, well, you "feel" it. Emotion is just something that affects you, your mood, how you are, etc. That is why feelings are easier to identify, because they are more intense. Emotions are deeper, however, when someone becomes emotional you can't just snap out of it instantly, it hangs around in your system. That is why they are probably made up of more parts than feelings are.

The reason feelings are both more intense yet shallower than emotions is probably because your system can only handle so much intensity at a time, so you can only experience shallow things intensely. If you compare it to a river, emotions would have a lot of water and be going slowly, and feelings would have less water, but be going faster. The feeling is therefore going to touch more things in your mind shallowly, and the emotion is going to touch more things in your mind deeply.

Why then do some simple things cause us to become more emotional if emotion is a deeper experience? That is because the feeling must trigger emotions, the simple thing is actually a feeling itself, but it triggers emotions. Like how color can be more emotional than black and white. It is actually that color causes more feeling, and we become emotional then about that feeling. But while you are looking at the color it is a feeling which you are feeling, not an emotion. The feeling made you feel good, however, and that good feeling infects the rest of your feelings and emotions, and then you become emotional.

In fact, all feelings make someone more emotional. The only difference between feeling and emotion is that feeling is the immediate feeling you get from something. It is the thing which you are experiencing currently. Feeling is another word for current stimulation. You can only feel something that you are either thinking about or experiencing. Otherwise you aren't really feeling it, and it is an emotion. That is why the word feeling is the word feeling, because you can feel it intimately, closely.

How is it then that emotions are generally considered to be deeper? That is because with emotions you are actually feeling more, you just aren't as in touch with what it is that you are feeling. So you would experience the effects of having a lot of feeling, such as heavy breathing, crying, laughing, they would be things that make all your other feelings and emotions feel the same way. However your mind isn't intensifying that experience because it would be too much for you to handle. Therefore emotion is just many feelings (or one strong feeling) that is dulled down, and it would actually be a stronger feeling(s), you just can only experience it fully as an emotion. You can also probably experience parts of that emotion as feelings since parts of it are going to be less intense than the whole, and you can "feel" them then.

So people can basically only "feel" or focus on small amounts of feeling. If it is a feeling that is very large it becomes an emotion with more parts. It isn't that this emotion isn't as deep as the feeling, it is actually deeper, but you simply cannot comprehend the entire emotion at once to "feel" it like you feel feelings. You can bring up feelings from memory (by thinking about sensory stimulation) but those types of feelings are going to be less direct and therefore more like emotions (less intense) than current, direct sensory stimulation that you are feeling in the real world.

Just as feelings can generate emotions, emotions can also generate feelings. For example, something like a fly buzzing might generate the feeling of annoyance, and this feeling might generate the emotion sad. You respond to the feeling first because feelings are faster and more immediate than emotions. An example of an emotion generating a feeling would be being sad that you are depressed. The depression is more of an emotion than the sadness because it is deeper and "slower" but the sadness is more like a feeling because it can be more immediate (it can also be an emotion, but in this example it is a feeling).

How This Chapter shows how Intelligence is intertwined with Emotion:

- If emotions are dulled feelings then your mind is capable of taking feelings and making them into emotions, and vice versa. That means that a part of intelligence is your ability to control your own feelings and emotions and thoughts.

7.12 Emotions and Feelings are Broad Thoughts

Any emotion or feeling can be broken down into the sensations and real events that caused it. And you can think about any of those things (with thoughts).

A thought is thinking about something in specific. You can have a thought about an entire paragraph, but it is going to be just a thought, it is going to be about one thing, and that one thing might be a summary of the paragraph - but it is still a thought. So what we think of as thought is really just a short period of thinking - one unit of thinking that lasts for a short period of time. An essay is composed of many thoughts, but just one thought would be "I went to the store".

Then again, "I went to the store, and Jason followed me" might be considered one thought as well. So how long exactly is a thought? If it is longer than "I went to the store, and Jason followed me" then it is probably going to be considered multiple thoughts. Thus humans use the word thought as just a short period of time in thinking.

Thoughts are in general talked about as being verbal, people rarely think of emotions and feelings as thoughts. But emotions and feelings are thoughts if you think about that emotion and feeling. The short period of time in which you think about the emotion or feeling is a thought. So thoughts can be about emotions and feelings. They are just harder to identify because they aren't verbal.

The reason that verbal things are easier to identify is because they are distinct sounds (that we have definitions for). Distinct sounds, different sounds, are easy to separate. It is easy to identify one sound from another sound, and that is all words are, different sounds. So it could be that someone is talking and you don't have any thoughts about them talking, or you are not thinking about them talking. In that case you just aren't listening to them, or you are not paying attention to the sounds they are making.

So thought then is really just any short period of high attention. And thinking is long or short periods of high attention. So if you are thinking for more than a few seconds, then you are probably going to be thinking about several thoughts. Since you can think about emotions and feelings too, however, you can think about your emotions or feelings for long periods of time.

Just as thinking is made up of individual components of thought, feeling, or emotion, each of those components is made up of their own further components. In fact, when you think about an emotion or feeling you intensify that feeling or emotion a lot. Each emotion, however, is made up of experiences in the real world. The real world can include thoughts and feelings in your head as well.

So emotions, feelings and thoughts are made up of real experiences. A thought isn't just a thing in your head, but it is something that has components that are real in the world. Those things might be sounds (when you think about someone speaking, you make that sound in your head). A sound in your head is just like a sound in reality, you are mimicking the emotion that the sound in reality is causing in your head by yourself, without having the real sound be there. Just try it and think about any sound, it produces the same emotions as when the sound itself occurred outside your head.

So a thought in the end boils down to you thinking about sensations, any sensation, taste, touch, sound, smell, feeling, or emotion. How can a thought be of emotion? Aren't thoughts supposed to be specific and quantifiable? Well a thought about an emotion is basically a summary of that emotion. If you played Frisbee and you get an emotion from playing Frisbee, then that emotion is a summary of the things in which you remember about playing Frisbee. The same goes with feelings. The feeling you have about something is really all the feelings that that thing causes in you, and when you focus on different aspects of that feeling, you are focusing on different aspects of the real experience which caused the feeling.

So when you think about an emotion you are intensifying the feeling of those real experiences. You have no conscious idea of which parts of the feeling you are thinking about, however. Maybe if you think about directly different parts of the real experience you can link it up to different parts of its emotion.

Thus any emotion or feeling can be broken down into the sensations and real events that caused it. And you can think about any of those things (with thoughts). You can also think about those things as individual thoughts. A thought isn't just a short period of your attention, but it is a short period of your attention during which you are trying to think about something (at least it feels like you are trying, you could not be trying and have a thought). Your natural attention span varies, but if you think about something you can boost that attention, you are trying to boost that attention on something specific or something broad (like an emotion).

Emotions and feelings are so intense, however, that it is like you are trying to focus your attention on them. So emotions, feelings, and thoughts are all periods of focused attention. A thought is just more focused attention than a feeling or emotion (unless it is a thought about a feeling or an emotion, in which case it is going to be even more attention than the feeling or thought or emotion by itself since it is a combination).

So emotions, feelings, and thoughts are all related, they are all things that you pay more attention to. And since emotion and feelings are made up of stuff which occurs in the real world, you could label each one of those things which occurs in the real world a thought, and say that emotions are made up of thoughts, or are broad thoughts. That is, you pay attention to your thoughts, and you pay attention to your emotions, so you could say that emotions are just a bunch of individual thoughts squished into one thing.

What then is the difference between a thought and an emotion? Emotions are usually more intense and therefore last longer in your brain when you think about them, or "bring them up". You usually can only bring them up by thinking about them, however. Other things might bring up an emotion, like other emotions or other feelings, consciously or unconsciously. The same with feelings and thoughts.

People "bring up" emotions, feelings and thoughts in various ways. One way to bring up an emotion would be using thought, such as thinking "I like my dog" would bring up the emotion of the dog. You could also think directly about the emotion of the dog without using the verbal discourse, however. This could also be described as just "feeling", "feeling out" or "being emotional about" your dog. A feeling could also bring up a thought (and all the other combinations of "bringing up" between thoughts, feelings and emotions). They might also be concurrent, that is, when you have one emotion there is an associated feeling with it (and the other combinations of that with feelings, thoughts and emotions). Don't forget that one of those combinations is that thoughts can also bring up or be concurrent with other thoughts (as with feelings and emotions).

How This Chapter shows how Intelligence is intertwined with Emotion:

- Since emotions are made up of many parts which are real, then intelligence is ultimately just your ability to manipulate real things, and therefore your emotions are going to determine what it is is in your mind, and give a larger pool of things for your intellect to explore.

7.13 Emotion vs. Logic

What is the difference between logic and emotion? When someone says that they are "emotional" which emotions do they mean? I guess they mean that they experience all emotions more. They could specify further, however, and say which emotions they experience more, which emotions they are more prone to.

If someone is emotional does that mean that they enjoy life more? What if someone was emotional, but only experienced positive emotions more than most people, and didn't experience negative emotions. Then that person would be happier I guess. Unless they separated out the emotions joy and sadness and just talked about those. Can you be an emotional person and just have excess amounts of the emotion happy? So anyone just "happy" is therefore being emotional. You'd probably be a lot more emotional if you were happy and sad at the same time however (the mix of the two would drive someone mad most likely, however).

Happy and sad seem to be the two strongest emotions. They are stronger than fear, anger, surprise, disgust, acceptance, and curiosity. That would make anyone bipolar (experiencing swings from happy to sad) very emotional. Does the swing mean that someone is more emotional than just experiencing one at a time? The emotional change is hard I think and that is more of an experience than just being very happy all the time, so the change from happy to sad is what adds the emotion in. That is, your body goes through changes as it experiences major emotional changes.

There are two degrees of change in emotion however; one is a major change from depression to mania (which is what bipolar is). Another is just your ordinary change from sad to happy, which can occur many times in a day. So if someone is manic or depressed are they being more emotional than someone who is just happy or just sad?

Symptoms of mania ("The highs"):

- Excessive happiness, hopefulness, and excitement
- Sudden changes from being joyful to being irritable, angry, and hostile
- Restlessness
- Rapid speech and poor concentration
- Increased energy and less need for sleep
- High sex drive
- Tendency to make grand and unattainable plans
- Tendency to show poor judgment, such as deciding to quit a job
- Drug and alcohol abuse
- Increased impulsivity

The symptoms of bipolar depression are the same as those of major depression and include:

- Sadness
- Loss of energy
- Feelings of hopelessness or worthlessness
- Loss of enjoyment from things that were once pleasurable
- Difficulty concentrating
- Uncontrollable crying
- Difficulty making decisions
- Irritability
- Increased need for sleep
- Insomnia or excessive sleep
- A change in appetite causing weight loss or gain
- Thoughts of death or suicide
- Attempting suicide

I don't think that people with the two extremes of mania and depression are any more emotional than people who are just happy or sad. That is because being too happy or too sad shuts off the other emotions people would experience like anger, fear, disgust, surprise, acceptance, and curiosity. Why does it? Because with all the other symptoms of mania and depression, there isn't really any room left for emotions other than happy and sad, a person's system can only handle so much emotion. If you are crying all the time (like you would if you were severely depressed) there isn't any more room for you to experience other emotions. Or if you are as happy as you can be, you're probably too out of it (in your happy land) to think about anything else.

A person could be happy or sad and be less emotional than someone with mania or depression, however. But a person (if they were experiencing the other emotions other than happy and sad) could be just as emotional as someone with mania or depression. Although those people may be crying or have expressions of extreme glee on their faces, happy and sad are not the only emotions someone can experience and therefore they may not be as emotional.

Emotion means that you are feeling something; if you are feeling emotions other than happy and sad, then wouldn't the other emotions (if they were positive) increase the happy emotion and you then have a happy emotion that is larger than the other positive emotions you are experiencing? I guess that would be happy, but it would probably lead to overload. That is why it makes sense that people who are emotional experience a range of emotions from happy to sad ones, so that if they just experienced happy ones it would lead to too much happiness causing overload.

Why would emotions be balanced, why not just have only positive emotions? Because if you are curious, your curiosity is going to backfire when there is a failure (you'd be curious in a failure). Or if you are overly surprised, you would be just as surprised at a bad thing happening as you would as a good thing happening, leading to being happy and sad. Or if you got angry at something, you are then likely to become pleased by the opposite thing happening, so the emotions tend to balance out.

So is it really that the positive and negative emotions balance out? It is probably too hard for your mind to wait to become emotional at things that are only going to lead it to become happy. That is, you would have to consciously say to each thing, ah that is a positive emotion, I can have that emotion now. It seems more natural that when something bad happens, you get more upset, and when something good happens, you get happier. So you don't have to calculate and spend time to assess if you should "feel" in those instances.

That is a good way to size people up, assess how happy they get from what things, and how sad they get from other things. Why is it that happy and sad are the two strongest emotions? It seems that way because all the other emotions follow suit with them. When someone is happier they are likely to be more curious, or more accepting. When someone is sad it also makes him or her less reactive to things (the surprise emotion).

The other emotions don't occur as much as well. You can easily be happy or sad all the time, no matter what you are doing, but the other emotions need to fit into what you are doing. Like the emotion curiosity needs something to be curious in, and the emotion disgust needs something to be disgusted by. When you are doing nothing the emotion you are going to feel most of the time is just plain happy or sad, thus those two emotions are also our "idling" emotions (when we are idle we have them).

If the other emotions don't occur as much, then why would someone be happy or sad in the first place? Are the emotions happy and sad simply the result of other emotions in your body? If that is the case, how is it possible for someone to become manic or depressed? Mania and depression are such extremes of happy and sad that other emotions can't be experienced as well. What then is the source of that extreme happiness or sadness?

Either it seems like life has enough in it to justify being manic or depressed or it doesn't. If it doesn't then the mania and depression would arise from people just being unstable and fragile creatures, easily upset and disturbed. If it does then by a logic process one should be able to figure out the cause of their mania or depression is and solve it.

How This Chapter shows how Intelligence is intertwined with Emotion:

- It could be viewed that emotion is entirely driven by intellect, that everything that you feel you feel because you are who you are, and who you are is determined by your thoughts and your own intelligence. Or it could be rephrased the opposite way, that intelligence is entirely driven by emotion for the same reasons, those viewpoints are obvious when you take emotional highs where it seems like you are acting out of control - because then you realize why it is you are having those emotions, and you are having them because of something you did (which was driven by your intellect) or something you were feeling (which is driven by your emotions). Your intellect determined how you felt the emotion, because you are your intellect, and that (you) would then determine how you feel about something that happens. Someone's emotional template (who they are, how they respond to the world) could be viewed as being an intellectual template because intellect is understanding real things, and your emotions determine what it is that you process and how you process them.

7.14 Emotion and Attention

How does emotion influence attention? If you think about it, humans probably have a complicated mix of emotions occurring all of the time, and this emotional make-up is somehow going to impact their attention. If someone is in a state of pure pleasure, then they probably aren't going to be paying as much attention to their environment then if they are in a normal or negative state. That I think is because there is no reason for the person to pay attention to their environment because they are satisfied within their own minds.

The sensory input that a person is receiving is going to be related to their emotional state as well. People can be in touch with their senses, with their thoughts, or be focused on their external environment. People often look to sensory stimulation in order to relax themselves - such as taking a bath or eating food. My guess would be that this changes their focus from their own internal thinking to their environment or their senses. There is a complicated mix of emotions, senses, and thoughts occurring all of the time.

So an important question is if someone can pay more attention to sensations if they wanted to. There is going to be some sort of complicated sequence of attention occurring, a person might naturally focus on one thing more and then switch to something else without awareness of themselves doing that.

Also, which emotions are triggered by which sensations? Some people buy scented candles in order to induce an emotional response, but are they aware that a much more complicated psychological response could be being created that they aren't aware of? If you think about it, someones entire network of sensations, thoughts and feelings could be manipulated by sensory feelings.

Someones thoughts are going to impact how much attention they are paying, and what they are paying more attention to. If you think about it, if you spend your time thinking about one thing, then your attention is going to be changed significantly. You might pay more attention to the thing you were just thinking about (obviously), but there might be other ways your attention could change.

People know that they can go into different moods for different things (such as being in the 'mood' to go shopping or the 'mood' to have a romantic encounter), but the question is, what triggers these moods? It isn't as if people randomly start to want to experience different things in life and therefore go into a different mood (or you could call it a mode). Your thoughts and thinking probably plays a large role in what you are feelings and therefore the moods you might go into.

Think about it this way - in each mood or mode you go into, your attention is probably focused more on whatever the mood is for - i.e. the mood you are in is a happy one, so you want to go out and have a picnic, or the mood you are in is a sad one, so you want to chill out. You want those things, so you begin to focus on them more, your attention changes. When people pay attention, there isn't just one thing they are focused on, their is everything in life they can focus on. All of the things that person who is paying attention can pay attention to, or usually pays attention to, are going to be things which are going to be factors in how their attention is functioning.

For instance, if a person cares about such and such things, and spends a lot of time thinking about those things, then those things are probably going to be a permanent part of their attention. When that person is in a mood for one thing, the other things they care about are also going to impact how their attention is behaving. For instance when a person is relaxing, the high-stress elements in their life are going to play a role in how their attention is even during the time when they are relaxed. You aren't ever completely in one state - so when someone is in a relaxed state, how they are when they are in a high stress state, and things they pay attention when they are in that other state, is going to have an impact on what they are like when they are in the relaxed state. You might pay attention to some things that you think you only care about when you are stressed when you are relaxed, and this is probably because all of your emotional states are mixed. You might also experience emotions and have a similar or associated experience during the time when you are relaxed as when you are stressed, because these two different states are related and connected to each other.

Humans have many different emotional states, or you could call them moods, ways of behaving, ways of thinking, ways of feeling, etc. All the different ways that people can feel and think are obviously going to be connected to one another. A simple way to think about it would just be to say that if you are stressed then you might want to relax later on, however that is missing the complicated emotional subtlety involved. There are emotional states, ways and levels of feeling, ways and levels of thinking, and these different things are going to play a role when you are relaxing or whatever it is you are doing. Your feelings, behavior and thoughts are going to be under the influence of more subtle tones of feeling and thought that are related to the previous things you have done and your other emotional states when you are doing other things.

I am just using the different things people do so I can describe what a different emotional state is like. Different emotional states are obvious if you consider the two most extreme examples - a high stress state and a relaxed state. However there must be many many more ways of feeling that people can experience. For instance people probably experience many feelings, sets of feelings, modes, moods, etc during an activity. I am suggesting that people have different ways of 'being' whereby their feelings and thoughts are influenced by their mood, their emotional state, whatever you want to call it.

My theory is that for a certain period of time people are influenced by certain ways of being. So say someone is doing any activity - during this activity they might change modes and for a few seconds or a few minutes feel more like the activity is like another activity that they have done. Or maybe they just adopt a different way of feeling for that activity that they are doing (feel differently about it in some way).

So there are many different layers of feeling, ways of feeling, modes people can go into where they feel differently for a certain period of time, or ways in which their thinking and feeling interact to help them have a unique experience that is dynamic, shifting, deep and complex.

Emotion is influenced by thoughts, moods, experience, previous activities, your environment, your physical condition - and there a levels of emotion and thought that make this experience much more complex. When one can adopt a set of feelings for one activity for a few seconds or minutes during a not related activity, it makes you wonder just how complex emotional and intellectual experience is.

7.15 Life Occurs In Sharp Spikes

Life occurs during the brief periods of time when people are actually paying attention, in spikes.

People need to pay attention to things in order to keep their minds alive and active. They need to pay attention to little things all the time. That is why spikes occur, when people refocus their attention on little things over and over it occurs as a spike, because the new object needs to be processed as a whole and this processing takes energy in the form of a "spike".

Humans cannot pay attention to everything, and the things they do pay attention to they need to "spike" their attention initially to get that object into their attention and focus. It is possible to not use spikes of attention, but if you did that then life would be boring. In order for life to be interesting people naturally spike their attention on certain things every so often (once a minute or so) to make life more exciting. Life would be boring if you never paid sharp attention to anything. Spikes of attention keep life "crisp".

If life occurs in sharp spikes, why then doesn't it feel like life occurs in sharp spikes? It seems pretty smooth to me. If it seems this way, then you aren't realizing or paying attention to the complicated emotional and cognitive processes that are going on in your mind, life is not "all smooth" but there are changes in attention going on all the time. Each little thing you pay attention to (actually pay attention to that is, not just "absorb") actually occurs as a spike in attention. This is because most of the time your attention isn't extremely directed, but you need to make it extremely directed sometimes (once a minute or so) in order to properly stay awake. It is also because you don't absorb every little thing, you only absorb a few things once in a while, and these things that you do absorb are the spikes. They are spikes because they are relative to most of your activity which isn't absorbing things intently or deeply. Every minute or so you need to absorb something. That thing is the spike.

When you pay attention to your attention (or what you are paying attention to) how does life feel to you? Does it feel smooth or rough? Life seems rough if you pay attention to it like that, with occasional spikes of interest in things. It is rough because there are many little fluctuations of interest in various things, but intensity is needed somewhere. This intensity comes from the spikes, otherwise life would just be rough and there wouldn't be anything smooth. The top of the spike is smooth, however because it is clear and it lasts a little while (a few seconds or a few dozen seconds). Paying sharp attention to things allows you to have a clear mind for the time you are giving that sharper attention. It separates out all the other things and you focus more on what it is you processed. This clears your mind because you just received a lot of stimulation. In this way spikes can make life be smooth. Without spikes life would always be rough because of all the little things. But if you use a spike then life is smooth afterwards because you are satisfied.

Life is many small variations in attention over time. There are periods of focused attention and periods of non-focused attention. The periods of focused attention are the spikes. This is very complicated if you try to follow your own spikes because there are so many things you are "spiking" and paying sharp attention to all the time. There are three groups of things, things you pay sharp attention to, things you pay attention to, and things you don't pay attention to. You pay sharp attention to things much less often than the other two categories, and that is why the sharp attention is a spike, because it is uncommon and doesn't last as long as the other things, so it looks more like a spike when compared with the other two categories than a leveled plain.

Also, people's emotions change all the time. The change probably occurs both gradually and like a series of steps. There are so many emotions in a person's head that some of them are going to interact with each other suddenly, causing a sudden sharp change in emotion, and others are going to interact more slowly, causing gradual changes in emotion.

It might be that the changes are just sharp, however. You could look at the mind as a system that only changes when it gets a trigger, and that would probably mean that it only has sharp changes of emotion. However those changes wouldn't just be sharp changes. Large, sharp changes of emotion don't just happen by themselves, but deep emotional experiences are often followed by similar emotions that are less intense. That is, if you experience emotion A, emotion A is going to linger in your system.

That excludes the staircase model, but there still could be something like a staircase, only instead of steps at a 90 degree angle they would be something like an 100 degree angle. With 10/360 percent being the emotions that hang around after an initiating event. That would be just emotion changes resulting from large events, however. Either a large event within your own system (something like a thought or a feeling, or a mix of thoughts and feelings), or a large external event (like something happening outside your body). That's because your mind needs to understand, "ok now I am sad". As intellectual, thinking beings all major emotional events that occur in the mind need to processed intellectually (unless you're sleeping). So in other words if you just get sadder and sadder and are not aware of it you are not going to get nearly as sad as when you realize that you are getting sadder. The points when you realize (at some level) that you are getting sadder are going to be when you start feeling a lot sadder (the steps on the downward staircase of sadness and depression).

There must be other stuff going on in the mind, however. While a clash or mix of two feelings or emotions or thoughts could be figured out, and that would probably result in a noticeable emotional change (the staircase or spike model). There are probably other things going on in your conscious or unconscious mind. That is, some things that happen to people take a long time to recover from. But the main point is, everything, whether or not is a slow, gradual change or a sudden, quick change, resulted from some mix of emotions and feelings and thoughts and external events happening.

Furthermore, any mix of those things, when they interact, is going to be a large change. That is because it is a large change relative to your normal state, which is most of the time feeling nothing, because nothing is going on most of the time. People experience events in life and things in life and they occur in individual units.

Thoughts, emotions, and feelings are the three main components of the brain. "Everything" isn't stimulating enough to cause sharp spikes. There is vision, that is, you see things all the time, but your emotion doesn't go up or down a lot when you close or open your eyes. Unless you are looking at something that is causing a feeling, of course. But even then that feeling is only going to last a few seconds before it dies off. Therefore vision clearly functions with the sharp spikes pattern.

The same with hearing, if you hear something interesting, there is a sharp spike of initial interest, and then it dies down to almost normal. That must mean that feelings and emotions are probably a combination of thoughts, feelings, and emotions. That you almost think about the event that is occurring, and that when you think about it there is a large spike upwards. That the combination of feeling and emotion with thought results in large spikes, which form our best and common regular life experiences.

That is, you can't really tell you are thinking about it because it isn't verbal. But it feels like you are thinking about it during that brief time. That means that your attention is going to be focused on it, basically. Sometimes when someone is in a depression these spikes can be very large because that person is very upset. A large spike would result in emotional damage, furthering the depression, thereby causing the depression to go down like a staircase. It is easy to do emotional damage, but it can't be repaired in a series of spikes, as it would go up gradually (still small compared to the spikes however).

Just think of it as fabric; damage needs to be mended, and mending takes time. It is easy to do damage to the fabric, you can only mend it slowly. No one just "snaps out" of a depression. Furthermore it is easy to stimulate the fabric, just poke it. That poke would be similar to a life experience, the poke has ripples, but the main event was the poking.

The sharp spike occurrences show just how short of attention span humans have. That for brief periods we are capable of almost perfect attention, and during those periods is the height of the spikes. These spikes actually look more like lumps since they go up gradually and cause a stay in attention for a few seconds, but they are so fast that they are best called spikes. Say looking at an attractive girl/guy causes a feeling. The first few seconds you look at her/him, you are going to have perfect attention, but then it is going to die off. Everything else in life is somewhat like that, whether you are looking at your pencil, or your computer, or whatever. The item you are looking at needs to be initially processed, and your attention needs to be directed to it first off.

Everything in life needs to be processed before it enters your system, and that process is going to be a sharp spike of emotion, feeling, and thought. After you process looking at the computer you can move along to just wandering your eyes throughout the room. If you pause at any one of the things you are wandering your eyes around, you will experience a sharp spike of emotion/thought/feeling. That is, looking at things also causes emotion as well as the thought needed to direct your attention to it, if you are paying more attention to something which causes emotion, then logically you are going to feel more emotion from it.

This doesn't mean that you aren't thinking/feeling when you don't pause or stop. You could say that people are thinking, feeling, and are having emotion all of the time just in amounts so small it is hard for them to detect. That these amounts only go up in sharp spikes when they actually pay attention to something either in their mind or outside it. This "paying attention" doesn't have to be conscious or deliberate. If two feelings interact within your mind it could cause you to pay conscious or unconscious attention to them.

Something like, your girlfriend meeting your ex girlfriend would cause a clash of feelings for your new girlfriend, with feelings for your old girlfriend (possibly). But that clash of feelings wouldn't occur in a thought spike, it would occur in an emotional spike. It would also be a slight rise of tension in the feeling between which one you like more. Also, the rise in that feeling wouldn't be significant compared to if you thought about that feeling at the same time. When you think about the feeling it would result in a sharp spike, and that spike would last a few seconds, then die away. That is because that feeling was a potential explosive one, one that exploded when you thought about it, resulting in a spike. Also, thought about anything else, a feeling, a vision, whatever, results in lesser spikes of thoughts/feelings/emotions. That anything and everything, when thought about, is interesting for the first few seconds, but then that interest dies off. It is the same principal when you pinch yourself. When you pinch yourself the first time, it hurts the most. That is because the first time you are thinking about it a lot more, after that your interest in it dies off. Amazing how much our attention can fluctuate to cause life to occur in short, sharp spikes. The girlfriend example is different than spikes that occur more frequently all the time, when you pay attention to little things. The girlfriend example was an example of when a spike can happen, but that is a spike that you are going to notice a lot more then something like, you just refocusing on what you are typing. It is spikes like that which happen all the time so you stay focused.

Although there are spikes of emotion and feeling, spikes of thought are needed to direct attention. Not thought in the verbal sense, but thought in the sense that it is under your control and feels more similar to thoughts. Thought occurs as basically a bunch of spikes, and since people think all the time and about everything, life occurs in those spikes. They don't feel intense because it is just thought. But basically whenever something new comes into your vision or your attention there is an initial sharp spike of interest. And if you are going to be doing the same thing for a long period of time, then it is going to take additional sharp spikes every couple of seconds or every minute to keep your attention. It is easy to test that, try and read something with the same bland expression as when you start reading it (but after your initial interest at the beginning when you notice the piece) and you just can't do it. To maintain attention your mind needs to snap back to what it is paying attention to. Feelings and emotions are going to follow the thought, however (that is emotions and feelings are imbedded in thoughts). That is why people need to think all the time, to maintain a healthy level of mental activity, it is a part of life. Emotions and feelings can also be described as thoughts, however, so those spikes continue even after you stop thinking, just in the form of emotion-feeling-thoughts (they are still more similar to thoughts however since they are short and spiky).

Basically your attention needs to be initially "grabbed" for anything that you are going to pay attention to. That grabbing is the initial period of paying attention to it. During that first period of paying attention to something is where the spike is because you are processing the item/object. You need a spike to grab your mind and attention, otherwise you wouldn't be paying attention to anything. You can still process most of life without the spikes, but that is only because spikes had brought you back to reality in the first place in order for that attention to be grabbed. Furthermore it is going to be easier to process new things based on what the spike was about, that is, it is going to be easier to process similar things more related to the spike then to other things in the area. If you focus on a school bus, then you are going to be more attentive to the other school buses you see for the next few seconds or minutes because you were just paying attention to one school bus, and your mind is wired to notice school buses.

Furthermore there is a similar way in which your mind processes each spike. For spikes that are under your control, first the spike would be a period of thought about something, say a school bus or a coffee machine. Then what you just saw or thought about becomes an emotion, or an unconscious series of thoughts. That is you are less focused consciously on what it is you are seeing or whatever but your mind is still processing it. Next, after your mind processes the unconscious thoughts it becomes a feeling, you then feel something about what it is you were focusing on. So it isn't when you look at something you immediately get a feeling, that doesn't make any sense. First you think about it, then you feel it in a general way (an emotion) then after you understand what that feeling is, you feel it (but that basically happens instantaneously so in a way you do feel it right away - also, that same process can happen over a longer period of time). That is because you know what it is, you know where it is, and you know what to focus your attention on. An example of unconsciously processing something you see is when you look at match you then think about fire. Then after you think about the fire you can almost "feel" the fire, following the pattern of thought to emotion to feeling (you think about the match, then something happens unconsciously (this unconscious thought process is emotion (remember emotion is unconscious thought) which then causes you to feel the fire – a feeling).

It could be that a few minutes passes before a conscious spike occurs (that is a spike that is under your control). A spike is basically just anything that you are going to start paying attention to. During those first few seconds of when you are going to pay attention to something there is a sharp spike upwards. Without these periods of attention humans/animals would never pay attention to anything. Basically once every few minutes or so you need to pay attention to something or your brain is going to be too inactive. After you pay attention to one thing, however, your general attention is grabbed and you don't need to have another spike for at least a few minutes.

Everything that is processed, not just spikes, follows the sequence of thought to emotion to feeling. That is because thoughts are clearer than emotions and feelings, and emotions are more similar to thoughts than feelings are (discussed previously) so when you see something or hear something or whatnot for the first time, it is clearer in your mind. Then it becomes less clear and you think about it unconsciously. You think about it unconsciously because it takes further processing in order to isolate the feeling that that things gives you. Some things are just too complicated to feel them right away. Other things, however, can be felt right away, say if you are touching something the feeling arises right away. That is because the physical stimulus is more immediate than emotional stimulus.

Emotional things, however, are simply to complicated to "feel" them right away, they need to be processed first. That is logical, just take looking at anything, say a book. In order to feel the feelings that the book causes in you, you are going to have to at least unconsciously think about it first (that is, after you start paying attention to it, which you do by starting to think about it or just see it and notice it more than you usually notice things in the area). Since you don't need to think about physical stimulus since it is just a physical stimulus, (not something like vision) you don't really unconsciously process it.

Spikes are dramatic rises in attention. They can be assisted by load noises or something dramatic visually, but they don't need to be. In other words they can be internal or external. You can pay sharp attention to something in the real world or something in your own head. If there is a load sound in the environment, it is most likely that your spike in attention is going to occur during that period. It doesn't have to, you could pay attention to something else in spike form, but the main point is that you have to have about one sharp spike in attention a minute at least. That is, you have to pay attention to something in your environment or something in your head, sharp attention in the form of a spike (lasting a second or a few seconds) every minute or so.

Otherwise the world would just go by you and you'd be completely out of it. You don't just need to pay attention to things, you occasionally need to pay sharp attention to things. Furthermore this attention in the form of a spike can't be dissipated and spread out, it is always going to occur in a spike. If, in between the spikes, you are trying to get the highest attention you can in an attempt to spread the spike out, (that is, if you are trying to spread out your attention instead of having spikes) the normal spike would still be a spike relative to even the extra attention you gave to the non spike period, because that attention would still be too low, so you couldn't give it that high of an attention level, as it would be very low compared to the spike still. Spikes of emotion and feeling also need to occur every few minutes or so. The human system needs to be "shocked" into reality because you need to pay attention to life.

Say it is time for another sharp increase in attention (that is you waited too long without focusing on anything) and something occurs like a dog barking. Then you are going to focus on that dog barking intently in the form of a spike. So if the dog continues to bark for the next few seconds or minutes, your attention will be on that more because you paid attention to it initially more so than other things in your environment. This is very important because if someone doesn't use their spikes say to someone they are talking to, they could be talking to that person and not be paying attention at all. You could hear what they are saying but not really be interested in it nearly as much as you would in a normal conversation (if you choose not to think about the person talking to you – remember if you do think about the person talking to you then naturally you are going have a thought spike because that is how thought initiates when thinking about new objects, the new object needs to be grabbed and processed first).

If you direct your attention spikes away from the things you don't want to hear (say if there is a loud noise in the background, just don't pay sharp attention to it) then most of your attention will follow along suit. If attention was uniform then people wouldn't be able to direct their attention easily. In order to ignore the other things in your environment and just focus on one thing, the only way to get just that one thing into your focus would be to use a spike in attention. After that spike the thing you "spiked" would be in your attention at a low level, but the other things around you would be at an even lower level. The spike is necessary to differentiate what you are paying attention to, to differentiate the new thing which you are paying attention to from everything else. You can't just go to a slightly higher rise in attention for one thing (you can pay attention to something new, but you wouldn't be paying more attention to it than other things in the environment already, you'd just be isolating that thing, it wouldn't be a rise in attention, or an insignificant one), because people can only focus on one thing at a time for this reason. Because of the spikes in attention, people can isolate (focus intently on) one or a few things.

That limitation (of only being able to focus intently on a few things) happens because each spike eliminates the other things which they were paying attention to previously. You can spread out one spike to different things, however (if you do it at the same time), that is how your attention can be spread. You can't do a series of smaller spikes because that confuses your mind, it is like saying, pay attention to this, then pay attention to that, and then pay attention to that. It is too confusing. It is easier to say at once, pay attention to this that and that, and then you can do it.

That explanation also explains why spikes occur at all – because it is much easier to pay a lot of attention in a short period of time then to keep jolting yourself over and over at each thing that you want to pay attention to. That way is too jarring and much less smooth. You don't notice the spike when it occurs because it is more like a refocusing than a spike. People basically need to be focused on little things continuously, and this focus is directed by short periods of refocusing labeled here as spikes. One way in which these spikes occur is that when something is first presented it takes more energy and brain power to process it at first because it is new. It is easier to try and comprehend the entire thing at once than to comprehend it in pieces, as the latter just doesn't make any sense. People comprehend things as wholes not as parts added up over time. The other reason these spikes occur is to initially catch your attention and hold it at a high level on something. That is, in order to go from a state of inactivity to a state of activity, you cannot just go up to the level of activity, but you need to motivate yourself to get there by having a spike (this spike is also the initial processing of the new object/event and occurs because of that as well).

In order to get someone's attention they can't just lazily look at you like they are looking at everything else, but they need pay sharp attention to you for the first instant (this is the initial "grabbing" talked about). Otherwise people would be paying attention to anything and everything at the same time. There has to be a way of separating out what it is that is in someone's attention field. That method of separating is by the use of the spikes.

Spikes work for emotional things and feeling as well as for thought. That is things that are emotional occur in the same spike pattern, as well as things you feel (feelings). Another way to note this would be that your attention is only focused on things that change (things that change, the change usually occurring in spike form). It might be that something grabs your attention a little, and you only put a spike in after it initially grabs your attention a little to then pay full attention to it. Lots of time something happens, like a loud noise, that you only process after it occurred, or slightly after it occurred. So there might be a delay in when you process it, or spike it, or you might not spike it at all. You might also not need to spike something if a similar spike occurred with a similar thing previously.

How This Chapter shows how Intelligence is intertwined with Emotion:

- Someone's attention determines what they see and figure out about the world, if someone is paying more attention then they are probably going to realize more things, or notice more things visually and intellectually. Since attention varies based on emotion, your intellect is going to vary based on your emotions. If you are emotionally interested in things then it might make you pay more attention to them and then you might realize more about those things. If something causes more of an emotional impact (or more of a spike) you might retain understanding it longer (memory is also a part of intellect) or it could increase your emotional intelligence about that thing.

- Everything that is processed follows the sequence of thought to emotion to feeling – that shows how everything in the world is real, and these real things all cause feelings, you recognize what it is (a thought) and then you feel that thought, your emotional processing of your thoughts is part of your thoughts themselves – this is obvious with emotional spikes because when you feel something strongly that strong feeling clearly aids in you understanding things about what it is you are feeling.

- People also only comprehend things in their entirety, because if it isn't completely understood then you cannot verbalize it and make a thought process of it, therefore things that aren't completely understood or verbal are going to be emotional and you are going to "feel" them, not think them.

7.16 Angry, Upset, and Depressed?

Angry and upset feelings often accompany sad feelings, as it is natural to be upset and angry that you are sad (or became sad).

If someone is sad or depressed, it is natural that they are going to be upset that they are that way. Therefore it is probable that all depression or sadness has feelings of anger and agitation mixed in. In fact it is easy to see a combination of those three feelings as when something bad happens to someone their reaction is an intense feeling of sadness/anger/agitation. Like if you punch someone in the face, or shoot him or her, they aren't going to be just sad, they are going to sad, angry, and upset.

After the event occurs (such as getting punched in the face) the sad/angry/upset feeling only lasts a few seconds on that persons face, to various degrees of visibility to other people. What happens after that is more interesting however. After the first few seconds of sad/upset/angry their mind loses focus on what happened and it no longer is a single emotion. They are focused on the event and that is why it shows up on their face, after they lose focus, however, the emotions become unconscious.

In their unconscious form the emotions are like a depression. A depression is something that affects someone's mood, his or her entire system. When the angry/sad/upset emotions go into the unconscious, they start affecting the other emotions around them, and your entire system becomes sad, angry, and upset. This might not be visible on your face because it isn't as intense, you didn't just get punched, or something bad didn't just happen to you, but it has left a mark.

It seems like the angry and upset emotions are more temporary, and the sad feeling is retained longer. That is because you forget why you are sad, you forget the event that caused the sadness, but your emotions remember the impact of the upset and anger, and that impact was to make you sadder. The emotion sad is simply easier to remember. It is marked in your mind for vengeance, you associate the sad emotion with being bad for you, but the anger and the agitation are more hormonal, temporary emotions.

That is, it is hard to be angry if you don't know why you should be angry. You need to be able to logically justify your own feelings. It is more common that sadness occurs for a long period of time than anger. There are still elements of anger and agitation remaining mixed in however, just less so than the sadness. So after an initiating event there are the three emotions equally present for a few seconds, and after that mostly the sadness remains, still with elements of the other two emotions.

It is hard to be angry or upset when you don't remember what it is you are angry at. It is easy to be sad because you don't need to remember anything to be sad at something, the sad feeling simply stays in your system because you are used to sad feelings and you don't need to justify them like you would an angry feeling. Or it could be that being angry and upset takes up more energy than being sad does, being sad lowers how energetic you are because it brings you down. When you are angry and upset you are much more energetic and agitated.

So it is like, ok that really pissed me off, but I am too tired to be pissed, I can be sad though. The sadness in your system isn't even an individual emotion after the first few seconds from the initiating event, however. It becomes mixed in with the other emotions and feelings in your body because you no longer remember what caused the sadness. So it is like a depression because it affects your entire system and mood like a depression does.

So there is really a difference between being sad, and being upset. You might even call that period after the few seconds for that person "the person being upset" instead of them being sad. That is how much the upset and agitation emotions are mixed in, that after someone is punched you could say either they are upset, or they are sad, or they are agitated, it depends on the person and the circumstance. That is a lot of proof to show that all three are often mixed in together.

You might say that they are upset, but they are probably going to be more sad, however, because if you are upset and angry then you are going to be sad about that, just like you are going to be upset and angry that you are sad. But I think the sad is going to dominate because no one has enough energy to be upset and angry for very long. When you are upset and angry your tone is louder, you are moving faster and more agitated like, you are more aggressive and looking for retribution. Anger and agitation almost need something to take vengeance on, while sadness you don't attribute to someone else causing it. You do attribute anger and agitation to something external, however.

How This Chapter shows how Intelligence is intertwined with Emotion:

- If it is hard to have emotions if you don't remember something, then that shows how your emotions are based off of your intellect as well. What your memory (which is a function of intellect) remembers is going to bring up emotions, which are then in turn going to determine (to some extent) your emotional intelligence.

7.17 Emotion is a Combination of Feeling and Thought

Emotion is such a strong feeling that it must be the combination of thoughts and feelings. If you think about it, if you combine positive thoughts and positive feelings, you're going to have a general overall greater experience, (if the thoughts and feelings are on the same idea or the same thing, you are going to have a greater positive single emotion about that thing). Just take the strongest emotion you can experience, it would have to be a combination of all the positive things in your mind, and people can control their thoughts to a large extent.

By a combination of feeling and thought I mean a combination of what it feels like to have a thought, with the feeling of what it feels like to have a feeling – I don't mean the combination of actual verbal thoughts with feelings, but non-verbal thoughts which are like verbal thoughts in that they are about something, you just can't identify what it is all the time because it is non-verbal.

Since thoughts are conscious and unconscious, emotion could be redefined as the combination of feeling and thought - that you only have emotion when you are thinking about something, and feeling something at the same time, and the combination of the two results in individual emotions. There is evidence for this from the facts that you can only experience one strong emotion at a time, and you can also only think about one strong emotion at a time. That shows how emotions are pulled up by thoughts, or controlled and generated by them. It might be that this only applies to strong emotions, but it depends on each individuals definition of emotion (it might vary), but I don't think anyone can experience two strong emotions simultaneously. You can feel it for yourself, try and feel any combination of the following emotions (strongly) at the same time - anger, fear, sadness, disgust, surprise, curiosity, acceptance, or joy. You just can't do it. A slight feeling of curiosity is exactly that, a feeling and not an emotion. Emotions are stronger than feelings, and stronger than thoughts, but what are they made of? The only logical conclusion is that they are made up of thoughts and feelings.

The type of thought that makes up emotions isn't just words or sentences or verbal ideas in your head, but basically any period of thinking. It doesn't have to be intense thinking, in fact, if you are intensely thinking there probably isn't enough room left to process a strong emotion, but rather emotion arises from periods of very low intense thinking, and less intense feelings (you still have to be trying to be thinking, that is why negative emotions don't exist, because people just don't try to think about them). During those periods of low intense thinking (from which part of emotion arises) you don't have to even understand what you are thinking about, just understand that to some degree you are more thoughtful than usual. Feelings are generally considered to be shallower than emotions, and thought is considered a deep experience, so in order to have the strong, deep feeling of emotion, it must be made up of the part of your brain that experiences deep things, (the thought part) (remember feelings feel like feelings from sensory stimulation, which isn't "deep" at all).

Furthermore, emotion isn't just a strong feeling, a strong feeling can give rise to an emotion, just like a strong idea can give rise to an emotion, but an emotion is the combination of a lesser feeling and a lesser idea or thought process (this thought process might be unconscious, leading the person having it to just know that they are thoughtful during the experience). You can't have a strong feeling and a strong emotion at the same time because there just isn't enough room or processing power in your mind to do that (it's easy to feel that in your mind just by testing it).

Is a thought sensory input? No it isn't, you can think about sensory input, and that would give rise to a feeling of the sensation itself, but a thought is much faster in the brain. A thought is like a fast firing of neurons while a feeling or a sensation is an experience that actually takes some amount of time longer than it takes for a neuron to fire, which (it feels like anyway) is the length of a short thought. So basically, emotions must be the result of feelings and thoughts in your brain because there isn't anything else left that they could be made up of. All that is in your brain is feelings and thoughts. It is obvious how you can turn off a thought automatically, but you can also do that to some feelings. This is so because feelings are in large part triggered by thoughts. That's because feelings are experiences of sensory stimulation. If you are feeling something that you don't want to feel, however, because that sensory stimulation is present in your environment, there is nothing you can do. But if it results from a memory or something in your mind, you are going to shut it off automatically. This way feelings and thoughts work together; you have your present experience of the sensation, and your mental direction of thinking about that sensation. The latter part you can turn on if you want to make that natural, environmental feeling a strong one. It is hard to experience a strong feeling just by bringing the feeling up in your head, to have a strong feeling you need to have some type of direct sensory input and be thinking about that sensory input at the same time.

So a strong feeling is just like a strong emotion, only you need direct sensory input and thoughts to feel it, while with emotions you just need a feeling (which can result from the memory of a sensation) and some thoughts. So, very simply, everything in the brain is either a feeling or a thought. And emotions are combinations of feelings and thoughts.

Thinking about things generates feeling because you are simulating the emotions of that thing in your head. Although you are not experiencing the stimulation in real life, you still understand what it feels like to be in that situation, and this memory of that stimulation you can feel almost like being in the real situation itself.

If you have emotion about something then you are feeling that thing. Thus you are directing thought about that object, and directing thought is what thought is. Thought is just directed to something specific, while feeling is more generalized, you have only a few feelings for many many things, and thought is only a way of categorizing those feelings. For example, you can simulate many feelings by thinking, "I am going to go to the store then I am going to come home". Instead of feeling "store" which you feel in the store, you are adding the feeling of traveling to the store and being home. Those feelings are less intense than actually traveling to the store and actually being home, but they are still there and present in the thoughts. So when you have a thought about the store, you feel the store because you are simulating the idea of being in the store in your head.

Emotion always precedes thought; thought is always just going to be an explanation of emotion. Everything in the end turns out to be an emotion in your system, so therefore everything is really an emotion. When you say "I want to leave" the feeling of you wanting to leave is always going to precede the thought. Actually first you quickly understand what it is that you are feeling when you realize what it is you are feeling as an unconscious thought process, then you have a more regular feeling about it, and then you are able to verbalize that feeling into a thought. Unless something is said to you instead of you thinking it, in which case the process is reversed. First it is a thought because it is expressed that way, then it is a feeling, and then it is a quick unconscious thought process to think about what was said.

When the thing is said or thought of verbally it is most clear what the meaning is. In this way words assist understanding. This is probably because the combination of adding the stimulation of sound to the stimulation of the visual (or other sense) of the object/idea enhances understanding and forces you to think deeper about it because sound is an enhancing mechanism for thought.

Feelings are fast, you don't pause and think about them. Emotion you could say, since it is deeper, that you almost "think" about it.

How This Chapter shows how Intelligence is intertwined with Emotion:

- Thoughts also contribute to what it is you are going to feel, and what you feel and how you feel it is then going to determine your emotional intelligence, and over the long run would help determine other aspects of your intelligence as well.

7.18 Self-Regulation: A Definition and Introduction

What is self-regulation? Which mental processes compose it, and how do those processes work together? Self-regulation is the conscious and nonconscious processes by which people regulate their thoughts, emotions, attention, behavior, and impulses. People generate thoughts, feelings and actions and adapt those to the attainment of personal goals. Behavioral self-regulation invovles self- observing and strategically adjusting performance processes, such as one's method of learning, whereas environmental self-regulation refers to observing and adjecting environmental conditions or outcomes. Covert self regulation involves monitoring and adjusting cognitive and affective states, such as imagery for remembering or relaxing. Someones performance and regulation is going to be changed by their goals, motivations, and decisions, People self-regulate their own functioning in order to achieve goals or change how they are thinking.

Someones actions and mental processes depend on one's beliefs and motives. Self -regulation is cyclical - that is, feedback (information, responses) from prior actions and performances changes the adjustments made during current efforts. Adjustments are necessary because personal, behavioral, and environmental factors are constantly changing during the course of learning and performance. Someones performances are constantly being changed by their attention and actions. Forethought is the phase that precedes efforts to act and sets the stage for a performance. A person self-reflects on performances afterwards, and this reflection influences their responses.

Forethought Phase

In the forethought phase people engage in a) task analysis and b) self-motivational beliefs. Task analysis involves the setting of goals and strategic planning. Self motivational beliefs involves self- efficacy, outcome expectations, intrinsic interest/value, and goal orientation.

Performance Phase

In the performance phase people perform self-control processes and self- observation strategies. Self- control involves self-instruction (various verbalizations), imagery (forming mental pictures), attention focusing and task strategies (which assist learning and performance by reducing a task to its essential parts and organizing the parts meaningfully. For example, when students listen to a history lecture, they might identify a limited number of key points and record them chronologically in brief sentences. People do those things while learning (say in education), and in non- educational settings.

Also as part of someone's performance they do self-observation. This refers to a person's tracking of specific aspects of their own performance, the conditions that surround it, and the effects that it produces. You can set goals in forethought about how you are going to do self- observation.

Self-Reflection Phase

Bandura (1986)[9] has identified two self-reflected processes that are closely associated with self- observation: self- judgment and self-reactions. Self-judgment involves self-evaluating one's performance and attributing casual significance to the results. Self-evaluation refers to comparing self-monitored information with a standard or goal, such as a sprinter judging practice runs according to his or her best previous effort. Previous performance or self-criteria involves comparisons of current performance with earlier levels of one's behavior, such as a baseline or the previous performance.

People also make casual attributions about the results of their evaluations - such as whether poor

9. Bandura, A. (1986). *Social Foundations of Thought and Action.* Englewood Cliffs, NJ: Prentice-Hall.

performance is due to one's limited ability or to insufficient effort. Self-satisfaction involves perceptions of satisfaction or dissatisfaction and associated affect regarding one's performance, which is important because people pursue courses of action that result in satisfaction and positive affect, and avoid those courses that produce dissatisfaction and negative affect, such as anxiety.

Adaptive or defensive inferences are conclusions about how one needs to alter his or her self-regulatory approach during subsequent efforts to learn or perform. Adaptive inferences are important because they direct people to new and potentially better forms of performance self-regulation, such as by shifting the goals hierarchically or choosing a more effective strategy (Zimmerman + Martinez-Pons, 1992)[10] In contrast, defensive inferences serve primarily to protect the person from future dissatisfaction and aversive affect, but unfortunately they also undermine successful adaptation. These defensive self-reactions include helplessness, procrastination, task avoidance, cognitive disengagement, and apathy. Garcia and Pintrich (1994)[11] have referred to such defensive reactions as self-handicapping strategies, because, despite their intended protectiveness, they ultimately limit personal growth.

An Introduction

I said in the beginning of this chapter that "Self- regulation is the conscious and nonconscious processes by which people regulate their thoughts, emotions, attention, behavior, and impulses. People generate thoughts, feelings and actions and adapt those to the attainment of personal goals." But what is meant by terms such as self-regulation, self-control, self- awareness, and self-monitoring? The difficult thing to figure out I would think would be how much of self- regulation or what is going on mentally is conscious or not conscious. When someone is doing any action, how much of the control they are employing is conscious and how much of it is unconscious? That is a very complicated question. To a certain extent it is like you are unconsciously saying to yourself various things while you are doing something, but you also might be saying things to yourself consciously at the same time that also helps direct your behavior.

Other important questions are - how does a persons goals and motivations influence their feelings, behavior, self-control and actions? How much of feeling, impulses and impulse control, motivation and goal creating is conscious or unconscious? If you think about it, your goals, motivations, and the natural impulses that result from your emotions (which are to a large extent determined by your goals and motivations) are going to be fluctuating and changing all of the time.

People can alter the goals they have, however there is going to be an incredibly complex set of unconscious goals that one is not aware of. These goals create multiple motivations as well as multiple concerns. Also, doing well at approaching an incentive is not quite the same experience as doing well at avoiding a threat. If you think about it, your emotions are going to be different if you achieve something you are striving for then if you are threatened and respond because you are under pressure. It makes sense that approach is going to have such positive affects as elation, eagerness and excitement, and such negative affects as frusturation, anger and sadness. (Carver, 2004[12]; Carver + Harmon-Jones, 2009[13]). Avoidance involves such positive affects as relief and contentment (when someone avoids a threat, they are relieved and content) and such negative affects as fear, guilt and anxiety.

Goals can be changed by how motivated someone is to have that goal. Some goals can be brought into conscious awareness at various times for various reasons. Simon (1967)[14] reasoned that emotions are calls

10. Barry J. Zimmerman, and Manuel Martinez-Pons. (1992). Perceptions of efficacy and strategy use in the self-regulation of learning. In D. H. Schunk + J. L. Meece (Eds.) *Student Perceptions in the Classroom: Causes and Consequences* (pp. 185-207). Hillsdale, NJ: Earlbaum.
11. Garcia, T. + Pintrich, P.R. (1994). Regulating motivation and cognition in the classroom: the role of self-schemas and self-regulatory strategies. In D.H. Schunk and B.J. Zimmerman (Eds.), *Self-Regulation on Learning and Performance: Issues and Applications* (pp.132-157), NJ, Hillsdale, Lawrence Erlbaum Associates.
12. Carver, C. S. (2004). Negative affects deriving from the behavioral approach system. *Emotion, 4,* 3-22.
13. Carver, C. S., + Harmon-Jones, E. (2009). Anger is an approach-related affect: Evidence and implications. *Psychological Bulletin, 135,* 183-204.
14. Simon, H. A. (1967). Motivational and emotional controls of cognition. *Psychology Review, 74,* 29-39.

for reprioritization: that emotion regarding a goal that is out of awareness eventually induces people to give that goal a higher priority. The stronger the emotion, the stronger the claim for higher priority. Affect pulls the out-of-awareness into awareness.

Simon's analysis applies readily to negative feelings, such as anxiety and frustration. If you promised your spouse you would go to the post office today and you've been too busy, the creeping of the clock toward closing time can cause an increase in frustration or anxiety (or both). The stronger the affect, the more likely the goal it concerns will rise in priority until it comes into awareness and becomes the reference for behavior.

Therefore, it makes sense that the main goal you have and you know you have can reliquish its place. You are constantly shifting the goals you have, you simply might not be aware that you are doing this. If you think about it, people unconsciously might create many goals that they don't think about because they don't understand that they are motivated to do those things. They simply don't know that they are trying to reach certain objectives clearly. Take for instance sexual goals - people probably do many things to enhance sexual feelings without being aware that that is the motivation behind other goals they are consciously striving to achieve.

Emotionally people have many desires - all of these emotions are going to create and alter the various goals that people have (conscious and unconscious). If you think about that further, on a moment-by-moment basis your emotions are going to be altered continuously by various goals - your emotions are going to be creating goals, objectives and whatnot. For instance, even with simple activities you may have an emotional goal that you aren't aware of. Say you are opening a door - maybe a previous event caused you to slow down when opening the door and going into the next area because your motivation was decreased so you weren't as excited about moving onto the next activity in your life.

A Review

So before someone does anything, their previous thoughts and emotions are going to determine how they perform during the action/activity. They have many goals that they created unconsciously and consciously that determined to some extent the emotions they are feeling, and they thought many things which (in combination with their emotions) helps determine how they are thinking. During the action conscious verbalizations and mental imagery help assist performance, and reflection of the performance afterwards helps to determine a persons response.

Further Thoughts

The process of self-regulation is not completely understood, nor do I think it ever will be, because it is basically asking the question of how exactly does the mental processes behind thinking and feeling work. When 'mental imagery' is used, how exactly does that work? Which associated images come up with each image you bring up for a specific purpose? When people monitor their affective state, how much does that enhance what they are feeling or change what they are feeling? When someone uses a strategy such as a verbalization to help learning, why does that work exactly the way it does?

There seems to be a large unconscious factor that is too complicated to be understood. The unconscious is so complicated, as it has many factors that are interacting with each other all of the time. When those factors mentioned in the previous paragraph are brought up (mental images, monitoring, cognitive strategies), along with the natural unconscious emotion and motivation that occurs always with humans, it becomes obvious that there is no telling what could be influencing your thinking and feeling (on a detailed, moment to moment basis and even just considering the obvious factors).

7.19 How are Arousal and Stimulation Processed in Emotional Processing?

If you think about it, emotion is going to be related to everything in life. Things that inspire us generate emotion, things that arouse us generate emotion, and ordinary stimuli generates emotion as well.

But what is arousal? What is inspiration? If everything in life has some combination of arousal and stimulation, and this combination generates an 'emotional response', then are there other factors present that are also significant?

Arousal is a physiological and psychological state of being awake or reactive to stimuli. Arousal is important in regulating consciousness, attention, and information processing. It is crucial for motivating certain behaviours, such as mobility, the pursuit of nutrition, the fight-or-flight response and sexual activity. So in order to understand what arousal is, it helps to recall what sexual arousal is, since the two are related. Arousal is basically being stimulated, when someone is stimulated in a powerful way, they are aroused. This doesn't need to be sexual arousal, although sexual arousal is one type of arousal. You could say that there is 'intellectual' arousal or arousal from other types of stimulation.

When a person is aroused, he or she may find a wider range of events appealing [15] The state of arousal might lead a person to view a decision more positively than he or she would have in a less aroused state. So therefore arousal relates to inspiration, if one is inspired then they might also be more aroused.

How can inspiration relate to emotional processing? Arousal clearly relates, when someone is aroused, it influences their perception and determines if they are feeling strongly or weakly. If someone is aroused, then it is likely that they are feeling stronger emotions because they are more stimulated. But what if someone is inspired? Is someone going to be feeling stronger emotions if they are inspired? Can someone be inspired when they are feeling poorly?

Could someone be 'stimulated' or 'aroused' and not be experiencing strong emotions? Why would it matter if those emotions are 'inspiring' or not? Inspiration is related to imagination more than to stimulation. It could take only a little stimulation to get someone inspired because inspiration is something you make up or create in your mind. It takes a lot of stimulation to get someone aroused because arousal is more of a physical response and is less intellectual. It is as if the most obvious form of arousal is sexual arousal, because that is clearly biological and powerful.

Is arousal just 'stimulation'? If someone is stimulated, then they are likely to be aroused. Arousal implies a response so strong that it generates a physical response. Arousal involves the activation of the reticular activating system in the brain stem, the autonomic nervous system and the endocrine system, leading to increased heart rate and blood pressure and a condition of sensory alertness, mobility and readiness to respond. It should be obvious that a stronger emotional response will lead to a stronger physical response. The mind and body are linked, when someone has a reaction, they also move in a certain way to reflect the nature of that reaction (such as a facial expression, or a body expression or gesture), and this physical reaction is not always controlled. That example is one way of demonstrating the link between mind, body and arousal.

Arousal is a difficult concept to understand. It becomes more simple when someone thinks of sexual arousal. Sexual arousal is obvious - someone feels strongly in a sexual way. This makes the person more alerted and possibly results in a faster reaction time because they are stimulated and 'aroused'. Non-sexual arousal works the same way only it is not sexual. It is non-sexual things or stimulation generating a physical response in the body. Imagination also can generate a physical response, which is interesting because it is as if imagination is something you are just making up.

This makes it more clear how emotion is processed - an emotional reaction causes various factors in your mind and body to interact with each other, producing a more complex reaction. Arousal, stimulation, imagination and various thoughts and ideas (which are in the same category as 'imagination' because they are made up by the mind) all interact.

7.20 Intentions

When someone has an intention, or does anything such as thinking something or doing something without thought, what is the exact mental process that lies behind that action? What combination of emotions,

15.   Ariely, D; Loewenstein, G. (2006). "The heat of the moment: The effect of sexual arousal on sexual decision making.". *Journal of Behavioral Decision Making* 19 (2): 87–98.

feelings and thoughts makes that happen? Here is what is at the bottom of the "Emotion is a Combination of Feeling and Thought" chapter:

"Emotion always precedes thought; thought is always just going to be an explanation of emotion. Everything in the end turns out to be an emotion in your system, so therefore everything is really an emotion. When you say "I want to leave" the feeling of you wanting to leave is always going to precede the thought. Actually first you quickly understand what it is that you are feeling when you realize what it is you are feeling as an unconscious thought process, then you have a more regular feeling about it, and then you are able to verbalize that feeling into a thought. Unless something is said to you instead of you thinking it, in which case the process is reversed. First it is a thought because it is expressed that way, then it is a feeling, and then it is a quick unconscious thought process to think about what was said."

So there is an unconscious thought process before everything you think/do, however there are also patterns of feelings which are also there. The feelings described are an important part of it, when you do something there isn't an unconscious thought right before you do it. You first have the unconscious thought when you have the original feeling that caused you to want to do that thing - you first have a feeling that you want to do something, then you understand what that feeling means as an unconscious thought, and then that is translated back into a feeling which remains there until you do the action. So the unconscious thought is not right before you do the thing, the feeling is there before you do it because feelings are faster than thoughts, so your mind has the feeling ready at hand to act on the unconscious thought process. That is because once you realize what it is you are going to do as a thought process, you don't need to spend the time to think the entire thing through again, but it is stored in the instinctual part of your brain where your feelings are. Remember from the instinctual frog example that feelings are faster than thoughts, and feelings are also unconscious thoughts so they can also store information to do. This is the frog example in the chapter "Thoughts":

"The definition of intellect and thoughts is almost understanding (those concrete things). Emotion is feeling, completely separate from facts or information. All facts and information are going to be about things that cause feeling, however, since all things that happen cause feelings and all facts and information are about things that happen. So facts and information are just feelings organized in a logical manner. Intellect and thought also generates feelings when those thoughts are processed in your mind. Since thought is really only about feelings, it is logical that thought actually has root in feelings. For example, all events are really feelings in the mind, so thoughts are actually just comparing feelings. You take two feelings and can arrive at one thought. Take the feeling of a frog moving and the feeling of a threat of danger. The two feelings combined equal the idea or thought that the frog needs to move when there is danger - the thought is actually just understanding how feelings interact. All thought is is the understanding of how feelings and real events interact with themselves. Feeling is what provides the motivation to arrive at the answer (the thought). If you just had the facts, there is a threat, and the frog can jump, you aren't going to arrive at the conclusion that the frog should jump away. You need to take the feeling that there is a threat and the feeling that the frog can jump and then combine the two sensory images in your head to arrive at the answer.

That shows how all intellect is powered and motivated by emotion. It also shows that frogs have thoughts; the frog has to have the thought to jump away when it sees a threat, as a thought is just the combination of two feelings resulting in the resulting feeling of wanting to move away. That process of feelings is like a thought process. Thoughts are a little different for humans, however, because humans have such a large memory that they are able to compare this experience to all the other experiences in their life while the frog only remembers the current situation and is programmed (brain wiring) to jump away. The frog doesn't have a large enough memory to learn from new information and change its behavior. That shows how humans are very similar to frogs in how they process data (in one way at least), and that one thing that separates a human from a frog is a larger memory which can store lots of useful information and potential behavioral patterns."

It would be too slow for you to just do something based on an unconscious thought process, you would have to wait to have this unconscious thought right before you do the thing, instead of having the thought at one point in time and storing it, and then doing the thing later on. If it is just an instinctual reaction, however, it is just a feeling that you are responding to because it is too fast to have an unconscious thought process. It is just a manner of the definition of what an unconscious thought is - that it is going to be more like a thought than a feeling - which is also an unconscious thought, so it depends how you view it.

If it is an instinctual, immediate reaction, say if you slam a door on your hand then you are going to say "ouch" - that is a thought that resulted from two feelings, the feeling of pain and the feeling that you need to express that pain. The thought is so fast you might consider it unconscious, that is also like in the frog example.

It gets even more complicated than that - this is in the "Life Occurs in Sharp Spikes" chapter of the book:

"Everything that is processed, not just spikes, follows the sequence of thought to emotion to feeling. That is because thoughts are clearer than emotions and feelings, and emotions are more similar to thoughts than feelings are (discussed previously) so when you see something or hear something or whatnot for the first time, it is clearer in your mind. Then it becomes less clear and you think about it unconsciously. You think about it unconsciously because it takes further processing in order to isolate the feeling that that things gives you. Some things are just too complicated to feel them right away. Other things, however, can be felt right away, say if you are touching something the feeling arises right away. That is because the physical stimulus is more immediate than emotional stimulus.

Emotional things, however, are simply to complicated to "feel" them right away, they need to be processed first. That is logical, just take looking at anything, say a book. In order to feel the feelings that the book causes in you, you are going to have to at least unconsciously think about it first (that is, after you start paying attention to it, which you do by starting to think about it or just see it and notice it more than you usually notice things in the area). Since you don't need to think about physical stimulus since it is just a physical stimulus, (not something like vision) you don't really unconsciously process it."

That shows that it is really all mixed in - thoughts, emotions and feelings - that there isn't just an unconscious thought process but you could also just say that feelings or thoughts are first - this is because when you process something you might think about it first, and it certainly feels this way because when you are processing something it is a very intellectual experience, it is clear in your mind and it feels like you are thinking about the thing so clearly that you must be using thoughts instead of emotions. I say that things are first clear in your mind when you first see it or whatnot, - that would be the "thought" but then it is an emotion, and you do that (make it into an emotion) to isolate the feeling the thing causes in you, so then you feel it (after you isolate the feeling) - thought to emotion to feeling.

So when you have an intention to do something could it be that first it is an unconscious thought and then you just do it? First you are going to have an unconscious thought about it, then you are going to have a conscious thought about it (because it is an intention) and then you are going to do it. Your conscious thought about it may or may not be verbal, you don't have to think about everything verbally in order to do it. You do have a conscious thought about it because that is almost the definition of intention, your intent. If you don't have a conscious thought about it then it is more instinctual, or it could be a mix of the two. Everything someone does is going to be on the spectrum somewhere between complete intention and completely instinctual.

Intentions and instincts (or things you do) aren't just thoughts, but feelings and emotions are often involved as well, where do they fit in? First an emotion could start an intention, and then it would be an unconscious thought process, and then it might become another emotion because you can feel everything (you are going to feel the thought, or have a feeling about it) and feelings are very fast so this feeling can fit into the time after you think about it and before you do the action, or after the initiating event and before the unconscious or conscious thought process. When you do think it is very fast, in fact your thinking might be slow, but there is one point in time where your thinking leads to a conclusion and that is culmination is considered to be when you had the "thought" because it is a conscious thought that your mind understands, but leading up to that conscious thought (which could be verbal or not verbal) was unconscious thoughts (or thinking) because it is hard to reach difficult conclusions instantly. This thought is then held in your mind until you do the action, it prepares your mind for the action, and during that time that thought might generate a certain feeling – maybe fear or a lack of confidence. This feeling is then used when you do the intention, because when you do something you do it so fast that you don't "think" about it right before you do it, but you use the feeling that is "storing" the thought. You might not have feelings about it and your action might not be swayed by feeling, but if it is then your thoughts might be under the influence of your feelings. Your feelings might cause you to stop doing the thing if you are too afraid, for example.

So there is an unconscious thought before every intention, that is what thought is, it is figuring out what you are going to do, and you are going to have to figure out what it is that you are going to do first before you do it. Unless it is like the frog example where you just feel it at the same time that you do it, but in that case the feelings are mixed in with the thoughts, so then it is a matter of how you define "thought". Thought is really a conclusion (not a partial thought, which could be an emotion), so you take two feelings and come at a conclusion, which is the thought, then you do the thing, and that means that you do have an unconscious thought right before the intention, the feeling really is a thought, it is just so fast that it is a feeling and a thought. So right before you do something there can be a feeling - which is also a thought, that causes you to do it finally. So is it a thought or is it a feeling? The feeling is the drive behind the thought (or thinking), which builds up along with the feeling. The feeling is powering the thought (or thinking) because it is so instinctual. So things that are more instinctual are going to be faster and involve more feelings, feelings can speed up thoughts (this is obvious with the instinctual example, where instinct then is really just powerful feelings causing you to think very fast).

So if you do anything there is going to be unconscious thoughts before you do it, because thoughts are just understanding real things. That includes if you have intentions, only intentions (since they are more conscious) are going to involve conscious thoughts as well as unconscious ones, unless it is an intention you intended to do unconsciously. The reason intentions involve unconscious thoughts as well is because you need to think to arrive at the conclusion, and most thinking isn't completely consciously understood. How many people can think without using words, yet understand what it is that they are thinking? You can understand that you are going to do a certain thing without using words, but you can't think for a long period of time without using words and still follow your thought process. Complicated non-verbal thought processes are unconscious. And almost all thoughts and everything you do is going to be complicated - and therefore they are going to involve long unconscious thinking about them (by long I just mean longer than instantaneous, which would be what you would do if it was instinctual).

So right before you do something there is going to be something in your mind that understands what it is you are going to do, this is a thought because it is real (versus feelings which are things which you just feel). You might even "feel" the thought really. That is what happens right before you do something. However, leading up to that final thought/feeling it is going to be like described before; first you might have a feeling. If humans were computers I would say that first it starts with its programming and then it has the thought, but for humans feelings are their programming – so humans first have feelings and then we have thoughts. Feelings can originate from thoughts however, so it is then a which came first, the chicken or the egg debate. But if the original feeling started because of a thought, the thought was more further away in time from the feeling -by a few seconds at least – that is because conscious thoughts (verbal ones) have space of time around them, if you think, "I am going to shoot" you don't shoot as quickly as you would if you just understood that you were going to shoot, the conscious verbal thought slows you down. So when you have an intention or when you are going to think something (which is what thoughts are - they cam be verbal because you can express anything verbally almost, including all intentions) then that follows the process of feeling to unconscious thought to feeling again to store it. I said before "a feeling, then an unconscious thought process, then a more general feeling".

I said that because the first feeling is just the real feeling of the intention you are going to have - which you could say is an unconscious thought because as discussed previously all feelings are unconscious thoughts - and it is clear they are when you realize it is an intention, which is going to be doing something real, and intellect is understanding things that are real. So the first feelings/thoughts are when you first feel that you want to do something, then you need to unconsciously think about it to realize what it is you want to do exactly (this is not a conscious non-verbal thought, but an unconscious one), and then you have a more specific or general feeling about it (by general there I really mean larger or more clear) to store that clear thought, the general feeling then is going to be more clear because you now unconsciously understand what it is that you are going to do, and then it is a real conscious thought and then you could translate that conscious thought to a verbal thought or an action.

So to explain the statement, "first it is a feeling, then it is an unconscous thought process, and then it is a more general feeling and then you are able to make that feeling into a conscious thought (or do an action which would stem from that clear thought)" - that was originally said in the book at the end of the "Emotion is a Combination of Feeling and Thought" chapter in this form - "actually first you quickly understand what it is that you are feeling when you realize what it is you are feeling as an unconscious thought process, then you have a more regular feeling about it, and then you are able to verbalize that feeling into a thought". Whether someone's state before they have that thought is one that started with an emotion or without an emotion, that state must have originated from a previous state, or from some other previous stimulus. In terms of someone's first feelings, their first feelings probably came from physical feelings before the brain was developed in the womb. First people would have just physical feelings, not deep emotional ones because all there is in the beginning is sensory stimulation - mostly feeling your own body and your surroundings.

So the first thoughts/feelings originated from physical stimulus, like, "ouch that hurts". Or "that looks cool". After the human develops they can have thoughts and feelings that can originate from sensory stimulation, physical stimulation, or other thoughts and feelings. But that doesn't explain what happens right before someone thinks something or does something. It explains that originally there are those things which would cause the intention, but not how the intention is formed. Since humans have strong emotions, many intentions are going to be formed from emotion. Intentions are also going to be formed from conscious / unconscious thinking. Feelings are also going to have elements of thoughts, however (so it isn't either feeling or thought that originated the intention, it might be both at the same time). Say if you want to switch a switch - it is going to be a progression of feeling/thought. That is, it is going to take time for you to realize what it is you want to do, so it could be feeling and thinking all along, and at some point in that feeling/thinking you are going to realize fully what you want to do, and then you could call it a thought because it is completely formed (this thought might be conscious or it might remain unconscious and only later become conscious). When you realize you want to switch a switch it isn't instantaneous, but it takes time. But when you do switch the switch instantaneously, are you acting off of the thought or the feeling? You are probably acting off of the feeling, the thought was a period in time a while ago, but that thought started the feeling of you wanting to do it, which lead to you switching the switch off of the feeling instead of the thought. Unless you happen to do the thing right after you finally figure out what it is you want to do, then you could say that the thought made you do it.

That reveals that you are always going to have some feeling about what it is you are going to do right before you do it, because then you "think" or "feel" what it is you are going to do. It isn't going to be as strong in terms of thought as when you first thought of what it was you were going to do, because you don't need to think as much to realize what it is you are going to do. You are probably going to be feeling more than thinking right before you do it because you are going to be excited about doing something, you already realized what you were going to do which was the thought part, now it is time for the feeling part. The thought is still there of course otherwise you wouldn't know what to do, however right before you do it feeling is probably going to dominate.

Right before you do something your mind needs to get ready to do it, and you need to remind yourself what it is you need to do and that you need to do it. So that means your mind probably feels something based on what it is you are going to do. This feeling can be simulated if you read a book and then later reflect on how you feel about the book. Reading the book in this instance would be the original thought process, and reflecting on it later would be simulating the feeling right before you do something. You don't need to think about everything in the book to understand the feeling that the book causes you. You don't need to think as hard to understand the same things because it was already understood at one point. The second time it is easier. That is like when you first have an unconscious thought process to understand what you are going to, when you are going to do it later you already understand what you are going to do, you simply then "feel" what it is you are going to do because it is more clearly understood, it is understood emotionally now (more instinctual) so you don't need to "think" as much as you did before. Emotion replaces thought because emotion is easier than thought. Someone isn't going to think unless they have to, you basically have already done the hard part, so the second time you bring it up the thought would be reduced and the emotion would remain. The further excitement of being about to do the thing would raise the emotion even more. But here learned is another thing, if you think about something once the next times you bring it up (especially if you bring it up right after you figure it out) it is going to be much easier to understand so thought is going to be reduced and feeling raised relatively.

So in other words, before the thought or your understanding of what it is you are going to do is complete, you are going or are not going to be having emotions that are encouraging this thought process or affecting this thought process. Emotion and intelligence are intertwined. That is why first comes the emotion, then the complete thought, and then you might have an emotion about that thought itself as well, - in other words the state of the emotion you are feeling is probably going to evolve as the thought does. This reveals that while emotion is unconscious thought, not all unconscious thought is emotion.

Humans don't just say things without thinking about them first, so everything is going to be unconscious first. Speech is much much slower than your thoughts are, and unless you start saying something and don't know the complete sentence before you say it, you are going to have the entire thing thought out first. So technically everything starts with an unconscious thought. However this thought has levels of understanding, there are levels to which you understand the thought, that is why you can't just say everything all at once, you usually have to think about it for a bit first. When people think, it takes time to think, and they don't think unconsciously in sentences. They think unconsciously with emotions, thoughts, visualizations, anything your mind can simulate. When they think unconsciously with emotions you could be taking large emotional experiences and trying to analyze them, or little ones, you could be combining different experiences, or combining emotion with thought or emotion with visualization (etc.). Your mind doesn't just use sentences to figure out what it wants to do, that would take too long. Sentences are actually just sounds that represent things, you don't need to simulate a sound in your head in order to think. It might be that you simulate tiny sounds, or however it is your neurons fire to organize the thoughts, the point is the thoughts are not fully formed instantly. It isn't the firing of one neuron once that makes a complete sentence. There is a progression of thought. This is obvious because when you are doing a problem, say a math problem, you often can reach the answer without having to say anything. What is happening is that you are thinking about things unconsciously, maybe you are visualizing the number of things you need to visualize to find the answer (say adding 1 to 1 you have to visualize the separate objects, and then visualize the two objects together).

7.21 An Overly Optimistic Attitude towards Life Leads to a Dulling of Emotion

When you go into a situation or an event the attitude you have is going to impact your emotional experience. If you think something is going to be fun, when in reality it isn't, and you continue to think that that thing was fun afterwards, it is going to make you feel worse than if you had the right understanding of how much fun the event was. This is because an overly optimistic attitude causes you to consciously focus on things which you enjoy more, but your conscious mind can only recognize a tiny amount of things which you enjoy. So you are amplifying a disproportionate amount of emotion in your own mind. That throws things off balance in your head and you start to wonder (consciously and unconsciously) why you are enjoying some things more than others, and it throws off your responses to natural, ordinary events. In other words, your mind compares the positive things which you are amplifying to the things you aren't amplifying (like how it compares how you work during the day to how you rest at night – that is your mind compares the work during the day to resting at night and therefore you feel more rested because your mind is comparing those things to if you didn't work during the day). Furthermore ordinary events start to become duller because you are amplifying a few events you just think are fun, when in reality all of life is fun if you give it an equal chance.

What those people fail to realize is that basically everything can be viewed as fun, they don't need to grab onto a few things with their overly optimistic attitude. Emotions are fun, and life is so full of emotions that any scene or event in life can be broken down into its many emotional parts. Emotion just means how something makes you feel, and that in turn means what kind of reaction things make you have. In fact, each individual object in life gives an emotion, and makes you react in a certain way.

If you have an optimistic attitude towards life, or an overly optimistic attitude, then most of the emotion that you get is going to be undercut (undermined, etc, because it is going to be outweighed by the few things which you are praising, or have an optimistic attitude for) and therefore overall be leading to a dulling of emotion. That is because this overly optimistic attitude is a conscious thing that only enhances a few of the events in life and doesn't understand that everything in life can be viewed as being fun (if you take the same attitude and just twist it that is).

You're not still being optimistic because you're dismissing the verbal discourse whereby you rate some things in life as higher than other things. You are still being optimistic in a way but now you understand that you shouldn't be over inflating some things more than others. It is like saying, wow that duck tape is really really cool. But then you are missing all the other things in the room which are also cool, maybe a lot less cool than the duck tape but they can still be viewed as being cool. So instead you'd say, hey that duck tape is cool, to keep it more in line with how cool the other things are. This doesn't mean that you are less optimistic towards life, it just means you are more aware and considering of the whole.

Similarly, an overly negative attitude can bring down how cool an object is. You can basically manufacture false emotions about things. While you might feel a temporary sensation of elation (if you're being optimistic) or a temporary down feeling (if you're being pessimistic) afterwards you are going to feel bad because you basically insulted all the other feelings in your mind as being weak compared to it. Either that or you feel bad because you inserted an emotion that was too hard to deal with in your mind because it was so strong, and you feel bad afterwards because that strong emotion lingers in your mind and takes up room that it shouldn't, in addition to throwing your system off balance.

That is what an overly optimistic attitude does, it takes all the things in your mind that you might verbally over inflate, and inflates them. That creates a tension in your brain because then most of the ordinary things which you should also be enjoying seem dull. The reverse is true with an overly negative attitude, which is also bad.

How This Chapter shows how Intelligence is intertwined with Emotion:

- Your attitude is determined by your thoughts, and your thoughts are going to be determined by your intellect because your intellect is who you are, and you decide what it is that you are going to think. Your attitude is going to lead you to have different emotions, and these emotions are then also going to change how it is you understand the world emotionally, or your emotional intelligence.

7.22 Smaller Emotions Follow Brief, Intense Emotions

Extremely deep feelings and emotions, like sadness or anger, usually only last a few seconds. However, those deep feelings often trigger lesser feelings of sadness and anger for the period afterwards. This intense, brief period of emotion can trigger a long array of smaller, similar emotions afterwards. Say if the deep emotion was you being sad, the following emotions that person is going to experience would be lesser sad emotions. These emotions aren't just by themselves, but are often accompanied by thoughts, behaviors, or environmental stimulus.

If you have a brief period of being extremely happy it is more likely to be followed by extremely optimistic thinking, like thinking, I am great, I am amazing, and wow I really did a good job. A brief period of extreme sadness is likely to be followed by pessimistic thinking because that is how your brain is wired. Your brain is programmed to associate sad with failure, and success (or happy) with optimism.

Why do intense emotions only last a few seconds? They do because emotions work in accordance with thoughts. Thoughts only last a few seconds, and therefore it is logical that the most intense emotions you experience are going to be periods of intense thought and intense emotion at the same time. These periods are so intense that they are probably capable of being noticed by the person experiencing them.

Such an intense emotional experience is going to leave a mark, however. That is why those brief periods of intense emotion are going to be followed by lesser, similar emotions. Say if you were extremely happy for a few seconds, then you'd be slightly happy for a while afterwards.

Why does the brief period only last a few seconds? Can't it be longer? If life were great, I guess the positive intense emotional experiences would last longer, and the short negative emotional experiences not even exist. But the attention span of the average human/animal is actually very short, and they can only handle so much intense emotion in a certain period of time.

That leads to another phenomenon called overload. A person or animal can only experience so many intense periods of emotion in a certain amount of time. Say you made someone laugh really hard, and then would tell an equally funny joke right after, that person wouldn't laugh as hard because the laugh brain circuitry is already exhausted. It is like being jaded, only in the short term. This theory is easy to test, just pinch yourself, then pinch yourself again, and you'll realize that it hurts a lot more the first time. That is because pain is an emotional experience as well, and that first pinch is exactly similar to the brief periods of intense emotion mentioned before. Furthermore, the pinch is followed by lesser amounts of pain. When all that residual pain is gone you can pinch yourself again and it will hurt just as much as the first time.

In other words, the brief, intense emotion was so intense that it leaves an aftereffect of lesser amounts of that same emotion. I could also just change the word emotion with thought. If you think something strongly, then similar thoughts are likely to follow, only less intense. The intensity of the emotion/thought goes downhill after the main event solely because your mind is exhausted by the intensity of the intense experience of emotion or thought. Humans/animals simply don't have the capacity for a more intense experience then an intense emotional or intellectual experience.

People just don't have very, very, very intense emotional or intellectual experiences. The mind just can't handle it. People can have very, very, very intense physical experiences, however. That is only because evolutionarily humans and animals evolved going through very intense physical experiences, but there just isn't any need or purpose to go through intense intellectual/emotional experiences. It would even be boring after the first few seconds. That's because most emotion and intellect is originally from sensory stimulation, which is found in the real world and not in your head.

There are many examples of the intensity of intellectual and emotional experiences dying off. It is simply because something repeated over and over in your head becomes less and less interesting as its newness dies off. You could take any idea and repeat it to yourself over and over and you'll notice how doing that becomes less and less interesting.

In fact, sometimes it is better to not initiate thinking about something that would lead to you to continue to repeat it (or similar ideas or emotions) because it is unhealthy to repeat things (or experience emotions that last too long) because the intensity of the experience dies off and you are stuck in a pattern of thinking about something, or feeling something, that you don't want to be thinking or feeling because it isn't providing enough stimulation. But you are still stuck feeling/thinking it because for whatever reason your mind doesn't let go of it easily.

It is healthier to not be so interested in the thing in the first place so your mind doesn't over inflate it and you wind up going through a period of over-excitement, which you don't really enjoy, followed by a period of under-excitement, which you don't really enjoy. It is like an addiction to emotion that would lead to this behavior. Or an overly optimistic attitude towards life. Someone that is overly aggressively approaching life, trying to grab onto whatever positive emotions or thoughts they can. Or someone overly upset about something and, just being persistent, doesn't realize that it becomes less and less interesting to be upset about that thing, but continues to persist in thinking about it. They just need to move on.

In fact, you could view this two different ways, one is to not experience the more intense thoughts/ emotions and try to spread it out over time. The other way to view it is the sharp emotional spike is a good thing. It is probably only a good thing if you like hurting yourself, however. It is a bad thing because it is so out of character with your everyday emotions/thoughts, which are much less intense. Such a drastic change from the ordinary would cause a violent mood swing. Your mind is going to be upset that things around it are changing so fast, and it would lead you to continuously try and figure out what is going on (consciously or unconsciously). Your mind has in it an automatic thing which tries to figure out what is happening to it, and that device is going to short circuit if you put in short, brief periods of intensity. It is like the brief period of intensity jolts your entire system. Like a hot wire.

If you are going to go for the brief period of intensity then that is a way of looking at life, it is a philosophy that you need to grab on to anything that throws its way to you. Or if you are looking for the brief period of negative intensity then that philosophy would be looking to grab onto (really anything, not just anything positive) that comes your way. Someone with those attitudes would think something like, "ok there is a positive experience, lets do it, I mean lets really go and do it that would be really really really fun". They are so upset about life that when they see a positive thing, they cling onto it desperately. What they don't realize is that clinging onto something positive (or negative) or any clinging, causes your mind to stop liking it due to repetition and overload.

How This Chapter shows how Intelligence is intertwined with Emotion:

- When you have a strong emotion it just doesn't disappear, but it disappears gradually. This shows how your emotions are going to determine your thoughts and therefore your intellect. It shows that emotions cannot be completely controlled and therefore are going to change your thoughts and therefore possibly the reliability of your intelligence.

7.23 Visual learning

Things that are easier to picture are easier to understand.

Things that are easier to picture are easier to understand. Take the difference between understanding, we are going to play with the Frisbee, and if you throw the Frisbee twice as fast, it will arrive at its destination in half the time. It is clearly easier to understand what playing with the Frisbee is then it is to calculate how soon it will get to the other person. That is because the emotional event of playing with the Frisbee is large and distinct, and involves many things.

One thing was an emotional event; the other thing was a precise calculation. You could also view that backwards, that the calculation is actually an emotional event, and the emotional event is actually a calculation. The emotional event of playing Frisbee is in fact a calculation; you are calculating everything that there is involved with playing Frisbee. When someone says, "let's play Frisbee" you imagine and picture in your head everything that playing Frisbee involves.

Thus for anything that is said you bring up a picture of it in your head. Even if it is a sound or a smell, you always try to picture what is causing it. That is because the vision enhances the experience and makes it more enjoyable to think about and therefore it is also going to be easier to remember. It is like vision is tied in with everything, and that if something can't be visualized, it simply doesn't exist.

Empty space is the absence of vision. But when you think hard about just an empty space, you'd like to imagine something there because you know that you would enjoy looking at that space more that way, that it just isn't right for something to be empty like that. Even blind people visualize things because they can feel in three dimensions with their bodies and hands.

That is also why harder mathematical problems are harder to do, because they are harder to visualize. You have to memorize what 12 times 12 equals, but you can easily visualize what 1 times 2 is. Just one group of 2, that equals 2, you can picture that object in your head easily but when you picture adding up 12 groups of 12 the image gets too large.

Even if you think about a smell that is an invisible gas, you are going to picture something in your head like a gas outlet or a gas tank, or the air being filled with an invisible substance. Vision is in all of our thoughts and emotions, the other senses aren't. Only some things smell, only some objects make noise, but everything can be seen. Everything exists somewhere physically, that is, and if it exists somewhere physically, then even if it is invisible you are going to be trying to imagine the space in which it is in.

In that manner blind people can see. They have an image of the world similar to what we do (even if they have never seen) solely from feeling objects and imagining where everything is. If someone asked you what the properties of an invisible gas were, you'd be thinking about the empty space in which the gas was in. How is it that people can visualize empty space? If there wasn't empty space there, then there wouldn't be anything, just empty space. So when most people visualize empty space they probably think of something like an empty room, or the corner of an empty room and just not focus on the walls, trying to look into the empty space by having an unfocused look to their eye.

It also seems that the easier it is to picture something, the easier it is to understand and remember. That is because things that have a stronger visual presence cause more emotion to be invoked in a person, and it is has a larger presence in that persons mind, and therefore is easier to remember. So the easier the vision is to comprehend, the easier it is also going to be to remember.

Also, the more emotional the event, the easier it is to remember. (and all events and such things in life are visual, as well). That is why dogs remember the words they care the most about like walk, Frisbee, food, and their name. It isn't just easier to remember these larger things, but it is easier to understand them. The smaller and more complicated it gets, the harder it is to understand. So easier physics problems would be something like ball A hitting ball B, but harder ones would involve something like friction, which you can't see as well. For example what is easier to understand, what is the force of friction on the ball, or what is the force of my hand on the ball? Mathematically they would seem to take just as much physical work to write down the mathematical solution, but emotionally it takes more work to do the friction part of the problem. (because it is harder to visualize) That means, however, that it is going to be harder for you to do the mathematical problem, or the friction part of the mathematical problem.

The easier something is to visualize, the less the strain on your mind processing that thing is going to have. Things that are easier to picture are easier to understand as well.

There are also degrees to which you visualize something. Say you are doing a math problem that involves distances. You can focus on those distances when you think about them to varying degrees. That is, when you think of the word distance you have unconscious thoughts about something like, "oh was that a very long trip?" Or you think more or less clearly about how straight the line of the distance is because you are thinking about trips now. Or thinking about the force of friction on an object, you have to try and visualize the tiny particles rubbing against each other. There are degrees of effort you can put into thinking about each visualization. Fields like engineering and physics require a lot of visual intelligence. People who can focus more and visualize things better would probably do better in those fields. Since vision relates to everything, better visual ability could help in countless situations to varying degrees.

Is emotional intelligence visual? How does the statement, "boys are aggressive so they would be more likely to buy a book about aggresivity to encourage their own aggressiveness than if they weren't aggressive" relate to visual intelligence? You have to be able to imagine boys being aggressive and then you have to think about the response (which is visual) to boys when they are encouraged to be aggressive. Emotional intelligence is then just observing slight visual changes in affect. However to notice these slight changes in affect it is important to point out or lead one to notice better certain visual things by more intellectual observations, which are actually just visual observations themselves.

They are visual observations themselves because almost everything is a visual observation, the only things that aren't visual observations are observations related to the other senses, but those other senses might play a lesser role than visual since visual is the sense people are most in tune with since it occurs all the time.

Emotional intelligence, however, might also relate to understanding physical senses because you need to understand how people physically feel in order to understand their emotional state, as the physical contributes to emotion. You feel your own body all the time and the senses from your skin and muscles changes all the time as well. Those feelings play an important part in how you feel, and serve as a baseline for emotions. That is you can close your eyes and stop thinking, but you are still going to feel something. That thing you are feeling then must be mostly physical since you aren't getting any other inputs (other than unconscious emotional ones, but you can do things like focusing on your heart beat or breathing to eliminate more of that focus and focus more on your body).

How This Chapter shows how Intelligence is intertwined with Emotion:

- Emotional intelligence is sensory (or comes originally from sensory data), and your senses are directed by your thoughts and emotions (or you – and you are your intellect). So it becomes clear then that someone is their intellect, and their intellect then must comprise their emotions and their thoughts (since someone is only emotions and thoughts just behaving in a certain pattern).

7.24 Consciousness

Understanding the psychology of your feelings, emotions and thoughts is important because it leads to increased consciousness.

Consciousness occurs when feeling and understanding meet, this is because consciousness is shown in the ability to reflect on your feelings. In other words, when you understand what it is that you are feeling you are the most conscious. That is because during that time you are most aware of what is going on. This awareness could be described as an understanding of life, not just general understanding. That is you could be doing a math problem, but that math problem isn't going to increase how conscious you are, because doing it isn't going to increase your understanding of how it is that you are feeling. It could be that doing the problem makes you more awake, and as a side effect of that you understand how it is that you are feeling better, but that is just a side effect. Understanding how you are feeling makes you more aware of yourself because that increases how much you are thinking about yourself (or your feelings).

Since thoughts and emotions lead to feelings, the more you understand them as well the more conscious you are going to be. So if you are doing a math problem, the more you understand that you are doing a math problem, and the place the math problem has in your life, then the more conscious you are. That is, it isn't doing the math problem that is making you more conscious, but it is understanding the place of what it is you are doing and feeling (in this case a math problem) and where that fits into your life that determines how conscious you are. It is your inner reflection of how the math problem makes you feel as a whole that separates humans being conscious from other animals. Consciousness basically means aware. This means that the math problem actually does lead to increased consciousness, because you are becoming more aware of the place of that math problem in your entire life as you do the math problem.

So consciousness basically means how aware someone is of themselves (it means other things as well). The more aware of yourself you are the more conscious you are. In order to be aware of yourself you need to understand where everything in your life fits in. It is this awareness, or commonsense, that is more important to understanding who you are. In order to be aware of yourself, or have a concept of self, you have to have a concept of how yourself interacts in the world as a whole, not just as individual parts.

Even though you might be sleeping, you are conscious because you still understand who you are. Then again, during dreams you don't act in as rational a manner as when awake, as dreams tend to not make as much sense as real life. Therefore you wouldn't be as conscious during a dream as you would when you are awake. You are still conscious to some degree, however, since you are functioning in a somewhat reasonable manner. But you still aren't clearly perfectly aware of yourself or your place in the world since in dreams sometimes you do things and see things that don't make sense, but you apparently don't notice them. This indicates further that consciousness is more a matter of commonsense and how well you know yourself than just standard intellect like would be present say when doing a math problem. Your ability to reflect on yourself might not be related to normal IQ, but might more likely be more highly related to emotional IQ.

In other words commonsense can be measured just as standard intellect can be. But what leads to commonsense is emotional intelligence not intelligence that is more related to memory or something built up over time, like skill. The more commonsense someone has the more conscious they are because they know what it is that they are doing. This is a different type of consciousness then the type that makes humans human, this is the practical type of consciousness that makes someone aware of their environment and their ability to function, versus a deeper human consciousness. In dreams people have very little commonsense, for example, in a dream you might try to do the same thing over and over again even though it might be failing, and you just randomly appear in scenes or scenarios with no background knowledge of how you got there or where in the world you are. That suggests that during dreams you are solely emotional. So commonsense isn't just emotional intelligence, but it is a general awareness that would result from understanding your emotions, thoughts, and feelings all at the same time (and their place in the world). In order to understand the proper place of emotions, thoughts and feelings just a large assortment of knowledge isn't going to increase your understanding of who you are. What is going to increase your understanding of who you are however is understanding how your emotions, thoughts and feelings fit into the general assortment of facts and information which makes up the world.

In review, commonsense and a general knowledge of where you are leads to consciousness. Those things both are clear facts separated from a bunch of haziness (the real world). So something like a bee might act like it understands its place in the world, but it doesn't consciously understand it because if you put it in a glass cage it might just bat against the wall trying to get out over and over, not aware that it is ever going to get anywhere. The bee has no commonsense or knowledge. Knowledge in that case would mean understanding that it is in a glass cage, and commonsense would mean understanding that it is never going to get out. So to have commonsense you do need knowledge, but you need to take knowledge and appropriately configure it in order to gain common sense, or consciousness.

You need some knowledge and standard intellect (like memory) to attain commonsense (or consciousness). The more memory you have (random assortment of facts and information) the more information you have to put together in an organized way. It could be that it is easier to put together small amounts of information since it is less to process, leading to more commonsense than just being confused with a lot of memory. However, if you have a lot of data (or memory) and are also capable of putting it together effectively (like you wouldn't be doing in say a dream) then you would have more commonsense then if you had less data and put it together just as effectively, because overall you'd have more data that is properly processed. So commonsense (or consciousness) is your ability to organize the data in your head. This data is organized relative to yourself, therefore giving you a greater understanding of where you are relative to the data. Disorganized data doesn't count at all. A greater memory might increase your commonsense, but only if you can put that extra data together effectively. The bee didn't understand the data that it was in a glass cage, and it didn't understand that it wasn't getting anywhere by hitting against it over and over. If bees had some commonsense they would fly around a room trying to get out instead of trying to get out in the same place over and over. They just have no idea what they are doing. But that is because it probably doesn't remember what it just did. It might remember to some extent, but that memory might not be clear. So it isn't the bees fault that it has no commonsense, because it didn't have a large enough memory to collect enough facts to potentially use commonsense. A person with no commonsense in that example would be someone constantly running into the door without using the handle. You know the person has a large enough memory to remember that it just did that and it shouldn't do it again, but it is still doing it over and over. That human is not conscious at all.

That human is showing no understanding of its actions. Understanding actions leads to commonsense because it shows that you know your place in the world. That human apparently isn't aware of its current place in the world, which is that it is never going to get out of the room with that strategy. So the more sense someone has, the more likely they are going to understand their place in the world and what they are doing, therefore being more conscious.

The better one understands the statement "I am happy" the more that person understands how they are then relative to their condition at previous times. That would lead to them understanding themself better. The better someone understands themself, the more aware of themself they are, leading to increased consciousness. That is an example of how understanding feelings leads to increased consciousness. That is also different from what makes humans truly conscious, however. It is someone's own deep understanding of who they are and how they are happy at that specific time relative to their life, and the meaning of that which makes someone really aware.

So life is a bunch of data that needs to be sorted in some ways in order for a sense of self to be identified. One way to sort the data would be to identify things similar to yourself. A data point in the center would be you, the points closest to that would be the points most similar to you, and the points further out would be more different. That type of sorting would lead to a long term understanding of sense of self. The other type of sorting where the closest points are what is most relevant to you at the time would be a temporary sense of self. Take the bee example, the bee doesn't understand that hitting the wall over and over isn't getting it anywhere, so for it a temporary data point that it is missing that would increase its sense of self awareness is that it isn't getting anywhere by doing that.

The other type of sense of self is a more long term one. Things like what you like and dislike, and what emotions different things cause in you repeatedly would help you identify "who you are". So consciousness isn't just awareness of your environment, it is an understanding of yourself and who you are relative to your environment. That means a deep psychological understanding of your emotions, thoughts and feelings, an understanding of how you perform both in individual and general instances, and what your ability is to perform in those instances.

Putting together some data points doesn't increase self consciousness as much as if you put together data points that relate to yourself. It is when you relate data point(s) to yourself that even more increased consciousness occurs, because you are relating yourself to more information, increasing your interaction with the world and therefore understanding yourself better relative to the world. So doing a math problem isn't going to increase your understanding of yourself a lot, because those data points don't really relate to you. It is going to increase your understanding of yourself a little because you understand what it is that you are doing, which increases your understanding of yourself, but it doesn't increase how much you are thinking about yourself, which would increase your awareness of yourself even more. If you are trying to leave a room (the bee example) however, you linking your desire to leave the room and the fact that opening the door allows you to do that is linking a point about you and a point about the door together, strengthening your sense of self and how much you are thinking about yourself.

So basically any thought about oneself is going to increase ones sense of self. You have a permanent understanding of who you are that doesn't change, and that is your long term understanding of self, but when you think about yourself, or you doing something (like trying to leave a room) your sense of self is temporarily increased because you are thinking about yourself more. So consciousness fluctuates greatly based on thought. It also increases greatly if you are having feelings or emotions about yourself as well. It increases when you are thinking, feeling, or being emotional about yourself because during those times you are more aware of yourself.

Commonsense increases someone's ability to put data points (facts) together, but the more those facts (and resulting combinations of facts) relate to yourself the more that your consciousness is going to be increased. This leads to the conclusion that consciousness is just the awareness of the experience of oneself, and that experience includes ones actions, thoughts, feelings, and emotions (both long term and short term). It could be rephrased that consciousness is awareness of someone's life experience, both short term and long term. The more commonsense someone has the more aware of their life they are going to be because they are going to be able to organize their life and their actions in an efficient, clear manner (both short term and long term) by connecting facts to themselves (the more distant the fact, the less consciousness it leads to because it is less related to yourself causing you to think about yourself less). The more someone is thinking about themself (or experiencing feelings and emotions about themself) the more they are going to be aware of that life experience because their life is going to be temporarily elevated in their minds.

It is impossible to have a perfect understanding of self, or consciousness because to do that you would have to be aware of the exact effect of each emotion, feeling and thought you have. To do that you'd have to be aware of everything in your environment, and everything that you can remember all at the same time. This means that your consciousness evolves based on your memory, that is if your memory changes, who you are changes because you can't base yourself off the same things anymore. Who you are also changes based on your environment, and how aware you are of your environment.

You are going to be more aware of your environment if you are thinking more about your environment, or processing data about it (again this type of consciousness is more a functional one versus a deeper one). Processing data about your immediate environment leads to a greater sense of self because who you are is dependent on your immediate environment, because you automatically process what is going on in that environment. You get a lot of sensory stimulation from the environment you are in. That can be proved because when you think about your immediate environment your awareness of it increases much more than if you think about an environment you are not in. If you think about being in an environment you are not in your sense of self is going to decrease more than you would be if you weren't thinking about anything, because your minds awareness is going to be divided between two places, so you'd have two senses of self. That links into the idea that processing data that is more relevant to yourself leads to greater consciousness, if the data is physically in your environment it is going to increase your self awareness because that is where you are (so you'd be thinking more about yourself).

While thinking about yourself being in another environment leads to less consciousness then just thinking about nothing, thinking about another environment without yourself in it leads to even less self consciousness then either of the two. That is because you just aren't thinking about yourself at all. If you are processing data in your environment it is like you are thinking about that environment, only less so, so processing data in your environment would increase your sense of self more so than thinking about nothing in your environment, but less so than thinking about your environment directly. By "your environment" I mean the area directly around you, the closer it is to you the more related it is to you, so the more it is going to cause you to think about yourself. If you look at trees in the far distance you aren't going to be as focused as if you were looking at someone right in front of you because your attention is on something less related to yourself.

In summary, when you think about your environment, or you being in an environment, your sense of self changes, (listed from most positive to least positive amounts of change) a) if you think about you being in your environment, b) if you are processing regular data in your environment c) if you are just in your environment not thinking, d) if you think about yourself in another environment, and e) if you just think about another environment (because you are removing you from yourself). This thinking about oneself leads to greater consciousness because that is what consciousness is, awareness of oneself which is going to increase a lot when you think about yourself (or have feelings and emotions about yourself).

Those rules apply unless the environment has data which is similar to yourself, say if there is a painting of yourself far away that you are looking at, it would cause you to think more about yourself then if you were just focusing on your immediate environment. So if the environment is just environmental, sensory stimulation those rules apply, but if there is something in the environments that causes you to think deeply about something then you are going to be either even more removed from yourself (if you are thinking deeply about something not related to yourself like a math problem or a person who is different from you) or even more related to yourself (greater consciousness) if you are thinking about something deeply which is similar to yourself (say a person similar to yourself, or an experience of yours was a personal experience about you).

That shows that if you think about consciousness as a short term thing, your consciousness changes all the time and drastically. For instance, one might have barely any consciousness at all if they are completely out of it (drunk, really unfocused, laughing really hard). During that time you simply have little or no short term consciousness. There are multiple different time spans of awareness, however, one is of your life in the long term (many years), the other is of your life in the short term (a few years), and another is of your life in its immediate, current phase (days or so) (or any combination of time). People about over 50 might have a consciousness for each 10 year or so span of their life, and they would constantly remember all 5. People are aware of themselves and their lives at different periods. The only thing that is very consistent that people have of themselves is their understanding of who they are, how they interact in the world, and how their emotions, feelings, and thoughts respond in similar instances. Those are things which don't change a lot based on the environment they are in, and that sense of self, or consciousness, is a more long term one. So long term consciousness is based off of how well you understand the psychology of your emotions, feelings, and thoughts, and also how those three interact as a whole to produce your long term psychological state/condition.

So having a larger memory isn't going to necessarily increase your consciousness a lot because it isn't going to lead to a greater understanding of yourself. What you remember of yourself changes your consciousness, but it doesn't increase or decrease it a lot unless it is a dramatic amount of difference in memory, like the difference in memory between a dog and a human. Unless the greater your memory the greater your emotional experience and you'd need to constantly remember all prior experiences in order to maintain the most advanced level of emotional experience you have. In that case a decrease in memory would decrease your emotional experience, and the more advanced ones emotional experience the more likely it is they are going to have a better understanding of themself.

That leads to the idea that certain emotional experiences lead to a greater sense of self more so than other emotional experiences. If someone was in a war they would have the emotional experience of understanding how they respond in combat, and their sense of self would then forever (or as long as they can remember) be a more action oriented one. So the deeper the emotional experience, the more it contributes to your self consciousness. The more individual the emotional experience, that is, the more related the experience is to yourself, the more the experience is going to increase your self consciousness. That means that there isn't just self consciousness, but people can be conscious about the world around them and other people, and that there is an overlap between self consciousness and world consciousness.

That is, if you have an experience with another person, you then become more aware of that person as well as more aware of yourself. So you'd have more consciousness of that person, and more self consciousness. The same idea goes if you have an emotional experience with an object, or group of objects (in the case of a war it might be something like guns). Going to war might increase someone's consciousness of weapons or danger. Consciousness therefore means awareness in general, not just self awareness. If you are aware of something, then you are conscious of it.

Most dictionary definitions of consciousness just list it as being the things people are most aware of. There are things to be aware of that aren't major things, things which you aren't "most" aware of. Awareness just happens to center around the self. That is a selfish view of the world. Someone could be only most aware of wrongdoing, more aware of wrongdoing than they are of themself, that is possible. If that were true for most people then consciousness would be defined as wrongdoing, not someone's interest, or awareness in themself.

So the best definition of consciousness is therefore "everything that someone is aware of". People are aware of things in both the short term and the long term. A fly is probably only aware of things in the short term, since it has almost no memory compared to a human. A human's consciousness can change drastically, however (their consciousness, or what it is that they are aware of in total). Conscious just means, "Are you aware in general", but consciousness means, "what are you aware of exactly".

The next question is, what are people usually most aware of? Most dictionary definitions have as definitions for consciousness things like awareness of ones surroundings, ones feelings, ones identity, things that people are usually most aware of. Those definitions are people's long term sense of consciousness. Over the long run, most of the things you are going to be aware of are going to be related to yourself somehow; therefore most of consciousness is based on the self. However, you can think about things that aren't related to yourself, and your thought changes drastically, so during periods of thought about things that aren't related to oneself that person is almost completely not focused on themself. It is impossible to be completely not focused on oneself because you are experiencing physical sensations from your body all the time (which are going to be about yourself), not just mental ones.

So someone can have consciousness about something, the question "what is consciousness" is like asking "what is awareness". Awareness is when you focus on certain things and therefore think about them and/or have more feelings and emotions about them. In review, consciousness means "awareness", "everything that someone is aware of", "everything that someone is aware of currently", or "everything that someone is aware of currently or during a certain period of time (say their life)". So you could ask, "what was your consciousness over the last 5 years". That would mean, over the last 5 years, what have you been aware of. The response could be "wrongdoing", "myself", or a large list of things. A more specific version of that would be to ask, "what are you aware of, and when are you aware of it", or "over the last five years what were you aware of, and when were you aware of it". If someone wants to know someone else's life time consciousness they could ask, "what were you aware of throughout your life". If someone wanted to know if someone was conscious about something (or what their consciousness was of something) they could ask, "what is your awareness of that thing", or "what is your consciousness of that" (for example, "what is your consciousness of war"). You could also say, "what does it truly mean to be human" that could also mean what is consciousness.

How This Chapter shows how Intelligence is intertwined with Emotion:

- Explaining the definition of consciousness shows how intelligence isn't just random thoughts and emotions, but some parts of intelligence are directed thoughts and directed emotions, and that direction is what makes someone conscious.

7.25 Curing Depression

Depression arises from any negative emotion. Therefore, to eliminate depression, negative emotions need to be eliminated.

Depression arises from wanting things that you can't have. You basically need to be satisfied with your current state/condition. Even thinking that although things are bad now, but there is hope for them to get better means you're satisfied with your current condition. If someone wants something that they can't have, they get depressed. Therefore that is the logical cause of depression.

That works on the small scale too in addition to the large, if you are unhappy with yourself in general, that is probably going to result in a larger depression than if you can't go to the store right away. If you want to go to the store right now, but can't, then it might make you sad, but that isn't as large an issue as if you are dissatisfied with something like your personal life or who you are in general.

What if there is something that will make you happy but you don't know about it? That is ok because thankfully there are only a few general causes of depression. The human condition can be studied and similar things that people want arise in each instance. Just go through everything that you might want but can't have and say in each instance, it's ok that I don't have that, I don't need everything.

Wouldn't ignoring something that you want but can't have be imposing blocks on yourself, that if you want something, you should let your emotions run free and let the desire go? Well if you do that, you're going to be upset. You basically somehow need to justify that your current condition is the best thing.

The best way to do this is to realize that each person is an individual and unique, and that a difference should be viewed as an asset. That if you are different in some way, that that way is positive, not negative. That other people appreciate you for who you are. You need to have confidence in who you are and the state your life is in.

Is having too much confidence in yourself arrogant? Yes it is slightly arrogant, but it also means that you have what you want. If someone has what they want, they are going to be confident. That won't be bad however, because people like people that are confident in themselves because they are easier to be around. Lower self confidence would cause someone to act differently. This is because they would be unsure that each thing they are going to do is going to be ok, so they are going to be hesitant and unsure, causing them to act different and more uncertain. Therefore confidence is the most important thing for someone to have in order to combat depression.

Confidence also eliminates fear. When you aren't confident you are afraid that life is failing you, you are afraid that there is something out there that you want but can't have. It is very important to not be afraid of anything. What if there is something you're afraid of but you don't know what it is? You need to go through everything that you might be afraid of, and eliminate that you are afraid of them.

What if you're afraid of fighting a lion? Something like that would be a test of how fearful you are in general. Once you pull up the fear emotion by doing something fearful, if you are more afraid than you should be then something is wrong. That was just a test. You shouldn't have a lot of fear in life for anything. You should have a lot of self confidence. So you shouldn't be too afraid to do something like fight a lion, you should, however, realize that it is probably going to cause you to die.

How is it possible to not be afraid of death? Surely everyone is afraid to die. Well it is perfectly possible. Think about the situation if you were not afraid of death. What would you be, and how would you be acting, if you weren't afraid to die. If you can imagine that, then you know that it is possible. If you can't imagine that then go up step by step. Take something you are just a little afraid of, and imagine doing that without fear. Then keep going up. Eventually you won't be too afraid of anything, including death.

Fear isn't necessary. Part of logic is the understanding of facts. So if you logically understand that you are going to die, that is ok. If you get a weird feeling when you think about death (aka fear) then you should realize that you don't really need that feeling. The feeling of fear is almost completely unnecessary. You don't need strong feelings of fear to remind yourself that you are going to die if you fight a lion, or to motivate you to run away. Maybe the emotion fear can't be eliminated completely, but the more that is eliminated, the more self-confidence you are going to have.

In fact, logically, eliminating any negative emotions is going to help eliminate depression. That is the definition of negative after all, bad and likely to cause sadness and therefore depression. Just go through the negative emotions of anger, fear, sadness, disgust and surprise. Try to go through anything that might cause those feelings and eliminate them. Also you can do the test like we did with the death test for fear. If you have a larger amount of that emotion than you should for an extreme example, (like death) then that is indicative that there is too much of that emotion in your system, that you are too afraid in general and need to reduce how much of the emotion fear is in your system.

Logically only positive emotions are good, and all negative emotions should be eliminated. They basically don't do any good. The only reason to have minor amounts of them in your system would be to cause a small, healthy amount of anxiety to keep you on edge, but the key word there is still small.

Wanting things that you can't have counts as a negative emotion which is called dissatisfaction. Also a lack of self confidence is a negative emotion because that is more likely to cause fear. If you have 100% confidence when fighting a lion you aren't going to be afraid.

Basically psychology doesn't need to be complicated. If psychology is complicated, then things like depressions can arise easily because there are complicated factors going on. Psychology, however, is actually simpler than it seems. Just imagine a person standing anywhere. This person is not doing anything; there are no inputs in and no outputs. If there are no inputs in and therefore no outputs, then there is no possibility for error (or a depression). Life doesn't get much more complicated than just standing around and doing nothing, so where could a depression arise from?

It is logical then that something like a slight confidence boost (say imaging having enough confidence to fight a lion) should raise someone out of a depression and into feeling normal, like how they would in the situation where they were just standing around, getting no inputs in and therefore no outputs (output like a depression).

In fact, if you imagine yourself just standing around doing nothing, not only are there no outputs, but you probably feel good about yourself too. There is a simple pleasure in just absorbing the surroundings. That means that humans are like cars, when in idle they are set to go at a minimum speed. They don't stop when you put them in drive but the engine keeps running at a slow pace. From where can a depression arise if our natural state is a happy one?

7.26 Unconscious Emotion Regulation and its Determinant in Humans: Cognition

The proper term for 'unconscious' emotion regulation is actually 'implicit' emotion regulation. Emotion regulation is typically considered to be more conscious and deliberative, however I think that the interesting and complex aspects of emotion regulation are the unconscious ones. If you think about it, people don't know all the complex ways in which their emotions change. All of the emotional changes that people experience occur at the unconscious level because emotion is so subtle and complex - people basically have no idea what is happening to them emotionally. Knowing you are experiencing one emotion is much different from understanding exactly what is going on.

Many different factors influence someones experience of emotion. The biggest factor in the experience of emotion is probably the strength of the emotions occurring. I was thinking that there would many more factors to discuss (since I am talking about emotion and is obviously a significant psychological phenomenon) but I guess there isn't. There should be a lot of factors that impact how emotion is felt and how it changes.

Since strength seems to be the only significant factor of emotional processing to discuss I will start there. It appears to me that emotion is triggered often and starts and stops frequently. Humans have a whole set of cognitive thoughts or unconscious mental decisions that start and stop emotion. For instance when they see something significant their mind has this stimulus categorized and responds to it in a way that has been programmed in - either from at birth or by previous emotional development.

So one thing a person might respond to is just seeing another person. That stimulus would trigger a complex emotional response, immediately upon seeing the other person the cognitive unit of 'compare myself with this person' or 'analyze this person' is engaged. The things the other person represents in your mind, the way the other person is emotionally significant, what the other persons current attitude and manner is, are all things that your mind tries to think about and picks up on initially as a pre-programmed response.

These 'pre-programmed' responses occur because there is a natural, fast, and complex way humans interpret emotional information. The significant emotional dispositions of other people (who they are), whatever it is they are emotionally communicating at the time (what they are projecting), and how your mind is prepared to accept, look at, and interpret that information are the factors that determine these pre-programmed emotional responses.

The automatic emotional response occurs instantly and continues to give feedback. People then start to think on their own after the initial response and their thoughts influence the emotions that are felt and (obviously) their thought process and the ideas that they have about the other person. I just used people meeting other people as an example of strong, instantaneous emotional decisions/responses, however whenever your mind processes any object it makes calculations about that object that come from pre-programmed cognitive structures.

Attention can lead to complex thought. When someone experiences an emotion their attention changes based off of that emotion. The emotion triggers a set of thoughts. The emotion triggers cognitive units of thought, and this is going to impact someones attention because the thoughts (or cognitive units, whatever you want to call them) are associated with certain emotions.

7.27 Unconscious (Implicit) Emotion Regulation, Mental Representation, Principles of Emotion and Cognitive Determinants of Emotion

How do emotions fluctuate and change? What principles, mental processes, and cognitive determinants govern feelings? The most obvious factor behind how emotion varies from individual to individual, from situation to situation, and from moment to moment; is appraisal theory. However, it is a more complicated question to ask how appraisals and mental processes affect changes in the nature of feeling and mind.

A process of appraisal can be considered the key to understanding that emotions differ for different individuals. Assuming a process of appraisal that mediates between events and emotions is the clue to understanding that a particular event evokes an emotion in one individual and not in another, or evokes an emotion at one moment, and no emotion, or a weaker or stronger one, at another moment. (This is because the evaluations (appraisals) (for example, someone steals your car and then you think 'that is bad that my got stolen, this is going to make me feel bad' and then you feel bad, the thought involved an appraisal of if the event was good or bad for you and if it was going to cause negative or positive feelings in you) that people make about events influence how they feel about those events). A process of appraisal also explains why an emotionally charged event elicits this particular emotion, and not another one, in this particular individual under these particular conditions.

The process of appraisal accounts for the fact that the arousal of an emotion depends upon the meaning of the event for the individual and explains why the emotion that is evoked often depends upon quite subtle aspects of that meaning. Arousal of emotions is determined by the interaction between events, the individual's conceptions or expectations as to what constitutes well-being for him or her and the individual's expectations that he or she will be able to deal or cope with the event and, if so, in what manner or how effectively.

However, all of someones thoughts are going to influence their feelings, not just their appraisals of events. People think things about the events that occur in their lives. They don't just ask if the event is good or bad, they form opinions of it, compare it to other events, analyze it, struggle with it, etc. Also, the sequence of events in someones life causes emotions to occur in a certain way as well, if one event follows another, it might influence the emotions felt for the previous or next event.

Also, a thought may have an emotion associated with it that you wouldn't expect or don't know about. If you think about it, with each thought, an emotion is going to be a result of the thought or would have helped bring up the thought. This is because thoughts are more complex that just the verbal thought - there is a lot of things the thought represents in your mind that also could be emotional triggers.

Why are appraisals such significant thoughts then? People must really care about how good or bad the events in their life are. Your assessment of how good or bad an event is is going to influence how good or bad the event actually is. That basically means that your attitude and thoughts about the event is going to influence feelings about the event. These thought processes are the most significant ones someone has about an event.

That makes sense - what else would someone think about something that just happened to them other than if it is good or bad for them anyway. They could think practical things about an event, but in the end it all really results if it is good or bad for them. People get emotional about if something is going to hurt them or help them, it seems.

All thoughts represent something larger in the mind and are more significant than they might appear by themselves. People have hopes, desires, and fears about each thought they think. Thoughts are also related. One thought might bring up similar hopes and fears as another thought, therefore helping to trigger or inhibit the other thought.

But surely thoughts are related more than just emotionally. Emotionally thoughts are related because they bring up similar or related emotions. But thoughts are also related because they represent similar physical things or other thoughts and ideas. Desires are ideas and thoughts, and these might be triggered by similar thoughts. When someone sees a piece of art, the art could represent desires that they have (and therefore trigger thoughts).

A child might be afraid of an animal. Since animals are similar to humans, the emotional response of the child to the animal it is afraid of might be similar to being afraid of a human. Physical the animal might look somewhat like a human. Animals and humans are certainly more related in how they look than humans and physical objects. Animals and humans both have emotions, and animals think to a certain extent. My point is that thoughts and emotional reactions have things in common with other thoughts and objects. They all represent similar and related things in the mind (such as emotions like hope, desire, fear, and beliefs).

This complex network of interacting ideas, emotions, and representations is going to determine how the emotions of humans fluctuate. Emotions and thoughts are related to each other because they each represent ideas, other thoughts (such as beliefs or facts) or other emotions. A simpler way to say that would just be that one emotion, event, or stimulus triggers a complex reaction in the mind. It triggers an intellectual reaction whereby the person goes through all the things that that event represents to them. This can be other physical things, complex thoughts and ideas (such as beliefs or facts), or hopes and other emotions.

7.28 Unconscious (Implicit) Emotion Regulation

Implicit emotion regulation is how someone moderates and changes their emotions automatically, beneath their awareness. Goals and intentions are going to play a large role in how this process occurs because they are a large source of emotions and feelings. People form many intentions which they aren't aware of, and these intentions are going to influence their emotions and the potential thoughts they might have.

When someone feels better but they don't know why, or when someone thinks something but they don't know what motivated them to think it, then it was clearly from the unconscious (such as unconscious feelings, thoughts, intentions and goals) which caused them to want to think the thought and generate the new emotion.

What is the difference between an unconscious goal and an unconscious intention? It is clear what the difference between those two terms when referring to there conscious function is - a goal is a large objective, an intention however is something that you want or intend where you are thinking that you are trying to do something right then. You are trying to accomplish something - that what an intention is. You have the intent to do something. You are striving to do that thing.

A goal, however, you aren't necessarily trying to achieve in the present time. You can put a goal aside or lower its priority. An intention you usually wouldn't do that with. When someone forms an intention, they try to do it right away. So a goal is basically a more important intention. If you intend to do something, and it is important for you, then it becomes a goal because goals are longer term or just more important.

This distinction is important because goals and intentions can be unconscious. People make goals and intentions about things in their lives all of the time, consciously and unconsciously. However, there are two types of unconscious goals/intentions - one type is very subtle, and the other type is a larger more obvious type of goal or intention.

A subtle unconscious goal or intention might be something very insignificant emotionally. For instance you might not want someone to come closer to you, so emotionally you might freeze up. This is so subtle you probably wouldn't notice that it is occurring consciously. However what happened unconsciously was that you recognized that you didn't want this person to come near you, and you unconsciously regulated your emotions so you would be feeling less. You could say that the other person made you afraid and that caused the emotional freezing, or it could be that it was an unconscious intention of yours to block out the other person because you didn't like them or want them coming near you.

That is just one example of a subtle, unconscious emotional event. There are constantly emotional things going on beneath one's notice. All of those emotional processes are regulated unconsciously. People are much more capable of manipulating their emotions unconsciously than the are consciously because there is much more going on unconsciously than consciously.

Some other examples of unconscious goals or intentions are seeking pleasure, trying to feel any single or set of emotions, trying to increase, decrease, or maintain any single or set of feelings, or trying to achieve some thought you had at some other point - such as a conscious goal of some sort of success in your life or something like that.

7.29 How the Mind Works, Principles of Emotion, and Mental States

The mind works primarily through various emotional principles - for instance striving for pleasure is a natural emotional process that people have little control over, and this process is going to be influenced by stimuli and cognition. Striving for stimuli or pleasure is one of the more important principles of emotion since clearly emotion is going to fluctuate and be influenced by stimulation, which often (and hopefully) takes the emotional form of 'pleasure'.

What exactly is a principle of emotion then, or, if emotion is so important to a mental state, what is a normal mental state? What happens differently to someones mind when they are under stress then when they aren't? What is the difference between a mental state and a mood? If someone is happy - that is a mood, if someone's mind is more or less competent, conscious or capable of performing then that is more of a mental state. Meditation is like a mental state - in that state the mind is doing certain specific things   (such as being calm in a way that is induced by certain thoughts or feelings). A mood, however, is just your general way of feeling (which you can feel for a long period of time and doesn't necessarily impact your performance). Someone can be in a mental state to do work, or be in one of the two most obvious mental states - conscious or not conscious.

My saying that doing work is a mental state is theoretical. It depends on how someone defines the term 'mental state'. There could be a endless number of mental states, or someone could define mental states to be states just related to doing work. Maybe for one job they have their own defined mental states where they need to be in a certain mental zone or whatever in order to perform a certain task.

It looks like this is much more complicated than it seems. If you think about it, there are going to be a lot of factors that influence someones mental state. There are ways of going into a meditative mental state, people can prepare their minds to go to work, to go to sleep, etc. Everyone knows they are in different states at different times, however it would be interesting to know what exactly is going on. For instance, in each of these states what is the person focused on, what are they capable of doing, how are they feeling, what are they thinking about (consciously and unconsciously), how conscious are they and what are they paying attention to.

7.30 Concentration and Emotions are Important Factors in Intelligence

People can concentrate in various ways, and one of these ways is imbedded in how a person's brain functions (their emotions, feelings and thoughts all contribute to a certain "brain structure" which would enable some people to concentrate more than others). All things which are harder to do and require a higher intelligence really require more concentration. Concentration is best understood when it is compared to a person's emotional mind; that is, emotion and concentration are contrary to each other because as emotional development and temporary emotion increase, concentration decreases. As adults age their emotional development grows and how emotional they are increases as they learn to separate out the things they enjoy from the things they don't, (as this is a sign of good emotional development) but their intelligence decreases. This must mean that something (probably emotion and emotional development) replaces the decline in intelligence that occurs as adults age. Emotion replaces it because that is the natural thing to happen. As animals use less and less of their conscious mind, they become more and more unconscious. For an animal with as large a brain as a human's being more emotional would mean that they could be very emotional. The larger brain size increases emotional capacity. Since brain size doesn't decrease over age the emotional capacity becomes used more as intellect goes down. When people are less intelligent, they tend to be more emotional because they have a more direct connection (they don't have to "go through" or "think through" their intellect) to their emotions.

A good example of how concentration can have a large impact on intelligence is seen through the example of some people who cannot read and comprehend complicated sentences, but are capable of hearing and comprehending these sentences in real life (Durell, 1969). It may mean they just aren't concentrating enough when they read as when they are listening. Listening leads to them being more interested in what is being said so they can focus on it deeper. The sound and/or social factors "wakes" them up and focuses their attention naturally. That means that solely because they were motivated their intelligence increased; that shows how emotion can influence intelligence.

Concentration is relative to emotion, which is unconscious thinking about something. Concentration is also another word for consciously or unconsciously thinking about something, usually when it is normally hard to think about that thing. That is, you need to concentrate more if you are being emotional or not focused in order to stay in focus, so concentration might then be better defined as thinking under pressure, or thinking in the absence of emotion. That is, someone very emotional would concentrate and that would be thinking under pressure, the pressure coming from the emotion, and someone non-emotional might just concentrate without having to battle wild emotions or distractions.

While concentration means thinking against the perils of disruptions and emotion, you can also concentrate when you're not being disrupted. So any higher-level thinking can be viewed as concentration. This means that when you're not concentrating, you're doing more simple things, since those things wouldn't be higher-level intellect. People can't think about several emotions at once, so therefore emotional things are simpler than intellectual ones (so simple that you can't think about them consciously easily – too simple). That is, as emotion increases, conscious thinking decreases, therefore the number of things you recognize yourself as "doing" also decreases. This happens because people can only think of a few things at a time, and if one of the things you are thinking about is emotion (which you would do just by being emotional) then you wouldn't be capable of thinking as much consciously (remember emotion is unconscious thought) and that this lower thought capacity would be reflected in a lower intelligence. That is, unconscious emotional processes can replace the higher level functioning used in intelligence as your brain ages and physical factors in your mind decrease your intelligence you might accommodate that change by spending time and energy you'd otherwise spend remembering things and figuring things out by putting your mind into emotion. In the absence of thought you retreat into feelings because they are all your mind can physically handle. As people age their minds physically change to accommodate emotion more than intellect, which decreases. It could be that you understand how your brain is changing, and your emotional mind understands that as well, so you emotionally develop to accommodate your changing mental wiring. That is, as you get dumber (in certain ways) you learn to relax more because you don't have to think as much. You retreat to become more embedded in your feelings and more sensitive to them because the intellect that was covering them up (partially blocking them) is gone. Younger adults might be wilder than older adults, but this does not make them more emotional because emotional means being affected by your emotions, so the younger adults might have a lot of emotion but their intellect isn't affected by it, therefore they are less emotional.

That is, it could be that your emotional development happens to correspond with the physical changes in your brain. That is demonstrated by imagining an adult in a child's mind (say around 3) it simply wouldn't work because the mental wiring is so different. The child is simply too interested in the world and this greater interest is mirrored by faster learning connections in the brain. That is fitting because if you are interested in something, you want to learn about it. As you get older you want to learn less and your ability to learn mirrors your desire to learn. This coincidence is likely a product of good evolution. Learning uses higher level functioning because you need to draw conclusions based on data for the first time, and it is going to be harder to come to conclusions the first time you learn something then when you implement that learning later on. Using what you learned requires much less brain functioning because you aren't getting used to new material which may require a different way to think about that material (it would probably require a new way since by definition you are learning).

Emotion is really any disturbance from concentration, which can be seen as higher-level intellect. So as emotion increases, your conscious concentration goes down, and therefore your conscious intellect goes down (that is when emotion increases a lot such that your willpower cannot overcome it, say during any highly emotional time like crying). But what then is unconscious intellect? It seems that unconscious intellect would be things like emotional intelligence, that is emotional intelligence would be processed unconsciously, since it is emotional. You can think about how "cool" something is but you don't have a conscious thought process about it, you have an unconscious emotional one about it so therefore it is emotional intelligence and having more of that type of intellect might make you more emotional (because you are thinking and processing more things unconsciously, which means you are processing them with emotion). That means that emotional intellect is really just an understanding of things that make you feel, and therefore when you use this intellect you are having feelings so large you can usually identify that you are feeling something, like in the example where you identify how "cool" something is you probably are experiencing an emotion of enjoyment if the object is very cool. If the object is neutral (not cool or uncool) then you would still "feel" your emotions as your mind delves into the emotional part of your brain in order to figure out if you like it or not. You can test that for yourself; just think of a neutral object and ask, "How cool is that" – you become slightly more emotional when you ask the question because you have to think deeply in order to figure out the answer. If you ask the question of "how cool is that" to something cool then it makes you feel good because it is a cool object (this happens because it causes you to think deeply about how cool the object is, and think deeply means thinking more about how cool the object is, and since the object is cool you are going to enjoy thinking about it).

If you think about it emotion is really just things that distract you. Emotion and conscious concentration are completely contrary to each other; they are opposites. If something happens to you that is a disruption (like emotion) then you simply cannot concentrate as well, because you were disrupted. As in the cool example, when you think about how cool something is you start to have feelings about it, and this distracts you from other things that you might be thinking for that time period. That is, it feels like emotion "disrupts" you because it is unconscious, so it disrupts your consciousness because it causes you to feel which disrupts your conscious mind and you recognize your sense of self fundamentally as being a conscious being, not an unconscious one. In this way it is fitting that emotion would replace higher level intellect (as adults age), because it is clearly separated from it. That is, thinking about how cool the object is thought just like regular thinking is thought, you can feel that in your mind – this indicates that since emotion and thinking take up the same space they cannot exist concurrently.

Emotion feels like it is disruptions and unconscious thought (that is, because it is not logical so it disrupts your sense of logic and the rational continuity of life). When I say "rational continuity of life" I mean that you need to be logical in order to function in a way that would continue your life. You need to have a basic understanding of who you are and where you are and what you are doing (which having higher order brain processes as shown in a good learning ability helps). That understanding is often absent in dreams, where you are mostly emotional and you clearly don't know what you are doing because if you did, you'd be aware that the dream you are in doesn't make sense (as most dreams make little sense). Emotion doesn't just disrupt people in that way (less logical continuity of life) but it would also cause someone's mind to become more emotionally chaotic. In other words, emotion is unconscious because it cannot be understood. If emotion was understood, then it would be conscious and it wouldn't be emotion. That is why emotion disrupts consciousness and clear thinking, because it by nature is unclear and not understood. When something not understood such as emotion interacts with things that are understood (such as things in regular thinking and intellect) then the clearer thinking becomes disrupted, because something that is not clear and not understood in nature is only going to add components that don't make sense, instead of adding logical information which does make sense. That means that when emotion is on, thinking is off. Thinking and emotion cannot exist in the same space, because thinking by definition is something you understand, and emotion is something you don't (you understand emotion to some degree, that is people can say, "I like that" which shows understanding of their emotions, but emotion is less understood than non-emotion related thoughts such as math, which is much more exact). To deal with this your mind must turn off emotion in order to think, and thinking off in order to feel; thus your brain separates periods of thinking from periods of emotion. The two components of intellect and emotion never exist together, they are by nature they are separate (in terms of time and separate in terms of nature).

If you are disrupted, you think about what happened unconsciously, so emotions and disruptions are the same (that is because disruptions cause people to become more emotional since they get so upset that they got disrupted, which in turn causes them to think about the disruption unconsciously, which is why emotion is unconscious thought - or an unconscious control process of conscious thought that is the mechanism by which the disruption causes you to stop; but what drew your attention to the disruption in the first place, however, was something unconscious because it was so fast - this quick attention to the disruption is emotion, and that is why emotion is thinking unconsciously). That further shows how emotion is different from higher level, conscious intellect.

If you are more emotionally developed does that mean that you think more unconsciously and therefore think less consciously? Emotion or unconscious thinking would replace your decreased intellect, and this is fitting because emotion also takes away from conscious thinking anyway because you only have so much space in your mind (you can only think about so many things at once, and it is harder to think about more things than less). That is, it is fitting that emotion would replace intellect because you are still capable of thinking of the same number of things, so you'd need to replace brain power used for intellect with something in order to maintain the same mental activity overall. That is, your brain still has the same power (which could be thought of as your number of neurons) but they are just used differently. That could also be thought of as when you age the number of activities you do remains the same, so you still need to use just as much brain power. When viewed that way humans can be compared highly with other animals, that is, most of life is really just doing simple, animal like actions. Someone could do something intellectual, but this isn't going to result in a significant amount of more brain activity than non-human animals. Just because non-human animals don't think in words doesn't mean that they don't feel similar emotions and feelings as humans. If one animal likes another they have a feeling about that. A human's ability to put that feeling into words doesn't necessarily add that much emotion or feeling. Most of the feelings people have come from external sensory stimulation, not internal (such as thinking) so therefore most emotions humans have are going to be similar to other animals (dogs, cats, etc). Therefore it becomes obvious that humans maintain a similar level of activity when they age as when they are younger. And a human's intellect can be seen as just a mental blocking of their emotions; especially when compared with other animals in the world. Most emotions come from real sensory stimulation, not just sensory stimulation that you think of in your head say when reading a book. Doing the actions of the book in real life would generate more emotion than reading about them, for sure. So as people age they still get about the same stimulation, and this stimulation either needs to be felt or blocked out.

A good example of "blocking" emotional stimulation can be seen when certain behaviors of dogs are compared with that of humans. When a submissive (possibly younger) dog meets a more aggressive older dog (say the meeting between an American bull dog and a regular dog) the younger dog can show his/her submission by nipping the dominant dog's snout. That is because the emotional interaction is so intense (due to the dominant dogs aggresivity and potential to harm the younger dog, who it views as annoying) that the submissive dog would be viewed as ignoring the dominant dog if it didn't engage in a very friendly social interaction such as a nipping on the mouth. The nipping relieves the enormous tension between the two dogs, it is a way of saying, "it is ok we are friends". The need for such a nipping comes from too much emotion between the two animals. If humans were in the dogs' skins such an interaction wouldn't occur because the emotional intensity wouldn't occur in the first place. The humans' intellect would block the emotional interaction, they simply wouldn't be aware of it because they aren't as aware of their emotions, the dog is more impulsive and responds directly to his/her emotions. The human might be intellectually aware that one dog is dominant and that this might be a problem, but they ignore it. Ignoring it would cause anxiety for the human in the dog's body and the human wouldn't know why. The human cannot give into their emotions and accept that there is a problem, and that it needs to be resolved.

This problem (the problem is there is a dominant dog and a submissive dog, and the submissive dog would be upset that there is a dog more dominant than it, and the dominant dog would be preoccupied by how annoying the non-dominant dog is, because it is so inferior to it that it is annoying, also there is a need to establish dominance) of dominance can be seen with other animals as well. If there are two roosters and too few hens the roosters are going to fight. If a human was in the rooster's body (but had the rooster's emotions such as a desire for the hens) then it would have to fight it out with the other rooster in order to relieve that anxiety of desire for dominance. The human is simply less in touch with its emotions than the rooster. That is, the rooster is capable of such desire for the hens that it is going to fight over the hens each time, humans on the other hand wouldn't "have" to have a fight over anything that is emotional, they simply don't experience emotions as well because they have too much intellect. Even though the rooster's brain is much smaller than a humans, it is capable of much more emotion because of the lack of intellect. Emotional conflicts that aren't solved then generate anxiety because they aren't solved, so sometimes a lack of emotion leads to people being dumber instead of more intelligent. In fact more emotion means that animals would spend more time dealing with emotional issues, thereby causing less anxiety. It doesn't appear that animals other than humans have the same level of anxiety or depression as a human. How often do you see a dog with a depression or long term anxiety? From those examples it is clear how intellect is a block of emotional stimulation, so if intellect (or memory, which is a part of intellect) is removed the result would be that the animal (including humans) would become more emotional.

Instead of intellect blocking emotions, it could be that intellect is simply changing the emotions to make them go away. That is like with the rooster example, a human might not be aware that there is a problem because he/she isn't as in touch with its emotions (desire for the hens), or with the dog example he/she might not be aware that one dog is different from it and this causes a social issue consciously, but unconsciously he/she would be aware. So the tension still exists, only unconsciously, so the emotions related to the problem still exist. It is only that the human is blocking them out because of his/her conscious mind, which is capable of blocking the unconscious. He/she isn't aware of these unconscious emotions because he/she is thinking too much (and thinking is a conscious process, so humans are conscious because they think, but this leads to a blocking of emotion). That could be viewed as that humans think in a way fundamental to their psychology and consciousness, so fundamental and important that it interferes with their emotions. That means that intellect is intricately tied in with emotions. If something is tied in with something else then as one increases ones awareness of the increase increases he/ she is going to be aware directly proportionally of the larger portion (that is rather obvious). So as intellect decreases, the emotions that were always there from the large amounts of sensory stimulation and social factors become uncovered.

Just as emotion takes away from intellect, intellect also takes away from emotion. That is, if you are thinking about something you can't be feeling as many things, because you can only think about so many things at the same time, and emotion is really just unconscious thought. If you have less conscious thinking then your memory is going to be less because you are thinking less about stuff. That is, emotion uses processes in the brain to think that relate to emotional things, like feelings, not intellectual, concrete things which you would be capable of remembering. Emotional things are complicated things which involve feelings and people have a very hard time thinking about them consciously (for this reason when people feel emotion it is almost all unconscious, that is, you do not associate emotion with a sense of self). Unconscious thinking isn't as clear and defined as conscious thinking, so more unconscious thinking instead of conscious thinking would reflect less of an intellect (because it is less clear and defined, "cloudy"). What it might lead to is a greater emotional understanding, however. That is, it doesn't help with concrete learning, like in school, since its nature is not concrete, but it might help with emotional learning, since its nature is emotional. That is, if you spend more time being emotional it might be that you have more insight into how it is that you are feeling, and have a more direct connection to your feelings.

The reason that less intellect would lead to greater emotion is because emotion is by definition feeling. And people don't "feel" their thoughts. That is, thought doesn't lead instantaneously to feelings. Thoughts can lead to feelings, that is you can direct which feelings you are going to have by thinking about certain things, but the thoughts themselves are not feelings. The thoughts are instantaneous; the feelings take time and linger in your mind. That is why there is an almost endless source of feeling, because you feel them and this feeling is more profound than something you don't feel. It could almost be said that thoughts are just ideas, and feelings are real things. The ideas might generate feelings, but not directly. The reason that feelings are such a source of emotion and feeling is because feelings are more similar to direct feelings which you get from touching things, feeling things, smelling things, tasting things, hearing things and seeing things (the 5 senses). Stimulation of any of the 5 senses leads directly to feeling. It would seem like there would be an overabundance of such sensory stimulation if your intellect was taken away. That is why other animals' minds are smaller than humans, because without the intellect if they had such a large mind to just process sensory information it would lead to an overload of sensory data. That is why most of the human's mind is used for intellectual endeavors, and the feeling part of the brain is very small. In fact, how much people feel compared to how much they think is mirrored in the proportion of the size of the feeling part of the brain to the thinking part. That makes a lot of sense. People think much more than they feel. Animals other than humans tend to feel much more than they think. Just imagine you stopped thinking and just felt the world around you, like if you were a dog. That when you encountered a situation when you needed to think you instead just responded to feelings directly. If you did that then with the submissive/dominant dog example you would respond to the dominant dog (if you were the submissive dog) like the submissive dog does. You would feel the feeling "scared" when you encountered the dominant dog and feel that you would want to suck up, you'd do that by kindly nipping the dominant dog's jaw. Instead people don't respond directly to their feelings but they think about things. When they see the dominant dog they would think about the dog and not realize as well that they are scared. This would cause a tension in the relationship between dominant and submissive dog because it would appear that the submissive dog isn't scared when it should be, and is therefore threatening the dominant dog's dominance. That would cause both dogs anxiety and probably lead to the dominant dog growling at the submissive dog and the submissive dog running away.

In review, intellect disrupts emotion just as much as emotion disrupts intellect. This is because too much feeling or emotion can disturb an intellect because the intelligent mind is very powerful and can magnify the sensations and feelings it receives from the emotional/sensory part of its mind. Intellect also disrupts emotion because it blocks it out or minimizes it. It is capable of doing this because it is so much larger and more powerful than emotion. That is emotion is weak, but is capable of being large if allowed. It is like a river, emotion has a wide stream but it is moving slowly and has a weak current. Intellect has just as wide a stream but is moving much faster. Thus when intellect meets emotion, as it does in the mind, more "water" from the intellect comes in. If the water from the intellect is reduced, however, there is plenty of water from the emotion to take its place. The lake where the water from the emotion comes from is almost infinitely large, because people can feel anything, anytime. The lake behind the intellect however is more limited, so when you have nothing to think about you resort to feelings. This may make some people feel stagnant, (if they aren't thinking) because they otherwise wouldn't be moving around all the time. So for optimum enjoyment/health people either move around all the time, or think all the time, or do one or the other or both all the time. Before modern civilization people were hunter-gatherers and they moved around all the time, and probably thought less. In modern civilization it is more common for people to think all the time, and move around a lot less. That is a significant change. People might be more emotional and in touch with their feelings in pre-civilization time when they were exposed to more sensory and physical stimulation. Physical stimulation is a feeling, you get direct feelings from physical stimulation just as you get direct feelings from external sensory stimulation.

That is, either you are interacting with the world or you are thinking, and if you are interacting with the world you are receiving direct sensory stimulation, which leads directly to feelings. Sometimes intellectual topics lead to feelings, but they rarely lead to deep feelings (things like extremely intense arguments might generate deep feelings, and no one can handle those arguments all the time). Intellect leads to fewer feelings than real sensory input because intellect only leads to thought. How many thoughts can you think of that are more intense than doing the actual thought in real life? I cannot think of any. Real feelings in the brain mostly come from sensory stimulation and emotion, or unconscious thought. If a male sees an attractive female he might feel things and therefore get emotional, but he doesn't have to think anything consciously to feel those things. So even though there are complicated thought processes (unconsciously) going on about the female, it was still sensory stimulation which triggered the emotion. That is, the sensory stimulation lead to no conscious thought that would be related to having a higher intellect. So that same person could feel all those things even if they had a lower intellect or consciousness (conscious mind) because the thoughts generated from seeing the female in that instance were unconscious. You can only think of a few conscious thoughts when the female is seen because you can only think so fast consciously, but you can think much faster unconsciously, and if it occurs unconsciously it is going to lead to emotion, because that is what emotion is, unconscious thought. Emotion is unconscious thought because if it occurs unconsciously it is something you are going to "feel" instead of "think".

This emotional nature of emotion (separate from higher order thinking or learning ability) is best demonstrated during dreaming, where a person is entirely unconscious and therefore one can see how emotions (which are unconscious thoughts) function. Dreams are random, chaotic and rarely make sense – that is a reflection of the nature of emotion itself. During a dream you rarely know who you are and things occur which often reflect that you really don't know where you are. There isn't a strong sense of self in dreams because you can't think clearly about yourself. "Thinking" is something which doesn't really occur in dreams, because if you were thinking you'd realize that you were dreaming, and your mind would switch from its unconscious thinking which consists of making up an elaborate story for a dream to conscious thinking where you wouldn't do that, or be capable of making up such a complex story and complex visual data that quickly. Emotion can really be defined then just as complicated confusion, such as exists in dreams, which are almost entirely emotional.

Dreams are so out of the ordinary in order to generate more feeling and emotion. The out of the ordinariness in dreams, however, also makes them less logical and make less sense. This means that in order for something to be emotional, it needs to not make sense; if it made sense, then it would be conscious thought not emotion, and that emotion therefore could be defined simply as stuff that doesn't make sense that you think about, not just as unconscious thought. And "stuff that doesn't make sense" isn't going to be remembered because it isn't stuff that you can think about consciously because it doesn't make sense. Dreams still make sense to some degree, since there are events in them which are at least somewhat real. So while emotions make some sense, they still make less sense than conscious thought. That is, if you are feeling a lot then are you emotional, and if you are emotional then a lot of stuff is going on in your brain. It could be that emotional development causes people to focus more on things they enjoy as they get older and block out the things which they don't like (this makes sense as it would be good emotional development) and that therefore they get to be more emotional and experience emotions better. That is, maybe people can separate themselves from the things they don't enjoy and attach themselves to the things they do. Adults might even seem to be asking the question, "how does that relate to my emotions?" (Since they learn to separate out things they like from things they don't like better, they'd have to relate everything to their emotions more.) This might mean that adults are capable of being both more distant and more "close" than teens/younger adults because of their emotional development, they simply don't treat things as equal anymore and possibly as a result gain more feeling. The down side of getting older on the other hand is that the things you enjoyed before are now older and you potentially don't enjoy them as much because of that (they are less "fresh"). More unconscious thinking (emotion) probably also helps to maintain a more emotionally developed mind, as emotionally developed minds would need to think more about their emotions since they have more of them. This means that as people get older they would get more unconscious, but more intelligent emotionally.

Evidence for the idea that adults learn to separate out emotional events from ordinary ones and emphasize the emotional more comes from studies in autobiographical memory retrieval. In a study done by Dijkstra and Kaup (2005) younger and older adults were tested for autobiographical memory retrieval. Older adults were more likely to selectively retain memories with distinctive characteristics, such as being self-relevant and emotionally intense, particularly when remote memories were involved.

In another study by Charles, Mather and Carstensen (2003) the forgettable nature of negative images for older adults was tested. Young, middle-aged and older adults were shown images on a computer screen and after given a distraction task, were asked first to recall as many as they could and then to identify previously shown images from a set of old and new ones. The relative number of negative images compared with positive and neutral images recalled decreased with each successively older age group. Since it is clear people don't want to remember negative images as much, the study shows how age and emotional development cause people to select what they like more. This would cause people to "relax" more. That is, as adults get older and their intellect decreases, this lack of intellect enables them to be more in touch with their emotions and be more capable of selecting the more positive images.

Memory tests (R.t. Zacks, G Radvasky, and L. Hasher (1996)) show that young adults perform better than older adults when told to remember and forget data. The older adults remembered less than the younger adults when told to remember, and when told to forget data they remembered more than the younger adults.

The results show that younger adults have better control over their minds than older adults. A greater emotional makeup of the older adults is likely a consequence of this. Emotions would lead to less "mental willpower" which would enable younger adults to direct their thinking and to forget when told to forget, and remember when told to remember.

A paper by Einstein and Mcdaniel (1990) investigated the ability of old versus younger people to remember to carry out some action in a future time (known as prospective memory or PM). They suggested that different patterns might emerge between situations in which the PM target is triggered by some event (e.g. "when you meet John, please give him this message"), and those that are time based (e.g., "remember to phone your friend in half an hour"). Their work showed age-related decrements in time-based but not event-based tasks (Einstein, Mcdaniel, Richardson, Guyn & Cunfer, 1995). In my view that would indicate that the event based tasks were more emotional than the time based ones. That is, old people are programmed to work based off of emotional events that occur in real life, not based off something unemotional like time, which occurs all the time and isn't associated with emotional events. Since they forgot more on the time based tasks but not on the event based ones, it suggests that older adults are cued into emotional events more than the younger adults because there wouldn't be a discrepancy between the two. It is clear that the event based task is more emotional than the non-event based task because the non-event based task doesn't occur along with an event. That is, the event is a trigger for the old adult to remember the task. Even if the older adult is more motivated to remember the event in the beginning, they still aren't going to remember it later on unless this motivation is "triggered" again. That is, it is something unconscious (motivation, emotion) which helps them to remember the event. The motivation can be triggered better by the event based task because the motivation comes from the task itself, so they attribute a greater amount of emotion to the recipient(s) of the task. Events are simply more emotional than non-events.

You think of yourself as primarily conscious, therefore anything unconscious would take away from your consciousness because you can only think about so many things at the same time. If one of those things is unconscious that you are "thinking" about (and thinking about emotion is going to be difficult at best) then it would make you more confused because you would lose more of your conscious, clear, defined sense of self. That is, your sense of self is a clear and focused one (different from emotion, which is not clear). Your sense of self can't be an emotional one, because emotion doesn't really make any sense (already shown as in dreams) so you can't really think about emotion consciously, because it defies conscious thinking or logic. So since your sense of self is what you think about consciously, you are not going to think of yourself as emotional, you are going to think of yourself as more logical than emotional and if you do call yourself emotional that just means emotional relative to other people. That shows that emotion is clearly different in nature from higher order logical processes. And that therefore as intellect goes down as people age as adults it is possible and easy for emotion to go up, because it is clearly separate from intellect. The idea you have of yourself is as a functional being, not an un-functional and chaotic emotional one (that is, if you were solely emotional, not logical, you wouldn't be able to do anything, you'd just feel and not think – like a frog).

In review, as people age they learn to separate out what they like from what they don't like, and this ability causes them to gain more emotion, and emotion, being chaotic and unclear in nature, clearly works differently in the brain than intellect does. Emotions are chaotic; they permeate all your thoughts and have an affect on them, like a cloud. When someone is emotional it certainly seems like your entire mind is affected. Some emotions even have physical effects. More evidence that emotion doesn't use the same brain processes as memory and learning ability can be seen during very emotional times, like during sex or crying, where ones concentration is less. Concentration is needed to maintain intellect, and emotion is clearly different from concentration (as when you are very emotional during sex or crying you cannot concentrate). You can't memorize multiplication tables (which to do you'd need to concentrate) during sex or crying.

If an adult is intelligent at the same time that he/she is emotional then he/she is relatively less emotional because the intellect balances the emotion. So older adults would be considered to be more emotional because their intellect (or learning ability) is less (if older adults have more emotional intelligence then that wouldn't make them less emotional because to use emotional intelligence you don't "think" to figure out the answer but you feel. Emotional intelligence is therefore a sophisticated way of being emotional that animals other than humans might or might not have). That is, younger adults are wild and they are smart. They would still be considered to be less emotional though since a greater portion of their brain is intellect. Animals (other than humans) would be considered to be even more emotional than humans because they have almost no intellect. Emotional is acting instead of thinking, and all animals do is act, not think. Younger adults could then be viewed as acting and thinking at the same time with a higher proportion of intellect than older adults, if you don't think that older adults have a greater emotional intelligence than younger, that is.

The statement "people and their intellect are based on emotions" is a complicated one. They are based off of their higher emotions and their lower emotions. There is really no such thing as "no emotion" because people they are always thinking, consciously or unconsciously, and that is what emotion is. Sometimes it appears as if they have no emotion, but they are still thinking about things, they still have a memory and they are still using it, processing data and sensory inputs. Those things all cause thought and therefore emotion.

How then could someone be called non-emotional? It must be that they are feeling less, that is if they are concentrating deeply for a very long period of time then they might be a deep thinker that isn't really wavering in their feelings, just simply thinking about things and not really doing anything interesting that would invoke a lot of emotion, or unconscious thought.

Many older adults complain about being too occupied, both emotionally and physically. That is better seen in very old people whose brains are decaying, for whom even tiny mental tasks can wear out their mind. It isn't that their mind is being worn out; it is that they already lost most of their intellect but the pauses are filled with emotion. That is what animals are like, the experience you get from animals is an emotional one, not an intellectual one. Therefore animals spend more time being emotional. Emotional in that context means feeling, animals spend more time using unconscious thought and "feeling" the world around them. That is good evidence that as intellect, learning ability and memory decrease it is replaced with emotion. That is because emotion doesn't need to increase, it simply needs the block of intellect to be removed. People were already thinking about enough things consciously and unconsciously. That is, someone's unconscious mind is really being partly blocked at least as a younger adult, but when intellect is removed the unconscious becomes unveiled (like how animals are unconscious) and the person becomes more emotional as a result.

Evidence for the connection between higher amounts of emotion and a lower intellect can be found in test studies done on people with a depressed mood. In a meta-analysis done by Vreeswijk and De Wilde (2004) a confirmation of the connection between overgenerality and depression was done. The depressed patients were less specific in recalling their memory than the non-depressed.

Since being emotional is rated by how much proportionally larger the emotional part of your mind is than the intellectual part, older people do get more emotional since intelligence decreases over age. However they don't necessarily get more emotion as they age, they simply get more of it relative to their intellect. The lowering of the intellect, however, would make them more in touch with their emotions and capable of greater emotional regulation (as evidenced by the study where successively older age groups remembered more and more of the positive images). They aren't likely to get significantly more emotional, however because the amount of sensory stimulation they are receiving is going to be similar to what they received when they were younger. The only thing that would go down is internal stimulation or thinking which goes down from a lowering of intellect.

As adults age from 20-74 their IQ (Wechsler Adult Intelligence Scale) declines steadily (Kaufman, Reynolds and Mclean (1989). The verbal IQ actually stays about the same but it is performance IQ that decreases. From the postulates in this paper the conclusion would therefore be that verbal IQ is somehow related to emotions. Performance IQ is clearly not related to emotions because it tests mostly visual abilities. Verbal isn't likely to go down because the things it tests have to do with emotion and emotional control of attention. You cannot control how effective you are doing visual stuff, however because it requires concentration to visualize objects because there is less motivation to visualize then there is to just think. Thinking is easier than visualizing because people are used to thinking about anything, however they usually only visualize things they want to visualize, not things that are going to be tested on the IQ exam. That is, you can use emotion to control thought but you cannot use emotion to control your basic intelligence as would be reflected in visual ability tests (performance IQ).

The "willpower" of adults won't decrease as adults age. The willpower can direct a mind for under 20 second periods, and under 20 seconds is the time that it takes to do most intellectual tasks. Like a math problem. They could repeat the focus they put in every 20 seconds, "spike" their mind every 20 seconds or so to maintain this intelligence. The things on the performance test don't require that much focus, either you know them or you don't. Note that three of the verbal tests test mention attention or concentration specifically (which relate to willpower which relates to emotion as already stated). And the other parts of the verbal test measure things which are also going to relate to emotion such as information acquired from culture (you are emotionally interested in your culture) and ability to deal with abstract social conventions, rules and expressions (you are emotionally interested in social events) and verbal reasoning (tests things that occur in everyday life which you are emotionally attached to). The performance test on the other hand doesn't test things that are likely to go down because of increased emotion. The performance test tests things that are more intellect related than emotion related, that is visual things require a more intellectual, flexible mind to move objects around in your head. While the verbal subtests just require some motivation to perform (only one component of verbal tests working memory (which isn't that emotional and wouldn't be subject to changes in concentration) - one component wouldn't have a significant impact on the result).

Wechsler Adult Intelligence Scale

Verbal Subtests

Information

Degree of general information acquired from culture (e.g. Who is the premier of Victoria?)

Comprehension

Ability to deal with abstract social conventions, rules and expressions (e.g. What does - Kill 2 birds with 1 stone metaphorically mean?)

Arithmetic

Concentration while manipulating mental mathematical problems (e.g. How many 45c. stamps can you buy for a dollar?)

Similarities

Abstract verbal reasoning (e.g. In what way are an apple and a pear alike?)

Vocabulary

The degree to which one has learned, been able to comprehend and verbally express vocabulary (e.g. What is a guitar?)

Digit span

attention/concentration (e.g. Digits forward: 123, Digits backward 321.)

Letter-Number Sequencing

attention and working memory (e.g. Given Q1B3J2, place the numbers in numerical order and then the letters in alphabetical order)

Performance Subtests

Picture Completion

Ability to quickly perceive visual details

Digit Symbol - Coding

Visual-motor coordination, motor and mental speed

Block Design

Spatial perception, visual abstract processing & problem solving

Matrix Reasoning

Nonverbal abstract problem solving, inductive reasoning, spatial reasoning

Picture Arrangement

Logical/sequential reasoning, social insight

Symbol Search

Visual perception, speed

Object Assembly

Visual analysis, synthesis, and construction

Optional post-tests include Digit Symbol - Incidental Learning and Digit Symbol - Free Recall.

There is more evidence that emotion plays a role in intelligence. In a study done by Bartolic et al. (1999) the influence of negative and positive emotion on verbal working memory was tested. Their data showed significantly improved verbal working memory performance for positive emotions and a significant deterioration in verbal working memory during negative emotion. That shows how emotion can manipulate intelligence in the short term, as working memory is a short term ability. Therefore, however, long term intellect (like the rest of the verbal IQ test other than working memory) might be manipulated or under the control of long term emotions. It seems like your ability to learn all the rest of the verbal IQ tests would go up during the period of increased emotion as in this study, only it is hard to test for that. But that ability over the long run would be reflected in no decline in verbal IQ scores, and there isn't. That is, it isn't likely that just verbal working memory would increase due to increased emotion; that was just the only thing that they tested for. The subject probably became motivated overall and this motivation and good mood gave him/her greater mental powers, not just a better verbal working memory.

As adults age their explicit memory goes down Howard (1988) but their implicit memory stays about the same. Howard describes implicit memory as the ability to successfully complete memory tasks that do not require conscious recollection. Since emotion is unconscious, that lack of decline would provide further evidence that emotional process don't decrease with age, but more intellectual ones do. That itself provides evidence that the emotional part of the brain is separated from the intellectual. The emotional part of the brain and the intellectual part still interact, however.

Emotion can enhance or detract from intellect, and intellect can enhance or detract from emotions. In the long run intellect does not disrupt emotion, but in the short term intellect and emotions intermingle and disrupt each other. It was shown how emotions are separate from intellect, and how therefore concentration (which can be defined as thinking under the pressure of emotion [since to give undivided attention you couldn't be disturbed by emotional factors]) is an important part of intelligence (such as memory). When people's intellect is removed they become more emotional, as this is what is left. The source of emotion (sensory stimulation) is so large that it can never be ignored. Intellect, however can be ignored and emotion would rise up in its place. In the case of adults aging this "ignoring" of intellect happens as the mind physically gets older and some of the intellect is removed. This reveals the idea that humans have the ability to hold off emotion and do intellectual endeavors, or to indulge and bask in emotion if they want to (and switch between the two) sometimes as fast as a split second, and they can switch from one to the other for years.

BIBLIOGRAPHY

Bartolic et al., 1999 E.I. Bartolic, M.R. Basso, B.K. Schefft, T. Glauer and M. Titanic-Schefft, Effects of experimentally-induced emotional states on frontal lobe cognitive task performance, Neuropsychologia 37 (1999) pp. 677-683.

Charles, S.T., Mather, M., & Carstensen, L.L. (2003). Aging and emotional memory: The forgettable nature of negative images for older adults. Journal of Experimental Psychology General, 132, 2, 310-24, June.

Dijkstra, K. & Kaup, B. (2005). Mechanisms of autobiographical memory retrieval in younger and older adults. Memory Cognition, 33, 5, 811-20, July.

Durrell, D. D. (1969). Listening comprehension versus reading comprehension. Journal of Reading, 12, 6, 455-60, March.

Emotion-Focused Therapy: Coaching Clients to Work Through Their Feelings. Leslie Greenberg. Amer Psychological Assn; 1 edition (January 2002)

Howard, D.V. (1988). Implicit and explicit assessment of cognitive aging. In M. L. Howe and C.J. Brainerd (eds.), Cognitive Development in Adulthood. New York: Springer-Verlag.

Kaufman, A.S., Reynolds, C.R., and McLean, J.E. (1989). Age and WAIS-R intelligence in a national sample of adults in the 20 – 74 years age range: A cross-sectional analysis with education level controlled. Intelligence, 13, 235-254.

R.t. Zacks, G Radvasky, and L. Hasher (1996), Studies of directed forgetting in older adults, Journal of Experimental Psychology: Learning, Memory, and Cognition, 22, pp. 146-148 (experiment 1b).

Van Vreeswijk, M.E., De Wilde, E.J. (2004). Autobiographical memory specificity, psychopathology, depressed mood and the use of the Autobiographical Memory Test: A meta-analysis. Behavior Research and Therapy, 42, 2, 731-43, June.

7.31 More details about emotions

Humans think about things.

When someone thinks about something, they can form ideas in their minds. That means that they can think about stuff.

Is an emotion or feeling by itself?

How could a feeling feel without thoughts?

Humans have feel that they can feel because they can feel those feelings.

That means that people can think.

If people can think with ideas, words, sentences, thought processes, etc. Then what is the difference from experience and taste?

Table 7.0

Chapter

Intellect, Cognition and Emotion

Humans have emotions - feelings are tangible while emotions are - or could be considered to be deep and complicated. The idea that feelings are tangible basically means that they could be more sensory or less intellectual and deep. Emotions are more powerful than feelings; however, they could also trigger the human intellect.

What would it mean for emotion to be powerful? Would that involve physical feelings? Physical stimulation can also be deep or shallow, emotional or intellectual. If the feeling (physical, emotional) is intellectual then it could be emotional or it could also be tied in with sensory feelings (say when you touch something).

What would it mean for something to be intellectual? Would that mean that it is different from the persons emotions? Emotions can be tied in with feelings - however that means that the emotion could be shallow and thought provoking or deep, or a strong emotion that is also deep.

It is important to distinguish deep feelings from sensory feelings. Deep feelings are probably intellectual - they are tied in with complicated cognitions which include memory processes, executive functioning (control of thoughts, ideas and images) and understanding concepts.

Concepts can also be emotional since they are intellectual or intelligent. A concept is like an idea only it is general or generic. An idea is something that occurs to someone while a concept could be the definition of an idea or the idea that the person refers to or already understood. Those deeper concepts can trigger emotions that are related to the idea or concept. A single concept could be powerful or significant to the person.

A humans emotions could influence their thoughts - and their physical feelings can also influence either their thoughts or their emotions (or both at the same time). Thoughts could be complicated - they are a mix of goals and motivations with the persons environment and experience. Furthermore, a motivation could have complicated emotions, and their present situation could be causing complicated emotions.

The difference between feelings and thoughts is simple and complex - a thought could be complex because it could involve the persons motivations mixed in with the objects in their environment and their experience. They could have a thought for each object or each objective reality in their situation.

The difference between their feelings and thoughts then is that their feelings cause feeling, or stimulation and could be complex and intellectual while their thoughts could be unconscious or complex.

8.1 title

Humans have feelings. Humans can also think about their feelings. Other factors in reality help the thinking process - such as what is in the persons environment, and what they are paying attention to all assist the persons thinking process.

But what exactly is a thought process? Is it a sentence? Is it a single idea? Is it a few ideas that the person is trying to think about or understand?

The ideas someone is thinking about could be complicated and internal - or simple and related to their environment.

Humans have ideas - mulitple ideas can compose a thought process. The ideas can be about different things - stuff in the persons environement, other ideas or memories that they want to think about, and they can form thoughts or sentences about those ideas - they can also think about their feelings (with ideas or sentences).

For instance, a feeling could be an idea - or an idea could become a feeling

What does that mean an idea is? An idea is something that occurs to someone - it is a concept or intention, or an understanding of some sort.

Ideas can relate to a persons feelings - and to the persons thought process. That is, ideas can complete a thought process.

8.2 title

Ideas are thoughts that occur to people, 'that is an excellent idea' wold be the expression.

People have emotions. Their emotions are feelings that they feel. That means that they like to think about things

If humans think, then however it is more fun , however , it is not fun , however I now think that that makes sense.

Table 8.0

Feelings are triggered by cognition

A practical therapy would be for someone to learn how their thoughts trigger their feelings - how complicated can someones feelings be?

There are feelings like happiness and sadness, those are major feelings because humans care if they are happy or sad. Sadness is not a painful feeling, though it would seem to be a negative feeling - especially if it is a deep sadness that generates pain.

So sad can be a painful feeling. Any feeling could be a painful feeling if the person is in pain.

Emotions are important because they make humans feel stuff - humans have a wide range of feeling.

If humans have a wide range of feeling then there is a lot to analyze about what they are feeling. My previous articles discuss different ways in which feeling functions - like how it interacts with cognition. Humans can be delusional and their emotions could be influenced by their thoughts (and vice versa).

9.1 Analyzing emotion

There are lots of things to analyze about emotions and feelings - what their impact on people is, what it causes people to do, how it makes them think, and so on.

For instance feelings can be powerful - how is that supposed to be analyzed? Someone can know if they have a strong feeling, and they can know when they are thinking something, also.

How is a person supposed to know when their thinking is influencing their emotions? How could that process be described? Thoughts are about stuff - while feelings are simply how someone feels.

Table 9.0

Chapter

My theory of subjective analysis

Emotion is subjective - that means that the feelings that humans experience are unique to each individual person - if each person has their own experience then they are going to form different opinions and different ideas than the people they interact with.

But what is emotion? Emotion mean feeling - that someone is feeling something. If someone is feeling something then it feels 'like' something.

If someone is feeling something then they are experiencing emotions. Emotion is an experience - it is something that you feel.

Humans can also think about things - the things that they think about help to make their emotions more complex. However, this also applies to other animals such as dogs - if a dog thinks about their owner then they make their feelings more complex. They are focusing their feelings on their owner, and that generates those feelings. They could also look at their owner, and so on - in order to help to trigger those complicated feelings.

That seems fairly simple - how is someone supposed to know when they are generating an emotion? If they are aware that they are experiencing an emotion then they might notice the emotion.

This applies to all things in life - different objects and experiences cause humans and animals to have emotional reactions. The reactions that they experience could be complicated reactions, or they could be simple reactions.

What would make a reaction simple? What would make an emotional reaction complex? Emotion can have subtlety - so even though there might be a single emotion - say the feeling 'joy' - then the feeling could still be complicated.

10.1 Analysis of Emotions

But I am just talking about experiencing emotions and feelings. There is more to life than experiencing emotions. Humans have to think about things, also.

There are lots of things in life that humans think about. People think about physical stuff like food or other objects in their environment, or different environments that they are in. All the things in someones environment are physical things.

If an object that a person is thinking about is physical then they could imagine it in their mind - 'picture' it. That means that there are lots of things that people can think about - abstract concepts that cannot be imagined by a visual mental picture, and concrete objects that can be pictured. Some concepts can be pictured, however there is a large range of stuff to think about and much of it involves complicated objects or a lot of objects (making it harder for the person to make a picture in their mind of the concept or environment).

What would make an object a complicated object? Someone can picture a human in their mind - however that doesn't mean that they are going to make it emotionally complicated.

What is the difference between just picturing something or someone and thinking deeply about it then? When I say 'picture' what does that mean other than literally making a mental picture of something. Perhaps my use of the understanding of 'picture or mental image' just makes humans think more about whatever it is that they are thinking about.

Table 10.0

Chapter 11

How do Emotion, Attention, Thought, and Arousal Work

Together?

11.1 Unconscious and Conscious Processes

A Study by Douglas Derryberry and Mary Klevjord Rothbart titled "Arousal, Affect, and Attention as Components of Temperament"[1] concluded that "This study demonstrates that the general temperamental constructs of arousal, emotion, and self-regulation can be successfully decomposed into more specific subconstructs revealing interesting patterns of relations."

I believe that statement makes a lot of sense - there are several key factors that influence what a person is going to feel, and the main ones are probably affect, arousal and attention. If you think about it, when you are in a social situation, your affect is constantly changing, and so are your levels of arousal and attention. Those things constantly fluctuating is going to determine the emotions you are feeling on a moment to moment basis. Your attention can change and be directed at many different things in a brief time period - the only other significant factors other than the attention changes are going to be your affect (which shows your subtle emotions) and your arousal (which shows your more powerful emotions).

Actually your thinking and physical response is also going to be significant - in the study they had a number of items they defined - here is the "thinking" one:

- *Cognitive Reactivity (CR).* The amount of general cognitive activity in which the person engages, including daydreaming, problem solving, anticipatory cognition, and the ease with which visual imagery or verbal processes are elicited by stimulation. "A continuous flow of thoughts and images runs through my head."

In a way there is always a continuous flow of thoughts and images running through a humans mind. People are always processing information from their minds or from their environment. I would think that the cognitive thinking aspect directs the emotional and physical ones. Information or thoughts trigger you to feel different things or react in different ways all of the time, probably many different times in a minute. Every slight physical reaction, such as you looking at something different, or shifting your position, or a subtle change in affect, was somehow triggered by thought.

In this article I am going to analyze things such as... what types of emotion are generated in which high arousal situations, and what is the level of attention involved. For example, when you are in a high intensity social situation, your arousal and attention are higher, but there is also fear. By "arousal" in that example I don't mean sexual arousal, I just mean non-sexual arousal.

The thoughts someone experiences all of the time are incredibly complex, my understanding from observing my own thoughts is that you have natural impulses that cause thoughts to arise automatically all of the time. These thoughts usually aren't clear to the person having them that they are having the thought possibly because it directs a behavior or response that they aren't aware they are doing. For example if you experience an emotion generated by someone else in a social situation, your affect might change in a subtle way that you are not aware of. That change in affect is an unconscious thought because thought was

---

1. Derryberry, D., + Klevjord, M. "Arousal, Affect, and Attention as Components of Temperament"
Journal of Personality and Social Psychology 1988, Vol. 55, No. 6,958-966

necessary in order for your affect to change.

In the study they separated out these natural impulses (which I would say are unconscious thoughts) into the positive ones and the negative ones:

- *Inhibitory Control (1C)*. The capacity to suppress positively toned impulses and thereby resist the execution of inappropriate approach tendencies. "I can easily resist talking out of turn, even when I'm excited and want to express an idea."

- *Behavioral Activation (BA)*.The capacity to suppress negatively toned impulses and thereby resist the execution of inappropriate avoidance tendencies. "Even when I am very tired, it is easy for me to get myself out of bed in the morning."

Your positive emotions might cause you to want do something and because you are so positive about it there is that strong, impulsive drive which could cause you to do things. It is the opposite with negative emotions, if you feel very strongly these feelings are going to cause you to do things and think things automatically in order to satisfy the feeling.

This "impulsive drive" as I called it in the previous paragraph, is related to a persons level of arousal. Arousal would be someones stronger, more potent emotions and therefore would cause someone to become impulsive because the drive is powerful. If you are feeling very strongly (such as high arousal), then you are going to be consciously and unconsciously motivated to think and do things you wouldn't otherwise do. In addition, I already mentioned how even without feeling strongly, people have many different reactions in a minute (such as slight changes in affect). These probably increase if you are feeling more strongly. That makes sense, when you are talking to someone and you say something that gets a reaction, the other person usually changes their expression more or something.

The amount of arousal someone experiences can change from normal to high in a certain time period, or high to low in a similar time period - this was defined in the study:

- *Rising Reactivity (RR)*. The rate at which general arousal rises from its normal to its peak level of intensity. "I often find myself becoming suddenly excited about something."

- *Falling Reactivity (FR)*. The rate at which general arousal decreases from its peak to its normal levels of intensity. "I usually fall asleep at night within ten minutes."

So, as I have said, a higher arousal rate is going to result in more reactions from you, or as the people who wrote that study called it, "rising reactivity". A higher arousal rate is also going to cause your attention to change in some way, too. I would think it would cause your attention to increase normally, but it is possible that more excitement or arousal could cause you to pay less attention, though usually when people have more energy they are more attentive. Here is from the study again how they defined someone's ability to focus their attention and someone shifting their attention:

- *Attentional Focusing (AF)*. The capacity to intentionally hold the attentional focus on desired channels and thereby resist unintentional shifting to irrelevant or distracting channels. "My concentration is easily disrupted if there are people talking in the room around me."

- *Attentional Shifting (AS)*. The capacity to intentionally shift the attentional focus to desired channels, thereby avoiding unintentional focusing on particular channels. "It is usually easy for me to alternate between two different tasks."

Snygg and Combs speak of a "narrowing of the perceptual field under tension," which means that when people are tense and anxious, they tend to be less observant and less aware of their environment. As these authors say, "the girl too concerned over her appearance entering a room is only too likely to be unaware of the disastrous carpet edge in her path."[2]

There is likely to by many things that people do and think that they aren't aware of. I would say that each minute you have a few unconscious thoughts you aren't aware of. These thoughts probably influence your

---

2. D. Snygg and A. W . Combs, *Individual Behavior*. New York: Harper, 1949. Pp. 110-111.

emotions in subtle ways. These thoughts are going to be influenced anxiety, arousal, your attention, (and, obviously, what is happening). There are obvious unconscious thoughts, such as something you might notice you missed later on, and there are (I believe) more subtle unconscious thoughts, a great level of detail in emotion and thought that occurs every second. Analyzing that level of what is going on I think could reveal more about what someone is feeling and thinking.

The following passage by Lindgren, Henry Clay[3], shows how unconscious processes operate in everyday life.

- Even though it constitutes a denial of reality, repression often serves a useful function in that it enables us to adjust more easily to the demands of life, relatively unhampered by unpleasant thoughts and feelings and unaware of contradictions in our behavior. It enables us to perform tasks and operations that would be difficult or impossible if w e were bothered by recurring painful reminders of past faflures or by other disturbing thoughts and memories.

- ...our conscience or superego plagues us with guilt feelings whenever w e indulge in thoughts and actions that run contrary to the accepted standards of our culture. Tliese feelings often cause us to repress certain thoughts that might otherwise lead us to perform forbidden or disapproved acts. Some actions that are disapproved are violations of moral standards, while others involve certain patterns of behavior that are less acceptable than others. For example, there is a tendency in our culture to repress feelings that would lead to an emotional display. Under most circumstances w e disapprove of weeping in public, and this attitude leads us to repress feelings of deep sorrow, particularly when w e are with others. W e condone kissing in public on certain occasions, provided it is more or less formal and perfunctory. But if a nine-year-old girl throws her arms around her mother and effusively kisses her — sa\, on a streetcar or in a department store — the mother is likely to be embarrassed and to scold the child. These are examples of a cultural pattern which stresses emotional control and which regards the expression of strong emotions as babyish, immature, unmannerh', or even abnormal. Thus the typical American not only expresses less emotion than, say, the typical resident of the Mediterranean countries, but wfll often deny that he feels any emotion at all when faced by situations that would evoke considerable emotionality on the part of the Mediterranean person. In our " flight from emotion," w e often try to present ourselves as calm, reasonable, competent, and efficient persons, even though we may not feel this wa}'. W e stress the intellectual aspects of our behavior and attempt to deny to ourselves and others the presence of strong feelings.

- Unconscious feelings do not always reveal themselves through such obvious means as a slip of the tongue. Usually they express themselves indirectly through subtle little mannerisms, quirks, facial expressions, tones of voice, and so on.

But is that the full mystery behind unconscious operations? It couldn't be - there must be a lot more going on unconsciously that needs explanation. For instance, in each different social situation there are probably different emotional responses. Your anxiety, arousal, attention, perception and emotions could vary - I already stated that those were the main factors involved with psychological functioning.

The following passage (also by Lindgren) shows the importance of empathy, it also explains a little how it impacts your perception and anxiety:

- Empathy, as used in this sense, is the ability to be aware of the feelings and attitudes of others without necessarily sharing them. W e gain this awareness by observing the speech, facial expression, posture, and body movements of others. As one four-year-old said, " I k n o w m y M o m m y 's mad, 'cause she walks mad." Empathy is the result of sensitive and acute perception. Like other forms of perception, it m a y be sharpened or dulled, depending on the state of our emotions. Sometimes anxiety can serve to sharpen empathic awareness, but usually it operates to distort it.

---

3. Lindgren, Henry Clay , (1959). Psychology of personal and social adjustment (2nd ed.)., (pp. 44-65). New York, NY, US: American Book Company

Empathy, and its influence on anxiety and perception, is just one aspect of psychological functioning. It has to do with how connected people are to other people, but there are many aspects about how people are connected and a complex emotional and intellectual exchange that occurs moment to moment when people interact. Your perception, connectivity, anxiety, arousal, feelings and thoughts are constantly changing.

This next passage by Lindgren mentions how interactions are sort of like unconscious interchanges of feeling:

- Most of us are capable of empathizing most of the time, and as w e empathize with one another, w e find our actions and atdtudes conditioned or affected by one another's feelings. This amounts to a sort of communicadon or exchange of " feeling-tone " that takes place below the level of consciousness. In many, if not most, situations involving two or more persons, the interchange of feeling-tone at the unconscious level is of greater importance than the verbal exchange at the conscious level.

Lindgren shows an example of feeling-tone by a salesman who is hiding contempt for some of his customers. Even though his contempt isn't obvious in his tone and gestures, nevertheless those customers end up feeling tense and stressed. Here is another example he uses the shows how teachers do a similar   thing:

- Teachers, too, are in a position to use or misuse the communication of feeling-tone. Some teachers are technically competent, but so unsure of their relations with others that they attempt to " cover up " by being grim or pedantic or hypercritical. Teachers of this sort usually succeed in communicating the very feelings they are tr}'ing to hide, with the result that the class becomes tense, hostile, or just bored. Other teachers are able to empathize with their students to the point that they can determine whether students understand or are confused, whether they are recepti\-e, or whether they are in a m.ood calling for a change of pace and subject matter.

Lindgren also showed how some things are unconscious, people may come up with reasons for their behavior, but the real reason could be something that is unconscious and beneath their awareness. The feeling-tone that people convey is similarly beneath awareness most of the time. People could be acting one way, but be communicating something completely different unconsciously.

Here is another example he gives and a conclusion:

- The communication of feeling-tone is essential, too, in courtship. T w o people may meet accidentally and discuss the weather or the latest television program in a casual fashion. Yet whfle this desultory con\'ersation proceeds, there is an exchange of feelingtone, and each may begin to feel the effects of mutual attraction and warm feelings. This experience leads to other meetings, untfl the participants are sufficienth' a-ware of their feelings to make them a subject for communication on the conscious level.

- In the situations w e ha\'e described above, the words spoken at the conscious level do not necessarily give clues to the communication taking place at the feeling le\el. And, as we have indicated, the latter type of communicadon realh' plays the more important part in attitude formation, motivation, and the course of action people actually will take.

Here is another conclusion he makes, which shows that you cannot hide or act differently, your feelings are there and going to determine what occurs:

- The abihty to put oneself in another's place and sense his attitudes and feelings is an unconscious process termed " empathy." It is highly necessary- if one is to understand others and communicate with them effectively. If w e are not empathic, w e are in danger of being chronically disappointed in others. Thus we must be aware of h o w others feel, and of the fact that their feelings are frequently at odds with what the}' say. At the same time, w e must be aware of our own feelings, which have an effect on others. There is, in short, an exchange of feeling-tone.

Emotions lie at the heart of social interactions. Subtle changes in emotion occur all of time, and these changes are going to influence what you think and do, and also the larger, more potent emotions that you feel. Empathy is just one important aspect of how emotion works in a social interaction, without it there would be a disconnection, and much of the subtlety involved might not occur. For instance the "subtle little mannerisms, quirks, facial expressions, tones of voice, and so on" might not occur at all.

11.2 Cognitive Performance

Someones beliefs and views of the world are obviously going to influence how they socially interact - along with their personal history. Their personal history is going to matter because it is who the person is - people use knowledge of past events and especially experience from them to guide behavior in social interactions. Knowledge may be activated whenever the proper conditions for retrieval are met - that basically means when the time is right, your knowledge is going to be used accordingly.

So someone's knowledge about the world and their understanding of the world is going to be used in social situations (their semantic memory), and so is memories of their personal history (their episodic memory). Knowledge is contextualized, whatever someone knows, this knowledge was learned from some experience that may also be recalled (consciously or unconsciously) at various times.

People might also use knowledge of their attitudes and preferences, their abilities, shortcomings, behaviors or their identity as a whole. They use their knowledge of their own history and of the world around them. They use this knowledge on a moment to moment basis all of the time, in social interactions or otherwise.

When someone uses knowledge of their personal history (their memories), they may interpret this information in their own way. People have their own beliefs and understanding of what happened. Each memory has its own implication to the person, and what each memory means, how the person remembers it, what they learned from it, etc - is going to vary from person to person. Even for two people that were at the same event and remember the same details, the knowledge they learned is going to be different.

Sensory information is also remembered, people have a "feel" for each memory and what it was like being there. How someone learns from memory is something that will never be completely understood because it is so complicated. Different memories are linked in some way, people use all or some of their memories to interpret the facts and information they have. In that way, semantic and episodic memories are linked. People may bias facts and information, memories, and feelings and interpret them in their own personal way instead of a more truthful way or the truth.

Each memory, or even knowledge and information, is going to have a certain personal meaning and emotive power. Memories and knowledge make people feel in possibly deep, meaningful ways - or nothing at all. They may also impact judgement, perception of others, problem solving skills, etc. Memory is a resource for living, it impacts what you feel, forms who you are, and helps determine what you are and aren't conscious of. For instance if you had a personal history of something, say perhaps abuse, then you might be more conscious of such things.

Memories may provide a parallel model of everyone else's inner life. People are constantly interpreting and predicting the behavior of others and, as a result, adjust their conduct according to their analysis. We use our experience to explain the actions of others, or even our own actions. Our awareness of what is going on in a situation is going to to then be related to our memories and past experience. We might be more conscious of certain situations and certain feelings if we have experience of it, giving us more insight into our subjective state and more insight into others feelings.

How do people perceive and evaluate others? Obviously their autobiographical memory is going to play a role in how they do that. People make attributions and other daily explanations. Indeed, in order to analyze the situations in which we find ourselves, to make decisions, or to understand, evaluate and predict the behavior of others, everyday life often leads us to refer to these memories.

A self-schema is basically ideas someone has about themself that were derived from their experience (their interpretation of their experience). Therefore, since they are about the self, they organize information and processing related to the self:

- Cognitive-affective structures representing one's experience. They organize and direct the processing of info relevant to the self. We hold self-schema for particular domains, domains that are personally important for which we have well-developed self-concepts.(self-concept) Packages of self-knowledge derived from experience and our interpretation of experiences (I'm friendly, a people person, I don't trust others, "I'm shy) – vary in content and in how elaborate they are, some are interrelated (student athlete) and others are separate; they vary in their temporal focus (past, present, future) and in the extent to which they are congruent or discrepant from each other.[4]

These self-schemas can change the amount of attention someone gives things, for instance if there is something related to independence, someone may pay more attention if they are interested in being independent. There are many ideas about the self someone could have that could motivate them to pay more or less attention to things. Taking that further, someone's attention all of the time, on everything, is partially determined by the ideas they have about themselves - the ideas and thoughts they formed from their experience, and the ideas and conclusions they come to continuously from their knowledge and memory.

I should note here that this means people have a lot of ideas about themselves, or you could call them "self-evaluations", and that these ideas form their perception and how their memories are created. This also means that they might have certain expectations about their own behavior and the behavior of others based off of these ideas - which may or may not be accurate.

Autobiographical memory could help someone put themselves in the right or wrong emotional state. Based off of what someone would like to be and what their own self concept is, psychological states of emotional discomfort could result because they aren't corresponding their self-concept with their emotional state. Self-standards (such as standards of how they want to be, what they want their emotional state to be like) may have been internalized during childhood. So certain autobiographical memories are associated with certain emotional states. For instance, if you put yourself in the emotional state of happiness, or happiness with a little sadness, then the corresponding childhood memories (or recent memories) may be easier to bring up.

People can have many different things that they pay attention to at one time. There are going to be things people automatically, unconsciously pay attention to and things they do consciously. There is going to be a priority list of which things you want to pay more attention to in your mind (and how much energy you are going to devote to each task). If your controlled, conscious attention is going to take over a task that is usually unconscious, the person must 1) be aware of the automatic effect (what the unconscious is doing) 2) have the motivation or intention to think enough to dominate the unconscious and 3) have enough attention capacity to support the flexible, unusual type of unconscious attention usually given to the task.

If someone is trying to pay attention to something, and they are in the wrong emotional state, it may be harder to focus. For instance, if your emotional state is a happy one it may be harder for you to focus on something sad that is occurring. This gets even more complicated if you consider that the emotional state you are in is going to bring up memories related to that emotional state, which are also going to impact your ability to focus or pay attention to certain things. That being said, positive or negative emotions may help or hinder your ability to pay attention, depending on the type of emotion and the set of feelings it is, the memories or thoughts it brings up, and what you are paying attention to.

How does memory of ones past influence how someone thinks? First off, there are two types of memories that might influence thought, one is taxonomical categories (supplies, birds, sports) and the other is categories derived from goals (birthday gifts, camping equipment, things to do by the sea). Of course just regular memories of events could influence thought as well, but how exactly would that occur? If you are just thinking, "I want this for lunch", memories of certain items you wanted for lunch in the past may come

---

4. Retrieved from http://webspace.ship.edu/ambart/PSY_220/selfschemaol.htm 6/7/2012

up. Those would be a category that is goal related - each item in the goal related category is going to be goal related to a certain degree, some things more desirable than others. I doubt that when you think "I want this for lunch" that a memory of an event is brought up in your mind, it is more likely just items from the past are brought up.

That shows that a lot of your thought is derived from previous items that you have experience with. Your memories of your past aren't going to play an obvious, active role with most of your thinking. But maybe they do, if these memories are personally meaningful for you, then perhaps they influence your thinking in subtle ways. It obviously would if you bring up the memory and recall it while trying to think about something else, or recall the memory then do a related task.

Marks [5] has shown that people tend to think that their opinions are widely shared and their abilities unique, underscoring the existence of a false idiosyncrasy effect or a uniqueness bias. During social interactions, people develop a need for enhancement that turns performances, reinforcements and other events into episodes associated to their cognitive, emotional or behavioral consequences, such as mood and self-esteem. So basically people are constantly striving to increase their self-esteem and mood, by comparing themselves to others, trying to help their own thoughts and emotions and behaviors, and continuously trying to reward themselves. This probably means that self-esteem is a key feature for autobiographic memory - when something that triggers the feeling of self-esteem or wants to start the feeling of self-esteem, memories of the persons personal history may help (and self-esteem is wanted or triggered frequently in life and in social interactions). That makes sense, when I want to feel good I can recall memories. I meant that it was used more automatically and in a more subtle way, however.

For instance, when you are simply interacting with someone, you are probably bringing up lots of old memories. You are certainly using the experience you gained from studying those memories or thinking about them. If the conversation involves thinking about certain memories, then you may also bring up previous conversations or other subtle, little things from memory. If you think about it in terms of just experience, if you use experience all of the time, then there is going to be a lot of memories associated with that experience that may come up or are used unconsciously.

Wegner[6] has argued that cognitive control requires two mental processes: An intentional operating process, that searches for and implements a mental content consistent with the preferred cognitive state, and a monitoring process to search for mental content not consistent with the intended state. Wegner argues that the monitoring process is always active and constantly searching for material that conflicts with our intentions and goals. Botvinick and colleagues[7], on the other hand, believe the monitoring system becomes activated only when conflict arises. However, the basic goal of both system is similar: to reduce conflict and help achieve goal-oriented behavior. For Wegner that also includes an additional process: the operating process.

That basically means that whatever it is you are doing or want to do, your mind is going to support you doing that, at the same time, your mind is going to monitor what else it is that you are doing and see if it in line with the intended state. That makes sense, people have cognitive capacity, when someone does something, it is much more complicated than them doing one single simple thing - there are mental processes involved. These mental processes distract attention, use mental resources (such as attention and focus), and cause complex emotional and cognitive phenomena. It makes sense that the "monitoring system" focuses on other aspects than your conscious "operating system". I don't know when it operates most, when you are doing a conscious task with the operating system, or when conflict arises, such as Botvinick and colleagues suggested.

Under particular circumstances, this two process system may not function properly; we may not be able

5. Marks, G. (1984). Thinking one's abilities are unique and one's opinions are common. *Personality and Social Psychology Bulletin, 10,* 203-208.

6. Wegner, D. M. (1994). Ironic processes of mental control. *Psychological Review, 101,* 34-52.

7. Botvinick, M., Braver, T., Barch, D. Carter, C. + Cohen, J. (2001). Conflict monitoring and cognitive control. *Psychological Review, 108 (3),* 624-652

to think positively, inhibit certain thoughts, or focus our attention on particular items. We may, in fact, perform the exact opposite of our intentions. Wegner refers to this as counterintentional error, where, in given situations, instead of performing an appropriate behavior or response, we behave or think in an opposite manner. For example, when we need to receive a good night sleep for an important day, yet the more we want to fall asleep the more we fail to fall asleep. There seems to be an interaction, in these situations, between how much we think about something and the increasing amount of failure of that action occurring.

That makes sense, when you try to do something, you are creating a new cognitive task, your mind is doing something new, this new thing might detract from what you want your mind to do - trying to assert conscious cognitive control is going to change how your mind normally functions.

The ironic process occurs as a direct result of this two-process cognitive control, the monitoring process is sensitive to our failures and may operate in the opposite direction whenever the intended state is overwhelmed or undermined. This overwhelming or undermining of the operating process is due the mental capacity load of the two processes. The operating process is a conscious process that consumes greater cognitive processes due to the effort required to attend and control the desired ideas and thoughts compared to the normally autonomic, unconscious monitoring process. The theory of the ironic process states that the variable that separates successful from unsuccessful cognitive control is the availability of mental resources. The operating and monitoring processes work in tandem; while the operating process is searching for desired state and implementing goal-oriented ideas, thoughts or emotions to achieve the desired state, the monitoring process is insidiously searching for any mental content not consistent with the desired state. When an unwanted idea, thought or desire infiltrates working memory, it tries to reset the operating process to begin anew and filter out the unwanted ideas, thoughts, or desires. However, because the monitoring process is constantly searching for any material not associated with the desired state, it is exactly this type of mental material that may become sensitive and intrude upon the desired state.

So basically, while one part of your mind tries to put in place certain emotions, thought, or desires - another part is searching for the unwanted emotions, thoughts and ideas and is trying to filter them. When an unwanted idea penetrates and comes into consciousness, the system is reset. Because the monitoring process is constantly searching for material that is unwanted, it is exactly that type of material that is going to intrude upon the desired state. This makes sense, clearly there is going to be the state that you want to have, and the states that you don't want to have. You would have to be conscious of both states all of the time, your mind cannot simply have the desired state and it be clean and running perfectly, the rest of your mind is also there, while temporarily less conscious than the state you are in, there are still all the other states you may have. So each state you are in is only one state of many, the other states are still there in unconscious form producing desires, thoughts and emotions. The operating process is conscious and consumes more resources, and the monitoring process is unconscious. The monitoring process may work against the operating process if the operating process fails. That makes sense, if you are trying to do something consciously or have some sort of conscious state, then when you fail at that, your unconscious mind may take over and start to use the resources, directing you into a different state.

Obviously, the irony being in that a system that is intended to search for an undesirable state, in order to reinstate the operating process, actually brings about this undesirable state. This may occur under conditions of capacity limitations, as seen in both normal and clinical populations during times of stress or distraction, where the monitoring process may supersede operational processes and create more sensitivity to the opposite desired state because the executive resources needed to successfully avoid them, or initiate thought avoidance, are limited. When executive resources are limited, our ability to effectively control our cognitive abilities diminishes; our operating or monitoring system may not work properly. If cognitive control depends on operating or monitoring processes that rely on limited resources, it would be important to know how, and under what circumstances, those resources become limited.

For instance if someone is anxious they may not perform either conscious tasks (the operating system) or unconscious ones (the monitoring system) well. Saying, "when executive resources are limited" is basically like saying, "when you can't think clearly". Executive there means your main, primary thoughts that you are aware and conscious of and that are more primary than the other things your mind does, such as feel and focus attention. so when executive resources are limited, you might be stressed or distracted. The irony of the ironic process is that your unconscious functions, which are supposed to support your conscious ones, actual can hinder them. For instance you are doing one thing, but wind up with more anxiety or wind up being more distracted because unconsciously you were searching for some other state to be in.

Eysenck[8] also describes how an aversive emotional and motivational state that occurs in an adverse environment may negatively affect performance on cognitive tasks. He explains that a person who is highly anxious would need more resources to obtain a specific performance level compared to a person who is not highly anxious. This need for additional resources would result in negative effects on some cognitive tasks that are already demanding sufficient cognitive resources. Esyenck refers to this reduction of processing efficiency as, quite simply, the Processing Efficiency Theory. The Processing Efficiency theory involves two components: worry and motivation. Worry is characterized by concerns over evaluations and expectations of negative evaluation and may be observed in situations where a person is tested or evaluated. The motivational component involves an increased effort by the individual to minimize the aversive state. These two components would affect the monitoring process that was described earlier by Botvinick and colleagues and Wegner, Eysenck argues that this increase of worry and motivational activity interrupts normal processing of working memory by taking up additional attentional resources. Because attentional resources are limited, the two components consume attentional resources that would normally be available for other tasks; thereby, resulting in a reduction in cognitive performance.

It makes sense that anxiety decreases mental functioning and performance. There is also probably going to be automatic amounts of worry and changing levels of motivation. The motivation shows an effort by the person to automatically try to decrease the anxiety or worry, which are more unconscious processes (because it is hard to control your anxiety or worry). Worry, motivation, and anxiety are going to take up resources and impact working memory (cognitive performance).

Eysenck and colleagues[9] recently extended the Processing Efficiency Theory to the more specific Attentional Control Theory. The Attentional Control Theory posits that anxiety, defined as a negative emotional and motivational state under threatening situations, affects cognitive performance by affecting two components of attentional control: top-down and stimulus-driven processes. Posner and Peterson[10] described the top-down or goal-directed attentional system as the involvement of expectation and knowledge of current goals, while the stimulus-driven process involves detecting and responding to sensory events that are clear and obvious. The Attentional Control Theory states that anxiety disrupts the balance of goal-directed stimulus-driven processes by decreasing top-down processing and increasing stimulus-driven processing (Eysenck). Assimilating this information with Wegner's two-process theory, anxiety would decrease the operating process, which is conscious and goal oriented, and increase the monitoring process, which is automatic and stimulus driven. Anxiety reduces stimulus-driven processing by affecting the automatic processing of threat-related stimuli, but may also affect performance in any ongoing task. The rationale for this is that it would be harmful to the individual to focus on only threatening material; the best strategy would be for anxiety to affect attentional resources globally, not just towards threatening material. The idea is that anxiety may be affected by external and internal cues, with worry being an internal cue. Because anxiety involves emotion and arousal, it is important to understand how emotion and arousal, in general, affect cognitive control.

---

8. Eysenck, M. W. and Calvo, M.G. (1992). Anxiety and performance: the processing efficiency theory. *Cognition and Emotion, 6,* 409-434.
9. Eysenck, M. W., Derakshan, N., Santos, R., + Calvo, M.G. (2007). Anxiety and cognitive performance: Attentional control theory. *Emotion, 7*(2), 336-353.
10. Posner, M. I., + Peterson, S. E. (1990). The attention system brain. Annual Review of *Neuroscience, 13,* 25-42.

In my view, the theory is that anxiety decreases conscious thinking (such as goal-oriented thinking) and it increases sensory response (such as things you feel or just response to sensory stimulation). This makes sense to me, anxiety is going to make someone less conscious because it is an unconscious process itself. When you aren't thinking, you are going to be responding to the world more physically. Anxiety would thus actually increase your sensory response. For instance you might be faster physically - more aware of your body and your own condition. Anxiety is going to decrease your worrying or whatever it is you are thinking about because you have to deal with being anxious. At the same time, you are going to be at a higher state of alert, so you would respond faster to physical, sensory stimulation.

So anxiety can impact your attention, and your ability to shift your attention. It could also impact the thoughts you have and the emotions you are experiencing. Anxiety could cause your attention to shift to more sensory things, and make you less conscious about your thoughts or non-sensory things that you are thinking. People pay attention in different ways, and have different cognitive processes. There are conscious processes and unconscious ones. Unconscious ones can monitor for other thoughts and other emotional states, and the conscious processes are going to be the things you do that are more or less under your control. But the conscious is just a small part of mental functioning. People couldn't do everything and have it be completely conscious - that is why there is a monitoring or unconscious process that keeps track of the other options - the other thoughts and emotions you might experience. Anxiety, attention, emotion, thought, consciousness - all of these things are key factors in mental functioning.

11.3 Cognition and Emotion

Feelings, values and preferences are going to influence even simple perceptual judgments. Your judgments are thoughts, and your feelings, values and preferences are all highly emotional. This example demonstrates an aspect in the age-old quest to understand the relationship between the rational and the emotional aspects of human nature. Is affect or cognition primary or dominant? From this example it would seem that they are separate, you have values and feelings, and that is separate from when you make decisions and judgments. When you make those judgments, feeling influences the judgment and motivates it, but it is a separate system.

There is a growing recognition that there are different categories of affective phenomena and their role in social cognition is quite distinct. One crucial distinction is between emotions and moods. Both emotions and moods may have an impact on social cognition, but the nature of this influence is quite different. Emotions are usually defined as intense, short-lived, and highly conscious affective states that typically have a salient cause and a great deal of cognitive content, featuring information about typical antecedents, expectations, and behavioral plans. The cognitive consequences of emotions such as fear, disgust, or anger can be highly complex, and depend on the particular prototypical representations activated in specific situations. As distinct from emotions, moods are typically defined as relatively low-intensity, diffuse, and enduring affective states that have no salient antecedent cause and therefore little cognitive content (such as feeling good or feeling bad, or being in a good or bad mood). As moods tend to be less subject to conscious monitoring and control, paradoxically their effects on social thinking, memory, and judgments tend to be potentially more insidious, enduring, and subtle.

Powerful emotions often leave a lingering mood state in their wake, and moods in turn can have an impact on how emotional responses are generated. Emotions are obviously going to be intense and short lived compared to moods, if you consider that a mood is your overall emotional state, it is not specific like emotions are. You feel each emotion, a mood, however, is something that could just hang around for a while. Since emotions and moods are so different, they are each going to have a different impact on your thinking, memory and judgments. It is probably more clear what the impact of a specific emotion is then a mood, which is going to have some sort of subtle impact on what you do. For instance if you are cooking, a bad mood might have some impact, but if you experienced an emotion, say, excitement or sadness, the impact would be more obvious.

A major development in affect-cognition research in the 1980s was the realization that in addition to influencing the content of cognition - informational effects - affect may also influence the process of cognition; that is, how people think about social information. It was initially thought that people in a positive mood tend to think more rapidly and perhaps superficially; reach decisions more quickly; use less information; avoid demanding and systematic processing; and are more confident about their decisions. Negative affect, in turn, was assumed to trigger a more systematic, analytic, and vigilant processing style.[11][12][13][14] More recent work showed that positive affect can also produce distinct processing advantages, as people are more likely to adopt more creative, open, constructive, and inclusive thinking styles.[15][16] It now appears that positive affect promotes a more schema-based, top-down, and generative processing style, whereas negative affect produces a more bottom-up and externally focused processing strategy. This processing dichotomy has close links with the fundamental distinction between promotion-oriented vs prevention-oriented processing developed by Tory Higgins, a distinction that has deep roots in evolutionary theorizing as well as classic conditioning accounts.

It makes sense that when someone is in a good mood, their thoughts are also going to be more positive. They are less nervous, and not worried about the environment around them, also, they don't need to think everything through from the bottom up but instead can generalize and think more casually. When positive, people can even think rapidly and superficially. They are more relaxed. Pain causes people to do work - it puts them in a more demanding state. They have to think harder, and they are more vigilant in their thinking.

Having adopted early on the perspective that emotional reactions were organized and had evolved to serve largely adaptive functions, Magda Arnold was among the first of the the contemporary emotion theorists to recognize the difficulty and importance of addressing the processes by which emotions occur. Arnold[17] and virtually all subsequent theorists started with the assumption that different emotions served different sets of circumstances. The puzzle that appraisal theory set out to solve, then, was to describe the mechanism that had evolved to elicit the appropriate emotional reaction when a person was confronted with circumstances in which the functions(s) served by that emotion were called for. This puzzle was complicated by the fact that, as Arnold recognized and subsequent appraisal theorists emphasized, emotions are not simple, reflexive responses to a stimulus situation. It is relatively easy to document that the same objective stimulus situation will evoke a broad range of emotions across individuals. Thus, an evaluative exam that might be anxiety producing to a person who doubts his abilities might we a welcome challenge to one who is confident of hers, and yet elicit indifference in one who is not invested in the outcome. Rather than assuming that this heterogeneity or response reflected a disorganized or chaotic system (as did the conflict theorists), beginning with Arnold, appraisal theorists have assumed that emotional reactions are highly relational, in that they take into account not only the circumstances confronting an individual, but also what those circumstances imply for the individual in light of her or

11. Clark, M. S., + Isen, A. M. (1982). Towards understanding the relationship between feeling states and social behavior. In A. H. Hastorf + A. M. Isen (Eds.), *Handbook of social cognition* (2nd ed.), New Jersey: Erlbaum.
12. Isen, A. M. (1984). Towards understanding the role of affect in cognition. In R. S. Wyer + T. K. Srull (Eds.) *Handbook of Social Cognition* (Vol 3. pp. 179-236). Hillsdale, Nj: Erlbaum.
13. Isen, A. M. (1987). Positive affect, cognitive processes and social behavior. In L. Berkowitz (Ed.), *Advances in experimental social psychology* (Vol. 20, pp. 203-253). New York: Academic Press.
14. Schwarz, N. (1990). Feelings as information: Informational and motivation functions of affective states. In E. T. Higgins + R. Sorrentino (Eds.), *Handbook of motivation and cognition: Foundations of social behavior* (Vol. 2, pp. 527-561). New York: Guilford Press.
15. Bless, H. (2000). The interplay of affect and cognition: The mediating role of general knowledge structures. In J.P. Forgas (Ed.). *Feeling and Thinking: The role of affect in social cognition.* New York: Cambridge University Press.
16. Fiedler, K. (2000). Towards an integrative account of affect and cognition phenomena using the BIAS computer algorithm. In J. P. Forgas (Ed.) *Feeling and thinking: The role of affect in social cognition* New York: Cambridge University Press.
17. Arnold, M. B. (1960). *Emotion and personality* (2 vols.). New York: Columbia University Press.

her personal hopes, desires, abilities, and the like. The elicitation mechanism Arnold proposed to give emotion this relational character was one of "appraisal," which she defined as an evaluation of the potential harms or benefits presented in any given situation. She then defined emotion as "the felt tendency toward anything intuitively appraised as good (beneficial), or away from anything intuitively appraised as bad (harmful)" (p. 182).

So people make intuitive, unconscious appraisals about things that determine what the emotions they are going to feel are. You might unconsciously decide that something is going to be good for you, so therefore that thing is going to make you feel good. However, this unconscious appraisal process is probably a lot more complicated than that. There are many unconscious reasons why something might cause positive or negative emotions. Furthermore, each emotion has a different, unique feeling that could be described by describing whatever is causing the emotion, and how that cause is unique.

Beyond being relational, it is important to note that appraisal is also meaning-based and evaluative. the fact that appraisal combines both properties of the stimulus situation and of the person making the appraisal means that it cannot be a simple or reflexive response to the emotion-evoking stimulus. Instead the appraisal is a reflection of what the stimulus means to the individual. Appraisal is also evaluative, in that it does not reflect a cold analysis of the situation, but rather, as Arnold emphasized, it is a very personal assessment of whether the situation is good or bad-is it (potentially) beneficial or harmful for me? That this evaluation is meaning based, rather than stimulus based, provides the emotion system with considerable flexibility and adaptational power. Not only will different individuals react to very similar situations with different emotions (as illustrated previously), but also objectively very different situations can elicit the same emotions if they imply the same meaning to the individuals appraising them. In addition, an individual can react very differently to the same situation across time if changes in her or his desires and abilities alter the implications of that situation for his or her well-being.

So, everything has a different meaning for each person. That also means that each thing in life is going to evoke unique emotions in each person. Everyone is different, everyone experiences emotions differently, but on the other hand, people are also general and ordinary (and are going to experience similar emotions in similar circumstances).

A further assumption is that appraisal occurs continuously. That is, a number of appraisal theorists have proposed that humans constantly engage in a meaning analysis in which the adaptational significance of their relationship to the environment is appraised, with the goal being to avoid, minimize, or alleviate an appraised actual or potential harm, or to seek, maximize, or maintain an appraised actual or potential benefit. The reason for proposing that appraisal occurs continuously is that the emotion system is seen as an important motivational system that has evolved to alert the individual when he or she is confronted to adaptationally relevant circumstances. In order to serve this alerting function, the emotion-elicitation mechanism must be constantly "on guard" in order to be able to signal such circumstances when they arise. It is important to note that in making this assumption, appraisal theorists do not assert that the appraisal process need be conscious or deliberate; instead, they have consistently maintained that appraisal can occur automatically and outside of awareness. The importance and implications of this latter assumption is considered in more detail when I discuss process models of appraisal.

So, basically, there is something in people that is constantly searching and alerting people for significant emotional events. I don't know how to explain the complexity of the appraisal process that someone goes through in order to respond to emotions. People experience emotion constantly, there must be extremely complicated evaluations going on all of the time - you are constantly deeply thinking about the significance of what is going around you and how that is impacting your own emotions.

A final major assumption is that the emotion system is highly organized and differentiated. Appraisal theorists recognize that the same basic approach/avoid dichotomy associated with drives and reflexes and subscribed to by theorists endorsing two-dimensional conceptions of emotion, such as positive and negative affect, is fundamental to emotion. However, appraisal theorists describe emotion as being far more differentiated than a simple view of this dichotomy would allow. They argue that there are different major types of harm and benefit, and that these different types have different implications for how one might best contend with them. This is especially true for actual and potential harms, in which, depending on the circumstances, the most adaptive course might be to avoid the harmful situation, but could also range from active attach of the agent causing the harmful circumstances to reprimanding oneself if one caused the circumstances, to accepting and enduring the harmful circumstances if they cannot be avoided or repaired. Building on Arnold's definition of emotion mentioned previously, contemporary appraisal theorists tend to conceptualize different emotions as different modes of action readiness, each of which is a response to a particular type of adaptationally relevant situation ,and each of which physically and motivationally prepares and pushes the individual to contend with those circumstances in a certain way (e.g., at attack in anger, to avoid or flee in fear, to accept and heal in sadness). Within this differentiated system, the fundamental role of appraisal, again, is to call forth the appropriate emotion(s) when the individual in confronted with personally adaptationally relevant circumstances.

So when someone experiences an emotion, there is an adaptation taking place (at least if the circumstance is somewhat new). They have to process if this emotion is harmful or beneficial, and they respond to each in the appropriate fashion. People can learn each time they have an emotional response. The way their emotions respond to something each time changes. Not just in terms of if it is beneficial or harmful, but perhaps if it is cool or exciting. Though I would think that pain and pleasure (or beneficial or harmful) would be the dominant things by which people respond to, seeing as everything - even when it includes other complicated elements (such as other emotions or attitudes) - is dominated by our response of it is beneficial or harmful.

The existing appraisal models generally include some sort of evaluation of how important or relevant the stimulus situation is to the person, whether it is desirable or undesirable, whether and to what degree the person is able to cope with the situation, and who or what caused or is responsible for the situation (and thus toward what or whom one's coping efforts should be directed). Different patterns of outcomes along such dimensions are hypothesized to result in the experience of different emotions. Moreover, the specific pattern of appraisal hypothesized to result in the experience of a given emotion is conceptually closely linked to the functions proposed to be served by that emotion. To illustrate how these models are organized in this way, I draw on the model of Smith + Lazarus[18].

According to this model, situations are evaluated along seven dimensions: motivational relevance, motivational congruence, problem-focused coping potential, emotion-focused coping potential, self- accountability, other accountability, and future expectancy. Motivational relevance involves an evaluation of how important the situation is to the person; motivational is a key part of the term, however, in that importance is appraised in a subjective, relational sense, evaluating the relevance of what is happening in the situation to the individual's goals and motivations. Motivational congruence is an appraisal of the extent to which the situation is in line with current goals, which again is relational - to the extent to which the circumstances are appraised as being consistent with one's goals, they are appraised as highly congruent or desirable, whereas to the extent to which they are appraised as inconsistent with those goals, they are appraised as incongruent of undesirable. Problem-focused coping potential is an assessment of the individual's ability to act on the situation to increase or maintain its desirability. In contrast, emotion-focused coping potential evaluates the ability to psychologically adjust to and deal with the situation should it turn out not to be as desired. Self-accountability is an assessment of the degree to which an individual sees her/himself as responsible for the situation, whereas other accountability is the extent to which the individual views someone or something else as responsible. Finally, future expectancy involves an evaluation of the degree to which, for any reason, the person expects the circumstances to become more or less desirable. According to the model, different patterns of outcomes along these dimensions (having different adaptational implications) result in the experience of different emotions (serving different adaptations functions). Thus, these appraisal dimensions are held to be responsible for the differentiation of emotional experience.

18.   Smith, C. A., + Lazarus, R. S. (1990). Emotion and adaptation. IN L. A. Pervin (Ed.) *Handbook of personality: Theory and research* (pp. 609-637). New York: Guilford Press.

So, in other words, people care about the emotions they experience and therefore they are constantly evaluating if these emotions line up with the goals and motivations that they have. They evaluate who is responsible for the emotions and the situation they have, if the situation is going to get better, if they can do anything about it, etc. People make these types of decisions and think about these things all of the time - whether they are aware of it or not.

Reference

Affective and Cognitive appraisal processes. Craig Smith. Leslie Kirby. In Handbook of Affect and Social Cognition. Psychology Press; Reprint edition (November 3, 2001)

Table 11.0

Chapter 12

Emotions and Feelings and How to Change Them

Emotion is more similar to conscious thought than feelings are to conscious thought. Although emotion and feeling can be described as unconscious thought, one of them is going to be more similar to conscious thought. Feelings are more like sensations, when you touch something you get a feeling. Therefore feelings are faster than emotions and thought, because when you touch something there is a slight delay before you can think of something about it (thought), or feel something deeply about it (emotion). Emotion is therefore just unconscious thought. Actually it would better be described as unconscious feeling (so a feeling is like a conscious emotion because you can "feel" it better and easier but emotion is a deeper, more unconscious experience similar to unconscious thought, but emotions are also more similar to conscious thought because thought is a deep experience while feelings are intense or shallow, but not deep).

One definition of emotion can be "any strong feeling". From that description many conclusions can be drawn. Basic (or primary) emotions can be made up of secondary emotions like love can contain feelings or emotions of lust, love and longing. Feelings can be described in more detail than emotions because you can have a specific feeling for anything, each feeling is unique and might not have a name. For instance, if you are upset by one person that might have its own feeling because that person upsets you in a certain way. That feeling doesn't have a defined name because it is your personal feeling. The feeling may also be an emotion, say anger. "Upset" is probably too weak to be an emotion, but that doesn't mean that it isn't strong like emotions are strong in certain ways. Cold is also just a feeling. There is a large overlap between how feelings feel and how emotions feel, they are similar in nature. So there are only a few defined emotions, but there are an infinite number ways of feeling things. You can have a "small" emotion of hate and you could say that you have the feeling hate then, if it is large you could say you are being emotional about hate, or are experiencing the emotion hate. You can have the same emotion of hate in different situations, but each time the feeling is going to be at least slightly different.

You can recognize any feeling, that is what makes it a feeling. If you are sad that is a feeling, but if you are depressed that isn't a feeling it is more like an emotion. You can't identify why you are depressed but you can usually identify why you are sad. Feelings are more immediate, if something happens or is happening, it is going to result in a feeling. However, if something happened a long time ago, you are going to think about it unconsciously and that is going to bring up unconscious feelings. Otherwise known as emotion. So emotions are unconscious feelings that are the result of unconscious thoughts. Feeling defined there as something you can identify. So you can't identify the unconscious thought that caused the unconscious feeling, but you can identify the unconscious feeling (aka emotion).

Another aspect of unconscious thought, emotion, or unconscious feeling (all three are the same) is that it tends to be mixed into the rest of your system because it is unconscious. If it was conscious then it remains as an individual feeling, but in its unconscious form you confuse it with the other emotions and feelings and it affects your entire system. So therefore most of what people are feeling is just a mix of feelings that your mind cannot separate out individually. That is the difference between sadness and a depression, a depression lowers your mood and affects all your feelings and emotions, but sadness is just that individual feeling. So the reason that the depression affects all your other feelings is because you can no longer recognize the individual sad emotions that caused it. The feelings become mixed. If someone can identify the reason they are sad then they become no longer depressed, just sad. Once they forget that that was the reason they are depressed however, they will become depressed again.

That is why an initial event might make someone sad, and then that sadness would later lead into a depression, is because you forget why you originally got sad. You might not consciously forget, but unconsciously you do. That is, it feels like you forget, the desire to get revenge on whatever caused the sadness fades away. When that happens it is like you "forgetting" what caused it. You may also consciously forget but what matters is how much you care about that sadness. It might be that consciously understanding why you are depressed or sad changes how much you care about your sadness, however. That would therefore change the emotion/feeling of sadness. The more you care about the sadness/depression, the more like a feeling it becomes and less like an emotion. That is because the difference between feelings and emotions is that feelings are easier to identify (because you can "feel" them easier).

The following is a good example of the transition from caring about a feeling to not caring about a feeling. Anger as an emotion takes more energy to maintain, so if someone is punched or something, they are only likely to be mad for a brief period of time, but the sadness that it incurred might last for a much longer time. That sadness is only going to be recognizable to the person punched for a brief period of time as attributable to the person who did the punching, after that the sadness would sink into their system like a miniature depression. Affecting the other parts of their system like a depression.

In review, both feelings and emotions are composed of unconscious thoughts, but feelings are easier to identify than emotions. Feelings are faster than emotions in terms of response (the response time of the feeling, how fast it responds to real world stimulation) and it takes someone less time to recognize feelings because they are faster. Feelings are closer to sensory stimulation, if you touch something, you feel it and that is a fast reaction. You care about the feeling so you can separate it out in your head from the other feelings. "You care" in that sentence could be translated into, the feeling is intense, so you feel it and can identify it easily. That is different from consciously understanding why you are depressed or sad. You can consciously understand why you are depressed or sad, but that might or might not affect the intensity of that sadness.

If the intensity of the sadness is brought up enough, then you can feel that sadness and it isn't like a depression anymore, it is more like an individual feeling then something that affects your mood and brings your system down (aka a depression). Also, if you clearly enough understand what the sadness is then it is going to remain a sadness and not affect the rest of your system. That is because the feeling would get mixed in with the other feelings and start affecting them. The period of this more clear understanding of the sadness mostly occurs right after the event that caused the sadness. That is because it is clear to you what it is. Afterwards the sadness might emerge (or translate from a depression, to sadness) occasionally if you think about what caused it or just think about it in general.

The difference between emotion and feeling is that feelings are easier to identify because they are faster, a feeling is something you are feeling right then. An emotion might be a deeper experience because it might affect more of you, but that is only because it is mixed into the rest of your system. That is, a depression affects more of you than just an isolated feeling of sadness. In other words, people can only have a few feelings at a time, but they can have many emotions at the same time. Emotions are mixed in, but to feel something you have to be able to identify what it is, or it is going to be so intense that you would be able to identify what it is. Emotions just feel deeper because it is all your feelings being affected at once.

Since emotion is all your feelings being affected at once, emotions are stronger than feelings. Feelings however are a more directed focus. When you feel something you can always identify what that one thing is. When you have an emotion, the emotion is more distant, but stronger. All your feelings must feel a certain way about whatever is causing the emotion. So that one thing is affecting your entire system. Feelings can then be defined as immediate unconscious thought, and emotions as unconscious thought.

- When you care about an emotion, you could say that you have a higher attention for emotion or that emotional event during that time. You are probably going to be in a higher state of action readiness, that is, you are probably more alert and going to be able to respond faster to whatever it is you are focusing on, or just respond faster in general. You also are going to have a better understanding of the emotion if you care about it more - you make an assessment of the emotions strength and its nature when you think about the emotion (or the event that generated the emotion).

- Feelings are more direct than emotions and thought because they are more sensory – when you touch something you get a feeling. That shows further how emotions are really about things in the real world, only it more like you are thinking about them instead of feeling them in real time. Things that come from memory are going to be emotions and/or thoughts, not feelings because feelings are things which are more tangible, those memories might result in new feelings, but the memories themselves are not feelings because they are just thoughts. That shows how you can feel some things more than others, that thought and feeling are indeed separate and intelligence is sometimes driven by feelings and emotions, and sometimes it isn't. You can think about things and not have feelings guiding those thoughts Or your feelings could be assisting your thoughts.

- If you care about a feeling then it becomes easier to identify it – that shows how your feelings can help you to identify other feelings, so your emotions contribute to your emotional intelligence.

- If a certain emotion is larger than others then to your intellect it is going to be easier to recognize, and easier to think about (that is why a depression feels like it does, because you don't know the individual emotions contributing to it so you cannot feel a specific emotion of sadness from it.

An explanation for this chapter:

So feelings are easier to "feel" than emotions, that is probably why they are called feelings, because you "feel" them better. Maybe someone else thinks you can feel emotions easier, I don't know, the point is you can feel emotions and feelings with different levels of intensity and in more than one way, a feeling could be not intense but clear to you. So how conscious you are of the feeling or emotion influences the intensity of it and your conscious experience of it. A feeling could be more intense than en emotion if it is the only thing you are feeling as well. That makes sense, if an emotion is very complicated, then you probably couldn't feel the entire thing as clearly in a brief period of time. So my theory is that feelings are more simple, and therefore there are more shallow but possibly more intense than emotion because you can focus on a simple thing easier.

If you are having a deep emotional experience (experiencing an emotion) then it makes sense that you aren't as in touch with all of those feelings that are occurring. When you touch something you get the feeling "cold" - that is simple to understand. When you are in a depression you don't understand all the complicated emotions that you are experiencing. You could experience sadness all day. When you can say "oh, I really "felt" that", then you know you feel it and it is a feeling. When you feel something, it is a feeling. When you are emotional about something, those are feelings too, but it is more powerful and deeper, you aren't as in touch will all of it because it is more complex. You could be in touch with something complex and feel that too, I guess. Though I would argue that a feeling is easier to focus on if it is simple and clear to understand and feel to your conscious mind.

The significance of this chapter:

If someone is emotional, then they are feeling a lot. I could say that the emotions someone is experiencing could be brought up at different times and felt more - translated from somewhere in your strong emotions to something you feel more closely. So you can feel some things but that doesn't mean that the feeling is intense or clear - those things might become clear however at some point.

When those emotions become clear and you 'bring them up' - either by caring about the emotion or the thought that represents it or it just emerges by some other method (such as by doing an evaluation of your emotional state) - then they become feelings because you can feel them easier. These feelings are more clear, similar to when you touch something you get a feeling that is simple and tactile. That is why feelings are called the result of emotions, because emotions are like the basis for feelings (at least non-tactile ones). You might have a feeling that has a shallow source however as well I would say. It doesn't have to be that a feeling is first felt deeply, and then you feel it more clearly later on (the feeling being the result of an emotion). Maybe the feeling is simple at first and then it becomes more complex later.

What role does attention have to play? Being emotional or feeling something can make you pay more or less attention to things, including other feelings. Your attention can naturally rise just because of your emotional state.

People feel emotions, and they can feel feelings. Emotions are strong and the powerful source of human behavior, and while feelings are also powerful they are also diverse, curious, and unique - 'old feelings returning'.

12.1 How to Change Emotions and Feelings

An appraisal is when you assess something. People make appraisals or assessments of emotion all of the time, however they aren't aware most of the time that they are doing this. How much someone cares about an emotional stimulus is something that is probably thought about frequently during the experience. If you think about it people frequently are going to naturally analyze what is going on in every situation they are in and think about what the emotions occurring are.

I said in the previous paragraph that people make appraisals of emotional things but they aren't aware of themselves doing that. How is that possible or what does that mean exactly? If people care about emotion, which they clearly do, then they are going to want to know what is going on in the situations they encounter in life. So clearly people make assessments of how much emotion the things around them are generating, the only question is can they do this in a a way that is beneath their awareness.

People surely must make assessments since they often work on inducing or inhibiting feelings in order to make them "appropriate" to a situation. If you are going to be changing feeling, then obviously you are going to need to measure and assess it first. Sometimes people think this process through consciously, and sometimes they don't.

It makes sense to me that people are going to "know" how valuable certain things in their environment are. This is clear when you realize that people focus on some things very quickly - such a thing would clearly be something of interest to that person or something that generates emotion - which would make it interesting.

So you could say that a person whose attention gets alerted to something around them made an assessment about the stimulus or responded to it, the stimulus (the thing in their environment they paid sharp attention to) was clearly emotional for them. It could have generated any feeling - disgust, surprise, happiness, - or maybe an intellectual reaction such as 'that person has a bright coat'.

Does that mean that the person assessed if the bright coat generated emotion for them? What would it mean if it generated emotion? Could they respond in a fast way without being interested? Someone could respond quickly to something and not be in a mood that is very caring at that time, in which case maybe little emotion was involved. However if someone was interested in something then it makes sense that it is going to cause them to have feelings.

Is something someone is interested in going to cause them to have deep emotions or shallow feelings? What types of stimuli result in deep or shallow feelings? Just because something generates more emotion for you doesn't necessarily mean that it is going to cause you to respond to it faster or you would be more interested in it. Maybe your interest is more intellectual or maybe you are interested or responding to it quickly because you have to.

Under what circumstances do people care more about feelings? This relates to appraisals - if you care about something then you are going to make more assessments during the experience about how much emotion is being generated probably. People can care more about feelings but that doesn't mean that they are aware that they care more during that time. This is similar to people going into modes where they are seeking pleasure. My theory here is that people have levels of desire and need that fluctuate constantly.

This means that there are many different levels someone can experience an emotion or feeling. It is more complicated than simply saying that the feeling has a certain strength - each feeling or emotion is going to have a unique nature, represent unique ideas and objects, and have a unique significance on your psyche.

Maybe you can say that there are shallow feelings and deep emotions, and that there are certain properties that shallow feelings have and certain properties that deep feelings have. For instance you probably care more about deep feelings (unless the feeling is negative) and therefore they probably cause you to have a faster reaction time. However if the feeling is deep, sappy, and emotional then maybe your reaction time is slower because the emotion is weighing you down.

This relates to the 'emotions and feelings and the difference between them' section above because I am outlining further that deep feelings/emotions or shallow feelings/emotions are different and things happen to humans differently with each one. It shows that clearly emotion can make someone be different physically, as when you are motivated by emotion you often move faster.

This is just bringing up ideas of depth - some feelings are simple and some are complex - that is obvious, however I think people could notice a lot more if they grouped their emotions into a categories of strength and shallowness or depth and how they responded differently to each different category. - Also the person should note what the interest was, the reaction time, the negative or positive valence of the emotion.

Goffman suggests that we spend a good deal of effort on managing impressions - that is, acting. Your impression of other people makes you feel in different ways, and you try to manage this in a social situation. So therefore all of your strong feelings you try to influence by thinking about what caused those feelings - such as your impressions - and how you can change them.

So people are basically "emotion-managers", constantly thinking about their feelings and what caused them and how they can change them. Whenever you change an impression of someone, you are also changing your feelings. When you think about your own feelings you are changing them because you are changing how much you care about them. You set goals for yourself about your own feelings - 'if I do this I am going to become happy'.

When you think about your feelings you can make insignificant feelings large or large feelings small. When a feeling is small, you could say that it is more unconscious or beneath your awareness. Something (including yourself) could trigger this small feeling and it could emerge into something you feel more closely and more consciously.

So the question is, what circumstances and what type of thinking warrant that feeling of 'that sort'.

We assess the 'appropriateness' of a feeling by making a comparison between the feeling and the situation. We also have goals for how we want to feel that we don't know we are thinking, and we have goals for how we want to act as well. Is there a 'natural attitude' or a natural way of behaving and thinking? Not really - especially when you consider that you are unconsciously constantly creating goals, drives, thoughts and behaviors that are not fully under your control.

- In *secondary reactive emotions*, the person reacts against his or her initial primary adaptive emotion, so that it is replaced with a secondary emotion. This "reaction to the reaction" obscures or transforms the original emotion and leads to actions that are not entirely appropriate to the current situation. For example, a man that encounters danger and begins to feel fear may feel that fear is not "manly." He may then either become angry at the danger (externally focused reaction) or angry with himself for being afraid (self-focused reaction), even when the angry behavior actually increases the danger. Listening to this reaction, someone is likely to have the sense that "something else is going on here" or "there's more to this than just anger." The experience is something like hearing two different melodies being played at the same time in a piece of music, one the main melody and the other the background or counterpart.

- Secondary emotions often arise from attempts to judge and control primary responses.

- Thus, anxiety may come from trying to avoid feeling angry or sexually excited, or it may arise from guilt about having felt these emotions.

When someone rejects what they are truly feeling, they are likely to feel bad about themselves. Feeling or expressing one emotion to mask the primary emotion is a metaemotional process. Feelings about emotions need to be acknowledged and then explored to get at the underlying primary emotion.

Experiential therapists see clients emotional processing as occurring on a continuum with five phases (Kennedy-Moore + Watson, 1999[1]):

1. prereflective reaction to an emotion-eliciting stimulus entailing perception of the stimulus, preconscious cognitive and emotional processing, and accompanying physiological changes

2. conscious awareness and perception of the reaction

3. labeling and interpretation of the affective response; people typically draw upon internal as well as situational cues to label their responses

4. evaluation of whether the response is acceptable or not

5. evaluation of the current context in terms of whether it is possible or desirable to reveal one's feelings.

What role does the emotion 'interest' play in emotional responses? It is a baseline emotion of great importance - the action tendency of interest involves intending, orienting, and exploring. Interest is felt very frequently, probably without being noticed. If you think about it, to some degree interest is going to be present with each reaction to stimuli. With every response someone has, they are interested to some degree. You can look at interest further when you consider secondary emotional responses - what was the interest that came from the response that had some other type of interest?

Through each stage of evaluation of a response, or simple evaluations that aren't a response to things, there is interest involved as well. This 'interest' induces caring, and the interest and caring is going to change your emotions - emotions are going to be brought up, intensified, changed based off of your interest or caring or evaluations. When you think and make evaluations, you change the nature and intensity of the emotions that are related to what you are doing or processing.

Are people going to be more interested in clear, primary emotions or feelings that they aren't in touch with? When someone is interested in a feeling, how is that different from being interested in the source of the feeling? If someone is feeling sad, they might not care about the sadness if the feeling is unclear to them or they don't know they are sad. If someone is going to try to change a feeling of sadness, it clearly would be beneficial if they knew when the feeling is occurring.

Is it possible to experience deep emotions without being aware at all that these emotions are occurring? Yes it is, but there are times when people are conscious of those emotions - say when they are recalling them - that the deep emotions are more clear. There could be a deep emotion that occurs over a long period of time - say anger at someone, this anger could be in your body for a long time, during being the person, or while away from the person; the point is the anger is reflected upon or it occurs more deeply at certain points - and then you are going to be aware of the emotion.

That anger is a significant, primary feeling. The feeling is significant because it shows how large the emotion is that is behind it. People can feel feelings that are shallow or intense at the time, but these feelings don't necessarily mean more than that or are deeper than that because they aren't deep or primary - they don't mean anything else or occur at other times you aren't aware of (indicating that this feeling is significant). The feeling of shallow feelings is still potent (because you are feeling them in real time), but they aren't as powerful as feelings that have a special meaning or significance for you (which would make you feel deeper in real time and feel more effected).

If you think about it, people change their feelings by thinking all of the time. The way they could help manage this is probably by making assessments of their emotional state. If people think about what just made them happy or sad, then they might be able to do something or think something to change that. Some emotional responses are going to be more noticeable, and that is when people might try to figure out what went on.

---

1. Kennedy-Moore, E., + Watson, J.C. (1999). *Expressing emotion: Myths, realities and therapeutic strategies.* New York: Guilford Press.

There are subtleties of emotion as well. People probably respond in many ways that they aren't aware of consciously, but they might have responded because something beneath their notice occurred emotionally. You could say that the emotional world beneath your notice is the "unconscious" mind or the unconscious world.

Your emotions change all of the time, only sometimes are you going to notice when an emotion changes or when you are experiencing one. Furthermore, you might want or expect to experience one emotion but you are actually experiencing a different one because unconsciously that is how you are responding. For instance, maybe you have an unconscious bias against a group of people so you feel hate when you interact with them, but you consciously think that you like those people and feel like you should be happy and positive towards them. A feeling might be important to your unconscious mind, or a feeling might be important to your conscious mind - in which case you would probably 'care' about it.

Your attention is constantly divided between various things in your environment, your own internal thinking and your own emotions. Your emotions are going to determine and assist what you pay attention to. For instance, if something is emotional in your environment for you, then more of your attention is probably going to spent thinking about or focusing on that thing.

Or maybe something in your environment is just more interesting than something else, the point is something in your environment or something in your head (emotions, thoughts) caused an intellectual or emotional reaction in you, and that then caused you to pay more attention to it. That doesn't mean that you notice it more after you pay attention - this type of paying attention might be unconscious - i.e. - more of your attentional resources or just more of the focus that people have (not all of which they are aware of) is going to be directed at it.

References

Emotion-Focused Therapy: Coaching Clients to Work Through Their Feelings. Leslie Greenberg. Amer Psychological Assn; 1 edition (January 2002)

Table 12.0

Chapter 13

Advanced Ideas are Important Objects

Human beings can think simple ideas or they can think complex ideas. How is a person supposed to know if an idea that they are thinking is something that needs further consideration?

There are lots of things that people can think about. Some things that people think about are simple topics that they regularly bring up in conversation. Other things that people think about are things that they emotionally ponder.

How is a person supposed to know if something that someone ponders is something that is important for them? Humans could think about many topics throughout the day.

What is thinking for that matter? When a person thinks they are pondering stuff - they form ideas about life or what they are doing, and they try to make sense out of what is happening.

If someone doesn't make sense out of what is happening, then they might not process what is going on in a situation. Their understanding could be emotional or it could be a practical understanding. A practical understanding could be emotional - that is, if they have a feeling for what is going on then they might also be capable of interpreting that understanding in practical fashion.

13.1 Thoughts and Concepts

It doesn't really matter if someone interprets a situation in a practical fashion, as long as they understand what the significant factors are or if they can respond in an effective manner.

Different ideas that the person has could be emotional ideas (ideas about the feelings that they are experiencing) or they could be ideas about what is going on or what their thoughts are. If their thoughts are on their feelings then they could interpret things differently from if their thoughts are coming from the situation.

Therefore, there can be different amounts of focus on ones thoughts or the situation - people can direct their thoughts at life in general or they could direct their thoughts at what they want from a situation.

Situations or life-scenarios impact a humans feelings in various ways - the person could try to interpret what is going on by analyzing either the external sources or what the impact on their feelings is.

Table 13.0

Table 14.0

Chapter 14

Practical Realites are Symbols of Emotion

Different objects or experiences in life generate different amounts and kinds of emotion. These experiences or symbols can consistently generate the same emotions and feelings or they could be diverse and inconsistent.

All of life can be divided into different ideas or categories of objects. The different objects can be emotional objects that generate feeling, like someones pet - or they could be practical objects that someone uses for non-personal purposes.

Then would that just be a matter of analyzing which objects are most important to the person? People do different activities - that then is just a simple matter of managing their lives.

If a feeling is motivating someone to achieve a goal or objective - does that then make them look for an object that will fulfill that purpose?

Goals and objectives are the ideas that people form in their minds based upon what they think they will capable of achieving and what objects and objectives they will be capable of satisfying.

Feelings can motivate thoughts and ideas - how is a person even supposed to know what an idea is or what a thought that they have is? THere are simple thoughts that relate directly to what the person wants and their are more complicated thoughts that are harder to think about. There are also things that are unclear.

That means that an idea can be unclear, simple or complex. If an idea is simple and unclear then it could be understood better emotionally. If an idea is felt well - or naturally understood by the person, then it could be a simple idea because the unconscious mind is usually more simple than the conscious mind.

That doesn't necessarily mean that emotional ideas are simple - emotions can communicate complex concepts or ideas. That is dreams are often very complicated.

14.1 Ideas and Symbols

Humans can have an idea about life, or they can think about life in a more simple manner just by idle thinking or daydreaming. However it isn't necessary to daydream in order to ponder ones objectives and experiences.

Daydreaming would be the equivalent of understanding something in a simple emotional manner - however is daydreaming, idle thinking, or emotional feeling-based thought simple, unclear, or obvious?

Those are interesting questions, it means something about the unconscious mind - what does it take for a person to ponder their life - they don't necessarily need to think about their life in a simple or emotional fashion.

Table 14.0

Chapter

Table 15.0

Truth and Logic
Chapter

If something is subjective then it is subject to opinion, and isn't like a fact or solid piece of information. Truth and logic can determine how subjective something is, if someone is being accurate then it is logical and makes sense - or is the truth.

Why would it matter is someone was being accurate? What would that mean anyway - to be accurate about something?

It really depends on what the person is accurate about. Lots of stuff in life relates to peoples emotions, so therefore that information could be subject to personal opinion.

What sort of information relates to opinion or to human emotion?

Humans have a lot of emotions, feelings can mix with other feelings - for instance sadness and anger can mix together. It is a critical concept to understand that different feelings can combine to form a new, combined feeling.

Different attitudes can also combine with feelings - for instance sad can combine with a pessimistic attitude. An attitude differs from a feeling because an attitude is like an intention, while a feeling is simply how the person is feeling (the two can combine to produce a more powerful feeling/attitude).

In this way attitudes and feelings are separate - attitude is something that is more under the persons control - because they can control what they are thinking about and where they direct their hostility to some degree, while a feeling is the unconscious minds understanding and feeling of what is happening, which cannot be controlled, only influenced by the persons thoughts.

15.1 Tiger's Eye

What happens when someone has a feeling that they don't understand, but have a strong attitude about something? They can have an attitude and might know what the attitude is for - however that doesn't mean that the feeling that is associated with the attitude is as simple as the attitude.

Attitudes are simple because they are more something that the person is directing towards something - that is what an attitude is after all - something that the person is passionate or violent about.

Feelings can be complicated because they come from the unconscious - the unconscious mind is not as directed as the conscious mind. An attitude could be under control or directed because it is conscious, however that doesn't mean that it is going to be.

People know what the 'attitude' means, and they know what the word 'feeling' means, however these two words are critical to understand because attitudes are directed at something and are more of a force, while feelings are just emotions.

A human doesn't even necessarily need to have an attitude, they could just be feeling emotions. If a feeling or emotion is strong enough it could be considered to be an attitude because it would change the persons demeanor, however perhaps feelings and attitudes could be controlled and mixed in a desired fashion.

Table 15.0

Chapter

Table 16.0

Perception and Reality
Chapter 16

There is a reality to any situation. Different parts of the situation can be observed by the perceiver. Depending on what someone is feeling, different ideas and perceptions could be understood or looked at.

That, however, brings up the question of - what is a perception? If a perception is a way of looking at something then there are different ways of understanding a single experience or event.

Some experiences are unconsciously processed - the person simply feels that way based upon what their mind wants to feel and think.

The person in an experience can try to alter how the experience is felt by thinking about what their emotions are and what is happening in the situation. How is the person supposed to know if thier emotions are being influenced? Why would someone care about what they are feeling?

Some decisions are 'subjective' - that means that a decision that a person makes in a situation depends on their emotions and feelings. If they have an idea - then that idea might be something that is influenced by the person in the situation.

Depending on what is happening in a situation, different emotions and feelings are going to be influenced. The person can also influence their own emotions by think about how they want to feel - or what they are feeling.

What else might influence how a person is feeling in a situation that they can control by their own thinking? Why would a person thinking about their own feelings influence how those feelings are felt? They can try and manage their own feelings - or they could think about what they want, or how they are feeling.

Thinking about how they are feeling influences the feelings because the emotions that they are feeling are tied in with their thoughts. Thoughts influence feelings in different ways - a thought could assist a feeling, a thought could hinder a feeling, or a thought could change the nature or positive or negative orientation of a feeling.

Somw feelings can be influenced by the reality in a situation, while others are influenced by what the person is thinking about. Sometimes the feelings might be physical - however those feelings are also influenced by a persons thoughts.

16.1 Different Ideas

If a person thinks about an idea - then they are thinking a thought of some sort. That means that something is occurring to them. What could a person think about as an idea? They can think about anything basically, some ideas or thoughts might be partially unconscious or unclear.

Some ideas or thought are going to be linked to different feelings that a person has - and further more there could be groupings of ideas and groupings of feelings that are linked to the thoughts that a person has.

There can also be different ways feelings influence thoughts - positively, negatively, delusionally, optimistically, and with a different feeling that can also change the perspective of the thought.

Table 16.0

Chapter

Table 17.0

What is an Emotional Perspective?

A perspective can be a way of viewing something - that basically means that something in life can be different than from how it was previously, and different in many ways.

If something is different from how it used to be then what would the difference be? Humans understand different ideas in different ways, and things in life also change depending on the circumstances.

The situation that someone is in can effect how that person is feeling in that situation. What the person is doing could be something simple or something complex, and it could hard or easy for the person to achieve their goals and objectives.

Depending on the person a situation or difficulty could be viewed in various ways. The other people in the situation could also be dealt with in a different manner.

This means that in any situation there are multiple things that are changing. The people in the situation change, difficulties in the situation change, and the viewpoint from different areas around the environment is different, depending on where the person is standing.

If a person has a different viewpoint of an environment from different locations, and if they can see different people and different difficulties from spaces around the area, then that means that stuff happens in those areas that can differ drastically.

If things is life are different, or change then the motivations and desires that the people who are in those environments feel could also change.

That is a simple way of looking at it - in any room there are different objects, and in any environment there are also different objects. Different people can also be different - like how one object is different from another object, any one person is different from the next.

Life is full of objects and ideas - the ideas in life can be used to describe the different objects in life, and these objects can mean different things to different people. Objects can be symbols which can be important to a person, and these symbols can all fit in an environment or room.

17.1 Perspectives

That means that someone can look at a situation positively or negatively. If something is positive and beneficial, then it means that the different objects that comprise the objective or reward can be broken up into various parts and each part can be looked at for its motivational, emotional or cognitive components.

If an object is a symbol that means that it can represent different things in life. Something in life that is different could be something that is extremely dramatic or obtrusive. Something obtrusive is something that causes an emotional response.

An emotional response is something that the person feels - the person might notice that if they think about what they are doing in any situation. If a person is aware of what they are doing then they might be aware of the reasons behind what they are doing.

Table 17.0

Table 18.0

Chapter 18

Subjective Emotions are Perspectives (with logic)

There are ways of viewing the world - these ways can be called different perspectives. A perspective is a viewpoint. A viewpoint is a way of looking at something. Since there are different main emotions, then there are also only a few major ways of viewing things in life.

Emotions are feelings - perception is a way of feeling because it is like viewing a specific or related set of objects. What would it mean to 'look at something in one way'? What would be the different ways of looking at something? There are ways of perceiving things from emotional viewpoints - negatively, positively, and neutrally.

Information can be viewed from a positive perspective, some information is objective and it doesn't matter what the feelings are that the person who is thinking about the information has. Which feelings relate to what information then? There are some feelings that can slant how some information is looked at more than other feelings. Would those feelings be described as being key, important or basic?

When an emotion is basic or important, how does it influence the persons overall feelings? There can be an emotional state that someone is in - this state can come from many key feelings or just a few strong emotions or drives.

How is someone supposed to identify if an emotion is important? What is a single emotion anyway? There can be a single state of feeling or a single drive or motivation that is powerful. How would that relate to thinking or thought?

If there are multiple thoughts then there could be a different way of viewing something from each different thought. Thoughts can also have a viewpoint or perspective, basically. A thought could be an idea or understanding that a person has that reflects a viewpoint or feeling.

Different ideas can form a 'theoretical framework' for an emotion or perspective - the structure is theoretical because different feelings are subjective - that means that the ideas can change easily based upon the persons feelings, and in turn influence other thoughts or ideas - which all contribute to a certain perspective.

Perception

A perspective is more than a way of looking at something - everything is based off of what happens in life, so a perception is a way of looking at behavior or action in the real world (philosophers call this the 'life- world' or the 'horizon'). Reality can be viewed as a whole - or it can be looked at part by part. Similarly, feelings and perceptions and actions all can be looked at individually or as a whole.

Being aware of something means that the person is conscious of that object. A human could also be conscious of the entire world, the life within the world, or some of the world. What does all that mean - human think with words and thoughts and ask questions about themselves and the world - it doesn't necessarily mean anything if they do that kind of thinking - what would make such thinking productive? If they recognize which aspects of the world they are thinking about, how they are thinking about them, and what the feelings and perceptions of those things are.

Table 18.0

Chapter

Table 18.0

Subjective Perception and Logic

Logic is the ability to understand information in a clear way - when someone thinks about something, it can be simple or it can be complex. If it is complicated then it isn't necessarily clear, or something could be simple and it could also be unclear. What then would the difference be between something simple and something complex?

Complex information could be anything that is hard to understand. How does someone know when something that they think about is easy or hard to comprehend? Things that are hard to understand can be related to advanced topics - or they could be simple things in life that are just difficult to think about or are subjective.

If a concept is subjective then it could be an emotional concept - an emotional concept could be a concept that is dependent on a persons feelings or opinions. If someone has an opinion about something - for instance, if they are assessing how much they like something (desire) or if something is interesting (which could possibly be how cool something is) then that is a subjective concept or thought that is emotion or feeling based.

When someone makes a subjective decision or evaluation they are using their feelings to make that decision. That relates to intellect as well as to feeling because someones opinion is their intellectual assessment of how much they desire something.

19.1 Desire, Drive and Interest

How intellectual is desire or drive? Is an interest in something more emotional or is interest more intellectual? What does that mean exactly - for an interest to be cognitive/ Desire could be something that a person thinks about - someone can think about their own desires and motivations, and that could help to make those motivations more clear to them.

If a human understand what their feelings are then it becomes more cognitive and clear. However the unconscious is very complex so there could be a confusion of feeling or understanding - the unconscious mind gives signals and feelings about what a person really wants or dislikes.

Desire is a human drive - humans and animals drive themselves to have pleasure seeking-goals and motivations. They also think about things in life that relate to those goals. The things that humans think about are cognitive aspects of thought or mind, and the things that cause them to experience feelings are the emotional or feeling-based aspects of the mind.

How does the cognitive (thoughts and intellect) mix with the feeling or emotional aspect of mind? Humans have thoughts, and they have feelings - however how cognition and emotion relate is much more complicated than simply thinking about something and it having a component or aspect that is emotional (a feeling).

19.2 Logic and Emotion

There are different aspects of life that are emotional, different things that generate feelings, and these same things can also be thought about - can be understood. If something is understood then it is 'comprehended', feelings can be intelligent and that means that there is something to understand about the feelings.

When a human understands a feeling, what exactly is it that they are understanding? Feelings relate to certain things, and these things can help to classify and define the feeling. Feelings relate to the parts that makeup the feeling. The parts that makeup the feeling are usually simple and direct - if a person can label the feeling anyway. If it is hard to label or pick out the feeling then it would be hard to identify what the source of the feeling is.

Assessing feelings is very subjective because it is hard to label what a persons feelings are. It isn't even clear if humans have the appropriate ways or language to describe their feelings. They don't necessarily even need to be described - when someone is feeling something then it is obvious that they are feeling something - or even if it isn't obvious they still are experiencing emotions.

Emotions were described by Aristotle as being wild and uncontrollable - while reason is the opposite. That is a simple idea to understand - feelings are passionate, while logic is simply thoughts or ideas.

Feelings aren't necessarily passionate - a person can experience feeling and not be interested in their own feelings, however compared to reasoning (which could be understanding concepts and ideas in life, or thinking about things that are intelligent). How could someone define when thought is intelligent then? Feelings can be simple - or they could be complex feelings, while thoughts are also simple - it is the combination of many difficult thoughts that lead to more complicated understandings (a thought could be something like a sentence describing an idea or concept).

19.3 Is intellect clear?

How is someone supposed to identify if a thought or idea is intelligent? Humans think about lots of things all of the time, it isn't necessarily clear if those things are complicated or they are simple. Thinking about something to eat could be a simple idea - or could that be a complicated idea?

Dogs and other animals think about what they want to eat - and it helps to motivate them to get that food. The motivation or drive is a survival instinct. The instinct for survival motivates them to get the food - or is it the desire to eat something? That is a complicated question right there.

Assessing the reason behind different motivations is very complicated, or it could be considered to be simple. On on hand, when a human wants something it could be obvious what it is that they want and why they want that, if you consider the basic and important emotions then the basic instincts are rather obvious, however there are often subtle motivations and lesser feelings that humans can experience.

Table 19.0

Belief, Perception and Reality

In the SOPHIST Plato distinguishes between two kinds of belief - 'doxa' which is the process of thinking, and 'phantasia' - which is 'through sense perception'.

What is the difference between perception and reality? There are different processes of thinking about things. Humans think in different ways about different topics and objects.

For instance, people can think cognitively or emotionally. That means that they can sort of 'feel' stuff - or they can think about stuff (or some combination of the two).

What happens when a human thinks about something - this could be called a thought process or just a period of thinking. People can think as if in a day dream, which might be more of an idle type of thinking - or they could seriously consider different ideas in a logical fashion (which would be intelligent thinking).

What are the consequences of intelligent or serious thinking? If it is thinking about emotions then it could be considered to be emotionally reflective - or if it is thinking about a topic which is related to human beings then it could also involve an understanding of feelings. - For instance emotions and motivation are clearly important for an understanding of politics, any event that involves people, or anything basically - the details are complex.

When humans think they use their feelings to think about things - or the thoughts involve an understanding of feelings. An understanding of feelings could use feeling that the person could feel - or the feeling could simply be thought about.

20.1 Logical thinking

What are the different types of logical thinking? There could be ways of thinking clearly about things, or the thinking could involve different supporting points - or some combination of the two.

Thinking that is more logical would probably involve a greater understanding that simply thinking in a simple or inaccurate fashion - what would be an example of logical thinking then?

Some thinking corresponds with reality while other types of thinking are more motivation related. If the thinking is motivated then it is triggered by feelings and emotions -

For any idea there could by many logical or supporting points. A logical point is a point that makes sense or reveals a truth that is accurately represented. If a reality is misrepresented then it is probably not very clear - its 'misrepresentation could be clear however that would be disguising a more accurate truth or logical point.

What would be an example of an argument with supporting points that shows how logic works with the feelings that the mind uses to think? Any topic using different amounts of feeling to think about - in each situation the feelings are different and need to be analyzed.

So a clear idea would be an idea that is clearly understood - since everything in life is subjective then some ideas are going to be understood more clearly by some people than by others. Rating or cool something is or how much someone likes something is subjective - and that might not be clear. However that brings up the point of what a clear idea would be that is more of a fact - something that is not subjective or subject to opinion.

Most ideas are subject to personal opinion, whether it is a reality or it isn't a reality.

20.2 Perception vs Reality

There are ideas that humans can think about that involve their perceptions - and there are ideas that involve reality. How is a person supposed to separate out what their perceptions are from what the reality is?

There are perceptions, representations and objects that all correspond with logical or illogical thought. A representation is an object that is represented in a persons mind - for instance, if you see a basketball it is a simple object in reality but when you think about it in your mind it might be associated with playing a game or having fun - in addition to representing and thinking about the simple visual object in your head.

That means that humans can use representations to think about things. They can represent multiple objects or multiple ideas, and the ideas and objects can be thought about differently in the mind. Using my example of the basketball, if you have different objects and want to think about them all together then you need to consider how each object is thought about in the mind, and then how the mind combines thinking about the objects - because a representation is how something is represented - not necessarily what it actually is.

So what then is the perception vs. the reality? A single object gets represented in a rather simple fashion - usually someone can tell what they think about a single object in their mind if the concept is simple and easy to understand.

That makes sense - simple concepts are less subjective and therefore they are easier to understand. If a concept is easy to understand then it could be more easily figured out if it is emotional or non-emotional - logical or non-logical.

Ideas that are only opinions could be emotional or non-emotional. How much someone likes something is very emotional or related to feelings. What are all the topics or ideas in life that are important or significant? Humans do not think about an infinite number of ideas - there are only a few ideas that are the major categories - at the top of a tree structure of ideas.

20.3 Different Concepts and Their Understanding

Some concepts are emotional - these are concepts like desire and fear - and other concepts that relate to the basic emotions. Other concepts are intellectual and these concepts could also relate to emotions, but would relate to understanding emotions not just measuring how strong the feelings are.

Understanding emotions is different from feeling emotions because feelings are simple while understanding is difficult and complex. Intelligent understandings involve understanding the motivations that lye behind the feelings - motivations involve thoughts while feelings do have sources, they aren't necessarily tied in directly with the motivating thought.

Table 20.0

Chapter 21

How do our ideas influence our emotions?

Human beings get inspired by different types of information or different things. Some stuff in life is boring, while other stuff is interesting. That is significant because experiences or emotions that are fun or happy could be interesting - or would probably be interesting, but could also be boring, even though they are happy experiences.

That would seem rather obvious - what makes an experience a happy experience? There is cognition and emotion - human emotions are influenced by their thoughts and their understanding of events. The want something to be cool - and that then influences there emotions to want to the thing to actually be cool and generate positive emotions for them.

So there are happy things in life and sad things. Woody allen said that life is tragedy, with oasis of comedy. That is a significant statement. How do happy emotions combine with sad emotions? Humans cannot be happy all of the time - although it seems like dogs and cats might be.

Maybe there is no such thing as a single emotion. I previously understood that there could be multiple emotions, and possibly a single dominant emotion. However maybe it is more complicated than that - for instance maybe emotions could combine into each other in the mind. They would certainly influence each other.

That would mean that an experience has multiple emotions, that all come from the same experience. That would seem rather obvious, however it is complicated for various reasons. When something in an experience becomes an emotion it could be misrepresented - Heidegger wrote about how objects could be misrepresented.

Emotions emotions emotions are free - emotions emotions emotions for me - one one one one one one two three, emotion is for me. Emotion is extraordinary.

That was not a logical paragraph. Paragraphs are only logical if they have multiple supporting points.

If someone rambles on stupidly and emotionally then it isn't very logical. So that means that the persons emotions would be influencing their thoughts - or acting with their thoughts. That is significant informatoin becasue humans have emotions all of the time, and it is useful to know when their emotions are influencing their thoughts.

Emotions are feelings - feelings make humans motivated and to do things and think things. If someone is motivated to do something then they could do lots of stuff. Human emotion is powerful and their ideas are influenced by their emotions.

The ideas that humans hold are influenced by their emotions. Humans have lots of ideas, and each idea could be influenced by different motivations and drives and desires.

Table 21.0

Chapter 22

Is the field of Emotion and Cognition limited or already

understood?

Emotion and cognition is a significant field of study. I wrote articles about emotion and cognition and discussed how the mind thinks in various ways - there are different ways of thinking about things and different ways of feeling things.

There are ways that the mind learns new information. There are also ways that the mind forgets information. If I have written everything that is significant about how the mind thinks and feels then it shouldn't really be necessary to discuss other intellectual topics.

What other topic could be a significant field of study?

Medicine is obviously significant. Literature is also significant, however literature just relates to life and the important aspects about life are how people feel emotions and how they think - which I have already discussed in my emotion and cognition articles.

22.1 Is Life Subjective?

This article is a 'summary' article - and by that I mean that it is a summary of life. Humans need to understand different things in order to get along in the world. Is all of life subjective? How do people decide if something is cool or uncool, or other subjective decisions like if different celebrities are interesting in such and such a fashion?

It is a simple understanding that humans see items and then some of those items cause them to experience emotions. That is just the start of this article - it might seem obvious that different things cause people to experience different emotions.

What are the necessary requirements for a person to get along in life? How would I know that someone is even understanding these words that I am writing? If it is looked at that way, then the difference between animal intellect and human intellect is very simple and not a large difference.

Animals understand basic things about life and about emotions, and humans have a similar understanding except they can make the understanding verbal, and understand various logical points about the emotional experience in life.

Animals understand how to function in reality very well, they can move around and notice basic objects and how to go around them. They also note varoius intentions of other animals and humans - what else do they really need to understand?

If an animal understands basic intentions, then it knows how to get along in life because it is aware of the intentions of the other animals that it interacts with - which means that it knows what the other animals are going to do and can predict their behavior.

22.2 Emotion and Cognition

What is the influence of a persons emotion and cognition on their overall psychological health?

How someone thinks and feels is obviously going to be important for that person. However, how could I separate how someone thinks about things from how a person thinks about the same issues?

If it is an idea or life experience, then how does the conscious mind process, understand or 'feel' that experience differently from the unconscious mind?

It is subjective to decide how 'aware' someone is of their own thoughts and feelings about an event - if it is just processed or if it is really understood.

How then could someone define when an experience is felt or thought about? If there are different components to the experience then it could simply be viewed by its different components and if each of those parts is processed by the subject.

Therefore an experience should have different components that can be measured - there is the number of significant feelings involved, the 'emotional intelligence' of the feelings, the unconscious implications of the feelings, the amount the feelings are thought about consciously - the amount of 'meta' reflection, and the influence of the experience on other feelings and thoughts or ideas the person might have.

22.3 Meta Reflection

In the previous section I used the word 'meta' reflection, which hasn't really been defined academically yet, however if you think about it then if there is a meta-cognition and meta-reasoning then there is also a meta-reflection.

After all, reflection is when a person thinks about their ideas, thoughts, emotions, etc. Therefore it is basically like the term 'meta-cognition' except it is implying that the person is 'reflecting' on something instead of thinking about their thinking. So they could be just thinking about experiences and their own thinking at the same time.

I have talked about cognition and emotion in many previous articles, and how thoughts relate to feelings is very important for people to understand because they will be capable of influencing their own emotions and their own intellect - which is basically their conscious mind, while their emotions are basically their unconscious.

22.4 Abstraction, Logic and Thoughts

How could a thought be 'abstracted'? What would it mean to abstract a thought? Thoughts are related to feelings, and some thoughts are more logical than other thoughts - so if a thought is abstracted then it could be made to have more feeling.

What would that mean, however - to 'give a thought more feeling;? If thoughts have feelings attached and associated with them, then their associated feelings could be made to be stronger or contain more information.

The idea that a thought could be made to have more feeling is interesting - it is obviously true, however it might be hard to define what a single thought is or what a single feeling is. Thoughts and conscious, cognitive thinking have feelings that are associated with the thinking.

I mean, how is someone supposed to identify a single feeling - if they are holding a apple they can say 'I can feel this apple' - that would be like a single feeling. Apples are red.

Table 22.0

Chapter 23

Mental Processes and Cognition

What are the significant mental processes? That question is basically asking how the mind works. The mind thinks in various different ways, and it feels in complex ways also.

Humans have different ways of thinking about things – there are ways of framing something from a different emotional or objective perspective. An objective perspective could be an intellectual viewpoint, however, emotions could also be intellectual (combining viewpoints with non-biased information and biased information).

Emotions are basically feelings – emotions are theoretically the basis for feelings, when someone is motivated to do something – then that comes from an emotion, which is a strong feeling. Feelings are shallow because they are more sensory, however when someone feels strongly that should be labeled as an emotion. So I could simply define an emotion as 'any strong feeling'. That is why emotions are the base of human behavior, and feelings are shallow, sensory and stimulation is also a type of feeling.

Humans aren't motivated to do things because of shallow, sensory feelings. That is why emotions motivate people and make them feel more strongly. People don't feel everything deeply – there are an infinite number of feelings, however there are only a few defined emotions. Feelings are how we feel things; while emotions are also how humans feel – they also are more complex because they are deeper than feelings and require more resources for the mind to process.

Feelings and emotions also relate to the other cognitive functions.

Such as the regulation of emotion through the modification of attention, which is a significant mental process.

Humans can change their attention, and what they are paying to - depending on what they are paying attention to and how much and what kind of attention they are giving - their emotions are going to fluctuate accordingly.

What are the different types of attention? Emotions could theoretically tilt someones attention in certain ways.

Attention relates to the different cognitive abilities.

Attention, memory, emotional processes, thinking, and arousal (which is more physiological) are the main ways in which human minds perform. Emotional processes and arousal evokes feelings, while attention, memory and thought are cognitive.

1. Life and Subjectivity

Life is subjective – everything is dependent on human feelings, they determine our perceptions and our emotions, and how everything works. Life is basically just feelings interacting with each other, or is it an intellectual understanding that comes from the experience of life? This is obvious is you look at lesser animals like dogs, who basically just feel and are obviously very emotional or feeling-based. Humans intellectualize their feelings and that is why they are human.

Feelings comprise life – what makes feelings complex? Different objects alone wouldn't seem to be very complicated or intellectual. It must be the emotions that make people intellectual such as love, disgust, contempt, anger, sadness, surprise, and joy. Those emotions come from very complex feelings and understandings. The 'understandings' are basically of other things in life that also comprise feelings.

Emotions are very significant, however there are an endless number of ways of feelings things. Feeling is how something feels, while emotions are the minds intellectualizaitons. Emotions are more intellectual than feelings. There is the surface way of feeling life and experiences – and there is the deeper way of experiencing life – which basically consists of thinking and experiencing emotion, not feeling.

How could an animal like a dog be described as experiencing life then? Could a dog be described as being emotional, or just something that experiences feeling? It would seem to experience emotions, however they just aren't as intellectual as a humans. They probably also experience feelings, however those would be more basic than a humans and be about food, basic behaviors, interaction, etc.

A humans feelings could be about lots of simple things, or many complex things. A humans emotions could be compared to a dogs.

23.1 Personal Goals, Motivation and Emotion

"When people perceive a discrepancy between how they think are and how they would like to be (i.e., between their actual and ideal selves), dejection related emotions such as disappointment, sadness and depression predominate. In contrast, a contrast between how people think they are and how they think they ought to be, (i.e., between their actual and ought selves) leads to agitation related emotions such as guilt, fear and anxiety." - "Self-Awareness and Self-relevant Thought in the Experience and Regulation of Emotion" Mark Leary and Dina Gohar. 2014. In (Ed.) James Gross, "Handbook of Emotion Regulation" Guilford Press.

How a person perceives themself is important, however it doesn't necessarily cause agigitation related emotions or dejection related emotions. There are other factors that lead to those emotions such as social influence or other goals that the person might be failing. Their emotions come from there general motivation, which is determined by their interpersonal goals and their pleasure goals - which is the goal they have to achieve pleasure.

That would be Freuds sex instinct, and he also mentioned a death instinct. Those two instincts manifest themselves in interpersonal goals, personal goals such as how they would like to be and what they want to achieve, and other motivations that relate to death and sex.

Basically when I describe the death and sex instinct of Freud as 'motivations', it makes it more clear what is going on - if you relate the other goals and objectives that people have such as how they would like their personalities and behaviors and mannerisms to be then you can form a complete picture of the human motivational/emotional/intellectual psyche.

What ideas influence a persons emotions? I just described that the drives for pleasure or the desire for destruction (the sex and death instinct) could motivate people to achieve those desires - however there are certainly other desires that humans have.

So that means that basically all human thoughts, feelings and drives come from the basic desires of pleasure and pain. These could be extremely high cognitions that influence the persons emotions. How could simple thoughts influence emotion? What is so special about the higher cognitive functions?

Dogs have simple emotions - however, could a dogs emotions be described as being deep without the cognitive functions that a human has? A humans stimulation or physiology must be very psychological.

This means that essentially emotions are tied in with thoughts, and that emotions influence our physiology, sensations and stimulation. This occurs because emotions are tied in with physical feelings - they are unconscious while thoughts are merely cognitive.

So what do thoughts achieve then? I described in previous articles that they can be directed and can influence emotions. They also inspire, motivate and direct many complicated, simple or even ordinary feelings.

Ordinary feelings could also be complicated, maybe the multiple objects in life can be misrepresented to form more complicated symbols or representations - this helps to make thought and cognition more advanced - and that in turn makes human feeling more intricate.

23.2 Thought and Self-Reflection

What would a 'direct' thought be? Humans self-reflect all of the time, the question is, how complicated is that process?

23.3 What is the influence of the unconscious on mental processes?

The unconscious mind is powerful, most processes could actually be viewed as just being unconscious because humans can only exert a small amount of control over many processes, for instance pulling up a memory could be considered to be a conscious process, however since it takes time to pull up many memories that means that the persons unconscious mind needs to think about things like other associated memories and emotions in order to think more about the memory and bring it up.

Humans have different mental processes. Emotion interacts with thoughts, and it also interacts with physical stimulation. What are the ways in which emotion interacts with thoughts? Emotions and feelings can be intellectual - the way in which they are intellectual influences the persons thoughts - intelligence and thoughts in the mind are basically the same thing.

There is no point to emotions that aren't intelligent - that is basically just what dogs are like.

Table 23.0

Chapter 24

Can Artificial Intelligence be Artistic?

Can a computer be built to be as intelligent as a human being? What intellectual superiorities do humans have over any advanced artificial intelligence computer?

Computers could not be programmed to analyze emotional responses in an adaptive fashion. They could be programmed to respond to emotions individually - for instance they could program a feeling into a computer and have the computer respond to that feeling, however there are many different subtleties to any feeling.

Can the different subtleties to any feeling be described and programmed? There are different components to any feeling in the real world or internal stimulation (such as thinking or physical feelings). Computers will never really have any feelings because they are not biological, or they are not 'alive'. Feelings come from physical stimulation - or feelings are simply physical processes.

Feelings are physical processes that come from emotions that people experience. The emotions that people experience come from stimuli in the world or internal cognitions. So the question then is, what makes a feeling subtle? Is it a deeper way of feeling or is it a more complicated way of feeling?

If it is a more complicated way of feeling then it could be programmed into a computer, but what kind of information does a complicated feeling convey that is different from a more deep or intense feeling? Maybe a deep feeling has more information that is related to that single feeling that is connected in the real world.

So feelings that are simple might have more details that are just related to one thing in the world. Feelings that are complicated could relate to more detailed objects in the world, or multiple objects that are grouped together. Multiple objects grouped together could result in multiple feelings for each object, or one feeling altogether, for instance if someone goes into a room they get a feeling for that room.

If a robot had to look at a line of houses on a street, then the robot couldn't possibly recognize one street from another street because it would have to recognize all of the different houses on the street - and then label that street as the street that had all of the different houses in that order. Furthermore, each house would have to be 'abstracted' so that it could be more artistic or easily programmed and so that the robot could recognize the simple features of the house.

24.1 Ideas, Objects and Artificial Intelligence

So feelings have associated ideas, an idea can contribute to a feeling, or multiple ideas can contribute to feelings or a feeling. If humans have feelings then they use their feelings to think about their ideas, however, what then is the difference between ideas and feelings? Why wouldn't a human simply have ideas then, and not need to experience feeling?

Feelings certainly separate out ideas in terms of the time that the idea occurs to the person, and it could also have associated ideas, however, how do two ideas interact in terms of feeling? If a person has the idea of 'orange' and the idea of 'apple', then what happens when the person thinks of appples and oranges at the same time? And how would that be different from seeing an apple and an orange together on a table?

How are the feelings separate in the persons mind? They must be linked to other related objects in the persons mind like the category of 'fruit'. Things in the mind are associated with each other based upon their real life associations, but also based upon how the mind learned to associate those 'thought units' - or whatever you want to call them.

The mind works by association chains, basically.

How would two dissimalar items be related to each other then? The mind might have a feeling of 'fruit' if they thought about both an apple and an orange at the same time, or they might think of other individual fruits, or if the feeling that the fruit produces is similar to the feeling of a completely different object then it could be related in terms of similar feelings.

Heidegger wrote that objects in life can be missrepresented. That is a significant concept and is related to artificial intelligence and idea associations. Some ideas can be 'misrepresented' while other ideas are more simple and can be felt and understood easily - and obviously their association chains could be understood.

What does it mean to 'misrepresent' an object, then? Objects mean what they mean, it is very simple. How could it be a complex thing to misrepresent an object? Would that mean confusing one object with another object? Or would it mean confusing the feeling of an object?

So how would the details of idea and object associations play out? Furthermore, what would be considered to be 'advanced' thinking, if the mind only thinks with ideas and objects? It would seem like the mind thinks mostly with simple ideas and objects, and the ideas and objects each having associated and direct feelings.

Perhaps the feelings that certain groups of ideas or objects have lead to greater intellectual categories, for instance fruit could be related metaphorically to furniture, that could be a more intellectual and less direct association - that would be associated in the mind but would be more of an intellectual association. If someone thinks about fruit, then it could be related to furniture because they are both physical objects, but fruit is soft and furniture is hard.

How would that be intellectual? It doesn't seem like that would lead to any advanced thinking. However, it could lead to advanced thinking because all metaphors or comparisons that aren't direct could be harder to figure out or related via less direct associations.

Does that mean that all less direct associations are more intellectual, however? Maybe multiple feelings combine into categories that overlap and the entire thing becomes complicated and intellectual, or   something like that.

Idea Associations

So the ideas related to each other with things called associations. Associations relate ideas to each other - they are connected through relationships in real life or cognitive relationships. If someone thinks about something then that could relate to something else that they think about, or the idea in their head could be different from how it is in reality - there is emotional realities and physical realities that could be related.

If it is an emotional reality then it could be dificiult to figure out, obviously since emotions are subjective, and hard to measure. For instance if you want to relate how cool two different things are it would be impossible because one person could think that it is cool and another person could think it is not cool.

What kinds of emotional reality are measurable and less subjective then? How does emotional reality relate to artificial intelligence? If robots just need to assess objects and how objects are related to each other then they don't need to necessarily have any emotional intellignce.

If a robot needs to understand stuff, it doesn't need to assess emotions, it just needs to understand how to get around in reality. Understanding emotions is too complicated and only a human being could make subjective judgements.

Designing Robots

Just have the robots do stuff - it can't be that difficult to have them function properly. On one hand humans perform very simply -their actions are 'artistic' and can be performed by understanding their own feelings. On the other hand, their actions could be considered to be complex and cognitive and requiring conscouis effort and thought.

If it requires conscoius thought then the person needs to think about what is happening and how to perform in each instance - unless it is already learned (but metacognitive theories already addressed those ideas).

How is a robot supposed to understand that a house is a house, and that houses are where humans live? That seems like something a person would understand, however a robot wouldn't need to understand something like that. What would a robot need to understand that is difficult or complex then, in order for it to be intelligent?

It needs to be capable of abstracting more, robots can be programmed to do lots of things - however that does not make them very intelligent. How could 'abstraction' be programmed into a robot? Abstraction is artistic and uses a humans feelings.

Robots need to be capable of organizing objects in an efficient manner, they don't necessarily need to understand emotions. How could understanding emotions be related to organizing objects, however? Maybe significant objects could generate more emotion, so the significant objects could be related to other significant objects and the insignificant features of an area be disregarded.

The significant features of an area are the features that are, well, significant. They can be significant for different things, different categories such as houses, interiors of houses, a category of objects that consists of things related to human beings, and so on.

What about the definitions of objects? An object could be recognized and its definition looked up by the robot. That way they could form associations - and human minds could be looked at to see what the typical associations are - does this object relate to that object - it has it in its definition after all.

How could a robot relate one object to another object? It looks up the definiton of the object then compares the related features of the two different objects by looking at visual similarities - what about the amount of light shed on objects in a three dimensional space? If the robots can see in three dimensions then they can at least figure out the spacial significance of objects.

If a robot knows the spacial significance of objects then it should theoreticaly be capable of doing anything.

The definition of each object can be programmed in, and how it would relate to other objects and the significance of each object. If the definiton can be described to the robot properly, then the robot should understand everything - however, some things are very hard to understand and it could be dificult to describe it to the robot.

The robot can relate different things to each other, and fit them together spacially so it knows what to do in reality.

Table 24.0

Chapter 25

Is Life Subjective?

This article is a 'summary' article - and by that I mean that it is a summary of life. Humans need to understand different things in order to get along in the world. Is all of life subjective? How do people decide if something is cool or uncool, or other subjective decisions like if different celebrities are interesting in such and such a fashion?

It is a simple understanding that humans see items and then some of those items cause them to experience emotions. That is just the start of this article - it might seem obvious that different things cause people to experience different emotions.

What are the necessary requirements for a person to get along in life? How would I know that someone is even understanding these words that I am writing? If it is looked at that way, then the difference between animal intellect and human intellect is very simple and not a large difference.

Animals understand basic things about life and about emotions, and humans have a similar understanding except they can make the understanding verbal, and understand various logical points about the emotional experience in life.

Animals understand how to function in reality very well, they can move around and notice basic objects and how to go around them. They also note varoius intentions of other animals and humans - what else do they really need to understand?

If an animal understands basic intentions, then it knows how to get along in life because it is aware of the inteions of the other animals that it interacts with - which means that it knows what the other animals are going to do and can predict their behavior.

Table 25.0

Chapter 26

How powerfull and developed is the unconscious?

How powerful and significant is the unconscious mind?

The Phenomenological Realism of the Possible Worlds: The 'A Priori', Activity and Passivity of Consciousness, Phenomenology and Nature Papers and Debate of the Second International Conference Held by the International Husserl and Phenomenological Research Society New York, N. Y., September 4–9, 1972 (Analecta Husserliana)

edited by Anna-Teresa Tymieniecka

Anna-Teresa Tymieniecka / Imaginatio Creatrix: the creative versus the constitutive function of man, and the possible worlds

1. Human being appears as the major dynamic factor within this system not only with the respect to the progress onwards but also at the level of introducing the essential and basic level of meaning through the structurizing work of his consciousness.

1. the cognitive object and the cognitive act 'self-given' presence

2. imagination and expectation, the flow through which - as it seems

3. revindicating the basic role of the impulsive, emotive and affective dimensions of the passions

Those quotes by tymieniecka are basically just different ways of cognitive functioning - there is sensations, imaginaitons and expectations, and impusive drives, emotional drives, and affective drives - I would assume an affective drive differs from an emotional drive in that the affective is what is expressed and the emotional could be hidden and more unconscious. 'Revindicating' could mean the conscious mind reanalyzing and affirming the passions and tensions of the unconscious.

Mary Rose Barral / Continuity in the perceptual process:

1. but should we expect that phenomenology open to us every door?

1. this will therefore lessen the chance of witnessing a truly original perceptive experience which it may be possible to investigate phenomenologically, without presuppositions.

Those two quotes were separate in her article - but it brings up the question - what is an 'orignial perspecitive'? There can be conscious perspectives and unconscious perspecitves - how the mind views the world conscoiusly is completely different from how it sees the world unconscoiusly - what does that mean anyway - for consciousness to 'see' something? Barral described it as a 'perceptual process' or an 'original perspectie experience" that you can 'invesiigate phenomenologically without presuppositions'. However the conscious mind always slants or views life differently from the unconscious mind - a persons unconscious mind is basically a different being from who they understand themselves to be.

Mario Sancripriano - The activity of consciousness - Husserl and berguson He

is referring to writing by husserl

1. The central chapter of Erfahrung and Urteil is dedicated to the general structure of the predication and to the genesis of the principle categorical forms. The detailed examination of the 'relation' has predisposed the reader to the most imtimate process whereby concscouness rises from interests in perception to analysis of predicative activity in general in its diverse modalities and in its objective

reference, to the comprehension of the same modalities (departing from their costituent origins) as modes of defining to themselves the ego. This analysis brings us nearer to amore accurate apporoximation to things, insofar as it may be conceded where the object was placed at a certain 'visual distance'. The full resoluation of the cognitive tensions is thereby brought about.

Sancripriano put the words 'visual distance' in quotes - what could he mean by visual distance then? People can see the object of their perceptions at different distances, it is basically saying that perception can change how someone views the world or any individual object - there are also 'cognitive tensions, constituen origins, and differeny modalities - what could all of those things be cognitively?

The mind needs to intellectualize everything that it processes - the unconscoius mind first recognizes inputs from the external world and its internal processes and all of those processes are intellectualized and thought about in a more deep fashion. Is the conscoius mind just a way of understanding the unconscious? There must be different levels of presence of mind - as Tymienieca said that there were different levels of 'self-given' presence. Barral said that the mind has 'suppositions' and that there are different perspecitves.

So what is going on exactly - what is the difference between the conscious mind and the unconscious mind? The unconscious mind is already understood by normal people as being the drives and thoughts that people have that they aren't fully aware of - however did people typically think of the unconscious mind as possibly being a different person? When someone is sleeping they are certainly like a different person, and often don't even remember what they were dreaming about - that is because there is a difference between the two consciousnesses and the people who arise from those consciousnesses.

What would it mean for the mind to 'intellectualize' something? Could that mean that the conscous mind - or who the person of the conscious mind is - understands something in recognition of itself and its own personality traits and characteristics?

I said in a previous article that 'consciousness can cause feelings and intellectual stimulation' - however what does that mean exactly? Is it the unconscoius mind that causes the feelings and the stimulation. or is it the conscious mind, or is it the two together? It would be described as how someones mind respond to external stimulation - the stimulation triggers a reaction in the mind which helps to determine the responce. The reaction is conscious and unconscoius, obviously - but what are the conscious and unconscoius components?

So some of the components would be different factors from reality - the unconscious mind could recognize some factors while the conscoius mind only recognizes others - it was already understood that people absorb somethings unconsciously and don't recognize them consciously, however there are more details that could be looked at like if the unconscoius mind 'understands' what is going on and is processing information and emotions with a greater understanding of the persons feelings, ideas and other associations and thought and feeling structures.

26.1 The Mind - its Information and Emotions

Rationality is how rational someone is - or the term 'logical' could apply, and rationality relates to how someone processes information - or the philosophical field of epistemology. How a person uses their logic or rationality can help to determine how they think and understand information in the world.

What is a logical or rational understanding then, however? In a previous article i pointed out that there are different types of emotional understandings, and that these understandings are linked to cognitions and thought structures. Some thoughts are rational thoughts and are linked to emotional understandings, while other thoughts are normal thoughts or illogical thoughts and more simple 'understandings' - which i could call a 'unit of thought' or something of the sort.

What would a 'normal' thought be then however? Maybe some people think many more illogical or emotional thoughts than other people. If a thought that is logical could be defined by not being influenced by the persons emotions. A logical thought could have been developed because of irrational emotions, however it is more likely that logical thoughts that are more intelligent or practical were developed from experiences or thoughts = or some combination of experiences and thoughts that were uhm, interesting. Or not interesting, it doesn't really matter. It might matter if the experiences that developed the thoughts were interesting or not because salient experiences are more significant for the mind to understand and build upon.

26.2 Knowledge and Mental Representations

People have knowledge, and they use representations in order to process the information that they have. A mental representation could be of different objects. Is a mental representation a vision then, or is it just a 'unit of knowledge'?

What objects in life need to be analyzed different from other objects? A word or object might have a definition that the person understands, and if the object is hard to comprehend then it might have a more complex vision or knowledge structure attached to it.

Some things in life are harder to understand than other things, however the question is what makes one thing harder to understand than something else? Is it an emotional understanding? Understanding emotions involves thinking about different subtleties that have emotional information - such as understanding human motivation.

Human motivation is certainly an emotional topic because it relates to peoples emotions and feelings. Anything that someone likes is going to trigger emotions because the person is emotionally interested or attached to it. Therefore analyzing something that relates to human interests is going to be emotional - doing mathematics isn't going to necessarily engage many emotions or be an emotional or feeling type of thinking - it is probably more visual, or unconsciously visual.

26.3 Emotions, Sensations and Knowledge

What is the relationship between feelings, sensations and knowledge?

Humans use feelings and sensations in order to understand the world, they then store this information in their minds as knowledge.

Feelings help humans think about the things that they think about. Everything that someone thinks about probably has an associated feeling.

'People have feelings and they think' - that may seem like a simple statement, however it is actually very complicated. There are many different feelings that humans can have, and they can think about many different things.

When a feeling triggers a thought, it is an extremely complicated process if you look at the details - on the surface it is a simple process, a feeling simply cause the person to feel something for a certain period of time, and during that time different and more subtle feelings are evoked that are associated with the main feeling.

So if there are smaller feelings involved with any major feeling, that means that the smaller feelings are going to be related or associated with the main feeling.

Different feelings can be logical or illogical - but what is a 'logical' feeling? Maybe some feelings people bias with their own personal emotions, these feelings could be more unconscious feelings because the unconscious is more emotional than the conscious mind.

So a thought could be influenced by unconscious feelings, and this could be considered or labeled as being more unconscious than a thought that the person thinks more clearly and consciously to themselves.

26.4 Perceptions and the unconscious

How could i describe the different ways of perceiving life or anything in it? Would there be a 'psychotic' way of perceiving it and a non-psychotic? a logical or a non-logical? a conscious or an unconscious? What might other ways of perceiving life be?

If someone perceives life from a psychotic viewpoint they might slant some of the information depending on their perspective. They might the slant the information in a non-logical manner so they can see the world the way they want to see it. Or perhaps emotional conditions placed upon them cause them to create a greater emotional emphasis on some things - probably the things which they are psychotic about.

So there is clearly a psychotic way of viewing the world - however this 'emotional bias' towards certain things in life can be applied to non-psychotic people, who could also put an emotional bias on different things. There could be something in specific that they put an emotional bias on, or a group of related or dissimilar things.

Therefore some thoughts that a person might have could be illogical, and that could be compared to a psychotic person viewing something completely differently. What would the difference be between viewing something completely differently and viewing something only slightly differently then?

Maybe there are degrees to which something can make sense, and different amounts of logical can be used in viewing something.

What would be examples of something that could be viewed differently? Any experience or even an individual object could be made to not make sense or viewed in a psychotic fashion, it would seem.

26.5 Visual Distance and Consciousness

Sancripriano mentioned a 'visual distance' in an above quotation, however, what could the mind be perceiving exactly? Different things in life are perceived in different ways, and people are conscious of those things in different ways also.

Different things that people see are linked to different cognitions, and they trigger different mental representations.

A mental representation is a 'unit of thought' or some sort of understanding that the mind has. What is the nature of this understanding? The mind could be considered to be made up of different units of understanding.

How could the mind be made up of understandings? People simply understand different things, they understand how a car looks, they understand how the car makes them feel. There must be an understanding of how the car and looking at an automobile makes them feel and the 'actual' feeling. There is going to be a relationship between the unconscious feelings involved and the conscious feelings involved. If the person is using their consciousness to think about the understanding of how the car makes them feel at the current time then that is probably more conscious, and less of an unconscious endeavor or feeling.

What is an 'actual' feeling?

An actual feeling is one that is probably fully harnessed by the unconscious mind. that means, however, that there must be some sort of interaction with the conscious mind. Depending on the feeling it might be that there needs to be some sort of conscious processing - in order for the feeling to coincide with conscious feelings you might need to think about the feeling or develop consciously in order to properly experience the feeling.

Which feelings and thoughts are 'actually' conscious?

SO which feelings and thoughts are 'actually' conscious then? It really varies a considerable amount depending on the circumstances in reality - however the conscious mind builds and changes its response to the feelings it receives in reality. Would the feeling-responses be defined as being conscious or unconscious then? Consciousness i have already stated is being understood as an iceberg, with most of the feelings and processes being beneath the surface.

Table 26.0

Chapter 27

Are Religious and Political Ideas Delusional Manifestations of the

Human Psyche

Different ideas that humans hold help shape their psyche over time. Some ideas occur simply- for instance the interaction between cognition and emotion can influence a single thought in a few seconds or minutes. Other ideas are much more complex and can influence a person over a long period of time. These ideas can be political, religious and spiritual or just common ideas related to how they manage their lives.

The different types of ideas that people hold can be grouped into different categories. I already mentioned how there are religious ideas and common daily ideas - but there are more categories that can be described such as delusional ideas, ideas related to emotional speculation and ideas that are more concrete and mathematical.

People can make instinctual and deliberative decisions, and similarly, there are deliberative and instinctual ideas. A deliberative idea can be more or less concrete (like mathematics) and an instinctual idea can also be more or less concrete. The question then is what combination of deliberative and instinctual classifies the different ideas, and how much emotional speculation is involved.

If an idea is held and it becomes reality then how it influences the person changes significantly usually. For instance, someone may have the idea that they want freedom of speach, however obviously if the government is restricting their actual freedom of speach it might greatly impact their emotions. So the interaction between the ideas and goals that people have with how these goals occur in reality is significant for a persons psychological, spiritual and emotional well-being.

27.1 Are Religious Beliefs Political Ideas?

Religious beliefs are different from political beliefs - although in order to incorporate some beliefs into society they might need to be political policies.

For instance, Jesus's message of an earthly and heavenly kingdom could be viewed politically as democratic or 'positive' governments to take over the earth. Jesus's message was just a religious way of phrasing a political message - there are different ways of thinking about certain concepts. One way is religious - but that often relates to more practical beliefs that people think about every day.

Maybe the trinity in Christianity of God, the Son and the Holy Ghost can be seen as a division of power like how the government of the united states tries to have a balance of power between the presidency, the congress and the supreme court.

However, how God influences peoples lives is very different from how the government influences peoples lives. God created the world, Jesus was sent to bring a kingdom to God's world - and the holy spirit resides in each person.

So does an earthly kingdom mean that all government policies could come from god? What about the ways in which people treat other people - perhaps that could be considered to be like the holy spirit - something that guides our actions and behaviors. God creating the world at the beginning of the universe is very different from a current earthly kingdom or a spirit residing in each person.

Perhaps someone can be just spiritual and reach their own conclusions of how they should act and interact and the values they hold instead of being taught by a religion. That could be classified as personal values with spirituality and religious values if they follow the values of their religion.

27.2 What Religious Ideas Mean

Religious ideas such as immortality and a spirit can actually be translated into more common or practical words or terms. I already mentioned how religious ideas were just a different way of thinking of things. Being in touch with your spirit or with reality could be described in a different way that is more understandable to people - such as how in scientology people can repeat painful experiences on purpose people who are Hindu could get in touch with the 'ultimate reality' through suffering and sacrifice.

27.3 Pain and the Unconscious

Pain is an important part of the unconscious mind. If you think about it, since emotion is unconscious then pain is extremely unconscious because pain is both physical (instead of intellectual) and emotional.

Many religions involve dealing with pain and pleasure and the influence of those feelings on people's lives.

27.4 What exactly is a religious idea, a value, or a political policy?

Religious ideas can be political policies. But the important question really is - what kind of ideas are religious ideas? Are they psychological ideas or morals that guide someones life? Not all religious ideas can be described exactly as values. I am not just suggesting a debate about the definitions of the words 'political policy or theory' 'value' 'moral' and 'religious idea' but I am also suggesting that entire doctrines can be described in that fashion.

27.5 Are Religious Values Psychological Constructs?

In order to start this section first I need to ask the question - what is a mental construct? The unconscious mind can construct or manifest many ideas that the conscious mind holds. A humans imagination is largely unconscious because it is too difficult to think clearly about such things. Dreaming is unconscious and uses a significant amount of imagination, but I am not suggesting that the conscious minds ideas that come from an unconscious imagination are false or not accurate.

An example of an unconscious motivation generating a mental construct is a religious value - a religious value can mean different things to different people and be interpreted in different ways because it is an abstract concept. There are many ideas and concepts that people think about every day that are abstract; however some are very powerful concepts and have a long term hold over a persons mind. A single value can tilt or modify how more regular emotions are felt throughout a day. An example of such a value could be depriving oneself of excessive amounts of pleasure - there is the real emotional effect (the reality) - and there is how that person thinks about that experience, both could both help determine the feelings involved.

So there are different religious values. Different religions value different things, ideas and values. They also have different ways of worship. Ideas about how much pleasure someone is supposed to experience in life is one of the major concepts. What is a spirit? What is reality? Who is god? These are some of the important religious questions that different religions ask.

Sacrifice is an important part of religious values because it relates to how much pleasure people experience in life. If someone sacrifices, then their understanding and experience of pleasure can change. This could include personal sacrifice and sacrificing something to god - sacrificing something to god is a more historical form of sacrifice, possibly because those objects were more valued and scarce and activity in life was different so more attention and value was placed on rituals. However, personal sacrifice such as fasting is also difficult and something that changes someones values and forces them to think.

So there must be some combination of perspective and reality that is constantly interacting and changing. The different types of reality are emotional reality, physical reality, and intellectual reality. Physical reality is extremely powerful and emotions are physical in many ways - and that is perhaps why they are so potent. It is subjective to label an experience as being physical, emotional or intellectual. However, if those three classifications can be related to religion then more detail can be found.

For instance sacrifice or fasting or prayer worship could be considered to being physical realities because all involved a lot of physical effort. Prayer worship is a physical effort because it involves speach. Obviously, since the intellectual and emotional combine those physical activities could also be extremely intellectual. It is easy to see how they are physical = however the important and even spiritual question is to ask how they are intellectual.

27.6 Spirituality

Saying that the intellectual is spiritual is comparing ghosts to spirits - a ghost is like a spirit because it has no physical form, and similarly, the physical is extremely real and emotionally potent.

What is the definition of spirituality? I like this definition: predominantly spiritual character as shown in thought, life, etc.; spiritual tendency or tone. Something needs to be added to that what this "spiritual" character is, however. I would say that it is the same attitude that a religious person would have about being religious, that is, by "spiritual character" they mean someone who is likely to be religious. Spirit is someone's soul, so spirituality would be focused on the self, but focused on the self in a manner in which they can understand it more deeply than just standard cognitive thinking about it, so religion might help you understand yourself in that "higher" manner. That is, it is almost like faith to believe in yourself like that, so it is like religion. The relationship between faith/religion and spirituality then is that both are "higher" methods of understanding the world. Spirituality is just focused on the self, while religion is focused on god. So there is an inner peace that spirituality brings because spirituality is about yourself. You can also say it is about your soul, not just your state of being, because soul is who you really are, the core of yourself, and if you are more connected to the core of yourself you are going to be more at peace, and therefore have more of that spiritual connection, which is one that is a "higher" connection to yourself, like how religion is a "high" connection to god. This "high" connection is higher because it is connected to who you really are, which is the spirit part of spirituality which implies a soul, because when you imagine someone as being a spirit or a ghost you take away their physical form and focus more on who they are mentally, or the core of their being or soul. Also use of the word soul, like that is using energy from your soul, appeals more to your higher morals which you would consider to be more consistent with who you are at the core.

So people can compare reality with intellectual and religious questions that they can ask themselves. Does it matter how a person perceives how much pleasure they experience? If someone experiences a certain experience (which would be a combined emotional, physical and intellectual reality) then how would it matter how it is perceived? It can be perceived over the long term and over the short term by a person - and perceived cognitively and emotionally.

27.7 Connecting Religion, Politics and Psychology - and possibly Physics

How could the study of Physics, religion and psychology be related?

Physics is about the connection of matter to matter - and psychology is about understanding abstract emotional concepts. It would seem that it would hard to find a connection between the two subjects. However it is probably easy to find a connection between religion and psychology and politics.

Politics consists of political theories that governments use to govern their populations. These ideas and political policies can help influence the lives of the people in the population of their respective governments.

Could a person want their government to tell them what to do with their life? Not all religions don't necessarily tell someone what to do with their lives - if someone has freedom of religion then they can decide whatever beliefs they want to follow - whatever religion or religions those beliefs come from.

But that certainly doesn't relate to the study of physics. Physics is simply physical objects interacting with each other - while politics and religion are both about the ideas that people hold about life - such as how to live their lives and what to think about life in general and their individual lives and how they are being led.

This raises the question of the point of such thinking - how would it matter if someone thinks that they are being sinful (in Christianity for example) - or how would it matter if someone thinks that they are living a peaceful and pleasure-less life (in Buddhism and Hinduism for example)?

Religions certainly have a set of ideas that they follow - if you link up all of their studies, prayers and sacred texts then a more concise set of ideas about their beliefs could be formed that is easier to understand. Religions do a ton of stuff that could be reinterpreted into a more simple form or set of ideas that describes what those religions do for each person who follows that set of beliefs - if that is the best way to describe a religion anyway - as a set of beliefs.

Maybe someone could simply believe in the policies of their government instead of believing in a religion. At least the policies of their government have a real impact on the persons life. However, perhaps some religious ideas have a real impact on a persons life also - each religious idea would have to be analyzed and thought about - then the impact of that idea on the persons life could be further explored.

27.8 How Can Physics and Religion be Connected?

How can physics be connected to religion? Religion matters because it influences how people feel and the things that they think about. Physics doesn't really relate very much to it. It relates in a way - that religious ideas can directly impact a person and matter directly impacts matter. That is the only way that physics and religion really relate.

What does it mean to believe in God? Does it really matter how the events of our lives unfold anyway? Life

doesn't really matter anyway so it doesn't really matter how our lives could be influenced by a god.

Those previous statements weren't even really that significant - it is obvious that the events of life are significant or not significant - some events in peoples lives are significant and other events aren't as significant. It could be viewed as being a bunch of little details or bunch of moderately small details.

God can be portrayed as being mighty or the universe as being everywhere and god as being all powerful. Are those ideas delusions? Why would it matter that much if god was all powerful? It seems like that idea is delusional - every religion believes in an all powerful god. While different religions have differing views of how they view god they all believe in an omnipotent being of some sort.

IF you think about it, people have delusions all of the time, and god would certainly seem like something to be delusional about. But what is the person being delusional about exactly? Are they being delusional that life is grand and extensive, or are they being delusional that god is going to help them in some magical or realistic way?

These are all important questions - how can an idea influence the human psyche so significantly? What emotional or cognitive processes are being influenced when people frame things in different ways?

27.9 Religion and the Unconscious

To what extent is religion unconscious? Religion seems to be extremely unconscious because it involves ideas that are powerful and emotional.

When i say that religious ideas are emotional does that mean that they are delusional? Whenever someone thinks that their life is going to be a certain way and that it is going to happen magically that way then they would be both delusional and emotional - I am not suggesting that people who follow religion are delusional - or more delusional than people who are just planning out their lives anyway.

Why would the understanding of how much pain or pleasure someone is in need to be cognitively interpreted? Does that mean that it needs to be verbally interpreted or does it just need to be understood more consciously? If something is understood consciously does that mean that they are going to be less emotional about it or more emotional about it? The unconscious can deviate from the conscious mind, and, in that case, could be the opposite of what the conscious mind wants to think or believe.

I would think in that case doing something like reciting a prayer or thinking about something religious could be done consciously but the persons unconscious emotions wouldn't follow. Perhaps that is what it is like for someone who doesn't believe in a religion who tries to follow it but fails.

I suppose it doesn't really matter if the people who follow various religious beliefs and values care excessively about them. I am just wondering what the point of repeating certain values or beliefs to oneself is. Having not practiced any religion or prayer worship consistently I cannot speak from personal experience. However, if you think about it, religion is sort of like therapy in that the person repeats the things that are occurring in their lives - or at least repeating the things or ideas that lie behind what is occurring in their lives. That is what religious values and ideas are - they are the foundation for someones life - and you don't need to necessarily discuss your life with a therapist in order to enhance it or think about it. If the idea that lies behind your life is that you need to be pleasure-less or dutiful to your society or family then you ca think about those values to yourself or in prayer worship and don't need to discuss them in therapy.

27.10 Religious Concepts and Messages

What influence do religious ideas have on a persons life? Why does a religious experience over time influence a person?

Are there similar comparable experiences in a persons life that a religious experience could be compared to? Perhaps that is why some of tales that are preached in different religions try to relate a certain type of life experience through the tale. Fiction can modify how life is viewed - and in religion many of the tales are fictional and these are often used to communicate morals or messages.

So the fictional tales in many religious writing or preached in religious temples are significant and a large part of a religious experience. Even if the story is one of the history of the religion - false or truthful - is a part of the religious experience.

What then is the difference between fiction and reality? The religious stories told are often very different from reality. Or what is the difference between religious fiction and reality?

The messages communicated through the stories are usually messages that center around ideas that are central to the religions beliefs. The tales portray the proper or improper thing to do - or could tales of their religious gods or figures - which would be a different type of example or tale.

So, every religion has core ideas or messages that it tries to communicate. However, what is difference between a story and a single idea? A single story can communicate different ideas - however it might be debated which ideas are being communicated in different stories. Each religion has its own story, and its own stories it tells - both of which could communicate messages or concepts about life to the followers of those religions.

27.11 Religion and Consciousness

Religious ideas are often values such as kindness and compassion or a different world-view or perspective on those values. But what is a world view of a value? Say the value is kindness - then there is a way that the manner of kindness can be perceived - maybe simply a different way of describing the kindness, for instance it could be a simple honest kindness or a more complicated and less caring kindness. Perhaps the other qualities and values that people have can change the nature of the simple adjective 'kind'.

For instance, if someone is kind but doesn't value kindness that could be different from someone who isn't kind but values kindness. Confusists value being kindness and it is one of the hindu virtues. It isn't discussed as a Christian or islamic value - however the ten commandments could imply a kindness and following the laws of your religion in islam could be considered being kind or honoring your society like how confusists value their family and society.

Perhaps different ways of discussing the religious values lead to different ways of personally being. Discussing kindness in different ways could lead to a different way of being kind for each religion.

However, what does a different way of being - or I could call that having a different personality orientation - have to do with consciousness? Is it a matter of understanding your own personality or beliefs in what your personality should be? Or are religious beliefs more about someones understanding of the world?

Obviously there are going to be various types of religions beliefs - beliefs and understanding of the world, people and social structure, and an understanding or how people interact with the world. Beliefs of the world could be ideas about consciousness or enlightenment - because consciousness, enlightenment or 'revelation' is obviously related to a persons understanding of the world - so it relates to humans and world. Some religious ideas can relate to the world and to a person - and to how the world interacts with people and how ideas are shared and more or less dependent on either someones personality and intellect and how much of the intellect is shared or developed or interacts with the rest of the world.

If it is an understanding of a person in the world, then clearly the idea is connecting the human to the world, however, if it is just an understanding of the persons own personality traits or preferences then it is just an understanding of the person - some personality traits are more related to interpersonal qualities and some are more 'inter-global' qualities.

27.12 Are Religious Ideas Motivating?

If religious ideas are often delusional - which I have discussed in previous articles that the idea of God or other religious beliefs could be delusional or manufactured by the unconscious - then it makes sense that they are also motivating. That seems fairly obvious because people become delusional in the first place because they want to feel good. However, feeling good from verbal cognitions is a feature that is unique to humanity.

Animals get excited about reward and punishment also - however they only get excited like that when they see a direct reward or a direct punishment. Human beings cognize various ideas and motivations so they can bring up the same feelings of reward and punishment at different times or in different ways than animals do.

Similarly, religious ideas work in a similar fashion - they are ideas about how people are going to be rewarded or punished from all the events and occurrences in their lives. Whatever someone thinks is going to happen in their life a reward and punishment system is going to change the motivation involved - and that obviously is going to relate to religious beliefs because religions discuss reward and punishment that is determined by God.

That is why many religious beliefs are beliefs about what God does for people. In prehistoric times it might seem like a coincidence if an animal appears at the right time that they could kill - or it if something else happens that uncomforts or hurts someone because the living conditions were more simple and easily effected by coincidence. It is in this environment that the idea of God originally came into being.

In modern times, many more things happen to human beings because their lives are much more complicated. How could their idea of God be similar to how it was in prehistoric times when there was a more simple and obvious reward and punishment motivation system? People in modern times get rewarded and punished all of the time - perhaps their lives are simply more chaotic to focus so much and so simply - almost in a meditative way - on religion or beliefs about God rewarding and punishing them. Perhaps a change in thinking of that sort could change how humans cognize their beliefs and motivations.

27.13 A Physics Work in progress - the beginning

I have only studied physics a little - however theoretical or philosophical physics is a subjective topic that could be speculated upon by lay people - some of this article could relate to how the universe was formed.

It would seem to me that physical particles have to combine in manner that makes sense, but the question is - what is logical physical connection? Is it logical for one particle to bond or interact with a different particle?

What is inside empty space? Could it be that there are small particles in empty space that aren't visible or have any interactions with other particles?

Maybe I can say that a 'particle' is the smallest unit of matter or the smallest unit of something that can be physically observed or actually exist - I don't know if someone else has defined something like that before.

There are different ways that different particles interact - they have charges and strong and weak forces - however, are those all the ways in which they can interact, bond, attract and repel each other, and so on and so forth?

What is the difference between energy and matter then? Energy is matter (or could be viewed as being matter), and matter is energy because both are physical substances. I could define the smallest particles as physical substances - but if they don't exist anywhere then maybe they can be transformed into different types of matter because they are pure energy - but does that statement even make any sense - all energy has to be matter because it has to physically exist.

27.14 Why is understanding the world important for human beings - and

how does that relate to religion?

Why do human beings need to understand the world intellectually?

Instead of calling human consciousness intellectual I could call it verbal, 'more conscious', 'awareness' or any other term that would indicated that something or some understanding is being understood in a more intelligent manner.

What would happen to a human if it didn't understand something intellectually? Wouldn't that just be what animals are like? Animals could be described as simply not being verbal - they might understand emotionally what humans understand - but they simply aren't capable of intellectualizing or 'cognizing' it.

Perhaps that is all religion is about - intellectualizing things in their lives and making life seem more grand or important to themselves - or is it about changing their emotions in a more basic and important way?

People often do things for intellectual satisfaction. It is interesting that there is such a large mix of the emotional reality and the intellectual reality that is present with human beings. It seems that with humans intellectualizing (being verbal, thinking about, etc) is needed in order to direct and motivate their emotions.

That is what therapy is about also - people think about their psychological problems and it helps them work through those problems. Religion is about thinking about the basics of their lives and what they want to achieve - it is a more simple form of therapy where the focus is to improve and focus on life in general. If someone has a specific problem that is related to their brains psychological make-up then therapy might be the answer, however if they are simply trying to think about or improve their life in a more simple fashion then religious or spiritual thinking could help enhance their 'human' emotions.

What is necessary in order to enhance human emotions? I would think that in early history there were grand tales told of the deities in order to inspire awe and admiration. In modern times, such tales wouldn't create as much awe because modern technology is what inspires the awe - not deities that have 'magical' powers. God is still viewed in a similar fashion to after early civilization developed after Jesus. There wasn't much technology back then - however there was still considerably more than when there were just tribes and no civilization.

Inspiring awe and admiration in the population must have served to change their emotions - the stories were enough to motivate them to think and change - because the significant factor of the time was that humanity was just beginning and humans had power and were like the divine. By the time of Jesus more was needed to motivate people - so Jesus - who was a very motivational personality - helped to motivate the population and was much more realistic than stories told about multiple deities who did magical things.

Some symbols or stories are told of Jesus - and this helps to motivate some Christians. The early deities were just ways of thinking about creation and how powerful humans were - at the stories were enough to inspire people and change the way they think and feel.

The History of Religions

So stories can influence someones ideas and motivations. The history of someones religion could be comparable to being the history of their own family - their were only a few Hebrews that made it out of Egypt so they could all be seen as being a single family - and stories of Abraham and Isaac and the other Hebrews could relate what their culture and human history was.

The old testament is also included in the beginning Bibles - with the new testament only coming after - but every religious text is really just a different way of explaining sets of values and ideas about God and what he does for the world.

The 'story of god' is complicated and can be told in many different ways. It can be interpreted what the correct thing to do is many different ways also - does God teach the correct thing or does interacting with Him teach the correct thing to do? God doesn't necessarily communicate directly to people so interacting with what god does on earth and learning from what he did in the past is the only way to interpret what life was like - and what life should be like.

Table 27.0

Chapter 28

The Will and its Relation to Feelings

Every thought that a human has is motivated by a feeling. However, which feeling would be the feeling behind that? It would seemingly be a selfish feeling, however, perhaps it is just at its core a selfish feeling. That is, humans have selfless feelings, however they are probably motivated by a more basic instinct that seeks to only respond to the human that is doing the action.

That makes sense - human being have instincts, and this can be compared to the human will. That brings up a question of definitions - what is the difference between the definition of instinct and the definition of 'will'?

In general, "will" does not refer to one particular or most preferred desire but rather to the general capacity to have such desires and act decisively based on them, according to whatever criteria the willing agent applies. However, instinct is an impulse, usually an innate impulse. So a human could have the will to follow an instinct, or a decision could be 'willful', 'instinctual', 'determined', or 'decisive'. They basically all mean the same thing - if someone is intending to do an action, then their feelings are going to be motivating the action - and if feelings are motivating an action it is going to be more decisive or driven.

28.1 The Influence of Feelings

Feelings are important to human beings because it makes them feel. That is a rather simple statement, however that doesn't necessarily mean that feelings are simple or that understanding feelings is simple.

If a feeling is simple would that mean that it is easier to understand? How could a feeling be understood, or what does that mean, to 'understand' a feeling? Humans can feel feelings, or they could understand them, or some combination of the two.

If a feeling is understood then it is probably a salient or powerful feeling. However, a feeling could be powerful but the person experiencing it might not know that it is a large or significant feeling. What then is the difference between a 'significant' feeling and a large feeling?

A feeling could be large but that doesn't necessarily mean that it is a salient feeling - salient means that the feeling is significant - however what makes one feeling important and another feeling not important?

If a feeling is important it probably has a greater impact on cognition. The persons thoughts are influenced by the feeling more, basically.

28.2 Feelings Interact

Some feelings interact with other feelings, or it would probably be better described as drives interacting with other drives, because a feeling could be small and there could be many feelings, while there are probably only a few drives or strong desires a person can have at any one time.

A drive is like an emotion because it is powerful, however drives could be driven by thoughts while emotions could have any cause.

A feeling could be complicated, and have elements of thoughts and other feelings interacting. However some of this information about feelings isn't completely necessary for someone to understand in order to properly experience feelings.

While feelings can be complicated, and thoughts can be complicated, drives are often simple because they are basic emotions that are driven by simple thoughts - such as the drive that most humans and animals have to eat food - it is a strong emotion or feeling that is powered by cognition, i.e., the idea that they are hungry.

28.3 Experiencing Feelings

Humans experience feelings all of the time.

How could a feeling be described? It is basically something that someone feels - different things in life evoke different feelings. Therefore thought is really an insignificant component, because feelings occur continuously with human beings.

If a feeling isn't continuous, then it could get interrupted suddenly. Feelings mix in complicated ways, and if it is complicated it might create a weird feeling because simple feelings are easy to understand. If it isn't simple then you might not know what is going on or it could be strange, which could cause the feeling to be weird. This could be compared to other weird feelings or things in life that are also weird. However there is a difference between something being weird because it is unknown, and it being weird because the feeling is unknown.

Normally someone would just describe something weird as being strange or unusual - however then it is possible that the unusual feeling is more powerful because it is different from what the person is accustomed to. New and different feelings or stimulation could be more powerful because the mind hasn't experienced it before and needs to adapt.

Feelings that are powerful could be considered to be tangible components of the mind, or be part of life experiences, life experiences that generate feelings are called 'experiential' phenomena.

Feelings that are the result of experiences are different from feelings that are the result of someones inner thoughts. Humans can think to themselves all of the time, and this inner type of thinking can also cause feelings. However, experiences can cause a different type of feeling because it is stimulation, and stimulation is more of a physical feeling. Thoughts are just thoughts in your mind, while stimulation from the world or from the external senses could seem more 'real'.

Thinking of things in terms of if they are strange could also help to identify what the feeling is or what it is like. Would an external feeling from the world feel more strange than someones thoughts? How could a thought seem strange, and, how would that be different from stimulation from outside in the world seem strange? What does that mean exactly - a thought being strange? That wouldn't seem to make any sense because people think to themselves all of the time, so it wouldn't seem like thinking would be out of the ordinary, and it is usually strange types of stimulation or things in the external world that are different - not someones internal cognitions or thinking.

28.4 Feelings and Drives

I stated previously that emotions could have any cause while drives could be driven by thoughts. Emotions could also be the result of thoughts, or drives could be the result of thoughts. However drives come from powerful emotion so it is unlikely that simple thoughts would cause a strong emotional drive.

I also basically stated that you can look at how strange a feeling is in order to understand it better. However, what about the strength of feelings? If drives come from strong emotion, then the drive would probably not be a strange feeling because drives are basically never strange. That is because people are only motivated by selfish desires, and there is nothing strange about a selfish desire. Either that or the 'strange' feeling is a feeling and not a strong emotion.

Feelings are shallow - when you touch something you get a feeling that is simple (and tactile), however emotions are strong and deep and more related to thoughts because thoughts are intellectual. What about drives? If drives are strong then they too would be intellectual. That makes sense because it is something that you are driven by - hence the word 'drive'.

Table 28.0

Chapter 29

Phenomenology and Reality

Intentions are gradual because they are emotional. While a person might do something instantaneously, it isn't obvious when their intention to do that action started. Some cognitive processes are very fast, like vision is fast however the emotional processes that accompany vision are often slow. It makes sense that vision is tied in with consciousness and emotion because vision is a large part of how humans and animals see - whether or not they are blind.

So how can someone separate out basic vision and the basic emotional processes that are tied in with vision with more complicated or slower emotions? A vision could immediately invoke a feeling - or a feeling could be more stored and come from deeper or more complicated emotions - the feelings that come from someones consciousness can come from their immediate environment or from what they are feeling and thinking.

Sometimes what people see matches what they are thinking and feeling, and sometimes it doesn't. Obviously it is going to vary on the situation i.e., what they are seeing and what they are thinking and feeling, that is going to determine what they are conscious of and what they are feeling and thinking.

Some stimuli is more stimulating and rises to consciousness easier than other stimulation. Vision in combination with what the person is thinking helps to determine what the person is paying attention to at any given moment.

There could be a question of if the person is aware of the stimulation before it happens or is thinking about something that prepares them for the stimulation what effect that might have on the stimulation. They could be paying attention to something initially and then that object could respond, or it could come into attention suddenly. If you think about the thoughts and feelings that are involved it adds more detail about what is going on - because they obviously are a factor in the feelings and thoughts before, during and after a stimulus - and if that stimulus has a 'leading-up' lesser stimulation.

29.1 Mental Processes and Reality

There can also be unconscious and conscious processes. The mind has feelings and thoughts that are complex, and there are different levels of conscious and unconscious attention.

How does the mind perceive reality? Is reality the environment, culture or nation that someone is in?

The country that someone is in could have a large impact on how the person perceives the world, there are different values that 'hold sway' in different places - such as different morals and beliefs and abilities.

How does that differ from a humans conception of other human beings? People can conceive of different people differently, and similarly, they can think about different nations or culture groups differently.

How does a babies conception of reality or other human beings differ from an adults conception? I don't really think it would matter to a baby or even a small child what country they were in - though maybe that is because they are just being influenced and it isn't under their control.

So a humans perception of reality must be formed since birth - and initially when the child is young 'reality' is simply imposed on him. If reality is imposed on humans when they are born, then how could they possibly determine their own reality?

However, what is reality? What is the reality that is imposed upon humans, as children or as adults?

Children theoretically have less cognitive ability than adults, however that is simply related to how intelligent they are - they might have a similar level of technical ability, or even greater skill and ability to learn technical things - by technical ability there I mean an amount of competency that deals with the management of physical objects. They also might have greater skill that is adaptive, like the ability to play video games. That skill requires a lot of ability to understand what is going on in the game, and what the rules are about how the game is played that adults might not be able to figure out because it requires a more creative type of intellect that is also adaptive.

Or perhaps the 'reality' in video games is one that is simply more attuned to the world of a child and isn't suited for adults. The young adults hand-eye coordination is faster and that is obviously why they could perform better at the video games, however if you consider what a 'reality' is then a 'reality' could be any world that needs to be understood, imaginative or real.

29.2 What is Reality - and what influences it?

What is reality? And what influences reality? Human beings are in reality, human interaction is an important part of human emotion - however, how could I define what 'reality' is?

Is reality simply human beings and the ideas that they hold? Or is reality interpersonal communication? Why does phrasing reality that way mean what it does? On that account, what would even be the definition of reality?

Reality would usually mean what is considered to be 'real'. The world is real, human beings are real, and the physical objects in the world are real. I wrote a lot of articles about emotion and cognition, and clearly emotion and what influences human thought is incredibly significant for how they feel, and how a human being feels and his or her consciousness is going to be what the reality is for them - however reality usually refers to the external elements in the world which happen to determine the persons thoughts and feelings, instead of implying that the person determines their own thoughts and feelings, using the word 'reality' implies that the world imposes order on them from their environment and then that is what determines their reality.

29.3 Intentions

Interpersonal interaction is a large part of life, or 'reality'. People function and part of that cognitive functioning involves interacting with other humans. Other humans are part of peoples visual field (what they see) and their minds influence how emotions and feelings from the other person are interpreted.

How does someones mind 'interpret' emotion? Is feeling simply felt, or is feeling interpreted? What does that mean exactly anyway? If feeling is interpreted, then it isn't literal - by that I would think that that means that feeling things isn't simple. What would be gained by determining if feeling something is simple or complex? What would be the difference between a 'complicated' feeling and a 'simple' feeling?

Feelings are obviously tied in with a higher 'cognitive' type of understanding, and that could help to make the feelings more complex - because the thought structures and idea groupings influence which emotions are felt. In that way emotion and thought are intertwined - people think things, and those thoughts are linked with emotions that influence their feelings.

29.4 Feelings and Reality

What would happen if reality influenced someones feelings? Could that be compared to the world 'pressing' in on someone? How could that be visualized? Can 'reality' be visualized? There could be artistic representations of the world, however I wouldn't think that the image of a globe or map or an image of the planet from outer space would properly represent 'reality'.

Table 29.0

Chapter 30

My Take on Einsteins Theory of Relativity

Einstein described that if a rock falls from someone on a train down the ground outside the train then it would appear to the person on the train as falling in a straight line - but it would appear to the person on the ground watching the train as a parabola. That is because the person on the ground isn't moving, and the train is moving away from the person (so they see it from different angles). Air resistance makes the rock move in a parabola - the train is moving fast so when it drops it goes in a parabola. The person on the train simply sees it from an angle that doesn't reflect the entire nature of the parabola - if you look at some things from only one angle you might not be able to see everything that is going on. If you look at something from all angles so you can account for its movement in all three dimensions.

Time would be the same from both perspectives only the speed of the objects for both people would be different relative to how fast they were traveling. If one person is travelling fast then it is moving at a different speed relative to that person, so the person would be travelling faster away but the speed of the object could be viewed as being two speeds because everything in the universe is moving relative to something else.

30.1 The Gravitational Field

If the brakes are applied to the train, then the train stops and the person experiences a sudden jerk forward.

The person jerks forward because of gravity - the friction of the wheels of the train are influenced differently by gravity than the person sitting on the seat. The person is not pinned down to the seat, so his force is not stopped as well as the force of the train is stopped.

Gravity helps to determine the force of friction on the wheels of the train, and considering the speed of the train and the person on the train (which are the same before the train starts to stop) the train simply stops faster than the person because the persons motion is harder to stop because it is only the train that stops. If different elements of the body that is stopping its motion (like the element of the person in the train and the body of the train, or perhaps something else that is loose in or part of the train) stop at different times then they are going to move separate from the other different elements, and appear disjointed.

30.2 My ideas about the nature of time

Time is only measured based upon what can be observed changing in a certain period of time. Some things move faster than other things, and if you take into account how everything moves at different speeds then everything can be changing relative to a 'normal' constant.

But what would be moving at a normal speed? How could someone define 'normal'? Everything on the earth moves relative to the ground of the earth, but the entire earth is spinning. So everything could be 'normal' compared to the center of the earth, or other places on the earth and how things are moving there - that is how time and speed on earth is measured and compared and contrasted - and that is because everyone on the earth is only on earth and we don't really care very much about stuff outside the planet - because people live on the ground of the planet.

So what would be a 'normal' speed? Everything moves relative to something else. That is what reality is about - physical objects that move in a certain pattern, sometimes the pattern is organized, and sometimes it is chaotic.

Table 30.0

Chapter 31

Concept, Mind and Reality

How do our concepts influence our conclusions? That was a question posed by Kant, however with a deeper understanding of the mind that question can be looked at further.

For instance, there are emotional drives that influence what our thoughts are, however concepts in that sense refers to all the persons ideas that they have formed since birth.

That is another interesting question - I don't think that Kant asked the question "which idea or concept exactly influences which conclusion" - i would have to describe various concepts and how they influence differing other concepts, assessments and understandings.

Different concepts can change based upon the persons emotional development over time, and you could view a concept that a person has about life based upon different stages in their emotional development.

For instance if the stage of development is 'identity recognition' in the persons youth then the concepts that the person has is going to be influenced by their struggle for an identity (whether it is a question of masculinity or other personality traits that determine who the person is).

This articles relates to some of my other 'truth and reality' articles because i discussed in other articles how thought is related to feeling and how the unconscious mind influences the conscious mind through feelings, drives and unconscious thoughts influencing and driving conscious thoughts.

So feelings are part of who a person is and a part of how they perceive reality. However, how does something like an interpersonal feeling change how someone perceives reality? How the universe is structured has to do with feelings and how a person views the world. What then is the relationship between how reality is formed and how the mind views reality?

Some objects and structures in reality are concrete, but all are perceived emotionally and cognitively by the mind. What would a structure in reality be that is concrete other than a literal physical building or other physical structure? There is the physical world and the mental world, and these two worlds interact all of the time.

So is that just someones experience of the physical world influencing their feelings? Or is it just describing feelings and thoughts as being physical or elated? Perhaps thoughts and feelings 'feel' supernatural and they can be then described as being weird or surreal. It is interesting that feelings can take on so many forms - like trying to describe a feeling as a physical object.

That would basically equate to describing a feeling as being very real, or perhaps it would be describing how a feeling is tied in with certain thoughts making it either a surreal intellectual experience, a surreal emotional and intellectual experience or an ordinary experience.

It would seem that simple feelings are just described in more simple terms than advanced feelings and that is all that is going on. If you think about simple animal like feelings that do not have any advanced components, and therefore all advanced components to life could be considered to be surreal or spiritual.

Table 31.0

Chapter 32

Emotional and Intellectual Preferences

Life is more than thoughts and emotions - humans perceive life in different ways. They perceive individual objects differently and therefore they perceive everything differently as a whole.

It seems obvious when I say it that way - each person is different and is going to perceive life differently and experience emotions differently. What is behind that difference, however?

Is it that people emotionally develop in different ways or is it that they were born that way? Perhaps a certain perception could be achieved in the persons 20s that is more academic or intelligent than the perception that the person achieved in youth. This difference in perception would be different from how teenagers or young children view the world..

However, how could i describe the difference in development as children age and as young people in their 20's age? I have described that it is basically the same emotional preferences only a maturation - the emotional 'orientation' getting more advanced and developed, possibly changing a slight to moderate amount depending on the type of emotional interest.

So humans all have various emotional interests - that is what makes them human - wait, animals also have emotional interests - they simply aren't as intelligent as human interests. What makes an emotional interest intelligent, however? Humans have a more complex reaction that shows that they are capable of much more advanced thought, however that could be hard to describe what that difference is exactly.

I twice saw my dog have a basic reaction to a painting - however in retrospect i realize that the reaction was a simple reaction - the painting was very simple and emotional. Dogs probably wouldn't have a reaction to paintings that have complex scenery or involve complex ideas. I also noticed my dog responding to a basketball player on television making a slam dunk - which is a dramatic emotional experience if you think about it.

So animals clearly have basic emotions and basic intellect - but the basic intellect is basically just tied into the basic emotions. Which ideas and types of intellect are more considered to be human then? I said that 'advanced' intellect is human - but how could that be described? Just saying 'concepts or topics that require further thought' isn't really describing it perfectly.

That is basically all it is, however. Thinking provides humans with a more advanced way of viewing the world - the compare, contrast, analyze, etc. Some of these categories of advanced thinking involve human motivation, some involve human emotional preferences (which is related to motivation, but doesn't involve the motivation drives as much), and human intellectual preferences (which is basically their emotional preferences only they could be described as a more mature type of pursuit).

Table 32.0

Chapter 33

Thoughts and Feelings in the Mind

There are emotions and thoughts and feelings and they interact. I don't think it really matters what the difference is between an emotion and a feeling. It doesn't really matter - that is just picking hairs. Emotions are basically feelings, so it doesn't matter if it is an emotion or if it is a feeling. In a previous article i stated that feelings are more direct and are clear and you can feel them in a more simple manner - similar to when you touch something you get a feeling that is simple (and tactile). But if you can feel both of them it doesn't really matter as long as you can feel it.

It doesn't really matter because of life is feeling - life is full of feeling. There are also thoughts in life that impose and structure feelings. Thoughts are significant - and they impose order. Thoughts impose order over feelings, that is why they are significant. Feelings are wild and natural, while thoughts are calm and controlled.

There are automatic thoughts, which are not so controlled. However automatic thoughts come from feelings, from the unconscious mind in combination with the conscious mind. However automatic thoughts don't come often, many thoughts might be assisted by the unconscious mind that people aren't aware of as semi-automatic in any way, however they could be described as being that way.

Feelings are important because they make people feel things. Do thoughts make people feel things - or is it the feeling? The feeling associated with the thought could be causing the feeling or it might possibly come more from verbal sentences and thoughts - but then thoughts are really just triggers for feelings. Everything results in a feeling, thoughts are just points of information in a world of feelings (the unconscious).

That is why there are feelings, because there are things like thoughts. Thoughts cause feelings, and feelings can motivate someone to think a thought or two. That is it, that is all there is to life - feeling feelings and emotions and thoughts. But why would a thought be significant also? I said feeling 'feelings' - and that is obvious because feelings are obvious; however thoughts are also important components of the mind.

Thoughts could be considered to be the intellectual aspect of the mind - however why would someone need to have a thought at all if they can just feel things? What is a thought then - a thought would just be something that imposes order and gives logical direction, and isn't necessary for feeling. Perhaps that is why animals are also significant.

So thoughts impose order, give logical ideas and that is it - they don't serve and function in terms of biological feeling. That is interesting; however it is not obvious to see how that functions in life.

Table 33.0

Chapter 34

Deliberate and Intelligent Consciousness

Decisions can be instinctual or deliberate - they can be something that the person thinks about a lot (making it deliberate), or something that is immediate and instinctual. So that means that thought and intellect can be immediate and instinctual or a type of thought that using more processing power or is simply more intelligent.

Could someone have a thought that is intelligent that is more immediate and instinctual, however? It would probably have to be very learned - but wouldn't that make all adults learned then since they have been using the same words in the same contexts for years and years?

That is definition of experience - to use a word or do something in a similar context - or to learn from different dissimilar contexts. However it doesn't have to be how people use words - it is the nature of changing experience, it doesn't have to be just verbal.

When i describe how it works verbally it becomes more clear - however, and also if i use words or sentences about emotional development as examples it could make it more clear how people develop other types of competency also. For instance if someone says 'walk slowly if the path is cluttered so you don't trip' then the persons competence of walking could increase because they learned from the verbal statement.

It is both a verbal, cognitive sentence and an experience in real life. In that way words and other types of cognitive intellect are tied in with real experience. Maybe all of life has a verbal or cognitive aspect that is reflected with the persons intellect. Or maybe there is also a physical or sensory quality to life that can be reflected with a persons intellect - not just an experiential one.

Thats how people think -they use their unconscious mind and their physical power - which helps to power their will, and they use thier conscious intellect, sometimes less conscious and sometimes more instinctual and unconscious, and they reach conclusions and do stuff.

Table 34.0

Chapter

The Mind's Comprehension

There are mental models and mental associations, and there are thought association chains that are usually what a mental model is like. Does that describe all of the significant features of how the mind functions, however? I already pointed out in previous articles that thoughts and feelings can interact - but certainly it is more complicated than that.

The unconscious mind has a different power than the conscious mind, and the unconscious mind understands the world differently. The unconscious mind is the world that is absorbed by our senses while the conscious mind is the world that we understand. The unconscious doesn't really 'understand' anything the same way that the conscious mind does - it mostly stores information and feelings, while the conscious mind mostly does the intellectual work.

That relates to Descartes famous quote "I think therefore I am" which i stated in a previous article that the thought and intellectual component over someones entire life helps to determine the persons emotional development also. Emotional development is deliberative - or who the person is is deliberative - so that means that they are determining with their thoughts who they are and their development - or is that not the case so much?

Maybe someones emotions determine who they are more so, and it isn't really a conscious endeavor. This is what the will and the spirit is about - who someone is and how they respond to the world. The way a person responds to the world could be considered to be emotional and unconscious or intellectual and conscious. They respond both ways obviously, It could be compared to my analysis of how emotion works with intellect - emotion takes a long time and can have many points, while thoughts or intellect are just singular thoughts and intellect is driven by the will - so it takes power and direction. The unconscious mind does not take much deliberative conscious direction or willpower (the 'will').

Or maybe there is an action-sense and it isn't either intellectual or emotional - it is both combined in an action sense. That would be tying in the physical factor or perhaps the sensory quality of the unconscious - making experience largely unconscious because there is a sensory quality. Or is that more how animals experience the world (animal senses are considerably greater than human senses).

Table 35.0

Chapter

Conscious Attention
Chapter

What is conscious attention and how could that term be defined? Is that just simply consciousness that you are focusing on? What would that be - if someone is conscious then they are paying attention, and if they are less conscious then they are paying less attention - so saying 'conscious attention' would just be implying that the person is paying close attention - so it would be like saying 'attentively paying attention' instead of saying 'consciously paying attention'.

If someone is paying attention to something then what other mental processes are going to interfere with their attention process? Their mind could be trying to pay attention to other things unconsciously. That makes sense that attention is multifaceted - if someone is trying to pay attention to something it could be difficult or easy - their thoughts and feelings could be assisting them - or certain thoughts and feelings could be assisting them or hindering them.

What might cause someone to pay less or more attention to something other than the obvious factors such as how interested they are in the object or whatever they are paying attention and how hard they are working to pay attention to it.

People can pay attention to something and have their unconscious assist their mind or they could have their consciousness assist their mind. If their unconscious is assisting their mind then they might pay attention more efficiently because they are naturally paying attention - their feelings and drives and unconscious thoughts are all assisting their attentional process. However, if someone is paying conscious attention they they aren't necessarily using all of their minds power to focus.

Someone can try to focus on something but that doesn't mean that they are necessarily focusing as much as they can. This is probably a large issue with sports players that want to perform well - many cannot perform perfectly because their performance varies - it is because their biology limits them from focusing and paying attention as much as they would need - if they try to pay better attention then it could increase their physical performance - however it is also a conscious and unconscious battle and in that case also related to a third factor - their physical endurance or ability.

So paying attention is then mostly an unconscious and conscious battle - with possibly a third factor that would be dependent on what the activity is - what the person is trying to pay attention to. So paying attention also relates to mental associations because these could influence the persons unconscious mind and their performance. The idea would be for the person to become as unconsciously performing as possible so that their ability is enhanced by their unconscious mind. The conscious mind is limited compared to the power of the unconscious because more feelings and thoughts can be triggered if the person isn't trying to trigger them.

Table 36.0

Chapter 37

Mental Abstraction and Associations

I wrote in previous articles that mental representations and thoughts are tied in and associated with each other - and that the feeling of one thought could interact with the feeling of another thought. However, how exactly does that work? It is obviously an association structure of some sort. Those can be called a 'mental model' or a 'mental architecture' - so is the mental model for the entire brain just a simple association chain?

If some drives are more powerful then it is likely to bring up an association that is most highly related - that seems rather obvious, however what if someone is thinking something that they want to be associated with another thought or related representation? An association could be tied in from previous emotional development. There 'emotional' development could mean long term emotional development or something that was learned at one time in an experience or interaction.

So does one emotional drive or motivation have a set of related or associated images or feelings? What if an emotional drive has multiple feelings - or conflicting feelings? That could be related to secondary emotions - a secondary emotion is when someone tries to mask their primary emotion with the emotion they want to feel (for example, if someone is embarrassed because of a shy emotion and they want to be more masculine they could try to replace it with a tough, masculine emotion but the real emotion was something shy (masculinity being the secondary emotion).

So what would the mental model or association chain be with that secondary emotion? Is this just a detailed way of looking at simple emotional interactions? I could label all of the ideas associated with the primary emotion and see what their associations and triggers are and what is going on with them, and then think about the secondary emotion and figure out what is going on with that - if the person is actual masculine and tough then maybe they could replace the primary shy emotion with a secondary emotion - or maybe not.

So an artist could have an association chain that could bring up something completely different from what an expected association would be. There could be 'feeling-thoughts' and direct and guide certain feelings or thoughts to be related to other feelings and thoughts in the mind. These could be called guided feelings or thoughts..

A complex mental model or association chain could be referred to as mental abstraction because the person is being abstract - however people could be abstract with all of their thoughts all of the time - why does one thought pull up another? Why does one feeling pull up another thought? They are usually associated or tied in with feelings that formed and developed them - or maybe the feeling was unconscious and the association or model cannot be figured out.

Table 37.0

Chapter 38

Ideas, Emotional Speculation and Reality

What does an idea consist of? An idea is a thought - and a thought is usually a sentence. An idea could be about any topic - but that is obvious.

So it is obvious that an idea can be about anything, but are all ideas obvious?

People often don't understand other peoples ideas so it isn't necessarily that all ideas are obvious.

Which ideas are hard to comprehend then? Subjective ideas that are personal opinions or that involve emotional speculation could be more difficult for some people to comprehend. There is also an emotional bias that makes it hard to understand some seemingly simple concepts.

An example of such a bias would be not understanding human motivation - if someone doesn't understand the desires and needs and motivations of people then they cannot reach the conclusion of what they are likely to do - this is a common subjective evaluation that people make with frequent decisions.

If someone didn't understand that another person wants to do something, like manage a store or keep customers satisfied then they would not be capable of functioning well in society. Many of these ideas may seem like obvious things to understand - however - most people take these ideas completely for granted.

So assessing any type of motivation that someone may have in life could be completely subjective because it involves an emotional analysis and emotion and feeling is difficult to assess sometimes.

Table 38.0

Chapter 39

Truth and Reality

What is truth? Does it come from our senses and the external world around us or can we trust our internal senses?

Intelligence is subjective and truth is subjective, truth is really just discovering what the most accurate emotional reality is - and measuring emotion is extremely subjective.

All the words the people use are really subjective then - anything complex that isn't scientific would be subjective - or could be considered to be subjective. there are different emotional concepts that are tied to different words - if Jung found out that everything in life was a mental construct or an archetype I don't knŏw how he would react. There aren't just a few words that are significant that are archetypes - but practically every word that is psychologically significant or a mental construct is significant in some way.

When someone says the word 'god' that is significant as an exclamative or declarative word - they are making a statement or trying to convey emotion or distress. So the word 'god' is probably the best example for a word that is used to convey emotion because people say it when they are emotional - similar to using a swear word only swear words are more vulgar. So the word 'god' is used in a similar fashion to using swear words only it is less vulgar and possibly more emotional.

So when someone says the word 'god' what are they being subjective about? they are simply being emotional - it could be subjective to decide if they are emotional, however it might be obvious because of their facial expression or tone which could help convey if they are being emotional or what their feelings are.

So how emotional people are or how much they are feeling might not be so subjective because humans can see facial expression and tone of voice, etc. The more complex subjective feelings and ideas that people have might be harder to understand or prove, however.

How could all of reality be perceived? It would be perceiving everything all at once - in previous articles I mentioned that there was unconscious and conscious and emotional and cognitive perception. If someone views something emotionally then they are just looking at their emotions and how they look at it unconsciously - but if someone is perceiving something consciously it is a more conscious and deliberative attempt to view the world.

However, how is everything then perceived? What is the 'minds eye' so to speak? People don't just see the visual world but they perceive everything emotionally and cognitively. How could someone understand what they are taking in from the world around them?

There are different ways of understanding concepts and experiences intellectually - emotionally how life is experienced in rather simple because everything could just be described in emotional groupings - this event evoked this this and that feeling, etc.

However the intellectual is much more complicated - animals could just experience emotions and feelings however if you think about an experience you could frame it in very different ways. Different experiences might evoke similar emotions - because there are only a few basic emotions, however someone could think about the experience in rather different ways.

What does that mean - to think about something in a different way? Someone could think about something with a different emotional perspective - for instance think angrily or pessimistically (sad); however that would just be thinking with the different emotional groupings that I already mentioned someone can feel with.

Any idea could tilt how someone views something intellectually. There might only be a few basic ideas just like there are a few basic emotions; however there are probably a lot more basic ideas than basic emotions because when someone thinks about something it is very different than from when then feel something.

An idea could be tied to an emotion or feeling - that is why feelings and emotions differ - because their associated ideas also differ.

Table 39.0

Chapter 40

How Does the Mind Process information?

A mental model could mean any kind of mental model. There are models of how emotion functions and models of how intellect functions - and models of how intellect functions and is processed in the mind with emotion.

SO what is the mental model for how the entire mind works then? First there is a sensory input -and then it is processed emotionally and cognitively by the mind. That seems rather obvious. Sensory inputs cause a reaction in the mind. That is what happens - there is some sort of stimulus - and then that stimulus causes a human to think about what that stimulus does for the person.

Different stimuli trigger mental reactions that can be cognitive or emotional. That happens all of the time when someone sees something that triggers a reaction. Vision helps humans to notice various kinds of stimuli. That means that the stimuli must be processed first by one of the human senses. That is only for external stimuli or stimulation, however. A stimulus or trigger could come from within the mind from memory or what the person is thinking about.

40.1 Emotional and Cognitive are intertwined

If there is an emotion stimulus (like seeing a dog) then that could trigger a cognitive or emotional reaction in a persons mind.

So what kind of reaction does it trigger? A cognitive reaction or an emotional reaction? A cognitive reaction would be considered or viewed as the person thinking more - while an emotional reaction would be the person feeling more. Since dogs are emotional it would probably trigger an emotional reaction and not a cognitive one - however, what if an emotional stimulus starts something cognitive? It might start off as emotional since the person is seeing a dog and dogs are cute and they are animals (and animals think less and are more feeling-based than humans) but that doesn't necessarily mean that it converts into being more emotional.

What kinds of thoughts would seeing something emotional (like a dog) trigger? What kinds of emotions would it trigger? If thought about that way then it seems simple - seeing something emotional would 'probably' trigger a more emotional reaction in the mind but could also just simply cause the person to think more depending on the mood that they are in. It would seemingly produce an association of similar ideas or feelings that the dog is associated with. However, the person might see dogs all of the time and in that case it wouldn't generate much more or different stimulation for the person.

40.2 Emotional and Cognitive Stimulation

So mental stimulation can be either emotional or cognitive. If the stimulation is emotional then it produces feelings; however cognitions can also produce feelings - an example of that would be someone laughing after hearing a good joke.

So what is the relationship between knowledge structures and emotional and cognitive stimulation? There must be some sort of emotional-cogntive relationship between each mental process or mental node that produces a combination of feelings or thoughts (i could call the thoughts 'intellectualizations')

Consciousness can also cause feelings or intellectual stimulation. What is that saying - that 'consciousness' can cause stimulation? That is basically just saying that someone is in a state of feeling in which they are largely aware of what they are feeling. So the question then is can someone direct what their feelings or thoughts are aware of? People have important feelings and less important thoughts and feelings. Can someones consciousness feel certain feelings better than other feelings? That person might more largely be aware of some types of stimulation more so than other types of stimulation then.

Different types of information could also be processed by the mind - not just different types of feelings. Feelings are also just communicative so they could fall under the title of 'information' in the mind. So feelings and thoughts are processed as information by the mind.

40.3 Mental Representations

Different ideas, concepts and thoughts can interact in the mind. One idea can be a 'meta-idea' - an idea of another idea, or an idea could simply be associated with another idea. If different ideas produce different feelings and different amounts of feeling then an idea that is a meta-idea of another idea could produce a similar or associated feeling.

The ideas don't even have to be of each other - one idea could be a further reflection of another idea without the person being aware that that is occurring. Meta-representation (meta-ideas) do not have to be conscious - humans naturally reflect on stuff and feelings and thoughts or 'intellectualizations' naturally reflect and build on each other.

David Rosenthal proposed that a representation is only conscious if it is presented by a higher-order thought. However, I don't believe that to be completely accurate - representations could be simply thought about more without the person consciously thinking about it to themselves. Thoughts that aren't conscious naturally reflect on other thoughts or ideas or experiences and these concepts or 'understandings' build in the mind naturally by themselves. Furthermore, Any time someone becomes more conscious of something it could be the result of a feeling enhancing another feeling - not necessarily a thought enhancing another thought.

For instance - if someone 'has a feeling' for something and they then think more about it they don't need to necessarily be consciously directing that feeling (the further 'meta' feeling) because humans minds naturally reflect on things all of the time and they don't need to consciously say to themselves 'I need to think more about that'. It could simply be a feeling in their mind that triggered another feeling or there are possibly 'reflective feelings' whose purpose is to reflect and build and make more conscious other feelings. These feelings could be understandings of experiences or understandings of anything in life (though i would think that most understandings would be of experiences).

40.4 Florid vs Pastel Representations

Daniel Dennett suggested that there are representations that involve a sense of action or agency which he called 'florid' representations while 'pastel' representations are more basic intentions that do not necessarily involve as much intention.

However, how does a representation have an intention? A representation could be an idea - and in that case, the representation could have intentions attached. If the representation is a feeling it could also have intentions attached. An intention is a strong feeling - so it could be obvious that some representations have strong feelings or other thoughts attached.

Why do they need to even be labelled 'representations' then - I could just say that some ideas have stronger motivations and feelings attached than other ideas, and that some ideas form ideas or 'understandings' of other ideas that could be objects in the world or other concepts in the persons mind. However, when some object or idea is 'represented' as or in another idea or object in the mind it is called a meta-representation, or just a 'representation of another representation'.

So the term representation does have some use - because people represent things in the world that are happening all of the time. There is a difference then between the definition of an 'understanding' and a 'representation'. Humans could have understandings of anything basically, some of the stuff in the world is going to be represented in their mind as a single object, and other stuff is just going to be 'understood' as an 'understanding' to the person. 'Understandings' could involve multiple representations and 'understandings of understandings' could involve multiple meta-representations.

The important question then is - which components of our representations or understandings have strong feelings attached? That is what Dennett suggested by his distinction between 'florid' and 'pastel' representations. The word 'florid' by definition means elaborately or excessively intricate or complicated or excessive - so that makes it obvious that some feelings have components that are more motivated or salient.

40.5 The Use of Representations

Dennett also pointed out that there is knowing and a use to representations - if someone simply has a representation that is different from it being a practical representation. This is different from 'symbols' in my view because some symbols have a greater significance on the human psyche. That makes it seem simple - obviously different objects in the environment are going to have a greater psychological impact than other objects, and different objects are going to be represented differently.

Take is a step further and it becomes obvious that different mental constructs interact with each other within the mind. Mental constructs have been defined a long time ago - Carl Jung talked about mental constructs when discussing dreams and other significant psychological phenomena. I would think that much could be understood if it could be sorted out the different mental constructs - these are different from simply grouping ideas and subjects and experiences and 'understandings' in life into different categories - but the significance of each would need to also be understood.

The question then is - which subjects or categories or experiences could form a significant mental construct? Do different emotions form mental constructs? Can different thoughts or constructs be formed from significant life experiences and the emotions that these experiences generate? Then is it simply an emotional world that needs to be analyzed? If complex mental constructs can be formed it is certainly more complex than a few simple categories in life evoking certain emotions.

This is obviously going to be more complicated than simple symbols, a physical symbol is going to be more simple than a mental symbol - if you could call a mental symbol a representation anyway. Jung called significant mental constructs or symbols 'archetypes'. However - those a just single symbols or constructs - what would happen if a mental construct combined with another mental construct? A representation is just a single object - but a representation can be of a mental construct which could consist of multiple representations, and different mental constructs can combine and influence each other in the mind - and obviously are going to be emotionally significant.

40.6 Object Representations

One form of a mental representation is simply objects from the world forming a mental representation - either multiple objects in someones vision or a single object in someones vision - this is called the 'object- based attention' model - Montemayor and Haladjian (2015)[1]:

- Such diverse theories and studies give us good reason to believe that different attention systems work together in complementary ways to process perceptual information, and that object-based attention is an evolutionarily newer processing strategy that developed after the more basic feature-based and spatial forms of attention. The usefulness of the object-based model of high-level representation is that it provides a structure wherein low-level information from the various visual pathways can be integrate to form a coherent and persisting representation of a visual object (Ballard et al. 1997, Kahneman, Teisman, and Gibbs 1992, Noles, Scholl, and Mitroff 2005). Some studies, however, suggest that this binding can happen even when pairs of features are simply

1. Consciousness, Attention and Conscious Attention. (2015) Montemayor and Maladjian. The MIT Press.

superimposed spatially (Holcombe and Cavanagh 2001) and thus not necessarily bound in an object file format. Nevertheless, such forms of 'conjunction attention' enable the crucial integration of multiple features. This ability is particularly important for guiding actions and for conscious attention, which we discuss further in chapter 4. Our position is that before you can have a conscious representation, visual information must be organized in some useful way. Object file representations provide this organization, especially since visual features usually belong to discrete objects. Without the ability to select an individual object and bind its feature, an agent could not sustain a persisting representation of the object.(

- We are particularly drawn to the object-based attention model because it provides a nice structure for the integration of information from the various visual subsystems to form a coherent representation of a visual scene, in a way that allows mental representations to refer to external objects. Whether or not mental representations truly are organized via object files remains debatable, but for our purposes the form in which features are integrated is not problematic as long as there is some account for this integration. we believe that object files are theoretically important for providing the content of mental representations and for integrating perceptual information from multiple modalities, as well as from other forms of attention, in order to produce a cohenerent representation. It is these representations that most liekly make up the contents of conscious experience

I already mentioned in a previous article that vision was like the base-line cognition. They stated that vision is necessary for mental representations, which I pointed out before them that vision was the baseline cognition which is basically saying the same thing. People that can see use their vision to think, and when they aren't looking with their eyes open they are visualizing things which they are thinking about. That is going to influence their cognitions greatly because vision is always needed and is a part of the thought process.

I also pointed out in my previous article that vision is tied to more simple cognitions - which seems fairly obvious on the surface but could be extremely complicated if someone wanted to analyze it because it would basically be analyzing all of a humans thinking and where that thinking comes from. Does it come from vision, emotion or feeling or other thoughts or memories?

40.7 Measuring Emotion and Subjectivity

So far in this article I discussed mental representations and how they influence the mind cognitively and emotionally. The question that comes up when trying to measure how reality is expressed and represented in the mind is how could such subjective mental functions be measured?

Some things in life are obvious and their influence on the human mind is obvious also - however it isn't really that simple. Things in life have an unconscious and a conscious influence on people. If the influence is unconscious then it could be completely unknown what the influence is. Alvin Goldman phrased meta-representations on a simple lower level 'first order representation level' and a higher level a 'meta-representational' level. There are simple beliefs and desires on the first level and the second level is more reflective - it is a meta-representational level by which people think about their attitudes and their basic representations of the world - their basic beliefs and desires.

He talks about 'mental attitudes' and these attitudes are different from concepts. If someone has an attitude then it is different from a concept that they can form. Attitudes come from beliefs and desires and intentions and other mental attitudes - however - how do these attitudes become concepts?[2]

- What concepts do the folk have of mental representations? How do they conceptualize or represent to themselves such states as belief, desire, intention, and the other mental attitudes? What properties do they endow these states with, in their fundamental grasp of them? These questions should be

2. The Mentalizing Folk. Alvin Goldman. (2000) In Dan SPerber (Ed.) Metarepresenations. Oxford University Press

contrasted with questions about the essential nature of mental states......do not conceptualize beliefs and desire as neural states. How do they conceptualize them?

So they conceptualize by looking at their first level representational state - their basic beliefs and desires - then they form higher or more complex representations of those basic needs. This might be related to a hierarchy of needs because it has to do with different levels of thinking. Thinking is basically the same as different levels of representation, because, just as the world is represented simply and more complex, so too can thinking be simple and complex - and it can be about the world or about the self and world intertwined.

Table 40.0

Chapter 41

The Components of Consciousness - Mental and Phenomenological

Processes

41.1 Subjective Perception

How are various experiences in life perceived mentally? What does that mean anyway - to perceive something mentally. I wrote in a previous article that life can be viewed or perceived cognitively and emotionally. If life can be perceived in different ways then it can give rise to different experiences. Different emotional and intellectual experiences.

Different 'things' in life can be phrased in different ways. How can the experiences or phenomena in life be divided? People usually simply use the term 'thing' but phenomena could be experiences or occurrences. How does that relate to verbal phrasing, however? If someone uses a different word then it could mean something completely different then using another word or phrasing something differently. You would need to look closely at the definition of the word and see what it does for someone psychologically - and assume that it would have a similar psychological impact on different or similar people.

There are also conscious and unconscious phenomena - that makes sense - if something can be conscious or unconscious it is also going to be tied to its conscious or unconscious phenomena in the real world.

41.2 Unconscious Perception

What is an unconscious perception? If there can be unconscious perception and conscious perception then what is the difference between the two? Is that the same as asking what the difference is between consciousness and unconsciousness?

If something is unconscious then it isn't conscious - but what does that mean? If you understand something consciously then that means that you are aware of it - you understand it and are possibly aware of that understanding. However where is the line between being aware of the phenomena and a meta-awareness (aware that you are aware)?

There could be an endless number of degrees of awareness to different things - and different types of awareness - some of the awareness is going to be meta-awarenesses - awareness of other types of awareness - and some of the awareness is going to awareness of stuff that doesn't require further reflection or you already know you are aware of.

If someone already knows that they are aware of something then it doesn't require further reflection.

41.3 Consciousness is multifaceted

There are different ways of being conscious - the two most obvious are unconscious vs aware or conscious. Other ways are emotionally conscious, verbally conscious, semi-conscious or conscious in a speculative way, intuitively conscious, immediately conscious, more fully conscious, slightly conscious, visually conscious, some combination of visually conscious and emotionally or cognitively conscious, or some combination of all of those ways.

Different ideas or objects in life are mental constructs - so a simple object could represent a more complex mental representation. That idea significant because it can be applied to all mental cognitions or architectures. All mental or intellectual interactions in the mind have their own mental representations and are linked to other thoughts or representations. A representation of a park could be tied in with the representation of a picnic - or I could simply say that the events or meaning or definition of someone having a picnic is tied in directly or in a more complicated way with the persons conceptions of parks - it could be much complicated than simply tying in the ideas of 'picnic' and 'park' and arriving at the conclusion that 'you have picnics at parks'.

Some stuff in life is obvious and can be more conscious than stuff that isn't obvious. That relates to how conscious or unconscious ideas or experiences are. How is an experience emotionally or intellectually absorbed? How else can an experience be processed by the mind? Maybe it can be stored more visually or more unconsciously - so it might be stored unconsciously but stored intellectually even though it might seem like the experience should be stored emotionally since the unconscious is emotional.

If an experience is processed emotionally what does that mean? Would that mean that it makes the person happier or is it possible to process pain in an emotional way - pain is more physical so I don't know if you could say that humans process pain emotionally. It is different to say that there is an emotional component to pain than to say that pain is processed emotionally. Obviously it is processed physically but that doesn't necessarily mean that it processed cognitively and felt more deeply. Clearly someone in physical pain is feeling a lot - but they probably aren't as emotional as when they are having fun or experiencing more pleasurable physical stimulation.

41.4 Subjective Reality

What is an emotional reality? The physical reality is obvious - that would simply be what happens in the world physically - how that affects a persons mind is much more complicated, however.

A single physical reality can influence the different components of consciousness - how someone is aware of the different components of reality. Those components become a part of the persons mind in various ways - with the other major factor being what the persons mind is thinking and feeling independently and how that changes based upon the different inputs from reality.

People need to be aware of what the reality is otherwise their minds could simply determine how they interpret reality unconsciously - instead of it being something more under your control or that you are at least aware of.

So the question then is - how does someones mind influence the reality in their mind - or how does their understanding of reality or how they are influenced - influence their own mind?

41.5 Defining Components of Mind

In order to sort out the task of 'discovering the mental and physical reality' first the different components of mind and reality need to be defined.

Components of Reality
- Unconsciousness or the elements of your unconscious that someone isn't aware of

- The feelings and thoughts that someone is aware of

- More complicated aspects of consciousness such as the ideas their reality is making them or leading ('influencing') them to think

- The conclusions people reach based off what they think the reality is - not just the 'background' ideas that are ideas that people have that influence them significantly that they aren't aware of - such as delusions or not-so-delusional delusions

- That means that there are different levels of ideas that people hold with different amounts of influence over their minds - some ideas are more delusional and they have different amounts of influence over their feelings and other cognitions

- The rest of physical and emotional processing and how that ties in with their higher cognitions -

much of the physical stimulus might be obvious but it can be emotional or intellectual as well (like how the ideas that people hold and think about can be different degrees of emotional and cognitive)

41.6 Is Mental Reality Subjective?

First off - what could be a 'mental reality'? It could mean different things or be perceived in different ways. Is the mental reality in peoples minds the physical reality that they interpreted from the real world? Or is the mental reality subjective and something that their minds created?

There are different components of the intellectual. There is obvious intellectual - some things are more obvious or important intellectually while other ideas or understanding is more detailed or less important - or less detailed and sort of important, etc.

Some ideas or understandings are very important - but what are some of those understandings? It wouldn't be like the understanding of how to do cooking or solve mathematics problems. Perhaps it could be an understanding of how to interact with other people or a persons understanding of their own emotions.

Some understandings are going to be more related to consciousness or the self. This would incorporate a hierarchy of needs relevant to what is most important to someones sense of self or core emotions. It is different from a hierarchy of needs for survival - it is a hierarchy of needs for personal satisfaction and the attainment of higher consciousness - which is a key goal that human development has focused on for millennia.

So there are different intellectual things that humans can focus on at different times. There are different intellectual skills that they can have and different understandings of those skills. Once a birdy, twice a wordy, once a birdy, twice is there, once a birdy, twice a wordy - once a birdy, twice is there. Twice is here, twice is there, twice twice twice, over there. That is an intelletual understanding of a rhyme. How could that understanding possibly be significant? It doesn't even make any sense - it just sounds rhythmical. How could a song influence someone intellectually? It wouldn't really matter that much I suppose. Songs can make people feel what the emotion is behind what the song is - that is obvious if you look at a song and analyze it and think about the feelings that it generates. Songs could generate a humorous mood or a sad or happy mood. But are all intellectual cognitions like songs? With songs it seems obvious - songs are emotional and carry emotion easily - but would a certain conversation or environment create emotion in the same obvious manner that a song would? A song conveys the emotion of the theme or message of the song (or the rhythm) - however other emotions are much more complicated - the question that brings up is that perhaps making more complicated emotions makes the emotions dulled down because there are so many emotions - it isn't a simple emotion like how a song has one simple emotion.

So, if there are many different emotions and complicated ways of feeling is mental reality then subjective and diverse - or concrete and obtuse?

41.7 How is Intellect Processed in the Mind?

I stated in previous articles that different feelings and thoughts are connected in the mind - and that the feeling or thought of one thought can influence the feeling or thought of another.

However, that means that certain ideas or thoughts can have a tangible presence and influence the feelings of other ideas and thoughts. They can also be grouped into categories - for instance a humans delusional or emotional thoughts could be exerting feelings while their logical or non-emotional and intellectual thoughts are producing conflicting feelings with the more intelligent thoughts at the same time. Such an interaction would be an example of cognition interaction with emotion - a humans cognitive or more intellectual thoughts could be exerting a certain type of feeling while their less intelligent or emotional thoughts could be producing a different type of feeling.

Cognition and emotion are always in balance - just like the left brain is theorized to be more logical and right brain is theorized to be more emotional and those two brains are always in balance - so tp emotion is always in balance with intellect or cognition.

WHy would a thought balance an emotion? If more intellectual thoughts are more conscious - and more emotional thoughts are less conscious - than that makes sense because thoughts are single points of information while emotions would probably take a longer time to experience than a thought - so say someone is experiencing an emotion - they could suddenly stop experiencing that emotion and think certain thoughts or even just initiate a period of more intellectual thinking which could stop the emotion, assist the emotion or hinder the emotion.

So certain types of thoughts are going to be more emotional and possibly assist emotion more than other thoughts that people can think. If the thoughts are delusional that might make the person more emotional than thoughts that make sense and are logical. There are also ideas and thoughts that can be grouped together - if someone thinks something through more clearly then maybe they can make the idea or thought structure more intellectual and less emotional. If it is more intellectual it could interfere more with emotional processes because thinking too much stops emotion or feeling.

It is obvious how thinking or thoughts could interfere with emotions = if someone is feeling good about something and they then think - 'I hate that thing' then it could stop the feeling good about the emotion completely. If someone continues the good emotion with thoughts that assist the positive emotion then the intellect or thoughts would be encouraging the emotion. However, if they think too much then they might become less emotional about it because they would be interfering the emotional process.

So someones emotions could be feeling one thing (that would be like a thought or group of ideas - but they would being conveyed by the persons emotions) and their intellect (which is more conscious) could be thinking about or conveying something completely different. The emotional is unconscious - so unconsciously someones emotions could be making the person feel stupid and telling them that they are emotional and stupid while their intellect could be trying to override their emotions and make them think clearer.

The persons emotions could be telling them one idea unconsciously while they could be trying to communicate or enforce a different idea to their mind consciously.

41.8 Ideas can be cognitive or emotional

Ideas that people have can be conscious ideas or not conscious ideas - they can come from the conscious mind or they can be more unconscious. If they are conscious they it is probable that the person thought about them more consciously to themselves then an idea that came from their unconscious mind. How could a thought even stem from the unconscious anyway? Some ideas people simply absorb or learn from their environment and the person doesn't necessarily need to think about as consciously.

If the person doesn't think about the idea as consciously then it could still be understood consciously - they just might not be able to verbalize it as clearly. That makes sense - it depends on what the ideas and concepts are basically. Some ideas could be very conscious while others could be very unconscious - that brings up the point of how someone would define a 'conscious' idea versus an 'unconscious' idea or concept.

Other than the fact that the unconscious concept the person wouldn't be described as being as consciously aware of anyway - some concepts a person could be aware of in a different way yet could still be described as being conscious of. Some concepts don't need that much conscious thinking about either - if someone is hungry they don't really need to think that much about that in order to understand that they are hungry - their body is communicating the information about how hungry they are and they become aware of that because they are in touch with their physical senses - that is all that is required to be aware of that in that circumstance - a slight physical awareness.

Other things that people might be aware of could require large amounts of intellect, however. All animals know when they need to eat and when they are hungry - so that isn't a very complicated desire. What about social cues - those might be hard for a person to process consciously and could be unconscious for a long period of time before they become more absorbed consciously. All of a persons emotions could be unconscious to different degrees and further thought could influence how much they 'absorb' or understand those emotions.

Table 41.0

Chapter 42

Ideas can be cognitive or emotional

Ideas that people have can be conscious ideas or not conscious ideas - they can come from the conscious mind or they can be more unconscious. If they are conscious they it is probable that the person thought about them more consciously to themselves then an idea that came from their unconscious mind. How could a thought even stem from the unconscious anyway? Some ideas people simply absorb or learn from their environment and the person doesn't necessarily need to think about as consciously.

If the person doesn't think about the idea as consciously then it could still be understood consciously - they just might not be able to verbalize it as clearly. That makes sense - it depends on what the ideas and concepts are basically. Some ideas could be very conscious while others could be very unconscious - that brings up the point of how someone would define a 'conscious' idea versus an 'unconscious' idea or concept.

Other than the fact that the unconscious concept the person wouldn't be described as being as consciously aware of anyway - some concepts a person could be aware of in a different way yet could still be described as being conscious of. Some concepts don't need that much conscious thinking about either - if someone is hungry they don't really need to think that much about that in order to understand that they are hungry - their body is communicating the information about how hungry they are and they become aware of that because they are in touch with their physical senses - that is all that is required to be aware of that in that circumstance - a slight physical awareness.

Other things that people might be aware of could require large amounts of intellect, however. All animals know when they need to eat and when they are hungry - so that isn't a very complicated desire. What about social cues - those might be hard for a person to process consciously and could be unconscious for a long period of time before they become more absorbed consciously. All of a persons emotions could be unconscious to different degrees and further thought could influence how much they 'absorb' or understand those emotions.

Table 42.0

Chapter 43

How is Intellect Processed in the Mind?

I stated in previous articles that different feelings and thoughts are connected in the mind - and that the feeling or thought of one thought can influence the feeling or thought of another.

However, that means that certain ideas or thoughts can have a tangible presence and influence the feelings of other ideas and thoughts. They can also be grouped into categories - for instance a humans delusional or emotional thoughts could be exerting feelings while their logical or non-emotional and intellectual thoughts are producing conflicting feelings with the more intelligent thoughts at the same time. Such an interaction would be an example of cognition interaction with emotion - a humans cognitive or more intellectual thoughts could be exerting a certain type of feeling while their less intelligent or emotional thoughts could be producing a different type of feeling.

Cognition and emotion are always in balance - just like the left brain is theorized to be more logical and right brain is theorized to be more emotional and those two brains are always in balance - so tp emotion is always in balance with intellect or cognition.

WHy would a thought balance an emotion? If more intellectual thoughts are more conscious - and more emotional thoughts are less conscious - than that makes sense because thoughts are single points of information while emotions would probably take a longer time to experience than a thought - so say someone is experiencing an emotion - they could suddenly stop experiencing that emotion and think certain thoughts or even just initiate a period of more intellectual thinking which could stop the emotion, assist the emotion or hinder the emotion.

So certain types of thoughts are going to be more emotional and possibly assist emotion more than other thoughts that people can think. If the thoughts are delusional that might make the person more emotional than thoughts that make sense and are logical. There are also ideas and thoughts that can be grouped together - if someone thinks something through more clearly then maybe they can make the idea or thought structure more intellectual and less emotional. If it is more intellectual it could interfere more with emotional processes because thinking too much stops emotion or feeling.

It is obvious how thinking or thoughts could interfere with emotions = if someone is feeling good about something and they then think - 'I hate that thing' then it could stop the feeling good about the emotion completely. If someone continues the good emotion with thoughts that assist the positive emotion then the intellect or thoughts would be encouraging the emotion. However, if they think too much then they might become less emotional about it because they would be interfering the emotional process.

So someones emotions could be feeling one thing (that would be like a thought or group of ideas - but they would being conveyed by the persons emotions) and their intellect (which is more conscious) could be thinking about or conveying something completely different. The emotional is unconscious - so unconsciously someones emotions could be making the person feel stupid and telling them that they are emotional and stupid while their intellect could be trying to override their emotions and make them think clearer.

The persons emotions could be telling them one idea unconsciously while they could be trying to communicate or enforce a different idea to their mind consciously.

Table 43.0

Chapter

Chapter 44

Is Mental Reality Subjective?

Chapter

First off - what could be a 'mental reality'? It could mean different things or be perceived in different ways. Is the mental reality in peoples minds the physical reality that they interpreted from the real world? Or is the mental reality subjective and something that their minds created?

There are different components of the intellectual. There is obvious intellectual - some things are more obvious or important intellectually while other ideas or understanding is more detailed or less important - or less detailed and sort of important, etc.

Some ideas or understandings are very important - but what are some of those understandings? It wouldn't be like the understanding of how to do cooking or solve mathematics problems. Perhaps it could be an understanding of how to interact with other people or a persons understanding of their own emotions.

Some understandings are going to be more related to consciousness or the self. This would incorporate a hierarchy of needs relevant to what is most important to someones sense of self or core emotions. It is different from a hierarchy of needs for survival - it is a hierarchy of needs for personal satisfaction and the attainment of higher consciousness - which is a key goal that human development has focused on for millennia.

So there are different intellectual things that humans can focus on at different times. There are different intellectual skills that they can have and different understandings of those skills. Once a birdy, twice a wordy, once a birdy, twice is there, once a birdy, twice a wordy - once a birdy, twice is there. Twice is here, twice is there, twice twice twice, over there. That is an intelletual understanding of a rhyme. How could that understanding possibly be significant? It doesn't even make any sense - it just sounds rhythmical. How could a song influence someone intellectually? It wouldn't really matter that much I suppose. Songs can make people feel what the emotion is behind what the song is - that is obvious if you look at a song and analyze it and think about the feelings that it generates. Songs could generate a humorous mood or a sad or happy mood. But are all intellectual cognitions like songs? With songs it seems obvious - songs are emotional and carry emotion easily - but would a certain conversation or environment create emotion in the same obvious manner that a song would? A song conveys the emotion of the theme or message of the song (or the rhythm) - however other emotions are much more complicated - the question that brings up is that perhaps making more complicated emotions makes the emotions dulled down because there are so many emotions - it isn't a simple emotion like how a song has one simple emotion.

So, if there are many different emotions and complicated ways of feeling is mental reality then subjective and diverse - or concrete and obtuse?

Table 44.0

Chapter

Subjective Reality
Chapter 45

What is an emotional reality? The physical reality is obvious - that would simply be what happens in the world physically - how that affects a persons mind is much more complicated, however.

A single physical reality can influence the different components of consciousness - how someone is aware of the different components of reality. Those components become a part of the persons mind in various ways - with the other major factor being what the persons mind is thinking and feeling independently and how that changes based upon the different inputs from reality.

People need to be aware of what the reality is otherwise their minds could simply determine how they interpret reality unconsciously - instead of it being something more under your control or that you are at least aware of.

So the question then is - how does someones mind influence the reality in their mind - or how does their understanding of reality or how they are influenced - influence their own mind?

45.1 Defining Components of Mind

In order to sort out the task of 'discovering the mental and physical reality' first the different components of mind and reality need to be defined.

Components of Mind
- Unconsciousness or the elements of your unconscious that someone isn't aware of

- The feelings and thoughts that someone is aware of

- More complicated aspects of consciousness such as the ideas their reality is making them or leading ('influencing') them to think

- The conclusions people reach based off what they think the reality is - not just the 'background' ideas that are ideas that people have that influence them significantly that they aren't aware of - such as delusions or not-so-delusional delusions

- That means that there are different levels of ideas that people hold with different amounts of influence over their minds - some ideas are more delusional and they have different amounts of influence over their feelings and other cognitions

- The rest of physical and emotional processing and how that ties in with their higher cognitions - much of the physical stimulus might be obvious but it can be emotional or intellectual as well (like how the ideas that people hold and think about can be different degrees of emotional and cognitive)

Table 45.0

Chapter

Consciousness is multifaceted

There are different ways of being conscious - the two most obvious are unconscious vs aware or conscious. Other ways are emotionally conscious, verbally conscious, semi-conscious or conscious in a speculative way, intuitively conscious, immediately conscious, more fully conscious, slightly conscious, visually conscious, some combination of visually conscious and emotionally or cognitively conscious, or some combination of all of those ways.

Different ideas or objects in life are mental constructs - so a simple object could represent a more complex mental representation. That idea significant because it can be applied to all mental cognitions or architectures. All mental or intellectual interactions in the mind have their own mental representations and are linked to other thoughts or representations. A representation of a park could be tied in with the representation of a picnic - or I could simply say that the events or meaning or definition of someone having a picnic is tied in directly or in a more complicated way with the persons conceptions of parks
- it could be much complicated than simply tying in the ideas of 'picnic' and 'park' and arriving at the conclusion that 'you have picnics at parks'.

Some stuff in life is obvious and can be more conscious than stuff that isn't obvious. That relates to how conscious or unconscious ideas or experiences are. How is an experience emotionally or intellectually absorbed? How else can an experience be processed by the mind? Maybe it can be stored more visually or more unconsciously - so it might be stored unconsciously but stored intellectually even though it might seem like the experience should be stored emotionally since the unconscious is emotional.

If an experience is processed emotionally what does that mean? Would that mean that it makes the person happier or is it possible to process pain in an emotional way - pain is more physical so I don't know if you could say that humans process pain emotionally. It is different to say that there is an emotional component to pain than to say that pain is processed emotionally. Obviously it is processed physically but that doesn't necessarily mean that it processed cognitively and felt more deeply. Clearly someone in physical pain is feeling a lot - but they probably aren't as emotional as when they are having fun or experiencing more pleasurable physical stimulation.

Table 46.0

Chapter

Subjective Perception
Chapter

How are various experiences in life perceived mentally? What does that mean anyway - to perceive something mentally. I wrote in a previous article that life can be viewed or perceived cognitively and emotionally. If life can be perceived in different ways then it can give rise to different experiences. Different emotional and intellectual experiences.

Different 'things' in life can be phrased in different ways. How can the experiences or phenomena in life be divided? People usually simply use the term 'thing' but phenomena could be experiences or occurrences. How does that relate to verbal phrasing, however? If someone uses a different word then it could mean something completely different then using another word or phrasing something differently. You would need to look closely at the definition of the word and see what it does for someone psychologically - and assume that it would have a similar psychological impact on different or similar people.

There are also conscious and unconscious phenomena - that makes sense - if something can be conscious or unconscious it is also going to be tied to its conscious or unconscious phenomena in the real world.

47.1 Unconscious perception

What is an unconscious perception? If there can be unconscious perception and conscious perception then what is the difference between the two? Is that the same as asking what the difference is between consciousness and unconsciousness?

If something is unconscious then it isn't conscious - but what does that mean? If you understand something consciously then that means that you are aware of it - you understand it and are possibly aware of that understanding. However where is the line between being aware of the phenomena and a meta-awareness (aware that you are aware)?

There could be an endless number of degrees of awareness to different things - and different types of awareness - some of the awareness is going to be meta-awarenesses - awareness of other types of awareness - and some of the awareness is going to awareness of stuff that doesn't require further reflection or you already know you are aware of.

If someone already knows that they are aware of something then it doesn't require further reflection.

Table 47.0

Chapter 48

A Physics work in progress - the Beginning

I have only studied physics a little - however theoretical or philosophical physics is a subjective topic that could be speculated upon by lay people - some of this article could relate to how the universe was formed.

It would seem to me that physical particles have to combine in manner that makes sense, but the question is - what is logical physical connection? Is it logical for one particle to bond or interact with a different particle?

What is inside empty space? Could it be that there are small particles in empty space that aren't visible or have any interactions with other particles?

Maybe I can say that a 'particle' is the smallest unit of matter or the smallest unit of something that can be physically observed or actually exist - I don't know if someone else has defined something like that before.

There are different ways that different particles interact - they have charges and strong and weak forces - however, are those all the ways in which they can interact, bond, attract and repel each other, and so on and so forth?

What is the difference between energy and matter then? Energy is matter (or could be viewed as being matter), and matter is energy because both are physical substances. I could define the smallest particles as physical substances - but if they don't exist anywhere then maybe they can be transformed into different types of matter because they are pure energy - but does that statement even make any sense - all energy has to be matter because it has to physically exist.

Table 48.0

Chapter 49

A Discussion about the Mind and Consciousness

How does the mind decipher meaning?

Or I might ask another question - what exactly does that mean? What is meaning in the mind anyway?

An example would be an expression or any saying basically - say someone says 'red apples taste good'. That statement has a certain significance for both the listeners and the person making the statement. Depending on their experience and understanding of how red apples taste their understanding of the statement is going to differ.

That was just a verbal example, however. The mind also gets meaning from its surroundings and physical phenomena. The red apples by themselves, for instance, might give the person an experience from just seeing the apples but probably more of one when they eat one of the apples.

So there is verbal or intellectual experience and physical or phenomenal experience - the important question then is how do these two types of experience relate to each other - here Heil states Davidson's theory (Heil, J):

- Davidson argues that ... every mental token is identical with some physical token. Your being in pain at midnight is (let us imagine) identical with some physical (presumably neurological) event occurring in your body at midnight, although there is no prospect of translating talk of pain into neurological talk.

That theory received a lot of criticism, and I can see why. It doesn't seem like that would ever be literally true - as a guideline it might make some sense that mental events or states correspond with what is going on physically with the body at any time, however they probably aren't exact because different factors are going to be determining someones mental cognitions than the factors determining their physical biology.

49.1 Concepts

According to the classical theory of concepts, concepts have are complex mental representations that have a definitional structure (the concept fits properties according to its definition).

Other theories developed such as the prototype theory and the dual theory. The prototype theory suggests that concepts fit a stereotypical prototype (kind of like Jungian archetypes). The dual theory developed later and suggests that concepts have a 'core' and an 'identification procedure'. However 'Conceptual Atomism' suggests that concepts don't have any structure and they just correspond with what they represent - be that casual or historical.

In another article of mine **m52492** I reference James Sully (1892) who points out that concepts have three parts - abstraction, comparison and generalization. That suggests that people go through a process of thinking for each concept - they compare the concept to other concepts, generalize the concept - but first just have an abstract picture of the concept.

His simple explanation basically just points out that concepts involve thinking 'more' about each concept - including generalizing it. The other theories of concepts all have valid points as well however. The prototype theory suggests generalization is involved (as prototypes are generalized). And the dual theory suggests that identification is involved (which is similar to comparison). While the atomism theory suggests that it is just a simple thought process - which would be the 'abstraction' phase of understanding the concepts.

Concepts and experiential qualities

So how would a thought process of a concept occur in the mind? First you would think a little about the concept - an abstraction - then you would think more about the concept and possibly compare it to other concepts or even the real experiences involving the concept (such as when the concept occurred in a real life situation) and then you would come to a conclusion about the concept and generalize it as this or that type of concept (It doesn't necessarily occur in that order, however - these are my theories).

How might someone know when a concept is being thought about? Humans probably think about a lot of advanced concepts all the time. They might only know about their thoughts or concepts some of the time however, and certainly not the full implications or experiential aspects of them (much of this must be unconscious).

Some Questions about the Mind

- One question is about perception - is its aim to provide accurate perceptions? When you consider how the unconscious mind thinks versus how the conscious mind thinks then the answer is no because many things you simply want a feel for and therefor couldn't possible have an accurate perception of.

- What is the relationship between attention to action and awareness of mind? Clearly being aware of ones physical actions gives a sense of self or agency - and that that therefore is a part of 'being present' or getting a feel for yourself and the people around you.

- How subjective is pain introspection and emotional introspection? Are pain and emotion second hand representations that come from thoughts of the original pain or are they direct feelings? Is a model of pain or emotion needed in mind in order for these feelings to be processed?

- Are there different levels to representations? Is a meta-representation a representation of another representation or is it the same representation just thought about more? What happens when someone thinks more about a representation or compares it with other representations? Can the mind be divided up that way - based on individual representations or do representations 'merge' into each other (i.e. the feeling or thought of one representation influencing the feeling or thought of another).

Some Questions about Concept and Image Associations

- When a concept is thought about more than its initial abstraction, is it thought about verbally or non-verbally - or some combination of both?

- When a concept is compared with other concepts that are related or similar - or not related and dissimilar - is it compared by using words or by using comparative images?

- I would think that when a concept is thought about 'more' it is automatically compared to similar concepts because similar things in life are naturally associated with each other.

- Is visual processing (processing of visual images or visual thinking) unconscious or conscious? That is, when the mind uses images to think does it do so unconsciously or consciously?

- Images naturally accompany thought all of the time, both consciously and unconsciously. It is hard to figure out or explain how exactly this occurs, however.

- For instance, there could be fast, more unconscious images or slow, deliberate and conscious images that accompany thoughts.

- Would the unconscious images be as useful or informative as conscious images? How is it even possible to 'partially' visualize an event or idea or experience?

Words provide management of images

Words manage and direct the imagination process. It would be hard to go through a sequence of thinking about one or multiple things simply by visualizing their occurrences. Here (Paivio, 1979) talks about the two processes of images and words and how they relate:

- One important hypothesis concerning the interaction of the processes is that imags are particularly effective in promoting rapid associations while verbal processes give them direction. something of this kind has been suggested, for example, by Rugg in connection with the requisites of the creative act, which are said to include "a well filled storehouse of imagery to guarantee richness and freedom of association, and of ordered key concepts to guarantee organization of thought" (1963, p. 311). Imagery is characteristic of autistic thinking in general and in that context is free of logical restraints; verbal processes superimposed on such imagery presumably contribute order and direction. These hypothesized, mutually supportive functions of images and words can be viewed as a consequence of the relative weighing of parallel processing and sequential processing features in the two systems: Imagery having both spatially and operationally parallel properties, is likely to be characterized by freedom and speed of association, whereas the sequentially organized verbal system is capable of providing organization to the associative process.

Some Questions about Representations, Images and Abstraction

- Are there different levels of the complexity of mental images?

- Can an image be thought about more by making a more complex or sequentially next image of it?

- If one image fits one representation, then it could be said that there are 'images' and 'meta- images (or visualizations)' and that those are comparable to representations and meta-representations.

- How do visualizations and images relate to the concreteness or abstractness of mental concepts?

- Would an abstract concept be harder to visualize or easier than a concrete concept?

- For instance, visualizing numbers might be simple but visualizing an abstract concept might be challenging if its symbol is difficult to understand (but it might be 'understood' unconsciously.

- So visions or images can take on a simple, unconscious form perhaps like in dreams with dream symbols and images.

- I guess that unconscious image processing is more simple than conscious processing - like how the images in dreams are more simple than images people have when they are conscious.

Conclusion

Images are used to compare and contrast conceptual information. People think about their experiences with these unconscious images and thoughts. A concept could be a summary or example of a certain type of experience, and using images would probably create more detail for the concept. Words obviously trigger and direct conceptual thinking, however the content of conceptual thinking comes from feelings or visualizations. Visualizations might be tied in with fast thinking or slow, emotional thinking. Doing math doesn't require emotional processes but would require complex visual processes but not necessarily complex conceptual thought - since most advanced thought is actually emotionally based and might or might not use emotional processes when thinking.

The question then would be when is an emotional process used in thinking. I mentioned that math doesn't require emotional processes and was just visual. Many concepts are just visual even if they are emotional concepts, however - so this could be difficult to figure out.

Bibliography

Heil, J. (2003) 'Mental Causation'. In Stich, S and Warfield, T. (Eds) The Blackwell Guide to Philosophy of Mind. Blackwell publishing

Paivio, A (1979) Imagery and Verbal Processes. Lawrence Erlbaum Associates

Table 49.0

Chapter 50

How do Modularity theories of mind work? - Some Ideas

How does modularity in the mind work? If the mind is composed of modules, is it composed of a suite of specialized learning systems ('massively modular') or just a few (not 'massively' modular)? Here (Carruthers, 2006) references Samuels:

- Samuels (1998) challenges the above line of argument for massive processing modularity, however, claiming that instead of a whole suite of specialized learning systems, there might be just a single general-learning/general-inferencing mechanism, but one operating on lots of organized bodies of innate information. (He calls this "informational modularity," contrasting it with the more familiar form of computational modularity.) However, this would surely create a serious processing bottleneck. If there were really just one (or even a few) inferential systems - generating beliefs about the likely movements of the surrounding mechanical objects; about the likely beliefs, goals, and actions of the surrounding agents; about who owes what to to whom in a social exchange; and so on and so forth - then it looks as if there would be a kind of tractability problem here. It would be the problem of forming novel beliefs on all these different subject matters in real time (in seconds or fractions of a second), using a limited set of inferential resources. Indeed (and in contrast with Samuel's suggestion) surely everyone now thinks that the mind/brain is massively parallel in its organization. In which case we should expect there to be distinct systems that can process each of the different kinds of information at the same time.

If there was a set of learning systems in the mind, each doing it own thing (for instance maybe a system for language, a visual system and an auditory system each processing its own information) then would the information be encapsulated for each system? By encapsulated I mean the information being not related or influenced by other information in the mind. Carruthers suggested that this theory suggests not a suite of learning mechanisms but 'one operating on lots of organized nodes of innate information'.

Each one of those individual systems would have to input and output information to other systems and such - which is why Carruthers suggested that this might 'surely create a serious processing bottleneck'. However with any computational model this would have to occur as well - all the processing in the mind can't be completely parallel because there are surely multiple systems each doing its own thing - for instance there is a small section of the brain where language is processed.

I would think that this suggests that Samuels' theory of modularity is correct. Just because there would be a few systems by which the mind works that gather information - 'about the likely beliefs, goals and actions of the surrounding agents' doesn't mean that the mind can't be massively modular as well. The mind can work like a computer and still be composed of various regions where certain information is processed. That makes sense considering that various regions of the brain are thought to be associated with various mental functions.

Categorizing information in the mind

What kinds of modules would the mind consist of then? I would think that it simply works emotionally - that is, an idea or feeling that consists of a certain set of feelings triggers where those feelings are 'felt' most in the brain.

For instance if someone triggers aggressiveness then the area or areas of the brain that processes that feeling would be triggered respectively.

This would work for ideas as well - if an idea or concept consists of a certain set of emotions or feelings then the mind would simply process it by activating the respective feelings it represents.

Of course, certain types of information would require different amounts of 'thought power' to compute, and this might be done consciously or unconsciously. If it is done unconsciously then the information is not readily available to consciousness - but may become available when the processing is done or at some other point.

How does it work?

So there wouldn't be a processing bottleneck because the computational processes would be done by non-modular areas of the brain (various regions being triggered by respective feelings) and the modular-function related regions would interact very quickly in many instances but also slowly (since it takes time to process many environmental stimuli).

Bibliography

Carruthers, Peter. (2006) The Case for Massively Modular Models of Mind. In Stainton, R (Ed) "Contemporary Debates in Cognitive Science". Blackwell Publishing

Table 50.0

Chapter 51

The Scope of Consciousness and the Conceptual

There are many ways in which the mind represents the world as a whole and the individual objects in it.

I could say that mental states have been determined by the minds representations of all internal and external data.

At any time humans are in some various mental state - i.e. happiness, curiosity, anger, excitement, dread, or passiveness. I guess a question could be why is it hard to have a mix of some mental states - such as a combination of happiness and anger? Some combinations of mental states are common and make sense, while others (like being happy and sad at the same time) are hard on a person or difficult to acquire.

That is why concepts and consciousness has a scope and a limit - because there are only so many combinations of mental states, and it is hard to achieve many of these states.

51.1 Concepts, Perceptions and Beliefs

How are concepts, beliefs and perceptions related?

I suppose it depends on which type of each of those is being referred to. For instance 'perception' could mean just simple visual perceptions or it could mean how the mind perceives emotional or conceptual phenomena. 'Belief' could mean beliefs that are independent of stimuli (that you think about at a random time) versus beliefs a person forms from current incoming stimuli.

Conceptual phenomena can vary considerably. There are simple concepts like understanding the purposes of objects - those are definitional concepts. Other concepts concern human or animal behavior and an understanding of how they achieve certain goals. Other concepts are more emotional and concern beliefs and motivated goals, or abstract emotional concepts like in politics, history or the news (such as human events and affairs).

I guess the important question to ask then is how do those three ideas - conceptual thinking, perceptions and beliefs relate to each other considering the differing topics involved.

For instance, for any perceptual stimuli a concept, belief or abstract perception could be formed.

Table 51.0

Chapter 52

Consciousness: Perceptions and Concepts

Beliefs are a large part of how the mind functions since they help form desires and drives. How could one carve out the mental faculties and processes responsible for belief formation and revision? Here is (Goldman, A):

- An initial phase of this undertaking is to sharpen our conceptualization of the types of cognitive units that should be targets of epistemic evaluation. Lay people are pretty vague about the the sorts of entites that quality as intellectual virtues or vices. In my description of epistemic folkways, I have been deliberately indefinite about these entities, calling them variously "faculties," "processes," "mechanisms," and the like. How should systematic epistemology improve on this score?

- A first possibility, enshrined in the practice of historical philosophers, is to take the relevant units to be cognitive faculties. This might be translated into modern parlance as modules, except that this term has assumed a rather narrow, specialized meaning under Jerry Fodor's (1983) influential treatment of modularity. A better translation might be (cognitive) systems e.g., the visual system, long-term memory, and so forth. Such systems, however, are also suboptimal candidates for units of epistemic analysis. Many beliefs are the outputs of two or more systems working in tandem. For example, a belief consisting in the visual classification of an object ("That is a chair") may involve matching some information in the visual system with a category stored in long-term memory. A preferable unit of analysis, then, might be a process, construed as the sort of entity depicted by familiar flow charts of cognitive activity. This sort of entity depicted by familiar flow charts of cognitive activity. This sort of diagram depicts a sequence of operations (or sets of parallel operations), ultimately culminating in a belief -like output. Such a sequence may span several cognitive systems. This is the sort of entity I had in mind in previous publications (especially Goldman 1986) when I spoke of "cognitive processes."

- Even this sort of entity, however, is not fully a satisfactory unit of analysis. Visual classification, for example, may occur under a variety of degraded conditions. The stimulus may be viewed from an unusual orientation; it may be partly occluded, so that only certain of its parts are visible; and so forth. Obviously, these factors can make a big difference to the reliability of the classification process. Yet it is one and the same process that analyzes the stimulus data and comes to a perceptual "conclusion." So the same process can have different degrees of reliability depending on a variety of parameter values. For purposes of epistemic assessment, it would be instructive to identify the parameters and parameter values that are critically relevant to degrees of reliability. The virtues and vices might then be associated not with processes per se, but with processes operating with specified parameter value.

So various mental faculties might be responsible for belief formation like memory and vision. I would think that emotional processes also would obviously be responsible as well (as beliefs are emotional). Unconscious or conscious processes could help form beliefs, and that in turn could determine what the persons goals and drives are like.

How does the mind process sensory inputs? Sensory experiences in the mind have the label 'qualia' (Kim, J):

- Sensations have characteristic qualitative features; these are called "phenomenal" or "phenomenological" or "sensory" qualities-"qualia" is now the standard term. Seeing a ripe tomato has a certain distinctive sensory quality that is unmistakably different from the sensory quality involved in see a bunch of spinach leaves. We are familiar with the smells of roses and ammonia; we can tell the sound of a drum from that of a gong; the feel of a cool, smooth granite countertop as we run our fingers over it is distinctively different from the feel of sandpaper. Our waking life is a continuous fast of qualia- colors, smells, sounds and all the rest. When we are temporarily unable to taste or smell properly because of a bad cold, eating a favorite food can be like chewing cardboard and we are made acutely aware of what is missing from our experience.

How do these sensory qualities determine how we feel overall? Does the physical match up with the mental? (Kim, J):

- On the functionalist account, mental states are realized by the internal physical states of the psychological subject; so for humans, the experience of red, as a mental state, is realized by a specific neural state. This means that you and I cannot differ in respect of the qualia we experience as long as we are in the same neural state; given that both you and I are in the same neural state, something that is in principle ascertainable by observation, either both of us experience red or neither does.

So some aspects of mental states are physical and some are mental - here is another quote from the same author (Kim, J):

- In any case, is seems plausible that there are conscious mental states with no special phenomenal character. In general, mental occurrences that we call "experiences" appear to be those that possess phenomenal properties. Sensing and perceiving are experiences, but we do not think of believing and thinking as experiences. If this is so, the idea of phenomenal character and the idea of there being something it is like may come apart, though only slightly. For it certainly seems that there is something it is like to believe something, to suspend judgment about something, to wonder about something, or to hope for something. But as we saw, at least many instances of these states do not seem to have any phenomenal character.

How does someone know when they are conscious of something or in a conscious state? A good way to answer that would be to compare animals to humans, as that might illustrate how humans are more conscious. - Can you attribute intentionality without attributing consciousness? Here (Gennaro, R) asks that question:

- Can significant explanatory power be achieved by making intentional attributions without attributions of consciousness? It seems to me that the answer is clearly yes, as the animals' case in the previous paragraph shows. We would, I suggest, still rightly attribute all unconscious intentional states to such animals. would or should we withdraw intentional attributions to an animal if we later come to agree that it is not conscious? I don't think so. Such attributions are useful in explaining and predicting animal behavior, but it does not follow that they have merely "as-if" intentionality. In some cases, we may not know if they are conscious. The same i suggest, would hold for advanced robots. This is not necessarily to embrace some kind of antirealist Dennetean "intentional stance" position (Dennett 1987). For one thing, we might still agree that those systems have genuine internal mental representations.

I would say that animals have perceptions or even higher-order perceptions (HOP) but don't have thoughts or higher-order thoughts (HOT). A perception or thought is higher order when it takes another perception or thought as its object - such as you being aware of your thought or perception on a certain thing. Animals might have thoughts or perceptions then, but probably not higher order ones since they are basically functioning unconsciously if you were to compare them to humans.

You could say that animals don't really have 'conscious' thoughts since they don't think about what they are thinking about. They don't really have higher-level thoughts since they just have simplistic thoughts or thoughts that don't involve complex representations (or they don't make the representations complex).

For instance when someone thinks 'I just did this' then they are thinking more consciously about what they did and the thoughts that were involved. That enables further action or introspection that animals don't

Gennaro, R. (2012) The Consciousness Paradox. Massachusetts Institute of

have.

Is the mind physical or mental?

Physicalism is a philosophical position holding that everything which exists is no more extensive than its physical properties; that is, that there are no kinds of things other than physical things. Knowledge or concepts, however, are mental constructs not physical ones, so it follows that physicalism leaves something out.

How are words processed with concepts and knowledge?

When someone thinks of a word their mind automatically compares it to other things and makes associations with other words and other concepts your mind understands. It could be viewed that a word is a set of related mental nodes, and that similar or associated nodes are explored or activated when one thinks of the word. That is saying that a process of comparison occurs with each word that is thought about - which i mention in another article of mine - m52495 - where I reference James Sully (1892) who points out that concepts have three parts - abstraction, comparison and generalization.

Other propositions about the word are inferred, of course - and those related nodes are also activated.

So then words and concepts are actually very simple when you think about them as computationally processed. However, when someone 'infers' something it isn't simple at all. They are making a guess as to what that concept is like and how it might be like other concepts.

'Inferring' then is basically analyzing levels of emotional subtlety. You get an idea of an idea or concept and this idea triggers you to think more about it and guess or infer other properties related to it.

Is understanding that simple then? How much of this 'inferring and relating' process is emotional? someone could do mathematical calculations, which would involve activating networks like a computer does - but it wouldn't process the information exactly like a computer at all. The nodes connecting the mathematical equations would be emotional nodes or nodes with feeling and the consequences of feelings attached, not like a computer that is programmed with 1s and 0s.

Concept aquisition

A concept can be an association between a mental representation and a perceptually represented object, or a concept could be an association between a feeling and an object (both are basically the same thing).

Concepts are formed when unconscious feelings become linked to an object - this makes the object more able to be verbally described and conscious.

If animals formed concepts then they would be able to adapt their behavior in more creative fashions because they would be capable of more complex thought. The concepts they form are merely unconscious - A leads to B,, so don't do A - which is less sophisticated than a humans ability to manipulate concepts which goes something like 'maybe I can do this instead of that because of this or that reason'.

Concept categorization

Concepts are going to be categorized differently. Sometimes concepts fit several categories and are grouped or associated with other concepts.

Concepts are complex mental representations - that is why they go into so many different categories - because each word or concept in life is related or belongs with other events, experiences and ideas.

My guess would be this might help explain how the mind functions - different areas of the brain are going to be more biased for certain types of experiences or concepts and when a concept is thought about that region of the brain gets more activated than the other regions of the brain the concept is less associated with. That also explains how brains can function without the organs being fully developed in a 'final' state - because a lot of the brain can still work just with less functionality.

Bibliography

Gennaro, R. (2012) The Consciousness Paradox. Massachusetts Institute of

Goldman, A (1993) 'Epistemic Folkways and Scientific Epistemology". In Goldman, A. (Ed) Readings in philosophy and cognitive science. Massachusetts Institute of Technology.

Kim, J. (2006) Philosophy of mind. Westview Press.

Table 52.0

Gennaro, R. (2012) The Consciousness Paradox. Massachusetts Institute of

Chapter 53

The Role of Consciousness in the Mind

What is the role of consciousness in the mind? Consciousness uses the functions of cognition and emotion to operate the mind. Cognition is basically all of a minds mental abilities related to knowledge and thinking. While sensing and feeling physical feelings are the more emotional functions of the mind.

People use their cognitions to understand the world around them. Emotions can assist in understanding as well, however they often slow down or inhibit cognition (such as when someone is drunk). Here is (Trigg, J and Kalish, M):

- In a nontechnical sense, perceiving, remembering, believing, and judging are examples of cognition; imagining, idle thinking, wondering, and intending are not. In this sense, cognition is what happens when someone takes in how things are or becomes cognizant of some thing, event, or fact. Conversely, if something is cognized it becomes known somehow to someone. To say of someone that his cognitive faculties were impaired by drunkenness on some occasion would be to say that his capacity to attend to, take in, or get to know his surroundings was impaired by drunkenness on that occasion.

James Sully wrote in a book published in 1892 titled "The Human Mind" that there are three different mental functions - knowing, feeling and willing:

- By help of such a process of analysis carried out on a variety of psychological phenomena psychologists have come to distinguish between three radically different mental functions. These, which are pretty clearly recognized in our everyday distinctions, are known as Feeling, Knowing, and Willing.

- In order to illustrate the difference between these modes of mental manifestation, we may select almost any example of a familiar mental experience. For instance, I see an apple on a tree. I may be affected by the beauty of its colour glowing in the midst of its cool green surroundings. Such a mental state of delightful admiration would be properly described as a feeling or affective state. Or, again, if I happen to be a connoisseur of apples my mind may be stimulated by the site of the object to note its peculiar characteristics with a view to characterize the particular variety to which it belongs. Such a direction of mental activity would come under the head of knowing, cognitive process of intellection. And, lastly, if I happen to be hot and thirsty the sight of the apple may very likely insight a desire to pluck and eat it and prompt the corresponding actions. And in this case what goes on in my mind would be a process of willing, volition or conation.

- It can easily be seen that there is no mental process which cannot be brought under one or more of these three heads. Whatever state of mind we happen to be in, we shall always find that it is fully described by help of these three fundamental or primary functions. To be affected by some feeling, as wonder, love, or grief, to be following out some process of intellectual inquiry, or to be actively engaged in doing something or preparing to do something, this seems to exhaust all known forms of mental operation.

What he said about the three states of mind makes sense - of course there is more to mental functioning than knowing, willing or intention and feeling however those three functions could describe most of the surface functions of the mind - that is, what is simply going on not necessarily how the mind is doing it.

Later in the book he talks about concepts - it is important to point out that concepts are first then they move to being more complex concepts as one thinks more about them. The three stages he talks about are abstraction, comparison and generalization:

- The common account of conception here followed, as made up of a sequence of three stages, comparison, abstraction and generalization, rather describes the ideal form of the process as required by logic than the mental process actually carried out. As we saw above, a vague analysis or abstraction precedes that methodical comparison of things by which the abstraction becomes precise and perfect, that is to say, definite points of likeness (or unlikeness) are detected. With respect to generalisation, is has already been pointed out that this is to some extent involved in abstraction. To see the roundness of the ball is vaguely and implicitly to assimilate the ball to other round objects. It is to be added that an imperfect grasp of general features as such commonly precedes the methodical process here described. The child realises in a measure the general function of the name 'horse' before he carries out a careful comparative analysis of the equine characters. At the same time the use of the word 'generalisation' is important as marking off the clear mental grasp of the class-idea as such, that is, the idea of an indeterminate number of objects, known and unknown, answering to a certain description.

That is a simple explanation of concepts, however. Concepts that involve the self are more complicated, and concepts also have personal intentions involved and associated with them. In this next quote Don Perlis talks about intending with expressions and intentions (such as when coining an expression and using self-reference). When someone says an expression they are intending it to refer to something (its referent), and they also intend for the listener to understand that they intend the intending. They also are referring to themselves - to their present, past and future activity:

- What is it then, for an agent to "take" one thing to "refer" to another? Consider a primitive case: coining an expression, explicitly linking a symbol s to a referent r. This would seem to be no more nor less than an intention to use s as a stand-in for r in certain contexts. Following this trail, we now ask what it is to intend something, and we are smack-dab in the middle of both philosophy of language and philosophy of mind. And to reinvoke Grice, every utterance is a case not merely of intending, but also of intending listeners to understand that the utterer intends that intending. Can all this happen in the absence of a fairly sophisticated (and quite possibly conscious) cognitive engine? Moreover, the natural languages that we use for expression of intentions are-as noted-their own metalanguages, allowing loopy self-reference made possible by our intentions to so refer: We speak of ourselves, not just past or future, but our immediate present self and present activity including the activity of noting that activity.

- So, once again, does meta have a me? If meta involves reference, and if reference involves agency with intentions, including intentional self-referring activity, and if that in turn is at least a hint of a self, then yes.

Bibliography

Perlis, D. (2011) There's No "Me" in "Meta" - Or Is There? In Cox, M and Raja, A (Eds). "Metareasoning". Massachusetts institute of Technology.

Sully, James. (1892) "THe Human Mind. Longmans, Green and Co. London.

Trigg, J and Kalish, M. 'Explaining How the Mind Works: On the Relation Between Cognitive Science and Philosophy' Topics in Cognitive Science 3 (2011) 399–424

Table 53.0

Later in the book he talks about concepts - it is important to point out that concepts are first

Chapter 54

The Definitions of Meta- Representation and Meta-Cognition

Meta-cognition is 'knowing about knowing'. When a person knows what strategies their mind is using, or knows what they are thinking or how they are thinking - then they are thinking about their own thinking - and that is 'meta-cognition'.

Nelson and Narens (1990) proposed a conceptual framework that has been adopted by most researchers. According to them, cognitive processes may be divided into those that occur at the object level and those that occur at the meta-level: The object level includes the basic operations traditionally subsumed under the rubric of information processing – encoding, rehearsing, retrieving, and so on. The meta-level is assumed to oversee object-level operations (monitoring) and return signals to regulate them actively in a top-down fashion (control). The object-level, in contrast, has no control over the meta-level and no access to it.

So the object level does the automatic processes that are directed or monitored by the conscious mind. For example - text-processing is automatic and therefore it is at the object or unconscious level - however (obviously) the text is also understood consciously. This is because there is a difference between what someone understands unconsciously and what someone is understanding consciously.

Everything the mind does without conscious awareness is by definition unconscious. Therefore, most of the mind and its functions are unconscious. For instance you may remember many things you don't know about - or even understand many things you don't know consciously (but at times that knowledge might rise to consciousness).

54.1 Meta-Representations

If meta-cognition is thinking about thinking, then meta-representation is thinking about your representations.

Strictly speaking a meta-representation is a representation about another representation. In this article I use examples of representations and meta-representations, but that is subjective. Someone could label any detail as being a meta-representation of another detail it represents - it just depends what you think is representing what.

For instance if you say 'my dog is green' then you could say that is either a representation of your dog or a meta-representation since you are thinking about the representation of your dog being green.

Representations are basically something in the world that is represented in your mind in some way - Here Sam Scott explains Von Eckardt's definition of representations:

- I will use the term "representation" to mean mental representation as defined in Von Eckardt's (1999) MITECS entry. Her definition of mental representation is (I hope) sufficiently broad and uncontroversial to be acceptable to most of the various competing currents in cognitive science. According to Von Eckardt, a (mental) representation has four important aspects: "(1) it is realized by a representation bearer; (2) it has content or represents one or more objects; (3) its representation relations are somehow 'grounded'; (4) it can be interpreted by (will serve as a representation for) some interpreter." (p. 527) Points (1) and (4) in the above establish that a (mental) representation requires a subject that both bears and can interpret the representation.

So meta-representation is actually a type of meta-cognition then (unless it is about an external representation (I explain more about this later) - it is really just a matter of defining the terms) because someone is thinking about their own thoughts. You have a representation in mind, and when you think more about this representation it becomes a meta-representation. For instance, if you think the thought 'I have a dog' then you have a representation of 'having' your dog. If you think 'I am thinking about the fact that I have a dog' then you are thinking about your representation of your dog, so it is more 'meta' then just having the simple representation of your dog.

That makes it sound confusing, however. It seems like all representations are 'meta' because a representation is a representation that a person thinks about to themself - and whenever someone has a representation they automatically think about it to themselves. Some representations are more second- hand, however, and these are more considered to be 'meta' representations.

Hybrid metarepresentations are representations of external objects, like a drawing on a piece of paper. Here Sam Scott references Dennett's theory:

- Following Dennett (1998), it stands to reason that if a representation exists as an object in the world, then it too can be represented. Dennett's examples of metarepresentation tend to be of a hybrid nature. For instance a drawing on a piece of paper is a type of non-mental representation, which is represented in the mind of the person viewing it. The mental representation is of the drawing, but since the drawing is itself a representation, the viewer has a (mental) metarepresentation of whatever it is that the drawing represents.

When someone 'believes' something they don't necessarily have to think about it - they don't have to say to themselves 'I believe this'. When someone does say to themselves 'I believe this' then they are forming a meta-representation because they are thinking about some belief they have - they are forming a meta-represenation of it. The belief is the representation, however when they think about it they become aware of it and form a higher - 'meta' representation of it.

For instance if you think 'I believe I have a dog' then you are thinking about the representation of your dog and your belief of that - so you formed a meta-representation of a representation (your dog).

That example also shows what I said previously - that metarepresentations are a type of metacognition. That is because they are thoughts about your own thinking (the thinking being representations). Unless it is a representation of an external object such as a drawing, in that case you aren't really thinking about your own thinking you are thinking about something that doesn't necessarily require that much thought or is already represented.

So it seems there could be some confusion with the terms 'metacognition' and 'metarepresentation' then. For instance, what exactly is the difference between a thought and a representation? When exactly is someone thinking about their own thoughts? When exactly is a representation a representation of another representation if they are both just individual thoughts in the mind by themselves? Could a meta-representation be a thought of another thought?

Whenever someone thinks they could be considered to be forming representations and meta- representations (or cognitions and meta-cognitions). If you think about it, as a natural part of the thought process some representations or thoughts are going to be capable of being thought about more or in another way - and those could be the 'meta' cognitions or representations about the original thoughts or representations.

What is the difference between representing beliefs vs other thoughts?

Is there a difference between belief and thought? Beliefs are more like attitudes because they are propositions - hence the term 'propositional attitude' - A **propositional attitude** is a mental state held by an agent toward a proposition. Propositional attitudes are often assumed to be the fundamental units of thought and their contents, being propositions, are true or false. An agent can have different propositional attitudes toward the same proposition (e.g., "S believes that her ice-cream is cold," and "S fears that her ice-cream is cold").

So propositional attitudes are different from propositions - what a proposition is, is one thing. How we feel about it, or how we regard it, is another. We can accept it, assert it, believe it, command it, contest it, declare it, deny it, doubt it, enjoin it, exclaim it, expect it. Different attitudes toward propositions are called propositional attitudes, and they are also discussed under the headings of intentionality and linguistic modality.

So when assertion differs from belief is a topic of concern. For example, we frequently find ourselves faced with the question of whether or not a person's assertions conform to his or her beliefs. Discrepancies here can occur for many reasons, but when the departure of assertion from belief is intentional, we usually call that a lie.

So any proposition is a thought, and any thought could be considered to be a proposition. What role does attitude or beliefs play? If you believe something, then it is likely you have an attitude about it. That is probably why you came up with the proposition in the first place - because you had an attitude or desire to think or do something. So all propositions really have attitudes attached, but thoughts that aren't propositions don't necessarily have.

So what is the difference between a representation that is of an object in the world, an internal representation, a belief or other thoughts? Here Sam Scott references Dennett:

- In Dennett's Making Tools for Thinking (Dennett, 1998), he invites us to speculate along with him on the difference between what he terms "florid" and "pastel" representations. Florid representations are those that become explicit as objects in the world, by being encoded in language or some other physical medium (drawings on paper, for instance.) He notes that the capacity to form florid representations seems to imply the ability to manipulate the representations themselves, which leads him to raise the slogan "no florid representation without metarepresentation." He further speculates that "belief about belief" may not be the same thing at all as "thinking about thinking" – that is, having the ability to self-consciously reflect, compare notes with other thinkers, and so on.

I would say there is a big difference between thinking thoughts that are emotional and have attitudes attached, between representing things that are emotional, and between representing and thinking things that don't have much to do with beliefs or emotion.

Bibliography

Nelson, T. O., + Narens, L. (1990). Metamemory: A theoretical framework and new findings. In G. Bower (Ed.), The Psychology of Learning and Motivation: Advances in Research and Theory (pp. 125-173). New York: Academic Press.

Scott, Sam. Metarepresentation in Philosophy and Psychology. Retrieved from http://conferences.inf.ed.ac.uk/cogsci2001/pdf-files/0910.pdf 12/24/14

Table 54.0

Chapter 55 | The Nature of Consciousness - Perceptual, Representational or First Order - or are People as Confused as their Definitions of Conscious States?*

266

Chapter 55 | The Nature of Consciousness - Perceptual, Representational or First Order - or are People as Confused as their Definitions of Conscious States?*

267

Chapter 55

The Nature of Consciousness - Perceptual, Representational or First Order - or are People as Confused as their Definitions of Conscious

States?

There are many different definitions and words describing consciousness and conscious states such as phenomenological consciousness (which is basically the experience of conscious objects or states). There are other terms that define consciousness as being merely first order or not representational or higher order and only being representational. By 'representational' I mean that an object or experience is only conscious when someone has a higher order perception, thought or representation about it in ones mind.

Maybe consciousness isn't really like anything anyway. If you think about it - if it can be argued that lesser animals like dogs and cats can be conscious - then what makes a human a human isn't really that big of a deal.

Lesser animals think and feel. They don't have a large vocabulary, but I might postulate that they feel colors and objects in a similar fashion as humans do. What makes a humans capacity for thought such a greater achievement?

55.1 Explaining Consciousness

Materialism suggests that consciousness is the result of material interactions - which is obviously true, however there is a quality of consciousness that is surreal and could be described as being above the material.

I mean, people know what it is like to experience events. Certain things might be done to make the emotions involved more or less salient however, and that could be complex to achieve.

There is a difference between the real world and how ones mind represents the world to itself. This concept is called intentionality (not to be confused with the word 'intention') which is like the word intention, only so far as it implies that a mind has an intent to capture the essence of something in the world. It is defined by the Stanford Encyclopedia of Philosophy as "the power of minds to be about, to represent, or to stand for, things, properties and states of affairs"[1].

The question that then follows after hearing the definition of intentionality is - what if someone misrepresents the world? That doesn't really make much sense; however. The way your mind 'biases' or 'represents' the world is by definition how you are perceiving it. Over time you can perceive the world differently, and then it could cause different emotions in you. Because the color red doesn't necessarily have a strict bio-neurological reaction, it is dependent on your emotional and intellectual perception of the world.

What are the factors of perception, then, of perception and representation in conscious experience - and

---

1. http://seop.illc.uva.nl/entries/intentionality/ Retrieved 12/16/2014.

Chapter 55 | The Nature of Consciousness - Perceptual, Representational or First Order - or are People as Confused as their Definitions of Conscious States?*

268

can someone 'misrepresent' the world? Here is Robert Brandom:

- For what an organism is doing to be intelligible is representing, there must be room also for misrepresenting, for representation that is incorrect. One of the hallmarks of the normativity of intentionality is that what one commits oneself to in applying a concept outruns in principle what one takes oneself to be committed to. The norm of correctness one thereby binds oneself by goes beyond both the dispositions of those understaking those commitments and what they consciously envisage themselves as committing themselves to thereby. Because it does, a question arises about how to understand the features of the intentional state or meaningful utterance that settle which determinate conceptual norm one is bound by - exactly which standards for the assessment of correctness or success one has implicitly put in play - by being in that state or producing that utterance. If what one is committed to is not settled by what one consciously envisages (because one never so envisages enough), nor by what one is disposed to accept as such (because one can be wrong), how is it settled?

He brings up a couple of points in this passage. If someone is misrepresenting the world, how would that change what the feelings are vs if they represented it accurately? What does that mean anyway - to misrepresent the world? It isn't like people can expect how exactly something is going to or supposed to feel, or understand completely how something feels. It seems there is a conscious filter of sorts that is conscious in the sense that it is unique to humans because humans have such a developed sense of emotion and breadth of feeling, but is unconscious in the sense that it is how their mind naturally functions (how it interprets and feels emotions, thoughts, experiences etc).

Phenomenal or 'Experience" Consciousness vs Functional Consciousness

What if someone only had phenomenological experiences without consciousness? Ned Block distinguishes between what he calls 'access' consciousness and 'phenomenal' consciousness. He states that A-consciousness is representational and has direct control of thought and action (A-consciousness is the functional aspect of mind while P-consciousness is the experiential aspect). If A=P then information processing theories are right and the mind can be made that way. If, however, a humans realizations matter then there is a more subjective element and experience cannot be described or programmed. Something with only A-consciousness would be a zombie or robot - since it would be functioning like a human but it would have no experience or sensation of experiences.

That makes sense, if someone only had feelings and had no rationality (similar to an animal) then it would only be phenomenally aware. If someone had direct control over their consciousness, and didn't experience things very much then it would be easy to create a machine that duplicated that behavior since machines don't feel. Searle, 1990 mentions Blocks theory of access consciousness and criticizes it for confusing levels of attention and consciousness:

- There are lots of different degrees of consciousness, but door-knobs, bits of chalk, and shingles are not conscious at all... These points, it seems to me, are misunderstood by Block. He refers to what he calls an "access sense of consciousness." On my account there is no such sense. I believe that he .. [confuses] what I would call peripheral consciousness or inattentiveness with total unconsciousness. It is time, for example, that when I am driving my car "on automatic pilot" I am not paying much attention to the details of the road and the traffic. But it is simply not true that I am totally unconscious of these phenomena. If I were, there would be a car crash. We need therefore to make a distinction between the center of my attention, the focus of my consciousness on the one hand, and the periphery on the other ... There are lots of phenomena right now of which I am peripherally conscious, for example the feel of the shirt on my neck, the touch of the computer keys at my finger-tips, and so on. But as I use the notion, none of these is unconscious in the sense in which the secretion of enzymes in my stomach in unconscious.

It makes sense that there are lots of degrees of consciousness - that is fairly obvious actually. What makes it more complicated is to find out what exactly is going on - i.e. how emotionally focused are you on one thing, how much of the focus is intellectual, how much of it is planned or intended vs automatic.

Chapter 55 | The Nature of Consciousness - Perceptual, Representational or First Order - or are People as Confused as their Definitions of Conscious States?*

269

I mean if you are unconsciously focused on something then is it more emotional since the unconscious is more animal-like? How much does it matter if it easy to process or is high in information? Those concepts relate to system 1 and system 2 dual process theories and how those theories relate to consciousness vs. unconsciousness (which I talk about in another article m51859).

The unconscious mind gives largely the experience or feeling of life because when you think you can only focus on a little compared to how much you can focus on unconsciously - of course you can't really 'focus' on something unconsciously because by definition it is unconscious - so you could be doing more automated activities related to it but not really focus on it clearly like when you consciously focus on something.

So in my view theories of consciousness can be described by how conscious or unconscious various aspects of them are. This includes functions of the mind and how the mind experiences life - both are either conscious or unconscious, or some combination of both.

The mind is often described as an iceberg with only a small portion on the surface. The surface part is what people are conscious of, and beneath the water lies the unconscious. The important question then is what does an unconscious experience feel like? Dreams are entirely unconscious because you are sleeping - but what aspects of experience and functioning are unconscious when a person is awake?

All automatic mental processes are unconscious - all non-automatic ones that need conscious thought are conscious, though they may have unconscious aspects of experience. So a conscious thought can guide an unconscious experience. How do you define if a feeling is conscious or not, however? Feelings are a large part of experience, and the conscious mind can guide them, trigger them or inhibit them.

Conscious vs. Unconscious "Consciousness"

So there is a big difference between the unconscious and the conscious mind. This difference is outlined with system 1 and system 2 dual process theories. It seems like the unconscious mind is more emotional and animal-like, while the conscious mind is more logical and human.

The function of the unconscious is regulate physical activity, and give your mind the feelings related to this physical action. People aren't ever completely using their conscious mind since there are always automatic processes occurring. Those could be considered to be being done unconsciously.

Feelings and thoughts are the primary things that are either conscious or unconscious - but all a minds processes are conscious or unconscious to different degrees.

In another article I talk about what processes are conscious or unconscious in any environment m51883. People can be aware of the world physically or mentally, and this difference also relates to the different mental processes (which each could be considered to be conscious or unconscious, physical or mental).

Physical vs. Mental Consciousness

What is the difference between a type of 'physical' consciousness and a sort of 'mental' consciousness? Is it strictly the difference between being physically aware of your body - or experiencing thoughts or other cognitions that don't pull up a physical feeling? Are some thoughts more 'physical' than other thoughts? Here is (Davidson, Donald):

- On the proposed test of the mental, the distinguishing feature of the mental is not that it is private, subjective, or immaterial, but that it exhibits what Brentano called intentionality. Thus intentional actions are clearly included in the realm of the mental along with thoughts hopes and regret (or the events tied to these). What may seem doubtful is whether the criterion will include events that have often been considered paradigmatic of the mental. Is it obvious, for example, that feeling a pain or seeing an afterimage will count as mental? Sentences that report such events seem free from taint of nonextensionality, and the same should be true of reports of raw feels, sense data, and other uninterpreted sensations, if there are any.

I guess there are some sensations people 'interpret' to themselves and thus think more about the physical. However, all thinking could be considered to be physical since sensations are the minds inputs and all

Chapter 55 | The Nature of Consciousness - Perceptual, Representational or First Order - or are People as Confused as their Definitions of Conscious States?*

270

thought is visual to some degree. Maybe it is a constant mental balance, where a sensation triggers or balances a thought that is free of the physical and makes it more physical or emotional.

It could be that physical sensations are much more emotional than thoughts that are tied to mental representations (vs thoughts that are tied to physical feelings). However, which thought would be tied to a physical feeling vs a thought tied to a mental idea or concept? Or is there some sort of mix? People can internalize things and that is perhaps thinking more mentally and not physically = how could someone internalize a physical feeling? That doesn't seem to make sense - a person could experience a physical feeling, but the deep aspects of mental reflection seem more cognitive and not necessarily tied to the physical (if it is even possible for a thought to be entirely physical (even though it is a thought of a sensation, which is physical)).

55.2 The Nature of Consciousness

What are the roles of the different mental processes in the nature of consciousness?

What is the role of vision in thinking? If vision is a large part of thought processes, how does that change the nature of how an experience feels?

Judgements require concepts, however visual representations don't necessarily use concepts - you could just represent something in the world to yourself without thinking about it - so they don't *require* concepts but they probably use them in most cases. That is - most visual representations require thought, which means that they would require concepts. I would think that when concepts are used would be when an attitude is triggered - then you might start thinking about how you feel towards certain concepts. How does an image get conceptualized? Fodor asks that question here but doesn't offer an explanation (Fodor, 2007):

- Judgement requires conceptualization even if (as I suppose) representation doesn't; and, of course, there's no conceptualization without concepts. The question how (for example, by what computational process) iconic representations might get conceptualized is, of course, very hard and the answer is unknown for practically any of the interesting cases. On the way of looking at things of which I've been trying to convince you, that is a large part of what the psychology of perception is about.

Phenomenal states are perceptual - their vehicles belong to one of the 5 senses. So when you experience something, it is physical and sensory in nature. However, a mental image is inside your head and that is different from physically seeing something. In this quote (Prinz, 2007) says that "perceptual formats may have a kind of content that is not representational" that means that "conscious states comprise mental representations, but notice that it does not entail representationalism":

- I will define a perceptually conscious mental state as a mental state that is couched in a perceptual format. A perceptual format is a representational system that is proprietary to a sense modality. To say that phenomenal states are conceptual is to say that their representational vehicles always belong to one of the senses: touch, vision, audition, olfaction, and so on. This assumes that conscious states comprise mental representations, but notice that it does not entail representationalism, the thesis that every difference in phenomenal qualities is a difference in representational content. Perceptual formats may have a kind of content that is not representational, such that two perceptual representations can represent the same thing even though they are phenomenally distinct. With Peacocke (1983) I suspect that this is right. For example, I think we can phenomenally represent the feature of being located to the left of us, by vision, audition, touch, and probably smell. There is very good evidence that there are multiple modality-specific spatial maps in the brain (e.g., Gross and Graziano, 1995), and these may underwrite distinct phenomenal qualities even if they sometimes represent the same spatial features. So, in my definition on perceptual consciousness, I am committing only to the thesis that perceptually conscious states comprise mental entities that are in the business of representing. This definition would need to be amended only if we discovered that perceptual format includes components that are not representational in nature. It is sometimes

Chapter 55 | The Nature of Consciousness - Perceptual, Representational or First Order - or are People as Confused as their Definitions of Conscious States?*

271

suggested that there are words in languages that don't serve a referential function. Some expletives, particles, and logical operators may fall into this category. Perhaps perceptual symbol systems contain such things as well, and perhaps these things can contribute to the phenomenal quality of an experience. I am willing to accept that possibility. The key point about perceptual consciousness is the claim that perceptually conscious states have a perceptual format.

What does he mean in the final line of the passage - "perceptually conscious states have a perceptual format". That is being a little redundant - I mean, if the input from the world is perceptual then it makes sense that it is going to be perceptual in your mind. How the mind interprets, biases, thinks about, changes etc sensory inputs is an interesting question. Also does the mind convert sensory inputs into conceptual ideas? How does the vision of something outside the mind change when you think about that same vision independent of the stimulus? Does the mind use the same representations for different stimuli? - How are representations categorized, identified, utilized and felt by the mind?

55.3 Categorizing Functions of the Mind

The mind has many functions, and thinking takes many forms.

The mind thinks with words, visions and feelings. Any combination of those things could be used in thinking.

Some feelings the mind thinks with are strong feelings, and these probably communicate more information to the person. In fact, unconsciously there could be many strong feelings that are felt to some degree that are also informative.

So I would think that simply a simple sequence of feelings is what lies behind how the mind thinks - and each feeling could trigger thoughts, visions or other associated feelings.

So an example of this would be - 'feeling of friend' followed by 'image of friend' followed by the words 'my friend is coming to visit'.

How are stimuli expressed in the mind?

How are external stimuli expressed in the mind? Thoughts, feelings and words are all used to express ideas and feelings for internal thinking. How then does internal thinking differ from thinking that is the result of sensory inputs? Is a visual input broken down into categories and each of those categories expressed differently in the mind?

So if someone sees a white dog they can categorize it at least two ways - 'an object the color white' and 'a dog'. Each of those properties of the dog might trigger a category in the mind.

How is that different than when you just think of a white dog to yourself, however? Are the same mental nodes triggered or does it have a different mental reaction?

The difference between real world stimulation and internal thinking could be compared to hearing someone speak versus thinking or reading the same material. How the persons mind responds differently might be explained by how their brain processes external vs internal stimuli.

Recalling Experience

Thinking must be more complicated than a series of thoughts, words and visualizations that are either internal or external, however.

When an experience is recalled those things might be brought up - but each experience has a different character and that could bring up or trigger a different reaction entirely (that might be separate from the individual stimuli related to the experience).

Of course the stimuli in the experience help make that experience feel like what it feels like - however there are more complicated things occurring. For instance if three visions come from the experience maybe your mind would generate another vision that would be an internal representation of those three images from the experience.

Sensory inputs and internal outputs all are going to combine to form an experience, and the physical inputs might be recalled at various times to assist internal thinking.

Mental Reality and Physical Reality

That means that there is a mental reality and a physical reality. Each has inputs and outputs from the mind.

My guess would be that each input or output has a 'experiential' quality and a cognitive quality. The cognitive quality would be how the factor is understood by your thinking and the experiential quality would be how the factor is understood by your feelings.

So experiences are understood by the mind more unconsciously and understood with feelings, while more temporary inputs from sensory stimulation are felt and understood by a persons thoughts.

Feelings are unconscious - so that is why the complicated aspects of the physical and mental world are going to be experienced and understood there (unconsciously).

Cognition and thought is more simple, so more temporary processes are going to be cognitive such as images and words - however the experience of an event and its experiential qualities are going to felt and processed unconsciously.

Bibliography

Brandom, Robert. Modality, Normativity, and Intentionality. In Lycan, G and Prinz, J (Eds.) "Mind and Cogntion" Blackwell publishing, 2008.

Davidson, Donald. (2002) Mental Events. In Chalmers, D. (Ed.) "philosophy of mind: classical and contemporary readings" Oxford University Press.

Fodor, J. (2007) The Revenge of the Given. In Mclaughlin, B and Cohen, J (Eds). "Contemporary Debates in Philosophy of Mind" Blackwell Publishing.

Prinz, J. (2007) All Consciousness is Perceptual. In Mclaughlin, B and Cohen, J (Eds). "Contemporary Debates in Philosophy of Mind" Blackwell Publishing.

Searle, J. (1990) Who is computing with the brain? *Behavioral and Brain Sciences* 13, 4:623-642.

Table 55.0

Chapter 56

Emotion and Reason - How We Decide

People decide what to do depending on the options they have and the information they are presented with. Someones feelings may be guiding them person or leading them to think a certain thing - and that person could be completely unaware that their mind is doing that.

John Heil maintains that conscious thinking need not be linguistic but is imagistic or 'pictorial'.

Take the two ideas that people are subject to emotion and that conscious thinking is pictorial and I arrive at the conclusion that that is why people like going to movie theaters. The images there are large and that helps make it a different experience - the movie overrides their thinking with images and sounds. That is the difference between going to the theater and just watching the movie on your home television anyway.

'Understanding'

John Campbell maintains that the ability to know the reference of our singular and general terms is based, ultimately, on our ability to focus our conscious attention on objects and properties.

I think that that isn't saying much, however (or that it is rather obvious). I mean that is sort of by definition how people gain experience or understanding - by having a better or more developed understanding of the objects involved with whatever the knowledge is of.

I don't know if this means that understanding is visual or verbal - it is probably a combination of both and varies depending on what the understanding is of. Understanding is also emotional - conscious and unconscious emotions, visions and words all assist the understanding of ideas and objects.

'Deciding'

People make decisions based on two factors - what they want and what they are most likely to actually get (or is actually going to happen).

So if someone wants something a lot, and it is very likely that they can get it; then it is a very easy decision.

Different emotional properties might interfere with a logical decision making process. If someone is very aroused they might not be able to reach logical decisions - it might help with the speed of the decision - but not necessarily its accuracy.

'Truth'

What is the 'truth'? It might be the truth to find out what someone wants the most - that is one thing that someone could be true or accurate about. Or finding out someones motivation behind a behavior - 'person a did this because they were motivated by factor x and y' - could be something else someone might try to be accurate about.

So human motivation is a subjective topic that is very important in understanding ordinary, daily events. It therefore is probably important behind a lot of the thinking people do. If you think about when you think about anything, or even the stream of someones thoughts is going to be influenced by current motivations and drives.

What else might make thinking emotional? Motivation obviously generates emotion, but motivations are cognitively triggered more so than emotions that simply lie in your body - such as moods and background feelings (background feelings were described by Damasio as the feelings people have when they wouldn't be feeling anything else). Those feelings are going to be less tied to motivation because they aren't as connected to goals.

Feeling and motivations are also going to be tied to emotional biases (heuristics) and thinking biases (schema). Basically humans can be biased from more emotional drives or drives that are more related to goals and certain thoughts they may have.

56.1 Is Thinking Automatic?

How much of thought or feeling is consciously derived vs. derived from a persons environment? Humans don't 'create' the world around them - the world around them gives inputs for their minds (not the opposite).

Depending on the input (or the situation) a human mind could interpret the inputs in different ways. They could cause the person to feel emotions that they didn't expect to feel or that they didn't ask for. Their mind also biases the information that it thinks. It seems like the mind could structure new ways of thinking about things and how the feelings are generated when thinking about those things by practicing new ways of thinking.

Old habits die hard; however. When thinking about things feelings are automatically triggered - and these feelings have real sources in the world (which is perhaps why it is hard to change how they make you feel).

It probably depends if the thinking is context independent or context dependent - for instance if you are thinking in a different environment or have different emotions when you do the thinking. The context I am talking about here must be more complicated than 'background' feelings because the content is highly informational. There are a only a few background feelings someone could experience however there are many more ways of feeling in your mind if you combine the feelings with thoughts or specific situations.

Unchangeable Feelings

A person could practice going into a situation repeatedly - then the experience for them would gradually become more understood and the feelings generated more automatic. But how could their mind influence what feelings are felt? Maybe if they focused on different aspects of the situation or thought about different aspects differently they could change the feelings involved.

So feelings aren't entirely based on the environment or external stimuli - what the person thinks or who they are probably influences the feelings to a great degree.

How does that work exactly; however? It probably depends on what the situation is and what the inputs and thoughts are. Also, what aspects are unchangeable from situation to situation - or how does the mind construct feeling and thought from an environment?

Engaging Stimuli

The human mind responds to stimuli - it is for that reason that zombies aren't possible because zombies don't respond highly to stimuli - however that is how the human mind functions, by responding, recognizing and adapting to stimuli.

Stimuli from thoughts, emotions and the environment all help keep the mind active and alive. That doesn't necessarily mean that a person needs strong motivations all of the time, however. In order for the brain to function a complex set of inter-actions needs to be occurring. Emotions, thoughts and stimuli must be continuously triggering complex feelings that form a sort of 'feeling base' for the unconscious.

That is different from Damasio's 'background feelings' which could be viewed as just being simple feelings. The feeling the unconscious mind generates is complex and constantly dependent on stimuli and also (necessarily) constantly feeds the mind with its own stimuli.

56.2 Implicit Knowledge

Some knowledge that people have is unreportable - that is, they know or have the knowledge but are unable to report it verbally.

Sometimes there is a mismatch between conscious understanding and unconscious understanding. That has to do with mental representation - which is how an object is represented in a persons mind. There is going to be a partial or complete match between what the object is, how it is understood consciously and how it is understood unconsciously.

Someone can 'represent' an object to themself by thinking about it. How much they understand is going to vary depending on the object and how much they think about it. Their unconscious and conscious understanding of course is going to influence decisions made related to the object. Unconscious and conscious understanding also would help form how the feelings are related to the object and how decisions are formed related to the object.

How do thoughts and emotions work to trigger a mental experience? They must combine in some sort of 'cognitive architecture' or brain wiring. The total workings of the different processes the human brain brain uses is termed in cognitive science a 'cognitive architecture' (Thagard, Paul):

- A cognitive architecture is a general proposal about the representations and processes that produce intelligent thought.

- A cognitive architecture is a proposal about the kinds of mental representations and computational procedure that constitute a mechanism for explaining a broad range of kinds of thinking.

- A complete unified general theory of cognition would provide mechanisms for explaining the workins of perception, attention, memory, problem solving, reasoning, learning, decision making, motor control, language, emotion and consciousness.

Thinking seems fairly simple; however. Everyone thinks, and humans didn't need to study what thought was in order to understand how to think - so it couldn't be that complicated. Thoughts influence our view of the world, however (and therefore help shape our reasoning and decision making). - Here is (Prinz, Jesse):

- Thoughts are mental episodes that require the use of concepts. Thoughts may be unbidden or automatic, but they are not merely copies of the stimuli that impinge on our senses. They go beyond mere sensations and present the world as being a certain way. Thoughts can occur through processes of deliberation and can be affected, in many cases at least, by reasoning.

Thoughts can cause emotions. Typical thoughts that might cause emotions are appraisals and evaluations. If someone has a strong attitude about a thought it will probably generate more emotion than a thought that is more neutral. Thoughts are cognitive; however. Non-cognitive causes of emotion are primarily perceptual states like a smell causing disgust or a sudden change in vision (since perceptual is by definition what we 'perceive'). The non-cognitive correlates of emotion is theorized to be physiological arousal (like taking drugs or listening to music for example (other examples are weather and exercise)) (however some theories attach a cognitive component to the physiological aspect (Spinoza for example says every emotion comprises both a judgment and either pleasure or pain)).

So a lot of things cause and affect emotions in the brain. It is important to understand these causes (especially thoughts - since those are most under your control) if someone is to understand how your emotions influence your decisions and how your decisions influence your emotions. - (Prinz, Jesse):

- In sum, we have seen that there are several possible candidates for the constituents of emotions: cognitive states, such as appraisals, levels of arousal, emotional valence, perceptions of bodily change, action tendencies, or some combination of these.

56.3 Consciousness

Consciousness is hard to define - it arises from perception of the stimuli generated from an environment, the stimuli generated from our senses and the stimuli generated from our thoughts and feelings.

But what is the 'perception' of our own internal states and feelings? That would be a higher-order theory of consciousness. Higher order theories state that one is only conscious of a state when one reflects on that state. So if someone was constantly more reflective, then they could be considered to be more conscious in general.

Consciousness is obviously highly related to how people make decisions then. - If someone is conscious of a certain thing, or how they are conscious of that thing is going to determine how it feels for them and how they are going to make decisions from that conscious awareness.

Perceptual vs. Action Consciousness

Perceptual consciousness suggests that consciousness arises from our perceptions - this would include things like imagination and vision. Action consciousness suggests that consciousness arises from awareness of bodily actions - and thoughts can fall under that species of consciousness - or are our thoughts perceptions?

Two chapters on that debate are in the book "Contemporary Debates in Philosophy of Mind" Mclaughlin, B and Cohen, J (Eds). Blackwell Publishing, 2007. One chapter is by Jesse Prinz - "All consciousness is perceptual" and the other chapter is by Christopher Peacocke "Mental Action and Self Awareness".

Peacocke writes about action-awareness with schizophrenics:

- What the schizophrenic subject lacks in the area of conscious thought is action-awareness of the thoughts that occur to him. To enjoy action-awareness of a particular event of thinking is to be aware non-perceptually of that thinking as something one is doing oneself.

Peacocke postulates an idea about intentions:

- Is a thinker's knowledge of what he is doing really explained by his knowledge of his intentions in acting?

Prinz mentions that "there are conscious feelings associated with action". He talks about if Peacocke's view that action-awareness is different from perceptual awareness, and he talks about what Peacocke means by 'action'.

I would say that the debate is just a matter of defining the terms. The debate cannot really be solved empirically either. It is subjective to decide if something is a perception or is an action. I would say that there is a type of physical awareness of ones body and a type of mental awareness - awareness of ones own thoughts and emotions.

So that is it - there is the physical world and there is a mental world, and awareness or consciousness of both I would say is almost equally divided. That makes sense if you consider that if the physical overwhelmed the mental, physical feelings would dominate and vice versa.

People with left brain damage might have their emotions dominate (since the right brain is theorized to be more emotional). And similarly, emotional and intellectual; physical and mental are constantly in or out of balance.

Bibliography

Prinz, Jesse. Emotion. In Franish, K. and Ramsey, W. (Eds.) 'The Cambridge Handbook of Cognitive Science'. Cambridge University Press, 2012.

Thagard, Paul. Cognitive Architectures. In Franish, K. and Ramsey, W. (Eds.) 'The Cambridge Handbook of Cognitive Science'. Cambridge University Press, 2012.

Table 56.0

Chapter 57

Consciousness, Emotion and Cognition - How the Mind Works: An Overview from different

Approaches

How does the mind think? Attention and feeling are two processes that play a role with any thought a person may have. A feeling could encourage or inhibit a thought or an attentional process (or both). There are many questions to ponder about thoughts, feelings and how they work in the mind. - For instance, how does the content of the thought influence the experience of the thought? If you think a happy thought does that always bring up a happy feeling, or does it bring up a negative one? Does it make you think faster or slower? How does it change your experience of time and emotion? Finally, if a thought is harder or easier to understand, how does that change the nature and experience of the thought (or thought process)?

Executive functioning is by definition how the mind manages its own cognitive processes. Executive functions (also known as cognitive control and supervisory attentional system) is an umbrella term for the management (regulation, control) of cognitive processes[1], including working memory, reasoning, task flexibility, and problem solving[2] as well as planning and execution.[3]

Is Attention Necessary for Consciousness?

This question is related to executive functioning because you could say that a humans mind pays attention to all of its cognitive processes, and that this attention is part of the same attention capacity that a human notices it has. People can notice what they are looking at, if they are focused on their emotions or thoughts, or what they are doing and if they are paying attention to that.

The type of attention people have that they aren't aware of is the more scientific cognitive abilities their mind has that it is doing while they are doing something they can notice themselves. For instance if your mind is inhibiting a feeling you might not notice that, or if you are pulling up information or experiences from memory you might not notice that either.

A more complex cognitive ability that uses attentional resources is thinking. You might be using words consciously or unconsciously to think about something. You might also be using experiences or memories or visions (all consciously or unconsciously) to think about something. People use a term psychologists and cognitive scientists termed 'schema' to help think (schema are sort of the 'already learned' aspect of thinking):

Schema
- In psychology and cognitive science, a schema (plural schemata or schemas) describes an organized pattern of thought or behavior that organizes categories of information and the relationships among them.[4] It can also be described as a mental structure of preconceived ideas, a framework

1. Elliott R (2003). Executive functions and their disorders. British Medical Bulletin. (65); 49–59
2. Monsell S (2003). "Task switching". TRENDS in Cognitive Sciences 7 (3): 134–140
3. Chan, R. C. K., Shum, D., Toulopoulou, T. + Chen, E. Y. H., R; Shum, D; Toulopoulou, T; Chen, E (2008). "Assessment of executive functions: Review of instruments and identification of critical issues". Archives of Clinical Neuropsychology. 2 23 (2): 201–216.
4. DiMaggio, P. (1997). Culture and cognition. Annual Review Of Sociology, 23263-287. doi:10.1146/

representing some aspect of the world, or a system of organizing and perceiving new information.[5] Schemata influence attention and the absorption of new knowledge: people are more likely to notice things that fit into their schema, while re-interpreting contradictions to the schema as exceptions or distorting them to fit. Schemata have a tendency to remain unchanged, even in the face of contradictory information. Schemata can help in understanding the world and the rapidly changing environment. People can organize new perceptions into schemata quickly as most situations do not require complex thought when using schema, since automatic thought is all that is required.[6]

- People use schemata to organize current knowledge and provide a framework for future understanding. Examples of schemata include academic rubrics, social schemas, stereotypes, social roles, scripts, worldviews, and archetypes. In Piaget's theory of development, children construct a series of schemata to understand the world.

- Through the use of schemata, a heuristic technique to encode and retrieve memories, the majority of typical situations do not require much strenuous processing. People can quickly organize new perceptions into schemata and act without effort.[7]

So basically people use preconceived notions of the world (termed 'schema') to help themselves think. It makes sense that it is easier to think if you have the experience or thought (or some of the experience or thought) already thought out.

Implicit Processesing and Attention

Dual process theories often have a controlled (or explicit) process and an automatic (or unconscious, implicit process). Here is Jan De Houwer and Agnes Moors (Houwer, Moors):

- We propose implicit processes are processes that possess features of automaticity. Because different automaticity features do not necessarily co-occur, we recommend specifying the automaticity features one has in mind when using the term implicit.

- The starting point of our analysis is the postulate that the meaning of the term implicit is identical to the meaning of the term automatic.

- For instance, all automatic processes are assumed to be unintentional, uncontrolled, unconscious, efficient, and fast whereas all non-automatic processes are assumed to be intentional, controlled, conscious, inefficient, and slow. According to this view, it is relatively easy to diagnose a process as automatic. It suffices to demonstrate that the process possesses one of the automaticity features. If it has one of the features, it can be assumed to have all other automaticity feature and thus to be fully automatic.

- It became clear, however, that the different automaticity features do not always cooccur. Evidence from Stroop studies, for instance, suggests that the processing of word meaning is automatic in that it does not depend on the intention to process the meaning of the word. At the same time, word processing is non-automatic in that it depends on the allocation of attention to the word

Rainer Banse and Roland Imhoff outline some social cognitive dual process theories:

- Unlike the psychoanalytic notion of the unconscious as a powerful monitoring system that strategically decides whether pieces of information are allowed to become conscious or not, contemporary social cognition theories rather assume that implicit content can operate outside

---

annurev.soc.23.1.263

5. http://www.psyctherapy.com/Enrolled/glossaryBody1.htm Retrieved 7 March 2013.

6. Nadkarni, S., + Narayanan, V. K. (2007). Strategic schemas, strategic flexibility, and firm performance: The moderating role of industry Cclockspeed. Strategic Management Journal, 28(3), 243-270. doi:10.1002/ smj.576

7. Kleider, H. M., Pezdek, K., Goldinger, S. D., + Kirk, A. (2008). Schema-driven source misattribution errors: Remembering the expected from a witnessed event. Applied Cognitive Psychology, 22(1), 1-20. doi:10.1002/acp.1361

of awareness because it is automatically activated. Contemporary dual-process theories postulate two distinct information processing systems. For example, the Reflective- Impulsive Model of social behavior by Strack and Deutsch (2004) distinguishes a reflective and an impulsive system of information processing. The reflective system is based on propositional knowledge representations (i.e., information in the form of declarative sentences that are either true or false) and can perform complex, logical operations. This system is flexible and powerful, but it requires cognitive resources and allocation of attention. The impulsive system is based on an associative network and operates by the principle of spreading activation. Unlike the reflective system the impulsive system operates in an automatic fashion and does not require cognitive resources or the allocation of attention.However, the fact that automatic or implicit processes do not require attention does not imply that the content or outcome of implicit processes are ipso facto unconscious.

They mention that the impulsive system (which would be the unconscious) "operates in an automatic fashion and does not require cognitive resources or the allocation of attention". However, if your mind is doing something then in a way you are giving it attention. It really depends on how you define attention. They say it doesn't require cognitive resources or the allocation of attention because they mean conscious attention that people notice. And by 'cognitive resources' they mean conscious cognitive resources, which are more limited than unconscious resources.

Unconscious resources are more limited than cognitive resources because when you think consciously it requires more effort then if you just do something unconsciously. To make a process conscious you have to think about it more consciously and deliberately to yourself. If your mind is doing something by itself and it comes easily and naturally then you don't have to think about it as much and it is then more automatic, faster, and requires less resources. - However, that doesn't mean that you aren't paying attention to it. In experiences where basketball players get a 'hot hand' and experience what is termed 'flow' in psychology, then they are operating more unconsciously because the unconscious is more efficient than conscious processes. They can ignore things bothering them or disrupting a high performance better.

So when they say 'the impulsive system operates in an automatic fashion and does not require cognitive resources or the allocation of attention' they really mean it just doesn't require as much, if you think about how such processes would play out in reality - then they clearly use cognitive resources and the allocation of attention - the impulsive system never acts alone, conscious effort is always involved with any action, just not as much or maybe only a little when the impulsive or unconscious system is engaged.

So if a human mind is using explicit and implicit processes (by that I mean conscious and unconscious processes) how much attention is the person giving the process, and are they consciously or unconsciously directing it (in other words, how 'meta' or how much are they consciously thinking about their unconscious and conscious cognitive processes)? Here is Sun and Matthews on metacognition and dual-process theories:

- Thus, combining these two points of view, we may argue that both implicit and explicit cognitive processes are involved in metacognition. Reder (1987) took a view similar to this, in that she posited that a two-stage process was involved in judgment that invoked implicit similarity-based processes first and then a more explicit, deliberative, and analytical process that examines individual dimensions of stimuli. Narens et al (1996) also appeared to indicate that metacognitive judgments (such as feeling of knowing) might be the result of both explicit and implicit processes, because such judgments are equally predictive of explicit and implicit memory.

- Norman and Shallice's (1986) view is more akin to our view here. They posited the coexistence of two kinds of processes: (1) fast, automatic processes, which are triggered by stimuli and are inflexible; (2) slow, conscious processes, which are independent of stimuli and are flexible. The former is used in skilled performance, while the latter deals mostly with novel situations. In the former, different schemata can be triggered by stimuli and, through lateral inhibition, compete to be activated (which is termed "contention scheduling" by Norman and Shallice). In novel (nonroutine) situations, however, a supervisory attentional system decides on schemata selection and overrides automatic processes and their contention scheduling. Shallice and Burgess (1991) divided supervisory processes into four cate- gories: (1) plan formulation and modification, (2) marker creation and triggering, (3) goal articulation, and (4) memory organization. (These aspects are encompassed by our model.)

- Note that our view of top-down influences here is opposed to the view of Reder and Schunn (1996), which believes that metacognitive strategy selection cannot be taught explicitly. Our emphasis of bottom-up influences is also contrary to the view that metacognitive activities are necessarily implicit. Our view is that metacognitive processes are implicit in a variety of circumstances: such as during initial learning of such skills through trial and error, when such processes are well practiced (so that no explicit deliberation is necessary), or when cognitive load is high (so that explicit metacognitive processes may interfere with regular processes and degrade performance). In other circumstances, they may become explicit.

The last three quotes about dual-process theories explained that there are unconscious processes that are not controlled - when first learning a skill or a material, conscious direction and metacognitive processes are more necessary, however as it becomes more automatic it becomes more unconscious.

But what does it mean when they say that 'metacognitive processes are are implicit in a variety or circumstances'? What does that mean exactly? I would say that thinking directly about something too much interferes with processing - it is clearly easier and more efficient to do something more unconsciously. However, you aren't necessarily learning as much or you might not understand what is going on as much if you are doing something unconsciously.

57.1 How the Mind Works

Through a discussion of schema and dual-process theories I introduced a little of how the mind thinks. The mind conceives notions of the world and stores these notions or ideas in their mind as schema. The mind also works consciously and unconsciously - from the ideas of dual process theories 'system 1' is the unconscious; which is low effort, large capacity, rapid, automatic, non-verbal and non-logical while 'system 2' - basically the conscious mind - is the opposite.

I guess the question is when exactly is system 1 and system 2 engaged? Are some thoughts strictly 'unconscious' while other thoughts strictly 'conscious' - or can a thought have unconscious components? Similarly, can a performance or action have conscious and unconscious aspects?

Whenever a behavior is more automatic it is then more learned and unconscious because you don't have to think about it as much as when you learned it or are thinking about it in a new way or something. I already mentioned how this is similar to understanding what in psychology is termed 'flow' or in sports is simply termed being in the 'zone'. Conscious thinking and feeling can be difficult or easy - it is probably easier when you are using unconscious processes and influences because then the thinking or feeling is more automatic.

How the Mind Thinks

People automatically use metaphors and analogies to compare and contrast ideas and information in their mind. Obviously visions or images are going to be used to help describe some of the concepts that are being compared. A concept might not need a vision; however, if it doesn't have a simple vision tied to it. For instance if you think of a person then the vision of a person might be connected; however your description of that persons personality - if they a nice or mean, smart of stupid - wouldn't have a simple vision tied to it because you are describing behavior. You might pull up various visions of them being nice or stupid in order to reinforce the concepts - however they are probably less tied to vision than concepts that are more simply visual.

Humans minds use schema to store complex sets of information or ideas. In this way understanding of the world can build and change when your current ideas and concepts are challenged by new information. Schema are not likely to change easily, however, as people are biased and more likely to notice things that fit into their currently held ones.

My guess would be that some schema are more unconscious and some are more accessible to consciousness - probably depending on what you were doing recently and if it related to some of the schema you hold. In this way your thinking can be influenced by the ideas that you learned and formed in your mind into schema.

Your unconscious mind holds many preconceived notions ('schema') and uses metaphors and analogies and visions all of the time. Depending on the circumstance different aspects of the world are going to be more accessible to consciousness. In this way the unconscious mind and conscious mind work together to help guide thoughts and feelings - depending on how unconscious a thought or feeling is helps to determine if it is logical, verbal, or easy to process (all of those are aspects of 'system 1' or the unconscious) or not.

Bibliography

Houwer, J. + Moors, A. In Proctor R, Capaldi J, editors. Implicit and explicit processes in the psychology of science. New York, NY, USA: Oxford University Press; 2012

Rainer Banse and Roland Imhoff In J. A. Simpson and L. Campbell. The Oxford Handbook of Close Relationships. Oxford University Press.

Sun, R. + Mathews, R. C. (2003). Explicit and Implicit Processes of Metacognition. Advances in Psychology Research. Pp3-18. Nova Science Publishers, Hauppauge, NY

Table 57.0

Chapter 58

Dreams Rarely Make Sense Because They Are Usually More Emotional

Than Logical

Dreams in general tend to be weird. This would suggest that whatever engine is engineering, or designing the dreams is a weird and/or stupid one. Things in dreams often don't make any sense in reality, but dreams are often incredibly sophisticated at the same time. This would suggest that dreams are emotional, not logical. Emotion is very complicated, but it often doesn't make any logical sense. Dreams convey feelings very well, they amplify feelings, they don't amplify logic.

For example, say you were thinking about a toothbrush that day, or had a lot of thoughts about brushing your teeth, or had some trouble with the dentist and it was bothering you. In your dream that night, you wouldn't think about the events of the day, or logically think about how you could fix your tooth problem. In fact the logical thing would probably never occur in your dream, that would be out of character since dreams are more emotional, you'd probably never dream thinking "ah I should brush my teeth more thoroughly". Instead you'd dream of a really big toothbrush or something immature, childish, and extremely emotional. Or maybe get a large sensation of your teeth being brushed. See how one is more emotional than the other?

Dreams are so emotional that there is little room for anything logical, it's as if all your brain power is being converted into it's emotional essence. This is easy to prove, think of any dream you've ever had, or ever heard of, whatever it was, it didn't make complete sense. The fact that NO dream EVER makes complete sense must mean that the higher, logical part of your brain is shut off during sleep. That makes sense since if you were actually thinking, you'd want to experience real emotions and move your body around to get that experience, not just think about them.

This might make dreams more sexual or Freudian, but more importantly anything that is most strongly emotional to the person having the dream. Take this dream for example "I was at a type of arena-ish thing but it had balconies like a theater would." Notice first off that it doesn't make sense, arena's don't have balconies like a theater would. Clearly if the person was thinking clearly she/he wouldn't have been able to put theater balconies in an arena. Now there sometimes are balconies in an arena, but this person must have been referring to balconies that were pretty like they are in theaters with strong contrast to the arena, say like a stone arena with pretty wooden balconies in pink and stuff in them. That description I gave sounds like a typical dream because it doesn't make sense, and due to the contrast/mix of the arena and the theater, it is very emotional.

The mix of the two things makes it more emotional because it is something which you wouldn't find anywhere in reality. Things that stand out tend to be more emotional, and anything that doesn't make sense, like doesn't make ANY sense, is going to be emotional because it stands out from your everyday experience. Something like a giant gumball rolling over and over in your head, that doesn't make any sense, and its emotional. But why is it emotional? It is because you never find giant gumballs (that are chewed just standing around outside) so if you found one, you'd be in shock, and very emotional.

There are things that are emotional and can be found in real life of course. Take this dream "I was a warrior in a med-evil battle with Mel Gibson and we fought some kind of beasts with our golden swords lol Mel got his head chopped off and I awakened when I was being choked by a med-evil beast. " It would probably be more emotional for the dreamer to be doing something with Mel Gibson, since it's not likely he'll ever do something with Mel and therefore would find it rare when he did, so it's a not realistic, out of the ordinary, emotional experience. Furthermore they are using gold swords, how often are gold swords used? Gold is a more emotional color than steel as well. Color is emotional, so color, a dramatic color, or large color contrasts are often found in dreams to further amplify emotion.

Take this dream, see how emotional it is, emotional, not realistic, and amplified for dramatic content.

"I am the best student in a hard science class of some sort. Every day before class I hold study sessions. Everyone fails the first test but me. We are all milling about in the hall after class. The teacher and some other students express interest in the study sessions, but I say I don't really need them. They seem disappointed. Then I tell everyone "Hey, all those study sessions that I've been having... BY MYSELF... will still be there next week" inviting them. The professor asks anyone with a disease to hang around and see her in ten minutes, saying she has the shakes. She's very concerned with her health, which has been strange for some time. I think about staying, but I leave. I see Joe Horvath in the hall and hug him, but I see that he has a finger the looks like it was smashed and healed flattish and deformed. There are flecks of blue paint or nail polish or the nail is flecked blue. When I ask him about it he says he didn't even notice and doesn't know what happened, but it doesn't hurt."

The dreamer thinks he is the best in the class, not just any class, but a hard science class. He is so much better than anyone else, that he has "study sessions" by himself. Of course that doesn't make any sense, the people were asking him about a study session, implying that a study session would involve more than one person, like they usually do. But in his dream he forgets logic and all of a sudden he is the only person needed for a study session, in real life he wouldn't have said that because it just wouldn't be a proper thing to say - he wouldn't say something that silly in real life. To make the dream even more emotional another out of the ordinary event is occurring: the teacher is feeling sick, and her health has been "strange for some time" not bad for sometime, but strange for some time, the word strange would imply something really out of the ordinary going on, like an extraterrestrial disease or something weird, the weirdness and out of the ordinariness being added for extra emotional content, of course. Does this mean that the dreamer is afraid of a strange disease? No it just means he is trying to entertain himself in his sleep by adding extra dramatic content by using the word strange, instead of bad. (it's extremely rare to use the word strange when describing that one is sick, so what I suggested about extraterrestrial implications makes more sense). When you say, "oh I've been feeling strange lately" you are implying that something really weird is going on with you (or in this case your health) which would bring up further rise for concern, or a further rise in emotional, dramatic content!

Take this dream "We're in a hotel. We all have rooms, but we're in Steve's room. There are multiple beds that may be stacked. We are trying to make music. A boy starts playing guitar and it's fantastic. Steve holds up my cell phone, it's recording, he hands it to me. Steve asks me to play it back. There is a lot of music. One song my clarinet is so sharp. Steve says 'if you can't hear that...' condescending. Steve leaves the room. We are competing for his attention, girls and boys. I am on a bed that is high. I know I'm the favorite and they're asking me about it and I decide to leave. I slide off the bed, then reach up under the rail and grab a black candle (handmade) and a cigarette and something else." That is also very out of the ordinary, in fact that would probably never actually happen in real life because everyone in the hotel would hear the music. The dreamer obviously wasn't logically, clearly thinking. If she/he was then the dream would have ended with the people next door complaining about the noise, or there being somewhere in the dream something about checking to see if the hall was clear, but even then someone might walk down it. The point is it is very out of the ordinary, which, since it is rare, is probably more emotional solely because it's a new and exciting experience that you furthermore can't have in real life, so it also has that "I want it since I can't have it" emotional feel. This is the real kicker, you can sense that the dream wouldn't have made any sense if they actually checked to see if there were other people in the hall. It is only an ordinary, regular dream, if it doesn't make sense. And you can sense that that is true.

Let's see how out of the ordinary this dream is. (All this so far proves that dreams are out of the ordinary, probably just to add emotional content because of the contrast with reality). "We are rehearsing. Instead of a lyrics sheet there is a flat piece of 3D art. It's a series of concentric circles. One of the circles is made to look like a brick wall. That's the verse I am supposed to sing. I get singled out and have to sing the verse alone. It's about life going around and down forever. There's an infinity symbol."

For starters there is no such thing as a flat piece of 3D art, 3D is 3D, but you can see how that would be fun for the dreamer to think about, entertaining for him to think about how it could be 3D, yet not 3D at the same time. This emphasizes the emotional content, but it low on the logical content. Why is the emotional content emphasized? Because dreams are for entertainment, you're trying to have fun in your dream. So he/she mixes the lyrics sheet, 3D art, and flat together. That's a fun thing to do. Dreams in general are going to be more on the fun side, less on the logical, ah this makes sense side. Take the line "one of the circles is made to look like a brick wall". That just doesn't make any sense. Exactly, that's what is fun about it, trying to imagine something that doesn't make any sense. Trying to put together in reality, things that just can't be put together. It's like you're trying and trying to do something that just can't be done. That's behavior typical of an immature child that just won't give up. It's fun to try and break reality and put things together that don't belong together. That way you create something new and different, something you'd want to dream about. People don't want to think clearly in dreams, they want to relax, have fun, and do things that they never could in reality. See things they've never seen, and experience emotions that they aren't going to be able to experience in other places.

58.1 Dreaming and the Brain

"Although the details of human hopes are surely beyond the imagination of other creatures," writes Jaak Panksepp in Affective Neuroscience: The Foundations of Human and Animal Emotions (1998), "the evidence now clearly indicates that certain intrinsic aspirations of all mammalian minds, those of mice as   well as men, are driven by the same ancient neurochemistries."

Panksepp describes the SEEKING system as follows:

- This emotional system is a coherently operating neuronal network that promotes a certain class of survival abilities. This system makes animals intensely interested in exploring their world and leads them to become excited when they are about to get what they desire. It eventually allows animals to find and eagerly anticipate the things they need for survival, including, of course, food, water, warmth, and their ultimate evolutionary survival need, sex. In other words, when fully aroused, it helps fill the mind with interest and motivates organisms to move their bodies effortlessly in search of the things they need, crave, and desire. In humans, this may be one of the main brain systems that generate and sustain curiosity, even for intellectual pursuits. This system is obviously quite efficient at facilitating learning, especially mastering information about where material resources are situated and the best way to obtain them. It also helps assure that our bodies will work in smoothly patterned and effective ways in such quests.

When the mesolimbic pathway from the dopamine-producing VTA to the nucleus accumbens is stimulated, SEEKING behavior ensues. Panksepp writes: "For instance, stimulated rats move about excitedly, sniffing vigorously, pausing at times to investigate various nooks and crannies of their environment. If one presents the animal with a manipulandum, a lever that controls the onset of brain stimulation, it will readily learn to press the lever and will eagerly continue to 'self-stimulate' for extended periods, until physical exhaustion and collapse set in. The outward behavior of the animal commonly appears as if it is trying to get something behind the lever."

The mesolimbic pathway is activated trans-synaptically by normal rewards (food, water, copulation) but it can also be activated directly by the induced rewards of intravenous drugs or electrical or chemical brain stimulation (Wise).[1] The mesolimbic pathway is one of the dopaminergic pathways in the brain that modulates behavioral responses to rewarding stimuli. It originates in the VTA and connects to the limbic system via the nucleus accumbens, the amygdala, and the medial prefrontal cortex. A number of drugs are rewarding when they are injected into the nucleus accumbens and act as mesolimbic dopamine terminals,[2] and the axons of the mesolimbic dopamine system have high thresholds for stimulation

1. Wise RA. "Brain Reward Circuitry: Insights from Unsensed Incentives." Neuron. 2002; 36:229-340

(Wise).

Panksepp points out that when animals are in an appetitive state, anticipating a reward such as food or sex with a receptive mate, dopamine levels increase. But once an appetitive state turns into a consummatory state, dopamine levels immediately begin to decrease. So increasing levels of dopamine are not associated with consummatory, pleasurable activity. Rather the opposite is true. Pleasure is associated with decreasing dopamine levels. This does not mean that "reward" circuitry does not exist. Panksepp writes: "Temporal and frontal cortices contain an abundance of neurons that fire only in response to stimuli that have acquired meaning by being predictably associated with rewards."

That just means that once someone gets a reward they are satisfied. Most types of reward increase the level of dopamine in the brain, however pleasure apparently decreases dopamine levels.

Since humans think less when they are dreaming, it makes sense that dreams are emotional and not logical. I could say that they are driven by their 'reward system' when they are dreaming - the higher intellectual functions of their brain are shut off. They retreat into a more simplistic emotional state where they turn normal daily activity into some sort of silly movie.

During dreams, connection to your voluntary muscles is disabled. However, the person you are in your dream can move and it is as if then you can move your muscles in your mind. - REM sleep, the stage of sleep during which dreaming occurs, is characterized by paralysis of the voluntary muscles. Why? The phenomenon is known as REM atonia and prevents you from acting out your dreams while you're asleep. Basically, because motor neurons are not stimulated, your body does not move.

While dreams are often heavily influenced by our personal experiences, researchers have found that certain themes are very common across different cultures. For example, people from all over the world frequently dream about being chased, being attacked or falling.

So not only are dreams emotional, they also have a physical presence. - In your dreams you are really there and you can feel what is happening to you. That is why dreams of being chased, attacked or falling are fun, because you can 'feel' those sensations.

So in your dreams, not only are you using your imagination to run or move around, you are using your imagination to create worlds to run and move around in. Furthermore, these generated worlds are mostly from life events that are easily recalled in memory or simply more emotional.

So why does your mind make the dreams it makes? Does it select more emotional things to dream about or things that are simply more fun to dream about? (Apparently it does both)

So dreams are more emotional, and I think they also achieve stimulation from a more basic, reward based brain chemistry. The nature of emotion is reward based and simplistic, so it makes sense that dreams are that way since you aren't thinking.

58.2 Images in Dreaming

How does the mind construct images in dreams? What do dream images look like? This is a much more complicated question than simply asking if someone dreams in color or black and white. The mind could reconstruct video - like if you watched a movie clip and then your mind replayed it in your dream. But how would your mind reconstruct the movie clip? It would surely alter it in a way similar to how dreams are different from ordinary experiences.

---

2. Lassen et al. "Brain Stimulation Reward is Integrated by a Network of Electrically Coupled GABA Neurons." Brain Research. 2007 ; 46-58.

Loch Leven and Pap of Glencoe mountain By Mark Pettinelli

The above image represents what seems to me dream images are like. They are dulled down - since in dreams you are thinking less - but they are more emotionally potent. So the glowing colors make this image more emotional (similar to how gold is an emotional color), and they make it easy to see the image without thinking, as if seeing something glow in the dark.

My guess would be that when someone closes their eyes the patterns people can see on their eyelids (kind of like glowing outlines of abstract objects) help them to go to sleep because they are similar to dream   images - it is dark because your eyes are closed and the faint lines or colors are very abstract so this low level of abstraction - similar to a dream - helps induce relaxation and sleep.

Dreaming and sleeping unlocks and uses the power of the unconscious mind. The unconscious is not as clear as things that are conscious, in order to think something and understand it it has to be clear, if it is more abstract or artistic the the thing could be described as being more unconscious.

Table 58.0

Chapter 59

What is Logical or Rational Thinking, and how does it relate to Reasoning, Heuristics, Biases and

the Rationality Debate?

There are two different types of intelligence - one type can be measured objectively (i.e. perceptual speed and memory), and the type of intellect is subjective and, although it can be measured, is still subjective. The subjective type of intellect consists of things like reasoning ability and verbal comprehension.

I stated that something like verbal comprehension is subjective; however that statement is actually a big idea (if you think about it). It is basically saying that every words definition is up for debate, or subject to opinion. That is true, however - for instance the meaning of each word for each person may be different. When someone says the word 'dog' maybe they mean to use the word as a metaphor and really mean, 'that person is like a dog' not 'that is a dog'. Maybe even when someone says 'that is a dog' they are making a subjective statement, even though it seems pretty objective. - I mean a dog has a strict definition and most people have the same thing in mind when they think of that word, therefore making its meaning rather straightforward.

My point is that different kinds of emotional understanding (which are largely things in life that are 'subjective') make up life, the words people use, and common human understanding. Therefore nothing is ever really 'objective' because it is subject to human biases. Mathematical equations are objective, however if a animal were to look at a math problem they might not understand it as being objective - they might interpret the problem to mean something else (since it wouldn't mean anything to them mathematically).

People have beliefs of various sorts. These beliefs influence their thinking and how they feel.

What else is to be said about subjective reasoning?

What else is to be said about what I have called 'subjective reasoning'? I am labeling reasoning ability as being biased and subjective in any case where emotional information is handled, which is all the time unless something is completely objective. However, nothing is completely objective because even a math problem is going to cause someone to be emotional or process it emotionally in some way. That is why I am saying that all reasoning ability is actually a sort of 'subjective reasoning'.

I mean, if you think about it, most if not all of life involves dealing with your own personal feelings - whether you are aware of it or not. Feelings are always present, they bias your decisions, and they motivate your behaviors and thoughts.

Feelings effect our lives

How is someone supposed to know when their feelings or other ideas they have (such as a belief about something) influence their decisions or thinking?

Is most of thinking emotional and biased? Or is most of the thinking people do fairly straightforward and not involve making complex (and potentially influenced by feeling) decisions?

the most emotionally relevant factor is the motivator

Goals can be changed by how motivated someone is to have that goal. Some goals can be brought into conscious awareness at various times for various reasons. Simon (1967)[1] reasoned that emotions are calls for reprioritization: that emotion regarding a goal that is out of awareness eventually induces people to give that goal a higher priority. The stronger the emotion, the stronger the claim for higher priority. Affect pulls the out-of-awareness into awareness.

Simons analysis was just referring to goals. However, if you think about it, all of someones thoughts might follow a similar logic - the logic being that the most emotionally relevant thought has the highest claim to priority.

So if someone wants something, then they are emotionally motivated to think certain things because thinking those things will generate more pleasurable emotions.

computational components underlying intelligence

What are the computational components underlying intelligence?

To begin, I ask the question - is thinking straightforward or is it complicated?

When people think, they are constantly making emotional assessments of various sorts. They think about their own motivations, i.e. how they feel about different things, and what their goals are going to be based on those motivations.

Individual thoughts also mean something emotionally. Anything someone thinks is going to be associated with different feelings and preferences.

Does this mean that thinking is simple and logical? People think all of the time, what guides their thoughts are emotional preferences that were formed from previous development or at birth.

59.1 Semantics versus Cognitive Representations

Louis Narens[2] presents the idea that there is a difference between descriptive semantics (the words people use to describe something) and cognitive representations (which is basically the image or idea your mind makes up in your head (kind of like an abstract thought)) in evaluating evidence for judgments:

- Support Theory has an empirical base of results showing that different descriptions of the same event often produce different subjective probability estimates. It explains these results in terms of subjective evaluations of supporting evidence. It assumes that events are evaluated in terms of subjective evidence invoked by their descriptions, and that the observed numerical probability judgments are the result of the combining of such evaluations of support in a manner that is consistent with a particular equation. The processes of evaluation are assumed to employ heuristics like those of Kahneman and Tversky, and because of this, are subject to the kinds of biases introduced by such heuristics.

- This article provides a New Foundation for Support Theory. The New Foundation makes a sharp distinction between semantical representations of descriptions as part of natural language processing and cognitive representations of descriptions as part of a probabilistic judgment. In particular, judgments of probability employ a complementation operation that has no counterpart in the semantics. The complementation operation is used to construct cognitive events that are employed in the computation of the estimated probability.

So when someone evaluates a piece of information, they describe it in their mind (unconsciously or unconsciously) with words. Then they probably come to a conclusion from the evidence that the description provided.

So describing something with words would be something like, "Linda is a bank teller", or "Linda is a bank teller and is active in the feminist movement" Here is the explanation from Narens:

- Kahneman and Tversky found that over 85% of participants believed it was more likely that

1.   Simon, H. A. (1967). Motivational and emotional controls of cognition. Psychology Review, 74, 29-39.
2.   A New Foundation for Support Theory. (2004) Louis Narens. University of California, Irvine

Linda was both a bank teller and a feminist than just a bank teller. This is an example of what has become known as the conjunction fallacy. According to Kahneman and Tversky, it is due to representativeness: "bank teller and is active in the feminist movement" is more a "representative" description of Linda than just "bank teller."

So a humans mind has the verbal description given to them in words, and then their mind forms a representation based off of what they heard (i.e. - possibly an idea of Linda in their minds).

So that means that there must be lots of words use people use to describe things, and also lots of cognitive 'ideas' or 'representations' they have in their mind that might assist these words.

So words, ideas and representations are all things a human's mind uses to think. I don't know when exactly a human mind might use words instead of abstract, non-verbal thoughts - that would be getting unnecessarily detailed into how thinking works, I would say.

59.2 So what exactly is a 'Subjective Evaluation'?

A subjective evaluation is exactly what those words describe - an assessment or evaluation of something that is biased, opinionated, and even possibly highly influenced by the persons feelings.

Subjective evaluations are important because people make them all of the time, whether or not they are aware of it. For instance anytime you see another person your mind makes an opinionated assessment of them. You might or might not be aware of your unconscious assessment - maybe you make a conscious assessment of the person that is different from your unconscious one, in which case you could feel confused about the person or something.

Since earlier in this paper I stated that everything in life is actually subjective, that means that people are constantly making subjective evaluations whenever they think about anything. Any thought about something could be subjective in some way.

If you see a photograph maybe you have an unconscious opinion of that - or even if you think about something you wouldn't typically consider to be emotional your mind could still have a strong unconscious feeling or interpretation.

59.3 How to develop a logical reasoner

The human mind (and animal minds, though the process is different) comes to conclusions by weighing evidence. This process could be done unconsciously or consciously; for instance people might make if - then statements to think about material. Part of that might be considering evidence from examples that easily come to mind (this is called the 'availability' heuristic), or examples that are harder or take longer to come to mind.

People often have a tendency to rely on the first piece of information gathered, this heuristic is called 'anchoring and adjustment' - During decision making, anchoring occurs when individuals use an initial piece of information to make subsequent judgments. People might adjust away from the anchor to get their final answer, which would be the logical thing to do; however studies show people tend rely on the first piece of information - whether it is right or not (instead of using it as evidence and explain away from it when the information is false)

So it depends on the cirumstance if people try or don't try to explain (adjust) away from an incorrect piece of evidence. They might try to justify the first piece of information offered (the anchor) even though it wouldn't be the logical thing to do.

So this relates to thinking logically - when weighing evidence, people need to consider if they are being falsely influenced by information and are biasing different pieces of information in their mind. They might be biasing the first piece of information offered 'the anchor' and be relying too heavily on that instead of looking more objectively at all of the evidence.

So how exactly does the human mind weigh different pieces of information or construct an argument based off of evidence? It uses mental models to 'model' an argument, I would say. So there are different ways material or evidence can be considered by your mind, and these mental models weigh this evidence differently each time. Depending on the set of material or evidence, your mind might consider it differently (a 'mental model').

How could someone learn to reason more logically? I just explained two heuristics and how they effect thinking - by the speed and order of information made available to your mind. People bias the information they are given or don't consider it logically in many cases, but all that could be done about that to become a more logical thinker would be to be aware of your personal biases and be more reflective.

Hypothetical reasoning

What is hypothetical reasoning? It is creating imaginary worlds to test out our thinking. Here Stanovich [3] explains this type of reasoning in terms of carrying out goals, though I would say this type of thinking is critical for more complex thought as well:

- When we reason hypothetically, we create temporary models of the world and test out actions (or alternative causes) in that simulated world. In order to reason hypothetically we must, however, have one critical cognitive capability—the ability to distinguish our representations of the real world from representations of imaginary situations. For example, in considering an alternative goal state different from the one we currently have, we must be able to represent our current goal and the alternative goal and to keep straight which is which. Likewise, we need to be able to differentiate the representation of an action about to be taken from representations of potential alternative actions we are considering. But the latter must not infect the former while the mental simulation is being carried out.

If you think about it, humans must have a large imaginary world in their minds where they think and test out what they are thinking. This probably applies to everything - if you are trying to figure out which team is going to win a soccer match you might simulate the game in your head. If you are thinking about anything, you simulate the emotions, actions, behaviors, mathematical equations, or whatever it is - and this helps you think about it.

Heuristic vs. Rule-based processing

Heuristic processing is low-level, more unconscious and doesn't require as much thought as systematic processing. [4] Systematic processing requires active, careful scrutiny of relevant information and is more cognitively taxing.

Heuristic processing makes use of low-level decision rules such as 'analysts are always right' or 'statistics don't lie'. However, even though that type of processing makes use of rules, it is a lower-level processing than when rules are used by the systematic type of processing - which is more cognitive and leads to attitude change that is more enduring (because it is more conscious).

These different ways of processing are related to conscious and unconscious processing, or what is called in psychology a 'dual process theory' which provides an account of how a phenomenon can occur in two different ways, or as a result of two different processes. Often, the two processes consist of an implicit (automatic), unconscious process and an explicit (controlled), conscious process.

So rule-based processing usually refers to higher-level logic and casual inference. It follows rules, instead of merely conforming to them like how weight conforms to the law of gravity. So the unconscious could be considered to be doing its own thing, however the conscious mind actively thinks and therefore

3. Stanovich, K. E., + Stanovich, P. J. (2010). A framework for critical thinking, rational thinking, and intelligence. In D. Preiss + R. J. Sternberg (Eds.), Innovations in educational psychology: Perspectives on learning, teaching and human development (pp. 195-237). New York: Springer.
4. Chaiken, S. (1980). Heuristic Versus Systematic Information Processing and the Use of Source Versus Message Cues in Persuasion. Journal of Personality + Social Psychology, 39(5), 752-766. Retrieved from SocINDEX database.

'consciously' follows rules or thinks more about rules, more so than simply using a rule as a guideline. An example would be the rule-based decision rule example I used before to explain heuristic processing. If the rule or thought is 'analysts are always right' then your mind might unconsciously follow that when listening to an analyst and then you would believe that he or she is right. However if the process is more conscious then you might think 'well maybe this person is wrong'. The rule wouldn't be as unconscious.

Anyone could really define 'heuristic processing' as being conscious or unconscious, controlled or automatic actually. Different people have termed the processes of the conscious mind and the processes of the unconscious mind differently - these are called 'dual process' theories. Here Moshman[5] lists all the combinations of the different types of processing as possibilities:

- Central to S+W's analysis is a distinction between automatic heuristic processing (characteristic of what they call System 1) and explicit rule-based processing (characteristic of what they call System 2). I believe this dichotomy confounds two orthogonal distinctions. Specifically, the distinction between automatic and explicit processing is conceptually orthogonal to the distinction between heuristic and rule-based processing. Crossing automatic versus explicit with heuristic versus rule- based suggests four possible types of processing: (a) automatic heuristic processing (System 1),
  (b) automatic rule-based processing (not represented in the Stanovich/West analysis), (c) explicit heuristic processing (also not represented), and (d) explicit rule-based processing (System 2).

The two types not represented probably weren't because they don't make complete sense - rule-based processing is more conscious and controlled, so saying it is automatic would be putting it in the unconscious category - which is possible, however that is not how it is defined. Explicit heuristic processing doesn't necessarily make much sense either because heuristic processing is defined as being automatic and not cognitively taxing, however explicit or controlled processes are cognitively taxing because they are more deliberate and conscious.

Conscious vs. unconscious intuitions

In the 'authors response' section of a Stanovich and West article (the same article as the previous quote (the Moshman commentary in that article)[6] the authors discuss the difference between intuitive feelings and ideas and conscious analytic analysis of people. In the article 'System 1' is more unconscious, forms intuitions, and the conscious mind then acquires these intuitions. They give the example of a statistics instructor who, though initially draws conclusions about students and infers probability about their personalities ('for whom the basic probability axioms are not transparent'), he or she eventually becomes no longer able to emphasize with them. Basically the unconscious, intuitive mind helps form our conscious understanding of people and of the probability judgments we make:

- We agree with Kahneman that some people may make more nuanced System 1 judgments than others, and that individual differences in this capability are of some importance. This is related to Teigen's point that when System 2 analytic abilities fail, well-framed intuitions may come to our assistance in narrowing the normative/descriptive gap, and the better those intuitions are the narrower the gap. But, following Reber (1992a; 1992b; 1993), we would conjecture that the variance in these System 1 abilities might well be considerably lower than the more recently evolved structures of System 2. Note, however, that this variability could become larger through the mechanism discussed above – instantiating of automatic System 1 algorithms through practice strategically initiated by System 2. Thus, some of the "well framed intuitions" referred to by Teigen may well be acquired intuitions – having their origins in capacity- intensive serial processing, yet now having the encapsulated, automatic characteristics of modular processes. Some statistics instructors, for example, become unable to empathize with their students for whom the basic

5. Diversity in reasoning and rationality: Metacognitive and developmental considerations. David Moshman. Commentary in Stanovich, K. E., + West, R. F. (2000). Individual differences in reasoning: Implications for the rationality debate? Behavioral and Brain Sciences, 23, 645-665.
6. Stanovich, K. E., + West, R. F. (2000). Individual differences in reasoning: Implications for the rationality debate? Behavioral and Brain Sciences, 23, 645-665.

probability axioms are not transparent. The instructor can no longer remember when these axioms were not primary intuitions.

It is obvious that the unconscious mind helps forms our conscious understanding. People have two ways of thinking about the world, one is unconscious and one is conscious. These two systems must interact all of the time and influence each other in different ways.

Ways of thinking

The algorithmic level of analysis of mind is the level that just analyzes the details of what is occurring - it doesn't reflect and ask 'why' questions. There are different types of thinking dispositions, or ways people think - these ways of analyzing how someone thinks can help determine if a person is thinking rationally or irrationally. Here is Stanovich + Stanovich (2010):

- The difference between the algorithmic mind and the reflective mind is captured in another well-established distinction in the measurement of individual differences—the distinction between cognitive ability and thinking dispositions. The former are, as just mentioned, measures of the efficiency of the algorithmic mind. The latter travel under a variety of names in psychology—thinking dispositions or cognitive styles being the two most popular. Many thinking dispositions concern beliefs, belief structure and, importantly, attitudes toward forming and changing beliefs. Other thinking dispositions that have been identified concern a person's goals and goal hierarchy. Examples of some thinking dispositions that have been investigated by psychologists are: actively open-minded thinking, need for cognition (the tendency to think a lot), consideration of future consequences, need for closure, superstitious thinking, and dogmatism (Cacioppo, Petty, + Feinstein 1996; Kruglanski + Webster, 1996; Norris + Ennis, 1989; Schommer- Aikins, 2004; Stanovich, 1999, 2009; Sternberg, 2003; Sternberg + Grigorenko, 1997; Strathman, Gleicher, Boninger, + Scott Edwards, 1994).

- The literature on these types of thinking dispositions is vast and our purpose is not to review that literature here. It is only necessary to note that the types of cognitive propensities that these thinking disposition measures reflect are the tendency to collect information before making up one's mind, to seek various points of view before coming to a conclusion, to think extensively about a problem before responding, to calibrate the degree of strength of one's opinion to the degree of evidence available, to think about future consequences before taking action, to explicitly weigh pluses and minuses of situations before making a decision, and to seek nuance and avoid absolutism. In short, individual differences in thinking dispositions include assessing variation in people's goal management, epistemic values, and epistemic self-regulation—differences in the operation of reflective mind. They are all psychological characteristics that underpin rational thought and action.

So there are bunch of subjective things a human's mind does that determine how it thinks. I mean in any single situation how could someone think about their entire 'goal hierarchy' or their 'belief structure'? Does that matter if the person is open-minded? How much do you need to think about the future consequences of your actions or weigh the pluses and minuses of a situation? All of these processes are very subjective and hard to measure on standard IQ tests; however they are all 'psychological characteristics that underpin rational thought and action'.

59.4 The Nature of Reasoning

Deductive reasoning is the same as top-down reasoning, where someone looks at generalizations first and then figures out what the details of those would be.

Often it could just be a guess what the details are since you might be inferring the details instead of finding evidence.

I would say that this type of logic can apply to any type of thinking. For instance, even if I am just moving the mouse of a computer I could think of it in two ways (deductive or inductive). The deductive way of thinking would be something like 'I am moving the mouse of the computer, my arm causes it to move and those are the movements it makes' and the inductive way would be 'these are the movements my computer mouse is making, I must be deciding to move the mouse - I am directing its movements'. With the deductive method, the idea of you came before the realization you were making detailed movements, and with the inductive method the opposite occurred.

My example is different from more obvious or straightforward examples of deductive and inductive reasoning, where it is clear what the generalization is and what the details are. I would say that it is still a good example, however, it is just more subjective. The idea 'I am moving the mouse' is the main idea, and the detail is 'the mouse is moving, those are the movements it is making'. The reason the movements of the mouse are the details is because that is where more description can be described.

That example of deductive reasoning is subjective, however. A more typical example would be one with a concretely broad idea and it would be clear that detail was inferred from it. With my example, however, you could say that the opposite is true and that the general idea is that 'the mouse is moving', and the detail is that 'I am moving the mouse' (instead of the opposite). It looks like it depends on which idea comes first. Whichever idea comes first the human mind would assess is the more generalized idea that needs to be supported. - That idea itself is significant because people could form delusions, or imagine what the details are or what the other side of the story is simply because they heard one idea first.

Things can be viewed in more than one way

A fundamental element of reasoning is that a different idea can be viewed many different ways. This is different from simply listing the significant factors - viewing something differently means changing the subjective perspective you have on something, while listing significant factors could be categorized under one perspective. Therefore the two elements of information is content and angle (subjectivity). This painting is an example - the dramatized colors change how the painting is perceived.

Figure 59.1 A modified painting   Wc Piguenit - An Australian mangrove, ebb tide (modified by Mark Pettinelli) Notice how the dramatized colors change the nature of the painting.

All art is subjective

All of art is subjective, actually since it is highly dependent on subjective opinions. This doesn't mean that art isn't scientific and conveys information, however. Notice how in the image below there are obscure, abstract patterns yet the detail works together to convey more complex patterns and images.

Figure 59.2 Abstract art inverted eye by Mark Pettinelli   Notice how abstract yet detailed this image is.

Table 59.0

Chapter 60

An Outline of Consciousness

The internet encyclopedia of philosophy has a good entry on higher order theories of consciousness. Here[1] they reference a theory of Rosenthals:

- According to Rosenthal's higher-order thought theory (1986, 1997, 2005), a mental state is conscious when there is a higher-order thought about it. I am conscious of the pain in my knee when I have a thought to the effect that I am in that very pain state.

- ... A third important feature of higher-order thoughts on Rosenthal's account is that they are assertoric and occurrent. The higher-order thought must assert, rather than hope, fear or speculate that I am in a particular mental state. Moreover, the higher-order thought must occur at roughly the same time as the mental state it represents. The content of the higher-order thought should be, for example: "I am now feeling pain," not "I might have felt pain yesterday" or "Perhaps I will feel pain in a few minutes." Rosenthal (1997) has argued that higher-order thoughts must be occurrent in order to distinguish between non-conscious and conscious states. If the mere disposition to produce a higher-order thought were sufficient for a mental state to be conscious, it seems that all one's mental states would always be conscious.

Of course if someone has a thought about the pain they are experiencing the pain is going to be more conscious. It obviously depends on the situation if the thought makes the pain worse or less. I suppose a thought could make the pain less, but it would also make you more conscious and more aware of this lessened, (but more conscious) pain.

A model is proposed in the below image (B. Timmermans, et all), this is in the abstract of their paper:

- Metacognition is usually construed as a conscious, intentional process whereby people reflect upon their own mental activity. Here, we instead suggest that metacognition is but an instance of a larger class of representational re-description processes that we assume occur unconsciously and automatically. From this perspective, the brain continuously and unconsciously learns to anticipate the consequences of action or activity on itself, on the world and on other people through three predictive loops: an inner loop, a perception–action loop and a self–other (social cognition) loop, which together form a tangled hierarchy.

---

1. Higher-Order Theories of Consciousness. Internet Encyclopedia of Philosophy. Entry by Paula Droege. Retrieved from http://www.iep.utm.edu/consc-hi/ 7/2/14

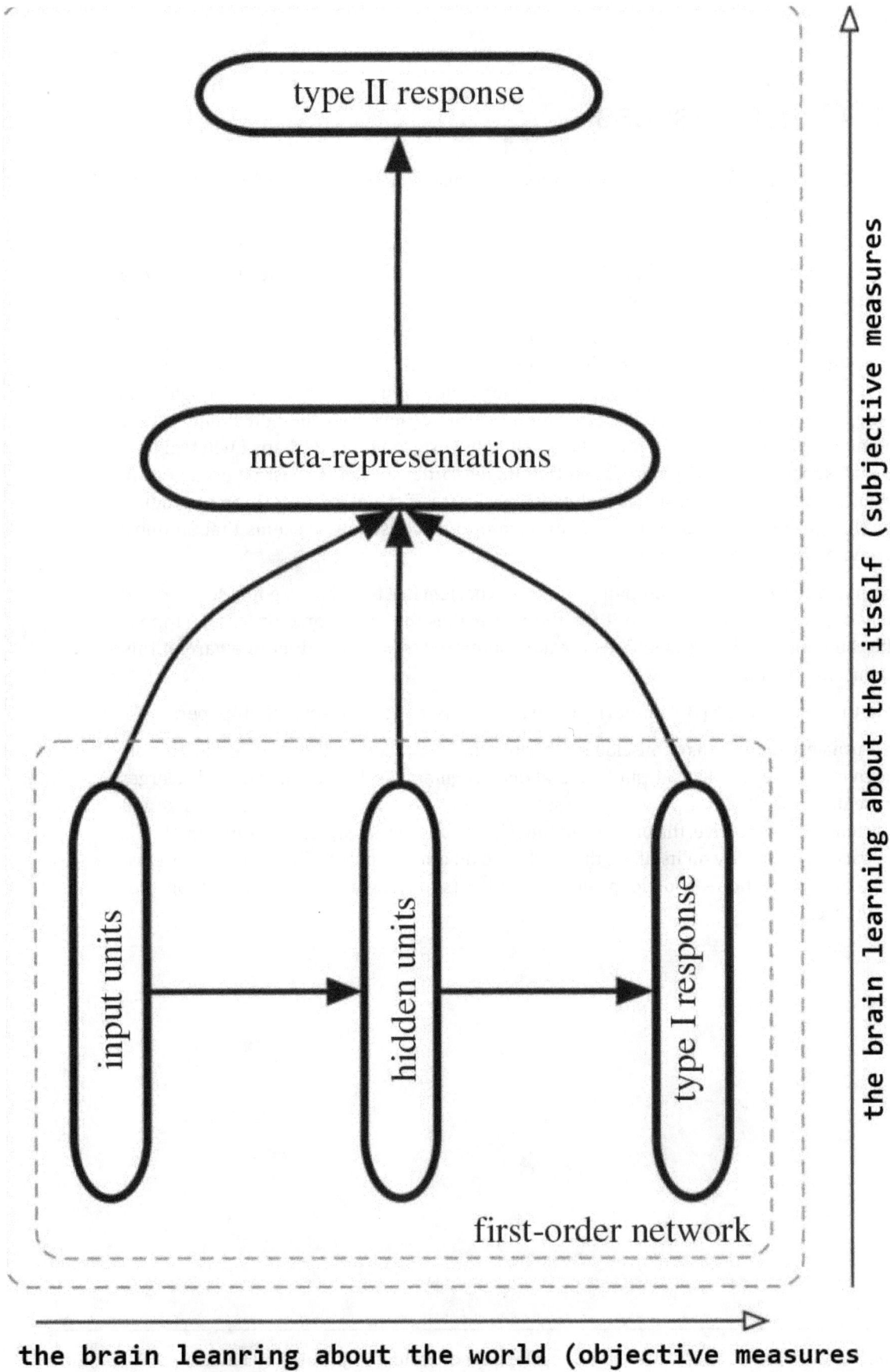

type II response

meta-representations

input units

hidden units

type I response

first-order network

the brain leanring about the world (objective measures

the brain learning about the itself (subjective measures

```
One can think of the
first-order network as instantiating cases where the brain
learns about the world and of the second-order (outside box) network as
instantiating cases where the brain learns about itself. Reference - "Higher order thoughts in
consciousness as an unconscious
re-description process" Phil. Trans. R. Soc. B (2012) 367, 1412-1423 B. Timmermans, L Schilbac
and A Cleeremans
```

My interpretation is explained a little differently from their explanation, but is still similar to theirs. The inner loop of the first order network is about the brain learning about the world, first there is stimuli and then brain thinks about the stimuli. When the brain thinks about the stimuli it forms meta-cognitions and has a secondary response from its initial response.

The 'inner loop' or their first-order network, is basically the brain thinking about the stimulus, and part of the meta-cognition (the 'thinking about the thinking') is two other loops, a perception-action loop and a self-other loop (social cognition). This means that the brain thinks more deeply about everything a second time, basically. Two of the things that it thinks more deeply about are perceptions of actions, and general social cognitions about the self and other people.

It makes sense that the mind has different levels of thinking. There is a more simple way of thinking about the world and there is a more complicated way of thinking. When anything is thought about, there is a more simplistic way of thinking about it and a more complicated way of thinking about it. It might be that a human cannot understand the idea or whatever you are thinking about if it is too complicated, in which case the simple level of your mind would be the only level that understands it.

I would say that the lower level of mind which isn't as intelligent or sophisticated as the its higher level is the initial, more animalistic response. What does that mean for sensation versus thought, however? Is there are lower level of feeling pain and a higher level? When someones mind is in the lower mode, how would it think different from its higher mode? It would probably have its higher-level social cognitions shut off. - So it wouldn't be capable of responding intelligently to other people, etc.

Two types of consciousness

So there are two different types of consciousness - one type is awareness of physical sensations, and the other type is high-order or lower-order thought. So the mind could not be thinking clearly and not be responding intelligently to other people, and it could not be aware of the pain, pleasure (other physical sensations, etc) that it is experiencing. In that case it would be in a lower level state.

So it makes sense that pain medication would also make someone think less clearly - that is because they are in a lower physical and mental state (both physical sensations and mental thinking are dulled).

60.1 Types of Thinking

The two different levels of mind (a dulled, more simplistic level and a sophisticated, higher order thought level) mean that in each level, a person is thinking differently. How does a person think differently when they are drunk, on pain medication, or otherwise not thinking clearly vs when they are thinking clearly? Is their thinking more top-down or bottom-up?

Or I could just simply ask the question - is an animals thinking (such as a dogs) more top-down or bottom-up compared to a humans?

Does that statement make sense? A dog doesn't necessarily look at any details, so you couldn't say that dogs look at broad conclusions first and then analyze down to the detail or vice versa (top-down vs. bottom-up thinking).

I am proposing that some peoples thinking is more top-down or bottom-up in general than another persons. It isn't clear what that means exactly though. Top-down or bottom-up thinking usually refers to a specific way of analyzing something, not to how someone thinks in general. Though if you consider how someone might think if they aren't being as intelligent, it makes me wonder if they might be more abstract and reach broad, not supported by any evidence conclusions first ('top-down') and ignore details. I could say that some people do that without thinking less than they usually do as well, however.

What are the higher levels of thought that are shut off when someone can't think clearly? I mentioned before that they might not respond as intelligently to other people (social cognition). But is that the full mystery behind the differences in these levels of thinking or is more analysis necessary?

When the higher intellectual functions of a humans brain are operating less efficiently, or are more shut off, (such as when someone is drugged, drunk or on pain medication) they are less under control of their cognition. In this way they are more like lesser animals since they cannot think as well.

Maybe when people can't think as clearly they make statements that don't necessarily make sense, or aren't supported by facts. I could say that those statements are a more top-down type of thinking because they reached conclusions first without looking at the details.

Making conclusions without looking at supporting details is both related to top-down thinking and subjective thinking. If you analyze the details of an idea or argument, you are probably making it less subjective and more scientific and objective.

60.2 A Thinking Consciousness

Levels of thinking is going to be related to consciousness. If people have a hierarchy of thought and feeling, some of that is going to be conscious at different times.

Some belief someone has formed in the past or near-present could be influencing their consciousness. That would be different from an attitude influencing how someone is thinking, or their 'consciousness'.

Here I am defining consciousness as someones current state of thinking and feeling. At any moment, different beliefs, attitudes, ideas, emotions, drives, feelings etc could be influence your current state of feeling and thinking (your 'consciousness').

Since some of the ideas that people have are going to be subjective, they might be ideas that make the person more emotional. Or an idea could simply use more unconscious emotional processes, but not make the person feel any more (be more emotional) than they currently are.

Philosophers have talked about an 'inner sense' or how consciousness feels to someone. The question I want to bring up is - which mental processes influence our consciousness and in what way do they do so?

How does a belief someone has influence what they are thinking or how they are thinking? Similarly, what does having an attitude do to someones thoughts, 'thinking' or consciousness?

When you are talking to someone else, you could have an 'attitude' that they are worthless, be thinking that they are worthless and not have an attitude about it, etc.

So, obviously, attitudes are influenced by beliefs and emotions (thought and feeling).

60.3 Higher order representations

Does a humans mind make representations of the world? I would say that your minds biochemistry determines what you are going to feel when you experience anything. You see the color red, and your minds biology determines how that makes you feel, not necessarily what you are thinking about it. However, since emotions and feelings are very complex then what influences your feeling when you see the color red might be mental, psychological factors. For instance, you get mad when you see red because it reminds you of blood, or something.

The internet encyclopedia of philosophy also has a good entry on "Consciousness". They talk about higher order representation – which is basically a person being aware of their own consciousness at any given time, or aware of anything at any given time. For instance, if I am aware of my feelings on a certain matter, then I am more conscious of that matter. That seems fairly obvious, I mean if you think about something more you are going to be more conscious of it. This relates to the two different levels of thought and feeling – the lower level is more unconscious and immediate and less under control, and the higher level of consciousness is part of conscious experience and people are more aware of because it isn't 'unconscious' it is 'conscious'. So what separates out the two different levels of consciousness is one is mostly beneath awareness and would be defined as being unconscious, and the other is largely in awareness and would be defined as being conscious. There is clearly an overlap between conscious thoughts and feelings and unconscious thoughts and feelings, however – there are degrees that someone's awareness is 'awake' and 'clear'. Have I presented here a theory of consciousness? It is obvious that there are degrees to awareness, and all I have said is that consciousness is basically a combination of feelings and thoughts - that is a rather simple explanation of consciousness. Is there more explanation that is needed in order to answer what consciousness really is?:

- As we have seen, one question that should be answered by any theory of consciousness is: What makes a mental state a conscious mental state? There is a long tradition that has attempted to understand consciousness in terms of some kind of higher-order awareness. For example, John Locke (1689/1975) once said that "consciousness is the perception of what passes in a man's own mind." This intuition has been revived by a number of philosophers (Rosenthal, 1986, 1993b, 1997, 2000, 2004, 2005; Gennaro 1996a, 2012; Armstrong, 1968, 1981; Lycan, 1996, 2001). In general, the idea is that what makes a mental state conscious is that it is the object of some kind of higher-order representation (HOR). A mental state M becomes conscious when there is a HOR of M. A HOR is a "meta-psychological" state, i.e., a mental state directed at another mental state. So, for example, my desire to write a good encyclopedia entry becomes conscious when I am (non-inferentially) "aware" of the desire. Intuitively, it seems that conscious states, as opposed to unconscious ones, are mental states that I am "aware of" in some sense. This is sometimes referred to as the Transitivity Principle. Any theory which attempts to explain consciousness in terms of higher-order states is known as a higher-order (HO) theory of consciousness. It is best initially to use the more neutral term "representation" because there are a number of different kinds of higher-order theory, depending upon how one characterizes the HOR in question. HO theories, thus, attempt to explain consciousness in mentalistic terms, that is, by reference to such notions as "thoughts" and "awareness." Conscious mental states arise when two unconscious mental states are related in a certain specific way; namely, that one of them (the HOR) is directed at the other (M).[2]

So a mental state can be unconscious or conscious. If someone is sleeping and dreaming, then their mental state would be considered to unconscious. I would say that there is a lot to say about how 'aware' someone is at any time. If someone is drugged or drunk, are they less aware of their interactions with other people? I said previously that they might not be responding as intelligently to other people. I wouldn't guess as to how exactly their cognitions or emotional response is dulled – there could be a wide range of emotional, personality and intellectual dispositions that someone could have that could be affected. That shows how awareness in general, not necessarily when someone has lower general awareness like when they are sleeping or drunk, is influenced to different degrees.

What is the difference between our unconscious awareness and our conscious awareness then? Here again is the internet encyclopedia of philosophy – they address the question of differences between HO (high order) and LO (lower-order) mental states, which I have said is basically the difference between conscious states and unconscious ones:

- A fourth important objection to HO approaches is the question of how such theories can explain cases where the HO state might misrepresent the lower-order (LO) mental state (Byrne 1997, Neander 1998, Levine 2001, Block 2011). After all, if we have a representational relation between two states, it seems possible for misrepresentation or malfunction to occur. If it does, then what explanation can be offered by the HO theorist? If my LO state registers a red percept and my

---

2. Consciousness. Internet Encyclopedia of Philosophy. Entry by Rocco J. Gennaro. Retrieved from http://www.iep.utm.edu/consciou/ 7/8/14

HO state registers a thought about something green due, say, to some neural misfiring, then what happens? It seems that problems loom for any answer given by a HO theorist and the cause of the problem has to do with the very nature of the HO theorist's belief that there is a representational relation between the LO and HO states. For example, if the HO theorist takes the option that the resulting conscious experience is reddish, then it seems that the HO state plays no role in determining the qualitative character of the experience. On the other hand, if the resulting experience is greenish, then the LO state seems irrelevant. Rosenthal and Weisberg hold that the HO state determines the qualitative properties even in cases when there is no LO state at all (Rosenthal 2005, 2011, Weisberg 2008, 2011a, 2011b). Gennaro (2012) argues that no conscious experience results in such cases and wonders, for example, how a sole (unconscious) HOT can result in a conscious state at all. He argues that there must be a match, complete or partial, between the LO and HO state in order for a conscious state to exist in the first place.

The mind must have an unconscious understanding of the world and a conscious understanding of the world, and that is what accounts for differences in higher-order (conscious) and lower-order (unconscious) mental states. Or I could say that there is simply a difference between how a human responds unconsciously, and how a human responds consciously to experiences and stimuli.

What is the difference between an unconscious response and a conscious response then, however? Unconscious responses are affective - they are faster and more immediate than conscious responses. Unconscious responses are also what your brain has programmed in from previous development. Conscious responses, however, are more so under your control and thoughts can help to change a conscious response.

What if someone's conscious response differs from their unconscious response? What would be an example of that happening? All responses are unconscious unless someone tries to change their response. For example, people often try to change their feelings by inhibiting them or encouraging them.

Saying all responses are higher-order or conscious doesn't make sense, because people are constantly influenced by natural emotional processes. First comes natural unconscious responses, and if you want to change or think about your situation, you 'think' and make the response more conscious.

So basically humans have emotional and intellectual responses to experience and stimuli. It is hard to influence your emotIONS WITH THOUGHT; HOWEVER PEOPLE ATTEMPT TO DO THIS ALL THE TIME (CONSCIOUSLY AND UNCONSCIOUSLY).

Table 60.0

Chapter 61

What is Reasoning Ability? - A Subjective Article Relevant to the

study of Cognition and Emotion

Is reasoning ability emotional intelligence, or is it mathematical intelligence? The general answer to what is reasoning ability would just be to say 'problem solving skills' or 'analytical ability' or 'deductive and inductive reasoning', however how much is that really saying about what analysis is or what reasoning really is?

There are an endless different types of intellect. For each topic, category, job, etc in life there is a different type of intellect or way of analyzing the material for that subject. Is there a generic 'reasoning' ability that applies to all of these categories or does one need to be defined?

Intelligence is very subjective, so it is hard to define emotional intelligence. However, I personally have found useful various tools that help my thinking:

- Categorize the information and make lists outlining the significant phenomena.

- That means that if you are thinking about something emotional, what the significant phenomena are is going to be subjective, it might be useful to make two lists, a list with the significant subjective factors and a list with the significant objective factors.

- Then you can analyze the information and say, 'well that is pretty subjective, I don't know if that is true, however if I consider this and that objective factors I realize that this and that subjective factors are more like x'.

How could someone figure out how subjective vs. objective something is? Facts are theoretically objective if it is a concrete fact that isn't, well, subjective. That is what subjective means by definition - something that is subject to opinion.

So therapy is subjective. When a psychologist assesses that someone has a problem, that is subjective. How is someone supposed to know if they are overly emotional in a certain way. Bipolar is a mental condition. If someone is bipolar they experience emotional swings from extremely happy to extremely sad. Does that mean that subjectivity is just about someones ability to measure emotion?

When someone says, 'this soda tastes good' you are measuring how much emotion drinking the soda causes you. That shows that a lot of the things that people say are subjective.

So subjectivity and objectivity relate to how the mind works, and the study of cognition and emotion. When people think things that are opinions of emotional states, or opinions of how much emotion something causes them, they are changing their thinking and possibly making their thinking emotional.

Why would it matter if a thought or just the words someone used was emotional or not? Are

the words people choose the primary factor behind what cognition is?

People have beliefs, attitudes, personality dispositions, goals, drives etc that all don't have to be thought about with words necessarily. Someones attitudes (along with the other unconscious processes mentioned) are going to determine what they think to a certain extent. If you have a strong unconscious attitude towards a certain type of person, this might influence what you say when you meet that person, for example.

So when someone thinks about facts, these might influence their attitudes and other subjective unconscious beliefs more or less so than when someone thinks about subjective information.

Table 61.0

Chapter 62

An Idea of Mental Abilities - Cognition, Language and

Development

What is the relationship between cognition and language, and how do those processes develop?

When someone learns something new they are going to think about it in some way. Words assist learning, and the choice of words that someone uses is going to influence the meaning behind what is learned.

That isn't necessarily the case, however. It could be that your unconscious mind has an emotional understanding of the knowledge, and the words you use simply point to this understanding - and if you happened to use different words it could point to the same understanding.

Words Assist Learning

- Words assist learning everything - for whatever topic in life you think about with words, the fact that you use words to think about the experience or whatever it is helps understanding.

- Although that doesn't mean that in every case if you think more with words you'll understand something better.

- Life is about various types of emotional understanding, and words can assist or even possibly hinder this understanding.

- So when a baby uses a word like 'goed' - that has an emotional understanding for the baby. The word might not seem to make any sense, but it means something to the baby.

- Etc.

- Etc.

Emotion is a powerful motivator

Not only does emotion provide information and drive for our thoughts and the words we use, it also motivates our behavior at the same time. Harré (1981a) claims that in the 'real' world, explanations are functional in a self-presentational sense. They function as a ritual display, as rhetoric, as show: they are designed to impress, and affect others impressions. And that people operate in a 'rhetorical impression manipulating manner'. There is a self-presentational motivation for peoples explanations (that is, someone has in mind their own presentation of themselves, what they look like, how they are perceived by others, etc when they make any explanation). Here Harré (1981b) tries to subsume all human affairs into a self- presentational motive:

- What sort of statements are being made in concrete social activities, such as strikes, riots, parties, working breakfasts, overtaking in the inner lane and so on? Starting with these as rough guides: modern strikes can hardly be seriously taken to be economically motivated. They are best understood as claims to recognition and dignity, as displays of worth: riots too may be something like that: look at me, and take me seriously.

So when people think in social situations, their thoughts are probably mostly emotionally driven by self-presentational goals. This doesn't mean that all thought is driven by emotion, it simply means that a lot of thought is motivated. So I have brought up a slightly different question here - how much of thought is emotional? What is it like to have a thought be motivated by feeling vs. not?

Classifying types of mental information

What are the different types of mental information? There are abstract concepts and objective facts - which relates to emotional information and numerical ability respectively. There is reasoning ability, and there is associative memory (which is basically linking similar objects together for faster recall). Reasoning ability doesn't necessarily relate to the amount or speed of someones memory - reasoning is something someone can think about by choice, while memory is less under someones control. A person could think of this or that in order to help remember something, however that wouldn't effect their measured I.Q. memory. Reasoning, however, is very subjective and someone could do a lot to increase reasoning ability.

What is subjective about reasoning information? It is that the information is about emotional material. Historical fact is about emotional material, and you could be considered to be using your reasoning ability when thinking about history. In fact, any idea related to human motivation is emotional and therefore subjective and subject to someone's reasoning ability. Unless someone uses reason to solve a math problem, or something objective, then reasoning is using emotional information and is subjective.

Bibiography

Harré, R. 1981a. Expresive aspects of descriptions of others. In C. Antaki (ed.), *The psychology of ordinary explanations of social behavior.* London: Academic Press

Harré, R. 1981b. Rituals, Rhetoric and Social Cognition. In J. Forgas (ed.), *Social cognition, perspectives on everyday understanding.* London: Academic Press

Table 62.0

Chapter 63

How does Cognition Influence Emotion?

Some mental factors (processes) are the link between cognition and emotion - such as basic imagery (body images), thoughts, and other cognitive associations and structures.

How exactly does the mind 'think' however? I could say that it uses images to think, and that these images are mostly unconscious. That would be similar to having a dream, in a dream simple images represent larger psychological ideas and life experiences. The images your mind uses to think are probably basic, similar to how a computer works with simple switches at the most simple level. The most basic and important mental images are used to represent more significant psychological 'code' or life experiences (like body images - since social interaction is important humans would be broken down in the mind into simple visualizations).

So I think that the mind basically thinks by breaking down the psychological factors of life into more simple images. If you have an interaction with someone, then that interaction is broken down into more simple body-images and other images that represent what occurred in the interaction. These images are probably unconscious, you would not notice in what order your mind is going through them or what they are exactly.

This means that your minds cognitions (such as images and thoughts) are going to influence your emotions. The real world is broken down into thoughts and visualizations (or psychological 'symbols') in your mind, and these mental processes influence your emotions.

63.1 Introduction (Part 2)

There are two major types of emotional experience - one is the obvious one which people experience daily and that is the major emotions they are experiencing as a result of their activities. The other type of emotional experience is one that is driven by deep unconscious factors, and it relates to your strong inner motivations, hopes, fears, expectations for the future, and how you perceive reality.

If you think about it, this makes sense. Emotion is generated by obvious factors - such as person A causes an emotional reaction in person B - and less obvious factors - such as person A has a strong inner desire to save lives, so when they see things that remind them of this, strong emotions are invoked. Emotions that are generated by strong, possibly hidden inner desires are much less obvious than emotions that are the direct result of experiences.

It is hard to measure emotion in both cases though. You can guess that if someone is doing a fun activity they are going to experience the emotion of 'fun' or other 'happy' emotions, but guessing what someones inner desires and motivations are is probably going to be much more

This relates to important concepts that influence how you perceive life, and how your emotions are generated. If you think about it, it makes sense that there are going to be emotional reasons you do things that you aren't aware of the motivation for all of the time. One of these important factors is a concept called "consciousness" - something could feel differently to you simply because you became more aware of it. The thing is new or different now. This concept of consciousness applies to all emotional things, you can become more conscious of one thing or feeling, or more conscious of yourself as a person as a whole.

I would say that how someone is processing their emotions changes how time feels, - their perception of time. If you are more conscious of certain emotions or just more conscious in general it could make any activity more difficult because you have to work to attain that consciousness. This is similar to saying that you should do an activity that is hard when it is least hard for you to do it. There are going to be certain conditions when things are going to be easier - - then your perception of reality and time might be

Another way of describing consciousness is just how clear a feeling or something is to you. If a feeling is more clear, then you are more conscious of it. This is like understanding why you like some things more than others, some things you know better how much you like after you spend time

I guess the question then is how is someone supposed to know when something emotional is more clear to them. Your emotions could be making you feel a lot of things that you aren't aware of you are experiencing. This is similar to having a hidden bias against someone or a group of people that you aren't aware of you have. I would say that you can observe these emotional phenomena through behavior, probably subtle behavior. That is similar to a painters strokes being influenced by their emotions. You can see how the painter is feeling by how they paint - their unconscious emotions are probably going to influence how they are feeling about the painting.

There are ways of interpreting cognitive information emotionally. Something can be imaginative, logical, happy, persuasive, or other ways in nature. For instance, something imaginative is going to make you feel differently from something that persuades you to do something by force. The 'imaginative' art or whatever it is is probably going to be much more pleasant than when your emotions and thoughts are forced or persuaded to think and feel a certain way. With imagination the thoughts seem more pleasant because your basically creating whatever it is you want to feel by imagining something. Even if you are imagining a nightmare the emotional process is still something you created and therefore subject to your personal bias (and people naturally want themselves to be happy). However, someone can easily repeat painful experiences to themselves, however that is different from imagination. With imagination you create the experience or magnify a real one. Magnifying a real experience emotionally is a part of what imagination is - maybe my point was just that things you create yourself and are more imaginative and probably going to be more pleasant.

There are other factors that make unconscious operations more complicated. kfkkkkffkdldkflldlkfkfk

63.2 Decision Making, Memory and Emotion Regulation

Emotion regulation refers to the set of processes used in response to emotional experiences and how we express our reactions to emotions (Gross, 1999). - This means that decision making and memory are going to be used in the emotion regulation process. A humans decision making ability and his or her ability to use their memory is going to be affected by the emotional nature of their experiences. Also, someone's personality might influence those processes as well. Someone who is action-oriented or harm-avoidant is going to respond differently than someone who might be more lazy.

63.3 Unconscious Processing

How does the mind think? I said previously that it uses images to think, and that these are basic images like body-images or other symbols.

But how does that information reveal other significant facts about thought? If your mind uses images to think, then a human's perception of the visual world is going to influence their mental thought processes.

Or maybe you don't need a visual representation, if someone feels something around certain nature scenes, like a pond, you don't necessarily need to visualize the pond. Being near the pond is enough to evoke the emotions that scene brings up because the pond creates a certain atmosphere, it changes the humidity in the air, and the life around the pond is different. So perhaps vision doesn't create most of the strong emotions people experience anyway.

Is it Simple?

There is a way a human's mind prioritizes information. Certain objects in life represent different things and trigger different emotions for people.

People are also sensitive to different types of emotional information. For example there might be something difficult to understand emotionally that someone understands unconsciously because it is important or more obvious to their unconscious mind.

What types of information are understood unconsciously vs. consciously then? Clearly there is going to be a difference - I can think of many examples off the top of my head. There are simple things in life people do like knowing their schedule for a day, that could be considered to be emotionally simple, and there are more complex ideas emotionally that people consider during a day like how to handle a debate or argument.

Is there a type of 'emotional speculation' where someone guesses what something might feel like? You could say that people do this all the time when they make any type of emotional assessment (for instance how cool or uncool something is, or if they like or dislike someone). What is emotional subtlety then? It is defined by levels of conscious and unconscious importance, and degree of difficulty in understanding and absorbing the information.

What information is absorbed consciously vs. unconsciously?

That is a critical question because there are many different types of emotional information. Something can be more important emotionally if the person simply cares about it more, or they could have a better understanding of the information because they have experience in that field.

What would be 'emotionally complex' pieces of information then? If the information is complex is it easier to understand consciously or unconsciously? Dogs often understand beforehand when their owner is going to go on a vacation, or many other complex ideas about social interaction. Dogs also understand if a person is being nice or cruel to them - does that mean that a humans understanding of kindness is at the same level as that of a dog? There must be more complicated ways a human understands what 'kindness' or 'cruelty' means than the understanding a dog has.

Maybe information that is 'subjective' is information that is consciously speculated. Unconsciously you simply get a feel for things, but you can guess about a lot of things verbally - are those guesses instinctual, 'gut' guesses or are they measured assessments? Is anything subjective a measured assessment? Saying 'that coat looks nice on that person' is subjective - the person isn't doing an analysis of who likes the coat on the person and who else thinks it looks good. They think it looks good - they didn't do a study of what type of person thinks it looks good. The information is subjective, it was triggered by their own emotions and motivations.

Is Conscious Understanding Subjective or Objective?

When someone thinks something is funny, how accurate are they? How can someone measure how funny a movie or a joke is? Can you measure that by the amount of time spend laughing or the amount of 'smiling' the person does as a result of hearing the joke? Conscious understanding of our own feelings is subjective. That information also means that all conscious understanding is subjective - when someone thinks they understand something, they are going to bias it in some way.

What if someone tries to be as objective as possible when making all of their decisions. Then possibly all decisions that are objective in the first place (non-emotional decisions) and not subjective might be fairly non-biased. But then what types of assessments are non-emotional and which types are emotional? Math isn't emotional - scientific fact isn't emotional. That isn't to say that there isn't a type of bias someone has when they do addition. Maybe they are thinking about something else at the same time and this biases possible interpretations of the objective data.

So it is clear that something objective is objective, and something subjective is subjective, however how could someone measure differences in how subjective something is?

What Classifies Material as Conscious vs. Unconscious?

Theoretically all the information someone absorbs is going to be consciously vs. unconsciously absorbed to different degrees. I would say that if the information is easier to remember then you are using your unconscious mind (like how songs are easy to remember). Songs are easy to remember because they are fun, a persons emotions are evoked and that helps increase mental processing of the song so they can recall it. The emotion 'fun' from the song (even if it is a sad song the fact that it is a song is positive) or just emotion from the song helps you to remember it.

Information that you don't need to think about that much consciously is unconscious information as well. If you think about it, if you have to do a lot consciously - like think of this and that in order to remember something or think or do something, then it is more conscious. If it is done more automatically then it is more unconscious.

I would say that all emotional information is more unconscious. Dreams are emotional because you are not conscious during them. That is why they don't make sense, because you are not thinking (lol). Does this mean that someone thinking a lot is going to be less emotional? That is hard to say because you can't really define when someone as thinking a lot or not. If someone is watching a movie, they are probably thinking less then when during a history exam.

So my theory is that knowing how emotional something is can help classify if it is intellectually intense or not. For example - which would use more thought, a math test or a history test? In history you use emotional information to help remember the facts. What happened in history is emotional and social. Math is logical, it is clear how to get the result if you understand how things work in a concrete, straightforward way. (I am not saying that calculus is straightforward, I am just saying that it makes sense why it works that way because math makes sense). History is a social subject, however, so ones understanding of emotion and human interaction is going to influence your ability to do well in that field.

So which subject uses more unconscious processes? History or math? I would say that history does since it is emotional, and math doesn't necessarily engage any emotions. I mean, you are just doing numbers, it could cause someone to become emotional if it brings up something indirectly, but that would not relate directly to the math problem like how historical fact relates to social interaction.

Emotional Material is Unconscious and Factual Thinking is Conscious

So therefore emotional material is unconscious and factual thinking is conscious. This is so because when you think about something you are thinking consciously, and that is a single point of information that you think as a 'thought'. If it is emotional or important it is unconscious because you can't think about your emotions, when emotions occur, they are physical processes that cause feeling. Thoughts can cause feeling, but only because they trigger emotions. So math is very logical, you can have a lot of thoughts about it but none of those thoughts necessarily have to trigger emotions because they aren't directly related. Historical fact is social, so it is probably going to be more emotional because it is more directly related to social interaction.

So a process like memory retrieval can be unconscious. When you are helped by your mind to remember a song, that is unconscious memory retrieval. When you try to remember something, that is more conscious. What is the line between unconscious and conscious then? Historical fact relates to a lot of things in your unconscious mind. If it relates to a lot of unconscious things, like emotional things or other things in your life you don't think about immediately, then it is more of an unconscious process. If it relates to things you easily remember then it is more of a conscious process.

63.4 Representation in the Mind

Since different objects represent different things to different people, and there are different types of emotional speculation (like deliberative decisions vs. instinctual ones), and various degrees of cognitive load (how intellectual or how emotional something is) then it isn't clear to me how these would function in the mind - which images, objects or experiences in life would do what to someone emotionally and intellectually?

63.5 Points made in this essay

- Mental images are possibly more simple in the mind than the full experience of them in reality. They are sometimes dulled down and made less intellectually intense like how dreams are more simple (and there are often simple images in them) than real life experiences.

- There are obvious and less obvious life factors that influence your emotions. This relates to having to do work to attain consciousness of something. If something is obvious or more significant, it is probably going to be more accessible to consciousness (how 'clear' something is).

- Someones memory and decision making ability is going to be influenced by their emotional reactions and their personality type.

- A persons perception of the visual world is going to influence those mental processes (decision making and memory) because vision is a large factor in how emotion is generated, though not necessarily that significant.

- People are sensitive to different types of emotional information and absorb some things better consciously vs. unconsciously. Some things are also more or less emotionally complex, in addition to being unconscious or conscious.

- Unconsciously people can get a feel for things - that is what the unconscious is - more automatic - you could have a more conscious feeling for something but it is easier to respond instinctively. This relates to understanding information consciously or unconsciously, if feelings are involved it could be considered to be an unconscious understanding, like how dogs understand if someone is being nice. If it is conscious then you aren't necessarily correct, you are using intellect to guess at something. You could be using your unconscious feelings as well, however.

- Information that is emotional (such as historical fact) isn't necessarily conscious thinking. One can think objectively about emotional information, and therefore it would be non-emotional to them. However, it makes sense that someone would use emotional information to help remember historical fact, since history is related to life and social interaction information (which are both emotional phenomena).

63.6 A Related Article

Chris Fields (2010) wrote an article explaining about 'hyper-systemizers' - "Hyper-systemizers are individuals displaying an unusually strong bias toward systemizing, i.e. toward explaining events and solving problems by appeal to mechanisms that do not involve intentions or agency.". And how they are different from their opposites 'mentalizers'. That relates to this article because I described how some information is more emotional than other information. It seems that some people process more emotional information, and other people process information more subjectively or are just less sensitive to emotional cues:

- Scientists, technologists, engineers and mathematicians rely heavily on a problem-solving and explanatory strategy or orientation, termed "systemizing" by Baron-Cohen (2002, 2008), that is characterized by appeals to natural laws, physical mechanisms, algorithms, formal inference rules, or other concepts of causation that do not involve autonomous agency or intentions. Systemizing or "mechanizing" (Crespi and Badcock, 2008) solutions and explanations are explicitly distinguished from "empathizing" or "mentalizing" solutions and explanations, which do appeal to intentional, 2 autonomous agency and to actions guided by beliefs, desires, goals, fears, worries and other "folk psychological" attributes associated with agency by a theory of mind (ToM) system (Frith and Frith, 1999; 2003).

Fields describes the proposition of his paper:

- Based on a review and synthesis of relevant literatures, the present paper proposes that pre-existing personality and cognitive demands interact to progressively sensitize the attentional and motivational systems of some individuals toward systemizing and away from mentalizing, resulting in hyper-systemizers who are not deficit in mentalizing capability, but rather relatively insensitive to cues that ordinarily induce mentalizing.

So some people are more driven by emotional processes - and their thoughts are influenced by emotion - but with other people this is less the case. I mean if your actions are being guided by beliefs, fears, goals, worries, etc. then it would seem to me that the person would be more emotional. That isn't necessarily the case, however. Someone could have their thoughts be driven by those things, but not be an emotional person. Would that person be thinking with more unconscious emotional processes, but not actually be more emotional? Emotion can be present in thought and used to assist thought, but might not actually make the person more emotional than someone whose thinking is more objective. Maybe they are emotional for a different reason.

63.7 Theory of mind

Theory of mind (often abbreviated "ToM") is the ability to attribute mental states—beliefs, intents, desires, pretending, knowledge, etc.—to oneself and others and to understand that others have beliefs, desires, and intentions that are different from one's own. (Premack, D. G.; Woodruff, G. (1978)).

In my view, ToM relates significantly to how emotional people and their thoughts are. If someone's actions are being guided by beliefs and desires (a 'mentalizer'), then it makes sense that their understanding and assessments of other people and themselves are going to be influenced by beliefs and desires. If someone has greater desires when making assessments (so the emotion would be related to their thoughts) would they be a more emotional person? Someone might be capable of thinking non-emotionally, even if they have greater desires and beliefs, though I would think that in general someone with more emotional thoughts would be a more emotional person. It probably depends what they are more emotional about, etc.

63.8 Consciousness?

A theory of consciousness is outlined by (De Luca, A Tony and Stephens, Newman L (2010)) - this is what they postulate - "To understand consciousness we have to understand the mechanism of its function, which is to effectively organize sensory inputs from our environment. Consciousness is the outcome of the process of organizing these sensory inputs. This implies that organization is an act which precedes consciousness:

- My hypothesis is that consciousness is the emergent outcome of several linked processes (outcomes for sensory systems) which are organized to form specific neuronal architectures. The most elemental of these processes is the electrochemical input to the brain cells which originated as external stimuli on specific receptors that in turn generate electrophysiological phenomena such as action potentials to occur in specific areas of the nerves system. These ascend to multiply loci in different parts of the brain. According to some investigators, i.e. Crick and Koch, it is the synchronization of these actions that results in consciousness. Crick termed this the "Astonish Hypothesis" In this book and subsequent articles awareness and perception were used interchangeably with consciousness. However, my hypothesis states that perception is different physiological construct from that of awareness and are elements of the subconscience and consciousness is the process of organizing awareness; its manifestation is the emergence outcome from this process.

In my view, it makes sense that perception is different from awareness. Perception is fast because vision is fast. Vision seems to me to obviously be linked to different cognitions than awareness. To figure out how awareness and perception are different, however, we first need to figure out what 'awareness' is (though I would think that an advanced cognitive process is slower than a fast visual process, as it takes a long time to think complex thoughts). When someone is aware of their environment, is that awareness emotional? A deer or other animal doesn't necessarily need to engage emotionally with other species in order to be aware of its environment. Even frogs posses basic emotional processes (I noticed a from responding emotionally - when you go near it you could possibly try to be nice and not scare it away). What is awareness then? Is it just awareness of ones environment, or awareness of the social cues needed to interact with other species? This is in the abstract of the paper by Deluca and Stephens:

- Consciousness is "something" which the majority of humans know that they posses, they use it when they want to understand their environment. However, no individual human knows whether other humans also posses consciousness. unless some tests such as she is looking at me, he is talking etc., are performed. We are caught in an intellectual sort of recursive carousel – we need consciousness to understand consciousness.

So awareness is complex - you have to be aware of other people, what they are doing, what is going on in your environment. Vision, however, is simple. First people need to see their environment in order to reach conclusions about it (or whatever the equivalent that is that a blind person would do). If someone stops thinking, they could still be able to see. I am just saying it seems to me that vision is a more simple process than advanced awareness. First you see your environment, then you think about it. I would guess that when you aren't thinking, you are still looking around and responding to more simple cognitions that enable you to behave normally. Advanced emotional and intellectual thinking is probably slower than simple thinking and vision.

So no wonder Crick and Koch used the words sensation and perception interchangeably, when someone fist is able to see their environment, when they wake up or whatever, it is as if that is when they are first aware. (Vision being the 'baseline' cognition). This relates to emotional and intellectual complexity, some things are simply more advanced than others to think about. When a baby is born can it think? It can see, and it understands how to interact, but then again, a frog also knows how to interact and I notice they can respond emotionally.

63.9 Consciousness in the brain

Wallace, Dr. Rodrick (2011) sums up an argument by Atlan and Cohen (1998) about how information systems work in the mind:

- Atlan and Cohen (1998) argue, in the context of a cognitive paradigm for the immune system, that the essence of cognitive function involves comparison of a perceived signal with an internal, learned or inherited picture of the world, and then, upon that comparison, choice of one response from a much larger reper- toire of possible responses. That is, cognitive pattern recognition-and-response proceeds by an algorithmic combination of an incoming external sensory sig- nal with an internal ongoing activity { incorporating the internalized picture of the world { and triggering an appropriate action based on a decision that the pattern of sensory activity requires a response.

When someone sees something does it 'require a response'? Seeing another human being might require a response, but what about biological or neural responses? What objects trigger which responses? Are there sets of 'brain wirings' that sort out different activities? Here Wallace cites a model - (Baars, 2005):

- ...it is clear that different challenges facing a conscious entity must be met be diferent arrangements of basic cognitive faculties. It is now possible to make a very abstract picture of the brain, not based on its anatomy, but rather on the linkages between the information sources dual to the basic physiological and learned unconscious cognitive modules (UCM) that form Baars' global workspace/global broadcast. That is, the remapped brain network is reexpressed in terms of the information sources dual to the UCM. Given two distinct problems classes (e.g., playing tennis vs. interacting with a significant other), there must be two different `wirings' of the information sources dual to the physiological UCM,

It is fairly obvious that there are different ways of responding to the world - social, emotional, intellectual, etc. - but the important question is: what are the similar ways in which different aspects of the world cause similar or different feelings? That way you could say - this is that are grouped in the mind because they have the same feeling (physical) response. Or is there "no room in any model for feeling" (Harnad, Stevan (2011))? I could use a emotional / intellectual division of world responses. While intellectually thoughts may cause feeling, it makes more sense that the mind is divided into emotional groupings not intellectual ones. That is because thoughts trigger feelings - a feeling can cause someone to have a thought, but that is only because you realized you had that feeling or it motivated you in certain way (while thoughts cause feelings directly). So it isn't someone's knowledge that causes feelings, I think the mind works by a more simple division of the world and biological responses - simple emotional groupings. That makes sense since humans evolved from lesser animals where that is more obvious. When an ape interacts with his friends, the emotion he feels is a simple one that derived from simple aspects of the world and the interaction he in engaged in. So while simple feelings might be the logical result of their corresponding thoughts, deeper emotional aspects of the mind are probably simple responses to the persons environment i.e., you went to a movie so you feel happy, etc. So my theory is basically only a few emotions are the end result of all our activities, and from these basic emotions more complex intellectual responses can be formed. Harnad, Stevan (2011) seems to feel that humans have little room for feeling in their intellectual responses:

- And perhaps it is indeed not worth fretting about the fact that, at the end of the day, the successful total explanation of our know-how will always be equally compatible with the presence or the absence of feeling. For unless we are prepared to be telekinetic dualists, according a separate, unique causal power to feeling itself ("mind over matter") -- for which there is no evidence, only overwhelming evidence against it – there is no causal room in any model for feeling. Yet, although it may be an illusion that some of the things I do, I do because I feel like it, it is certainly not an illusion that it feels like some of the things I do, I do because I feel like it. And that feeling is as real as the feeling that I have a toothache even when I don't have a tooth.

63.10 My Theory

Paul Ekman did a study that found that when participants contorted their facial muscles into distinct facial expressions (e.g. disgust), they reported subjective and physiological experiences that matched the distinct facial expressions. His research findings led him to classify six emotions as basic: anger, disgust, fear, happiness, sadness and surprise.[1]

So there is a physiological correlate for each of the 6 basic emotions - my theory is that from different stimuli, different intellectual cognitions (such as thoughts, dreams etc.), and one or more of those 6 basic emotions (or possibly other feelings) consciousness arises. It doesn't necessarily have to be right away, it could take hours for neural centers to respond (in that way more complex emotional responses can be formed since they are possibly a build up of a few hours of mental experience).

This way, from a simple emotionally triggered response (not just emotional, but also intellectual stimuli and external stimuli) in the brain complex feelings arise. The answer must be that different chemicals are stored up over time. In that way only a few basic emotions could give rise to a rich conscious emotional and intellectual experience. Emotions trigger thoughts, thoughts are triggered from external stimuli (in any order thoughts, emotions and external stimuli can trigger each other) (which was triggered by such and such stimulus) could trigger this and that feeling over the next few hours.

Humans must develop a way of organizing the three inputs of emotion, external stimuli, and thought (the intellectual input) over time, and the way their mind organizes the data forms their 'consciousness'. - For instance, if you respond to seeing this object this way emotionally and intellectually - then that was how your mind organized your emotional/intellectual response. It is subjective to decide whether or not you were 'aware' of your response - humans respond to things all the time and they aren't necessarily aware of those responses.

So someone emotions could be sending signals to the part of the brain or body that registers those feelings. Your mind (thoughts, etc. - the intellectual part of your brain) could also be sending similar or different signals about emotion (i.e. 'I want to be happy' or 'I don't want to be angry'). As a third input, the person could be getting signals from their external environment telling their emotions to be happy, sad, etc.

How can Intellect in the brain be categorized?

It is more clear how emotion works in the brain than intellect - the different 'main' emotions are obvious

1. Handel, Steven. "Classification of Emotions". Retrieved 30 April 2012.

mentally and physically. However, how does a humans mind work intellectually? There must be certain types of attributes it associates with itself, and some of these are going to be more intellectually 'stimulating' to your mind than other attributes. This might also be true of other animals with less intellectual functioning than a human, however it is probably very different.

Just like how different types of sensory information can be stimulating to someone, different types of intellectual information are probably also stimulating to various degrees. School can be academically (or intellectually) rigorous, but what pieces of information from academic material are more rigorous? The same information probably is just as rigorous outside of a school environment. Can I separate out information that is accompanied or 'forced' into someone by other emotional stress like if someone was under pressure at school to do well, or under pressure to figure out a solution otherwise?

Different types of information must be associated with different emotional architectures - i.e., when I think about this I feel this way. Some types of information are going to be more or less emotional or related to your personal identity. That is different from if the information uses more unconscious emotional processes. Information could use emotion to help to think about it (like my historical fact example), or the information could be emotional to the person or not as well.

63.11 Subjectivity and Emotion

(Vaknin, Sam) Proposes that emotions are either sensory or internal:

- Actions are sense data and motivations are internal data, which together form a new chunk of emotional data.

- If more sense data (than internal data) are involved and the component of internal data is weak in comparison (it is never absent) – we are likely to experience Transitive Emotions. The latter are emotions, which involve observation and revolve around objects. In short: these are "out-going" emotions, that motivate us to act to change our environment.

- Yet, if the emotional cycle is set in motion by Emotional Data, which are composed mainly of internal, spontaneously generated data – we will end up with Reflexive Emotions. These are emotions that involve reflection and revolve around the self (for instance, autoerotic emotions). It is here that the source of psychopathologies should be sought: in this imbalance between external, objective, sense data and the echoes of our mind.

So obviously emotions are going to be generated by either one or both inputs - internal and external. If you feel like (or are) responding to your internal motivations and feelings, then you are responding more internally. If someones environment is putting pressure on them (people in the environment, or other sensory inputs), then they would by definition be responding more externally.

What makes an emotion subjective? People feel emotions all the time, its just how they are - "Thats just how I feel" someone might try to communicate. It is too hard to assess where the emotion came from, if it was a logical one that made sense or an emotion that was subjective. What would an example of a 'subjective' emotion be vs. a 'logical' emotion?

An emotion that is strongly influenced by a motivation or desire is probably subjective. An emotion that is sensory, like a physical emotion, is more objective because you aren't influencing the emotion with your mind. People respond differently to different situations because they are different people and have different background beliefs, ideas, feelings, experience, etc.

I suppose you could say that some people respond to social situations more 'logically' than other people. If they aren't as influenced by their internal beliefs - earlier in this paper I cited the definition of 'mentalizers' - people who have their actions guided by beliefs, desires, goals, fears, etc. vs. 'systemizers', who rely on a problem solving strategy instead of intentions - then does that mean they are responding more logically? Someones emotions could be influenced by logical data just as much as someones emotions could be influenced by internal intentions (though I would guess in general the mentalizers are more emotional).

Do emotions arise from a persons problem solving strategy? One that is logical (systemizers) or one that is based on internal motivations (mentzlizers)? If that were the case, then systemizers would be distinctinly different emotionally than mentalizers. Or do emotions arise from perceiving external actions differently? Perceiving actions would be learned from experience, while someones problem solving strategy is based upon what they are thinking about. - So emotions could arise from perceptions of bodily changes (which is Damasio's theory) which I suppose could be observing other people in your environment, or they arise from a more internal, mental process which is based upon what you are thinking about, how you are   thinking, etc. (systemizers vs mentalizers for example).

63.12 Observation vs. Inference

When someone observes their environment they think about it in some way. This type of thinking is different from thinking that isn't based off of immediate vision. How do the two types of thinking differ? What is different when you think from when you are observing your environment, versus when you think about things that aren't dependent on what you are looking at (a more 'inferential' type of thinking)? Fodor (Fodor, Jerry (1990)) states - "For one thing, observationally fixed beliefs tend, by and large, to be more reliable than inferrentially fixed beliefs."

Based upon the same visual observations, will two organisms reach the same conclusions? Why don't I try to compare a deer and a human. There is a similar way in which both species process basic information about the environment (along with the animals in it), for instance if someone is attacking them both species recognize that as a threat. And i'm sure both species process data about environments without other animals or humans in it in a similar fashion as well. They both need to function in the environment, to look at the flora and fauna and decide what they want to eat, etc. It must be more complicated or 'theoretical' ideas that humans hold which separate our thinking from that of other animals (like deer). Here Fodor states that two organisms will reach the same observational beliefs 'however much their theoretical commitments may differ':

- The claim, then, is that there is a class of beliefs that are typically fixed by sensory/perceptual processes, and that the fixation of beliefs in this class is, in a sense that wants spelling out, importantly theory neutral. A a first shot at what the theory neutrality of observation comes to: given the same stimulations, two organisms with the same sensory/perceptual psychology will quite generally observe the same things, and hence arrive at the same observational beliefs, *however much their theoretical commitments may differ.*

Is there a difference between perception and cognition? How someone perceives the world is based off of - and influenced by - how they think of the world. Perception is the organization, identification and interpretation of sensory information in order to represent and understand the environment[2]. Cognition is how our minds use sensory data, in addition for being a name for all of a humans intellectual faculties - language, learning, reasoning, problem solving, and decision making. So what is the exact relationship between perception and cognition? Here again is Fodor:

- Precisely parallel to the philosophical doctrine that there can be no principled distinction between *observation* and *inference* is the psychological doctrine that there can be no principled distinction between *perception* and *cognition.* The leading idea here is that "perception involves a kind of problem solving--a kind of intelligence (Gregory 1970). Perception, according to this account, is the process wherein an organism assigns probable distal causes to the proximal stimulations it encounters. What makes the solution of perceptual problems other than mere routine is the fact that, as a matter of principle, any given pattern of proximal stimulation is compatible with a great variety   of distal causes; there are, if you like, many possible worlds that would project a given pattern of excitation on the sensory mechanisms of an organism. To view the mental processes which mediate perception as inferences is thus necessarily to view them as *nondemonstrative* inferences. "We are forced ... to suppose that perception involves betting on the most probable interpretation

2.   , Daniel (2011). *Psychology.* Worth Publishers

of sensory data, in terms of world objects" (Gregory 1970). It is worth stressing the putative moral: what mediates perception is an inference from effects to causes. The sort of mentation required for perception is thus not different in kind - though no doubt it differs a lot in conscious accessibility--from what goes on in Sherlock Holmes' head when he infers the identity of the criminal from a stray cigar band and a hair or two. If what Holmes does deserves to be called cognition, perception deserved to be called cognition too, or so, at least, some psychologists like to say.

So observation is similar to perception, and inference is similar to cognition. When someone interprets or infers information, they are thinking - and when someone observes the world around them they could likewise be viewed as just seeing (or 'perceiving').

Which visual objects generate which cognitions? Or, which visual environments generate which types of cognitions? My guess would be there are visual environments that put a high cognitive demand on someone, or alerts them to a higher degree than less threatening or stimulating environments. It is interesting that vision plays such a large role in what a human or other animal might be thinking. For instance, a forest environment might make a human feel like it was under threat, or at least more so than a grassy environment where the human could see far around itself.

From the Fodor quote I concluded that it seems like the observations and conclusions reached from perception or vision are simple ones. Investigation into what is going on visually is just linking the vision of a scene (like a crime scene in the Holmes example) and with the knowledge you need to make the proper links. An understanding of of deep human emotional factors isn't necessary. However, a complex understanding of human motivation might be needed to understand complex ideas. Complex ideas might be linked to vision, however most things that people just see visually they don't need a complex emotional background to understand. There are many 'worlds' that each visual environment might represent. Those are also simple, however. In the visual field there are simple things like effects and causes (this causes that, etc). To understand the environment, much of the information of what is happening doesn't have to pass through consciousness since it is usually fairly simple. A deeper reflection, esp. a deeper emotional reflection is capable with complex thought, probably at a separate time from when one reaches the immediate conclusions they do about the environment.

Bibliography

- Atlan, H., I. Cohen, 1998, Immune information, self organization, and mean- ing, International Immunology, 10:711-717.

- Baars, B., 2005, Global workspace theory of consciousness: toward a cognitive neuroscience of human experience, Progress in Brain Research, 150:45-53.

- Baron-Cohen, S. (2002). The extreme male brain theory of autism. *Trends in Cognitive Sciences 2(2),* 248-254.

- Baron-Cohen, S. (2008). Autism, hypersystemizing, and truth. *The Quarterly Journal of Experimental Psychology 61(1),* 64-75.

- Crick Francis and Koch Christof (1994) – The Astonishing Hypothesis. *New York: Scriber.*

- Crespi, B. and Badcock, C. (2008). Psychosis and autism as diametrical disorders of the social brain. *Behavioral and Brain Sciences 31,* 241-320

- De Luca, A Tony and Stephens, Newman L (2010) *A New Theory of Consciousness: The Missing Link - Organization.* (Unpublished) Retrieved from http://cogprints.org/7022/ 12/31/13

- Fields, Chris (2010) From "Oh, OK" to "Ah, yes" to "Aha!": Hyper-systemizing and the rewards of insight. [Preprint] Retrieved from http://cogprints.org/7220/ 12/31/2013

- Fodor, Jerry A. (1990) "A Theory of Content". MIT Press.

- Frith, U. and Frith, C. (1999). Interacting minds – A biological perspective. Science 286, 1692-1695

- Frith, U. and Frith, C. (2003). Development and neurophysiology of mentalizing. *Philosophical*

Transactions of the Royal Society of London B 358, 459-473.

- Gregory, R. 1970. *The Intelligent Eye.* New York: McGraw-Hill Book Company.

- Gross, J. J. (1999). Emotion regulation: Past, present, future. *Cognition and Emotion,* 13(5), 551- 573.

- Harnad, Stevan (2011) Doing, Feeling, Meaning And Explaining. [Conference Paper] Retrieved from http://cogprints.org/7335/ 12/31/13

- Premack, D. G.; Woodruff, G. (1978). "Does the chimpanzee have a theory of mind?". Behavioral and Brain Sciences 1 (4): 515–526

- Van Der Velde, Christiaan D. (2004) **The Mind: Its Nature and Origin.** Prometheus Books. Amherst, NY.

- Vaknin, Sam. "The Manifold of Sense". Retrieved from http://samvak.tripod.com/sense.html 1/13/14

- Wallace, Dr. Rodrick (2011) *Consciousness: A Simple Information Theory Global Workspace Model.* [Preprint] Retrieved from http://cogprints.org/7288/ 12/31/13

Table 63.0

Chapter 64

Actions and Explanations

There are different ways of knowing how to do something - you can think you know how to do it, and understand everything about how you should do it properly in your mind, but when it comes to doing it, it doesn't actually work out that way. This is important because it shows different ways of understanding how the world works, one way is a practical one and the other way is an internal one that you can think about to yourself.

For example, when you are doing something that you know how to do, you might do it automatically without thinking, or you may pause and think about how to do it or what you are doing throughout the process.

People seek reasons and explanations for their intentions. When you intend to do something, you usually know why you want to do it, however you might also seek additional reasons and explanation. Sometimes you are in a state of mind where it is more appropriate to seek reasons. If you are intending to do something, then you might be looking for additional reasons why you want to do it.

When you intend to do something, some combination of beliefs and facts goes through your mind. You have reasons to do it, and you are thinking about the beliefs and facts that you will use when you do it. For instance even something simple, like turning on a light switch, you have the belief that switching it on will turn on the light, and you have the fact that almost every time you did that before the light did indeed turn on. That is a simple example, there are much more complicated and even unconscious beliefs and facts that you understand before doing certain actions.

1. *Actions, simple or compound, are events.* For instance, anything that happens takes a certain amount of time to happen - this is an event. People label a certain complicated number of things happening into an 'event'- such as a game or a meal or a party. Every action can be a part of a larger whole - drinking is a part of the event 'meal'. The 'meal' is part of the event 'visiting friends'. Everything in life is part of something larger, and everything has its own smaller components. Practically people keep this simple and don't overly analyze the details, but it can be done.

2. *One action may have many significant properties.* This would be the different ways of describing events or the parts in them. So for instance while drinking is a part of a meal, the drink tasting good is a property of the drink or 'drinking'. Furthermore, there is a certain relationship between the descriptions - 'tasted good' - and the events - 'drinking'. The relationships are always casual, conventional and circumstantial. In the casual case the drink tasting good is made true because drinks are liquid and liquid often tastes good. In the conventional case drinks taste good because of a rule - all food or liquid has a certain taste. In the circumstantial case the drink tastes good because you happened to find a drink that tasted good. So, as you see, there are these different ways of looking at and analyzing how the properties of an event or action relate to the event or action. Also, these properties are ways of describing the action.

3. *Actions are events that are intentionally performed by agents.* Actions are events that are brought about immediately by the agent. If they aren't brought about immediately, then something else is doing the action, and it isn't the action of the original agent, it is the action of the second agent or third or fourth, etc, agent. An action is performed intentionally if it has one intentional description - you can describe how it was the intention of the agent. If you foresee that you are going to do an action, it still wouldn't be intentional unless you desire to do the action (have a pro-attitude about it). If you don't desire to do an action you might knowingly be doing the action, but that doesn't mean that you are intentionally doing it. When you do something with intent, you have a better understanding

that you are doing that action - there are many things you could do with little understanding that you are doing it, but then it isn't really intentional. If, on the other hand, you have a desire to do the action, then it is probably more intentional.

4. *Actions may be intentional under various aspects.* So one action may be the best option for you, it is more intentional than other things you might have intended. An action might also be partially not intended, for instance some of the action you are doing could be a more automatic process (such as the movements of your muscles), and if viewed that way that part of the action isn't as intentional.

5. *Any intentional description can be quoted in explanation of an action.* Explanations are relative to background knowledge. Explanations may start off more basic and simple, and progress towards more complex ones or the final, satisfactory explanation that shows the goal.

An explanation for an action is best when it eliminates the other possible explanations for that action. An explanation should point towards causes, not otherwise irrelevant factors. However, if the background knowledge of the person you are explaining the action to is insufficient, it may fail to count as an explanation because of the way in which it engages with the background knowledge of those seeking enlightenment. A statement which explains an event must give us a casual understanding; and the understanding it gives us must be an advance on the cognitive status quo. In a phrase, the explanation of an event must advance us in the search for the event's causes.

Three sorts of advancement in casual understanding, and there may well be others, can be characterized as causal embedding, casual excavation and casual enrichment. We embed an event casually when we point to its immediate origin; we excavate it when we turn up its remoter springs; and we we enrich it when we see how one or another features is the legacy of its ancestors.

A description provides a good explanation when it advances us in our search for the causes of the action. The first explanation of an action is most simple - it points to its obvious or immediate origin - the further explanations progressively reveal more and more. The explanation of an action also shows how the action was the desire or belief of the person doing the action. They desired to see that action done, that is why it was intentional on their part. It may also be the belief of the person doing the action that the action is being done. Furthermore, as the action progresses, so too will the desires, beliefs and understanding about it progress.

The desires and beliefs people have when performing actions can vary from very simple ones (usually for instance when someone is performing a simple action), to very complex ones (for instance some sort of complex motivation or goal). There is also the potential appeal of promise-keeping. With some actions the goal you have is very strong or motivated, and you 'promise' to yourself that the goal is going to be achieved.

What we seek now is a feature in the perceived appeal of promise keeping which would let us understand the surprising property in the desire it occasions, that the desire prevails over powerful competing urges. What feature in the cause could have passed on this property to the effect?

There are at least four different ways in which the casual enrichment required in this question is provided. All of them have in common that they locate the operative feature of the prompting cause in the agent. The first would relate it in a long term policy or commitment on the agent's part, the second to the agent's motivational profile, the third to his character or personality, and the fourth to his social position. The idea is that the perceived appeal of promise keeping, granted that is has the feature of engaging someone with such and such a policy, profile, personality or position, passes on to the desire occasioned the property of outweighing certain opposed desires. Some remarks will be useful on the invocation of the factors mentioned since the explanations in which they appear constitute the major action accounting varieties over and beyond the explanations, i.e. the explanations of (non-ultimate) desires.

So some motivating factors are long-term policies or commitments on the part of the agent, his or her motivations, character or personality, and their social position. These desires might overcome various opposed desires.

An agent has a policy, such as the policy of keeping promises come what may, when he makes an unconditional judgment in favor of those actions which he sees is future offing for him, that fulfill promises. It is not just that he finds them qua fulfillments of promises attractive or compelling, a state which would leave him free not to perform them, finding them unattractive under other aspects. He selects in all their particularity those actions that he foresees; he decides resolutely for them. Such a policy resembles a state of intending something in this regard. What distinguishes it is that whereas the intending is fulfilled by a single action, however complex, the policy remains intact and directive no matter how many actions have satisfied it.

So, basically, a person has the same motivations for the actions he or she does over time. He intends one thing, and then does many actions that will fill this intention. Even when he accomplishes his intention, the drive behind the intention is still there.

An agents motivational profile is constituted by the state of his emotions and drives. Emotions are passing states of feeling which are not associated with any very restricted class of action: fear and jealousy, shame and joy, despair and sadness, may sensitize agents to any of a number of promptings and may lead to any of a variety of actions. They are associated with characteristic circumstances of arousal and they usually issue in distinctive involuntary expressions. Drives on the other hand are passing states of feeling which are pointed much more definitively towards particular tracks of behavior: avarice and envy, revenge and ambition, hunger and lust, are primarily identified by the promptings to which they make us responsive and the actions which they lead us to perform. Like emotions they have characteristic circumstances of arousal but they do not have such distinctive involuntary expressions. As states of feeling, emotions and drives have in common the fact that it does not make sense, as it would with a policy, to think of an agent revoking them: they are conceived of as unwilled, if sometimes welcome, visitations.

Clearly emotions and drives are going to lead people to do various actions. They would also help motivate and power certain actions while the person is doing them. Drives might prompt us to do things, and emotions might also make us more responsive to our desires to perform actions.

An agents character or personality consists in deeply enduring and only partially controllable habits of mind and heart whereby he may be distinguished from other individuals. It is often described by the use of words associated with certain emotions and drives, the implication being that the agent has a susceptibility to those states. Thus we have fearful and jealous, avaricious and envious, people as well as having the emotions of fear and jealousy and the drives of avarice and envy. Personality is often characterized too, not by habits of the sensibility but by habits of thought. When we speak of someone as obsessional or judgmental, or when we characterize his belief patterns as fascist or xenophobic, we are ascribing personality just as much as when we describe his affective dispositions. In either case we are focusing on something in the agent which, like his policies or her motivational profile, may mean that a given prompting occasions a distinctively powerful desire.

So, depending on a persons personality, different triggers are going to elicit different drives and motivations. When you describe someones beliefs, actions and values you are describing their personality as well. You could label certain characteristics of a response that is associated with certain emotions or drives.

Finally, an agent's social position, in a slightly unusual use of the phrase, is the frame constituted by the relationships with other people which constrain his behavior at any time. The traffic warden seeing children safely across the road, the bank clerk considering a request for credit, the tourist office attendant giving information to visitors: these are examples of people who so long as they exercise the activities described are in highly visibly social positions. Like the other factors mentioned, position is something on the side of the agent which can mean that a given stimulus to desire is exceptionally potent, and that the desire occasioned has the feature of readily prevailing over competitors.

Bibliography

Pettit, P. "On Actions and Explanations". In Antaki, Charles (Ed). 1981. "The Psychology of Ordinary Explanations of Social Behavior". Academic Press, Inc. London.

Table 64.0

Chapter 65

How are Arousal and Stimulation Processed in Emotional Processing?

If you think about it, emotion is going to be related to everything in life. Things that inspire us generate emotion, things that arouse us generate emotion, and ordinary stimuli generates emotion as well.

But what is arousal? What is inspiration? If everything in life has some combination of arousal and stimulation, and this combination generates an 'emotional response', then are there other factors present that are also significant?

Arousal is a physiological and psychological state of being awake or reactive to stimuli. Arousal is important in regulating consciousness, attention, and information processing. It is crucial for motivating certain behaviours, such as mobility, the pursuit of nutrition, the fight-or-flight response and sexual activity. So in order to understand what arousal is, it helps to recall what sexual arousal is, since the two are related. Arousal is basically being stimulated, when someone is stimulated in a powerful way, they are aroused. This doesn't need to be sexual arousal, although sexual arousal is one type of arousal. You could say that there is 'intellectual' arousal or arousal from other types of stimulation.

When a person is aroused, he or she may find a wider range of events appealing [1] The state of arousal might lead a person to view a decision more positively than he or she would have in a less aroused state. So therefore arousal relates to inspiration, if one is inspired then they might also be more aroused.

How can inspiration relate to emotional processing? Arousal clearly relates, when someone is aroused, it influences their perception and determines if they are feeling strongly or weakly. If someone is aroused, then it is likely that they are feeling stronger emotions because they are more stimulated. But what if someone is inspired? Is someone going to be feeling stronger emotions if they are inspired? Can someone be inspired when they are feeling poorly?

Could someone be 'stimulated' or 'aroused' and not be experiencing strong emotions? Why would it matter if those emotions are 'inspiring' or not? Inspiration is related to imagination more than to stimulation. It could take only a little stimulation to get someone inspired because inspiration is something you make up or create in your mind. It takes a lot of stimulation to get someone aroused because arousal is more of a physical response and is less intellectual. It is as if the most obvious form of arousal is sexual arousal, because that is clearly biological and powerful.

Is arousal just 'stimulation'? If someone is stimulated, then they are likely to be aroused. Arousal implies a response so strong that it generates a physical response. Arousal involves the activation of the reticular activating system in the brain stem, the autonomic nervous system and the endocrine system, leading to increased heart rate and blood pressure and a condition of sensory alertness, mobility and readiness to respond. It should be obvious that a stronger emotional response will lead to a stronger physical response. The mind and body are linked, when someone has a reaction, they also move in a certain way to reflect the nature of that reaction (such as a facial expression, or a body expression or gesture), and this physical reaction is not always controlled. That example is one way of demonstrating the link between mind, body and arousal.

Arousal is a difficult concept to understand. It becomes more simple when someone thinks of sexual arousal. Sexual arousal is obvious - someone feels strongly in a sexual way. This makes the person more

---

1. Ariely, D; Loewenstein, G. (2006). "The heat of the moment: The effect of sexual arousal on sexual decision making.". *Journal of Behavioral Decision Making* 19 (2): 87–98.

alerted and possibly results in a faster reaction time because they are stimulated and 'aroused'. Non-sexual arousal works the same way only it is not sexual. It is non-sexual things or stimulation generating a physical response in the body. Imagination also can generate a physical response, which is interesting because it is as if imagination is something you are just making up.

This makes it more clear how emotion is processed - an emotional reaction causes various factors in your mind and body to interact with each other, producing a more complex reaction. Arousal, stimulation, imagination and various thoughts and ideas (which are in the same category as 'imagination' because they are made up by the mind) all interact.

Table 65.0

Chapter 66

Emotional Processing, Mental Representation, and How the Mind

Works

Various factors are going to impact the 'impact' of an emotion on someone. When an emotion is experienced, there are various ways that it could have been triggered (what caused the emotion to start), and, resultingly, there are various ways it can make a person feel.

The experience of emotion is more complicated than emotions just being the result of cognitive triggers. When someone thinks something as a cognitive unit (which is a 'unit' of thought), an emotion might be triggered or influenced.

The difficult question then is what types of thoughts (and experiences) trigger which emotions or emotional responses?

Thoughts that are of emotions are going to trigger those emotions. For instance if you think of something that makes you afraid then you might feel the emotion of fear. It is possible that thinking of something that is fearful makes you happy, however you would have to have that fearful object somehow linked to being happy instead of being fearful (or possibly be in a weird state or condition when you are thinking this resulting in non-normal, intuitive or logical thinking) in order for it to generate the emotion 'happy' instead of the emotion of 'fear'.

So, essentially, it is very complicated to figure out why someone feels the way they do, or why they are feeling one of the emotions that they are experiencing. Your mind has a whole network of associated thoughts, emotions, and feelings that might help trigger or inhibit other feelings and thoughts.

But this is more complicated that just things in your mind (cognitive 'units') being related to each other and triggering each other. Some responses are developed. Your mind or neurons need to be formed or developed over time in order for a certain response to be appropriate or natural.

That is just simple emotional development - for instance exposing yourself to happy feelings might make the person more happy. How could someone exposing themselves to happy feelings make the person more sad? If you think logically, the mind would develop more positive associations with everything it contains, all the representations and thoughts that it has. Why would someone going to happy events (experiencing more happy experiences) become more depressed over the long term? How is that logical?

Maybe for that person happy events make them sad because they formed a link in their mind (somehow) that happy things are actually sad ones. It seems weird that a person would interpret such events in a negative light when they really should be viewed as they are - positive experiences. However the mind is more complicated than that. Previous development could have caused the person to be so sad that a change is not possible, for instance.

Table 66.0

Chapter 67

Mental Representation and Cognitive Determinants of Emotion

How do emotions fluctuate and change? What principles, mental processes, and cognitive determinants govern feelings? The most obvious factor behind how emotion varies from individual to individual, from situation to situation, and from moment to moment; is appraisal theory. However, it is a more complicated question to ask how appraisals and mental processes affect changes in the nature of feeling and mind.

A process of appraisal can be considered the key to understanding that emotions differ for different individuals. Assuming a process of appraisal that mediates between events and emotions is the clue to understanding that a particular event evokes an emotion in one individual and not in another, or evokes an emotion at one moment, and no emotion, or a weaker or stronger one, at another moment. (This is because the evaluations (appraisals) (for example, someone steals your car and then you think 'that is bad that my got stolen, this is going to make me feel bad' and then you feel bad, the thought involved an appraisal of if the event was good or bad for you and if it was going to cause negative or positive feelings in you) that people make about events influence how they feel about those events). A process of appraisal also explains why an emotionally charged event elicits this particular emotion, and not another one, in this particular individual under these particular conditions.

The process of appraisal accounts for the fact that the arousal of an emotion depends upon the meaning of the event for the individual and explains why the emotion that is evoked often depends upon quite subtle aspects of that meaning. Arousal of emotions is determined by the interaction between events, the individual's conceptions or expectations as to what constitutes well-being for him or her and the individual's expectations that he or she will be able to deal or cope with the event and, if so, in what manner or how effectively.

However, all of someones thoughts are going to influence their feelings, not just their appraisals of events. People think things about the events that occur in their lives. They don't just ask if the event is good or bad, they form opinions of it, compare it to other events, analyze it, struggle with it, etc. Also, the sequence of events in someones life causes emotions to occur in a certain way as well, if one event follows another, it might influence the emotions felt for the previous or next event.

Also, a thought may have an emotion associated with it that you wouldn't expect or don't know about. If you think about it, with each thought, an emotion is going to be a result of the thought or would have helped bring up the thought. This is because thoughts are more complex that just the verbal thought - there is a lot of things the thought represents in your mind that also could be emotional triggers.

Why are appraisals such significant thoughts then? People must really care about how good or bad the events in their life are. Your assessment of how good or bad an event is is going to influence how good or bad the event actually is. That basically means that your attitude and thoughts about the event is going to influence feelings about the event. These thought processes are the most significant ones someone has about an event.

That makes sense - what else would someone think about something that just happened to them other than if it is good or bad for them anyway. They could think practical things about an event, but in the end it all really results if it is good or bad for them. People get emotional about if something is going to hurt them or help them, it seems.

All thoughts represent something larger in the mind and are more significant than they might appear by themselves. People have hopes, desires, and fears about each thought they think. Thoughts are also related.

One thought might bring up similar hopes and fears as another thought, therefore helping to trigger or inhibit the other thought.

But surely thoughts are related more than just emotionally. Emotionally thoughts are related because they bring up similar or related emotions. But thoughts are also related because they represent similar physical things or other thoughts and ideas. Desires are ideas and thoughts, and these might be triggered by similar thoughts. When someone sees a piece of art, the art could represent desires that they have (and therefore trigger thoughts).

A child might be afraid of an animal. Since animals are similar to humans, the emotional response of the child to the animal it is afraid of might be similar to being afraid of a human. Physical the animal might look somewhat like a human. Animals and humans are certainly more related in how they look than humans and physical objects. Animals and humans both have emotions, and animals think to a certain extent. My point is that thoughts and emotional reactions have things in common with other thoughts and objects. They all represent similar and related things in the mind (such as emotions like hope, desire, fear, and beliefs).

This complex network of interacting ideas, emotions, and representations is going to determine how the emotions of humans fluctuate. Emotions and thoughts are related to each other because they each represent ideas, other thoughts (such as beliefs or facts) or other emotions. A simpler way to say that would just be that one emotion, event, or stimulus triggers a complex reaction in the mind. It triggers an intellectual reaction whereby the person goes through all the things that that event represents to them. This can be other physical things, complex thoughts and ideas (such as beliefs or facts), or hopes and other emotions.

67.1 Unconscious (Implicit) Emotion Regulation

Implicit emotion regulation is how someone moderates and changes their emotions automatically, beneath their awareness. Goals and intentions are going to play a large role in how this process occurs because they are a large source of emotions and feelings. People form many intentions which they aren't aware of, and these intentions are going to influence their emotions and the potential thoughts they might have.

When someone feels better but they don't know why, or when someone thinks something but they don't know what motivated them to think it, then it was clearly from the unconscious (such as unconscious feelings, thoughts, intentions and goals) which caused them to want to think the thought and generate the new emotion.

What is the difference between an unconscious goal and an unconscious intention? It is clear what the difference between those two terms when referring to there conscious function is - a goal is a large objective, an intention however is something that you want or intend where you are thinking that you are trying to do something right then. You are trying to accomplish something - that what an intention is. You have the intent to do something. You are striving to do that thing.

A goal, however, you aren't necessarily trying to achieve in the present time. You can put a goal aside or lower its priority. An intention you usually wouldn't do that with. When someone forms an intention, they try to do it right away. So a goal is basically a more important intention. If you intend to do something, and it is important for you, then it becomes a goal because goals are longer term or just more important.

This distinction is important because goals and intentions can be unconscious. People make goals and intentions about things in their lives all of the time, consciously and unconsciously. However, there are two types of unconscious goals/intentions - one type is very subtle, and the other type is a larger more obvious type of goal or intention.

A subtle unconscious goal or intention might be something very insignificant emotionally. For instance you might not want someone to come closer to you, so emotionally you might freeze up. This is so subtle you probably wouldn't notice that it is occurring consciously. However what happened unconsciously was that you recognized that you didn't want this person to come near you, and you unconsciously regulated your emotions so you would be feeling less. You could say that the other person made you afraid and that caused the emotional freezing, or it could be that it was an unconscious intention of yours to block out the other person because you didn't like them or want them coming near you.

That is just one example of a subtle, unconscious emotional event. There are constantly emotional things going on beneath one's notice. All of those emotional processes are regulated unconsciously. People are much more capable of manipulating their emotions unconsciously than the are consciously because there is much more going on unconsciously than consciously.

Some other examples of unconscious goals or intentions are seeking pleasure, trying to feel any single or set of emotions, trying to increase, decrease, or maintain any single or set of feelings, or trying to achieve some thought you had at some other point - such as a conscious goal of some sort of success in your life or something like that.

67.2 Mental Representation

A symbol represents an idea, a process, or a physical entity. People can think with symbols just like they can think with thoughts. For instance, they can think of a symbol and the symbol would represent the larger more significant idea(s) that the symbol means. That is also how thoughts work as well. A thought might mean something simple, however it might represent or stand for something much more complex that your unconscious mind might understand better in some way (because the unconscious is also capable of understanding concepts differently from the conscious mind).

The important questions to consider are:

a. Why does the conscious mind understand things differently from the unconscious mind, and in what way is this understanding different?

b. A symbol can represent something more significant or complex than the symbol itself, however do you always know everything a symbol in your mind stands for?

c. If your unconscious understanding is different from your conscious understanding, then how can someone know exactly what their unconscious understanding is (since by nature and definition it is not as capable of being understood consciously)?

d. If humans have an unconscious understanding that is different from their conscious understanding, then what is the significance of that? Why does it matter that people can understanding something in more than one way?

e. The unconscious mind must understand the truth better of the significance of the world for you. For instance if you are insulted it might make you feel bad because unconsciously you understand that there was truth to the insult, however consciously you might think that the insult was insignificant.

f. This is why emotional processing occurs unconsciously - because you couldn't possibly understand the full implications of everything that occurs consciously.

g. So is the unconscious then simply 'the truth' of what is going on in your mind? Consciously you might understand anything, or have any type of interpretation of what is actually happening to you, however unconsciously you know what is going on because that is how you feel - your unconscious is going to make you feel a certain way and that is how your mind is responding to the situation (unconsciously not consciously)

h. This is a simple idea - feelings are processed unconsciously because if you tried to process them consciously you would just make up the result instead of responding in a natural way that shows the full significance of what is going on.

i. Unconsciously the world means something different to you then what your conscious interpretation of the world (or a stimulus) might be.

j. When someone thinks of a symbol, thought or an idea it might mean something much more significant unconsciously because your unconscious 'understands' the full implications.

k. The unconscious also understands the full implications of everything that occurs in your life, this is why emotional processes occur unconsciously. Your conscious mind is simply not complex enough to comprehend the full implications of everything that is going on.

l. Therefore 'mental representation' really means 'things are represented to your unconscious mind differently from your conscious one'. You understand one simple thing (such as a thought, idea or symbol), and unconsciously it means something else or something more significant.

m. Also, the entire world and all of your emotional processing is represented differently to your unconscious mind, not just one single item (a thought, idea, etc.)

Table 67.0

Chapter 68

How the Mind Works, Principles of Emotion, and Mental States

The mind works primarily through various emotional principles - for instance striving for pleasure is a natural emotional process that people have little control over, and this process is going to be influenced by stimuli and cognition. Striving for stimuli or pleasure is one of the more important principles of emotion since clearly emotion is going to fluctuate and be influenced by stimulation, which often (and hopefully) takes the emotional form of 'pleasure'.

What exactly is a principle of emotion then, or, if emotion is so important to a mental state, what is a normal mental state? What happens differently to someones mind when they are under stress then when they aren't? What is the difference between a mental state and a mood? If someone is happy - that is a mood, if someone's mind is more or less competent, conscious or capable of performing then that is more of a mental state. Meditation is like a mental state - in that state the mind is doing certain specific things (such as being calm in a way that is induced by certain thoughts or feelings). A mood, however, is just your general way of feeling (which you can feel for a long period of time and doesn't necessarily impact your performance). Someone can be in a mental state to do work, or be in one of the two most obvious mental states - conscious or not conscious.

My saying that doing work is a mental state is theoretical. It depends on how someone defines the term 'mental state'. There could be a endless number of mental states, or someone could define mental states to be states just related to doing work. Maybe for one job they have their own defined mental states where they need to be in a certain mental zone or whatever in order to perform a certain task.

It looks like this is much more complicated than it seems. If you think about it, there are going to be a lot of factors that influence someones mental state. There are ways of going into a meditative mental state, people can prepare their minds to go to work, to go to sleep, etc. Everyone knows they are in different states at different times, however it would be interesting to know what exactly is going on. For instance, in each of these states what is the person focused on, what are they capable of doing, how are they feeling, what are they thinking about (consciously and unconsciously), how conscious are they and what are they paying attention to.

Table 68.0

Chapter 69

Unconscious Emotion Regulation and its Determinant in Humans:

Cognition

The proper term for 'unconscious' emotion regulation is actually 'implicit' emotion regulation. Emotion regulation is typically considered to be more conscious and deliberative, however I think that the interesting and complex aspects of emotion regulation are the unconscious ones. If you think about it, people don't know all the complex ways in which their emotions change. All of the emotional changes that people experience occur at the unconscious level because emotion is so subtle and complex - people basically have no idea what is happening to them emotionally. Knowing you are experiencing one emotion is much different from understanding exactly what is going on.

Many different factors influence someones experience of emotion. The biggest factor in the experience of emotion is probably the strength of the emotions occurring. I was thinking that there would many more factors to discuss (since I am talking about emotion and is obviously a significant psychological phenomenon) but I guess there isn't. There should be a lot of factors that impact how emotion is felt and how it changes.

Since strength seems to be the only significant factor of emotional processing to discuss I will start there. It appears to me that emotion is triggered often and starts and stops frequently. Humans have a whole set of cognitive thoughts or unconscious mental decisions that start and stop emotion. For instance when they see something significant their mind has this stimulus categorized and responds to it in a way that has been programmed in - either from at birth or by previous emotional development.

So one thing a person might respond to is just seeing another person. That stimulus would trigger a complex emotional response, immediately upon seeing the other person the cognitive unit of 'compare myself with this person' or 'analyze this person' is engaged. The things the other person represents in your mind, the way the other person is emotionally significant, what the other persons current attitude and manner is, are all things that your mind tries to think about and picks up on initially as a pre-programmed response.

These 'pre-programmed' responses occur because there is a natural, fast, and complex way humans interpret emotional information. The significant emotional dispositions of other people (who they are), whatever it is they are emotionally communicating at the time (what they are projecting), and how your mind is prepared to accept, look at, and interpret that information are the factors that determine these pre-programmed emotional responses.

The automatic emotional response occurs instantly and continues to give feedback. People then start to think on their own after the initial response and their thoughts influence the emotions that are felt and (obviously) their thought process and the ideas that they have about the other person. I just used people meeting other people as an example of strong, instantaneous emotional decisions/responses, however whenever your mind processes any object it makes calculations about that object that come from pre-programmed cognitive structures.

Attention can lead to complex thought. When someone experiences an emotion their attention changes based off of that emotion. The emotion triggers a set of thoughts. The emotion triggers cognitive units of thought, and this is going to impact someones attention because the thoughts (or cognitive units, whatever you want to call them) are associated with certain emotions.

Table 69.0

Chapter 70

Emotion and Attention

How does emotion influence attention? If you think about it, humans probably have a complicated mix of emotions occurring all of the time, and this emotional make-up is somehow going to impact their attention. If someone is in a state of pure pleasure, then they probably aren't going to be paying as much attention to their environment then if they are in a normal or negative state. That I think is because there is no reason for the person to pay attention to their environment because they are satisfied within their own minds.

The sensory input that a person is receiving is going to be related to their emotional state as well. People can be in touch with their senses, with their thoughts, or be focused on their external environment. People often look to sensory stimulation in order to relax themselves - such as taking a bath or eating food. My guess would be that this changes their focus from their own internal thinking to their environment or their senses. There is a complicated mix of emotions, senses, and thoughts occurring all of the time.

So an important question is if someone can pay more attention to sensations if they wanted to. There is going to be some sort of complicated sequence of attention occurring, a person might naturally focus on one thing more and then switch to something else without awareness of themselves doing that.

Also, which emotions are triggered by which sensations? Some people buy scented candles in order to induce an emotional response, but are they aware that a much more complicated psychological response could be being created that they aren't aware of? If you think about it, someones entire network of sensations, thoughts and feelings could be manipulated by sensory feelings.

Someones thoughts are going to impact how much attention they are paying, and what they are paying more attention to. If you think about it, if you spend your time thinking about one thing, then your attention is going to be changed significantly. You might pay more attention to the thing you were just thinking about (obviously), but there might be other ways your attention could change.

People know that they can go into different moods for different things (such as being in the 'mood' to go shopping or the 'mood' to have a romantic encounter), but the question is, what triggers these moods? It isn't as if people randomly start to want to experience different things in life and therefore go into a different mood (or you could call it a mode). Your thoughts and thinking probably plays a large role in what you are feelings and therefore the moods you might go into.

Think about it this way - in each mood or mode you go into, your attention is probably focused more on whatever the mood is for - i.e. the mood you are in is a happy one, so you want to go out and have a picnic, or the mood you are in is a sad one, so you want to chill out. You want those things, so you begin to focus on them more, your attention changes. When people pay attention, there isn't just one thing they are focused on, their is everything in life they can focus on. All of the things that person who is paying attention can pay attention to, or usually pays attention to, are going to be things which are going to be factors in how there attention is functioning.

For instance, if a person cares about such and such things, and spends a lot of time thinking about those things, then those things are probably going to be a permanent part of their attention. When that person is in a mood for one thing, the other things they care about are also going to impact how their attention is behaving. For instance when a person is relaxing, the high-stress elements in their life are going to play a role in how their attention is even during the time when they are relaxed. You aren't ever completely in one state - so when someone is in a relaxed state, how they are when they are in a high stress state, and things they pay attention when they are in that other state, is going to have an impact on what they are like when they are in the relaxed state. You might pay attention to some things that you think you only care about when you are stressed when you are relaxed, and this is probably because all of your emotional states are mixed. You might also experience emotions and have a similar or associated experience during the time when you are relaxed as when you are stressed, because these two different states are related and connected to each other.

Humans have many different emotional states, or you could call them moods, ways of behaving, ways of thinking, ways of feeling, etc. All the different ways that people can feel and think are obviously going to be connected to one another. A simple way to think about it would just be to say that if you are stressed then you might want to relax later on, however that is missing the complicated emotional subtlety involved. There are emotional states, ways and levels of feeling, ways and levels of thinking, and these different things are going to play a role when you are relaxing or whatever it is you are doing. Your feelings, behavior and thoughts are going to be under the influence of more subtle tones of feeling and thought that are related to the previous things you have done and your other emotional states when you are doing other things.

I am just using the different things people do so I can describe what a different emotional state is like. Different emotional states are obvious if you consider the two most extreme examples - a high stress state and a relaxed state. However there must be many many more ways of feeling that people can experience. For instance people probably experience many feelings, sets of feelings, modes, moods, etc during an activity. I am suggesting that people have different ways of 'being' whereby their feelings and thoughts are influenced by their mood, their emotional state, whatever you want to call it.

My theory is that for a certain period of time people are influenced by certain ways of being. So say someone is doing any activity - during this activity they might change modes and for a few seconds or a few minutes feel more like the activity is like another activity that they have done. Or maybe they just adopt a different way of feeling for that activity that they are doing (feel differently about it in some way).

So there are many different layers of feeling, ways of feeling, modes people can go into where they feel differently for a certain period of time, or ways in which their thinking and feeling interact to help them have a unique experience that is dynamic, shifting, deep and complex.

Emotion is influenced by thoughts, moods, experience, previous activities, your environment, your physical condition - and there a levels of emotion and thought that make this experience much more complex. When one can adopt a set of feelings for one activity for a few seconds or minutes during a not related activity, it makes you wonder just how complex emotional and intellectual experience is.

Table 70.0

Chapter 71

Emotion and Cognition: The Scope and Limits of its Analysis

How much can be said about the relationship between emotion and cognition? For the most part, people know how their thoughts influence their feelings. There are other cognitive processes such as attention and awareness of feeling - which fluctuate constantly and influence mental behavior significantly. However people don't need to know which activities, thoughts, or emotions change their attention or focus in such and such a way. For sure, there are significant emotional phenomena occurring constantly through various activities, but a fine-grained analysis of such events isn't necessary or helpful.

The principles by which emotion functions are fairly obvious and already part of the natural understanding that humans have. When an emotion gets large, one tries to reframe their thought(s) so that they place less emphasis on whatever it was they were overvaluing. Emotions get out of hand or large frequently, and when this occurs people have a natural way of making them small or managing them.

Of course humans have a natural way of managing their emotions, even the animals we evolved from have emotions. I don't think animals have to manage their emotions, they don't have complex cognition like humans do. Their emotions still might be considered to be fairly complex, however.

A dog might get out of control, in which case he/she might need to be calmed down. The basic principles by which emotion functions apply to animals as well as humans, because animals experience basic emotions in a way similar to humans.

Animals get happy, sad, angry, afraid, surprised etc. Those basic emotions occur in both humans and animals.

There are certain things a theory of emotion should explain. However there are only a few basic principles that govern how emotion functions. Such as the fact that large emotion needs to decrease after a period of time, otherwise your system would be overloaded.

However, there can't be that many things described in any theory of emotion, because how emotion functions is very simple. Emotions vary in intensity all of the time, and that is pretty much all that is going on.

Table 71.0

Chapter 72

Self-Regulation: A Definition and Introduction

What is self-regulation? Which mental processes compose it, and how do those processes work together? Self-regulation is the conscious and nonconscious processes by which people regulate their thoughts, emotions, attention, behavior, and impulses. People generate thoughts, feelings and actions and adapt those to the attainment of personal goals. Behavioral self-regulation invovles self- observing and strategically adjusting performance processes, such as one's method of learning, whereas environmental self-regulation refers to observing and adjecting environmental conditions or outcomes. Covert self regulation involves monitoring and adjusting cognitive and affective states, such as imagery for remembering or relaxing. Someones performance and regulation is going to be changed by their goals, motivations, and decisions, People self-regulate their own functioning in order to achieve goals or change how they are thinking.

Someones actions and mental processes depend on one's beliefs and motives. Self -regulation is cyclical - that is, feedback (information, responses) from prior actions and performances changes the adjustments made during current efforts. Adjustments are necessary because personal, behavioral, and environmental factors are constantly changing during the course of learning and performance. Someones performances are constantly being changed by their attention and actions. Forethought is the phase that precedes efforts to act and sets the stage for a performance. A person self-reflects on performances afterwards, and this reflection influences their responses.

Forethought Phase

In the forethought phase people engage in a) task analysis and b) self-motivational beliefs. Task analysis involves the setting of goals and strategic planning. Self motivational beliefs involves self- efficacy, outcome expectations, intrinsic interest/value, and goal orientation.

Performance Phase

In the performance phase people perform self-control processes and self- observation strategies. Self- control involves self-instruction (various verbalizations), imagery (forming mental pictures), attention focusing and task strategies (which assist learning and performance by reducing a task to its essential parts and organizing the parts meaningfully. For example, when students listen to a history lecture, they might identify a limited number of key points and record them chronologically in brief sentences. People do those things while learning (say in education), and in non- educational settings.

Also as part of someone's performance they do self-observation. This refers to a person's tracking of specific aspects of their own performance, the conditions that surround it, and the effects that it produces. You can set goals in forethought about how you are going to do self- observation.

Self-Reflection Phase

Bandura (1986)[1] has identified two self-reflected processes that are closely associated with self- observation: self- judgment and self-reactions. Self-judgment involves self-evaluating one's performance and attributing casual significance to the results. Self-evaluation refers to comparing self-monitored information with a standard or goal, such as a sprinter judging practice runs according to his or her best previous effort. Previous performance or self-criteria involves comparisons of current performance with earlier levels of one's behavior, such as a baseline or the previous performance.

---

1. Bandura, A. (1986). *Social Foundations of Thought and Action.* Englewood Cliffs, NJ: Prentice-Hall.

People also make casual attributions about the results of their evaluations - such as whether poor performance is due to one's limited ability or to insufficient effort. Self-satisfaction involves perceptions of satisfaction or dissatisfaction and associated affect regarding one's performance, which is important because people pursue courses of action that result in satisfaction and positive affect, and avoid those courses that produce dissatisfaction and negative affect, such as anxiety.

Adaptive or defensive inferences are conclusions about how one needs to alter his or her self-regulatory approach during subsequent efforts to learn or perform. Adaptive inferences are important because they direct people to new and potentially better forms of performance self-regulation, such as by shifting the goals hierarchically or choosing a more effective strategy (Zimmerman + Martinez-Pons, 1992)[2] In contrast, defensive inferences serve primarily to protect the person from future dissatisfaction and aversive affect, but unfortunately they also undermine successful adaptation. These defensive self-reactions include helplessness, procrastination, task avoidance, cognitive disengagement, and apathy. Garcia and Pintrich (1994)[3] have referred to such defensive reactions as self-handicapping strategies, because, despite their intended protectiveness, they ultimately limit personal growth.

An Introduction

I said in the beginning of this chapter that "Self- regulation is the conscious and nonconscious processes by which people regulate their thoughts, emotions, attention, behavior, and impulses. People generate thoughts, feelings and actions and adapt those to the attainment of personal goals." But what is meant by terms such as self-regulation, self-control, self- awareness, and self-monitoring? The difficult thing to figure out I would think would be how much of self- regulation or what is going on mentally is conscious or not conscious. When someone is doing any action, how much of the control they are employing is conscious and how much of it is unconscious? That is a very complicated question. To a certain extent it is like you are unconsciously saying to yourself various things while you are doing something, but you also might be saying things to yourself consciously at the same time that also helps direct your behavior.

Other important questions are - how does a persons goals and motivations influence their feelings, behavior, self-control and actions? How much of feeling, impulses and impulse control, motivation and goal creating is conscious or unconscious? If you think about it, your goals, motivations, and the natural impulses that result from your emotions (which are to a large extent determined by your goals and motivations) are going to be fluctuating and changing all of the time.

People can alter the goals they have, however there is going to be an incredibly complex set of unconscious goals that one is not aware of. These goals create multiple motivations as well as multiple concerns. Also, doing well at approaching an incentive is not quite the same experience as doing well at avoiding a threat. If you think about it, your emotions are going to be different if you achieve something you are striving for then if you are threatened and respond because you are under pressure. It makes sense that approach is going to have such positive affects as elation, eagerness and excitement, and such negative affects as frusturation, anger and sadness. (Carver, 2004[4]; Carver + Harmon-Jones, 2009[5]). Avoidance involves such positive affects as relief and contentment (when someone avoids a threat, they are relieved and content) and such negative affects as fear, guilt and anxiety.

Goals can be changed by how motivated someone is to have that goal. Some goals can be brought into conscious awareness at various times for various reasons. Simon (1967)[6] reasoned that emotions are calls

2.   Barry J. Zimmerman, and Manuel Martinez-Pons. (1992). Perceptions of efficacy and strategy use in the self-regulation of learning. In D. H. Schunk + J. L. Meece (Eds.) *Student Perceptions in the Classroom: Causes and Consequences* (pp. 185-207). Hillsdale, NJ: Earlbaum.
3.   Garcia, T. + Pintrich, P.R. (1994). Regulating motivation and cognition in the classroom: the role of self-schemas and self-regulatory strategies. In D.H. Schunk and B.J. Zimmerman (Eds.), *Self-Regulation on Learning and Performance: Issues and Applications* (pp.132-157), NJ, Hillsdale, Lawrence Erlbaum Associates.
4.   Carver, C. S. (2004). Negative affects deriving from the behavioral approach system. *Emotion, 4,* 3-22.
5.   Carver, C. S., + Harmon-Jones, E. (2009). Anger is an approach-related affect: Evidence and implications. *Psychological Bulletin, 135,* 183-204.

for reprioritization: that emotion regarding a goal that is out of awareness eventually induces people to give that goal a higher priority. The stronger the emotion, the stronger the claim for higher priority. Affect pulls the out-of-awareness into awareness.

Simon's analysis applies readily to negative feelings, such as anxiety and frustration. If you promised your spouse you would go to the post office today and you've been too busy, the creeping of the clock toward closing time can cause an increase in frustration or anxiety (or both). The stronger the affect, the more likely the goal it concerns will rise in priority until it comes into awareness and becomes the reference for behavior.

Therefore, it makes sense that the main goal you have and you know you have can reliquish its place. You are constantly shifting the goals you have, you simply might not be aware that you are doing this. If you think about it, people unconsciously might create many goals that they don't think about because they don't understand that they are motivated to do those things. They simply don't know that they are trying to reach certain objectives clearly. Take for instance sexual goals - people probably do many things to enhance sexual feelings without being aware that that is the motivation behind other goals they are consciously striving to achieve.

Emotionally people have many desires - all of these emotions are going to create and alter the various goals that people have (conscious and unconscious). If you think about that further, on a moment-by-moment basis your emotions are going to be altered continuously by various goals - your emotions are going to be creating goals, objectives and whatnot. For instance, even with simple activities you may have an emotional goal that you aren't aware of. Say you are opening a door - maybe a previous event caused you to slow down when opening the door and going into the next area because your motivation was decreased so you weren't as excited about moving onto the next activity in your life.

A Review

So before someone does anything, their previous thoughts and emotions are going to determine how they perform during the action/activity. They have many goals that they created unconsciously and consciously that determined to some extent the emotions they are feeling, and they thought many things which (in combination with their emotions) helps determine how they are thinking. During the action conscious verbalizations and mental imagery help assist performance, and reflection of the performance afterwards helps to determine a persons response.

Further Thoughts

The process of self-regulation is not completely understood, nor do I think it ever will be, because it is basically asking the question of how exactly does the mental processes behind thinking and feeling work. When 'mental imagery' is used, how exactly does that work? Which associated images come up with each image you bring up for a specific purpose? When people monitor their affective state, how much does that enhance what they are feeling or change what they are feeling? When someone uses a strategy such as a verbalization to help learning, why does that work exactly the way it does?

There seems to be a large unconscious factor that is too complicated to be understood. The unconscious is so complicated, as it has many factors that are interacting with each other all of the time. When those factors mentioned in the previous paragraph are brought up (mental images, monitoring, cognitive strategies), along with the natural unconscious emotion and motivation that occurs always with humans, it becomes obvious that there is no telling what could be influencing your thinking and feeling (on a detailed, moment to moment basis and even just considering the obvious factors).

Table 72.0

---

6. Simon, H. A. (1967). Motivational and emotional controls of cognition. *Psychology Review, 74,* 29-39.

Chapter 73

Attention and Thought Control

How does the attention process work? Do people who are anxious pay more attention to threatening things in their environment than people who aren't anxious? Do people who are depressed have less motivation and a slower reaction time or do they pay more attention to negative stimuli than positive? There is going to be emotional biases with mental illnesses or each time someone pays attention to something - if someone is experiencing an emotion, than that emotion is going to influence their attention in a certain way. For instance, if someone is experiencing the emotion of 'guilt' then clearly if they see something they feel guilty about they are going to pay attention to it differently (as they would associate and compare the guilt they are feeling with the guilt related to the object they are looking at).

Attention also relates to the thoughts someone experiences - if someone is paying attention to their own thoughts, then they might do things to control their thoughts. Some thoughts are voluntary and people direct or create them consciously, and some are more unconscious and instinctual - thoughts that they have less control over. Wells and Morrison (1994) [1] investigated dimensions of naturally occurring worry and intrusive thoughts in 30 normal subjects. They were asked to keep a diary and record their worries and intrusive thoughts, and they were also asked to rate each thought on the following dimensions:

   i. Degree of verbal thought/imagery involved

  ii. Intrusiveness

 iii. How realistic the thought was

  iv. How involuntary the thought was

   v. How controllable it was

  vi. How dismissable it was

 vii. How much the thought grabbed attention

viii. Degree of distress associated with the thought

  ix. Intensity of compulsion to act on the thought

   x. Degree of resistance to the thought

  xi. Degree of success in controlling the thought

Wells and Davies (1994)[2] have attempted to distinguish types of thought control strategy. They interviewed patients with a range of anxiety disorders to determine the types of strategy used to control unpleasant and/or unwanted thoughts. Seven types of strategy emerged from the pilot interviews: cognitive and behavioral distraction; punishment; distancing; re- appraisal; mood changing activites; exposure to the thought; worry about more trivial things. Sometimes people might think that their thoughts are likely to come true, or that their worries are not controllable. "Cognitive and behavioral distraction" probably means distraction by your own internal thinking or distraction by you doing something - such as behaving in a certain way. "Punishment" would mean punishing yourself for having a thought you didn't want, distancing would mean somehow separating yourself from the thought, and re- appraisal would mean thinking of the thought differently or assessing that thought in a different way.

---

1. Wells, A., + Morrison, T. (1994) Qualitative dimensions of normal worry and normal intrusive thoughts" A comparative study. *Behavior Research and therapy.*

2. Wells, A., + Davies, M. (1994) A questionaire for assessing thought control strategies: Development and preliminary validation.

Multiple dimentions of emotional control strategy have been found in other studies. For example Mayer et al. (1991) [3] identified three dimenisons of emotion management distinct from dimensions of mood, labelled "suppression" (including distraction), "thoughts of actions" and "denial".

We can to some extent distinguish worry, intrusive thoughts and negative automatic thoughts on criteria such as intensity, unpleasantness, realism, intrusivenss and controllability, but those things are hard to define. How does someone know when the thought they have is 'intense' or when they thought they have is clear and realistic? If the thought is realistic is it going to be clear? I would think that the more realistic the thought is - tied in with reality - the more clear it would be because it is linked to real information. If you are fantasizing your thoughts are more like in a cloud (for example a dream state). It is also hard to tell if a thought is unpleasant, how is someone supposed to know how positive emotionally one single thought is? That seems too hard to measure. Someone might know how easy it is to control their thoughts or how pleasant their thoughts are for a certain period of time, but not every single thought they experience, or even a single reoccurring thought.

Two categories of appraisal are important in determining emotional experience and influencing subsequent coping efforts: primary and secondary appraisal. Primary appraisal is the process of evaluating the personal meaning and significance for well-being of events, which may be irrelevant, benign-positive or stressful. Stress appraisals may be further subdivided into harm/loss, where the person has sustained physical or psychological damage; threat, where harm/loss is anticipated; and challenge, where successful coping may lead to gains. Secondary appraisal is concerned with what can be done to deal with a situation, and includes reviewing the range of coping options available and their likely success in the situation at hand. A third form of appraisal delineated by Lazarus and Folkman (1984)[4] is reappraisal, which refers to the changes in appraisal which follow as the event unfolds and new information is acquired, including feedback on the success of attempts to cope.

There are a few more things to consider related to appraisals. How does considering the personal meaning of an event change the feeling involved? How does it change your thinking, and subsequently, what you are paying attention to? How does your history or beliefs change how you make that appraisal? Do you make it with a bias or a unique significance to yourself? Whenever someone makes an assessment, that assessment is unique to themself. When someone makes a secondary appraisal, how does that impact their attention different from their primary appraisal? You first assess a situation (primary appraisal), and then you assess what can be done about it (secondary appraisal), however how do those two actions influence your attention and your thinking? Are the primary appraisal and the secondary appraisals separated out by time or by other thoughts (intrusive or voluntary)?

What types of thoughts do you have in between the first appraisal process and the second one? What occurres with your levels of feeling during this process? - i.e., what happens to you emotionally after a strong appraisal or a strong thought? Does that influence your subsequent thoughts and appraisals? How is your attention to external stimuli fluctuating during this process? What sequence does your significant thoughts/appraisals/emotions occur in, and how does that impact your attention? Do you focus on your emotions or your own thoughts when you pause to consider what happened after you had a significant thought or a significant stimulus input (experience).

It appears that anxiety is only positively associated with on-task effort under rather special circumstances, where there is a strong and immediate perceived threat, or, perhaps, where task performance is appriased as instrumental in effecting avoidance or escape (see Eysenck, 1982)[5] That probably means that the decreased performance from anxiety in most other circumstances is a result of people being distracted by the anxiety i.e., scanning their environment for threats or just being distracted by the pain.

Negative mood, which indicates that the environment poses a problem and might be a source of potential

3. Mayer, J. D Salovey, P., Gomberg-Kaufman, S., + Blainey, K (1991). A broader conception of mood experience. *Journal of Personality and Social Psychology, 60,* 100-111.
4. Lazarus, R.s>, + Folkman, S. (1984). *Stress, appraisal and coping.* New York: Springer.
5. Eysenck, M.W. (1982). *Attention and arousal: Cognition and performance.* New York: Springer.

dangers, motivates people to change their situation. Negative mood is then thought to be associated with a systematic elaboration of information and greater attention to details. Bodenhausen and colleagues (1994)[6], investigating the impact of negative affect of social judgment, showed that induced sadness promotes the use of an analytic, detail-oriented mode of processing, whereas anger induction leads participants to process information on a shallow or automatic mode. If sadness (negative valence, lower arousal) triggered a type of processing identical to that fostered by the negative mood usually induced, anger (negative valence, higher arousal) fostered the hueristic or global mode of processing commonly associated with positive mood states (e.g., happiness or joy). This last result suggests that mood states of opposite valence may have similar effects as they share the same level of arousal (like happiness and anger). Likewise, it has been suggested that motivational-related approach and avoidance behaviors are independent of valence, leading to evidence that both happiness and anger moods are approach oriented, whereas serenity and sadness are avoidance oriented (when someone is depressed they avoid).

A sad mood experienced at our own wedding or birthday party may result in attempts to improve the mood, thus triggering systematic processessing in order to understand why we are sad in a situation that should normally make us happy. The same motivations are less likely to be aroused when the sad mood is experienced in situations where sadness is socially expected (e.g., at a funeral). According to Martin's model (2001)[7] people not ask merely: "How do I feel about it?" They ask "What does it mean that I am feeling this way in this context?" In other words, people evaluate the targets by taking into consideration both their mood and some features of situation and doing this configurally. Moods are processed in parallel with contextual information in such a way that the meaning of the mood influences and is influenced by the meaning of other information. The meaning of a mood experience can change in different context, and therefore the evaluative and motivational implications of mood are mutable.

To sum up, the informational value of mood lies not so much in the moods themselves as in the interaction between mood and context. Moods provide input for evaluative, decisional and inference-making processes, and these processes determine the effects that one's mood will have on one's evaluations, motivations, and behaviors. This course of reasoning, known as the *context- dependent effect of mood*, implies that the influence of mood on one's evaluations, motivations, and behaviors depends on the interaction of mood and the situational conditions.

In accordance with the *context-dependent effect of mood*, one's mood is not synonymous with one's evaluation. Whether a positive or negative mood leads to a favorable or unfavorable evaluation depends on the meaning of one's mood in that context. The question about the meaning of one's mood in different contexts is therefore a crucial one. In order to answer it, the mood as input model relies on the role- fulfillment process (Martin, 2001), also known as the "What would I feel if...?" process. This process can be characterized broadly as follows: when people make evaluations, they act as if they were asking themselves the question "What would I feel if...?: (For example, "what would I feel if the horror movie I just saw was a good horror movie?"). An evaluation is rendered subjectively when the person compares his/her current moods with the expected feelings. Favorable evaluations arise to the extent to which the person's moods (positive or negative) are congruent with what would be expected if the target had fulfilled a positive role (i.e., if this was a good thing I would feel good, I feel good, so I think this positive thing about it). Unfavorable evaluations, in contrast, arise to the extent to which the person's moods are incongruent with what would be expected if the target had fulfilled a negative role (i.e., if this party was bad, it would make me feel bad, however I feel good).

When people make evaluations, they are thinking more about what is going on then when they don't make evaluations. That is why negative mood enhances attention to detail - because it puts you in the state where you are questioning why the event or environment you are in is making you feel bad. Asking how you

---

6. Bodenhausen, G,V., Shappard, L. A., + Kramer, G. P. (1994). Negative affect and social judgment: The differential impact of anger and sadness. *European Journal of Social Psychology*, 24, 45-62.

7. Martin, L.L.(2001). Mood as input: A configural view of mood effect. In J. P. Forgast (Ed.) *Feeling and thinking: The role of affect in social cognition* (pp.135-157). New York: Cambridge University Press.

might feel if something is felt a certain way is a good way of analyzing the situation. If you think about it, asking how something makes you feel is important - people probably constantly evaluate the events they experience for value or what they got from them. Your mood is going to help you to evaluate those things because those events caused you to have that mood. The mood provides the information of what that event or stimulus does to you - how it makes you feel. If people didn't evaluate how an event or stimulus makes them feel, then they wouldn't really be analyzing that input any further than they normally would.

You basically can be put into a state where you are thinking about what the event or stimulus you are evaluating is like. This state is when you are questioning what the feelings the event made in you are like or what you think about the event. It is interesting that someone can simply not think about those things if they wanted. On the other hand, it seems natural for people who experience negative emotions to think more deeply about the source of those emotions. I guess the trouble that the negative emotions causes them forces one to think more deeply.

Table 73.0

Chapter 74

How can someone benefit from an understanding of psychology?

What psychological information could someone benefit by? How does self-help or therapy work? Those two questions are similar because through many self-help or therapy exercises someone gains a greater understanding of psychology. Therapy and psychology can help someone because they reflect more on their thoughts and their emotions and this helps to change them. There isn't any advanced psychology in non-civilized populations (at least I don't think since they don't have any education system), however they also don't have the same mental health problems.

But psychological information can be used for self-improvement as well. I should say that I am not a licensed psychologist, however I have a lot of knowledge and experience related to this. Clearly people learn from thinking about their emotions. Therapy or self-help is a focus on things you find important, like your mental condition. You could say that meditation works the same way - when you focus on yourself you can benefit.

Attitudes can take a long time to change. Emotion is complicated and dynamic. If you think about it, so is experience. But an attitude is simple - it is an attitude, everyone understands what an attitude is. It is a display of some bias or opinion about something. You have an attitude about something - you are displaying how you feel about that thing. You feel strongly about something, that is an attitude.

So it would seem to me that things can go wrong mentally, resulting in a mental problem, if the feelings you have toward certain things are too large. You could say that the person has an 'attitude problem'. But attitudes are simple. How the mind functions is much more complex. But people don't care about how the mind functions, they only care about things that are important to them like attitudes.

It is like when someone has a psychological problem, their attitude is too large. This large attitude causes the emotions that the person is experiencing to go out of balance. Emotions need to work properly, if you are feeling too strongly about one thing this could disrupt how you feel in general.

So the important question is - how could an understanding of psychology possibly decrease a strong attitude? That doesn't seem to make any sense, it would seem like the only way to decrease an attitude would be to show the person the opposite attitude, which isn't really that deep an understanding of psychology, it is just a basic simple idea.

So then you could really call anyone that understands that 'exposure to the proper influence over time decreases dangerous attitudes and feelings' is a psychologist.

Is psychology really that simple though? I know that there are lots of subtleties, but what are these subtleties about? People can be nice or mean in the wrong way. Depending on the circumstances, there are many different ways that someone can act. Each different way of acting socially could be analyzed and the person could work on that.

It seems simple when I say it that way, but that is basically what this is about. You go through an experience of practicing exposure to the proper behavior. You need to also consider the reason the person developed the strong attitude in the first place as well, however. The person probably wants that attitude to be strong, that is why he or she developed it in the first place, you need to consider that the person doesn't want to change and likes being violent.

I am not suggesting that everyone with a mental condition is violent. Maybe they are the opposite, it is just more clear when I use violence as the example.

That is why I said before that the emotions need to be properly balanced - because something like someone getting too violent can throw how they feel out of function.

But surely there is an aspect of self-improvement that an understanding of psychology can give you. It might help you understand emotion better. The question then is, couldn't someone get an understanding of emotion naturally or by doing practically any type of other work?

By studying psychology you make your natural understanding of psychology more conscious. For instance you might notice to yourself certain points of observation when you are in the real world observing how emotion functions. You might be able to describe with words better the nature of emotion or an emotional response instead of just simply having a feeling for it.

Table 74.0

Chapter 75

Some Points on Emotion Theory

- There are two types of observations in emotion theory, one type is general common observations (such as sex is good for someones emotional health) and the other type is functional observations (when an emotion stops at one second and another one takes its place, what is happening there, what are the emotions, why do they stop and start, etc (for example, if someone thinks a happy thought it might stop the negative thought completely) also, what are the degrees to which the emotion or thought is felt, is it completely gone etc.

- Emotions stop and start all the time, this stopping and starting might occur as sudden transitions or slow transitions, one emotion gradually fading into the other. That is not a complete explanation for how emotion functions, however. Humans would probably have several emotions occurring at one time, each emotion interacting with one or more other emotions and potentially causing them to stop, start, fade or increase.

- For instance, the emotions hate, love, painful emotions, sexual emotions, hopeful emotions, and humorous emotions are probably all constantly interacting with each other and being felt to some degree all the time. Those are only a few of the emotions/feelings that are probably felt a lot everyday.

- There are going to be observable patterns that occur with those emotions, for instance pleasure might relieve pain and make painful feeling go away.

- Life is intense and ongoing, so therefore intense emotion is probably maintained in humans all the time. These emotions might stop and start, someone could go from brief periods of intensity to periods of low intensity, but the point is there is that intensity that is felt and the continuous flow of emotional processing is ongoing.

- There are different emotional states that can change your outlook on life or how you might respond to a situation. Fear, anger, kindness and admiration are all emotional states that change how you might respond to events. You can also be in a state of readiness for certain emotions, you could be prepared to experience pain or pleasure or be in one of those states.

- Emotions are experienced consciously and unconsciously, the extent to which someone clearly feels an emotion is the extent to which it is conscious. If an emotion is being experienced but isn't under the awareness of the person experiencing it, by definition it is mostly an unconscious emotion because they are not conscious of it. Someone can experience a large emotion but that doesn't necessarily mean that the emotion is going to be completely under the awareness of the person experiencing it. They might describe the emotion as feeling like it is very large, but they might not be in touch with it (making it mostly unconscious). It is in this world of "seemingly larger emotions" that emotional processing takes place. Unconsciously there are many more emotions experienced than you are completely aware of that are being experienced. Therefor it is there, in the unconscious mind, that emotions interact in great depth and complexity, barely being felt consciously at times and with the person possibly only slightly aware that something emotional might be going on (unconsciously).

- Emotion is experienced differently for each person. An emotion evokes a certain emotional response in a person because that person is who they are, however we all share the same world and there are going to be significant psychological things in it that are generally considered to be significant by most people, such as death or love. Any individual has peculiarities and specifics about what might trigger a large emotional response, it wouldn't necessarily just be something that they "like a lot" but mostly things they consciously or unconsciously find to be significant.

- When emotion can stop and start, and there can be periods of intensity and low-intensity, it makes one wonder just how many different emotional states there are. For every mood in a social situation you could say is an emotional state. If there is a certain mood present, then the people are going to be feeling certain things and responding in a way that is correspondent to that mood. But that is just social moods, there are many other ways people's emotional state can change, if you are working on something you enjoy working on you could be in a certain emotional state for that.

- An emotional state implies a certain set of feelings that come up with a certain activity or under certain circumstances.

- An important observation to note in emotion theory is that pain can stop the current flow of emotion or feeling and alert the person. Pain and anxiety are different from the other emotions because they are unpleasant. How often is an emotion like hope or fun tainted by the emotion of pain? Is fun even an emotion or is it an emotional state? Fun would imply that you are experiencing a set of emotions that makes that circumstance fun, joy is an emotion, "fun" is more of an emotional state.

- The flow of someone's feelings can stop suddenly, for instance, say you are relaxing in bed after waking up, then your alarm clock goes off - you went from feeling happy, relaxed emotions to those suddenly ending. Emotions and feelings stop and start like this all the time. In a conversation, for example, someone could be happy and the other person could show or adopt a negative expression and that could suddenly end the other persons happiness. There are many emotions someone could adopt in a conversation such as shyness, or an emotion expressing a thought or an idea, and these emotions could influence (or start and stop) emotions that the other person is experiencing. It should be clear that the many emotions someone experiences throughout the day changes all the time, stops, starts, transitions, and changes in complicated ways all the time. These changes may or may not be observed, however if you pay attention to these feelings and their behavior you could certainly notice a lot more.

- Emotion can motivate thought. People go into different states or 'modes' where they are driven to think a certain type of thought or do a certain type of behavior. When someone enters a different mode, such as a pleasure seeking mode, that mode in particular is motivated by emotion. It is clear that with pleasure someone is feeling more, so you would say that it is motivated by emotion. However, every state someone is in, every different subtle social emotional state or emotional state when someone is doing work is going to have some emotion or set of feelings behind it. But it isn't just a set of feelings, the feeling is unique each time, and this uniqueness communicates certain information that is also unique. The feeling tells you what you like and what you don't like, that would probably be the primary emotions (pleasure and pain). But each other emotion communicates something - if you feel guilty you know what that feeling means, maybe that feeling in combination with other feelings is communicating something different or unique based upon the set of feelings it is and what it means in that context.

- Therefore someone could enter into a mode such as an abusive mode, where, emotionally, they are being abusive. It makes sense that since this is a mode, it takes a reasonable period of time to experience. It isn't an expression or a gesture, which takes a couple of seconds, but a mode like this my guess would be at least a few minutes long. Another mode could be a humorous mode. Maybe that is clear by the person being observed as being amused - but maybe emotionally they are amused for a certain period of time before and after your observation of them being that way.

- That isn't to say that someone couldn't experience amused feelings for a few seconds. Clearly when someone laughs the feelings mostly only last for the period of the laughter. But they would probably still be amused for a period afterwards. You just laughed - and you become happy or amused for a short period after that. My point about the modes is that there are certain powerful sets of feelings that last for a while - like a pleasure seeking set of feelings. That is different from laughter or amusement, this is a strong specific mode that brings up a set of feelings for someone. Maybe someone else has a different sort of mode - maybe they have a strong mode where they feel guilty, and they have a unique set of feelings and thoughts that are with this mode.

- Some of these modes might be a reflective mode, where you are in period that is reminiscent of the activity you were just doing. Other modes might be powerful ones, abusive ones, submissive or dominant ones, calm ones. It is as if someone gets in a 'mood' for these modes. Moods are more quiet however, and there are only a few moods that people recognize. However, there could be many different unique moods as well. What then is the difference between a mood and a mode? In a mood you have different emotions, maybe someone gets in an abusive mood. That would be like getting in an abusive mode. I think it is just a matter of how strong the mood or mode is. Moods are probably less strong than modes, and modes are also ways of acting, not just ways of feeling. In a mode the emotions are so strong that they influence your behavior - the emotion motivates thought.

- One emotion can lead or transition into another emotion. For instance, someone can rage, then become angry instead of being in a rage over a certain thing, and then the emotion could die to down to the person just being hateful at whatever the cause is. That is similar to if someone is punched, they might be at first angry, then upset, and then depressed or sad. Anger can lead to hate, or 'being upset' - and then after that the emotion might transition into sadness or whatever might follow someone being hateful. Maybe the lesser emotion of hate is bitterness. So they would go from being hateful to being bitter. Or maybe if someone is talking to them positively, they could go from being hateful to being happy or optimistic.

An explanation for this chapter:

An emotional state is a very complicated thing. If someone knew completely their emotional state, they would know everything they were feeling right then. Then they wouldn't really have any "unconscious" emotions, because they would be perfectly conscious of what they were feeling. But then again, it is impossible to feel the full force of all your feelings at once, so it is not possible to be completely conscious of all your feelings. Your unconscious feelings must be dimmed down, or only large in a way that isn't completely conscious. Like you know you have a large emotion, but aren't in touch with it.

Emotional states are complicated, it would be easy to say, "my emotional state right now is really messed up" because that is what emotional states are like, people have several emotions they are experiencing all the time, it is just hard to identify that this is occurring because I would say that people can only identify when they have a large, clear emotion that they can understand.

Table 75.0

Chapter 76

My Theories about Mindfulness- based cognitive therapy

In 1991 Barnard and Teasdale created a multilevel theory of the mind called "Interacting Cognitive Subsystems," (ICS). The ICS model is based on Barnard and Teasdale's theory that the mind has multiple modes that are responsible for receiving and processing new information cognitively and emotionally. Barnard and Teasdale's (1991) theory associates an individual's vulnerability to depression with the degree to which he/she relies on only one of the mode of mind, inadvertently blocking the other modes. The two main modes of mind include the "doing" mode and "being" mode. The "doing" mode is also known as the driven mode. This mode is very goal-oriented and is triggered when the mind develops a discrepancy between how things are versus how the mind wishes things to be.[1] The second main mode of mind is the "being" mode. "Being" mode, is not focused on achieving specific goals, instead the emphasis is on "accepting and allowing what is," without any immediate pressure to change it.[2]

Based on Barnard and Teasdale's (1991) model, mental health is related to an individual's ability to disengage from one mode or to easily move among the modes of mind. Therefore, individuals that are able to flexibly move between the modes of mind based on the conditions in the environment are in the most favorable state. The ICS model theorizes that the "being" mode is the most likely mode of mind that will lead to lasting emotional changes. Therefore for prevention of relapse in depression, cognitive therapy must promote this mode. This led Teasdale to the creation of MBCT (Mindfulness-based cognitive therapy), which promotes the "being" mode.[3]

The idea is that in the "doing" mode someone is trying to get to a better state. Therefore tension is caused and they are likely to spiral back downward into a depression. If someone is in the "being" mode they let their negative thoughts flow and ignore the negative state. That way they can pass out of it easily.

I this that this theory behind MBCT is very interesting in terms of how emotion and cognition interact. If you think about it, your emotional state of being upset about something is driving you to be in a state that is seeking out an answer. I think this method of therapy is basically just telling the person to say to themselves, "its ok, i don't need to react to my feeling upset, I can let this feeling and the unwelcome thoughts it generates or wants to generate pass".

But is that the full mystery behind what is going on when your mind enters one of these states? Each of these states is responsible for your way of thinking and feeling while you are in them, everything you feel and think in these states is being influenced by you either being upset, or just "being" and letting the thing pass you by.

It seems to me like there are an endless number of other different "modes" someone can be in. They can be in a mode where they just want sex, for example. Is this just a different way of acting? It isn't. When someone is in a different mode, they want something, their feelings and their entire state is different, it is like they are a different person (for example 'bitch' mode).

---

1. Segal, Z., Teasdale, J., Williams, M. (2002). Mindfulness-Based Cognitive Therapy for Depression. New York: Guilford Press.
2. Segal, Z., Teasdale, J., Williams, M. (2002). Mindfulness-Based Cognitive Therapy for Depression. New York: Guilford Press. p.73
3. Herbert, James D., and Evan M. Forman. Acceptance and Mindfulness in Cognitive Behavior Therapy: Understanding and Applying New Theories. Hoboken: John Wiley + Sons, 2011. Print.

So I guess then a different mode could be characterized by what happens in this mode. There are thoughts and attitudes that are characteristic of each mode. It is almost like a different personality, maybe sometimes someone acts nice, and in this mode they are really very different. But surely there are more modes than that.

I would say that there is a mode where you expect pleasure from other people. There is a mode where you are abusive, etc. Your attitude can change in many ways, and, in each of these ways, you are really in a different "mode" or are a slightly different person.

This is really a social thing then - you can be in a nice or mean mode, a mode where you are getting along with the people around you in a certain way. When someone is in the 'driven' mode of MBCT the person wants to satisfy whatever it is they are upset about. My point is that is just one mode of many different modes that a person can enter. People want satisfaction in other ways, maybe it is just in this mode that you are in a more extreme state such that it is directing your thoughts and feelings it is so powerful.

Emotion is powerful - these 'modes' are so powerful that they direct and influence your thoughts, feelings and behaviors. Emotion causes people to do things they didn't think about all of the time. Emotion itself communicates information - if you are in this emotional state, you are being informed by your emotions that you feel that way, so you might learn why you might be feeling that way.

You could say that the unique feeling of each emotion communicates a unique understanding. Some emotions are so strong they make you go crazy and you really are in a different mode. I think this shows how emotion influences your thinking. People are motivated by their emotions, they think differently because in these modes, when they are experiencing different emotions, they want different different things, their desires and preferences are different for that short, emotional, possibly moody time period.

So in the "being" mode it is like you are just being, and letting the emotional power flow through you instead of having it control you and influence your thoughts and feelings and behaviors. You are not driven, you are simply being.

Table 76.0

---

1. Retrieved from http://en.wikipedia.org/wiki/Cognition

Chapter 77

What is Thinking - or as Scientists name it - 'Cognition'?

- In science, cognition is a group of mental processes that includes attention, memory, producing and understanding language, solving problems, and making decisions. Cognition is studied in various disciplines such as psychology, philosophy, linguistics, science and computer science. The term's usage varies in different disciplines; for example in psychology and cognitive science, it usually refers to an information processing view of an individual's psychological functions. It is also used in a branch of social psychology called social cognition to explain attitudes, attribution, and groups dynamics.[1]

There are various things people can do mentally that have been labeled as aspects of cognition such as processes like memory, association, concept formation, pattern recognition, language, attention, perception, action, problem solving and mental imagery. Traditionally, emotion was not thought of as a cognitive process.

Most of those seem obvious - it is clear how memory functions, you simply bring up a memory. Well, you might need to be in the right emotional state in order to bring up the proper memory. Sometimes certain memories are easier to recall than at other times, this is probably because you were thinking of closely associated things that helped you to recall the similar memory. Sometimes people might need to spend some time trying to pull up a memory.

Actually, now that I think about it, you could probably go into great detail describing how memory functions - however on the surface and for the most part it is simple and easily understood. People use their memories all of the time, so in a way everyone understands how memory works.

However, when you think anything aspects of memory are probably used because it is related to what you did earlier that day. When you say 'hi' to someone, or do anything really, you use your memory to compare that event to previous events in your life or earlier that day. Your mind is like a computer, there are lots of things it is comparing and contrasting all of the time.

How does this process work? It probably works emotionally as well as intellectually. Your emotions help you bring up other similarly emotional memories and associated thoughts. Each emotion means something - it has a symbolic representation like saying hi brings up the emotion for people or the idea you have of people in your mind.

But the interesting thing is how memory or thought relates to mental imagery. I said that emotion can be used to compare different thoughts and memories, but is mental imagery also involved there? There are going to be mental images associated with memories, thoughts and emotions. Therefore your mind is really comparing and contrasting lots of different thoughts, sensations, images, memories, and feelings all of the time.

An image means something. This is obvious if you think about art. People can 'think' visually basically. People can also think with their emotions, as it is clear that emotion can be informative. A thought could be of an event, a memory, a group of related ideas, a group of not related ideas, an emotion. How could a thought be of an emotion? All emotions mean something, a thought that is of an emotion is just then an emotion with special significance that you have drawn more attention to in the form of a thought.

So a conscious thought is something that is clear to you. An unconscious thought is something that simply

---

1. Retrieved from http://en.wikipedia.org/wiki/Cognition

means something to you - it could be anything really. Anything that communicates information to your mind. Thought is really then informative, and the function of emotion then is simply to experience feeling.

But what kinds of information does thought communicate? It can communicate visual information, mathematical information, emotional information, various ideas and concepts, sensations, experiences, physical feelings and actions, mental feelings and actions, sounds - everything there is in existence that your mind can understand.

Table 77.0

1. Retrieved from http://en.wikipedia.org/wiki/Cognitive_behavioral_therapy

Chapter 78

Unconscious Thinking and Feeling - And Cognitive Behavioral Therapy

- Cognitive behavioral therapy (CBT) is a psychotherapeutic approach that addresses dysfunctional emotions, behaviors, and cognitions through a goal-oriented, systematic process. The name refers to behavior therapy, cognitive therapy, and to therapy based upon a combination of basic behavioral and cognitive research.[1]

A major aspect of CBT is to use an analysis of someones thoughts and feelings - how their feelings lead to thoughts and how their thoughts lead to feelings - as a way to help the person understand how they can change their thoughts and how this might help them change their feelings. Obviously they also analyze how thoughts and feelings relate to behavior as well.

But how much of someones thinking is unconscious? Someone can have a thought that they aren't aware of. They could have some belief, attitude, or thought process that they aren't aware of. A belief is something you are thinking that isn't a fact - which would be something you know to be true (or think you know to be true). So when I say that you might have some belief you aren't aware of that means anything you think that you aren't certain of. I would say that everything in the mind that you think is either a fact or a belief, or a more complicated thought that is more like a paragraph which would be describing something.

Surely when you are interacting with someone there is potentially a lot of unconscious beliefs and ideas you might form about the other person. You could be biased against them and not know it very easily. In fact, there might be subtle shifts in how you are biased against them many times during a conversation.

But is that what the unconscious is about - beliefs, facts, and ideas that you have that you aren't aware of? Or is it about deep motivations and powerful emotions that are influencing your feelings, thoughts and behaviors?

There is a lot of mystery behind what is happening in your mind unconsciously. That is why it might take a lot of work thinking about your own thoughts and feelings in order to change them. If you have some strong attachment or drive that needs to be changed - it is a powerful unconscious one, and you would need to do a lot of work over a long time in order to change how you feel.

I am not a licensed psychologist, but it is obvious that certain behaviors or ways of being can only be changed over a long period of time. If someone feels passionately about something, this cannot change instantly. That shows how any behavior might take a long time to change. People get used to acting a certain way and this can only be changed by showing them or practicing new ways of acting. They have deep unconscious beliefs and attitudes that are strong and reflected in many aspects of their actions. Such complicated and subtle behavior cannot change instantly because it is too complicated to change instantly - if a behavior is complicated then it is going to take a long time to change because there are many things that need to be changed about it.

You might not notice all of the things that change, however if you think about it an attitude is probably going to have many associated beliefs and unconscious drives that need to be addressed. This is what experience is. It isn't simply that an attitude is large and needs to be decreased over time - there is also a learning process.

What can be said about this? If a motivation is large, then why does it take so long to change? It seems to

---

1. Retrieved from http://en.wikipedia.org/wiki/Cognitive_behavioral_therapy

me that if you describe the motivation as 'unconscious' it shows that it is very large, because most of the mind is unconscious. What does the word 'unconscious' bring up anyway? Is it merely a way of saying something is more significant than you would think because you aren't aware of its full impact?

Human beings aren't aware of a lot of things about themselves, that is why saying 'unconsciously' brings up so much. Even some action you would consider to be 'conscious' is really 'unconscious' because everything you do you don't know the full implications of.

Table 78.0

---

1. Retrieved from http://en.wikipedia.org/wiki/Cognitive_behavioral_therapy

Psychology for Self Help
Chapter

- People have a certain understanding of their own actions. This is true for specific, individual actions where you can understand to different degrees what you are doing and if you are conscious of what you are doing - and this is true with more complicated actions and behaviors (such as a behavior that you have to think about or reflect on in order to understand what your action was.

- People have various beliefs about themselves, about the world, about what they are doing in the present time. These beliefs can influence your actions at any time. A certain belief can be brought up consciously (recalled or a new belief initiated) or a belief could have an unconscious influence on what you are doing. For instance a belief that you forgot you had or some bias you have.

- There are only a few basic personality traits that people can have. There is their moral disposition - if they are nice or mean. There is their energy level, their nervousness, their type of intellect or way of thinking. There is their social dispositions - extroverted, agreeable, etc.

- You can try and measure emotions in social interactions. For instance the emotion of love might only be present between two people who are in love occasionally. You could also try to measure it over a longer period of time, and try to observe certain indicators that point to if that emotion is occurring.

- Furthermore, in every social interaction there are going to be various emotions interacting with each other. This is a part of the 'mood' or 'atmosphere'. For instance there could be a humorous mood or a romantic mood, or maybe those two emotions/moods are interacting with each other during the interaction.

- This brings up the point that there are various ways someone can be conscious of their emotions. Someone may have an emotion, but that doesn't mean that it is easy for them to feel or understand that it is occurring.

- A mood or emotional state consists of a certain set of feelings (happy, sad, exciting, etc), in addition to having its own unique feeling.

- Emotion can cloud intellect. The various ways of thinking can be related to someones social disposition (if they are an introvert or an extrovert). Jung discussed the introverted type of thinking - '"this kind of thinking easily gets lost in the immense truth of the subjective factor... the extraordinary impoverishment of introverted thinking is compensated by a wealth of unconscious facts." (Carl Jung, "Psychological Types".) He seemed to think that introverted thinking was defective somehow, yet more internal and possibly deeper unconsciously.

- Your thinking (conscious and unconscious) determines who you are and what you feel.

Table 79.0

Chapter

Being Kinder

Anything that you'd ever want comes somehow from kindness. Whether what you want is given to you by a person or something else in the real world, it was a kindness that you received it. The Kindness Association seeks to promote kindness of all types and shapes, whatever you can imagine as a kindness the Association seeks to find some, any way to give it to you. Everything that you ever got, anything that ever happened to you, was from a kindness. If you find money on the street, reality was kind to you. If you win the lottery, luck was kind to you. If someone else is nice to you, or helps you in some way, then they are being kind to you.

Philosophically and morally kindness is the greatest goal anyone could aspire to get, or if they wish to help others and look good, kindness is the greatest thing anyone can give. Kindness functions on two levels, one is socially, the other, still emotional, is more of a physical thing related to interpersonal relationships. If I give you a dollar in a business transaction, that is more physical than social. Thus kindness can be divided into two general categories, emotional and physical.

Sometimes we don't consider being kind if say we are doing business, and merely seek our current practical objective. Therefore it is the other aspect of life, the emotional, that the Kindness Association seeks to improve for you and everyone else.

If you adopt the ideals of the Kindness Association, to promote your emotional wellbeing by promoting kindness in yourself and others, so that they will be kind to you, you will help the Kindness Association achieve its goals. You of course need to promote kindness in yourself, not just others, because being unkind yourself makes you think about things which cause negative emotion, which makes you feel bad. In order to fully feel and get the benefit of kindness, you must promote kindness in yourself as well, otherwise you'd only get half the benefit. (If you just promote it in others)

Table 80.0

Chapter 81

Emotion and Logic

Some things in life cause people to feel, these are called emotional reactions. Some things in life cause people to think, these are sometimes called logical or intellectual reactions. Thus life is divided between things that make you feel and things that make you think. The question is, if someone is feeling, does that mean that they are thinking less? It probably does. If part of your brain is being occupied by feeling, then it makes sense that you have less capacity for thought. That is obvious if you take emotional extremes, such as crying, where people can barely think at all. This does not mean that emotional people are not intelligent; it just means that they might be dumber during the times in which they are emotional. Emotion goes on and off for everyone, sometimes people cry, and sometimes they are completely serious.

Some things in life can identifiably cause more emotion than other things.

1. Color causes more emotion than black and white. So anything with more color in it is going to be more emotional to look at, whether it is the difference between a gold or silver sword, or a gold or silver computer. In both cases the gold is going to be more emotional.

2. Things that are personal are emotional, personal things that people like and that they feel are "close" to them. Things like home or anything someone likes actually. That is a definition of emotion after all, something that causes feeling. So if you like it, it is probably going to cause more feeling. Other things aside from liking something could cause emotions from it, such as curiosity, but usually like is one of the stronger emotions. You could say that the two are directly proportional, the more you like something, the more it is going to cause feeling.

But there are things that people like that cause thought. You could like something and it causes you to think, and we previously defined emotion as feeling, not thought. That thoughts are separate from emotions because thought is a period of thinking. What exactly is thinking then? You can think about emotions, "how did I feel then?" etc. So is thought just a period of increased attention? Or is it a sharp spike in attention focused on one particular thing that is clear? It is hard to focus that much if you are feeling a lot, however. This makes me conclude that there is an overlap of feeling and thought, like a venn diagram. But there are still parts of thought that don't have feeling or emotion in them, and parts of emotion that don't have thought in them. That means that thought requires more concentration than feeling does, since we defined thought as a period of increased attention. You can be emotional and have more attention, but usually if you are emotional you are going to be less attentive than you would be if you were thinking more. Then again, if you are emotional you are being attentive to your emotions, whatever they may be, and if your emotions are on something like the sun, then when you see the sun you are going to be attentive to it, but not be thinking about it. So you can pay attention to something and not be thinking about it at the same time. But you aren't going to be paying attention to anything else. It seems that thought is more attention than emotion, however. If you try to "feel" your computer you still don't give it as much attention as if you were thinking about your computer. Then again, it depends what you are thinking about your computer, if you are thinking that your computer sucks, you are going to give it less attention than thinking that it is great. It also depends what your feelings are about that computer. If you feel that the computer is good, then you are going to give it more attention than if you feel that it is bad (possibly). The thoughts and the feelings correspond, however. That is, if you are thinking it is bad, then you are going to feel that it is bad. Thus thought and feeling are really one and the same. But thoughts are really clearer than feelings. Thought and feeling may result in the same amount of attention to something, but thought is more precise. It is more precise for you to think that the computer is good, then to feel that the computer is good. Who knows why you feel the computer is good, but if you were thinking the computer is good then you would know why you thought that. Emotions and feelings are more obscure.

So, the more you like something (or hate something, or have any strong emotional reaction to anything), the more emotional it is, but that doesn't mean that it might not also cause you to think about it. One can't label everything in life as either emotion or thought however. Life isn't a scale with emotion on one end and thought on the other. There are other factors involved, things like adrenaline and physical action, which might also cause increased attention that isn't either emotional or thoughtful. When you're running you have a lot of attention on the fact that you are running, and you're not thinking about it or being emotional about it. This means that just because you like something, doesn't mean that it is emotional. You might like running, but it doesn't cause emotions in you. What does emotion mean then? Emotions must be thoughts that you can't identify, when you feel something, it must be that you are thinking about something unconsciously. You just have no idea what it is, usually. Emotions and feelings are thoughts then. By that I mean that they can be broken down into parts and figured out what those parts are. And thoughts are just really parts that you can identify. So the difference between emotions, feelings and thoughts is that you know what thoughts are about, but you don't have as good an idea of what emotions and feelings are, as they are more obscure and harder to identify.

Thus once you find out what is causing the emotion, it is no longer an emotion, but it is a thought (that is, you now call the emotion a thought, so the thought is still probably generating emotion. In your mind then there is still an emotion, but this emotion is now "part" of a thought, it becomes part of the thought associated with it because you created this link, and hence you would call the emotion/thought just a thought because while thoughts can generate emotions, emotions cannot generate thoughts (by themselves), unless you realize what the emotion is (then you are generating the thought, not the emotion generating it), but you are realizing it is a thought, not an emotion: so this realization takes over and now the emotion is part of that realization (because you consider the emotion a part of you, and you generated the realization), instead of the realization being a part of the emotion (and since it seems like the emotion belongs to the realization (you), instead of vice versa, you call it a thought instead of an emotion, because you generated the thought (and hence it also seems that you are now consciously also generating the emotion (the emotion coming from the thought))). So that would mean that all emotions have route in real things, and these real things can be explained with thoughts, so all emotions then are really thoughts that you haven't realized; an emotion would just be a thought that you haven't identified yet, so the term "emotion" goes away when you realize it is a thought (because that is what it really was all along, a thought) (though this thought might still be generating a feeling).

So, since you perceive the emotion as belonging to you, and you generate thoughts consciously, you consider the emotion to be part of a thought, not vice versa (and hence call identified emotions "thoughts"). So when you identify an emotion, it is a thought because thoughts can generate emotions, so if the emotion is still there after you identified it you would say it falls under the category "thought", because the thought is making it. You might be lazy however and not want to spend time thinking, which are what emotions are for. "Ah that gold sword is pretty" might be the emotion, but to your conscious mind you would have no idea that you like the sword because it is pretty, you might just know that you like the sword and it is making you emotional about it. Therefore, emotional things are really any feelings that cause unconscious or conscious thought. Feeling is also another word for unconscious thought. That then leads to the conclusion that thought can be emotional (because thoughts are going to be about things that can cause emotion). I think that emotions can be more emotional than thought, however, because emotions can contain more than one thought (while thoughts are very slow consciously), therefore causing it to cause more feeling, or be more emotional. While you can only express a few thoughts a minute, your emotions can contain endless numbers of thoughts per minute – they are not as exact and hence don't make as much sense as thoughts do.

So thought is just a lot of attention on one little thing. And emotion is attention on lots of individual things, or possibly one thing. So things that are emotional are things that cause you to think, consciously or unconsciously. And therefore they would cause you to feel, consciously or unconsciously. So the more you like something you can't consciously identify as to why you like it, the more emotional it is, and the more you like something where you can consciously identify what it is, the more conscious thought it is going to cause, and the more logical that thing is going to be. Emotion is just unconscious thought.

How This Chapter shows how Intelligence is intertwined with Emotion:

- "Emotion goes on and off for everyone" – this statement shows how there are degrees to which someone can be focused on and feel thought, and degrees to which someone can be focused on and feel feeling. That then also explains the next statement in the chapter "some things in life can identifiably more emotion than other things".

- Since there are parts of emotion that don't have thought (assuming that emotion and thought overlap – but that is a logical assumption because thoughts generate feelings and are therefore less independent) then emotion (especially emotion without any thought) is going to need less focus or concentration, because emotion is a more pleasurable experience, but thought is one where concentration is usually used.

- Emotions can direct and control thoughts – if you are feeling that your computer is bad, then you might then give it less or more attention, and conscious attention is a function of thought because you need to think to start to focus on something. Or when you notice something you noticing it is a conscious experience because you "notice" it and thoughts are things which you are aware of which would then contribute to consciousness.

- Next mentioned is how emotions and feelings are just harder to identify then thoughts, and that therefore emotions and feelings are really thoughts themselves, or vice versa. If all thought is really emotion, and all emotion really thought, then all intelligence could vary and be dependent on emotions. This is further evidenced by the statement "thus once you find out what is causing the emotion it is no longer an emotion, but it is a thought". That shows how an emotion is a thought that you just aren't identifying. It is just a matter of definition of the terms. Thought is concrete things which are real in the world, and emotion is something that you feel but can't visualize. So therefore intelligence is just the ability to do things which are real, versus feeling something, which isn't as "real" as thoughts are.

An explanation for this chapter:

This chapter basically described the difference between thoughts and feeling (or emotion). Thoughts are things that you are conscious of, when you have a thought, you know you have it because it is your thought. Unless you aren't aware of the thought you are having (which would make it an unconscious thought), then the thought is something that is clear to you, it is usually a sentence, though you might not be thinking of it as a sentence. You might know you want to do something, but you might not express it very clearly to yourself. When someone has a clear thought, they know what it is. You can want to do things and be thinking things all the time, some of the thoughts are going to be more clear than others.

Emotion, on the other hand, isn't clear like clear thoughts. When you experience an emotion, you might not know you are experiencing it at all, and it is certainly a lot more complicated than a sentence, which could be your typical thought. Emotion could be described with a lot of thoughts, and this probably occurs in humans all the time. People have complicated emotions, and these emotions would give rise to thoughts that people are aware of (a conscious, clear thought such as a sentence in your head), and thoughts that people are less aware of, (for instance you are doing something but you didn't fully realize that you were going to or are doing it.

Table 81.0

Chapter 82

Psychological Types

In Carl Jung's book, "Psychological Types" he talked about intuition in an extroverted attitude:

- In the extraverted attitude, intuition as the function of unconscious perception is wholly directed to external objects. Because intuition is in the main an unconscious process, its nature is very difficult to grasp. The intuitive function is represented in consciousness by an attitude of expectancy, by vision penetration; but only from the subsequent result can it be established how much of what was "seen" was actually in the object, and how much was "read into" it. Just as sensation, when it is the dominant function, is not a mere reactive process of no further significance for the object, but an activity that seizes and shapes its object, so intuition is not mere perception, or vision, but an active, creative process that puts into the object just as much as it takes out. since it does this unconsciously, it also has an unconscious effect on the object.

Jung said that a person in whom intuition was dominant, an "intuitive type", acted not on the basis of rational judgment but on sheer intensity of perception. In the extraverted attitude, this function (intuition) is "wholly directed to external objects". That means that an extrovert aims his ability of insight outward, instead of a type of inner reflection, the extrovert probably thinks more about other people and the significant aspects of them (such as their archetypes) and how these aspects relate to themselves. It is difficult to grasp the nature of how this process works, because it is unconscious.

This intuitive ability is "represented in consciousness by an attitude of of expectancy, by vision penetration". I think this means that you get excited from your analysis of other people. Only this type of analysis occurs all the time and is unconscious, so it is going to have a continuous effect on your emotions. For the extrovert, this means someone being "expectant". If you think about it, if you had a great insight about someone by realizing they were like an archetype, then that would make an extrovert wanting to be with that person. If I was an extrovert and realized someone was like a magician, I might find that very intriguing and want to hang out with them or something. Since I an introvert, however, I wouldn't really care. These archetypes are aspects of people that are significant, when this significance is triggered it causes a reaction in people, especially extroverts.

The unconscious intuition is "not a mere reactive process of of no further significance for the object, but an activity that seizes and shapes its object". That statement is much more complicated than it seems. How could it be that your analysis of other people "shape" the people you are analyzing? Since this analyzing is automatic, it is really a part of how you interact with the person. That seems rather obvious, clearly when you interact with someone it is complicated. There are going to be things you can analyze about an interaction, and these things are going to influence the interaction. If you couldn't describe descriptive qualities of a person, then the interaction wouldn't be very dynamic.

Take dogs and other animals for instance, there are only a few adjectives you can use to describe them such as nice, cute, and sweet. You wouldn't call a dog "devilish" or "representing the mother figure". There isn't a complex unconscious with many archetypes and significant descriptors that dogs have. This more complex level of interaction influences the other person, when you seek this depth of analysis, by looking at the significant descriptors of a person, the interaction is effected. If you didn't associate the person you were talking to with grander things, or make them appear to be a certain type of person with certain strong, noticeable qualities then there wouldn't be much happening in the interaction.

In this next paragraph Jung outlines what he thinks the relationship between intuition and sensation (in extraversion) is:

- The primary function of intuition, however, is simply to transmit images, or perceptions of relations between things, which could not be transmitted by the other functions or only in a very roundabout way. These images have the value of specific insights which have a decisive influence on action whenever intuition is given priority. In this case, psychic adaptation will be grounded almost entirely on intuitions. Thinking, feeling, and sensation are then largely repressed, sensation being the one most affected, because, as the conscious sense function, it offers the greatest obstacle to intuition. Sensation is a hindrance to clear, unbiased, naive perception; its intrusive sensory stimuli direct attention to the physical surface, to the very things round and beyond which intuition tries to peer. But since extraverted intuition is directed predominantly to objects, it actually comes very close to sensation; indeed, the expectant attitude to external objects is just as likely to make use of sensation. Hence, if intuition is to function properly, sensation must to a large extent be suppressed. By sensation I mean in this instance the simple and immediate sense-impression understood as a clearly defined physiological and psychic datum. This must be expressly established beforehand because, if I ask an intuitive how he orients himself, he will speak of things that are almost indistinguishable from sense-impressions. Very often he will even use the word "sensation." He does have sensations, of course, but he is not guided by them as such; he uses them merely as starting-points for his perceptions. He selects them by unconscious predilection. It is not the strongest sensation, in the physiological sense, that is accorded the chief value, but any sensation whatsoever whose value is enhanced by the intuitive's unconscious attitude. In this way it may eventually come to acquire the chief value, and to his conscious mind it appears to be pure sensation. But actually it is not so.

So intuition "transmits images" which are "specific insights" that influences action. By image he means an understanding about something, so people reach intuitive insights about other people and these insights influence their behavior. "Thinking, feeling and sensation are then largely repressed", because these are obstacles to intuition. That means that this intuition comes from the unconscious mind, and thinking, feeling and sensation are conscious things which would tend to block out the unconscious. People can reach conscious conclusions about other people, feel and sense things about other people - when they do that it limits their intuition, their unconscious processing of the other people.

So all that basically means is that you have a conscious and an unconscious interaction with other people. The unconscious one is intuitive, which is suppressed by the conscious processes of thinking, feeling and sensation. I don't know when you are interacting with someone what is means to "sense" something about them - I would say that that is intuitive. By sensation Jung might mean physical sensation, an attention to what is going on in the physical world. The sense-impression must be established beforehand, he uses sensations as starting points for his perceptions. He "selects them by unconscious predilections". A sensations value can be enhanced by the intuitives unconscious attitude. So the things you observe via sensation can be noticed by your intuitive unconscious mind and you can change the value of it.

That seems rather straightforward, your conscious mind uses senses to observe things about other people, and your unconscious mind changes the value of the things observed and perceived, you then perceive it in an unconscious way. So someone might act a certain way, you make immediate conclusions about their behavior, and then your unconscious mind generates its own perception of the person, by using something like descriptive adjectives or archetypes. Your unconsciousness can label someone as "devilish" or a "trickster". This is beneath your awareness, your unconsciousness uses these types of descriptive adjectives and labels all the time to help you understand what other people are like and what they mean to you.

In his next paragraph Jung talks about how the extroverted type tries to think about the widest range of possibilities:

- Just as extraverted sensation strives to reach the highest pitch of actuality, because this alone can give the appearance of a full life, so intuition tries to apprehend the widest range of possibilities, since only through envisioning possibilities is intuition fully satisfied. It seeks to discover what possibilities the objective situation holds in store; hence, as a subordinate function (i.e., when not in the position of priority), it is the auxiliary that automatically comes into play when no other function can find a way out of a hopelessly blocked situation. When it is the dominant function, every ordinary situation in life seems like a locked room which intuition has to open. It is constantly seeking fresh outlets and new possibilities in external life. In a very short time every existing situation becomes a prison for the intuitive, a chain that has to be broken. For a time objects appear to have an exaggerated value, if they should serve to bring about a solution, a deliverance, or lead to the discovery of a new possibility. Yet no sooner have they served their purpose as stepping stones or bridges than they lose their value altogether and are discarded as burdensome appendages. Facts are acknowledged only if they open new possibilities of advancing beyond them and delivering the individed from their power. Nascent possibilities are compelling motives from which intuition cannot escape and to which all else must be sacrificed.

What does Jung mean when he says that extroverted intuition seeks to "apprehend the widest range of possibilities"? By possibilities does he mean social possibilities? What kinds of social possibilities? I suppose he just means any kind of social endeavor, something to say, something to do, someway to act. Sensation tries to "reach the highest pitch of actuality" - which probably means the extrovert tries to become as happy and fulfilled as possible. Probably through his intuition realizing social possibilities.

It makes sense that an extrovert would want to do more things socially. By definition, the extrovert is more social. You could say that extroverts are a lot more social than introverts, that they constantly try to explore new ways of interacting and are always looking for more things to say and more things to do socially.

For the extrovert, "objects appear to have an exaggerated value, if they should bring a about a solution, a deliverance, or lead to the discovery of a new possibility." By objects he is probably referring to the significant psychological objects of archetypes, which are aspects of a persons personality or behavior that are significant and represented as an archetype, such as "wise old man". So an extrovert analyzes other people and sees if their qualities can lead to new possibilities of them being social. If someone else is "devilish", how could that give them a new possibility for being social?

When you think about it that way, there are probably a lot of things that could enable someone to be more social. If you are more insightful, you could have more things to say in a conversation. If you think more about what is going on you could be more involved with what is going on and therefore more socially engaged. If your thinking is directed toward what is happening in the situation, instead of just thinking about yourself in your own mind, you are probably going to have a lot more possibilities to be social.

In the next paragraph Jung discusses how extroverts are enthusiastic:

- Whenever intuition predominates, a peculiar and unmistakable psychology results. Because extraverted intuition is oriented by the object, there is a marked dependence on external situations, but it is altogether different from the dependence of the sensation type. The intuitive is never to be found in the world of accepted reality-values, but he has a keen nose for anything new and in the making. Because he is always seeking out new possibilities, stable conditions suffocate him. He seizes on new objects or situations with great intensity, sometimes with extraordinary enthusiasms, only to abandon them cold-bloodedly, without any compunction and apparently no further developments can be divined. So long as a new possibility is in the offing, the intuitive is bound to it with the shackles of fate. It is as though his whole life vanished in the new situation. One gets the impression, which he himself shares, that he has always just reached a final turning- point, and that form now on he can think and feel nothing else. No matter how reasonable and suitable it may be, and although every conceivable argument speaks for its stability, a day will come when nothing will deter him from regarding as a prison the very situation that seemed to promise him freedom and deliverance, and from acting accordingly. Neither reason nor feeling can restrain him or frighten him away from a new possibility, even though it goes against all his previous convictions. Thinking and feeling, the indispensable components of conviction, are his inferior functions, carrying no weight and hence incapable of effectively withstanding the power of intuition. And yet these functions are the only ones that could compensate its supremacy by supplying the judgment which the intuitive type totally lacks. The intuitive's morality is governed neither by thinking nor by feeling; he has his own characteristic morality, which consists in a loyalty to his vision and in voluntary submission to its authority. Consideration for the welfare of others is weak. Their psychic well-being counts as little with him as does his own. He has equally little regard for their convictions and way of life, and on this account he is often put down as an immoral and unscrupulous adventurer. Since his intuition is concerned with externals and with ferreting out their possibilities, he readily turns to professions in which he can exploit these capacities to the full. Many business tycoons, entrepreneurs, speculators, stockbrokers, politicians, etc., belong to this type. It would seem to be more common among women, however, than among men. In women the intuitive capacity shows itself not so much in the professional as in the every social occasion, they make the right social connections, they seek out men with prospects only to abandon everything again for the sake of a new possibility.

Jung writes, "so long as a new possibility is in the offing, the intuitive is bound to it with the shackles of fate". He also writes that "he seizes on new objects or situations with great intensity, sometimes with extraordinary enthusiasms...". By objects he means any aspect of a persons personality, or any aspect of a social situation I would guess. Even though Jung says the extrovert seizes external objects, he means that he orients himself outward. An introvert could think about the aspects of someone else in his head, but an extrovert might seize on "new objects" - implying that he is more engaged with the other person than the internal thinking of an introvert. The extrovert obviously is more involved with what is happening in a social situation than the introvert - "bound to it with the shackles of fate". Both an introvert and extrovert could think deeply about the other person and analyze their characteristics and attributes, but the extrovert is enthusiastic and energetic about being social and engaged with the other person.

Jung writes, "neither reason nor feeling can restrain him or frighten him away from a new possibility, even though it goes against all his previous convictions." That shows that Jung thought the extrovert was impulsive, willing to change his beliefs in a moment if it means he can have more fun socially. "The intuitives morality is governed neither by thinking or feeling . . . consideration for the welfare of others is weak". Jung is showing the extrovert to also be immoral, like he abandons everything in order to explore social possibilities. I think this makes some sense, if someone is very outgoing, it is like they are really getting involved and putting themselves out there. I don't know if I would say they are willing to give up their beliefs and have no morality, and they sacrifice those things in order to be more friendly, but it gives you an idea of what extroverts are like.

In this paragraph Jung describes the general attitude of consciousness for the introverted type:

- Although the introverted consciousness is naturally aware of external conditions, it selects the subjective determinants as the decisive ones. It is therefore oriented by the factor in perception and cognition which responds to the sense stimulus in accordance with the individual's subjective disposition. For example, two people see the same object, but they never see it in such a way that the images they receive are absolutely identical. Quite apart from the variable acuteness of the sense organs and the personal equation, there often exists a radical difference, both in kind and in degree, in the psychic assimilation of the perceptual image. Whereas the extravert continually appeals to what comes to him from the object, the introvert relies principally on what the sense impression constellates in the subject. The difference in the case of a single a perception may, of course, be very delicate, but in the total psychic economy it makes itself felt in the highest degree, particularly in the effect it has on the ego. If i may anticipate, I consider the viewpoint which inclines, with Weininger, to describe the introverted attitude as philautic, autoerotic, egocentric, subjectivistic, egotistic, etc., to be misleading in principle and thoroughly depreciatory. It reflects the normal bias of the extraverted attitude in regard to the nature of the introvert. We must not forget-although the extravert is only too prone to do so-that perception and cognition are not purely objective, but are also subjectively conditioned. The world exists not merely in itself, but also as it appears to me. Indeed, at bottom, we have absolutely no criterion that could help us to form a judgment of a world which was unassimilable by the subject. If we were to ignore the subjective factor, it would be a complete denial of the great doubt as to the possibility of absolute cognition. And this would mean a relapse into the stale and hollow positivism that marred the turn of the century-an attitude of intellectual arrogance accompanied by crudeness of feeling, a violation of life as stupid as it is presumptuous. By overvaluing our capacity for subjective cognition we repress the denial of the subject. But what is the subject? The subject is man himself-we are the subject. Only a sick mind could forget that cognition must have a subject, and that there is no knowledge whatever and therefore no world at all unless "I know" has been said, though with this statement one has already expressed the subjective limitation of all knowledge.

Jung describes the consciousness of the introvert as "subjective", furthermore, "the introvert relies principally on what the sense impression constellates in the subject". I believe this means that the introvert really has his own way of thinking about what is occurring that is almost self-centered, he is described as "egocentric" by Jung later in the paragraph. Jung is basically saying that the introvert internalizes everything and biases it in his favor. "the world exists not merely in itself, but also as it appears to me" - that statement shows what Jung means when he describes the introverts thinking as internal. Furthermore, "only a sick mind could forget that cognition must have a subject, and that there is no knowledge whatever and therefore no world at all unless "I know" has been said" - that shows that when the introvert thinks, he must think of the outside, of the "subject" (or the person he is interacting with), he must say "I know" the subject, when he thinks, he needs to consider the other people involved, or he would have "a sick mind".

In this paragraph Jung tries to explain what he means when he uses the word "subjective" to describe how someone can think:

- This applies to all the psychic functions: they have a subject which is just as indispensable as the object. It is characteristic of our present extraverted sense of values that the word "subjective" usually sounds like a reproof; at all events the epithet "merely subjective" is brandished like a weapon over the head of anyone who is not boundlessly convinced of the absolute superiority of the object. We must therefore be quite clear as to what "subjective" means in this inquiry. By the subjective factor I understand that psychological saction or reaction which merges with the effect produced by the object and so gives rise to a new psychic datum. In so far as the subjective factor has, from the earliest times and among all peoples, remained in large measure constant, elementary perceptions and cognitions being almost universally the same, it is a reality that is just as firmly established as the external object. If this were not so, any sort of permanent and essentially unchanging reality would be simply inconsceivable, and any understanding of the past would be impossible. In this sense, therefore, the subjective factor is as ineluctable a datum as the extent of the sea and the radius of the earth. By the same token, the subjective factor has all the value of a co-determinant of the world we live in, a factor that can on no account be left out of our calcuations. It is another universal law, and whoever bases himself on it has a foundation as secure, as permanent, and as valid as the man who relies on the object. But just as the object and objective data do not remain permanently the same, being perishable and subject to chance, so too the subjective factor is subject to variation and individual hazards. For this reason its value is also merely relative. That is to say, the excessive development of the introverted standpoint does not lead to a better and sounder use of the subjective factor, but rather to an artificial subjectivizing of consciousness which can hardly escape the reproach "merely subjective." This is then counterbalanced by de- subjectivization which takes the form of an exaggerated extraverted attitude, an attitude aptly described by Weininger as "misautic." But since the introverted attitude is based on the ever- present, extremely real, and absolutely indispensable fact of psychic adaptation, expressions like "philautic," "egocentric," and so on are out of place and objectionable because they arouse the prejudice that is always a question of the beloved ego. Nothing could be more mistaken than such an assumption. Yet one is continually meeting it in the judgments of the extravert on the introvert. Not, of course, that I wish to ascribe this error to individual extraverts; it is rather to be down to the generally accepted extraverted view which is by no means restricted to the extraverted type, for it has just as many representatives among introverts, very much to their own detriment. The reproach of being untrue to their own nature can justly be levelled at the latter, whereas this at least cannot be held against the former.

"It is another universal law, and whoever bases himself on it has a foundation as secure, as permanent, and as valid as the man who relies on the object. But just as the object and objective data do not remain permanently the same, being perishable and subject to chance, so too the subjective factor is subject to variation and individual hazards. For this reason its value is also merely relative. That is to say, the excessive development of the introverted standpoint does not lead to a better and sounder use of the subjective factor, but rather to an artificial subjectivizing of consciousness which can hardly escape the reproach "merely subjective."" Jung suggested there that the subjective factor is "subject to variation and individual hazards", he probably means that when other people reach conclusions about other people, or think about their personality traits and their archetypes, their opinion is subject to variation - it is not very reliable and consistent. This makes sense, when you make a judgement about someone it is by no means set in stone, you may be completely wrong about the person, the system you have for making these decisions is one purely of opinion, your opinion, and it isn't necessarily going to be very accurate. In other words, the subjective factor is, indeed, "merely subjective" - "That is to say, the excessive development of the introverted standpoint does not lead to a better and sounder use of the subjective factor, but rather to an artificial subjectivizing of consciousness which can hardly escape the reproach "merely subjective.""

In this paragraph Jung discusses the differences between introversion and extroversion is consciousness:

- The archetype is a symbolic formula which always begins to function when there are no conscious ideas present, or when the conscious ideas are inhibited for internal or external reasons. The contents of the collective unconscious are represented in consciousness in the form of pronounced preferences and definite ways of looking at things. These subjective tendencies and views are generally regarded by the individual as being determined by the object-incorrectly, since they have their source in the unconscious structure of the psyche and are merely released by the effect of the object. They are stronger than the object's influence, their psychic value is higher, so that they superimpose themselves on all impressions. Thus, just as it seems incomprehensible to the introvert that the object should always be the decisive factor, it remains an enigma to the extravert how a subjective standpoint can be superior to the objective situation. He inevitably comes to the conclusion that the introvert is either a conceited egoist or crack-brained bigot. Today he would be suspected of harboring an unconscious power-complex. The introvert certainly lays himself open to these suspicions, for his positive, highly generalize manner of expressions, which appears to rule out every other opinion from the start, lends countenance to all the extravert's prejudices. Moreover the inflexibility of his subjective judgment, setting itself above all objective data, is sufficient in itself to create the impression of marked egocentricity. Faced with this prejudice the introvert is usually at a loss for the right argument, for he is quite unaware of the unconscious but generally quite valid assumptions on which his subjective judgment and his subjective perceptions are based. In the fashion of the times he looks outside for an answer, instead of seeking it behind his own consciousness. Should be become neurotic, it is the sign of an almost complete identity of the ego with the self; the importance of the self is reduced to nil, while the ego is inflated beyond measure. The whole world-created force of the subjective factor becomes concentrated in the ego, producing a boundless power-complex and a fatuous egocentricity. Every psychology which reduces the essence of man to the unconscious power drive springs from this kind of disposition. Many of Neitzche's lapses in tasts, for example, are due to this subjectivization of consciousness.

Jung discussed how things are subjective to the introvert and objective to the extrovert - "Thus, just as it seems incomprehensible to the introvert that the object should always be the decisive factor, it remains an enigma to the extravert how a subjective standpoint can be superior to the objective situation. He inevitably comes to the conclusion that the introvert in either a conceited egoist of crack-brained bigot.". Jung means that an introvert biases information for himself, my guess would be that this is because he just doesn't care about other people. If you aren't paying attention to the other people in an interaction, it makes sense that you would be more focused on yourself. If you interact with people less, you care more about yourself and less about other people. The extrovert would be objective, because that way he might win the favor of others (instead of being self-centered). This statement shows how selfish Jung thought the introvert was - "The whole world-created force of the subjective factor becomes concentrated in the ego, producing a boundless power-complex and a fatuous egocentricity.".

In this paragraph Jung talks again about how the introverted thinking type is subjective with data:

- In the section on extraverted thinking I gave a brief description of introverted thinking (pars. 578-79) and must refer to it again here. Introverted thinking is primarily oriented by the subjective factor. At the very least the subjective factor expresses itself as a feeling of guidance which ultimately determines judgment. Sometimes it appears as a more or less complete image which serves as a criterion. But whether introverted thinking is concerned with concrete or with abstract objects, always at the decisive points it is oriented by subjective data. It does not lead from concrete experience back again to the object, but always to the subjective content. External facts are not the aim and origin of this thinking, though the introvert would often like to make his thinking appear so. It begins with the subject and leads back to the subject, far though it may range into the realm of actual reality. With regard to the establishment of new facts it is only indirectly of value, since new views rather than knowledge of new facts are its main concern. It formulates questions and creates theories, it opens up new prospects and insights, but with regard to facts its attitude is one of reserve. They are all very well as illustrative examples, but they must not be allowed to predominate. Facts are collected as evidence for a theory, never for their own sake. If ever this happens, it is merely a concession to the extraverted style. Facts are of secondary importance for this kind of thinking; what seems to it of paramount importance is the development and presentation of the subjective idea, of the initial symbolic image hovering darkly before the mind's eye. Its aim is never an intellectual reconstruction of the concrete fact, but a shaping of that dark image into a luminous idea. It wants to reach reality, to see how the external fact will fit into and fill the framework of the idea, and the creative power of this thinking shows itself when it actually creates an idea which, though not inherent in the concrete fact, is yet the most suitable abstract expression of it. Its task is completed when the idea it has fashioned seems to emerge so inevitable from the external facts that they actually prove its validity.

Jung states that facts for the introverted thinker are secondary to his own thinking, "It formulates questions and creates theories, it opens up new prospects and insights, but with regard to facts its attitude is one of reserve. They are all very well as illustrative examples, but they must not be allowed to predominate. Facts are collected as evidence for a theory, never for their own sake.". Facts are secondary to thinking, "facts are of secondary importance for this kind of thinking; what seems to it of paramount importance is the development and presentation of the subjective idea". This seems straightforward, when the introvert thinks, he ignores reality and thinks what he wants to think about a social situation. This seems fitting for an introvert, if you are not interacting with other people then they aren't going to influence your judgement - instead you are the one who is going to be influencing your judgement. You can ignore reality because you are not engaged with it.

In this paragraph Jung discusses how the selfish thinking of the introvert is balanced by the power of their unconscious mind, which can override thought and speak the truth:

- This kind of thinking easily gets lost in the immense truth of the subjective factor. It creates theories for their own sake, apparently with an eye to real or at least possible facts, but always with a distinct tendency to slip over from the world of ideas into mere imagery. Accordingly, visions of numerous possibilities appear on the scene, but none of them ever becomes a reality, until finally images are produced which no longer express anything externally real, being mere symbols of the ineffable and unknowable. It is now merely a mystical thinking and quite unfruitful as thinking that remains bound to objective data. Whereas the latter sinks to the level of a mere representation of facts, the former evaporates into a representation of the irrepresentable, far beyond anything that could be expressed in an image. The representation of facts has an incontestable truth because the subjective factor is excluded and the facts speak for themselves. Similarly, the representation of the irrepresentable has an immediate, subjective power of conviction because it demonstrates its own existence. The one says "Est, ergo est"; the other says "Cogito, ergo cogito." Introverted thinking carried to extremes arrives at the evidence of its own subjective existence, and extraverted thinking that the evidence of its complete identity with the objective fact. Just as the latter abnegates itself by evaporating into the object, the former empties itself of each and every content and has to be satisfied with merely existing. In both cases the further development of life is crowded out of the thinking function into the domain of the other psychic functions, which till then had existed in a state of relative unconsciousness. The extraordinary impoverishment of introverted thinking is compensated by a wealth of unconscious facts. The more consciousness is impelled by the thinking function to confine itself within the smallest and emptiest circle-which seems, however, to contain all the riches of the gods-the more unconscious fantasies will be enriched by a multitude of archaic contents, a veritable "pandemonium" of irrational and magical figures, whose physiognomy will accord with the nature of the function that will supersede the thinking function as the vehicle of life. If it should be the intuitive function, then the "other side" will be viewed through the eyes of a Kubin or a Meyrink. If it is the feeling function, then quite unheard-of and fantastic feeling relationships will be formed, coupled with contradictory and unintelligible value judgments. If it is the sensation function, the sense will nose up something new, and never experienced before, in and outside the body. Closer examination of these permutations will easily demonstrate a recrudescence of primitive psychology with all its characteristic features. Naturally, such experiences are not merely primitive, they are also symbolic; in fact, the more primordial and aboriginal they are, the more they represent a future truth. For everything old in the unconscious hints at something coming.

The things an introvert thinks are really inside his or her own head, "it is now merely a mystical thinking and quite unfruitful as thinking that remains bound to objective data". Furthermore, "the extraordinary impoverishment of introverted thinking is compensated by a wealth of unconscious facts . . . a veritable "pandemonium of irrational and magical figures, whose physiognomy will accord with the nature of the function that will supersede the thinking function as the vehicle of life." That quote basically means that introverted thinking is balanced by the wealth of the unconscious mind. This unconsciousness is the vehicle of life, not the thinking of the introvert. Even though the introvert biases information his or her own way, and would tend to see the world the way they want, not the socially acceptable way, their unconsciousness balances that type of thinking because it is so large and powerful. The truth is still in their unconscious mind even though their thinking points to an egocentric attitude.

In these paragraphs Jung describes how the introvert is more concerned with ideas than with people, and is even "cold":

- Just as we might take Darwin as an example of the normal extraverted thinking type, the normal introverted thinking type could be represented by Kant. The one speaks with facts, the other relies on the subjective factor. Darwin ranges over the wide field of objective reality. Kant restricts himself to a critique of knowledge. Cuvier and Nietzsche would form an even sharper contrast.

- The introverted thinking type is characterized by the primacy of the kind of thinking I have just described. Like his extraverted counterpart, he is strongly influenced by ideas, though his ideas have their origin not in objective data but in his subjective foundation. He will follow his ideas like the extravert, but in the reverse direction - inwards and not outwards. Intensity is his aim, not extensity. In these fundamental respects he differs quite unmistakably from his extraverted counterpart. What distinguishes the other, namely his intense relation to objects, is almost completely lacking in him as in every introverted type. If the object is a person, this person has a distinct feeling that he matters only in a negative way; in milder cases he is merely conscious of being de trop, but with a more extreme type he feels himself warded off as something definitely disturbing. This negative relation to the object, ranging from indifference to aversion, characterizes every introvert and makes a description of the type exceedingly difficult. Everything about him tends to disappear and get concealed. Hid judgment appears cold, inflexible, arbitrary, and ruthless, because it relates far less to the object than to the subject. One can feel nothing in it that might possibly confer a higher value on the object; it always bypasses the object and leaves one with a feeling of the subject's superiority. He may be polite, amiable, and kind, but one is constantly aware of a certain uneasiness betraying an ulterior motive-the disarming of an opponent, who must at all costs be pacified and placated lest he prove himself a nuisance. In no sense, of course, is he an opponent, but if he is at all sensitive he will feel himself repulsed, and even belittled.

The introvert directs his ideas inwards (and by inwards this means towards himself not other people) - "He will follow his ideas like the extravert, but in the reverse direction - inwards and not outwards". He doesn't really care about other people either - "if the object is a person, this person has a distinct feeling that he matters only in a negative way". "His judgment appears cold, inflexible, arbitrary, and ruthless" All this described by Jung makes sense, if someone doesn't try to be social and pay attention to other people, they are going to be more inflexible and not really care about other people.

In this paragraph Jung describes how the introvert is clumsy and unsophisticated socially because his inner world of ideas cripples him:

- Invariably the object has to submit to a certain amount of neglect, and in pathological cases it is even surrounded with quite unnecessary precautionary measures. Thus this type tends to vanish behind a cloud of misunderstanding, which gets all the thicker the more he attempts to assume, by way of compensation and with the help of his inferior functions, an air of urbanity which contrasts glaringly with his real nature. Although he will shrink from no danger in building up his world of ideas, and never shrinks form thinking a thought because it might prove to be dangerous, subversive, heretical, or wounding to other people's feelings, he is none the less beset by the greatest anxiety if ever he has to make it an objective reality. That goes against the grain. And when he does put his ideas into the world, he never introduces them like a mother solicitous for her children, but simply dumps them there and gets extremely annoyed if they fail to thrive on their own account. His amazing unpracticalness and horror of publicity in any form have a hand in this. If in his eyes his product appears correct and true, then it must be so in practice, and others have got to bow to its truth. Hardly ever will he go out of his way to win anyone's appreciation of it, especially anyone of influence. And if ever he brings himself to do so, he generally sets about it so clumsily that it has just the opposite of the effect intended. He usually has bad experiences with rivals in his own field because he never understandings how to curry their favour; as a rule he only succeeds in showing them how entirely superfluous they are to him. In the pursuit of his ideas he is generally stubborn, headstrong, and quite unamenable to influence. His suggestibility to personal influences is in strange contrast to this. He has only to be convinced of a person's seeming innocuousness to lay himself open to the most undesirable elements. They seize hold of him from the unconscious. He lets himself be brutalized and exploited in the most ignominious way if only he can be left in peace to pursue his ideas. He simply does not see when he is being plundered behind his back and wronged in practice, for to him the relation to people and things is secondary and the objective evaluation of his product is something remains unconscious of. Because he thinks out his problem to the limit, he complicates them and constantly gets entangled in his own scruples and misgivings. However clear to him the inner structure of his thoughts may be, he is not in the least clear where or how they link up with the world of reality. Only with the greatest difficulty will he bring himself to admit that what is clear to him may not be equally clear to everyone. His style is cluttered with all sorts of adjuncts, accessories, qualifications, retractions, saving clauses, doubts, etc., which all come from his scrupulosity. His work goes slowly and with difficulty.

Jung describes the introvert as not sophisticated, "an air of urbanity which contrasts glaringly with his real nature". Although the introvert "will shrink from no danger in building up his world of ideas, and never shrinks from thinking a thought because it might prove to be dangerous, subversive, heretical, or wounding to other people's feelings" - there is a down side to that type of thinking, however, "he is nonetheless beset by the greatest anxiety if he ever has to make it an objective reality". So although the introvert has these negative thoughts, they are not useful socially, and would probably only cripple him. The introverts thoughts are clear to himself, however this comes at the price of them not being clear to others - "However clear to him the inner structure of his thoughts may be, he is not in the least clear where or how they link up with the world of reality. Only with the greatest difficulty will he bring himself to admit that what is clear to him may not be equally clear to everyone.".

In this paragraph Jung describes the thinking introvert as naive, yet difficult to get along with:

- In his personal relations he is taciturn or else throws himself on people who cannot understand him, and for him this is one more proof of the abysmal stupidity of man. If for once he is understood, he easily succumbs to credulous overestimation of his prowess. Ambitious women have only to know how to take advantage of his cluelessness in practical matters to make an easy prey of him; or he may develop into a misanthropic bachelor with a childlike heart. Often he is gauche in his behavior, painfully anxious to escape notice, or else remarkably unconcerned and childishly naive. In his own special field of work he provokes the most violent opposition, which he has no notion how to deal with, unless he happens to be seduced his primitive affects into acrimonious and fruitless polemics. Casual acquaintances think him inconsiderate and domineering. But the better one knows him, the more favourable one'es judgment becomes, and his closest friends value his intimacy very highly. To outsiders he seems prickly, unapproachable, and arrogant, and sometimes soured as a result of anti-social prejudices. As a personal teacher he has little influence, since the mentality of his students is strange to him. Besides, teaching has, at bottom, no interest for him unless it happens to provide him with a theoretical problem. He is a poor teacher, because all the time he is teaching his thought is occupied with the material itself and not with its presentation.

Here the introvert is presented as naive and incapable. Like he is a good person at heart that is innocent, but because he doesn't understand social things, so he comes off as being rude - "Casual acquaintances think him inconsiderate and domineering. But the better one knows him, the more favourable one'es judgment becomes, and his closest friends value his intimacy very highly. To outsiders he seems prickly, unapproachable, and arrogant, and sometimes soured as a result of anti-social prejudices.". If someone doesn't interact well, at first it will probably appear like this person is rude and ignoring, however they are actually just as nice as the next person, and if you get to know them will learn to understand that his apparent rudeness and unfriendliness was just a lack of social understanding.

In this paragraph Jung describes what happens to the thinking introvert when his personality develops (his relations deteriorate and he becomes even more internal):

With the intensification of his type, his convictions become all the more rigid and unbending. Outside influences are shut off; as a person, too, he becomes more unsympathetic to his wider circle of acquaintances, and therefore more dependent on his intimates. His tone becomes personal and surly, and though his ideas may gain in profundity they can no longer be adequately expressed in the material at hand. To compensate for this, he falls back on emotionality and touchiness. The outside influences he has brusquely fended off attack him from within, from the unconscious, and in his efforts to defend himself he attacks things that to outsiders seem utterly unimportant. Because of the subjectivization of consciousness resulting form his lack of relationship to the object, what secretly concerns his own person now seems to him of extreme importance. He begins to confuse his subjective truth with his own personality. Although he will not try to press his convictions on anyone personally, he will burst out with vicious, personal retorts against every criticism, however just. Thus his isolation gradually increases. His originally fertilizing ideas become destructive, poisoned by the sediment of bitterness. His struggle against the influences emanating from the unconscious increases with his external isolation, until finally they begin to cripple him. He thinks his withdrawal into ever-increasing solitude will protect him from the unconscious influences, but as a rule it only plunges him deeper into the conflict that is destroying him from within.

Over time, the introverts ideas become more destructive and he becomes more isolated as a result - "His originally fertilizing ideas become destructive, poisoned by the sediment of bitterness. His struggle against the influences emanating from the unconscious increases with his external isolation, until finally they begin to cripple him. He thinks his withdrawal into ever-increasing solitude will protect him from the unconscious influences, but as a rule it only plunges him deeper into the conflict that is destroying him from within." His internal world of thinking destroys him from within because it becomes increasingly destructive.

A slightly different definition of extroversion and introversion was put forward by Eysenck (1964):

- The typical extravert is sociable, likes parties, has many friends, needs to have people to talk to, and does not like reading or studying by himself. He craves excitement, takes chances, often sticks his neck out, acts on the spur of the moment, and is generally an impulsive individual. He is fond of practical jokes, always has a ready answer, and generally likes change; he is carefree, easygoing, optimistic, and likes to "laugh and be merry". He prefers to keep moving and doing things, tends to be aggressive and lose his temper quickly; altogether his feelings are not kept under tight control, and he is not always a reliable person

- The typical introvert is quiet, retiring sort of person, introspective, fond of books rather than people; he is reserved and distant except to intimate friends. He tends to plan ahead, "looks before he leaps," and distrusts the impulse of the moment. He does not like excitement, takes matters of everyday life with proper seriousness, and likes a well-ordered mode of life. He keeps his feelings under close control, seldom behaves in an aggressive manner, and does not lose his temper easily. He is reliable, somewhat pessimistic and place great value on ethical standards.

Table 82.0

Chapter 83

Archetypes and Dreams

Carl Jung, c. 1919 advanced the concept of psychological archetypes. An archetype is a model of a person, personality or behavior. Some example archetypes are child, hero, great mother, wise old man, trickster, devil, scarecrow, and mentor. These are just people or people described with adjectives, or could be just an adjective if you change it - for instance devil could be someone who is "devilish" and mother could be someone who is "motherly". What makes the archetypes more significant than just being descriptive, however, is that they are models, there is a deep significance to each archetype. They represent a certain personality, they imply certain traits and characteristics of a person.

For instance, "wise old man" implies that there is a lot associated with that archetype. You could call someone a wise old man, but you could take that further and realize that you are implying a lot about the person by saying that. There is a certain place in our psyche for "wise old men". They have had an impact on who we are, they are a big part of our lives, without "wise old men" society would be completely different. Similarly, without those other example archetypes I mentioned in the previous paragraph, society would be completely different.

For instance, without mothers, obviously society would be different. Maybe that is why mother is described as "a great mother". There is a value placed on mothers in my guess would be every culture on the planet. Old men are often considered to be wise, it is incorporated into our psyche, when we think of old men we might think of a "wise old man". There is an understanding or prejudice in the world that old men are smart, I suppose.

You could really say that a lot of stuff has entered into the psyche of different populations in the world. A new toy could enter into the psyche of american people. When someone mentions this toy, it could bring up a lot of emotion to people. That shows that this toy has entered the psychological makeup of the general population. It is like they have been brainwashed to like the toy. Of course, if someone has not heard of the toy, it would probably not mean anything if I mentioned it. That is why archetypes are significant, because for many many reasons, they are extremely important to people. Obviously the archetypes of mother and child are important, there wouldn't be anyone alive if there weren't mothers and children.

So an archetype is just something that means something to people. There could be a collective archetype, which means something to everyone, or maybe there is something in your life that means a lot to just you. You could have your own personal archetype if you want. Maybe something in your life is very important to you. If you really like dogs you could say that dog is an archetype. Other people might not consider dog an archetype, probably because they don't think it has entered the psyche of the general population, but if you think about it dogs probably have. Dogs are extremely important to people. So archetypes are just things that are complex and significant enough to have their own psychological model associated with them. By that I mean a bunch of various things you could associate with the archetype to show its significance to the human psyche.

So "mother" is obviously very important to people, there are a lot of things this could bring up for people. Mothers play a large role in everyone's life. This doesn't mean when someone says the word "mother" it necessarily triggers a lot right then. Different things in society and in life could trigger various amounts of reaction. The archetypes are archetypes because they are especially more significant than other things in life or culture.

I would think that "friend" or "lover" are more significant than the archetype "wise old man". I am going to stop using the word archetype from now on in this article and just talk about what things are more or less significant to people in their lives, and that is all an archetype is anyway (that is not how an archetype is defined (In psychology, an archetype is a model of a person, personality, or behavior.) it is how I am defining it).

Then there is just the question, "what are the most significant objects in life"? That is a pretty significant question. Clearly the family is important, probably the most important objects in someones life, especially for emotional development if you are an adult and no longer live with them. Maybe where you live is a significant object in your life. All the items of your house and the immediate location around the house. It could be that a few items in the house are very significant for you. I wonder if these items could be generalized and significant for everything, for instance a sports item, or a cooking item, or a picture. Though a picture would really relate to the object of a person, or perhaps an aspect of a persons behavior or an aspect of their personality.

So objects relate to other objects, or if one object relates to a more significant object, then the important object there is the more significant one, and you could say that the purpose of the insignificant object is to make the more significant object more pleasurable. An obvious instance of this is male comradery, you could say that male bonding is merely to further themselves so they can achieve success with females. The males talk about girls with other males, they really only care about the females. That is just a perspective, of course the males enjoy spending time with each other, however you could label one object (the male- male interaction) as subservient to the female-male interaction, or vice versa.

There are going to be degrees an object is significant and degrees that it supports another object. Objects in a house support the object of the house. There is another way of an object supporting another object. A friend could "support" a friend. That is different than talking about objects in a house supporting a house, or your same sex interactions supporting your opposite sex interactions. One type of support is direct, the other is indirect.

It is a matter of opinion how direct the support of one object to another is. It one object intends supports, it is going to be more direct (say a friend supporting another friend). If a friend doesn't support the other friend, there still is an indirect support because they are still friends and through the friendship there is support, even though it isn't intended. That is because I am referring to an emotional support, having a friend makes the other person happy, so it is supportive. Whether or not the friend intends to make the other person happy, making the support direct or indirect, isn't as important as if there is support or not (I don't think it matters if it is direct or not).

That being said, how could an object that isn't a person support another object intentionally? Non-living things don't have intent. They don't think. Your television doesn't purposefully support you by providing entertainment. It indirectly supports you because it can't think and provide "direct" support, but the indirect support of making you happy from entertainment is still there. If a person directly tries to make you happy, that is an example of one object serving the purposes of another.

The objects in a house serve the purpose of the house, without anything in a house the house wouldn't be very entertaining to be in. This type of support, where one object serves the purpose of another, is commonplace. All objects serve the purpose of other objects in life (and a person can be an object). So all people help and serve the purpose of other people. More specifically, certain aspects of people help and support other people - like if an old man is wise, his wisdom could be supportive. If someone is devilish, that could hinder another person because the devil-like person is being mean, or it could be supportive because it adds character to the persons personality.

So there are objects, and objects within objects, objects outside of objects, and objects may help or hinder other objects to different degrees. An object within an object might be a persons personality traits being within the person, or the objects in a house being in the house. How you might define or describe that is also a matter of opinion. A person could hinder another person, or a certain personality trait of one person could help another person because it makes the person who has the personality trait a certain way (for instance, devilish).

In your kitchen, the refrigerator could support the purpose of the microwave - the fridge provides the food that you put in the microwave. In life, everything is related to everything else is some ways. The statement seems obvious, but if you look closer to these types of relationships in life you could discover a lot.

Table 83.0

Chapter 84

The Function of the Unconscious

In Carl Jung's essay, "The Relations Between the Ego and the Unconscious" in the section "The Function of the Unconscious" Jung outlined many ideas he had about, well, the function of the unconscious:

- There are certainly not a few people who are afraid to admit that the unconscious could ever have "big" ideas. They will object, "But do you really believe that the unconscious is capable of offering anything like a constructive criticism of our western mentality? Of course if we take the problem intellectually and impute rational intentions to the unconscious, the thing becomes absurd. But it would never do to foist our conscious psychology upon the unconscious. Its mentality is an instinctive one; it has no differentiated functions, and it does not "think" as we understand "thinking." It simply creates an image that answers to the conscious situation. This image contains as much thought as feeling, and is anything other than a product of rationalistic reflection. Such an image would be better described as an artistic vision. We tend to forget that a problem like the one which underlies the dream last mentioned cannot, even to the conscious mind of the dreamer, be an intellectual problem, but is profoundly emotional.

Jung begins this paragraph by talking about how the unconscious isn't very intelligent - he says that "there are certainly not a few people who are afraid to admit that the unconscious could ever have "big" ideas." And he is right, the unconscious clearly doesn't think as clearly and logically as the conscious mind. For the most part, your unconscious mind does not reach decisions for you, it simply responds to the decisions your conscious mind makes. You are the one who does the complex thinking in your life, the advanced and intricate thoughts ranging from thinking about everyday things to more complex problems. When you read a book or think about anything complex, you consciously understand why it is significant. If you don't consciously understand why it is significant then your unconscious isn't going to understand either. Your unconscious may pick up on why it is significant - get a "feel" for the significance, but it is never going to actually understand how and why what you are thinking about is significant, the unconscious simply isn't capable of "big ideas".

Your unconscious mind usually isn't going to be the one reaching conclusions. When people think, they are usually aware of what they are thinking. A good question is how much of our thought is unconscious - how much thought occurs without our awareness. How much of that thought helps you reach conclusions and make decisions? What even is unconscious thought? Occasionally people might reach conclusions or make a decision without them being aware they are reaching that conclusion, the most obvious state of that is when someone is first waking up from sleep and they have a problem getting alert.

Jung describes the unconscious as "an image" that "contains as much thought as feeling" and better described as an "artistic vision" the unconscious creates this image "that answers to the conscious situation". But what is an unconscious image? Why is the word image used by Jung? I believe that it is used because the unconscious is incredibly complex and cannot be described completely with words - it is like an image. There is a picture in your mind or an understanding of the situation that you understand consciously. The image is there unconsciously, you cannot look at all the details of the image at one time, but the image is there in your mind influencing you.

It is very interesting that Jung uses the word image to describe how the unconscious functions. That is like describing thought by saying it is a picture or a piece of art. This makes sense, consciously people can only think with words. Your conscious understanding of a situation is partially defined by your ability to describe it with words. You cannot describe an image with words as well, however. That is why the image is unconscious, because it has a lot of detail like any picture, but you cannot describe all the detail in the image. Thought is a beautiful tapestry and only a small amount of it can be understood by describing the conscious situation with words.

Can someone's entire understanding of a situation be described? Clearly not. In any social situation, or any situation that might occur in life, you cannot describe everything that is going on perfectly. You have an image in your mind of what the situation is, or a memory or emotion of that situation. You could have an emotion for an event or situation or anything in life, this emotion is how you remember the situation or event. When you think of the event, you remember the emotion you got from it. That is how your mind understands everything that occurred. You don't remember the event by describing with a lot of sentences what happened, you remember it by the image or emotion you have of it in your head. This emotion-image contains a lot more information, mostly emotional information, of what happened during that situation.

These were the next sentences in that paragraph by Jung:

- For a moral man the ethical problem is a passionate question which has its roots in the deepest instinctual processes as well as in its most idealistic aspirations. The problem for him is devastatingly real. It is not surprising, therefore, that the answer likewise springs from the depths of his nature. The fact that everyone thinks his psychology is the measure of all things, and, if he also happens to be a fool, will inevitably think that such a problem is beneath his notice, should not trouble the psychologist in the least, for he has to take things objectively, as he finds them,   without twisting them to fit his subjective suppositions. The richer and more capacious natures may legitimately be gripped by an interpersonal problem, and to the extent that this is so, their unconscious can answer in the same style. And just as the conscious mind can put the question, "Why is there this frightful conflict between good and evil?," so the unconscious can reply, "Look closer! Each needs the other. The best, just because it is the best, holds the seed of evil, and there is nothing so bad but good can come of it."

Jung talks about a moral man with an ethical problem, for him the problem is "devastatingly real", he then mentions someone who thinks "his psychology is the measure of all things" (obviously thinking overly great things about himself arrogantly) and a fool and that this person would have to take things objectively without twisting them to fit his "subjective suppositions". He means by that that this foolish person would have to take things as they are, not interpret what happens in his or her own way. This is very important, he is saying that on one hand you have a moral man who takes an ethical problem to be very real, and on the other hand you have an arrogant fool who thinks "such a problem would be beneath his notice".

So one person is ignoring things like ethical problems and interpreting everything that happens in his own biased way. The other person is moral, and takes ethical problems very seriously, this person probably doesn't bias his interpretation of events but instead feels bad when something bad happens. The significance of these two approaches is in how emotion is processed. If one person thinks everything that happens is tilted in their favor, they are less likely to experience the emotions they should be experiencing because they are biasing everything. They might not care about someone else or if something they don't like happens, they might not recognize it and might not feel anything from it. In order to feel emotion, you need to recognize events for what they are, not dismiss them because you fit them to fit your "subjective suppositions", but take events in life seriously with the full weight they deserve. For instance, if something bad happens to someone else this person might not care because they might twist the event in their mind to think nothing really bad happened to that person so it doesn't cause them to care or feel bad for that person themselves.

The moral man, on the other hand, for whom moral problems are "devastatingly real" cares deeply about things that occur that are bad, and therefore would probably really feel and connect, experiencing the world as it is and feeling as much as he can from it. These two approaches illustrate something very significant about the unconscious, that whatever it is you are thinking about something, your unconscious mind is going to feel very strongly and respond in a very strong way. Of course it probably is that the person that is ignoring bad things will not feel for them as strongly as the person who isn't ignoring them, but the point is that if something really bad happens to you, your unconscious mind is going to make you feel very strongly. You have ideas and biases of what happens, and these might influence how much you care, but unconsciously you care in an entirely different way - either type of person might feel various things from a bad event occurring. Your unconscious mind is a separate entity.

A rich mind may be gripped by an interpersonal problem - that means they consciously will be troubled by it, and "their unconscious will answer in the same style" - this means that your unconscious will cause you to feel and respond in the same way your conscious mind did. For the foolish man who biases events, and wouldn't be gripped" by an interpersonal problem, his unconscious might be gripped by it and cause him to feel a lot, but that wouldn't be in the same style as his conscious was thinking. The foolish man might ignore the evil in people because he is twisting things his way, but his unconscious wouldn't - his unconscious would say, "'Look closer! Each needs the other. The best, just because it is the best, holds the seed of evil...'"

In fact, saying "look closer" is a great description for the unconscious, no matter what you think occurred in an event, the unconscious mind is going to "know", probably much better, what occurred in that event and make you feel the appropriate things (no matter what you want to feel). Your unconscious mind takes a much "closer" look at what happens and is much more refined and complicated than your conscious one. You actually have a much deeper understanding of events than you would think, however this understanding is mostly unconscious. *The point here is, no matter what you think happened or what your interpretation of events is, your unconscious mind is going to know, understand and respond by making you feel the appropriate things. You respond to situations largely from your unconscious, everything you feel isn't determined by your thought or your conscious mind - it is mostly determined by your unconscious.*

Your unconscious mind determines what you feel. People's feelings are so complicated that there is no way you could consciously, deliberately determine what emotions and feelings you are going to feel. People can control what thoughts they think for the most part, and to a certain extent that influences your feelings - however emotion is like a piece of art, it cannot be explained in a logical fashion that would be comprehensible to your consciousness.

There might even be large things that occur in your life that you are not aware of. These things might be under the awareness of your unconscious, however, if you could say your unconscious has awareness, by definition it being what you are not aware of. But your unconscious mind is so powerful that you could say it is different from who you are, you understand yourself and your consciousness, but do you understand what is happening in your unconscious mind? There could be many significant things about yourself you don't know because they are locked in your unconscious. There could be conscious things you once knew that your unconscious repressed and hid.

But this seems fairly simple, how much could you possibly be missing about understanding yourself? How much could you be missing about what is going on in your life? People have a great deal of feelings, and these too can be conscious or unconscious. But what does that mean, a feeling being unconscious? It is clear when a feeling in conscious, you feel it and that is that. But what happens when a feeling is unconscious? How does a feeling that is conscious feel? If you are not fully aware of it, why would it even matter if you are feeling it at all?

Dogs seem to experience emotions all the time they aren't "aware" of. Of course they aren't going to be aware of that because they are dogs. They don't have a higher consciousness. Dogs get sad and happy, and that is that. I wouldn't say that dogs have a large unconscious mind. What could possibly be happening in the unconscious mind of a dog? That question sounds absurd, dogs aren't complicated enough to have an unconscious.

In Jung's book "on the Nature of the Psyche" he outlines various things that are noticed by the conscious mind:

- So defined, the unconscious depicts an extremely fluid state of affairs: everything of which i know, but of what i am not at the moment thinking; everything which I was once conscious but have now forgotten; everything perceived by my senses, but not noted by my conscious mind; everything which, involuntarily and without paying attention to it, I feel, think, want, remember, and do;

Chapter

all the future things which are taking shape in me and will sometime come to consciousness: all this is the content of the unconscious. These contents are all more or less capable, so to speak, of consciousness, or were once conscious and may become conscious the next moment . . . To this marginal phenomenon . . . there also belong the Freudian findings we have already noted.

So that quote just basically says that some things are conscious sometimes, and you see a lot of stuff that doesn't all or maybe a small amount come to consciousness. That is pretty simple, of the world you perceive only a small amount is going to be conscious. Therefore what you care about isn't everything that is in your mind. There could be a lot of things you should be caring about but they are unconscious and beneath your awareness. There could be things very important to you that you don't know are important to you. No one understands the entirety of their own mind and psychology.

Then there is obviously the intensity of consciousness, things may be conscious to various intensity. Feelings can vary in intensity, and a conscious experience could vary in intensity. But what exactly is a conscious experience? If you experience an event what occurs in your mind is mostly feelings and thoughts. But saying that "all that occurs in someones mind in any experience is feelings and thoughts" is really shortchanging life. Life is much more complicated than "a certain set of feelings and thoughts, laid out over a period of time".

But that is what Jungian psychology is all about, the mysteries of the unconscious mind and how they are deep, significant, and warrant closer attention. Jung describes in his book "The Structure of the Psyche" the relationship between instincts and archetypes - I think this shows how there are many things about the experience of life that you can observe in the unconscious:

- a dead deposit, a sort of abandoned rubbish heap, but a living system of reactions and aptitudes that determine the individual's life in invisible ways . . . the archetypes are simply the forms which the instincts assume. From the living fountain of instinct flows everything that is creative, hence the unconscious is not merely conditioned by history, but is the very source of the creative impulse.

So there are archetypes and there are instincts and there is creativity. Archetype refers to a generic version of a personality. In this sense "mother figure" may be considered an archetype and may be identified in various characters with otherwise distinct (non-generic) personalities. That is what an archetypes is, then how are archetypes "the forms which the instincts assume"?

Archetypes show how there is a great depth of thought in people, that people simply don't have thoughts and feelings and that is it, but that thought is very complicated, involving intricate unconscious factors. The thought of an archetype, such as mother, child, hero, or devil - is a very powerful and significant thought. Furthermore, these thoughts are integrated into your unconscious mind, the unconscious is instinctual because it is powerful and innate. So the deep thought and significance associated with the archetypes is a powerful part of your unconscious mind, even though it is only thought (unconscious).

Table 84.0

Values - Relish and Enthusiasm

- *Life is something to be enjoyed to the full, sensuously enjoyed with relish and enthusiasm.*

Relish means to take pleasure in, and enthusiasm means a lively interest. These words have a much more complicated significance, however. You could describe someone who is enthusiastic as being over excited and irritable, instead of just having a healthy interest. Also, you could describe someone who is relishing something as being so actively interested in it that they might be acting off an impulse - an impulse is a wish or urge, particularly a sudden one. So I have shown that the words relish and enthusiasm could on one hand suggest that someone is just being interested in something or taking pleasure in something - which is pretty much what the words mean, or they could suggest a greater intensity, an obsession like interest and pleasure in something.

So someone relishing something could be enjoying it so much that it would be an impluse to get invovled with it - that they have a sudden wish or urge to enjoy it. Or when you say, "this person is relishing that" you could just mean what the word normally suggests, that they are taking pleasure in it, not suggesting that they have become so obsessed with it that they respond to it with an impulse.

When someone uses the word enthusiasm, they probably just mean a lively interest. "That person is enthusiastic about the sports game", they don't necessarily mean that this interest has gotten to a much higher level than that and the person is becoming over excited and irritable. It just goes to show that the words relish and enthusiasm could mean on one hand a mild interest and pleasure in something or on the other, an obsessive, violent, and impulsive interest and pleasure.

The value statement, however "life is something to be enjoyed to the full, sensuously enjoyed with relish and enthusiasm" doesn't imply that the person should become obsessed with life and start going crazy, getting over excited and irritable about it. The word sensuous is used, however which suggests that you   really feel life in a pleasurable fashion through the senses. Maybe using the word sensuous to describe how life should be enjoyed suggests a violent level of interest in life, or maybe it simply suggests a mild interest.

Table 85.0

Chapter

Values a Character and Honesty

• *Character and honesty will tell in the long run; most people get pretty much what they deserve.*

Character traits describe ways of relating to people or reacting to situations or ways of being. A trait will bring together references to the person's moral system (whether dishonest, a cheat, or a liar), to his or her instinctual makeup (impulsive), basic temperament (cheerful, optimistic, or pessimistic), complex ego functions (humorous, perceptive, brilliant, or superstitious), and basic attitudes toward the world (kind, trustful, or skeptical) and him- or herself (hesitant). So someone could be responsible (instinctual makeup), giving (basic attitude toward the world), fearless (basic attitude toward him- or herself), mean (moral system) and skillful (complex ego function).

So honesty is a character trait. Character traits describe how good or bad a person is such as innocent, loving, rude, rough, arrogant, apologetic, anxious, and wicked. As well as what that person is like (their temperament) such as warm, quiet, concerned, good, peaceful, pleasant. So character traits describe a lot about a person and what that person is really like. The simple way to describe character would be to ask, "is this person good or bad? What is their attitude towards the world or themselves? What is their demeanor and instincts? Are they gentle or dangerous?

All of the character traits point to if someone is good or bad really, clearly their moral system does, but also their temperament (such as cheerful, optimistic, or pessimistic) and instictual makeup (impulsive, responsible) do as well. Also clearly someones attitude toward the world or themselves is going to determine if they are a good or bad person. Character traits are traits that show how a person relates to other people or their way of being, so clearly these descriptions are going to indicate how that person is perceived by other people.

Personality traits show what a person is like in general, character traits show how a person interacts and who they are such as attitude, instints, intellect, kindness or cruely. When you say, "this person has a great personality" you mean that as a whole who they are is great - they have a lot of complex, dynamic traits that can describe anything about who they are. Character traits, on the other hand, refer specifically to how a person interacts with other people or who they are - so it is completely different when you say that someone has a good character than when you say someone has a good personality. When you say someone has a good personality you mean everything about them, when you say someone has a good character you mean they interact well with other people and who they are is a good person.

Table 86.0

Chapter

Value - Will Power
Chapter

- *No weakness or difficulty can hold us back if we have enough will power.*

Will power is the strength of will to carry out one's decisions, wishes, or plans. But what does that mean, the "strength of will"? It is referring how much power a person has over their own mind. If someone has power over their own mind, or a lot of self control and self-discipline, then they would have enough "strength" to carry out their own decisions, wishes and plans. Will power is used for those purposes, but that doesn't mean that the force of mind used in it is used only for those purposes (your own objectives). Someone could use their will, or we could just call it self-discipline - to do a lot of things in life. You could just say will-power is a focusing of sorts that enables you to perform certain mental actions that without such focus you wouldn't be able to do those actions, you need more "power" or "will power" in order to perform this activity.

It isn't referring to a physical power but a mental one. Someone might physically be capable of taking a walk, but they might not mentally be capable of it - maybe they are too lazy or troubled psychologically otherwise, or their mind isn't collected enough at the moment for them to do such a directed activity. Will power is basically the force your mind has, it is a mental force just like walking is a physical force that your body can exert.

Will power can increase if someone simply tries harder, it is easy to not do any work and not think, but that wouldn't be showing any mental power or strength. Also, it is even harder to do mental work if you are in a negative emotional state, distracted, tired or otherwise troubled mentally somehow. Your ability to perform complicated mental tasks probably varies throughout the day, at any one time you might be more focused than at any other time.

The most important aspect of will power is that it usually is referring to a type of inner strength that people could have all the time. Its most important quality is that of discipline - in contrast to being lazy, will power shows the personal achievement of getting what you want or what you wanted to do when otherwise you were being too lazy or lacking focus. That is why will power usually refers to someone carrying out their own wishes, decisions and plans - because those things are the most common thing you would need or want to focus on to do.

Table 87.0

Chapter

Value - Emotional Control

Chapter

- *Man should control his bodily senses, his emotions, feelings, and wishes.*

People want emotional control so they don't experience pain. If someone could control their emotions, then they would stop pain from occurring. That isn't completely true, however, since a negative emotion could serve a functional purpose. It could provide a source of stimulation or thought. High levels of distress might produce high levels of negative emotions. If someone is in distress, it would probably be harder to control your emotions since you are experiencing large amounts of the emotion pain - it would be hard to feel the experience of many other emotions at the same time.

There is some control that people can have over their emotions, irrational beliefs don't allow a person to be reasonable and express a situation as moderately negative. If someone is being irrational, they may think that something really bad is happening to them, and therefore feel strong negative emotions because they believe themselves to be in pain. Irrational beliefs are rigid, absolutistic beliefs, expressed in the form of "musts", "shoulds" and "oughts". Rational beliefs are based on flexible premises, being expressed as desires and preferences.

If you think about it, your desires and preferences alone could help direct a positive emotional experience. If you understand what is going on in your life or in the situation you are in and think about it positively in terms of your desires and preferences, then you might feel really good because you are thinking about the situation in a very positive light. It is like just repeating to yourself the positives in the situation and this may help you realize or be aware of your own positive emotions.

That being said, people mostly cannot control their emotions. If something happens to you then you are probably going to feel the appropriate emotion and there is nothing you are going to be able to do about it. No one knows how thought exactly influences what we feel, but for certain if you don't have irrational beliefs that make the situation look negative and you instead focus on your own desires and preferences you will probably feel better, in addition to being in a better position to change what happens in the situation, which would also probably make you feel better.

Table 88.0

Chapter

Belief - Purpose in Life

Chapter

- *No time is better spent than that devoted to thinking about the ultimate purposes of life.*

Everyone may seek their own meaning in life, if life had the exact same meaning for each person, then we would all be the same. The meaning and purpose of life could be outlined with a few descriptive words, describing the general main activities that people engage in, or it could be described in great detail, outlining the many things that people can do and the rewards they can get.

There are a great many activities that people can do, there are also a great number of intellectual and emotional pursuits people could have. People have motivations that are satisfied by the satisfaction of emotion, or intellectual needs that are satisfied by gaining wisdom. People could have fun and experience pleasure, or they could achieve some other goal that doesn't relate to emotional satisfaction, but an intellectual satisfaction such as doing good or the right thing or they could gain knowledge and wisdom.

People could also realize their potential and ideas, they could become the person they always wanted to be. This would be a type of intellectual satisfaction, though it would only be achieved if certain types of emotional satisfaction were met. You could have an idea of what you life should be like emotionally, and when you understand that your life is like this then you would be intellectually satisfied.

How is it that just "becoming the person you wanted to be" can be so fulfilling? It is really just a short way of describing everything in life and everything you could gain from it - you could easily be just as happy without understanding that you wanted to be that way, you don't need to have goals in order to live a fulfilling life. I would say that the only thing understanding if you have become the person you want to be brings is a conscious understanding of how meaningful your life is, it is possible that you could have a meaningful life without understanding that.

Table 89.0

Chapter

Value - Virtue
Chapter

- *To starve is a small matter, to lose one's virtue is a great one.*

Virtue (Latin: virtus, Greek: ἀρετή "arete") is moral excellence. A virtue is a positive trait or quality subjectively deemed to be morally excellent and thus is valued as a foundation of principle and good moral being. Virtue is a behavior showing a high moral standard and is a pattern of thought and behavior based on high moral standards.

Anyone could have their own idea of which qualities are virtuous, or certain societies could have their own set of qualities which they might deem virtuous. Some Hindu virtues are restraint, altruism, honesty, cleanliness, and peace. Some roman virtues were dignity, discipline, tenacity, frugality, and gravity. It all depends what you consider to be very moral. And of course something considered to be very moral is something that would be judged as being a very good quality in terms of goodness - the right and proper thing to do.

People value virtues, you could say that virtues are values because they are qualities held in high esteem. Each individual has a core of underlying values that contribute to his or her system of beliefs, ideas and/or opinions. Someone could value kindness, and since kindness is something which shows moral excellence, it would also be a virtue.

Why are some things considered to be virtues and others are not? Why does the person making the decision of what is a virute matter so much? Everyone has their own ideas of what the "good" and "right" thing to do is. In fact, one person or culture might think something really terrible and evil (from one persons perspective) is the right thing to do and a virtue. One persons perception of what evil is could be very unique, he or she could be one out of a million people that has that perspective - that doesn't mean that the perspective is wrong, however.

How would one go about outlining what someone thought evil was? If you can explain what your idea of evil is, then it could help you to realize what you think are virtues because it would help your understanding of both good and evil (since good is the opposite of evil). You could list all the things you considered evil and all the things you considered to be "good" for starters.

Table 90.0

Chapter

Value - Morals
Chapter

- *There is no worthy purpose but the resolution to do right.*

Morality (from the Latin moralitas "manner, character, proper behavior") is the differentiation among intentions, decisions, and actions between those that are good (or right) and bad (or wrong). So someone who might be considered to have morals would be someone who is considered to "do the right (not bad or wrong) things". What would this meabe for that persons personality as a whole? Not every action someone does could possibly be the "right" thing to do. Even if that were the case, what would someone with perfect morals be like?

How do people define what the right and proper action is in a society? There are norms of what the right things to do are, certain behaviors are generally accepted in each society as either right or wrong. Therefore someone that always did what was considered to be "right" would just be an ideal citizen, because he or she only does what his or her society believes to be the correct thing. It isn't that straightforward, however, because while they might agree on a few behaviors, most people would disagree on what most of the right or wrong behaviors are.

For instance, most people would agree that murder is wrong, and something therefore someone without morals might do, or without morals for those types of behaviors, at least. However, what about most behaviors? Not all behaviors are either labeled as "right" or "wrong", though they could be. In someones opinion, they could label anything someone else does as either "right" or "wrong", though it would be hard to argue how something like choosing one profession over another could be the "wrong" thing to do. By using the label "right" or "wrong" it is implied that a "wrong" thing to do is really bad, that the person doing it is being evil or breaking some sort of moral code or societal standard of goodness.

For certain someone that does the proper right thing all the time would be looked up upon, probably because doing honorable actions is "good". People like people who are nice because it makes them feel good. Someone perfectly moral would be one of the nicer types of people because everything they did would be considered to be kind and good. It should be obvious why someone doing the right thing would be looked up upon, I don't know of anyone who would want someone to destroy society - it is something we all live in and everyone wants at least what is best for themselves.

Table 91.0

Chapter

Value - Love
Chapter

- *There are no human problems that love cannot solve.*

Love can be a means to achieve peace between two people. If they see that there is love, then they might see that they don't have to be hostile anymore. Love could be a goal that gives both parties something instead of being hostile, which might not give either party in an encounter something.

Why would love give both people or sides in an interaction something? Love generates positive feelings, that is why. If people are being hostile to each other, being hostile alone isn't going to generate positive feelings. It may achieve some other objective, but it isn't going to make either person feel good. That is perhaps why love can solve problems, because it has the power to make people happy.

This doesn't mean, that if there is an interaction, the two people fall in love with each other. It means that the two people experience positive emotions toward each other instead of hostile ones. Love, being the most extreme positive emotion, is just the emotion used to represent all the positive emotions because it is so powerful. So when someone says, "just use love" they don't mean to actually fall in love, they mean use love to achieve a positive atmosphere or attitude and therefore experience the benefits of that, which are similar to the experience of love.

Why is love such a powerful positive emotion? If you think about it, just the emotion happiness isn't as powerful as love would be. Love is powerful because people really like romantic relationships, love represents the good and gentle aspect a romantic relationship could have, that is why it is so powerful.

Table 92.0

Chapter

Value Boldness
Chapter

- *Love action, and care little that others may think you rash.*

This statement is rather straightforward, it is simply saying to be bold and not care if others think you are being careless. However, it seems to be suggesting something more significant, "love action" implies that you are really doing something great, not just simply bold. This makes a lot of sense, if someone wasn't proactive, trying to do things actively, then life for them would be pretty boring, they wouldn't be seeking adventure or being invested in life at all.

So the words "love action" imply that you are really getting into life, that you aren't going to be stagnant you are going to love being aggressive and a go-getter. You are being ambitious and caring about life, to the point that you don't care if others think you are being rash.

It makes sense that the adventurous person would be the ideal our imagination can create. How interesting would someone be if they just sat around and did nothing and wasn't bold at all? People look up to people that are powerful and interesting. Even if it isn't realistic, people love heroes as well. A hero couldn't be a hero unless he or she "loved action".

The statement doesn't refer to heroes, however, it refers to the common person. Therefore, the common person can attain the qualities of a hero by being forward, showing an interest in action, and even idolizing himself to the point where it wouldn't matter if he was "rash".

Table 93.0

Chapter

Value - Time
Chapter

- *The past is no more, the future may never be, the present is all that we can be sure of.*

How does someones sense of time function? Are people constantly hoping for the future, or constantly dwelling on the past? Is someones entire life simply them just "being in the present"? The present is certainly the strongest time period because that is what we are currently in all of the time. The past has already happened as well, and the future might not occur at all or if it does you wouldn't know now what is going to happen exactly anyway. Therefore the most important time period is the present.

On the other hand, there is a constant conscious and unconscious thought process that involves reflection on the past and future as well as what is going on in the present. If you think about it, all the emotional development you have incurred over your life and your memories all contribute to what you are thinking in the present, so whenever you think you are really reflecting on the past to a certain degree.

Similarly, you are also constantly planning for the future, even in a conversation you are going to be thinking about what to say next, planning on how the conversation is going to be drawn out. You have an idea what is going to happen to you for the rest of the day, and this concept influences your behavior "in the present" for that entire day.

Also, someones sense of time can be moving slow, fast, or normal speed. If someone is experiencing pain then it seems like time is meaningless and there is no point in living, then time would probably be moving rather slow and in a painstaking fashion. Your sense of time probably varies all the time in complicated ways, it would be great if life was always fun and time drawn out in a way that was enjoyable - but I wouldn't think life is like that for anyone.

Table 94.0

Chapter

Value Chapter Inner Experience

- *The most rewarding object of study any man can find is his own inner life.*

People care mostly about themselves, so therefore they are going to be mostly interested in studying their own feelings and experience of the world, their "inner life". This concept is more complicated than it may seem - it is the entire concept of being aware of yourself and consciousness. How much about your own life do you actually understand? How can someone get a greater appreciation and understanding of themselves and their own life?

Many different types of reflection could help someone gain a greater understanding of their inner life. They can reflect on what they have done recently, simply think more about what is going on their lives. I don't know what the difference would be between saying you are "studying" you own life or just "thinking" more about it, however. People naturally think about their own lives and analyze what is going on their life all the time.

People actually engage in two different types of self-analysis: self-reflection (enjoying analyzing the self) and self-rumination (not being able to shut off thoughts about the self). Self-awareness represents a higher form of consciousness which makes it possible for us humans to become the object of our own attention and to acknowledge our own existence. When self-aware we actively examine our personal characteristics, that is, our physical appearance, typical behaviors, emotions, motives, personality traits, values, attitudes, thoughts, sensations, etc.

Differences in levels of self-focused attention deeply affect our behavior. For example, past studies suggest that if you are highly selfaware you will know yourself better than less self-aware people, engage more effectively in self-regulation (i.e., monitoring and modifying your behavior), feel emotions more intensely, behave more consistently with your attitudes, conform less to social pressure, self-disclose more in intimate relationships, and react more strongly to social rejection.

Maybe you personally know people who spend a lot of time analyzing themselves—they seem to constantly be "beating around the bush", re-evaluating themselves, always questioning their behavior and appearance, being unsure of themselves, nervous, etc. This is self rumination: anxious attention paid to the self, where the person is afraid to fail and keeps wondering about his/her self-worth. Then maybe you have other acquaintances who are also highly self-aware, but instead of being anxious about themselves, they have wisdom they know themselves very well, are the "contemplating" type, feel secure, have depth, and are philosophical about their shortcomings. This is self-reflection: a genuine curiosity about the self, where the person is intrigued and interested in learning more about his/her emotions, values, thought processes, attitudes, etc. So we all analyze our inner thoughts and feelings (self-awareness), but some of us feel anxious about what we might discover about ourselves (self-rumination) while others feel intrigued and fascinated about ourselves (self-reflection).

Table 95.0

Chapter

Value Chapterdualism

- *The individualist is the man who is most likely to discover the best road to a new future.*

Individualism is a social theory advocating the liberty, rights, or independent action of the individual. An individualist enters into society to further his or her own interests, or at least demands the right to serve his or her own interests, without taking the interests of society into consideration. The individualist does not lend credence to any philosophy that requires the sacrifice of the self-interest of the individual for any higher social causes.

Individualists are chiefly concerned with protecting individual autonomy against obligations imposed by social institutions (such as the state or religious morality). So what does this indicate the individual that believes in individualism is like? Would an individualist be someone more independent in general? Would an individualist therefore not like having strong social ties to people like friends? Probably not, but perhaps they would like less ties to the government.

With such a strong desire to achieve their own objectives, it makes you wonder if an individualist cares about the needs of other people. By disregarding what society wants them to do, an individualist is disregarding what "most people" in the society believe life should be lived in that society. This doesn't necessarily mean that the person doesn't care about his or her society, maybe they believe that their way of doing things would be best for everyone, or maybe they think both people's objectives can be accomplished simultaneously.

Someone that doesn't care if society functions better as a whole, and instead just cares about him or her self or the individual, might believe that each person seeking out his or her own objectives is the best way a society should function. That is what capitalism is, competition makes the economy function more efficiently. But what if it was that the government functioned better trying to make life equal for everyone (such as a system like communism)? Someone that wouldn't believe in such a system would, to put it shortly, "have no heart".

Table 96.0

Chapter

Value-Truth

Chapter

- *In the ultimate test, truth only comes from inner experience-from inspiration, mystical union, revelation, or pure meditation.*

The value statement above seems to suggest that truth only comes from within yourself and is something you really deeply understand to be true. The statement isn't referring to simple facts or opinions, but deep, complicated aspects of life that are so significant they must be "true". For instance, revelation implies you are reaching a great conclusion or discovery. Some examples of those discoveries might be an understanding of mystical union, inspiration, or pure meditation.

So basically, when something is "true" there is something really more powerful about how "truthful" it is, how it reveals something deep and complicated about life. This doesn't mean an advanced concept necessarily, it just means something that might reveal certain biases or false interpretations of the world. An example might be if someone was racist, but the truth was that all people are equal - then there might be a lot of information that comes with the revelation that all people are more or less equal - it is a statement of truth. This statement is striking because of its complication and also its overcoming of biases at the same time. The "truth" might be something not only hard to understand, but something you were not willing to admit previously because of a bias in judgement.

That is why the words "inspiration", "mystical union", and "pure meditation" are used as well as the word "revelation" to describe truth. It is because something true might be something you really need to think deeply about in order to discover. It isn't just something complicated, but you might need to overcome emotional biases - something pure meditation might help with - in order to discover the truth.

In order to overcome an emotional bias, someone might really need to experience something that is powerful, such as inspiration or a mystical union. This is so because the nature of emotion is such that you can only think clearly if you are personally involved in a deep, "true", powerful and clear way. This heightened emotional experience might help you to see the "truth".

Table 97.0

Chapter

Value - Contemplation

Chapter

- *Contemplation is the highest form of human activity.*

Contemplation means thinking about something, paying attention to something (in a thoughtful manner), or basically just considering something. Saying that contemplation is the highest form of human activity is basically like saying that thought is the most important human activity, but not exactly. Contemplation includes an appreciation, an effort of paying attention to something that thought alone doesn't include.

If you contemplate something, you do more than just "think" about it - you focus on it, consider it, think about it carefully and attentively. So contemplation is just a higher form of thought. Saying it is a high form of human activity is placing intellect above other activities someone could do, such as a physical activity, a physical activity with little thought, or just thinking a little and not really being engaged with that thinking - not "contemplating".

So saying that contemplation is a high form of activity is showing how contemplation is similar to meditation, you are really focusing when you contemplate - showing care and really considering something. However, just saying that the deepest, most significant aspect of contemplation is "just really considering something" is downplaying how significant people think deep contemplation can really be. The highest form of thought, which is basically contemplation, can be something the people consider to be very powerful, moving and (most importantly) intellectually significant. That is why contemplation is a word often used when referring to how someone could think about God, you can "contemplate" God and the meaning of life, this isn't a trivial activity, it is a high and meaningful form of thought.

Thought is very significant to human beings, so it makes sense that there would be a word for the highest form of thought and this word (contemplation) would be considered to be the highest form of human activity. It should be obvious why thought is important to human beings, without thought, humans would just be like other animals that aren't conscious as human are. Contemplation, being a high form of thought, demonstrates the power of the human mind.

Table 98.0

Chapter

415

Value - Honor

Chapter

- *An insult to our honor should always be punished.*

There is a difference between honor and glory (though they are similar). Glory is more like fame, you gloat in the admiration of other people - that is glory. Honor, on the other hand, is your own personal belief of how respected you are. That also includes your own respect for yourself, which is why honesty and integrity (and the belief you are like that) is another definition for honor.

It is possible that honor can be gained by achieving glory or fame, or having a high social status. Anything that increases the respect you have would increase your honor. Unless you consider it honorable to be disrespected, everyone could have their own definition of what is honorable to them, however there would probably be a similar ideal of an honorable person in each nation or culture group.

In fact, there could be many ways a society defines or appreciates what qualities would be honorable in a person. Possession of certain goods, doing certain activities, having a certain job might all contribute to the communities perception of how honorable or how much glory a person would have. There are also certain people you might wish to present as honorable to more than others, such as your friends or family. Honor and glory could be extremely important to someone personally or to a society. They are worthy goals that might be very meaningful or fun to many different types of people.

The possession of material goods as well as pretty women can be indicators of status. The concepts of honor and glory are critical to understanding the motivation of the heroes in Homer's Iliad. Glory was gained by great, heroic actions and deeds and was conferred upon an individual by others who witnessed and acclaimed the glorious actions. Major battles provided an opportunity for many to find glory at once. Honor was similar to glory, but while the public had to view actions and deem them glorious, each individual maintained their own sense of personal honor which did not always coincide with honor as defined or perceived by the masses. Honor was gained through heroism in battle, but also through compelling speechmaking, loyalty and other noble qualities that a person might demonstrate.

Table 99.0

Chapter 416

Value - The Immaterial
Chapter 100

- *The ultimate and true reality is above the senses; immaterial, spiritual, unchanging, and everlasting.*

Valuing things that are "above the senses" shows a more intellectual type of value instead of a physical, pleasure based one. It is interesting that the "true reality" would be this intellectual, above the senses world because that is a world you cannot feel physically, so you would think that the true reality would be a world you can actually literally feel instead of one that you only feel with your mind and imagination. However, considering different viewpoints, it could be viewed that the world you create in your mind is the true reality instead of the world which you can only physically feel.

So things in the real world you can physically feel, and these give rise to pleasurable sensations. From this physical world you create your own rich inner world in your mind, one of thought, intellect, imagination, and senses you feel "in your head". This could mean that emotions and feelings are in your head and above the physical senses like that of touch. So you can still feel things in your mind, it just isn't as tangible as things related to the senses. Which world is more real? The world created in your mind (your thoughts, feelings and emotions) or the world you experience with your senses (your physical reaction to the world)?

Of course there is a mix of emotion and physical, the two worlds combine in feeling. Stimulation is an example of that, if you are sexually aroused, it is a physical sensation but there are going to be associated emotions involved. Stimulation is like a combination of emotion and physical stimulus, which is a sensation. You could say there is at least a little physical sensation in any emotion. The world in which you feel attracted to other people is an emotional one, but there are also occasionally going to be physical sensations mixed in.

What about the immaterial being "spiritual, unchanging and everlasting"? The world of thought and intellect is one that stays in your mind forever. When you touch something, the physical feeling is there and then it goes away once you stop touching it. The feeling could be in your mind for recall, however it wouldn't be the real sensation. There is something wonderful about the world in your mind and how it is always there, surreal (spiritual) and constant (unchanging).

Table 100.0

Chapter 418

Values - Tenderness and Passion

- *Tenderness is more important than passion in love.*

Someone being tender or experiencing the emotion of tenderness is going to feel quite differently than when they are passionate or are experiencing the emotion of passion. Passion as an emotion could be sexual and stimulating in nature, or it could be an arousal, or a more intellectual passion.

An intellectual passion in love would be a strong appreciation for the target person that generates passion - you are passionate about the other person because you appreciate them for who they are. A sexual passion in love would be more stimulation based, you are passionate for the other person because they make you sexually stimulated. There might be a mix of these two things, in addition to the severity of each or both varying.

Tenderness, on the other hand, isn't either intellectual or stimulation based like passion. Tenderness is just emotional - passion or however emotional "being passionate" makes you comes from stimulation or intellect, tenderness is something you feel that isn't a stimulation or something to be intellectually passionate about (which are the two things passion is - so passion is more stimulating or intellectual, and tenderness is more emotional and soft). It would be hard to get sexually aroused from tenderness considering that tenderness is, well, tender and not passionate and stimulating.

Therefore the statement, "tenderness is more important than passion in love" would seem to imply that love involves less sexual, stimulating, violent emotions and more calm, tender and caring ones. You could have a relationship with someone and not feel tenderness and not be in love, just be passionate about the other person. I guess you need to be tender and caring in order for the emotion of "love" to be evoked.

Table 101.0

Chapter 420

Value - Independence

Chapter 42

- *It is the man who stands alone who excites our admiration.*

Can independence be considered a value? Is independence a core belief? How can independence be defined?

Independence, as related to a persons social interactions, isn't referring to someone being materially independent and able to provide for themselves. It is referring to someone having an inner strength that allows them to be by themselves, mostly. Calling someone independent can mean a lot of things, on the surface it just means they like to be by themselves and rely less on others, but there are many other hidden subtleties of what this word means, all applicable.

Independence could be someones personal belief, they may believe themselves to be independent. That is one way to assess how independent someone is, by what their own belief of it is. It is possible that the person doesn't have any understanding of their own independence, however they are still very independent. Someones understanding could even be wrong, it is possible someone doesn't want to interact with people but really is actually heavily reliant on it.

Someone could value independence, believing greatly in their own strength, they could consider being independent to be very important, and that someone not independent is weak and frail. But then how could you say that this person likes interaction with people? If one believes so strongly in their own independence, then would they even like interpersonal interaction at all?

What if separation from people causes anxiety? Is someone weak if they need to be with other people in order to avoid pain? Does the emotion generated from interpersonal interaction make someone weak? What if the people you depended on didn't like you. You could need someone emotionally but not like them very much, though that wouldn't seem to make a lot of sense. It would seem that if you liked them more, they would generate more emotion and provide you more support.

Being invested in life isn't silly or stupid. Being invested in other people is, however because people cannot be relied upon, physically or to generate support and emotion for you. It isn't like other people are there just to provide you with support, people have their own lives and you are just one tiny aspect of that life. It is hard to assess even how much you enjoy interactions, though this could play a role in perceived independence.

People assess how much they enjoy interactions, it is automatic, you "know" if you like someone and you "know" if interacting with them is fun. Your unconscious understanding of how good a relationship is is much more complex then your conscious understanding. Consciously you only have a vague description of how good the relationship is. You might think, "this person is really important to me, he or she is really fun and supportive emotionally". But that is very vague, there are countless ways to measure how helpful various people are to you, yet consciously you can only describe a sentence or two with your idea of how good the relationships are.

How much you enjoy interactions, and how much you need them, is going to play a role in how independent you actually are. That is different from perceived independence, someone may look very independent but actually not be independent at all. How is it that your unconscious assessment of an interaction is much greater than your conscious one? All the emotional benefits of a relationship are felt unconsciously, you only have a simple understanding of how much fun it is, but in reality the emotion it generates is very complex and dynamic.

Table 102.0

Chapter 103

What is Subtle About Social Interaction?

If social interaction / psychology was straightforward, then life wouldn't be complicated and it wouldn't take 18 years of emotional development in order to become an "adult". How people socially interact develops and changes throughout their lives, so there must be very complicated factors present in social situations. People can deceive, play mind games, say completely appropriate or inappropriate things, act retarded or sophisticated, be friendly or isolated - and all of those things are just a few aspects of all the psychological factors involved in social interaction. There are many things to consider that play a role in interaction.

Emotion plays a role in interaction, people could be feeling one thing and presenting another emotion. Emotions determine how people feel which could change what they might say or act like. Judgements, prejudices, self-concepts and other thoughts play a role in what people are thinking and that influences behavior and the emotions that occur. What happened to the people involved leading up to the social interaction plays a role in how they are feeling and what they might say, what they did that day or the last week. Taking that further, their entire life history plays a role in who they are and what they have to talk about. Social interaction could be considered subtle and precise or it could be considered rather simple. Once a child can talk he can socially interact rather well fairly quickly. Animals and babies even know basic social skills, they know to greet people (friendly or hostile), they know the basic emotions involved and act in sophisticated ways. They can run when afraid, be happy and respond to positive input and affection, or even play simple games. Advanced social interaction could be considered much more complicated than that or not that much more complicated at all.

People generally act in a similar manner socially, the ways they behave are fairly simple to understand. People can act in a hostile or gentle manner, be excited or happy or sad and angry. There are different ways of thinking (based on who you are), and different ways of interacting with people. Everyone wishes to be liked, chosen or respected, but to achieve this, one must be 'visible'. Social visibility requires in turn the adoption of points of view which are original, and which are maintained with constancy and vigor. People have an image of themselves that they wish to present to others.

It is possible that people enter into relationships and associate with each other because they are similar (or think that they are). In this perspective, similarity is considered the foundation of social bonds. Individuals enter into relationships and association when they discover - or assume - that they have something in common and are similar, at least in some respects. Individuals will engage in behavior aiming to bring closer to them those with whom they are comparing themselves. It is those who are the most different who must make the required effort to get close to others. People might like other people with similar attitudes to themselves more so than people with attitudes which differ greater. There is a social desirability of personality traits and attitudes (those that are similar or not similar). In sum, similarity appears to be linked to interpersonal attraction only so far as the consequences of this relationship are psychologically rewarding. So people like to be different in order to differentiate themselves, but they are also attracted to others with similar attitudes and ways of thinking as themselves.

People are similar and different, in social situations, difference and similarity are sought simultaneously. This is so in behavior which has been referred to as the 'superior conformity of the self' (or the 'PIP effect"). (PIP from *primus inter pares* (first amongst peers or equals)) The self-image is thus central in the determination of behavior tending towards both differentiation and non-differentiation. Everyone is normally able to establish a cognitive discrimination between the self and others, and also among other people. Consequently, the search for identity is made through the assertion of difference and its recognition by others.

Character Traits

For instance, character traits are subtle because they are more related to social interaction and personal behavior than personality traits, because character traits are more related to the consistent attitudes and behaviors of a person than personality traits are. Character traits are complicated because it can be hard to understand the nature of a persons various character traits. Consider, for example, someone who presents him- or herself as a generous person. He or she may truly care about others and wish to share with them or alternatively may have learned that the appearance of generosity will gain approval from others and therefore help him or her to deny their inner greedy, covetous, or angry nature. Since it can be hard to understand why someone has one character trait, it would therefore be even harder to understand why someone has all the character traits they have (as observed by other people) - and how those character traits result in their behavior in social interaction.

Character traits describe ways of relating to people or reacting to situations or ways of being. A trait will bring together references to the person's moral system (whether dishonest, a cheat, or a liar), to his or her instinctual makeup (impulsive), basic temperament (cheerful, optimistic, or pessimistic), complex ego functions (humorous, perceptive, brilliant, or superstitious), and basic attitudes toward the world (kind, trustful, or skeptical) and him- or herself (hesitant). So someone could be responsible (instinctual makeup), giving (basic attitude toward the world), fearless (basic attitude toward him- or herself), mean (moral system) and skillful (complex ego function).

The Communication of Emotion

Understanding what you are feeling is important in part because you might or might not reveal those feelings in conversation. Recognition of what we are feeling means that we acknowledge the significance of some event, which may also be an interpersonal interaction. There is a possibility of multiple emotions experienced virtually simultaneously or in rapid oscillation as we consider different aspects of the person or situation. Recognition of the different features that often interact with one another in a social situation allows for a richly faceted appraisal, and one's emotional experience is similarly more complex. Sometimes we might be aware that we are "unaware" of some of our feelings.

Just as understanding what we are feeling helps with self-disclosure of those feelings, knowing what the other people you are with are feeling also is obviously an important aspect in social interaction. The better we understand our own feelings, the more we can understand others because people have similar experiences of feelings. The better people understand how and why people act the way they do the more they can infer what is going on for them emotionally. One person in a social interaction may not be saying what they are feeling but the other people may be capable of figuring out or inferring what they are feeling. Showing an understanding of what other people are feeling shows an ability to empathize, as well as showing that you are sensitive and compassionate. How we infer others' emotions, and, for that matter, how we reflect on our own, depends on what we believe to be the causes of these emotional experiences. We identify certain emotions associated with certain behaviors and come to understand that if someone does this or that thing, then they are going to feel this or that as a response.

How emotion is communicated in a relationship is very important to social interaction. Based on the type of relationship, different types of emotion is going to be communicated. In a loving relationship, the emotion love is going to be communicated, for instance. This skill requires individuals to take into account several aspects of the relationship's dynamics (1) the interpersonal consequences of their emotional communication within the relationship for themselves and for the other, (2) how they maintain the relationship quality (e.g., equilibrium), or alter it (e.g., be deepening or attenuating it), and (3) how they apply power or control within the relationship. So if you express anger the circumstances might change based on the type of relationship. How you maintain the relationship will also be important after a display of anger. Also, obviously how power and control is applied in the relationship is going to be an issue when anger (or other emotions) are displayed.

How emotion is used by individuals to guide communication production is complicated. Some individuals disregard their own affective reactions until the level of arousal becomes so high that it cannot be ignored. They then may act according to their emotional response, but they might not know why. It is mere reaction, not considered communication production. Others might actively engage their affective state, readily recognize and consult their feelings in making decisions. Thus, some people orient to their communicative world through their emotions- hence the label "affective orientation".

Attachment Styles

If people differ in their motivation to maintain positive relationships with others, then we can expect people who show higher levels of such motivation to perform more positive, constructive behaviors in various ways more so than their peers. There is also something called attachment style - which is a persons characteristic pattern of expectations, needs, emotions, and behavior in social interactions and close relationships. Depending on how it is measured, attachment style characterizes the way people behave in a particular relationship (relationship specific style) or across relationships (global attachment style). Someone can be *secure* in their attachment style and find it relatively easy to get close to others and depend on them. Someone could not be secure but be *avoidant*, uncomfortable being close to others, doesn't trust them completely, and doesn't allow themselves to depend on them. Someone could also have an *anxious* attachment style and are nervous about how close people get to them and worry their partner doesn't love them or want them.

Gender Identity

There is a wide range of constructs that represent culturally based masculine and feminine self-definitions. These constructs can be recognized in terms of three facets of masculinity and femininity: representations of oneself as (1) possessing gender-typed personality traits and interests, (2) having male-typical versus female-typical relationships to others, and (3) being a member of the category of women or men, as that category is defined within a given society.

Gender identity, like gender roles, encompasses qualities that are regarded as typical or ideal of each sex in a society. Gender identity can thus refer to descriptive gender norms, defined as what is culturally usual for women or men in a society. In the descriptive sense, gender identity is the construal of oneself in terms of the culturally typical man or woman. Gender identity can also refer to injunctive (prescriptive) gender norms, defined as what is culturally ideal for women and men. In the injunctive sense, gender identity is the construal of oneself in terms of the best of male or female qualities.

Neuroticism

Neuroticism, as a fundamental trait of general personality, refers to an enduring tendency or disposition to experience negative emotional states. Individuals who score high on neuroticism are more likely than the average person to experience such feelings as anxiety, anger, guilt, and depression. They respond poorly to environmental stress, are likely to interpret ordinary situations as threatening, and can experience minor frustrations as hopelessly overwhelming. They are often self-conscious and shy, and they may have trouble controlling urges and impulses when feeling upset. (McCrae and Costa, 2003)[1]

Embarrassment

Embarrassment is the state of mortification, abashment, and chagrin that washes over us when social life takes an awkward turn and we suddenly face the prospect of undesired evaluations from others. It typically strikes without warning and causes startled, self-conscious feelings of ungainliness, conspicuousness, and befuddlement. Embarrassment is usually sudden, automatic, and brief; it hinges on the realization that one has made some misstep or that an interaction has gone awry, but such appraisals occur without deliberation or reflection, and embarrassment can be in full flower before one ever thinks things through.

Social Anxiety

1. McCrae, R. R., and Costa, P.T. (2003). *Personality in adulthood: A five-factor theory perspective* (2nd ed.). New York: Guildford Press.

In contrast, social anxiety is fretful disquiet that stems from the prospect of evaluations from others in the absence of any predicament. It occurs when we believe ourselves to be subject to real, implied, or imagined social evaluation, and it takes the form of nervous concern for what others may be thinking, even when nothing has gone wrong. Unlike embarrassment, social anxiety often occurs over long periods of time, gradually waxing and waning. It depends on contemplation of social settings that portrays them as daunting and intimidating, so it is usually gradual, prolonged, and mindful (rather than automatic).

Shyness

Shyness occurs when social anxiety is paired with reticent, cautions, and guarded social behavior. Shy behavior may range from mild inhibition, involving bashful timidity or wary watchfulness, to stronger distancing behavior that can include total withdrawal form social settings. That is a broad range, and no one pattern of behavior reliably distinguishes shyness form cooler, calmer states (such as those associated with introversion) that lead one to be quiet and reserved in the absence of any anxiety. Shy behavior may thus seem ambiguous to observers; it is obviously not gregarious and convivial, but whether it derives from shy trepidation, a mild manner, dullness, or unfriendly lack of interest may be hard to judge.

Proneness to Shame and Proneness to Guilt

How do people react to their own failures and transgressions? People vary considerably in how they feel when they recognize that they have failed or behaved badly. For example, given the same event--say, hurting a friend's feelings--an individual prone to guilt would be likely to respond by ruminating about the offensive remark, feeling bad about hurting a friend, and being compelled to apologize and make up for it. A shame-prone individual, instead, is likely to see the event as proof that he or she is a bad friend--indeed, a bad person. Feeling small and worthless, the shame-prone person may be inclined to slink away and avoid the friend for fear of further shame. When people feel shame they feel bad about themselves- "small", however when people feel guilt they feel their conscience and feel morally bad that they did something wrong or are "guilty". The two are so different there can be "shame-free" guilt and "guilt-free" shame.

People can also blame other people instead of feeling shame for themselves, or maybe people that suffer from the pain and self-diminishment of shame may become defensive and angry and attempt to deflect blame outward. Because shame and guilt are painful emotions providing negative feedback for wrong-doing, it is often assumed that both motivate individuals to do the right thing. That isn't necessarily the case, however, someone could experience a lot of shame and still do lots of bad things (or do lots of bad things and not experience any shame).

Goals, Motivation and Perception

Social interaction can be motivated by a number of different drives. Motivation will affect the perceptual activity that takes place. The social situation in which A sees B at a party, or in some other open setting, and is deciding whether or not to interact with B. The problem here is one of predicting B's behavior - will B be a sufficiently entertaining and agreeable person to talk to? Is he likely to be able to tell A the way? etc. The prediction here is about behavior which is relevant to A's goals in this particular situation, and whether B is likely to be able to help him to realize these goals.

If A decides to initiate an encounter with B, A's initial problem is to select an appropriate interaction style from his repertoire that is suitable for B. If A behaves differently to others of different sex, age and social class (as everyone in fact does), he needs to be able to categorize B in terms of these variables, and whatever others are salient for him. At this stage then A is concerned with certain demographic and personality variables in B; once this is done that particular perceptual task is over, though some revision be made in the light of further experience of B.

During the encounter itself, A is concerned with eliciting certain responses from B, or with establishing and maintaining some relationship with B. In order to do this, A needs continuous information about B's reaction to his own behavior, so that he can modify it if necessary. A may simply want B to like him, or he may have other quite personal motivations with regard to B, or A may want B to learn, buy, vote, or respond in terms of mainly professional goals which A has. In either case A needs to know what progress he is making with B. He may be concerned with B's attitude towards himself, with B's emotional state, with B's degree of understanding, or with other aspects of B's response.

In some situations A's main concern is with B's opinions, attitudes, beliefs or values. This is obviously true of social survey interviews, but in many more informal situations people want to find out how far their own attitudes have social support from others, and how far their ideas about the outside world are correct. People want positive reinforcement and feedback about their ideas and themselves.

In other situations, for example interviews for personnel selection and personality assessment, the main object may be to assess personality, either in order to understand its clinical origins, or to decide upon its suitability for a given job. In other situations, such as law courts, or interviews with administrators, it is more a matter of deciding what sanctions to apply; here the personality is matched against some social norm of the behavior that is required.

The effect of interpersonal attitudes

If A knows B well he will have already formed a detailed impression of B, and knows which styles of behavior to use with him. He will notice any deviation from B's normal behavior, and interpret it as a temporary state or mood. Similarly A will be able to interpret B's behavior better - he will know when B is anxious or cross better than could someone who has not met B before. Generally speaking the better A knows B the more accurate his judgments of B's personality are. This is not always so, since A and B become involved in an intricate relationship, and A's judgement can become highly distorted.

If A likes or dislikes B, his judgments of B become systematically affected. If he likes B he will perceive B as liking A, more than he actually does. If A likes B, he also tends to see A in a favorable light, and bias all judgments in a socially desirable direction. This may be the result of interaction: if A likes B he will behave more pleasantly towards B, and elicit more favorable behavior from B.

If A likes B he will see B as more like himself and having more similar attitudes than is really the case. This effect is called assimilation, or simple projection; it would be expected that if A and B are really alike, A's judgments will be more accurate.This kind of projection is quite different from the Freudian kind - in which people fail to see their shortcomings in themselves, and instead believe that other people suffer from them.

If B behaves aggressively towards A, this affects A's perception of B in an interesting way. The immediate effect is for B to be seen as aggressive, and to be judged unfavorably in other ways. However, this effect may be mitigated when the causes of B's aggressive behavior can readily be seen. This is an excellent example of the shift from personal to impersonal causation. If A thinks that he has done badly on a task, for which B could reasonably blame him, he will feel less negative towards B.

Sources of Aggression

Various environmental stressors can lead to aggression - when the social rules are broken or subjects are exposed to stressors such as extremes of heat or noise for long or unpredictable periods of time. Consistent invasions of a comfortable personal space, working under crowded conditions or living in a densely inhabited area can often lead immediately to aggression. The frustration-aggression hypothesis states that the blocking of goal-directed behavior leads to aggression. However, experimental results show that only when goal blocking is severe and arbitrary or unjustifiably enacted does it lead to aggression. The perception of why a goal was blocked may be inaccurate. The situational conditions that lead to heightened arousal facilitate overt aggression under certain circumstances (such as competitiveness, loud noise, social conditions with exercise (dancing), etc).

Sources of Altruism

The number and actions of bystanders can influence altruistic behavior. When a subject is alone he or she might be more likely to respond to cries of help than when in the company of others. Also the activity of the other people in the situation influences behavior. Observing others helping might make one more likely to help. Reinforcement in one situation can lead directly to helpfulness in a another situation afterwards, while negative reinforcement would probably lead to the person helping less in the second situation. If the situation is ambiguous and it is hard to define if the situation needs a helping response would inhibit altruism. Therefore the greater the familiarity with the situation and the greater feeling of certainty of the social rules would probably lead to increased chance of altruism. Cultural rules, characteristics of the victim, or cost of help are also obviously factors.

Sources of Assertiveness

The most important determinant of assertiveness is an individual's power or status. This may be based on his position in an organizational hierarchy or in an informal group, his social class, or his age. In general it seems that it is more difficult to be assertive (rather than passive or aggressive) with people of greater power, more dominant role and higher status than with people of lower power, etc. That is probably more true of negative assertion - refusing requests, disagreeing, responding to criticism - that of positive assertion (though that may also be difficult). People are more assertive and assume positions of leadership when they are more competent at the task in hand, or know more about the topic under discussion that the others present. Females may be less assertive than males in responding to members of the opposite sex.

Sources of Attraction

The probability of friendship or attraction developing is determined in part by the structure of the environment - the physical distances between people at work, in housing or at recreation, and the time periods between periods of interaction. Environmental conditions have a direct influence on our emotions which in turn affects our attraction to others. Gouaux (1971)[2] found experimentally that subjects in an elated mood tended to be more attracted to a stranger than subjects in a depressed mood, irrespective of the fact that the stranger was not responsible for the mood state of the subjects. Griffitt and Veitch (1971)[3] found that under conditions of high temperature and high population density, measures of liking or disliking were more negative than under more comfortable conditions. Veitch and Griffitt (1976)[4] found that the hearing of broadcasts of good news led a subject to like a stranger, while after hearing bad news, subjects showed dislike of a stranger. Role expectations may determine the circumstances under which certain behaviors lead to attraction.

Goffman's theory of self-presentation

Goffman's book *The Presentation of Self in Everyday Life* (1956) has rightly been very influential in the study of the effect of self on social interaction. His theory is that interactors need information about one another for a number of reasons; this information is not directly available but must be inferred from gestures and other minor cues; the impressions formed are however deliberately manipulated in order to create perceptions that are more favorable than is warranted; there is a considerable element of conscious deception. Interactors try to establish a 'working consensus' in which certain perceptions of each other are agreed and there is a common definition of the situation. This deception is often necessary for the maintenance of a working social system, and is in the interests of both parties. Impression formation is achieved in the course of quasi-theatrical performances by individuals and groups, in the 'front' regions of homes and places of work, for the relevant 'audiences'; there is collusion between team-members, e.g. the members of a family receiving guests; they interact informally in the back regions and do not manipulate impressions for each other; in the absence of the audience they discuss the secrets of their performance, and express attitudes towards the audience different from those expressed in the presence of the audience. There is constant danger of mistakes, in which the performance is discredited and reality shows through; this completely disrupts the interaction and causes embarrassment; the audience cooperates to prevent this happening by being tactful, and not going into the back regions.

This constitutes a theory about social behavior; it postulates that social behavior is like the behavior of actors, in that behavior is enacted to generate impressions for an audience. It is present very persuasively

2. Gouaux, C. (1971) Induced affective states and interpersonal attraction. *F. Pers. soc. Psychol.,* 20, 37-43.
3. Griffitt, W. and Veitch, R. (1971). Hot and crowded: influence of population density and temperature on interpersonal affective behavior. *F. Pers. soc. Psychol.,* 17, 92-8.
4. Veitch, R. and Griffitt, W. (1976). Good news, bad news: affective and interpersonal effects. *F appl. soc. Psychol.,* 6, 69-75.

by evidence from literary sources such as George Orwell on waiters and Simone de Beauvoir on women, and from sociological case studies and books about professional groups such as house-detectives and undertakers. For example he cites Orwell's book *Down and Out in Paris and London*:

- It is an instructive sight to see a waiter going into a hotel dining-room. As he passes the door a sudden change comes over him. The set of his shoulders alters; all the dirt and hurry and irritation have dropped off in an instant. He glides over the carpet, with a solemn priest-like air. I remember our assistant 'maitre d'hotel', a fiery Italian, pausing at the dining-room door to address his apprentice who had broken a bottle of wine. Shaking his fist above his head he yelled (luckily the door was more or less soundproof), 'do you call yourself a waiter, you young bastard? You a waiter! You're not fit to scrub floors in the brothel your mother came from.'

- Words failing him, he turned to the door, and as he opened it he delivered a final insult in the same manner as Squire Western in Tom Jones.

- Then he entered the dining-room and sailed across it dish in hand, gracefully as a swan. Ten seconds later he was bowing reverently to a customer. And you could not help thinking, as you saw him bow and smile, with that benign smile of the trained waiter, that the customer was put to shame by having such an aristocrat to serve him (Orwell, 1951)[5]

Goffman did not produce any evidence in the form of experiments or sociological field studies to support his thesis, nor did he present the elements of it in the form of clear, testable hypotheses. It may help to focus attention on the empirical predictions from the theory if we consider some possible lines of criticism, which could be settled by evidence.

a. Does social interaction involve as great an element of deliberate, conscious deception as is postulated? It is in fact people like waiters and undertakers who fit the model best, and there is no doubt that there is an element of window-dressing in most professional performances. This need not however be conscious, and Goffman admits that after a time the personality adjusts to fit the   mask. Self-enhancement on the other hand is based more of self-deception than on deception of others. It may be suggested that the dramaturgical model applies quite well to confidence men, has some application to some aspects of professional performances, and very little application to everyday life.

b. Are there really front and back regions is most establishment? Visitors to factories are usually shown over the entire establishment' hospitals and university departments have no obvious division between front and back. There are areas where people live their private lives and don't want to be disturbed, and there are comfortable board rooms for long meetings, but this is not a matter of front and back. Private houses are an intermediate case. Visitors are shown into the sitting- room and perhaps the dining-room and are allowed to use a lavatory; they are not usually (except in the middle West) so welcome in the kitchen, or the bedrooms. It may be suggested that the the distinction between front and back applies well to institutions offering a service to the public, such as hotels and shops, but not so much to other places.

c. Is the difference in behavior to other members of the 'team' and to the 'audience' correctly interpreted in terms of collusion over impression management? It is often the case that P behaves differently to person A and B, but this does not necessarily indicate that he is being bogus to one of them. He relates to each by developing a synchronizing social system (a 'working consensus', as Goffman would say), and those will be different in each case depending on the personality and position of the other. Impression management is involved in each. The waiter behaves with skill, in order to elicit the desired reactions form the customers; his behavior with the books is managed also, as they too have to be controlled. Goffman is probably right however in postulating an on-stage-off-stage dimension, in which behavior in the more off-stage situations is more spontaneous and relaxed, more vulgar and intimate than behavior on-stage.

---

5. Orwell, G. (1951) *Down and Out in Paris and London*. London: Gollanez.

d. Does the acting model fit ordinary social behavior? The actor follows a script which he has learnt; in everyday life behavior is more spontaneous. Again, professional performers such as salesmen are like actors, in that they do have a script, but even they have to improvise to some extent. Actors only respond to one another in respect of timing. All social situations have rules, but they do not have a script; indeed it is one of the unspoken assumptions of social interaction that what is taking place is entirely new and spontaneous.

So how much of social interaction is "natural"? People obviously can't act how they really want and reveal their true selves in ordinary social interaction. There has to be an understanding of equality in order to people to get along. If people acted naturally, they would try to be dominant over the other people present. There are many factors that occur that people need to adjust to and "act" accordingly to. You can't just go into a social situation and do everything you want and have everything your way - you need to act and change your manner to a certain extent at least.

The Looking-Glass Self

• As we see our face, figure and dress in the glass and are interested in them because they are ours, and pleased or otherwise with them according as they do or do not answer to what we should like them to be; so in imagination we perceive in another's mind some thought of our appearance, manners, aims and deeds, character, friends and so on, and are variously affect by it ...the thing that moves us to pride of shame is not the mere mechanical reflections of ourselves, but imputed sentiment, the imagined effect of this reflection upon another's mind. (Cooley, 1902)

The concept Cooley articulated in this passage is referred to as the Looking-Glass Self. According to him, just as we make contact with our image in a mirror by knowing that it is a reflection of ourselves, so when we make contact with others we see our own images reflected in their actions by the ways they approach and react to us. Here the term "contact" does not refer to direct physical touching, of course, but to a symbolic meeting of minds through the medium of imagination. Sometimes imagination alone, of how others would react to us, is enough to affect our behavior.

If you talk to your mother on the telephone and she tells you how lonely she is and how much she longs for you to visit her, you understand this request through your own qualities reflected in her request. The qualities may be ideas of your obligations toward your parents, or even more generally your views of kindness and being a good person. Your own feelings about being alone, and the opposite, of enjoying the comforts of companionship, are mirrored in her request.

You may decide not to visit, but you and your mother have contacted each other in a symbolic act. Although we rely on our own particular ways of knowing, the social sense of knowing, which Cooley called society, depends on the imaginative reflection of ourselves in others. When you imagine turning down your mother's request, you hear her disappointment or the disgust in her reply. What is heard really is your own understanding of how you would act if the positions were reversed. You hear over the telephone line your ideas about yourself as a good son or daughter, or as a responsible adult. Thus one way to think about society is as a result of individual minds in reflective contact.

This theory of the Looking-Glass self is basically just saying that there is a certain amount of inner reflection and thought about everything that happens to you socially and otherwise. You see everything about yourself when you interact with someone, you reflect on what happens and ask, "what does this mean to me", "how does who I am factor into this", "what qualities do I have that influence my feelings as a response to this person", "how does who I am and my life experience matter in this situation", "what aspects of my life and who I am matter to this interaction and my feelings about it". If someone is talking to you and they make you feel a certain way, you may reflect on that and say that it is a result of certain qualities you have, you may bring up various feelings you have that relate to the conversation or the situation that are relevant. There is an enormous amount of things meeting someone can cause you to think about, you can think about your entire life, who you are and your personal attributes and characteristics (especially those that are relevant in this instance). There is a large amount of self-reflection in any interaction. There is a deeper reflection of the conversation or what is occurring than may seem. You think about the significance of the topic at hand to your own life, to the life of the person you are talking to, to the interaction. You also think about your feelings and their feelings and how these matter in the context.

Your (and their) life, feelings, and attributes aren't the only things to think about more deeply in social interactions. You can think about the appropriate way to behave, what generalizations you are making about yourself and them, what the expectations of the other person are and how you should appropriately adapt your behavior, if it is "set" to see certain kinds of behavior in certain situations from certain types of people.

Maslow and Psychological Needs

Maslows hope was to develop a more inclusive theory on motivation that would find commonalities in seemingly dissimilar motives through the discovery of their common core. Such clusters of variables, Maslow felt, were based on five core elements that were related to each other in the form of an ascending hierarchy of prepotency. These five sets of needs, each of whose functional appearance was contingent on the relative prior satisfaction of those needs believed to be more basic, were termed the physiological, safety, love and belongingness, esteem, and self-actualization needs.

The Physiological Needs. On the first level, Maslow included a range of simple biological needs recognized by all physiologists. On this most basic level are the needs for food, sex, water, optimum levels of salt, oxygen, and temperature, as well as the need for sleep, relaxation, and bodily integrity. Maslow began with these organismic demands both in order to be complete in his accounting of the body's requirements and to point out the obvious fact that no further psychological development is possible if they have not been attained. Many fields, ranging from physiology to anthropology, describe the organism's behavior during the state of physiological deprivation. These needs are so basic, in fact, that little variation in complex social behavior can be accounted for in terms of the search for these rewards.

Unfortunately, Maslow's use of the term "physiological needs" hindered the recognition of his most basic proposition: All of the needs described in his theory have their origin in the human organism. This term was an unfortunate choice, because it is in the consequences of the reward history of the later stages that the more interesting types of social behavior can best be understood.

The Safety Needs. The safety needs center around the requirement for an understandable, secure, and orderly world. Maslow (1970)[6] categorized the various manifestations of the safety needs as the needs for: "security; stability; dependency; protection; freedom from fear, from anxiety and chaos; need for structure, order, law, limits; [and] strength in the protector" (p. 39). Underlying these apparently different states is the common factor of the "need for prediction and control," as described so well by Seligman (1975)[7]. When these needs are not satisfied, a large variety of cognitive, emotional, and motivational conditions are created. Individuals may see other people and themselves, as well as the world in general, as unsafe, unjust, inconsistent, or unreliable. Hence, they seek for, or attempt to create, areas of life that offer the most stability and protection. Therefore, deprived safety needs appear in personality as beliefs about the world, states of discomfort, and desires to create a situation that solves these discomforts.

Love and Belongingness Needs. The love and belongingness needs center around the desire to experience intimate relationships with other people. Individuals motivated on this level desire contact, intimacy, warm and friendly relationships, and they function well in interpersonal situations. The central expression of this need is a clear desire for a warm companionate relationship, which encourages congenial activities on the basis of approximate equality among peers. It is important to recognize that, in Erikson's terms, mutuality of involvement and concern is the central characteristic, rather than the behavioral criterion of two people spending time in close physical proximity to one another (e.g., Schachter, 1959). However, the expression of affection for those who take care of the person, or for those who are cared for, should be understood as a resultant of the satisfaction of other types of psychological needs.

---

6. Maslow, A. H. (1970). *Motivation and personality* (2nd ed.). New York: Harper and Row.
7. Seligman, M. E. P. (1975). *Helplessness: On depression, development, and death.* San Francisco: Freeman.

Esteem Needs The esteem needs center around the issue of firmly establishing a high sense of self-worth, which is achieved both through the appraisal of actual competence in one's own activities and through receiving the esteem of others because of one's actions. Maslow (1970) classified the manifestations of this need into two subsidiary sets. First, there is "the desire for strength, for achievement, for adequacy, for mastery and competence, for confidence in the face of the world, and for independence and freedom. Second,... the desire for reputation or prestige (defining it as respect or esteem from other people), status, fame and glory, dominance, recognition, attention, importance, dignity or appreciation" (p. 45). Other manifestations of these needs are indications or expressed desires for self-reliance, selfacceptance, power, confidence, competition, trust in one's own abilities or self, leadership, and autonomy.

The Need for Self-Actualization. The stage of self-actualization is the part of Maslow's theory for which he is most widely known. It refers to one's wish for self-fulfillment, after one's earlier needs have been satisfied, and is expressed in those idiosyncratic ways most desired by the individual.

TABLE 3.9 Definitions of Selected Peripheral Variables that Affect the Social Process (adapted primarily from Murray, 1938)

Dependency	The need to defend against anxiety by establishing predictable social transactions through constructing a care-receiving relationship with another person.
Abasement	The need to defend against anxiety by constructing self-deprecating and self-defeating modes of interaction with other people.
Approval	The need to defend against anxiety by constructing a deferential, participative, and admiring relationship with a protective superior.
Authoritarianism	The complex trait that defends against anxiety through the characteristics of conventional values, hostility, stereotyping, antidemocratic attitudes, strong defenses against intraception, and a submissive, uncritical attitude toward authority.
Order	The need to defend against anxiety by actively organizing tasks and social transactions in precise and detailed ways.
Affiliation	The need to establish intimate egalitarian involvements with another person in mutually satisfying social transactions.
Machiavellianism	A complex trait that achieves a sense of self-worth through constructing amoral, manipulative, opportunistic, and exploitative modes of interpersonal transactions.
Dominance	The need to establish self-worth through demonstrations of directing, influencing, and persuading others.
Nurturance	The need to establish self-worth by responsibly caring for the successful development of persons, generations, and institutions.
Achievement	The need to establish self-worth through successful competition with standards of excellence in the pursuit of task-oriented activity.
Recognition	The need to establish self-worth through personal displays that gain admiration, respect, praise, and prestige from others.

Abasement

Abasement is the tendency to establish control and prediction of others' actions by self-deprecating maneuvers. Feeling inadequate, inferior, incompetent, unlovable, unworthy, and "sinful," such people appear to atone for their weakness through self-punishment, compliance, and passive surrender, as well as confessions of inadequacy and helplessness. By acting in such a seemingly self-defeating style, the self-abasing person actually attempts to control the degree of pain that he or she experiences, while simultaneously invoking the sympathy and pity of others. The function of such behavior is to set limits on unpredictability and retain some degree of control over events by forcing a reliable pattern of responding from others.

Dependency

Dependency is another solution to feeling mistrustful, anxious, and insecure. This motive has as its goal the formation of a dependent bond with another person. Dependency is a psycho-social mode in which one passively or actively structures a stable subordinate relationship in order to feel secure, trusting, and calm. Extremely dependent people depend on others to help them "get" and "take" from the world in a predictable and controllable way, and they fear the loss of a powerful protector. Individuals with a strong motive for dependency fear being stranded to simply "get by" on their own. Thus, the safety motive of dependency will manifest itself in fantasy, emotion, and action as the need for union to restore or maintain some form of the basic sense of trust, which makes the world seem manageable.

TABLE 3.8 Erikson's Conceptualization of the Development of Ego Strength

Psychosocial Crisis	Ego Strength	Definition of Stage-Specific Ego Strength
Trust vs. Mistrust	Hope	The enduring belief in the attainability of fervent wishes, in spite of the dark urges and rages that mark the beginning of existence.
Autonomy vs. Shame and Doubt	Will	The unbroken determination to exercise free choice as well as self-restraint, in spite of the inevitable experience of shame and doubt in infancy.
Initiative vs. Guilt	Purpose	The courage to envisage and pursue valued goals uninhibited by the de-feat of infantile fantasies, by guilt, and by the foiling fear of punishment.
Industry vs. Inferiority	Competence	The free exercise of dexterity and intelligence in the completion of tasks, unimpaired by infantile inferiority.
Identity vs. Role Confusion	Fidelity	The ability to sustain loyalties freely pledged in spite of the inevitable contradictions of value systems.
Intimacy vs. Isolation	Love	The mutuality of devotion forever subduing the antagonisms inherent in divided function.
Generativity vs. Stagnation	Care	The widening concern for what has been generated by love, necessity, or accident; it overcomes the ambivalence adhering to irreversible obligation.
Integrity vs. Despair	Wisdom	The detached concern with life itself, in the face of death itself.

What I am going to do now is provide an integrative analysis of the last few sections which were Maslow's Needs, the peripherial variables that affect the social process, and Erikson's Psychosocial stages. First off people have basic needs such as listed by Maslow - physiological, safety, love and belongingness, esteem, and self-actualization needs. All of those are important to social interaction but they need to be considered in a larger psychological context. People want to feel good about themselves and achieve self- actualization, but they can do that through the discovery of Erikson's Psychosocial Crisis. Trust, shame, guilt, inferiority, identity, intimacy, generativity, and integrity (some of the factors Erikson mentioned) all are components in the social process, and they all relate to Maslow's Needs. This is so because in any interaction there is a deeper reflection of the self that occurs. Your primary motivations (Maslow's needs) seeks introspection and development in Erickson's psychosocial crisis (for instance, you seek belongingness (Maslows need) through the development of trust (Ericksons stage)). In addition, there are the peripheral variables of dependency, abasement, approval, authoritarianism, order, affiliation, machiavellianism, dominance, nurturance, achievement, and recognition.

On one hand someone could say about life or this book, "life isn't complicated - I don't need to know all this stuff about social interaction". On the other hand, when one thinks more deeply and clearly it becomes obvious that there are many factors present in social situations that could use reflection. You need to understand how you are behaving, you need to notice how the other person is behaving, and you need to do this on a moment by moment basis. You need to come to conclusions based on that observation as well - potentially a lot of conclusions. You might need to modify your behavior based on your observation of the other person and the conclusions you reach. Furthermore, you need to notice the effect of this behavior on each person, on their emotions, and on the mood of the situation. One person might want the other person to like them, and is concerned with the attitudes, emotions, and types of understand the other person may have. The mood of a situation can vary from painful, difficult and not funny to humorous, joyful, and exciting. People could be getting along as equals, with shared understanding, or one person could be trying to dominate the other. The dominant person might also be getting along as a subordinate at the same time. The conclusions you reach, your attempt to modify your own behavior, your goals and motivations as a result of the presence of the other person, the mood and the emotions involved (pleasurable, painful, or others) and the type of relationship (dominant, subordinate, friendly) are all powerful and key forces involved in social interaction and worthy of conscious reflection.

Someone could also say, "there is an amazing amount of information and complexity involved in life and in social interaction, the emotions involved are powerful and real". But what is this complexity and how do you notice when the emotions are present? Is there a simply way of describing the complexity, of summing it up? You can read this book and this chapter especially, that is the long version of the complexity involved. However it would be nice to have a more simple understanding for quick review. There are many different types of social situations that people can find themselves in. The location, people involved, and the setting are all factors that have a lot options and change the nature of the interaction in many ways (creating a lot of variety). You have to perform differently in each different situation and function at a high level each time. You have to be aware of the situation, of the behavior, emotions, attitude, mood, understanding, role, motivation, and needs of the people involved. Because of these factors (also the characteristics of the people, and if there is a conversation) there is a certain mood in every social situation - this mood would obviously be very complicated considering the number of contributing factors. Moods, therefore, are a lot more complex than just "happy" or "sad" or "angry" - there are tones and subtleties to situations and interactions that contribute to the feelings and atmosphere (or "mood") present (it is a created environment - created by complex psychological factors (which are the thoughts of each person, their motivations, attitudes, feelings, personal characteristics, other circumstantial factors (the environment, setting, etc), and -- obviously -- their behaviors)).

Persistent themes in interpersonal relations: Authority, Subordinacy, and Equality

We should stress at this point the idea that authority, subordinacy, and equality are not isolated or easily separable experiences. Any individual in the development of his relationships with others and in the elaboration of his role performances is experiencing simultaneously the relevant tensions imbedded in a matrix of authority, subordinacy, and equality. Sometimes one of these three themes appears dominant in an interaction, and the others appear as background. Yet if interaction persists, the astute observer will see the relevance of all three issues in the unfolding of interpersonal relations.

The Nature of Interpersonal Skills

Interpersonal interaction involves a complicated balancing act of the needs of the people involved, Phillips[8] discussed how a person is skilled in this regard:

- the extent to which he or she can communicate with others, in a manner that fulfils one's rights, requirements, satisfactions, or obligations to a reasonable degree without damaging the other person's similar rights, requirements, factions, or obligations, and hopefully shares these rights etc. with others in free and open exchange.

This next quote from Robbins and Hunsaker[9] is rather obvious, in order to get better at socializing and learning social skills you need to practice:

- To become competent at any skill, a person needs to understand it both conceptually and behaviorally; have opportunities to practice it; get feedback on how well he or she is performing the skill; and use the skill often enough so that it becomes integrated with his or her behavioral repertoire.

The goals we pursue are not always conscious, and indeed one feature of skilled performance is that behaviour is often executed automatically. Once responses are learned they tend to become hard-wired or habitual. When we know how to drive, we no longer have to think about actions such as how to start the car, brake, reverse, and so on. Yet, when learning to drive, these actions are consciously monitored as they are performed. In the successful learning of new skills we move through the stages of conscious incompetence (we know what we should be doing and we know we are not doing it very well), conscious competence (we know we are performing at a satisfactory level), and finally unconscious competence (we just do it without thinking about it and we succeed). This is also true of interpersonal skills. During free- flowing social encounters, less than 200 milliseconds typically elapse between the responses of speakers and rarely do conversational pauses reach three seconds. As a result certain elements, such as the exact choice of words used and the use of gestures, almost always occur without conscious reflection. In relation to the negotiation context, McRae[10] explained how: 'Expert negotiators become so proficient at certain

---

8. Phillips, E. (1978) *The social skills basis of psychopathology*, New York: Grune and Stratton.
9. Robbins, S. and Hunsaker, P. (1996) *Training in interpersonal skills: tips for managing people at work* (2nd edn), New Jersey: Prentice Hall.

skills in the negotiating process that they do not have to consciously think about using these skills. It's as if the response becomes second nature.' However, an awareness of relevant goals does not ensure success. As expressed by J. Greene[11]:

- action may not be so readily instantiated in overt behavior... the inept athlete, dancer, actor or public speaker may well have a perfectly adequate abstract representation of what he or she needs to do, but what actually gets enacted is rather divergent from his or her image of that action.

Skilled behaviours are goal-directed. They are those behaviours the individual employs in order to achieve a desired outcome, and are therefore purposeful, as opposed to chance, or unintentional. As Huang[12] (2000:111) noted, 'the purposes people bring into communication have important consequences on communication processes'. For example, if A wishes to encourage B to talk freely, A will look at B, use head nods when B speaks, refrain from interrupting B, and utter 'guggles' ('hmm hmm'; 'uh, hu'; etc.) periodically. In this instance these behaviours are directed towards the goal of encouraging participation.

Skilled behaviours must be interrelated, in that they are synchronised in order to achieve a particular goal. Thus the individual will employ two or more behaviours at the same time. For example, when encouraging B to talk, A may smile, use head nods, look directly at B, and utter guggles, and each of these signals will be interpreted by B as a sign of encouragement to continue speaking. Each behaviour relates to this common goal, and so the behaviours are in this way interrelated and synchronised.

Skills should be appropriate to the situation in which they are being used. The skilled individual adapts behaviours to meet the demands of particular people in specific contexts. Dickson[13] (2001) referred to this aspect of skilled performance as contextual propriety. In their review of this area, White and Burgoon[14] (2001:9) concluded that, 'the most essential feature of human interaction is that it involves adaptation'. Indeed, linguistic conceptualisations purport that skill is mutually constructed through dialogue and so can only be understood by an interpretation of how narratives develop in any particular context (Holman[15], 2000).

Competence, therefore, is more likely to the extent that communicators pursue both self-interests and the interests of the other person(s) involved. Persons who want to initiate a romantic relationship with another need to appear composed and expressive if the other person is to perceive them as competent. Composure displays the suitor as confident and focused, and the expressiveness leaves vivid impressions and helps the other person know them. These skills help people pursue their own goals. However, unless the other person is made to feel important through coordination and altercentrism, attraction is unlikely to follow. Coordination shows a concern for making the interaction more comfortable, and the altercentrism gets the other person's interests involved in the conversation, and perhaps, the relationship. Thus, to be competent, interactants need to use their communication skills to promote both their own interests and the interests of the coparticipants.

Mutuality of Control

Another way to look at conversational processes is to examine the types of messages exchanged by relational partners (positive or negative in orientation) and how these messages serve to sustain or alter perceptions of the relationship. Because ongoing interactions provide opportunities for partners to assess

10. McRae, B. (1998) *Negotiating and influencing skills,* Thousand Oaks, CA: Sage.
11. Greene, J. (2000) 'Evanescent mentation: an ameliorative conceptual foundation for research and theory on message production', *Communication Theory* 10: 139-55.
12. Huang, L. (2000) 'Examining candidate information search processes: the impact of processing goals and sophistication', *Journal of Communication* 50:93-114.
13. Dickson, D. (2001) 'Communication skill and health care delivery', in D. Sines, F. Appleby and B. Raymond (eds) *Community health care nursing* (2nd edn), London: Blackwell Science.
14. White, C. and Burgoon, J. (2001) 'Adaptation and communicative design patterns of interaction in truthful and deceptive conversations', *Human Communication Research* 27:9-37.
15. Holman, D. (2000) 'A dialogical approach to skill and skilled activity', *Human Relations* 53:957-80.

relational growth and evolution, researchers have described episodes resulting in relationship change as turning points. Turning point research tries to isolate specific events or occurrences that prompt a change in the trajectory of the relationship. Often these turning points are explored by examining the reminiscences of relational partners.

A final theme involving interactional processes emphasizes the ways relational partners struggle to negotiate the parameters of the relationship that play out in day-to-day interactions. These discussions may explicitly or implicitly involve issues of control and dominance or the management of disagreements. Ideally, the interactions lead to mutual acceptance or general agreement about specific decisions and the way in which those decisions are reached. This mutuality refers to partners having a shared understanding of the way their relationship works.

One specific kind of mutuality, control mutuality, reflects consensus in the relationship about who is to take charge of specific relational issues. Indvik and Fitzpatrick[16] (1986) noted that control involves relational partners' ability to influence one another. Canary and Stafford[17] (1994) defined control mutuality as the "extent to which couples agree on who has the right to influence the other and establish relational goals" (p. 6). They believed that information about control mutuality, along with trust, liking, and commitment, can be used to assess the nature of an interpersonal relationship and its stability.

This area includes legitimacy or the acceptance of one's partner's right to be controlling or domineering, exclusivity or the partner's commitment to the relationship regardless of control issues, and dependence or the recognition of the partners' interdependence in establishing control (Indvik and Fitzpatrick, 1986). Individuals in a relationship can exert control in ways that are adaptive and collaborative or they can manipulate both verbal and nonverbal messages to increase their own control of the interaction. Canary and Stafford (1994) maintained that a lack of "control mutuality or unilateral control is displayed in domineering behaviors" (p. 6) that are less productive for long-term relationships.

Dominance has been conceptualized as encompassing both verbal and nonverbal behaviors that are "recognized and interpreted by observers as part of an interactant's attempt to increase his/her control of an interaction" (Brandt[18], 1980, p. 32). Relational dominance has been characterized as "an emergent property of social interaction" and as having an immediate "relational impact" at the time the behavior was enacted during some "critical moment in the interaction" (Palmer and Lack[19], 1993, p. 167). This suggests that dominance or control can be a product of the interaction between relational partners where one partner demonstrates her or his ability to exercise power, as well as a product of the other partner's reactions to the dominance (Berger[20], 1994). This reaction informs the perpetrator about her or his own ability to exercise control or domination. Outcomes of this process might include legitimate power (the right to influence others based on one's status or role), linguistic power (providing reasonable explanations for the right to influence others), expert power (having specialized knowledge), referent power (others wanting to identify with the person), reward power (having the ability to meet others' needs), or coercive power (the ability to shape others' behavior; Berger, 1994).

The Emmers-Sommer[21] (chap. 17) meta-analysis on sexual coercion supports Berger's (1994) theorizing

16. Indvik, J., and Fitzpatrick, M. A. (1986). Perceptions of inclusion, affiliation, and control in five interpersonal relationships. Communication Quarterly, 34, 1–13.

17. Canary, D. J., and Stafford, L. (1994). Maintaining relationships through strategic and routine interactions. In D. J. Canary and L. Stafford (Eds.), Communication and relational maintenance (pp. 3–22). New York: Academic.

18. Brandt, D. R. (1980). A systematic approach to the measurement of dominance in human face-to-face interaction. Communication Quarterly, 28, 31–43.

19. Palmer, M. T., and Lack, A. M. (1993). Topics, turns, and interpersonal control using serial judgment methods. The Southern Communication Journal, 58, 156–168.

20. Berger, C. R. (1994). Power, dominance, and social interaction. In M. L. Knapp and G. R. Miller (Eds.), Handbook of interpersonal communication (pp. 450–507). Thousand Oaks, CA: Sage.

21. Emmers-Sommer, T. M. (1999). Negative relational events and event responses across relationship

on the reciprocal nature of social power and control. Results on the perceptual aspects of sexual coercion indicate that men and women agree on the nature of important features of the coercive episode. Both men and women perceived sexual coercion as more justifiable for women who initiated the date, went to a man's apartment, had a previous intimate relationship with the man, or consumed alcohol. In these situations, women tended to understand, if not endorse, men using control, power, and dominance to force sexual intercourse. Males' reactions to women's attempts to resist sexual coercion appear to be shaped by traditional sexual scripts. Women's verbal and nonverbal protests are viewed as being disingenuous and a motivation to continue the sexual pursuit. The Emmers-Sommer meta-analysis explores controversies regarding who has the right to exert control, the acceptance of control or dominance by a relational partner, and the use of coercive control and intimidation in sexual episodes.

Sexual coercion is a particularly onerous example of the conflicts that may arise in relationships. Disagreements about appropriate use of influence and the means and ends justifying force and coercion are not always likely to be resolved to the satisfaction of one or both parties. Retzinger[22] (1995) noted that "conflict does not always resolve differences, unify persons or groups or result in constructive change, sometimes it is destructive, erodes relationships, and ends in violence" (p. 26). Conflicts may result in enduring disagreements and profound emotions that warrant, in the view of one or both parties, the termination of the relationship.

A meta-analysis in this section addresses the use of conflict management strategies by men and women in intimate and nonintimate relationships. Gayle, Preiss, and Allen (chap. 18) examine the evidence for commonly held beliefs that men use controlling or competitive strategies in nonintimate relationships and withdrawal strategies in intimate conflicts, and women use compromising strategies in nonintimate relationships and coercive strategies in intimate relationships. They found that extraneous variables such as stereotypical attitudes and gender-role enactments may influence the contradictory pattern of effects in the primary studies. In addition to finding small effect sizes for sex differences in conflict management selection, Gayle et at point to emotional affect, situational constraints, and relational factors as areas meriting additional study. Much more research into interactional conflict processes is warranted.

In general, the research on control, dominance, and conflict reveals the necessity of a shared vision of the way a relationship is enacted. Partners negotiate the range of relational issues, including who has the right to exert influence, who may control relational resources, what goals and outcomes are preferred, and how conflicts or disagreements may be managed.

A Review of the information up to this point

The chapter began describing basic factors of interpersonal interaction. and everyone's desire for individuality and social visibility; next it discussed character traits; how emotion is communicated in an interaction; various definitions of types of social behavior such as neuroticsm, attachment, social anxiety, gender identity, shyness, embarrassment, and shame; sources of aggression, altruism, assertiveness and attraction; goffman's theory of self-presentation, which outlined how he thinks people are like actors on a stage, consciously and deliberately making their actions and behavior tailored for certain recipients; the theory of the looking-glass self, which demonstrated how there is a deeper inner reflection in any conversation of yourself, your life experience, your feelings, your qualities, and the other persons as well; Maslow outlined various major and basic needs people have such as physiological, safety, love and belonginness, esteem, and self-actualization; in addition to Maslows needs there were various peripheral variables that affect the social process of dependency, abasement, approval, authoritarianism, order, affiliation, machiavellianism, dominance, nurturance, achievement and recognition; there was Erikson's psychosocial crisis, which were qualities that people seek to achieve their major needs from (Malsow) - the qualities were trust, autonomy, initiative, industry, identity, intimacy, generativity and integrity. I then

---

type: Examining and comparing the impact of conflict strategy-use on intimacy in same-sex friendships, opposite-sex friendships, and romantic relationships. Communication Research-Reports, 16, 286–295.
22. Retzinger, S. M. (1995). Shame in anger in personal relationships. In S. Duck and J. T. Wood (Eds.), Confronting relational challenges (pp. 22–42). Thousand Oaks, CA: Sage.

showed the simplicity of social information by summarizing a lot of its content - by saying how that there are tones and subtleties to situations that contribute to the mood present, these are created by the thoughts, attitudes, motivations, feelings, personal characteristcs, other circumstantials factors (the environment) and (clearly) the behaviors of the people involved. Then I mentioned that autority, subordinacy, and equality are persistent themes in interpersonal relations. Next I discussed social skills, because at this point it should be obvious that they are important - behavior is goal-directed, interrelated, learned (conscious) or innate, and people can be very competence and composed or not so. Finally, I discussed "mutuality of control" - which shows the factors involved in authority, subordinacy and quality. People have an understanding of how dominant, influential, controling and manipulative each partner is - they can exert control in ways that are adaptive and collaborative or they can manipulate both verbal and nonverbal messages to increase their own control of the interaction.

Message Types in Communication

- There are greeting and leaving messages "hello" "goodbye" etc.

- There are polite questions, "how was your day", "how are you doing"

- There are compliments, "you look good", "nice to see you" etc

- There are messages of good-will, "have a good day", "wishing you well", "have a good one"

- Some messages can refer to the persons personality attributes or strengths and weaknesses - "he is nice", "man or iron man"...

- People can discuss relationships and how attracted people are to other people - "got his goat"

- Improving life messages - "let's reach higher"

- Positive, negative, and neutral comments

- Messages of doom, or hope - "The Dangerous Age"

- Messages that communicate someones experience

- Messages that talk about what someone did at some time (recently or not)

- Sentimental messages - "Home Is Where The Heart Is"

- Bitter-sweet statements or expressions - "it's ironic"

- Important or significant statements - "the big move"

- There are statements that reflect hurt (or emotion) - "A Woman Scorned"

- There are personality statements as metaphors that can simultaneously communicate occupation (among other things) - "The Wolf Of Wall Street", "Lady Of The House"

- Statements that suggest you do something (related to someone or something) - "Pity The Poor Working Girl"

- Romantic statements or discussions, "Burning Kisses"

- Statements of opinion - "It Shouldn't Happen To A Dog"

Harry Stack Sullivan (Sullivan 1953) outlined various developmental epochs in his book "The Interpersonal Theory of Psychiatry" (it is a little difficult to read, but I have put my analysis and interpretation after it):

- What we have in our minds begins in experience, and experience for the purpose of this theory is held to occur in three modes which i shall set up, one of which is usually, but by no means certainly, restricted to human beings. These modes are the prototaxic, the parataxic, and the syntaxic. I shall offer the thesis that these modes are primarily matters of 'inner' elaboration of events. The mode which is easiest to discuss is relatively uncommon--experience in the syntaxic mode; the one about which something can be known, but which is harder to discuss, is experience in the parataxic mode; and the one which is ordinarily capable of any formulation, and therefor of any discussion, is experience in the prototaxic or primitive mode. The difference in thses modes lies in the extent and the character of the elaboration that one's contact with events has undergone. (p. 28-29)

- The prototaxic mode, which seems to be the rough basis of memory, is the crudest-shall I say-the simplest, the earliest, and probably the most abundant mode of experience. Sentience, in the experimental sense, presumably relates to much of what I mean by the prototaxic mode. The prototaxic, at least in the very early months of life, may be regarded as the discrete series of momentary states of the sensitive organism, with special reference to the zones of interaction with the environment. By the term, sensitive, I attempt to bring into your conception all of those channels for being aware of significant events--from the tactile organs, in, say, my buttocks, which are apprising me that this is a chair and I have sat in it about long enough, to all sorts of internunciatory sensitivities which have been developed in meeting my needs in the process of living. It is as if everything that is sensitive and centrally represented were an indefinite, but very greatly abundant, luminous switchboard; and the pattern of light which would show on that switchboard in any discrete experience is the basic prototaxic experience itself, if you follow me. This hint may suggest to you that I presume from the beginning until the end of life we undergo a succession of discrete patterns of the momentary state of the organism, which implies not that other organisms are impinging on it, but certainly that the events of other organisms are moving toward or actually effecting a change in this momentary state. (p. 29)

- This is just another way of saying that absolute euphoria and absolute tension are constructs which are useful in thought but which do not occur in nature. These absolutes are approached at times, but almost all of living is perhaps rather near the middle of the trail, that is, there is some tension, and to that extent the level of euphoria is not as high as it could be. (p. 35)

- From the standpoint of the infants prototaxtic experience, this crying, insofar as it evokes tender behavior by the mothering one, is adequate and appropriate action by the infant to remove or escape fear-provoking dangers. Crying thus comes to be differentiated as action appropriate to accomplish the foreseen relief of fear. (p. 53)

- Thus the juvenile era is the time when the world begins to be really complicated by the presence of other people.(p. 232)

- This giving up of the ideas and operations of childhood comes about through the increasing power of the self-system to control focal awareness. And this in turn comes about because of the very difficult, crude, critical reaction of other juveniles, and because of the relatively formulable and predictable manifestations of adult authority. In other words, the juvenile has extraordinary opportunity to learn a great deal about security operations, to learn ways of being free from anxiety, in terms of comparatively understandable sanctions and their violations. (p. 233)

- I would guess that each of the outstanding achievements of the developmental eras that I have discussed will be outstandingly manifest in the mature personality. The last of these great developments is the appearance and growth of the need for intimacy- for collaboration with at least one other, preferably more others, and in this collaboration there is a very striking feature of a very lively sensitivity to the needs of the other and to the interpersonal security or absence of anxiety in the other. Thus we can certainly extrapolate from what we know that the mature, insofar as nothing of great importance collides, will be quite sympathetically understanding of the limitations, interests, possibilities, anxieties, and so on of those among whom they move or with whom they deal. (p. 310)

His discussion of the three "modes" of experience is important, it is similar to a discussion on consciousness. The prototaxic mode seems to be awareness of the senses, and this awareness of what you are feeling gives rise to an understanding from these feelings of your environment or whatever it is they are feeling. That is why babies mostly experience the world in this mode, because they are not capable of thought they mostly just feel and that gives rise to their awareness of the world. Saying that the modes are types of 'inner' elaboration of events is just saying that there are different ways of experiencing the world.

The prototaxic is the most basic and primitive, which is why it relates to the senses the most, the other modes are probably more thoughtful - derived from knowledge or thought.

Saying that there are absolutes of tension and euphoria is important. It is important to say that in order to help understand that people can be in extremely pleasurable states or extremely painful states. Most of the time for most people they are in the middle somewhere, but it is very useful to note the extremes in order to help recognize and understand that pain and pleasure are there to certain degrees and changing all the time.

He discusses that crying helps the baby avoid "fear-provoking dangers", because it gets tender affection from the mother. He is describing it as a learned process, the child learns to cry because it helps relieve fear and is also positively reinforced by affection from the mother. It is useful to think of social behavior in this kind of way, there are larger more important motives behind social behavior other than what may seem if you just look at the obvious motives. Certain things help relief fear or the "foreseen relief of fear", a lot of social behavior can be seen as avoiding fear and anxiety. Those components are not normally thought about as factors, but it makes sense that they are. Getting a friend, or saying hello could be seen as the foreseen relief of fear if you consider that otherwise you might be in pain without doing those things.

His type of thinking about social interactions, by relating it to anxiety and fear, is obvious is his explanation of the juvenile era as well - he postulates that "In other words, the juvenile has extraordinary opportunity to learn a great deal about security operations, to learn ways of being free from anxiety, in terms of comparatively understandable sanctions and their violations.", he is saying that the juvenile functions like the baby crying gets attention from the mother, the juvenile might feel threatened by authority and the rules they impose on him or her and therefore could learn a lot about how to be free from anxiety by learning how to navigate those rules. That is a deep analysis, usually when someone thinks of a parent imposing rules on a child they don't analyze it in terms of their social development, however it makes sense to think about it that way as well. The rules of the parents become a part of the child's life, it is how a child lives, there are authority figures in children's lives that are probably at least as important for their emotional development as their peers. And an important part of their interaction with these authority figures is the rules that are imposed upon them, it is an important part of how a child lives - the nature of how adults and authority figures interact with them.

In his discussion of what characteristics a mature person would have, he mentions that intimacy would be important, and again puts emphasis on anxiety, that they would be sensitive to the anxiety of the other person as well as limits, possibilities and interests. It makes sense that a more developed person would be more intimate because they are more developed and capable of greater intimacy, also, to be intimate you would need to be mature. He keeps bringing up the importance of anxiety - it is important for social development and it would be an important thing to be sensitive about as well.

Types of Communicators

Some people are more competent at communication than others, however, it is hard to assess this trait. It could be argued that some people are more competent because they are assertive, Machiavellian, rhetorically sensitive, versatile, empathic, or androgynous. Maybe some people have more knowledge, have better performance, or are more effective than others. There are some communication behaviors that are more competent or appropriate than others for a given situation, or the communicator may be more competent. A person who has trait-like communication competence is generally competent in communication across different contexts, receivers and time. A person who is context-based communication competence, however, is a person only competence within a given context (competent under some circumstances but not others) but (in that context) across receivers and time. A person who has situational communication competence is competent in a given context, with a given receiver or group of receivers, at a specific time. The individual may or may not be communicatively competent in any other context, with any other receiver or receivers, at any other time. So someone with context-based communication competence may be competent in clubs, someone who is has situational communication competence may only be competent on his birthday, in a club, with certain people. A person who has trait-like communication competence is generally competent everywhere.

Three personality traits were looked into for qualities of personal effectiveness in communication in a study done by (McCroskey[23] et all) - the traits were if someone was neurotic or non-neurotic, introverted or extroverted, or psychotic or non-psychotic:

- A consistent pattern emerged across the three studies. Specifically, the results seem to indicate that non-neurotic extroverts are not shy or apprehensive about touch, tend to perceive themselves as more competent, view themselves as assertive and responsive, and express greater degrees of self-acceptance. Neurotic introverts report apprehension about communication, perceive themselves as less immediate, rate themselves as having a lower affect orientation, and somewhat higher levels of verbal aggressiveness. Neurotic participants report less self-acceptance. Neurotic non-psychotics report a greater degree of affect orientation, more apprehension about communication, and lower verbal aggression. Neurotic psychotic extroverts tend to be compulsive communicators and report greater tolerance for disagreement. Psychotics are non-responsive, and tend to report higher levels of verbal aggressiveness, argumentativeness and assertiveness. Finally, psychotic non-neurotics tend to have a greater tolerance for disagreement and are less likely to identify themselves as compulsive communicators.

Some of the qualities measured were views of competence, affect orientation, aggressiveness, self-acceptance, and apprehension about communication. Being "competent" in communication would seem to be rather simple, if someone has an idea or thought then they can simply express it, there might be some things getting in the way of that like self-acceptance, apprehension, assertiveness, and having a positive or negative affect orientation. If you have negative affect, expressing an idea you have could become complicated because you would then be unsure if you are going to have a positive response. Communication then becomes a social thing, it isn't about the ability to express yourself, it is about you being nervous because of the social situation, which would then effect your ability to communicate.

How do you relate and compare what is going on socially to what is being communicated? In some situations there is little going on emotionally and it is just a straightforward conversation, like in a debate or formal conversation. In other situations there are a lot of emotional, social variables that complicate the situation and what is going to be communicated like at a party. There are a lot of circumstances that can vary greatly at a party that would effect what types of communication occur. A lot of social subtleties and complications. At a formal debate, or a business conversation, there might not be so many complications. The purpose there is clear and what needs to be communicated is simple, there aren't a lot of emotional factors that are going to influence what you say, it is just about business and you have simple, clear objectives (unlike in most social situations where the emotional, psychological factors of the situation can complicate what is going on). In a social situation you could potentially raise any topic for communication, you have to pick the right thing to say out of an endless option of choices (in addition, you have to factor in the people there and each of their complex psychological makeups). In a business interaction you only have a few options based on the business objective in the situation, and what type of person you are talking to isn't as complicated or as much of a factor. I'm not saying all business interchanges are simple, I'm just using it as an example to show how much easier interaction is when you know what needs to be said and you don't necessarily have to pick the exact right thing (or "entertaining" thing) from an endless number of options of things to say.

One of the goals of communication is to seek affinity, but how do people do this in an interaction? Do people pay close attention to the other person, show sensitivity, be responsive, or include them in their social activities? A study was done by (Richmond[24] et all) titled, "Affinity-Seeking Communication in Collegiate Female-Male Relationships" - here are two of the concluding paragraphs:

23. McCroskey, J, Heisel, A, and Richmond, V (2001) Eysenck's BIG THREE and Communication Traits: Three Correlational Studies. *Communication Monographs,* Vol 68, No. 4, December 2001, pp 360-366
24. Richmond, V., Gorham, J, and Furio, B (1987) Affinity-Seeking Communication in Collegiate Female-Male Relationships, *Communication Quarterly,* Vol 35, No. 4. Fall 1987, Pages 334-348.

- The results of the study indicate that there are differences in college male and female affinity-seeking strategies. Significant differences were found on all but three of the twenty-five strategies, with distinct female-male patterns emerging for approximately half of them. The interpretation of these differences in terms of dominance/submissiveness, proactive/reactive or self-oriented/other-oriented continua, however, must be approached with caution. Females were more likely to ask questions and elicit others disclosures, to pay close attention and be responsive while listening, and to show sympathy and sensitivity toward the other's problems and anxieties.Males were more likely to present themselves as an important figure able to reward association with themselves. Both males and females were concerned with "looking good" to the other, with females more concerned with physical attractiveness and males with presenting an interesting self through who they are, where they've been and who they know. These findings appear to characterize females as reactive and other-oriented and males as proactive and self-oriented.

- Males, however, were more likely than females to complement the other, treat them like an important person and engage in self-concept confirmation, and to give assistance-such as getting a drink or taking the other's coat-or advice (altruism), strategies which, although perhaps the more proactive of those categorized by Bell and Daly as "concern and caring" (along with elicit other's disclosure, listening, supportiveness, and sensitivity) indicate other-orientation on the part of the males. Females indicated a greater likelihood of inclusion of other in their social activities and groups of friends, introducing him to her friends and making him feel that he belongs; males indicated greater likelihood of setting up encounters with the other person and of "putting [themselves] in a position to be invited to participate in [the other's] social activities" (self-inclusion). It is difficult to assess whether the essential element differentiating male and female responses on these strategies was the female focus on the other (inviting him along) and the male focus on himself (putting himself in a position to be invited) or the females active vs. the males reactive approach to initiating encounters with other friends. Similarly, females indicated they would avoid playing "one-upmanship" games and would assume equality while males indicated they would try to reinforce similarity by expressing views similar to the other's, agreeing with the other and avoiding behavior which might suggest differences. The goal of these strategies is similar. Both females and males appear to be concerned with the similarity/equality issue with the male-selected strategy somewhat more reactive.

What I find interesting is that you probably can only do a few things well in a social interaction, females tend to focus on doing some things, and males on others. Females showed sympathy and sensitivity and males tended to present themselves as an important figure. You could try to do both of those things, but I think clearly if you focused on one instead of the other you would present a more cohesive personality then if you tried to show that you did two different things with communication. The lesson there is that if you present one side, the message is going to be more clear for that side then if you tried to present multiple personalities, attitudes or characteristics. Males put more focus on putting himself in a position to be invited, while females made the other feel like they belong (inviting him along). The male response shows a greater interest in power, by treating the other like an important person and trying to reinforce similarity (this would get them in a position to be invited), while the females indicated they would avoid playing "one-upmanship" games and would assume equality (instead of the interest in power by the males). So what is learned from this is that there are styles of communication and interaction, while there are an endless number of things to pick from to say in a social situation, what you do pick is probably going to go along with your personality and how you present that personality and its characteristics to the world.

Attitudes

Someone could have an emotional reaction to someone or something someone does, that is different from having an attitude change, or it could be that the emotional reaction causes a change in attitude. Also, people make evaluations about the other person or about what they are saying or is going on, which could call upon a set of stored knowledge the person already has or be a completely new idea or set of thoughts about the person or thing going on. It makes sense that evaluations would have occurred before, however, since everything in an interaction is not completely new each time - therefore people make evaluations and assessments (come to conclusions during an interaction) about other people's behavior or something else about what is going on - and they are assessments that are similar to ones they have made in the past in similar situations. When someone makes an evaluation, they are likely to have an attitude adjustment because their opinion or thoughts about what is going on has changed. An example of such an evaluation might be "this person is not easy to get along with, I don't know if I like him or her, I might have to stop talking to them" - once a person makes such an evaluation of the other person, their attitude is likely to change. They have probably made evaluations like that in the past with other people, so have learned how to change their attitude and what other conclusions to make once they make that assessment. They also take in new information and construct an opinion based on the current situation, in addition to having learned assessments that they call upon. People can consider readily available information (what is going on in the social interaction they are currently in) and integrate this information into an overall attitudinal judgement.

During the coarse of an interaction or, for example, a conversation, someone might change their attitude many times, there might be large attitude changes or small ones. They change their attitude when they have an emotional reaction (generated from the other person most likely) or make an assessment or evaluation of the other person, their behavior, or what is going on (the conversation most likely). The nature of their evaluation might be similar to evaluations they have reached in the past, so it is a learned response or attitude change. That person might just happen to change his or her attitude in such a way when someone does such a thing, it is just what they do. A person might also generate a new attitude based on a new situation and new information they have gathered in this situation. When I say people make evaluations during interactions, I mean they reach conclusions about the other person, form ideas and opinions of them, their behavior and the interaction. These "evaluations" occur all the time and, since they can be natural and unconscious to a large extent, are going to be influenced by the persons previous experience with forming conclusions, opinions and ideas during an interaction. This means that not all the opinions and ideas you reach during an interaction (and their resulting attitude changes) are going to be completely under your awareness (conscious). That makes sense, of course you don't know all the times you change your attitude and all the assessments of the the interaction you are making during the interaction, the point is, however, that you are making them and they are influencing you behavior. Your attitude can change without you directing it, that shows that you are reaching conclusions and having evaluations and assessments during an interaction that you aren't completely aware of.

People come to conclusions about how good or bad elements of the interaction are during the course of the interaction. These conclusions might result in an attitude change. The conclusion (assessment) might be stored, it may be a conclusion you come to frequently and each time you change your attitude in a similar manner. Or it might be that during an interaction you reach completely new conclusions about what is going on and change your attitude in new and different ways from how you changed it in the past. Of course each time is going to be at least a little different, it is really a matter of degree. Here I am discussing the "conclusions" people reach during an interaction, however, if you were to ask someone how many conclusions they reached during an interaction they would probably say none. The conclusions aren't completely conscious - in an interaction your opinion is changing about the interaction all the time, you change your attitude continuously, each time you don't take note of that. Sometimes they are conscious - an example would be you saying, "this person is bad, i'm going to have a negative attitude towards him or her from this point on in the conversation". Conclusions and evaluations like that occur all the time without your awareness, they are a natural part of an interaction. People might also change their behavior based off of these conclusions and evaluations they reach about what is going on, not just change their attitude or opinion (beliefs).

Some evaluations people can make can be of "approval or disapproval", or the "attribution of good or bad qualities". Your emotional responses and beliefs which help influence your evaluations and attitude changes might also have a history- your beliefs were probably formed from past interaction, and your emotional responses are probably mostly learned ones. Your beliefs may also change right then in the interaction, what is going on could change your opinions right then and have resulting attitude changes at that time. What are your motivations for having various attitudes? People naturally have attitudes, based upon what they are thinking at the time, they are going to have a certain attitude from their current mindset in an interaction. This mindset is formed by your reaction to what is going on, which is influenced by your beliefs and who you are (and "you are" a product of your behavioral history, so your beliefs and emotional responses are going to be mostly learned).

What does having an attitude do? It could facilitate the management and simplification of information processing, help achieve desired goals and avoid negative outcomes, maintain or promote self-esteem, or convey information about your values and self-concepts. An attitude might serve any one of those purposes, for example an attitude that comes from a core value belief you have might help you express your values, or an attitude that you formed because of a belief of your self-worth could help serve your self-esteem, for example. Your attitude can be favorable or unfavorable, it shows judgement and a goal - for instance if you are nice you have reached the judgement to be nice and you have a goal you plan on using your attitude for, your attitude is favorable.

Attitudes, Communication and Personality

- A persons attitude changes can be attributed to their unique personality and their personality type

- There can be multiple attitude changes in a short period of time during an interaction

- Attitude can change from various causes, such as the content of an interaction which might include a conversation, or other interpersonal behaviors (your attitude can change when you're not interacting with a person as well though, obviously)

- Attitudes can vary in strength and duration - also how noticeable the attitude is to the people in the interaction

- Attitudes are considerably more complicated than simple affect orientations such as being nice or mean, there is a whole host of psychological factors that contribute to a certain attitude (though on the surface it seems as if attitudes are simple - when you look at someone they are easy to read on one hand, but mysterious and complicated on the other)

What makes an attitude? Why are attitudes important?

There are many psychological factors that contribute to how an attitude is formed and how it functions in an interpersonal context:

- Attitudes can show a certain level of affect

- Attitudes are influenced by person perception

- Attitudes can be influenced by the emotions someone is feeling during an interaction, if you are feeling a certain way that is going to affect your attitude

- Attitudes are therefore related to feeling, what you are feeling helps contribute to your attitude - if you are feeling sad you might have a depressed looking attitude, for instance

- What the person is focusing on in an interaction is going to contribute to his or her attitude, if you are focusing on being mean then you are going to have a mean attitude, for instance. This means if you are not focusing you might not have an attitude at all.

- Attitudes have various levels of goodness and badness, directed towards various objects in a social encounter such as the other person, something they said, something they are being shown

- Attitudes therefore contain information, if you have a bad attitude, that shows your feelings towards the object that is the cause of your bad attitude. Also, simply displaying more affect is more communicative as well because you are being more intense.

- There are as many attitudes as there are emotions and feelings, if you are feeling one thing then you could say that that is your attitude. Feelings are very complicated, and therefore attitudes are equally as complicated.

- Sometimes an attitude can be very noticeable, obvious, annoying or not so.

- Interactions are basically people displaying some sort of affect or attitude continuously, but the affect/attitude is not constant and singular, it is complicated and multidimensional - it changes constantly and is on one hand very simple to understand, and on the other very complex.

- If you think about it, the entire interaction is displayed in someones attitude, what they feel and what they think about what is going on is displayed in their attitude, an attitude is therefore just a reflection of what that person is thinking, it is the personality they are presenting to the world.

- People are basically just deliverers of attitude, they think and feel, but those are expressed through their attitude and affect, which are very similar, the emotions you display (your affect) and your attitude are basically the same thing. This is so because your attitude is what you are feeling directed at the world, and your feelings are all directed at the world (to various degrees).

- Your feelings are directed at the world because other people can read your feelings to a certain extent. You could say that your attempt to communicate your feelings to someone else is your attempt to have an attitude.

- Attitudes and the feelings that make them up are therefore communicative, attitudes communicate what you feel - and sometimes you do this deliberately or you may have an attitude you are completely unaware of.

- In fact, feelings are present all the time in people, so therefore they are communicating their feelings all the time in complex ways, showing a complex, changing attitude all of the time.

- Whatever you are feeling at any time could influence your attitude at that time - your attitude is just the feelings you have that you are presenting or trying to communicate to someone (or some number of people) - or you could be putting on a fake attitude and not really be feeling those things, but I would say in such cases your "putting on" the attitude would generate feelings that come from that attitude even if you are making the attitude up.

- So attitudes come from your feelings and thoughts, they are composed of certain ideas or feelings that you wish to display in an emotional way. For instance, if you are feeling sad you may show an attitude of lack of interest. Feelings are thus related to attitudes, you choose to display an attitude that shows what you want to communicate - you want to communicate a lack of interest so you act like you are bored, that is an attitude, however, since this attitude comes from you being sad part of your "bored" looking attitude is going to have elements of sadness, you might also be feeling bored to some degree. So what you are feeling caused you to generate an attitude that reflected those feelings and what you wanted to communicate because you were feeling those things. Your attitude may be made up, you may not feel that way, or maybe you just wish to communicate something with an attitude and you don't feel anything about it - it is a non-emotional attitude, and maybe you aren't even emotional or have feelings for the cause of you deciding to generate this non-emotional attitude.

- *Attitudes are something that you are communicating to another person or other people that have associated and related feelings. If you want to be rude to someone you could have a "bad" attitude, you are communicating that you want to be rude and mean to them. There are also going to be certain feelings you have that are related to that attitude, you might feel like you really dislike the person, or that they are a loser - or maybe you don't feel anything at all about the person or people and just wish to show a negative attitude.*

Perception of social situations

Another important thing to note is a persons perception of social situations. Considering how complicated an interaction is, how someone assesses that interaction and what they thought occurred is going to be complicated as well. The individual's interpretation of different situations plays an essential part in his adjustment to reality, i.e., for his satisfaction and social relationships. How intense the person believes the interaction was in a big perception people can make as well I would think. What kinds of responses do individuals make with what intensity in which kinds of situations?

Conclusion

In the final analysis, then, the self is an interpersonal tool. More precisely, it is an instrument that people fashion and modify to improve their chances for being included by other people in desirable social groups, ranging from multinational corporations to marital dyads. The self does not exist in a vacuum, independent of social ties, nor does it develop out of itself alone. It is a remarkably sensitive and powerful adaptation to the unstable but terribly important world of interpersonal relations.

Table 103.0

Death, Hope, Humor, Love and Sex

Chapter 447

When someone is in a social interaction, a complex set of emotions and feelings are being evoked on a moment to moment basis. That is, they are constantly changing rather quickly - from one second to the next to the next you could have many different emotions start, stop or occur simultaneously. However the level to which these emotions are recognized or felt is hard to figure out, it is not like people are taking account of all the second by second experiences of their feelings, or even if they can observe those consciously. I believe that the reality is that unconsciously these emotions are interacting with each other and influencing the conscious feelings and thoughts that you do have. They are still very important even though they aren't felt in an obvious way (which is why they are unconscious), however. The most powerful of these unconscious emotions I believe are the emotions of death, hope, humor, love - and sex (though sex is more of a simulation and humor more of an excitement).

Love is the most obvious example - even with someone you are love with the emotion love isn't present consciously every second you interact with that person, in fact, you probably only feel it very infrequently. That does not mean, however, that you are not in love with the person the rest of the time. Love is an unconscious factor in the relationship and in your emotions the rest of the time. Even though you don't really "feel" it, it has tainted your feelings more towards love, it influences your feelings to maybe be more powerful and in that direction. The same is true for the other emotions I mentioned, they are constantly present and influencing your emotions and feelings even though you wouldn't say you are feeling (for example pain (death) or hope).

I called death an emotion but really it only gives rise to the emotion pain or painful emotions. So hope must taint all your emotions in a positive way, make them more happy in a hopeful sort of way. Pain makes your emotions difficult and painful in a doomed sort of way, similar to the experience of death. When you interact with someone, if pain or difficulty is present you could say that death is a factor in the interaction. The emotions you are experiencing are actually larger and more significant than you notice. You only notice obvious, clear instances when you experience emotion. The reality is, however, that you are partially in pain and partially in pleasure the entire time of an interaction, the death factor and the hope factor are there all the time, only unconsciously.

In classical Freudian psychoanalytic theory, the death drive ("Todestrieb") is the drive towards death, self-destruction and the return to the inorganic: 'the hypothesis of a death instinct, the task of which is to lead organic life back into the inanimate state'.[1] It was originally proposed by Sigmund Freud in 1920 in Beyond the Pleasure Principle, where in his first published reference to the term he wrote of the 'opposition between the ego or death instincts and the sexual or life instincts'.[2] The death drive opposes Eros, the tendency toward survival, propagation, sex, and other creative, life-producing drives.

Frued believed in a death instinct (or drive), and a sex instinct. Freud encountered the phenomenon of repetition in (war) trauma. When Freud worked with people with trauma (particularly the trauma experienced by soldiers returning from World War I), he observed that subjects often tended to repeat or re-enact these traumatic experiences: 'dreams occurring in traumatic have the characteristic of repeatedly bringing the patient back into the situation of his accident', contrary to the expectations of the pleasure principle.

In Freudian psychology, the pleasure principle is the psychoanalytic concept describing people seeking pleasure and avoiding suffering (pain) in order to satisfy their biological and psychological needs.

---

1. Sigmund Freud, "The Ego and the Id", in On Metapsychology (Middlesex 1987), p. 380
2. Sigmund Freud, "Beyond the Pleasure Principle" in On Metapsychology (Middlesex 1987), p. 316

I have my own ideas about the death and sex drives, and the pleasure principle of Freud. I believe that pain and pleasure are both necessary and present in many interactions, and therefore you could view it as there being a drive towards pain and a drive towards pleasure and sex. It is that simple, both pain and pleasure are always components in interaction, however they are so large and important that you could label them as instinctual and drives. They cannot be avoided - similar to how people can repeat traumatic experiences, even though it may seem like people only want pleasure, the reality is pain is just as natural and driven. People automatically cause themselves to experience pain - it is a part of life and your conscious and unconscious emotions.

Humor is also important. Life isn't just about doomful death feelings and motivations, or selfish pleasurable sex drives. There is hope and love, but those would be boring by themselves. People need to recognize that there is a lighter side to life, a fun and carefree excitement that is often found in humor. These emotions are all present in every interaction, they are balancing each other and interacting with each other all the time. Pain can balance pleasure, hope can change your expectations, sex can help you have "fun", and humor can cause you to think life is "fun" or "funny". How these emotions and feelings play out on a second to second basis is going to vary based on the interaction, but the point is they are all there all the time and are major conscious and unconscious elements.

Table 104.0

Chapter 105

Personality Theory

Table 1 Examples of adjectives, Q-sort items, and questionnaire scales defining the five factors

Factor		Factor definers		
Name	Number	Adjectives[a]	Q-sort items[b]	Scales[c]
Extraversion (E)	I	Active	Talkative	Warmth
		Assertive	Skilled in play, humor	Gregariousness
		Energetic	Rapid personal tempo	Assertiveness
		Enthusiastic	Facially, gesturally espressive	Activity
		Outgoing	Behaves assertively	Excitement Seeking
		Talkative	Gregarious	Positive Emotions
Agreeableness (A)	II	Appreciative	Not critical, skeptical	Trust
		Forgiving	Behaves in giving way	Straightforwardness
		Generous	Sympathetic, considerate	Altruism
		Kind	Arouses liking	Compliance
		Sympathetic	Warm, compassionate	Modesty
		Trusting	Basically trustful	Tender-Mindedness
Conscientiousness (C)	III	Efficient	Dependable, responsible	Competence
		Organized	Productive	Order
		Planful	Able to delay gratification	Dutifulness
		Reliable	Not self-indulgent	Achievement Striving
		Responsible	Behaves ethically	Self-Discipline
		Thorough	Has high aspiration level	Deliberation
Neuroticism (N)	–IV	Anxious	Thin-skinned	Anxiety
		Self-pitying	Brittle ego defenses	Hostility
		Tense	Self-defeating	Depression
		Touchy	Basically anxious	Self-Consciousness
		Unstable	Concerned with adequacy	Impulsiveness
		Worrying	Fluctuating moods	Vulnerability
Openness (O)	V	Artistic	Wide range of interests	Fantasy
		Curious	Introspective	Aesthetics
		Imaginative	Unusual thought processes	Feelings
		Insightful	Values intellectual matters	Actions
		Original	Judges in unconventional terms	Ideas
		Wide interests	Aesthetically reactive	Values

Notes: [a] Adjective Check List items defining the factor in a study of 280 men and women rated by 10 psychologists serving as observers during an assessment weekend at the Institute of Personality Assessment and Research (John, 1989a).
[b] California Q-Set items from self-sorts by 403 men and women in the Baltimore Longitudinal Study of Aging (McCrae, Costa, & Busch, 1986).
[c] Revised NEO Personality Inventory facet scales from self-reports by 1,539 adult men and women (Costa, McCrae, & Dye, 1991).

Sources:
(John O.P. 1989a November. Big Five prototypes for the Adjective Check List using observer data. In O.P. John (chair), *The Big Five: Historical perspective and current research.* Symposium conducted at the annual meeting of the society for Multivariate Experimental Psychology, Honolulu.), (McCrae, R.R., Costa, P.T., Jr. and Busch, C. M. (1986). Evaluating comprehensiveness in personality systems: The California Q-Set and the five-factor model. *Journal of Personality.*) and (Costa, P.T. Jr., and Dye, D.A. (1991). Facet scales for Agreeableness and Conscientiousness: A revision of the NEO Personality Inventory. *Personality and*

Individual Differences, 12, 887-898.)

The table above shows the five factors in the five factor model of personality along with some more descriptive adjectives associated with each of the factors. It has been noted that the five factor model can account for a large amount of personality information with this simple model alone. Does this model account for all the personality traits? Does it sum up what most of personality is about in a short and simple manner? When you meet someone or study people what are the most obvious personality traits that you notice about them? What are the most common personality traits people have? Extroverted or introverted (if someone is social or not) is clearly a big personality trait. Kindness or cruelty is also clearly a big personality trait that is shown in the big five traits of openness and agreeableness. If someone is detail oriented, organized and thorough or not would seem to be a big factor in their lives, and that is shown in the table above as conscientiousness. If someone is paranoid and anxious seems to be an important factor involved with what someone is like - that is shown above as neuroticism. I would say the factors in Table 1 above and in Table 3 below are all important personality characteristics. I can sum up this table (and therefore a large part of personality psychology) better, - it is important if someone is or is not social, nice, detail oriented and thorough, neurotic and anxious, or imaginative and open or not.

There are circumstances in which the ascription of a trait to a person serves as a partial explanation of that person's behavior. If someone does something is act someway, you can label them as having a certain type of personality or certain personality traits because you observed them doing those actions. If you are not acquainted with John and if you ask me why John pushed the boy on a certain occasion, I might reply that John is aggressive. In effect, I am saying that such behavior is not unusual or unexpected for John, and such an "explanation" might serve as an answer to your question. However, if you and I both know John well, my telling you that John is aggressive does not answer your question. Were I to inform you that the boy had pushed John yesterday, you might very well feel that I had provided a satisfactory account of the incident (because you already know that John is or is not aggressive).

Table 3 Some item definers of O, A, and C factors in the California Q-Set

Openness
    Aesthetically reactive
    Values intellectual matters
    Wide range of interests
    Rebellious, non-conforming
      —vs—
    Sex-role stereotyped behavior
    Favors conservative values
    Uncomfortable with complexities
    Judges in conventional terms
Agreeableness
    Sympathetic, considerate
    Arouses liking
    Warm, compassionate
    Behaves in giving way
      —vs—
    Expresses hostility directly
    Basically distrustful
    Shows condescending behavior
    Critical, skeptical
Conscientiousness
    Productive
    Behaves ethically
    Has high aspiration level
    Dependable, responsible
      —vs—
    Self-indulgent
    Interested in opposite sex
    Enjoys sensuous experiences
    Unable to delay gratification

Note: Adapted from McCrae *et al.* (1986).

262   *Trait approaches*

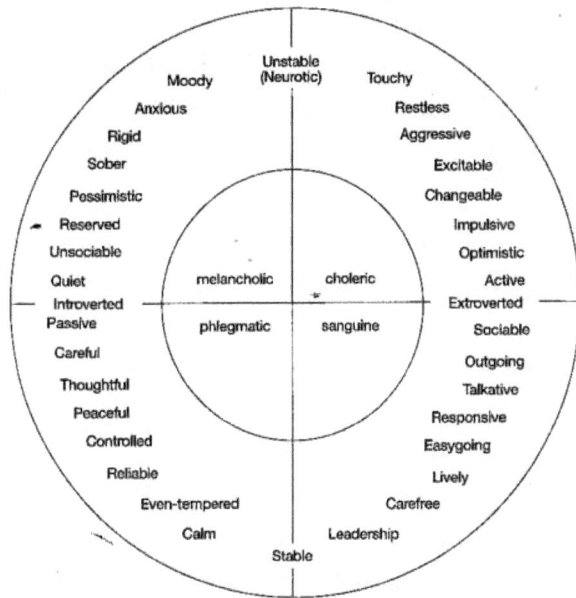

Figure 2 Two major dimensions of personality revealed by factor analysis compared with the four Greek categories
Source: From Eysenck, 1964, 27, by courtesy of University of London Press.

Source: Eyesnck, H,J, and Eysnck, S.B.G. (1964) *Manual of the Eysenck Personality Inventory.* London: University Press.

Table 105.0

Chapter 106

Interaction and Human Communication

Impossibility of not Communicating

Within an interaction, neither person can stop behaving, and each adapts to the other's behavior. Whether they are talking or remaining silent, being active or passive, they are behaving. Each person perceives the other's behavior and attaches meaning to some of it.

Those behaviors to which meaning is assigned become messages. Since any behavior can become a message, it is impossible to keep from generating meaning within an interaction. In this sense one cannot communicate.

In an interaction, anything you do or not do is communicating some message. If you move closer to someone when talking to them, you are communicating one thing, if you stay where you are, you are communicating something else. Depending on the role each person is in, who they are, what the current situation is, different actions and words could communicate different things.

Self-disclosure and Self-image

Self-disclosure in interaction is a revealing of the "inner" or "real" person to another, or the revealing or concealing of significant information about one's feelings or experiences. Self-disclosure relates to self-image, which is a persons image of him or herself that consists of a set of role images. In various different roles, you have an image of yourself as acting in some fashion or being yourself in some way. Self-disclosure could be an ongoing attempt to not disclose information about yourself and your feelings in an attempt to defend your self-image. If you disclosed all your personal feelings, you might perceive yourself as being vulnerable.

The self or self-image is the center from which all communication occurs. When there is a perceived threat to the self-image, communication will be characterized by defensiveness. Defensive communication involves a person's attempt to conceal some significant meaning in order to protect his or her self-image. For example, if someone criticized someone else by calling them incompetent, the other person may start to feel stupid, and would want to hide that. It might make them defensive and want to conceal their self, or self-image of being a stupid person. People try to defend their self-images. Someone could try to hide aspects of their self-image or hide feeling and decisions they have about their lives. These feelings and decisions may or may not be understood by other people. Someone could go a long time in a relationship with someone else and be hiding certain feelings because they are being defensive or they just don't want the other person to know.

Disclosure of Experience in the Here and Now

One aspect of disclosure is the expression of what a person is feeling, thinking, and experiencing in the "here and now". There is a sense in which healthy communication can be achieved only if both persons involved in an interaction are openly, freely, and spontaneously expressing to each other what they are experiencing in the immediate situation. Difficulties in communication occur when a person is trying to communicate one thing while actually feeling or experiencing something else. For example, homosexuals may be attracted to straight people but would probably hide their feelings when interacting with them because it isn't appropriate. There are probably incredibly complicated ways in which people's feelings are or are not being expressed in moment to moment interactions (between both friends and strangers, heterosexuals and homosexuals, etc).

Effective communication involves congruency between what a person is experiencing and what the person is expressing in an interaction. So if a person is feeling angry, they should express that they are angry in an appropriate fashion. Disclosure doesn't necessarily mean that the person needs to reveal all their secrets, it does, however, mean they need to reveal the appropriate amount of information at the appropriate times. For instance, a parent getting angry at a child without expressing why they are angry wouldn't be appropriate because the child wouldn't know what to do to stop the parent from getting angry at them in the future. The parent would appear to the child to just get angry and the parent wouldn't then be properly disclosing, or communicating, that they are angry and the cause of their anger.

Incongruency Between Role and Context

Major difficulties in interpersonal communication occur when a person assumes a role that does not fit in the context of the transaction. Suppose two army buddies go out drinking. Their evening is going pleasantly when Frank (a sergeant) says to bob (a corporal), "Get me another drink." "Get it yourself, I've had enough," replies Bob. Frank threatens, "Listen, i outrank you. Don't you forget that. And I ordered you to get me another drink." The role Frank assumes is appropriate within the context of conducting military business but incongruent with the context of two buddies out for a good time. Whether Frank spoke in seriousness or in jest, Bob will probably feel hurt and resentful. The incongruency between role and context, therefore, becomes the source of difficulties in communication between Frank and Bob.

This could be a source of great amusement. You could consider every interaction one in which each person is supposed to fit a certain role, or roles. If they don't fit those roles things could go dramatically wrong.

Incongruency Between Roles

Difficulties in interpersonal communication arise when two people in a transaction assume roles that are incongruent. If danny is trying to talk to Mary as a friend and Mary is responding to Danny not as his friend but as his supervisor, their roles are clearly incongruent.

Table 106.0

Chapter 107

Personality, Roles and Social Behavior

Role Theory

- The structural-functionalist perspective grew out of attempts to represent social structure. The basic assumption was that actions are patterned into coherent and ordered systems that govern both interpersonal interaction and society functioning. Actions are patterned, in this sense, because certain aspects of behavior seem more characteristic of the relationship of the setting than of the particular individuals involved. Thus, in an interaction between a police officer and a traffic violator, large parts of the behavior and expectations will remain the same even though the specific actors change from instance to instance.

- The symbolic interactionist perspective on roles, grew out of attempts to account for how an individual becomes a member of society. The essential answer was that the self does not exist, at least initially, without the social group. It is only through interaction with others that we learn to identify, label, and value objects. One of the objects that a person learns to identify is him or herself- the "me" as seen by others. The social self develops out of interaction and is defined by the process and results of that interaction. Consequently, there are multiple selves, as many, potentially, as there are interactions. Roles and identities, since they arise out of interaction, require a unity, but once acquired become a more independent self and guide behavior in future interactions. From a repertoire of identities, one can call up the self that seems most appropriate to present in a particular context.

- Cicourel (1970[1], 1974[2]) criticized traditional conceptions of roles and status as being abstractions that did not describe (a) what procedures an actor used to recognize and generate appropriate behavior, (b) how particular norms are recognized, selected and invoked in the context of a particular interaction, and (c) how innovation and change in the interaction alters general norms or rules.

An overview of the personality trait approach

- Gordon Allport (1937)[3] conceived of personality traits as inferred causes of behavioral consistency. Personality, he assumed, matured through increasing differentiation and increasing integration of behavioral tendencies. Traits reflect one level in a hierarchy of integration. With the maturation of personality, conditioned reflexes become integrated into habits. Traits, then, become "dynamic and flexible dispositions, resulting, at least in part, from the integration of specific habits, expressing characteristic modes of adaptation to one's surroundings. Belonging to this level are the dispositions variously called sentiments, attitudes, values, complexes, and interests" (pp.141-142).

Individual versus common personality traits

- Allport defines traits as either individual or common in nature. "Strictly speaking, no two persons ever have precisely the same trait. Though each of two men may be aggressive (or aesthetic), the style and range of the aggression (or estheticism) in each case is noticeably different. What else could be expected in view of the unique hereditary endowment, the different developmental

1. Cicourel, A. V. The aquisition of social structure: Toward a developmental sociology of language. In J. Dougles (Ed.) *Understanding everyday life.* Ney York: Aldine, 1970.
2. Cicourel, A. F. Interpretive procedures and normative rules in the negotiation of status and role. In A. V. Cicourel (Ed.), *Cognitive sociology.* New York: Free Press, 1974.
3. Allport, G. W. *Personality: A psychological interpretation.* New York: Holt, 1937.

history, and the never-repeated external influences that determine each personality? The end product of unique determination can never be anything but unique" (p.297).

- Allport noted there might be a deep assumption when comparing individuals about the underlying unity or sameness of the population measured. "For all their ultimate differences, normal persons within a given culture-area, tend to develop a limited number of roughly comparable modes of adjustment. The original endowment of most human beings, their stages of growth, and the demands of their particular society, are sufficiently standard and comparable to lead to some basic modes of adjustment that from individual to individual are approximately the same. To take an example: the nature of the struggle for survival in a competitive society tends to force every individual to seek his own most suitable level of aggression... Somewhere between the extremes of exaggerated domination and complete passivity, there lies for each normal individual a level of adaptation that fits his intimate requirements" (pp.197-298).

The Role Concept

The role concept was introduced in the book *The Study of Man* by Ralph Linton: 'A status, as distinct from the individual who may occupy it, is simply a collection of rights and duties..a role represents the dynamic aspect of a status... When (an individual) puts the rights and duties into effect, he is performing a role... Status and role serve to reduce the ideal patterns for social life to individual terms. They become models for organizing the attitudes and behavior of the individual so that these will be congruous with those of the other individuals participating in the pattern.'

In the book *The Cultural Background of Personality* Linton adds to his role explanation: 'The term role will be used to designate the sum total of the culture patterns associated with a particular status. It thus includes the attitudes, values and behavior ascribed by the society to any and all persons occupying the status. It can even be extended to include the legitimate expectations of such person with respect to the behavior towards them of persons of other statuses within the same system.'

Linton put forward a simple twofold classification dividing roles into those which are *ascribed* ('assigned to individuals without reference to their innate differences or abilities') and those which are *achieved* ('left open to be filled through competition and individual effort'). The criteria for ascribed roles must be evident at birth, making it possible to begin training immediately and eliminating all uncertainty. Such criteria are those of sex, age, kinship relations, and birth into a particular class or caste. Achieved roles, however, are given are given to the people whose individual performance qualifies them as the most meritorious. This classification is based on the mode of allocation of roles.

Roles are ranked in respect of prestige: the role of surgeon confers more prestige than that of chemist. Prestige is an abstract concept used to sum up the various little form of deference people show to those whom they respect socially and the devices they use to degrade those whom they consider inferior. Prestige is an attribute of roles: all surgeons enjoy the same prestige as representatives of an occupation. People distinguish, however, between outstanding surgeons and mediocre ones; this evaluation of how well someone performs a role is an assessment of esteem. Robertson will be highly esteemed as a radiologist and very little esteemed as a bridge-player. Esteem is thus a judgement of individuals not of roles. In any community or group of acquaintances a man is apt to be ranked on a basis of both these factors. If people could be given so many marks for the prestige of each of their roles, and more marks for the esteem they earn in carrying them out, and then all these could be added up, this would be an arithmetical measure of their social standing in the group. Some groups or communities value certain kinds of behavior more than others but this does not affect the general notion. In practice, such evaluations are made at times even if the process is not altogether conscious and the reckoning is far from arithmetical. It will be apparent that this kind of judgement can be made only in a fairly small community in which people are well acquainted with an individual's various roles and his fulfillment of them. To a certain extent the same procedure is carried out in larger communities or in the nation at large when it is referred to as an assessment of social status: because fewer factors can be taken into account when people are not acquainted with one another personally, judgments of social status are based upon roles held and not upon performance. Social status is therefore different from legal status. It is an evaluation of an individual's claims to deference in respect of the prestige of the various roles he plays: objective measures of social status can be based upon such factors as an individual's occupation, income, length of education, housing, etc.

Table 107.0

Chapter 108

Depression

- The first essential feature of major depression is either a depressed mood or anhedonia - that is, a pervasive loss of interest or ability to experience pleasure in normally enjoyable activities. The mood is usually sad, but it can also be irritable or apprehensive.

- Patients describe this mood as "living in a black hole or in a deep pit," "feeling dead," "overwealmed by doom," or "physically drained." However, many patients with major depression do not feel depressed or even dysphoric (dysphoria - any unpleasant mood, including dysthymia (the emotion or symptom of depression), but anhedonic. (Possibly start caring less about their lives and the things in them).

- The biological (also called vegetative) signs and symptoms of depression generally include, appetite loss, unintentional weight loss or gain, insomnia or hypersomnia, psychomotor retardation or agitation, a lack of energy or fatigue, and diminished libido.

- The psychological signs and symptoms of depression include a diminished ability to think or make decisions, negative thinking about the past (e.g., guilt), present (e.g., low self-esteem), and future (e.g., hopelessness), and thoughts about death and suicide.

- The acronym DEPRESSING can be used to help remember the criteria for depression. The letters represent Depression (sadness), Energy (loss of), Pleasure (diminished interest), Retardation (psychomotor slowing or agitation), Eating (changes in weight or appetite), Suicide (recurrent thoughts of death), Sleep (insomnia or hypersomnia, Indecisive (poor concentration), Negative thinking (worthlessness, hopelessness, or inappropriate Guilt).

- To a depressed individual, everything is bleak- their life, their world, their future, and their treatment.

- They ruminate over personal failures, real or imagined, often making mountains out of molehills. With a nearly delusional conviction, they may feel utterly hopeless, helpless, worthless, or guilty. A self-made millionaire declared that he was a "financial flop" who had "forced his family into the poorhouse."

In the chapter where I discussed mental disorders for children, I showed how kids become more energetic as a result of depression - they show more anxiety and anger, exhibit externalized behaviors as an expression of their feelings, and somatize their depression and experience physical aches and pains (vegetative symptoms are still a part of depression for children, only typically less so than with adults). While adults become more vegetative and relaxed and just give up, verbalizing hopeless more than kids. The adult response is less energetic, (but not necessarily more mature because they verbalize hopelessness more instead).

When there is a discrepancy between an individual's notion of an ideal interpersonal relationship and the actual state of that relationship, the individual may lose motivation to pursue self-regulatory goals, such as the promotion of positive interpersonal relations and the prevention of harm. This is important, if you aren't satisfied with what you have you are going to be depressed, obviously. That doesn't mean that just by changing your thinking you are going to not be depressed anymore, however. It could be that your notion of an ideal relationship holds some truth about what would help generate good emotion for you, and that you need that level of emotion generation in order to be happy. People need stimulation in life and a good way of seeing how good stimulation can be achieved is by looking at your ideal viewpoint of your relationships. So therefore just by lowering your ideal viewpoint of relationships doesn't increase the quality of your relationships which might be the cause of the depression (due to lack of emotional satisfaction) (so basically you might be at least in part correct).

Hammen (1991)[1] proposed that depressed people often provoke stressful events by their own actions and reactions to everyday life problems. Interpersonal difficulties are common in the lives of depressed individuals and are typically associated with negative appraisals of others and critical opinions about themselves. Although these negative appraisals may be a result of depressive biases in interpersonal perception, just as frequently they reflect an accurate judgment of the exasperated response of a relationship partner. States of mind commonly found in the midst of depression, such as self-loathing and fatalism, negatively influence the quality of existing relationships by inciting both avoidance and overtly negative confrontation from friends, family, and coworkers (Joiner, 2002)[2]

Table 108.0

1. Hammen, C. (1991). Generation of stress in the course of unipolar depression. *Journal of Abnormal Psychology, 100, 555-561*.
2. Joiner, T. E. (2002). Depression in its interpersonal context. In I. H. Gotlib and C. L. Hammen (Eds.), *Handbook of depression* (pp. 295-313). New York: Guildford Press.

Chapter 109

An Overview: How Social, Communication, Personality and

Well-Being Psychology Relate

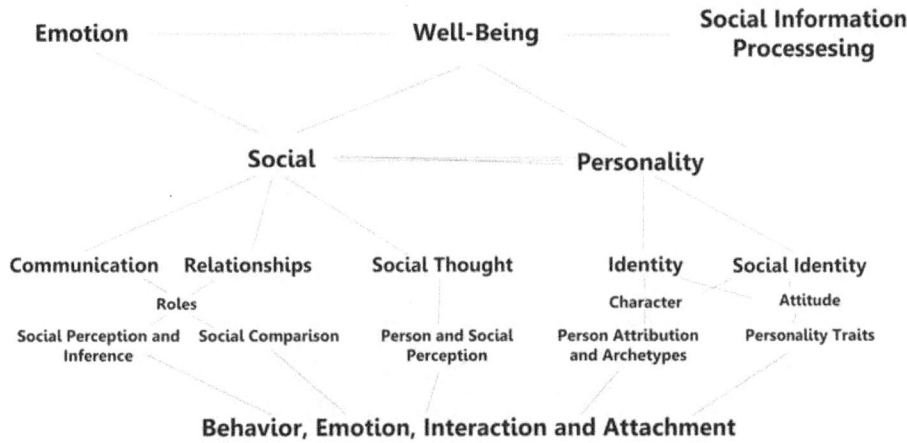

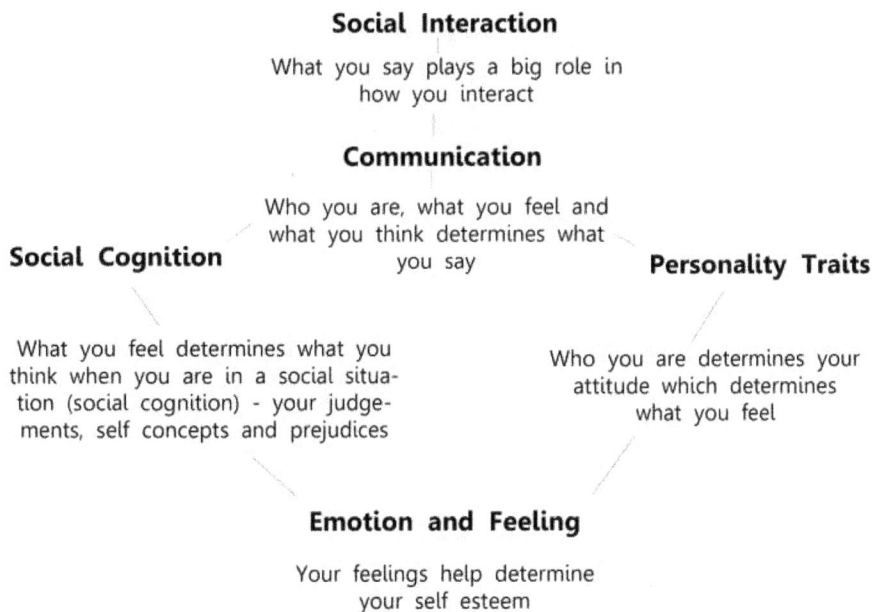

Emotion .... Well-Being .... Social Information
Processesing

Social .... Personality

Communication   Relationships   Social Thought   Identity   Social Identity

Roles   Character   Attitude

Social Perception and   Social Comparison   Person and Social   Person Attribution   Personality Traits
Inference   Perception   and Archetypes

Behavior, Emotion, Interaction and Attachment

Social Interaction

What you say plays a big role in
how you interact

Communication

Who you are, what you feel and
what you think determines what
you say

Social Cognition

What you feel determines what you
think when you are in a social situation (social cognition) - your judgements, self concepts and prejudices

Personality Traits

Who you are determines your
attitude which determines
what you feel

Emotion and Feeling

Your feelings help determine
your self esteem

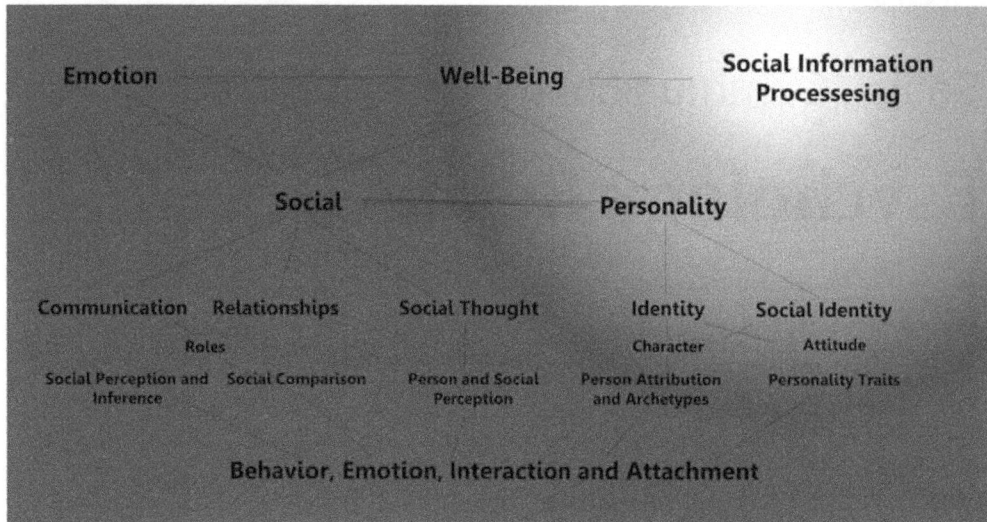

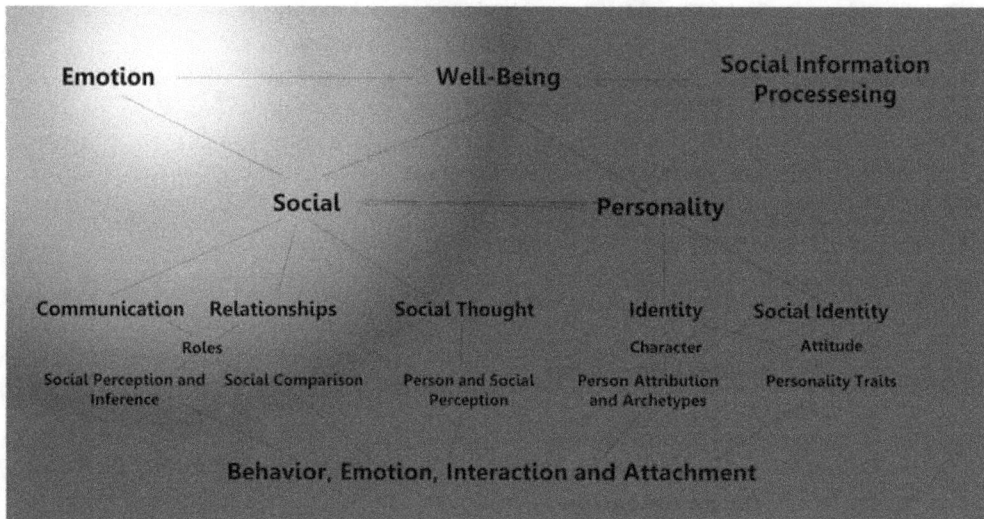

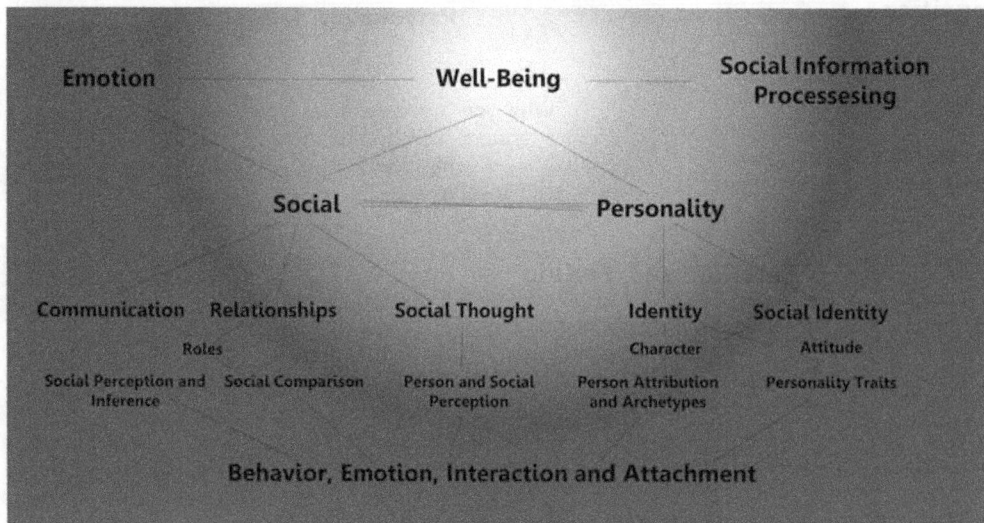

Table 109.0

Chapter 464

Emotion and Social Behavior

We should first start off with the question - what exactly is an emotion, and what are the properties by which it functions? It is by one definition any strong feeling, however that isn't a sufficient explanation of what emotion is. It is hard to figure out exactly what an emotion is and it could be defined in many ways. An example of this lies in a review of the evidence pertaining to Schachter's theory of emotion that appeared in the *Psychological Bulletin* (Reisenzein, 1983[1]): "It is concluded that there is no convincing evidence for Schachter's claim that arousal is a necessary condition for an emotional state, nor for the suggestion that emotional states may result from a labeling of unexplained arousal. It is suggested that the role of arousal in emotion has been over-stated." (p.239) People cannot figure out how much of a role arousal plays when someone has an emotion, that is how obscure and difficult it is to define and explain how emotion works. However, it is easy to point out obvious cases of when emotion is present and simple, clear things related to its functioning. It is easy to point out instances where it functions related to love or when strong emotion can be observed, for instance.

Emotion is complicated, so there are are problems defining it. Harold Kelley (1983[2]) has discussed at some length the terminological problems in the love area, and what he says about them is as true for emotion in general as it is for love in particular. That is, any general theory of emotion, like any theory of love, has associated with it a cluster of ideas that includes one or more of the following components (by "it" he is literally referring to a theory of love, but that comprises primarily the experience of love, and by "phenomena" he means things observed of the experience of love):

1. There are certain observable phenomena identified with it, particularly certain behavioral events that are believed to be the characteristic manifestations of emotion.

2. There are notions about the current causes believed to be responsible for the observed emotional phenomena.

3. There are ideas about the historical antecedents of the current causes and phenomena.

4. There are notions about the future course of the phenomenon.

So he is basically saying in order to outline a theory of how love functions properly, you need to identify the things that occur with love, the causes of those things, the history of them, and their future. So someone could notice how much emotion is generated in a love relationship, or the events that occur in that relationship (or as he says, "particularly certain behavioral events that are believed to be the characteristic manifestations of emotion"(since it is a love relationship, he is probably referring primarily to the emotion love)), and observe those things over time. I can rephrase all of that into just saying, in order to understand love (or emotion), track what happens with the emotions involved, and track the behaviors that occur as a result of those emotions. You could track those behaviors in different types of relationships where love occurs. Doing all this might help you form a theory of love or emotion, and a "theory of emotion (or love)" is a theory that outlines how love functions and its characteristics.

Table 110.0

---

1. Reisenzein, R. (1983) The Schachter theory of emotion: Two decades later. *Psychological Bulletin, 94*(2), 239-264.
2. Kelley, H.H. (1983). Love and commitment. In H.H. Kelley, E. Berscheid, A. Christensen, J.H. Harvery, P.L. Huston, G. Levinger, E. McClintock, L.A. Peplau, and D.R. Peterson, *Close relationships*. New York: Freeman.

Chapter 466

Person Perception and Attribution

Asch and Zukier (1984[1]) categorized the techniques used to resolve conflicts between contradictory characteristic traits of a target person. They distinguished between six techniques empirically - on the basis of descriptions of people formed when two discordant traits were present:

1. *Segregation:* The dispositions (e.g., brilliant-foolish) are each assigned to a different sphere of the person (e.g., to the intellectual and practical sphere).

2. *Inner versus outer (depth dimension):* One of the conflicting dispositions (e.g., sociable) is assigned to a surface manifestation of the person and the other (e.g., lonely) to a deep, inner layer.

3. *Cause and effect:* Two dispositions (e.g., dependent-hostile) are seen in a casual relationship (e.g., a person acts in a hostile way because of his futile efforts to break off his dependence on another person).

4. *Common source:* Two dispositions (e.g., cheerful-gloomy) are judged as resulting from the same basic disposition (e.g., moody).

5. *Means-end:* One disposition is interpreted as a means to achieve another disposition or end (e.g. with the pair strict-kind, strictness is regarded a manifestation of kindness).

6. *Interpolation:* The disparity between intelligent and unambitious is bridged by inferring from disappointing former experiences that a person has now lost interest. Interpolating a unifying explanation smoothes the contrast between conflicting dispositions.

Table 111.0

1.   Asch, S.E., and Zukier, H. (1984). Thinking about persons. *Journal of Personality and Social Psychology, 46,* 1230-1240.

Chapter 112

Emotional, Social and Personality Development

- In various studies, acceleration and deceleration in the aggressive behavior of nursery school children was shown to be linked to either positive or negative reinforcing reactions of other children. Positive reinforces for aggression were not approval or attention but crying, passivity, and defensiveness of the victim.[1]

- In other studies, the ability of a child to acquire friends was limited by coercive socialization in the family and peer group – acquired friends were likely to be aggressive and antisocial as well.[2] Among those children, communication with friends likely emphasizes deviant behavior[3] to involve conflict and assertiveness – this leads to acceleration of troublesome, antisocial behavior.

Obviously, emphasis and promotion of certain qualities will lead to those qualities developing over time. Over time certain characteristics or personality traits develop - they do so dependent on the age, special population, and environment of the person. So those studies were examples of how emotional development works. Because children talk to their friends about bullying, they become bigger bullies themselves. It is almost like they are consciously and deliberately forming their own development. Also, what comes along with becoming bigger bullies, is learning how to be good at bullying, almost a bullying competency. Such a thing is hard to measure, so my point is that the activities which lead to development become an integral part of the person and influences other aspects of their personality. Bullying might have the effect of making both the bully and the abused tougher as people, because they are exposed to harsh emotions and become more resilient because of that. Unless a bully constantly feels bad about what he/she did in the past, or the abused forever reflects in sadness on the bullying, the experience is probably going to be something for both parties to learn and develop from. Exposure to more emotion is probably going to lead to more development as long it doesn't hinder the person. People can grow (or have their personality traits change) from all types of emotion and experience.

- Piaget had the idea that children advanced more cognitively from conflict interactions with peers than with conflict interactions with adults. Children generally accept that adults have greater knowledge about the world than they do, and so yield to the adults point of view. In contrast, peer interaction forces children to coordinate or restructure their own views.[4]

Because children are at a similar intellectual and emotional level as other children, their confidence and smoothness in interacting is probably going to be higher. Also, similar interests and physical development would lead to greater identification. Kids could view adults to see how they can improve, and with children their own age they can identify and become more comfortable with themselves.

- In a volume titled "Identity: Youth and Crisis"[5] Erik Erikson asserted that close relationships with others are not possible until identity development is complete, because intimacy requires knowing and sharing the self.

---

1. Patterson, G.R., Littman, R. A., & Bricker, W. (1967). Assertive behavior in children : A step toward a theory of aggression. *Monographs of the Society for Research in Child Development, 32* (5, Serial No. 113).
2. Patterson, G. R., Reid, J. B., & Dishon, T. J. (1992). *Antisocial Boys*. Eugene, OR: Castalia.
3. Poulin, F. Dishion, T. J., & Haas, E. (1999). The peer influence paradox: Friendship quality and deviancy training within male adolescent friendships. *Merrill-Palmer Quarterly, 45*, 42-61.
4. Piaget, J. (1932) *The moral judgment of the child*. Glencoe, IL: Free Press.
5. Erikson, E. H. (1968). *Identity: Youth and Crisis*. New York: Norton.

I think that it makes sense that as self identity develops, relations with others will improve. Not necessarily that identity development needs to be complete – children of all ages can form close relationships even though they haven't fully developed yet. If animals like dogs can form close relationships, then young children shouldn't have a problem doing it even though they might not be strong in their identity.

- Three psychoanalytic writers - Harry Stack Sullivan, Peter Blos and Erik Erikson asserted that intimacy, empathy and loyalty in peer relationships emerge mainly in the second decade of life.

In order for close relationships involving empathy, intimacy and loyalty to occur, it makes sense that children would need to be confident with who they are first because without confidence it would be hard to be confident experiencing intimate emotions. Those emotions involve a sense of security that isn't present unless someone is confident in who they are. It is possible to be close to someone, like how animals can be close to people, but to experience real intimacy, empathy and loyalty a much larger amount of development would need to occur.

- A "behavior system" is a partnership whereby the individual is empathic to the needs and feelings of the partner, and functions to maintain ties between an individual and his or her partners. There are four types of systems believed to dominate interpersonal relationships –attachment, caretaking, affiliative and sexual/reproductive. In the early years the attachments system dominates parent-child relations but in adolescence it functions reconfigured and less prominently in peer and romantic relationships. The affiliative system includes play, cooperation, collaboration and reciprocity is present in initial parent-child relations but later dominates relations between childhood peers.[6] Romantic relationships in adolescence incorporate all four systems.

It is important how the people in relationships view these types of attachments. Someone could become more selfish in a relationship simply by considering the other person as contributing everything in the relationship, instead of viewing the relationship as reciprocal. There is an overlap and similarity between the types of attachment. For instance you could compare an affiliative relationship to a caretaking relationship, and learn from that that maybe even in play there is caretaking. Emotionally there might also be a large overlap, it might feel like a romantic relationship is like a friendship even though you would label the relationship as a romantic one.

- In the first weeks of life, infants can notice each other and respond to cries.
- 6 month olds can touch each other and toys held by peers.[7]
- Conflicts over toys and intrusions on physical space emerge in the last quarter of the first year of life.[8]
- By the end of the first year of life infants can communicate, share, participate in conflict, and form friendships. They can look at, gesture toward, and touch their peers. They can share things of interest with peers by pointing out, showing, and offering objects other children.[9] Infants at the end of the first year can participate in shared activities (spontaneous games) where distinctive actions (rolling a ball or hitting blocks together) in sequence, and alternating turns.[10]

How does interaction in the first year of life contribute to the infants development? The conflicts over toys

6. Weiss, R.S. (1986). Continuities and transformations in social relationships from childhood to adulthood. In W.W. Hartup & Rubin, Z. (Eds.), *Relationships and development* (pp.95-111). Hillsdale, NJ: Erlbaum.

7. Hay, D. F., Nash, A., & Pedersen, J. (1983). Interaction between six-month-old peers. *Child Development, 52,* 1071-1076.

8. Caplan, M., Vespo, J. E., Pederesen, J., & Hay, D. F. (1991) Conflict and its resolution in small groups of one- and two-year-olds. *Child Development, 62,* 1513-1524.

9. Eckerman, C. O., Whatley, J. & Kutz, S. L. (1975). Growth of social play with peers during the second year of life. *Developmental Psychology, 11,* 42-49.

10. Ross, H. S. (1982) Establishment of social games among toddlers. *Developmental Psychology, 18,* 509-518.

and intrusions on physical space in the last quarter of the first year is significant because it shows that infants are actively engaged with other infants. They are aware enough of their space and other people to feel intruded if their space is endangered. That means they have developed some sort of ego and attitude towards other infants – which must mean that the infants invoke noticeable emotion in each other in order to stimulate a response. The response to cries in the first weeks of life is the beginning of interaction, they begin to notice each other a little then. By 6 months they engage more heavily by touching each other and the other infants toys. Those interactions help to develop and form the infants sense of self, which would cause them to want to defend their space by the last quarter of the first year. By the end of the first year then, they must become cognitively aware of their peers (gesture toward and touch their peers) and cognitively aware of how to participate in trivial games (alternating turns) at the same time. The experience in play before teaches them so they become more intellectual and aware (cognitive) and become capable of more advanced games which involve knowledge and awareness of cooperation (such as alternating turns), and just more advanced games with distinctive actions (like rolling a ball or hitting blocks together).

- During around the pre-school years, it is theorized that play provides a forum for children's self-regulation and emotion regulation. It was theorized early that play can reestablish homeostasis by helping to deplete surplus or replenish expended energy.[11],[12] It was suggested by later theorists that play modulates arousal associated with excessively high or low levels of stimulation.[13] Freud suggested that play could be a medium for children to reconstruct and gain mastery over emotionally arousing experiences.[14] That idea is important in the study of the development of children's emotion regulation, which is a set of skills that help people to modify, monitor and evaluate their emotions to produce behavior that is adaptive for situations.[15] Self-regulation is an important skill in the promotion of positive peer interactions.[16] Play can help children master situations that involve intense emotional arousal, and help children regulate emotions and that can help reduce anxiety.

Importance: Emotion regulation is similar to regulation of energy states (excitement or arousal) because excitement and arousal are similar to and related to emotions. If someone is very happy, that is likely to contribute to excitement or arousal. So emotion regulation is similar to generic self-regulation. Emotion regulation must be developed at some point, and it makes sense that it is developed when children are first exposed to large amounts of emotion, which is likely to be during preschool play, where they have more increased cognitive, social, language, and social-cognitive skills than before. Those skills help contribute to more emotion being generated because they provide sources of emotion. Language adds a lot of things to get emotional about. A child isn't as likely to get excited as much being with his parents not playing. Emotion regulation is an important part of how people experience emotions. If you gain insight into your emotions from emotion regulation, your emotional experiences might be increased because you are more aware. Developing emotions in the preschool years contributes to how children feel and master emotions. In fact, play in those years is similar to adult interactions, it involves many of the ups and downs and uses similar cognitive abilities. It is like life is being experienced in greater depth, and these experiences form the starting point of feeling. With feeling comes emotion regulation, it is hard to have one without the other.

Describing Relationships

Hinde[17] (1979) suggested that many of the things that seem to be important about relationships could be classified into ten categories of dimensions (below). They move from properties of the interactions to those

11. Patrick, G. T. W. (1916). The *psychology of relaxation*. Boston: Houghton Mifflin.
12. Spencer, H. (1873). Principles of psychology (Vol. 2, 2nd ed.). New York: Appleton.
13. Berlyne, D. E. (1960). *Conflict, arousal and curiosity*. New York: Mcgraw-Hill.
14. Freud, S. (1961). *Beyond the pleasure principle*. New York: Norton.
15. Walden, T. A., & Smith, M.C. (1997). Emotion regulation. *Motivation and Emotion, 21*, 7-25.
16. Thompson, R. A. (1994). Emotion regulation: A theme in search of definition. *Monographs of the Society for Research in Child Development, 59*, 25-52.
17. Hinde, R. A. (1979) *Towards understanding relationships*. London: Academic Press.

of the relationship as a whole, and from primarily behavioral to primarily subjective issues.

1. *The content of the interactions* - This refers to the things the participants do together. Most sociological types of relationships are defined by the behaviors involved (the type of relationship e.g. doctor- patient, teacher-pupil, lover) Friendship and kin relationships are obvious exceptions, in that in our culture they are not identified by what the participants actually do together, but by aspects of quality, intimacy, interpersonal perception, commitment, etc.

2. *The diversity of types of interaction within the relationship* - The more things two individuals do together, the more aspects of their personalities are exposed; the more experience is shared.

3. *The qualities of the interactions* - For example, did the participants communicate constructively, competitively, loudly, softly, etc? Analysis of speech and nonverbal communication will provide data here. This is subjective, what someone might think of the quality of an interaction might or might not be a good relationship, this judgement could vary over time, between individuals, and between cultures.

4. *The relative frequency and patterning of interactions*- The extent to which interactions of different sorts or qualities are present; properties derived from the frequency of interactions relative to the frequency with which each partner attempts to initiate them (sometimes people try to ask to do something but it doesn't actually happen); the relations between differenct kinds of interactions, (the structure of the relationship) such as controlling, permisive, etc, and the patterning of interactions over time.

5. *The reciprocity vs. complementary nature of the interactions* - Reciprocal interactions are those in which the two partners do similar things, such as play the same sport; complementary interactions are those in which they do different things, but those things complement each other. Most close relationships involve a complicated mixture of reciprocal and complementary interactions.

6. *Power and autonomy*- Power and autonomy are complementary, if one increases in one partner the other is likely to decrease in the other partner. One partner could have power over the other if they can influence the consequences or impact of the other persons behavior. Frequently one partner would show power in some content areas while the other in different ones. The amount of power asserted can be measured and assessed (for instance persuasion vs. command). A power differential can be perceived differently be each partner, it can be seen as desirable by both or not. However, well-meaning moves towards closeness by one partner may be seen as constraining and decreasing the autonomy of the other. Lack of agreement or acceptance of where power lies leads to conflict.

7. *Intimacy-the extent to which the participants reveal themselves (emotionally, cognitively, and physically) to each other*- Intimacy requires the discloser to feel understood, validated, and care for and is thus related to trust. However intimacy has its limits as it may be important to maintain area of privacy.

8. *Interpersonal perception* This category includes things such as "Does A see B as B really is?" "Does A see B as B sees B, i.e., does A understand B?" "Does B feel that A sees B as B sees B, i.e., does B feel understood?" Feeling understood implies understanding at a deeper level and includes an interpretation of the verbal conversations the people have for a more true understanding (such that would lead to a "feeling understood" feeling. Also important is how the participants see the relationship, and also how they see the world, if they see it in a similar fashion they could be closer.

9. *Commitment.*- Do the partners strive to ensure the continuation of the relationship or improve its quality? Does each see the other as committed?

10. *Satisfaction*- Do the participants perceive the relationship as close to their ideal or preferable to alternative relationships?

I can express the above list in a more concise way that will show more effectively the properties of a relationship. Relationships are intimate, however there is power and autonomy involved. People have similarities and do similar things, or they do opposing things and are different. People might have expectations of satisfaction and an idea of what an ideal relationship might be like. That might influence commitment, if it isn't satisfying they are less likely to be motivated for commitment. This is likely to also be related to interpersonal perception, one person might view the other as poor or not the way they are because they want to see things their way. Maybe they find it interesting to see the person in a variety of ways, if a person was single faceted there wouldn't be any strong basis for commitment. Perception is very complicated, people don't just see someone completely accurately immediately or even after a long period of time. If they did see them accurately there wouldn't be any room for growth and change and dynamics. If you have problems in the relationship resulting from improper perception it could add a lot of content to the relationship. One person could want to see themselves as strong and the other as weak, causing a chaotic interaction which could prove interesting. The other person could constantly be trying to prove themselves. That is one way to put pressure on and provide one type of satisfaction. Or if they saw the person in a overly good light maybe that would influence how they feel and they'd feel good about the person because they think are very good, better than they actually are. Maybe the entire perception dynamic of all the persons traits is confused and their relationship is just a mess. Having things to work on adds content. Maybe the content, diversity, and quality of their interactions is perceived completely wrong as well.

Principles of dynamics

The next issue concerns the processes at work in the dynamic flux that every relationship entails. The processes can be understood at three levels- external influences on the relationship, the interchanges between the participants, and the internal processes that occur in each person.

1. *The social context-* The issue here involves social influences on the development of personality, the influence of third parties on relationships, and the dialectical relations with the sociocultural structure (how society communicates with groups, which could communicate to relationships, etc.)

2. *Processes of exchange and interdependence involving resources of various types.* There is an emphasis on the interdependence between partners, and on the manner in which an individual may include the partner in defining his or her goals and rewards. What is considered "fair" may differ based on the type of relationship, and "fairness" may not matter between close friends or kin. There are various types of resources that can be exchanged such as money, services, goods, status, information, and love. Obviously love should be placed in another category than the material ones. There is probably a lot you could say about each of those.

3. *Processes of positive and negative feedback-* Certain patterns of resource exchange (or interaction over a long term) may lead to increasing closeness or distance in the relationship.

Table 112.0

Chapter 113

Mental Disorders in Infants, Children, and Adolescents

- Bowlby described attachment as a process: a child produces behaviors in reaction to stress, and these behaviors in turn elicit other behaviors from the caregiver that reestablish a sense of security for the child usually through physical closeness or proximity. Therefore the quality of attachment in infancy is influenced by the nature of care.[1]

That is simply saying that some things might make an infant feel bad, however their caretakers might then compensate for that and make them feel better. That makes sense considering that young children can cry often. It also shows the importance of making the infant feel better, if it is just abused then it might not develop properly or with a strong sense of self or security. If a child has the proper confidence and mental stability then they are probably less likely to develop a mental disorder.

Attention-Deficit/Hyperactivity Disorder (ADHD)

- Predominantly Hyperactive-Impulsive Type

- Predominantly Inattentive Type

- Combined Type

- ADHD has an onset prior to age seven, is present in two or more settings (such as at home and in school), and interferes with social, academic, or occupational functioning.

- Symptoms of inattention include failure to give close attention to details, difficulty sustaining attention, poor follow-through on instructions, failure to finish work, difficulty organizing tasks, misplacement of things, distraction by extaneous stimuli, and forgetfulness.

- Hyperactive-impulsive behaviors include fidgeting, running about, difficulty playing quietly, acting as if driven by a motor, talking excessively, blurting answers, and interrupting.

- Therapists working with children with ADHD rely primarily on behavioral interventions. Behavioral treatments for children with ADHD are based on operant conditioning, the shaping of behavior through the use of positive reinforcers. Treatment most often addresses the behaviors of staying on task, completing work, and following directions. [2]

Finding the solution to ADHD seems to be very difficult if not impossible. I would argue that it is like trying to change who someone is. Those children exhibit those behaviors because that is what they want to do, they don't want to have a good attention because life is boring. Why would they want to be attentive to something boring or be calm when life is so much more exciting the other way? It is more than just something they "developed" or just an illness, it is how they feel they need to act and is how they experience and generate emotion for themselves. That is who they are, they probably can only function in that way because that is the best way for them. Life would probably be too boring for them the other way. You can't just say to them, your life is going to be boring now, stop acting out please.

Separation Anxiety Disorder

- The essential characteristic of this disorder is excessive distress upon separation from primary

---

1.   Blowlby, J. (1982) *Attachment and loss.* Vol. 1: *Attachment.* New York: Basic Books. (Originally published 1969)

2.   Rapport, M. D. (1995) Attention-deficit hyperactivity disorder. In M. Hersen and R. T. Ammerman (Eds.), *Advanced abnormal child psychology (pp. 353-375).* Hillsdale, NJ: Erlbaum.

attachment figures.

- Manifestations of that distress may include worry about caretakers being harmed, reluctance or refusal to go to school or be separated from caregivers, fear about being alone, repeated nightmares incorporating separation themes, and frequent somatic complaints linked to separation.

- Children with separation anxiety disorder frequently present with symptoms of other anxiety disorders and often report many specific fears, as well as feelings of sadness and of not being loved.

- The cause of Separation Anxiety Disorder varies, it could be precipitated by a stressful event such as a significant loss, separation from loved ones, or exposure to danger. The disorder may stem from an insecure attachment to the primary caregiver, or it may occur in families in which a parent is emotionally dependent on the child, and had been associated with enmeshed family relationships.

- Separation Anxiety Disorder can be classified as a phobic response (usually because there is a fear of leaving the primary caregiver but also might be related to fear of social situations). Consequently as a treatment the behavioral technique of systematic desensitization is good as it is highly effective in the treatment of phobias. That includes gradually bringing the child closer and closer to the school building and gradually extending his/her time in school.

- In young children, Separation Anxiety disorder is often characterized by features of depression, including crying, sulkiness, irritability, and a sad appearance.

This problem is more complicated than the child simply being too attached to their parents. They would probably need some sort of replacement for the emotion their parents give them. So I would think that if you transition the child to be more attached to his or her peers then they could begin to separate themselves from the parent. Or maybe it could be possible to maintain the level of attachment to the parent but not suffer the negative consequences of leaving them. The anxiety and fear caused by leaving the parent is a substitute emotion instead of receiving emotion from the situation they are currently in, or at least they could generate emotion from having their parents gone in a less anxiety related way. I am saying that the anxiety generated by the child works to provide a similar type of support that the parent gives because being anxious about the parent not being there is basically a substitute for the parent not being there. It isn't necessarily that they are too attached - they just might not be capable of finding an appropriate substitute emotion that could come from other people, activities, or maybe they could just think about it differently - possibly think of it as missing the parent instead of getting pain and anxiety from the loss.

Depression

- While reported feelings of sadness are characteristic of depression across all age ranges, children are more likely to exhibit externalized behaviors as an expression of their feelings.

- Carlson and Kashani[3] (1988), for example, found that depressed preschoolers typically displayed a sad appearance, sulkiness, crying, and social withdrawal but also tended to somatize (somatize: definition - To express a psychological process through physical symptoms such as pain or anxiety; to have a psychosomatic reaction to (e.g. a situation)) their depression and complain of physical aches and pains.

- Children and adolescents may show more anxiety and anger, fewer vegetative symptoms, and less verbalization of hopelessness than adults.

- IPT (interpersonal psychotherapy), adapted for adolescents (IPT-A) appears promising for the treatment of adolescent depression. About IPT-A - depression affects people's relationships and these relationships further affect our mood. The IPT model identifies four general areas in which a person may be having relationship difficulties: 1) grief after the loss of a loved one; 2) conflict in significant relationships; 3) difficulties adapting to changes in relationships or life circumstances;

---

3. Carlson, G. A., and Kashani, J. H. (1988). Phenomenology of major depression from childhood through adulthood: Analaysis of three stuidies. *American Journal of Psychiatry,* 145(10), 1222-1225.

and 4) difficulties stemming from social isolation. The IPT therapist helps identify areas in need of skill-building to improve the client's relationships and decrease the depressive symptoms. Over time, the client learns to link changes in mood to events occurring in his/her relationships, communicate feelings and expectations for the relationships, and problem-solve solutions to difficulties in the relationships.

So children get so upset about being depressed they show physical symptoms. That makes sense that they would show that more than adults considering how they are more energetic. The physical symptoms could distract the child from depression, loss of energy is a symptom for depression as well, however. Loss of energy in adults and children could be a way of them retreating from the world so they don't have to deal with it so much in a high energy state. Anti-psychotic medications also tend to lower energy levels. This symptom probably helps calm the person down and, by making putting a more relaxed state, they can deal with the world easier. That information gets more complicated when you consider that children show more anxiety and anger, exhibit externalized behaviors as an expression of their feelings, and somatize their depression and experience physical aches and pains. So why is it that children (largely (vegetative symptoms are still a part of depression for children) become more active from depression but adults become more vegetative? Maybe in general children respond to the world actively and physically and adults respond more intellectually because they are more mature. A child gets upset and sulks, cries, and socially withdraws (hides) while adults simply become vegetative / relax and give up (they verbalize hopelessness more).

Table 113.0

Chapter 114

What are Important and Significant Things to Know about Life

What are the important factors in life? It is important and obvious to note that "there is no doubt that emotions and feelings are in our midst". However, how large a background knowledge does someone need in order to navigate those feelings? Types of interpersonal relationships influence those feelings, and social interaction can be very complicated. An understanding of deep psychological factors might be needed to understand motivation in social interaction, and it might be important for high-level interactions. The psychological disorders are important, if someone is troubled then it could be useful to find a solution. Also even without those disorders someone could better themselves from understanding them because no one is completely psychologically healthy. Temperament and personality are important, they play a role in what people are like all the time, what emotions they feel all the time, and what their demeanor is all the time.

Going into more detail - what are the emotions people have about life, and how do they function on a moment to moment contextual basis? The basic emotions happiness, love, pride and lust probably are present in people all the time to various degrees. These emotions probably fluctuate based on the activity someone is engaged in. People are more open to positive emotions than negative ones, so they constantly try to promote pleasure in themselves and focus on the positive emotions. There are few things that are significant in life more than what most people already know about life. People know that jealously is bad, and that people like to be treated well. Those are important things to understand, but obvious. How important is it to understand developmental psychology? It is obvious that people can learn to like certain things as they realize their value – and that the value of things can be promoted in people. An obvious example of that would be a "sexual awakening".

There are emotions and how they function, but how important is it to understand what exactly happens when an emotion occurs in the mind? People can feel emotions for themselves, they know what it is like to feel emotions. If you cannot identify something that is happening in you, what is the point of having it explained? If it is large enough, its presence would be obvious and you would understand it and know its importance. It might be important to know that your attitude can change how you feel about a situation. If you go into a situation with a positive attitude, it might effect how you feel. Your thoughts also affect your emotions, but people have a rough enough idea of how that occurs. It should be obvious that a happy state is better than a depressed one, but maybe being depressed helps you reflect on certain things that you wouldn't reflect on if you were happy. It is also natural to be depressed if something bad happens. If something terrible happens you don't want to be happy about it.

It might be important to understand that people might have large unconscious drives that make them selfish or sexual, that are controlled partly by your conscious mind. Freud called those unconscious drives the id, and the conscious mind the ego, and your conscience the superego. People know what activities make them happy and sad, that they might be depressed in the evening because of something that happened to them during the day. It is usually obvious even if something small or hard to notice causes someone to become sad. The formula for happiness isn't that complicated, negative things cause people to become sad, and positive things make them happy. Also stimulation, or doing many activities, is important – but that is understood from the saying "busy hands are happy hands".

There is personality psychology – understanding different aspects of people and what they are like. But those qualities are usually observed over time because they are obvious. If someone has a relationship conflict it is usually obvious what the solution would be using good logic.

Table 114.0

Chapter 115

Highlights of Psychoanalysis (Freud and others)

- Freud had the idea of a prevailing role played by infantile sexuality in the development of human goals.

- Schools of psychoanalytic thought believe that the unconscious is never thought of as an isolated entity that can be studied independently of the total personality.

- The goal-directed quality of the unconscious was a Freudian concept.

- Freud believed that the ego (mainly rational) and the superego (mainly moral) were crystallized out of the id (primitive instinctual). Once crystallized out the provinces of the mind tend to function independently (to a large extent) and act in opposition to the id.

- Freud offered two categories of instincts, ego and sexual. The sexual instincts operate under the *pleasure principle*, or the pleasure-pain principle. Sexual instincts strive for pleasure or avoidance of pain always and in a very primitive manner. These sexual instincts created often immature sexual wishes (instinctual aims) that were largely unconscious (part of the *id*, biological impulse) and portrayed an underlying motivation or self interest. People often do not act on these underlying needs, Frued believed they were suppressed by an inner force called the *censor*, which represented the ego instincts which operated under the *reality principle*. Ego instincts included cognitive functions, personal ideals, self-protection, and social and moral restrictions. The superego was the conscience.

- Freud distinguished between a primary process, where instinctual drives manifest themselves psychologically, and a secondary process, where drives are ordered and controlled by rational thought and voluntary action. The id can be seen in the primary process, full of instinctual needs with desire for immediate gratification. It makes sense that it is called "primary" because basic desires come before rational thought and control, which could be considered secondary. The ego is a secondary process, which was the result of human development and was not inborn like the id. The ego maintains the whole person, it moderates demands from the id for instant pleasure gratification, and the desire for the superego to control to suppress the impulses of the id. The ego is mature and rational, the id is immature and impulsive. The ego also controls the relations among instinctual drives and between instinctual drives and the outside world.

- Freud's id, ego and superego were not considered the same as instincts, but were instead thought of as "institutions", aspects of the mind that develop through experience and function relatively independently, but constantly interact. A personality is considered by Freudians not only as instincts (the dynamic approach) but as forms of "institutions" and their relationships. They are called institutions because they function as separate aspects in the mind.

- The ego needs to take into consideration and balance and reach compromises between the needs of the id, the superego, and external reality.

Importance: What is the significance in saying that people have large unconscious sexual needs? The sexual drive is more aggressive, compulsive and powerful than ordinary motivation. Therefore saying that someone is sexually motivated means that there is a strong drive behind that person. The sexual drive could therefore motivate someone to simply be more aggressive in general, not just in terms of their sexual interest. The sexual theories of Freud indicate how selfish and aggressive people can be. The pleasure/pain principle can explain how every action (from the ego and the id) is a striving for pleasure and an avoidance of pain, and that people reach compromises to achieve a balance (for instance, avoiding social scorn (pain) while achieving getting pleasure). However, from the Freudian standpoint, the pleasure principle was only a part of the sexual instincts, and the reality principle was a part of the ego instincts. So with everything people do, not just sexual things, they want pleasure.

Freud wasn't clear as to exactly what the ego was (what it is and what it does), and this is because the ego is just a way of thinking about how people function, it doesn't represent accurately how people perform. Everyone is to some extent instinctual (id, so possibly overly sexual) and to some extent rational (ego), and these forces are balancing themselves all of the time. However, when people reach decisions, it isn't like there is literally a battle going on in their mind between the id, the ego and the superego. People don't think, "let me consider my instinctual drives, no wait let me stop that drive, no wait let me function by reality and see what is logical (the ego)". The ego is logical because it included social and moral restrictions. So it is like people have a range of ways to respond to the world, instinctively (the id), rationally (the ego), and hyper-rationally/cautious (the superego). These aspects of the mind may be considered to each be so strong that they can be considered separate things, however – and that is how Freud's classification helps.

- Freud used the term "defense" referring to a persons effort to protect himself from the dangerous demands of the id and the conflicts it causes.

- There are three possible sources of anxiety for the ego – threats from the outside world recognizable as a result of experience, demands of the id that the ego has to put down, and self-condemnation of the superego when the ego allows the id to get out of hand. Those three could also be turned around and looked at in an opposite light – for instance positive things can happen which wouldn't illicit a defensive response from the ego, such as viewing the external world as being pleasurable.

- Any type of blocking or avoiding sexual feelings and thought is a function of someones higher, more rational mind (the ego). The ego "defends" you against your own powerful unconscious sexual mind.

Importance of defense mechanisms of the ego: Defensive reactions (to protect your mind from "threats" such as self-condemnation from the superego and powerful drives from the id) are from the ego because the ego responses to reality and is rational and so are defensive reactions. If someone is acting defensively it is not like they are acting off their own instincts as much if they were to do something selfishly motivated, but instead from rationality, it is rational to be under control and reasonable. The ego represses the id by using defensive mechanisms. For instance - someone who is aggressive randomly probably is being more selfish in nature and more instinctual than someone who acts aggressively for rationally and is just being defensive (the ego). When someone acts for their own benefit it is more instinctual because people are driven by instinct to want various things that may cause them to become aggressive. Being defensive can be viewed as being instinctual, but it isn't nearly as instinctual as someone doing something from a large selfish motivation – because that is much more natural and innate – and large emotions, especially powerful ones (as used in aggression) are more instinctual than thought and rational action because they are more like automatic reflexes, similar to how instinct is automatic. It is like being aggressive for selfish reasons is so selfish that it is instinctual and automatic, however when someone is defensive they are just being logical, not acting off their natural instinct of desire.

Even just acting aggressive independent of triggers can be a power play that can make people feel better about themselves. That would be considered more a function of the id, whereas defensive mechanisms would be considered a part of the ego because a defensive reaction isn't instinctual it is logical and based in reality, not based off of immediate gratification. Someone that wants something passionately is driven by instinct to want that thing. The more powerful the emotion and the drive, the more instinctual it probably is. It is hard to have a large drive that you create consciously, however instinct can be a powerful force to aid conscious desires. When people are defensive they are being less selfish (and less driven) than when they act off of instinct and pursue their own objectives for immediate gratification.

- Freud thought there was a death instinct, *Thanatos*, and a life instinct, *Eros*. The death instinct was the desire for people to revert back to absolute zero, it wasn't a striving for pleasure but instead a desire to die and achieve nothingness. This could be considered achieving absolute pleasure in a sense, however, and was termed by Barbara Low "the Nirvana principle". Freud believed that you only observe the death instinct "after it has become diverted outward as an instinct of destruction"[1]– so basically as aggression.

- The life instinct represented the tendencies of people to bind together, preserve, unify and build up. The term libido was used to apply not only to sexual instincts but to "the whole available energy of Eros"[2] and that it neutralized destructive impulses. Eros also included instincts for preservation of the species and self preservation, self love and love of others, and the reality principle.

Importance: It is important that he labeled the life and death instincts as instincts because that word "instinct" alone suggests more information about them. It implies that people are constantly wanting to die and constantly wanting to live, and that people do all the actions and beliefs to achieve those two things. For instance, aggression is destructive and not productive, so it might suggest someone wants to die. But at the same time people want to live, they want to be productive and love. It suggests that these emotions of love and hate are with people constantly, that there is a complex dynamic going on that includes people having strong opposing emotions.

- The preconscious (also known as the foreconscious) is the various information available to people (such as memories and perceptions). Depending on the circumstance, certain information will be available to varying degrees. It might take different amount of effort to bring certain information to surface into the consciousness. The unconscious consists of information that cannot be brought up consciously.

- Freud noted that diametrically opposite meanings frequently stand side by side. For instance someone might want two opposite things unconsciously, and have no problem with that unconsciously because the unconscious is not logical. For instance someone might want to leave their parents and join the army to gain freedom, but the army might be more authoritarian. However, unconsciously they might want both the freedom of leaving their parents and the structure of the army even though that contradicts what the person might have been thinking consciously. Consciously they might only want one and not want the other (a secondary process), because the conscious is logical.

Importance: What the unconscious wants might seem not logical, but it probably is the truth and very logical because your unconscious mind knows what you want better than your conscious one. Your conscious mind is limited by your logic, but unconsciously feelings motivate your actions without the logic of the conscious but with purpose that is logical. So the person joining the army is actually being logical because it is fulfilling their unconscious desires, even though consciously they don't understand that. However, you might do also something stupid if you acted just off your unconscious, but it would have been for something you really wanted, so the action would have been logical in one way. An example for that might be shoplifting, you unconsciously want to get the item but you aren't aware that you might get caught. If the person was more conscious, they would have been more aware that they might get caught and not done the shoplifting (but the shoplifting might have still been considered logical because it would be getting you what you want). Or maybe you unconsciously want to get caught, that would further motivate you to steal the item. The unconscious desire might satisfy current feelings but it wouldn't be aware of the long term consequences of getting caught. Or maybe the opposite is true, your unconscious might be more aware of the long term result of stealing but not as aware of the short term benefit (it probably depends on what you are feeling at the time)– the unconscious isn't logical.

- Adler believed that every action reflects the central goal of the human personality: the goal of superiority.

Importance: It is very significant if the people around you are trying to be superior all the time. That

1. S. Freud, An Outline of Psychoanalysis, W. W. Norton & Co., p. 22
2. *Ibid*

could be viewed as being extremely bad, and that they have an inner monster. It could also be viewed as a strength, and that competition between people is healthy. There could be innocent competition or intense, hurtful competition. Some people may lightly care about their superiority and others more heavily.

- Hartmann outlined various ways the ego develops and adapts with patterns of behavior that he labels functioning with *secondary autonomy* (being secondary to the id or instinctual drives, which would be first). The primitive ego connections become more advanced reaction patterns. For example, an infant might walk not just for fun but because of the appreciation of his parents. He might also eat tidily and have bowel control for fear of parental disfavor.

Importance: Hartmann seemed to be labeling lack of bowel control and eating messily as instincts. Those aren't exactly instincts they are just functions a human does without thought. There is a relation between lack of thought and instincts, if someone does everything without thought it doesn't necessarily mean that they are doing everything instinctually, however. Instinct is something natural not just something unlearned. So things that are natural might be changed, it can become natural to control bowel movements. What makes a baby eat messily is just him not thinking about how he should eat, that doesn't make it the natural way of eating necessarily. For something to really be natural it would probably have to be a strong drive. It could be that the baby has a drive to eat tidily, it just doesn't understand that it has this drive yet. So it could be that the baby is acting un-instinctively first in his development simply because first he doesn't think about how he should eat. Just because someone does something first and it is unlearned doesn't mean that it is a natural tendency for someone to do something unlearned. People can have strong drives to do learned activities the drives just won't manifest themselves until the activity is learned because it can't manifest unless it is. On the other hand, childish sexual impulses can reflect the true nature of sexual wishes in adulthood because you can see what sexual impulses are like without the other intellectual development of adults, revealing their true nature. In fact, Freud believed that infantile sexuality played a large role in determining adult goals.

- At birth and early life people respond more instinctively, however attitudes change and build up against these instinctive drives – or counterneeds. The Freudian term for that is countercathexis, the changing of attitudes opposed to direct gratification. In the infantile period infants refrain from actions out of fear, and as biological needs develop punishment stops these impulses.

- As the ego and superego develop, some activities become acceptable to the ego that are not acceptable to the superego so in reaction the behavior of the ego is modified, similar to how the ego can modify the behavior of the id.

Importance: It is interesting to see that as people develop they learn the proper way to function in society, and that this way may be different from how they really wish to respond to the world. People have to conform to society in many ways, if everyone's inner animal was released society wouldn't function as properly as it does. It is almost as if for every action, there is a secondary motivation or desire that might not be being fulfilled. But if people just functioned from the id, they would be in a constant state of bliss, receiving large amounts of pleasurable emotions from their instinctual drives. There is a higher order of thought that moderates the unconscious mind and people's instinctual drives. What would people's emotions be like if there was no ego or superego? Would people be in a constant state of sexual bliss? Or would it be a constant state of happiness? I would say half of our emotions come from sexual drives, and the other half from happiness. Things leading to happiness can be relatively harmless, like good jokes, conversation, visual stimulus and other activity stimulus. Things that happen, such as sexual encounters, or conversations, can influence a persons emotions for the rest of the day. If the ego and superego were taken away, people would experience emotions in a pure form, because the unconscious is emotional and instinctual.

Table 115.0

Chapter 116

The definition and meaning of the words "idea", "thought" and

"sentence".

Why are the definitions of the words "idea" and "thought" important? Their meanings seem simple when first looking at it, an idea or thought is something you think that involves an action, it can be a strong idea   and a strong thought that is clear. If the thought is strong and clear it could be considered to have a higher level of consciousness, you are more aware of the thought if it is clear.

When you break a thought or a senctence down into its parts, it is broken down grammatically. There are parts of the sentence that correspond to real things happening in real life, some of the things are people,   some are objects, and the various parts of the sentence relate to each other. You are also conscious of either both the entire sentence, thought or idea or conscious of individual parts of it, or both. Each time you think something it is going to be different, each time you think one word such as "go" the meaning is going to be different depending on the context. There is a generic meaning for go that applies each time, but each time the meaning is going to be different because the cirumstance is different. Similairy the emotions involved and the conscoiusness and awareness of the word is going to be different each time. Different parts of the sentence could raise to consciousness in different ways and at different levels.

Also how well you understand the definition of each word in an idea or thought can change the level of consciousness involved. On one level a thought can be simple to understand, or a thought could be extremely complicated with many deep unconscoius factors. If you think of a thought as just a simple sentence involving one action that is done, then it seems simple. On the other hand a thought could have many unconscious implications or deeper meaning involved. One word in the thought or sentence could have a deeper meaning or the whole idea could.

How could someone break down a sentence? How do you describe how the parts relate? Can you say, this leads to that, and so forth? Is a sentence just a flow chart with each individual thing involved leading to something else and it is that straightforward? You can break it down into the things in it. The sentence, idea or thought "I am a person" consists of the idea of you, which is described with the words "I am" and the idea that you are a person, described with the words "a person". You could take it to the next level and say that the words "a person" influence the meaning of the words "i am" and say that you are describing yourself as a person, so you are a person. So the two parts of the sentence aren't individual and separate, the meaning of one part greatly impacts the meaning of the other part. In fact, that is the whole point, that is why the words were put together in the first place, so the meaning of one part would influence the meaning of the other part.

There are many types of relationships that can be formed in a sentence or an idea, basically every type of relationship that is possible in life can be described and contained in a sentence. A bad relationship can be described in a sentence, "This happened and it was bad" that is describing a bad relationship. It is saying that what happened was bad, so there is a bad relationship in the sentence. The relationship between what happened and your feelings about it. There is implied there that you feel bad about it. If something bad happened, it makes sense that you are going to feel bad about it. That would be a more subtle level of detail and meaning involved. On one hand it is obvious that if something bad happens you feel bad about it, on the other hand it could be a very complex thing that is hard to figure out the meaning of. That is what sentences, ideas and thoughts are like, they are very simple on the surface sometimes, but could be vey complicated in the details frequently.

1. is, are, was, or will be doing* (this is the relationship between a subject and a verb, the subject is doing the verb) so the relationship between I and run in the sentence "I run" is that you "are doing" the running.

There can be one part of a sentence or idea that is more important than another part, or only one part that has a deeper meaning.

Various parts of each idea relate to other ideas or different parts of that one idea itself in various ways. They are connected or not connected (independent) to various degrees.

In fact, you could spend a lot of time thinking about one idea, sentence or thought and break it down into all its parts, its obvious surface meaning and its more subtle meaning. The more subtle meaning could involve deep unconscious factors.

So if you are reading a sentence, or thinking about an idea and don't understand all of its parts, just isolate the part that you don't understand and think more about it. Another question to ponder is - is it a whole idea if you only don't understand the entire thing? You could read a sentence but does that mean that the sentence becomes a single idea in your head?

If a sentence has multiple parts and is very complicated, do you think about it in your mind as a single simple thing, do you summarize it to yourself to achieve faster recall? Say you had to remember a paragraph, even if you just read the paragraph there are all those parts you have to remember, in your mind you probably automatically summarize it or if not that maybe you automatically remember just a single part of it because that is what you were focusing on.

If you were taking a test and had to answer questions on the paragraph you would probably try to summarize the paragraph in your mind so that you could remember more of it. In fact, in order to understand the gist of what someone is saying you have to put all of the information together to understand the complete message. When someone is saying something there could be a few main things they are saying that you could understand, you don't have to remember every little detail they said most of the time.

It is obvious that sentences and paragraphs have multiple parts and each part their own meaning that might be more or less independent than the other parts. All the parts might contribute to one main idea or several main ideas. One person could have trouble recalling or understanding certain types of ideas. So it might not be that someone has a problem reading complex sentences, it could be that they have a problem understanding complicated ideas. Maybe they understand the ideas if they are spoken to them. What is the exact difference between their verbal learning and their ability to read the same material? That is something to think about that could help deceipher someones problem. It could be a way of isolating if the problem has to do with reading the words or a probelm with understanding the ideas.

This is a link to my connexions article titled "Emotions and Feelings and the Difference Between them" *cnx.org/content/m14334/*

Table 116.0

Chapter 117

Definition of Literacy

If someone can read and write, that means that they would then have to have a large cognitive capacity to understand the communication. The ability to speak conveys meaning, so the same intellect used in speaking would be used in reading and writing. However, words written down are usually going to be longer than normal conversations, so literacy would mean the ability to understand entire books, articles, or even something as short as a paragraph, which isn't used in speech in the same way the same meaning or message would be communicated if it was written. In fact, reading and writing is just speech but doing it for longer periods of time. It could be for the same period of time, but it is usually going to be longer. That means that different mental abilities are going to be used for reading and writing since you are dealing with something that usually has one theme or main idea, but is very long. You could have a conversation about one thing for a long period of time, but this conversation isn't going to be structured to maximize understanding of the topic. When something long is written, it is put down in a certain pattern or way that itself communicates a message from the author, even if the author just meant to put it down in the most logical way possible. So literacy would then include understanding what complicated messages (which can be understanding of any sort – math, fiction, etc) mean, and how they can be understood in different ways, and the best way to structure and order it so understanding is maximized. That is even more important if you are the writer.

At the sentence level that type of understanding might be aided by better understanding how the parts of the sentence relate to each other, or grammar. This is a link to my article titled "The definition and meaning of the words "idea", "thought" and "sentence" **cnx.org/content/m14812/**. But the rest of the piece relates to itself in other ways as well, and since it is going to be long and written down, each piece might contribute to the same idea. So literacy means understanding long passages, not just being able to read but a higher level of literacy would mean being able to put together a lot of information that is related to varying degrees and link it to a few ideas. So if you are reading a math book, and relate something in the end of the book to something in the beginning, you are a good reader, or more literate. That shows how the definition of literacy can vary greatly because math might be very different from say, reading a story of fiction. Literacy also means understanding the implications and subtle messages a text might convey – that would be a higher degree of literacy anyway. The math book example shows how literacy can cover any mental ability, so then what is the main idea of literacy, it is not just anything someone can understand. It is things that people can understand that is written down, or that they write down, it is the ability to structure large amounts of material in a logical fashion (or if it is a story, structure large amounts of material for emotional appeal, so really any fashion you want, but it is ultimately going to serve an end, or be logical). Unless you are the sentence level, then literacy is the ability to understand a sentence and relate each part of the sentence to other parts of the sentence. In terms of understanding a word (word level) literacy might mean understanding all the possible implications of that one word. The word "store" might mean any type of store. So things at the word level can be very complicated even if it is a simple word, it might be deceiving in context.

How would "literacy" if someone were reading a math book, be different from just the ability to understand math? It would mean how someone is comprehending that book, it would mean the way in which they understand math. How they put together the knowledge of the entire book. Math is just like reading a fiction book, different parts of a math problem relate to other parts in a logical way. If it is explained in that logical way, then someone would use literacy to understand it because literacy is putting together information in a logical manner so that one can read or write what meaning they want to convey.

So literacy isn't just the ability to read and write, it is the ability to understand what you are reading as well. One cannot read unless they understand what they are reading. So someone might not be literate in math if they cannot do any math textbook. In fact, if you cannot understand something written in specific, then you are not literate for that. In English this might mean that if you are more literate you would be able to get all the hidden meanings that could lie in the text. There is basic literacy and advanced literacy, there are levels to it.

In fact, that is all life is, figuring out how different parts of it relate to each other. This can mean emotional parts as well as physical, simple or complex parts. Unless it is just one part, and you don't want to know if it relates to anything else. But any one part is going to made up of it's own parts. Unless you are a physicist who thinks that if you break something down far enough at some level it is going to just be one part. But that really is made itself up of different parts that you can see of that one part, you can get infinitesimally small units of that one thing that is somehow bonded to the other parts, it is like a infinitely small number.

Table 117.0

Chapter 118

What Consciousness is: A Definition and Framing of the

Problem

Consciousness is the total awareness a person has about who they are and what their life experience is like. This paper will show the aspects of that total awareness, which include having and experiencing small and large life events, and how those events might lead to your total experience or awareness of life as a whole. There is a functional consciousness, which is someone being aware of their immediate environment and how to function in it physically and intellectually, and there is a consciousness of self, which is on a deeper level and is a psychological awareness of who you are and what your life is like emotionally. In that sense if you are "aware of yourself" you are aware of your feelings and your thoughts, are aware that you are experiencing feelings deeply in some way and thinking deeply in some way and that therefore you are an "aware" and conscious being, that has a rich inner life, world or mental processesing higher than that of less intelligent animals. Each single experience someone has, even an experience as small as seeing an object move, could have a larger intellectual and emotional impact because humans have a complicated intellectual makeup (both conscious and unconscious) that makes this experience deeper and richer and leads to people being more conscious of things. If an experience is deeper, then you are probably going to be more conscious of it. An experience can be small, but if you internalize it and make it more significant (possibly by comparing it to the other experiences in your life, or understanding a deeper psychological meaning behind it) then your inner world becomes larger for the duration of that experience - so you might have deeper feelings about it because it "means" more to you. It means more to you because you are comparing it to other events in your life which helps you understand it better, what it means, why you care about it, how it makes you feel (and understanding how you are feeling and being aware of those feelings is a part of consciousness).

There are more questions to ask about the nature of consciousness other than "how do I know I am aware" and "what kinds of awarenesses lead to consciousness". The only two things to be aware of are thoughts and feelings, if you are aware of something external that object is only real in the sense that it generates thoughts and feelings. So consciousness is also essentially awareness of your own thoughts and feelings. Feelings can happen that people aren't aware of, but these feelings are probably going to have unconscious consequences on other feelings now or later, or even thoughts. If consciousness is complicated, then the only way it could be complicated is though complicated feelings, because thoughts are only relevant because they generate feeling, without feeling thoughts wouldn't mean anything. However, thoughts can lead to complicated feelings. Your experiences lead to complicated feelings both during the experience and after, and all your experiences have an impact on your feelings during other experiences (a human's internal world of processesing helps make this happen). Unconscoius thoughts help an experience to be deeper they can generate feelings and could be labeled as feelings because that is what is important about them – that they cause feeling. If you know what a feeling is and label it with a thought then you can understand better how your feelings interact with each other. If you think about it that way, all your many feelings at any instant could be explained with many words, or thoughts. That is how an experience of a feeling can be more complicated, because it has a larger impact beyond the individual feeling and because it fits into a larger psychological whole of what is going on in the entirety of you your mind (or your life). These thoughts and feelings are what generate larger amounts of feeling and thought – and those components and your awareness of them help bring consciosuness to life. If you had a feeling that you didn't "feel" you wouldn't be conscious of it, but it might have an impact on feelings and thoughts later on.

The next question to ask is, although people have feelings and thoughts, and are aware of them, what is the difference between high awareness and low awareness, could you just say you feel or experience the high awareness one more? If we think of high awareness as a higher degree of feeling and focus (and possibly thoughts) on your state of mind, which is going to be its feeling makeup and its thoughts - then what exactly is the difference between that high awareness and a low awareness? You might "know" that you are experiencing a large amount of feeling, and that because of that you are in a higher state of awareness about those feelings – but what does that matter? What are the consequences of being in a higher state of awareness? It probably means that you are focusing on certain feelings more, not necessarily all your feelings. Also, at any moment you aren't going to be feeling all your feelings at once - depending on what you are thinking about or what you are doing, only a few feelings are going to be present. Higher states of awareness are probably going to be about certain things or certain select, focused states of feeling.

What would it mean to say that someone is just more conscious or more aware than someone else? Would this person generate more feeling in the people around them than other people because they are more present? Could one type of person cause another person to become more conscious because they cause that person to think about who they are more? Different people generate different types of feelings in other people and different ways of thinking about the world. Those feelings and types of thinking are a part of your consciousness because they alter what you are feeling and how aware you are of those feelings. They can alter how you look at the world by causing you to focus on different types and kinds of feelings and those feelings can alter how you think about the world. For instance, dogs could make a person feel happier and more relaxed because they are so nice and friendly and affectionate. This could make the person feel those types of feelings, and think about the world in that nicer way. Similarly other types of stimulation (other than dogs) can cause people to think and feel about the world and themselves differently. If humans are more conscious than dogs, does this mean that people pay more attention to humans, and that humans generate more emotion than dogs because they are more conscious? What if someone wasn't aware of the impact having a dog or being with a dog had on them? They could have a deeper life experience because the dog made them feel those affectionate feelings, and those feelings could relate to other feelings in thier life and make them feel differently about those - but how does that show what the nature of consciousness is? It shows that people can be very complicated, but does that make them aware? To some degree they are aware of their feelings around the dog, they are aware that the dog makes them happy, but might not be aware of the full impact on their feelings and their entire life that experience has. They are aware, however, that they have a complicated life, and have complicated feelings. If these feelings become more complicated, or better because of having a dog then consciousness of that larger impact from the dog could be shown in how the person feels toward the dog or treats the dog. The person understands that the dog is important because they treat the dog well. So consciousness isn't necessarily literally understanding the impact on your entire life something has, there are other ways people show awareness of emotion.

How people respond to the world shows how they are aware of things, they don't have to intellectually understand everything in order to respond and act in certain ways that show a much deeper understanding. Many actions people do show that they understand various things deeply but they aren't necessarily fully aware of that understanding. If you stop to think about the things you've done you can become more aware of why you did those things and what those things meant to you. Would that make someone more conscious in general? Does thinking about your feelings make you a more conscious person? Someone could reflect on one event for a long period of time, then they could become highly aware of that one event and the place it had in their life. What is the difference between that and being aware of all the events in your life? Do you need to understand how each event changes your thinking and feeling in general? So is consciousness a deeper awareness about the world or a deeper experience of the world? Does showing a literal, intellectual understanding of the feelings you experience indicate that you are more conscious?

People sometimes aren't aware of small things in their life or even aware of larger things in thier life.

If something important happens to someone emotionally but they aren't aware that it is important, does that mean they aren't a very conscious person? People obviously cannot be aware fully of everything that happens in thier life. They aren't aware of all the emotional things that happen or all of the other things that happen, like moving to a new house or moving to the other side of the room. Those physical things can have an emotional impact. What is the difference between understanding all the little things that happen to someone and their emotional impact and awareness of your life as a whole? There is a larger impact of any indidvidual event on your entire life, and that larger impact shows a greater awareness on your part because it shows you have a consciousness that interprets small events and changes your feelings toward other things because of those events. That processsesing where one thing influences something else in a complicated way that you aren't aware should be described as being an unconscious process because it is incredibly complicated and you aren't aware of the many factors involved. So people must have a deep unconscious psychology whereby they experience deep emotions a lot, and they are deep because they impact their life and feelings in various ways, but they aren't going to be aware of all their unconscious feelings fully. If you think about it, every time you respond to something in the world you are doing so because an emotion or feeling was triggered that caused the reaction. Awareness of that emotion isn't going to make someone that much more conscious of what happened then. Awareness of all of someones emotions isn't necessarily going to make the person more conscious in general anyway.

So there are small and large life events that people are aware of both in terms of how they are feeling right then and how they will be feeling later on. There could be events that happen that people aren't aware of emotionally or physically, but they might impact their life in other ways that they might be aware of. Understanding some small aspects of a persons life might lead to a better understanding of their life as a whole. "Understanding" your life as a whole might change your feelings about life. However people don't need to necessarily understand their feelings about life or their feelings in general in order to have deep experiences of feeling. Consciousness could be shown in the fact that people act in responce to the deep feelings in their life becuase it shows that in some way they understand how important their feelings are and what they should do as a reaction to them. So small and large life events contribute to small and large types of experiences that people can feel, and since they can feel them and respond to them they are at least somewhat conscious of those events, and since people are aware of all those little events that make up their life they are therefore aware of their lives as a whole, or conscious of their life.

People are conscious of the little things in their lives to different degrees, when they say hi to someone they are conscious that they are doing that but they can also be conscious of the feelings that event causes them to different degrees. That event might make them happy or sad for the rest of the day, and they might or might not be conscious of that. Say it made them happy for the day, they could be considered a conscious intelligent being whether or not they are aware of that. It made them happy for a complicated reason, it was a simple event that had a profound influence on their feelings for the rest of the day, possibly how they felt about everything else that day. That shows a deep internal processing of seemingly simple events. How does that example show how a person is conscious in general? Consciousness is awareness of all the many things in someones life, and the total awareness of everything in your life is your total consciousness - but how you define awareness is important. Someone can experience something and because that event impacts that person later on it shows that they were aware of the event happening because they were unconsciously aware and that awareness impacted their life. So unconscoius awareness can contribute to how someone feels, and since unconscious awareness is very complicated humans could be considered to be very aware and conscious.

Potential Research Implications

To fully understand consciousness, the psychological, emotional impact of everything in someones life on their mind / psyche would have to be understood. Then that data would need to be analyzed to see how aware that makes the person. That brings into question the definition of "aware" - someone could have deep emotional experiences, but it is a subjective judgement to decide if that makes them "conscious" or "aware". Dogs could be said to experience deep emotions because dogs are emotional, but since it doesn't seem like they think or understand their emotions at all they probably shouldn't be considered as conscious as humans. To understand the degree someone is aware of their feelings, you would first need to understand the depth of the feelings, the exact makeup of the feeling, how it interacts with all the feelings that person has, if it is grouped with other feelings that might also be influenced, and what the long term influence of the event is on their feelings exactly. When I say "exactly" I mean you would need to figure out the exact degree and depth of the feeling - which could be measured by verbally describing and rating what that person thinks or feels the weight of the feeling is in various ways and the weight the feeling has on their other many feelings. For instance if you wanted to measure how conscious someone was of the feelings someone generated in them by just saying "hi" you would have to measure what the depth of feeling it generated was first. You could do that by asking the person all the ways in which the event made them feel, and really put everything in a larger context. You could completely analyze what the person feels towards the other person, what they were feeling the day and the moment the person said hello, and how it might have impacted them. So to figure out how conscious someone is, analyze absolutely everything in thier life, and then assess how much of it they are aware of, and how deep their emotional experience is. It is subjective wether or not a deep emotional experience alone makes someone "aware" of it or thier life because you could say they experienced the deep emotions and it doesn't matter that they did because they are too stupid for it to mean anything to them, or you could think the opposite.

Table 118.0

Chapter 119

A Look beyond the 16 Personality Types: Why they aren't Sufficient

To every person there are going to be basic psychological traits that would say to compose the majority of who that person is, and these traits could be called the fundamentals of their psyche. At first glance it might seem like just a standard personality analysis would show what the fundamentals of their psyche are, but a deeper look into their mind is needed. There are only a few personality types, yet two people with the same personality type could be completely different. Therefore there needs to be more to analyze about someone other than what their personality type is. There needs to be more tests or questions available to lay people that they can use to analyze themselves in a way in which they can understand.

The 16 personality types don't address deeper questions people should asking about themselves that would truly separate out each individual, not just 16 different types. For instance the statement from the descriptions of the personality types "interested in how and why things work" could be made more elaborate. Interested in how and why what things work? That could be broken down into interested in how: politics, mechanics, psychology, cognitive science, math, English, history, foreign language, the sciences, any subject, any aspect of psychology, or any aspects of any of those subjects.

The statement "can be depended on to follow through" is included in a description of the personality types as well. But to follow through in what instances? In social ones? In a work environment? For personal goal setting?

The descriptions of the personality types are broad and could be misinterpreted and people could classify themselves as things that they aren't if they don't look closely enough. For instance, saying "detached and analytical" could be interpreted to mean "logical in all cases, cold and cruel". In reality that person might be slightly detached or slightly analytical, the two don't necessarily go together. And it could mean detached and analytical in only some instances or in some subject matters. Someone can be analytical in one subject area but not in another. Or only analytical when it comes to academics, versus social situations. A psychologist might be analytical when it comes to emotional things, but not analytical with say, science.

"Does not like conflict" could mean personal conflict, group conflict, or wars and even political movements, like say the conflict between being communist or being for democracy.

"Risk takers who live for the moment" could only be applied in certain situations. In fact, the questions "when does this apply exactly?" and "how does this go into effect" could be applied when analyzing everything said about the personality types.

"Loyal and faithful" – someone may only be loyal and faithful to their friends, and put down their enemies - does "loyal and faithful" mean weak?

"Uncomplicated in their desires" – Does this mean that the person doesn't like doing things as much since they have simpler desires? Or does it mean that they are simpler people? That when they want to do something, they aren't picky? What instances does this apply, someone might be picky in some instances, but not in others. If someone is uncomplicated in their desires, does this imply that they are simpler at analyzing things since they might not see as many details, like how they wouldn't see details in what it is that they want? Does it imply a lower emotional intelligence since someone with a high emotional intelligence would probably be more specific about what it is that they want, since they know more about what it is that they want. Or does it mean that they want to live a simpler lifestyle?

"Stable and practical" – those two might not necessarily go together, just because someone is stable doesn't mean that they are also practical. Someone looking at the description of the personality types might not question that if they read the description, they might just then start assuming that if they are stable, they are going to be practical. Analyzing a personality needs to be done critically, with caution and a questioning mind (especially when reading blanket statements about what that type of personality is – one shouldn't take a personality analysis and assume that they are going to be exactly like that). Also, it shouldn't be assumed that that analysis is all that that person is (if it is even accurate) one could go into much more detail, and no one is probably just completely one personality, (even if certain traits are likely to go together) but it is logical that they are mix of many, many different things.

"Well organized and hard working" – again, do the two necessarily go together - someone can be hard working but not be organized. Someone could be well organized in many different things, not just in academics and common life, but in specific fields and at specific tasks, that isn't specified. Also, hard working, but does this mean that they are passionate about their work or that they want to do it? Or just that they do it when they have to? Do they want to be organized as well?

"Extremely thorough, responsible, and dependable" – once again the three might not go together, but it should also be noted that maybe they do work well together in some people. Does the person like having those traits? That question ties into a larger question, what are their main goals with their personality? What are they trying to achieve socially with their personality, or otherwise with their personality? Just describing traits doesn't show the intent or motivation of the person. In fact, if you look at it that way, by asking "what is this person trying to achieve" you get a much closer and "together" or "whole" look at who that person is. All of the descriptions of the personality traits don't address if the person is trying to achieve that. People should take the personality traits and analyze if that is who they want to be. The more they think about who they are, the more answers they will find.

"Well developed powers of concentration" – does that statement mean that the person is also more calm and better at meditating? Does it mean that they are also more detached since they can separate themselves from emotional swings? Does it mean that they can perform certain tasks better because of this concentration? Which tasks?

"Usually interested in supporting and promoting traditions and establishments" – does this mean long standing traditions and establishments more so than new ones? That would make this person more conservative instead of liberal. Or is it just someone who likes things that are ordered and structured, which are likely to be things like traditions and establishments?

"They work steadily towards identified goals" – does this make this person more organized since it is identified goals that they are working towards, instead of more motivated which would mean working towards all goals. The fact that they work towards "identified" goals means that they also might make more goals for themselves? Does that mean that they are more motivated about life as well?

"They can usually accomplish any task once they have set their mind to it" – that statement shouldn't be taken literally, maybe it means that they are very determined, not necessarily that they are very skilled. It might be they can't accomplish any tasks in certain fields at all.

"Loyal to their peers and to their internal value systems" – does this mean that the two go together? That someone is just a better person if they are loyal to their peers, so then they are also therefore going to stand by their values? If you aren't loyal to your friends does that mean that you might not also be loyal to yourself (which might mean being loyal to your internal value system). If you are loyal to your own value system does that mean you respect your own ideas more? Someone could have not decided which values to take on in life but still might have the value of being loyal to their peers and is strongly attached to only that value.

The next statement following the last one - "loyal to their peers and to their internal value systems, but not overly concerned with respecting laws and rules if they get in the way of getting something done." So they might only respect their own opinions, but not other peoples opinions or the opinions of a law or a rule? So they respect their own opinions, their peers, but not the people who write the laws. What if they have a value that is also a rule or a law, and it gets in the way of something they want done? Why are they loyal to their friends but not loyal to laws? Does this make them evil or good people? What exactly is going on here?

"Have an exceptional ability to turn theories into solid plans of action" – does that mean that they are reliable people that are practical? Or does it mean that they act on what they say? Does it mean that they are less frivolous since they don't just theorize but also actually plan? Are they less silly then?

References

Quotes are from personalitypage.com (January 3, 2008)

Table 119.0

Chapter 496

Highlights of Cognitive Psychology

Chapter 120

Cognitive psychology is the scientific study of the human mind and how it processes information (including the mental processes of thought such as visual processing, memory, problem solving, and language).

120.1 Philosophical Foundations of Cognitive Psychology

Dualism proposes that mind and body are two different kinds of entities. Substance dualism (also called *Cartesian dualism*) is where mind and body are perceived to be difference substances. How can a mental experience have substance? Vivid sensory experiences could be viewed as being substantial, for example extreme pain or seeing red. Other emotions and ideas could also be viewed as being substantial, though they are more abstract than something like extreme pain.

Monism, in contrast to dualism, is the belief that there is only one type of stuff instead of two. There are two monist beliefs – *idealism*, people who think that believe that there is only a mental world full of ideas, and not material world and then there is *materialism* - the opposite of idealism (only physical things exist).

Behaviorism – is the position that the only way to discuss mental events is in terms of observable behaviors.

Functionalism – this position is like behaviorism in that it includes taking into account environmental inputs and behaviors, but it also includes mental states. So a functionalist might define happiness not just as a tendency to do things that show the person is happy, but also show what happiness is relative to other mental states.

Supervenience – this position holds that if there is a difference in conscious events, there is going to be a difference in neural activity, but that not all neural activity can be explained by conscious events (unconscious neural activity).

Importance

It is important to understand (from dualism) that some emotions carry a certain weight and therefore are similar to physical objects. It is also important to note that simple physical experience gives rise to extremely complicated emotions, but the two are still fundamentally different. Physical experience gives rise to emotions because although the physical may seem simple, one object can be a mental trigger for many other things, making that one physical object something extremely complex. In fact, all the philosophical foundations of cognitive psychology help to understand how someone could be conscious because they are about fundamental ways in which the brain works, which is going to be related strongly to how people process information and therefore consciousness. That is why the philosophical information presented is the foundation for cognitive psychology, because the ideas are broad and far reaching.

Table 120.0

Chapter 498

The Meaning of Life
Chapter 121

The meaning of life must come from something real. There are only a few things that are real that contribute to happiness and meaning:

- What activities you do and how fun they are.

- What the impact on your happiness those activities have after the time of the activity.

- How much respect and attention you receive during interpersonal activities.

- The intensity of interpersonal activities.

- The impact on how much you respect yourself, and how much interpersonal and other activities have on you.

- How clear interpersonal and other activities are as they contribute to intellectual enhancement - so how much impact on what you are thinking the activities have. Not just literally what you are thinking about but the impact the activities have on how you process the world. This would include their impact on your emotional development. If a situation happens that you learn from, the learning takes a spot in your mind for the next day, week, month, year etc and influences how good you feel about yourself because part of your mind is being occupied by learning.

- How much intellectual stimulation activities cause. I'm not referring to the type of learning you do in school. The type I am talking about has to do with the intensity of emotional interactions, more intense emotional interactions are going to be more intellectually stimulating because there is more data there. Therefore there is a link between emotional openness and positive reinforcement to how well you can process data. It is almost as if you have to have the right emotional circumstances in order to be intellectually stimulated by an emotional interaction. For instance, if someone is mean to you it might shut you down emotionally, causing you to not process data as well and hinder your feelings and intellect. There is a link between emotion and learning.

- Perceived meaning isn't necessarily always going to be meaningful. Something may seem fun and be exciting but that doesn't mean you got anything from it that was actually deep. Most people probably just continually reinforce how much they like themselves and how important they are so they feel like their life is meaningful all the time. I mean, since meaning can come from anything, it is easy to generate false meaning just by feeling good about yourself. Or if someone gives you a compliment and thereafter you feel better about yourself – does that one compliment really justify you being happy forever? Maybe all people need to be happy is enough positive reinforcement until they think they are awesome.

- Real meaning from life is more likely to come from actually events that provide happiness and stimulation, not simply feeling good about yourself all the time.

- A fun activity might be fun simply because it makes you feel good, and therefore it wouldn't be as meaningful as a more deep activity. Simply feeling good about yourself isn't going to lead to being truly happy. I believe the only real source of happiness comes from the intellectual stimulation you get from events, what you learned from them, how they improve you as a person. However, remember that positive emotions such as fun can facilitate this learning, since fun opens up a person to grow.

Table 121.0

Chapter 122

Levels of Emotion and Thought

I previously discussed how emotions were deeper than feelings, yet are "felt" less because it isn't as obvious they are occurring because they are deeper and more intellectual. Emotions therefore involve more thought than feelings. Sensations are more related to feelings because they are simple things that don't involve thought. So since feelings are less deep than emotions, could it be that certain emotions and feelings are more cognitive than others? Although feelings are more like sensations, they can be intellectual like emotions too. For instance, the feelings curiosity and frustration are both related to thought, but they are not deep enough to be emotions. Some emotions and feelings, however, are more primary (less related to thought) and related to instinctual reactions than others, which might make them more cognitive and intellectual. Since emotion, feeling and thought are mixed – and some of those are sometimes more intense than the rest – then it makes sense that some emotions might be more consistently less intellectual than others. I could say that immediate, shallow feelings are more instinctual than deep, pondering emotions and thought.

Silvano Arieti categorized emotions into three orders, the first order being the simplest emotions and the third order being the most complicated. He listed 5 types of emotions as first-order ones – tension – which he said was "a feeling of discomfort caused by different situations, like excessive stimulation and obstructed physiological or instinctual response", appetite, fear, rage, and satisfaction and said that satisfaction was "an emotional state resulting from the gratification of physical needs and relief from other emotions". (Arieti) He classified the first order emotions as being bodily, elicited by stimuli perceived to be positive or negative, have an almost immediate effect and if they have a delayed reaction the delay would be from a fraction of a second to a few minutes, and require a minimum amount of cognitive work to be experienced. Those emotions aren't as simple as sensations, which consist of just feeling things without thought. To me those emotions also seem very strong, and perhaps they are strong because if someone is going to have an instinctual reaction, it is going to have to be strong to interrupt their thought process. So those more instinctual emotions interrupt thought because they are so strong and almost physical. In fact, small amounts of any of those emotions would make it possible for the person to reflect on the emotion because they aren't being distracted by large amounts of it, therefore making the emotion less of a first-order emotion and more like a complicated emotion. If you take rage and think about your rage, you make rage into a complicated emotion and less like a simple emotion. You also make it into more a feeling since now it is shallower. So a full-blown rage would be much more instinctual than just having a little rage, the small amount of rage is more controlled and initiated by cognition, whereas the large rage was triggered instinctually (or more basically, emotion is more instinctual and powerful and distracts from thought).

Arieti thought that second-order emotions started not from an "impending attack on the system" but by cognitive processes which he believed to be visual symbols or representations in the mind of real things (images). He explains how important images are to humans "Image formation is actually the basis for all higher mental processes. It enables the human being not only to recall what is not present, but to retain an affective disposition for the absent object. The image thus becomes a substitute for the external object." If the image is pleasant it acts as a motivator, and if it is unpleasant it has the opposite effect. Then he explains how these images play a role in the higher order cognitive processes of some second order emotions. It is clear to me, however, that not only images play a role in thought, when people think of a word they don't always see a strong image. There is going to be an image associated with practically everything, but you don't always bring up that image all the time. He lists the following second-order emotions:

- He said that anxiety is "the emotional reaction to the expectation of danger", and that it isn't the result of simple perceptions or signals (which would mean anything real that initiates a reaction) but the result of images which enable a human to anticipate danger and its consequences, and that anxiety is image-determined fear (fear is a first order emotion because it is the result of direct stimulus).

- He stated that anger is rage elicited by the images of stimuli. Rage leads to an immediate reaction, however anger lasts longer and that is possible because it is mediated by images in the mind. Rage is useful for survival, and anger is useful to retain a hostile defensive attitude.

- Wishing is "made possible by the recall of the image or other symbols of an object whose presence is pleasant".

- The emotion security. He didn't know if security as an emotion actually existed or was just the absence of unpleasant emotions. You can visualize an image of security, an "image-determined satisfaction".

My take on this is that images make the second-order emotions higher cognitive processes. Without an image someone isn't really thinking, they are just responding to stimulus instead of conjuring up something in their mind, which is going to take longer. However, rage and the other first order emotions are going to also bring up images immediately in a more unconscious way (but also some might be conscious just very fast) before someone can respond to the stimulus. In that way rage can be intellectual. If you think about it, something in your own mind can cause you to be enraged, and therefore it was an intellectual process which started the rage and is associated with it when the rage is being experienced. It isn't like rage is completely mindless, it is actually driven by anger, which is a second order emotion. Rage is simply more related to direct stimulus because that is much easier to get upset about because it is real and requires less thought. So anger is a more intellectual emotion because it lasts longer than rage and is easier to maintain because it only needs thought to be maintained, but rage is somewhat of the opposite. Rage and anger overlap to certain degrees as well. The same can be said of the other first and second-order emotions. The important fact is that real world stimuli elicits more powerful emotions that are less cognitive in first order emotions than in second order ones, however both are cognitive (which also means might be assisted by images) and both might be assisted by events in the real world (stimuli). Things that happen in the real world are simply more likely to stimulate a stronger emotional reaction.

Arieti described that with third order emotions language plays a greater role. This follows from his explanation that third-order emotions "although capable of existing before the advent of the conceptual level, expand and are followed by even more complex emotions at the conceptual level". That means basically that words are conceptual instead of visual or simply automatic responses from stimuli. He states that important third-order emotions are depression, hate, love and joy. Depression contrasts to anxiety because anxiety usually caused by the thought that a dangerous situation is about to occur. Depression, on the other hand, was caused by factors a while ago. I believe that that shows how there are other emotions that can be placed as second-order emotions, like sadness. Basically any emotion that isn't a strong immediate reaction and isn't a complicated emotion like the third-order emotions would be a second-order one. Anything that is caused easily by thoughts or images (like sadness) could be a second-order emotion. However third order emotions are going to be even more complicated, taking many factors over a longer period of time to generate the emotion.

Arieti thought that depression followed "cognitive thought processes, such as evaluations and appraisals". For instance if someone is told of a death of a friend, what makes that person depressed is their ability to evaluate the news. Those ideas from Arieti make it clear that depression really is complicated and supported by thoughts, and therefore is a third-order emotion. Depression can bring up sad feelings at any time, so those sad feelings are still really second order emotions because they were generated by something real (unconscious depressive thoughts). The feelings of depression, however, are the third-order emotions because they are more complicated than simple feelings. Each feeling of depression is going to involve more complicated thoughts associated with it because it is going to involve more parts, like evaluations and appraisals. If looked at that way, sadness could have a lot of parts as well. However, for each circumstance of sadness you can usually identify why you got sad, even if you got sad because you were depressed. When you are depressed, however, it is often so complicated you don't know all the factors leading to that depression.

Arieti said the following about hate, "...hate is the third-order emotion which corresponds to the second-order emotion anger and to the first-order emotion rage. The three together constitute hostility, but hate is the only one among the three which has the tendency to become a chronic emotional state sustained by special thoughts. Thus a feed-back mechanism is established between these sustaining thoughts and the emotion." To me this shows how powerful third-order emotions can be. That they really penetrate your consciousness for a long time. It shows how emotions are really also intellectual things. That you might interact with someone, and this interaction could make you feel things for a long time after. That long term feeling isn't necessarily going to be just an emotion, however. If you think about it you cannot sustain and be able to identify an emotion from just one interaction or one relationship for a long time. However, if you consider that the emotion is also an intellectual experience, then you realize that you can sustain it for a long time because you are aware at some level of the relationship you have with this other person, so it is emotional and intellectual. Don't forget that the emotional/intellectual experience is going to be able to be described with the thoughts and experiences that are supporting it. Albert Wellek said this about deep emotions, "Love, friendship, faithfulness, are emotions of the heart; they concern, involve, and engage a man in his very nature; they may move, touch, stir, or shake him and even change or transform him in his identity. On the other hand, anger aroused by a trifle, or by hurt vanity, is superficial and shallow, not matter how intense." (Wellek)

Wellek also went on to show the difference between intensity and depth in emotions. That relates to Arieti's orders of emotions because each of the higher order emotions are more deep than the first-order ones. Wellek said this "A man's emotional disposition may tend predominantly or almost exclusively toward explosive affectivity or, on the other hand, may tend predominantly or almost exclusively toward profound experiences. When extreme, examples of the first type of disposition are said to demonstrate lack of sensitivity, toughmindedness, or even brutality; examples of the second type, sensitivity, emotional responsiveness, or tendermindedness" That shows how some emotions are very deep, while others very shallow. He also said "...if we say that a man is emotional, the question is: do we mean that is sensitive, excitable, or sentimental?". That shows how deep emotions may trigger those sentimental feelings. But remember deep emotions aren't just emotions, they are supported by thought processes making them an intellectual experience. So it isn't like the person is emotional all the time, you could say they are being intellectual all the time. What shows the nature of the difference between depth and intensity is two examples that aren't really either deep or intense, yet are profound – those examples are aesthetic experiences and strongly held convictions.

Wellek also said this about the nature of depth and intensity, " Depth is characterized by breadth and continuity, intensity by its temporal limitation and resultant discontinuity. Intensive emotions are usually shallow and blow over quickly. For the very reason that too much vital energy is consumed in a comparatively short time, the emotion is quickly spent and little or nothing is left. No normal man can rage for hours on end – though a maniac may. Intensive emotions are shock-like, eruptive, explosive, volcanic; they show organic drive." Those intense emotions would relate to Arieti's first-order emotions, and less to the third-order ones. The third-order emotions would be more deep instead of intense. I previously showed how feelings are intense but not deep, and emotions are deep but not intense. Feelings are more like those intense emotions described by Wellek because you can really "feel" them, while emotions are more intellectual and you might experience them more in a more satisfying, sentimental, thought provoking way.

References

Arieti, Silvano (1970). Cognition and Feeling. In M. Arnold (Ed) Feelings and Emotions: The Loyola Symposium.

Wellek, Albert (1970). Emotional Polarity in Personality Structure. In M. Arnold (Ed) Feelings and Emotions: The Loyola Symposium.

Table 122.0

Chapter 123

A Theory of Emotion

People respond negatively to pain or any negative emotion. Pain might also hinder development of emotions because it isn't encouraging. The right factors need to be applied to someone in order to get them to experience the fullest potential of their emotions. This could simply mean having the right people around you who are supportive of you and your emotions. In fact, the words "thrive" and "support" are really key for emotion generation. That being said, it cannot be ignored that emotional events which feel painful in the short term may be beneficial in the long term, and even cause a person to thrive and experience good emotions.

It needs to be clarified what is significant about emotions, or how are they meaningful. There can be an individual emotional event, but this event might impact everything else that occurs in someone's life. In that way everything is tied in. Even words, or therapy, might change how someone views the world and greatly influence how they experience emotion. For instance, understanding that a loved one likes you – or loves you – consciously would cause your emotions as a whole to change. So not just your understanding of that thing in specific would change, but also your experience with that person. A cliché saying that explains this would be "once you let love in, the world becomes a beautiful and sunny place".

That expression explains the importantance of positive encouragement, the impact of one event or person on someone's overall emotions all the time, and the importance therapy can have. That one statement might make someone realize they love someone else and what this love does for their life. [I apologize if this article is starting to sound cheesy, but it is important to realize that all emotions are tied into each other, and that small events or even your cognition (which could be influenced by therapy or words (as in the cliché example)) can greatly influence your life.] Conversely, if something very bad happens to someone, they might not care about their life anymore and start to experience all their other emotions less.

In fact, everything that happens to someone probably influences everything else that happens to that person. You could also just look at life as individual events that only have minor impacts on each other over the long term. I suppose I am asking the question, "what is everything, how does everything feel, and how does everything relate". Is there a way to describe all emotion other than, "you're feeling something"? Certain activities bring up certain emotions, individual circumstances and their emotional parts can be described as action-reaction relationships. If all of life is described in that way, does that explain everything? If you describe how everything feels individually then that would describe everything if you take into your account of each situation how all the other things that happened influenced how you feel for that one thing. So that means how you feel most of the time, the general emotions you have that are mostly independent of what is happening – and also how you feel for each thing that happens.

Analyzing anything, however, has many levels of complication. A kid playing a video game generates the emotion fun. That could be the first level of analysis of an event, stating the obvious emotions involved. The next level would be asking, "what are all the emotions involved". To do that you would have to understand that all emotions are mixed, that the emotion "fun" the boy has could be mixed in with the feeling anger or frustration if he lost a fight or something. Also, how a specific negative event playing the game (say losing a battle) influenced his feelings of fun after that event. Also, his cognition might play a role, did he say something to himself after he lost to make himself feel better? Did his therapy session talking about how to deal with defeat alleviate his pain at the loss?

To have a complete understanding of everything, you could analyze the degrees of fun the boy has during the game, when it elevates and when it decreases. Is all of life like this video game, with variations of fun and anger and cognitive influences? If viewed simply, then yes, however there are many many things that happen in life that can be analyzed and the emotional components explained. It would be useful if I could describe a few principals that would apply to all of these events:

- Negative events generate fear, which causes people to either flee or shut down.

- Positive events generate pleasure, which results in encouragement and motivation.

That's pretty much all I can think of, I suppose I could say that my theory has two parts, the pleasure instinct and the pain instinct, and that all emotions stem from these two instincts. Everything is going to generate some amount of pleasure and some amount of pain, causing reward and punishment, it is almost Pavlovian. However it is more complicated than that, while my theory works on the small individual direct event level (thing A causes you to be motivated to do thing B) it also works in small ways on everything, like one event might motivate you for something else entirely. Freud believed in a death instinct and a sex instinct, which, if you think about it, is similar to my theory.

The pleasure and pain instincts apply when any emotion happens. Every emotion is going to be a certain amount painful, and a certain amount pleasurable. Furthermore, the meaningful aspect of the emotion   is going to be how pleasurable or painful it was. Learning emotionally could be viewed as long term pleasure. So if an event is meaningful instead of just fun or pleasurable it would still be placed under the category of pleasure because this meaningful activity adds to your life overall, thus causing long- term pleasure. It is almost like intelligence is fun, only in a different more long term way. Also, an even that is fun is also going to contribute to long term intellectual emotional development as well, because a fun event is going itself to contain information, and be motivating and inspiring. That also explains why negative and painful events can be beneficial over the long run for both fun and emotional intellectual development. They can be because the event itself might communicate information to the person, or help them understand something. Almost like learning a lesson the hard way. The point is that pain or pleasure is the stimulus behind all fun, learning, and long-term fun and learning. In other words, the pain and pleasure you get from events helps you out all the time, not just for those specific events. Pleasure is inspiring and encouraging, while pain is more of a learning experience. So every emotion is going to inspire in some ways if it is pleasurable, and you might learn from painful emotions.

Pleasure and pain function in the mind in many ways. The influence emotions, thoughts and the long term conscious and unconscious impact on thoughts and emotions. There are different types of emotion and thought that are influenced by different types of pain and pleasure:

- Different types of thought can vary in how emotional they are, for instance moral decisions could involve a lot of emotion compared to simple decisions. Important thoughts about emotional things (like loved ones) might also be very emotional.

- Emotional thoughts are more intellectual pleasure than regular pleasure (because it is a thought instead of a real event).

- The more emotional the thought, the greater its long term impact and significance might be on your emotions. Like the thought "I love person x". Of course, a non-emotional thought might also have a long term impact on how much pleasure and pain you experience.

- For each different type of emotion, you could have a thought that is emotional in that way.

- Every emotion is going to be a certain type of pain or pleasure. This pain or pleasure will vary between being intellectual and emotional. The more aware you are of the pain or pleasure, the more intellectual it will be. That shows how you might be suffering or in pleasure but not know it. If you don't know how much pain or pleasure you are experiencing, how much are you actually experiencing it? There is an unconscious element of pain and pleasure. Also, the pain and pleasure, or the emotion generating those feelings, might itself be of a more intellectual type or emotional type. For instance, if you are picked on, it is because you understand that you are being insulted that results in the emotional pain. That makes the pain in part intellectual because it stems from your understanding.

- Just like every emotion is going to be a certain type of pain or pleasure, every thought is going to be as well. Like emotional thoughts or non-emotional ones.

- An insult affects emotions because you understand that it is an insult, but normal events (like working or interacting with someone) generate emotion because you have a large unconscious emotional understanding of the significance of the event. At birth they might generate emotion because that is simply how you experience emotions, however after a long time the emotion that events generate is going be based much more on your experience, and what your experience is going to teach you is how much you enjoy that event.

- The fact that thought can influence emotions, pain and pleasure is amazing if you think about it. Is a thought a real experience? Thoughts don't even last very long. However, you could think of thoughts as tied in with emotion (since thoughts can be emotional, that shows how they are real). For instance, if something bad happens, you are going to experience pain because of real reasons that could be thought about. You change the nature of the emotion by altering how you think it affected you because the emotion was really just thoughts about the event, so you change the emotion by changing the thoughts that make up the emotion.

- Since emotion is so tied in with thought, pain and pleasure can be long term because you are always thinking. Something bad might happen to you, but you unconsciously think about the event for a while after, causing you to experience pain.

- The type of pain and pleasure can be explained by explaining the thoughts that make up the emotion, or the emotions that make up the thoughts. Also, real events and their emotions can be explained with thoughts. It is like a real event causes a series of thoughts about the event that determine how you are going to feel about the event both during the event and after. The thoughts are so real (are based in emotion), yet only thoughts, so therefore you could control how you feel about events and how they affect you to some degree. That shows the importance of talking about your feelings. There are also learned responses which also show the importance of thoughts. The response might have been learned from thoughts or unconscious thoughts. Therefore, it could also be unlearned just by thinking.

- Thoughts can change the nature of emotion. For instance, if someone makes you happy, the more you highlight why they make you happy the more the relationship will be enhanced. Also, thoughts can direct a negative emotional response. For instance, if something bad happens to you, if you think that what happened was really bad then you might feel even worse then if you trained yourself to not care. In other words, your emotional response to events is really just an intellectual, learned response that is determined by thoughts and your thoughts over the long-term. If someone is insulted, they have learned that insults are bad over time, and that is why it makes them feel bad. It also causes them to think about the negative thing that was said, and if it is true, might make them think that they are a failure in some way. In that case, simply by thinking about the insult and why it isn't true, or why it shouldn't affect your feelings could make it so the insult doesn't carry weight the next time.

- Changing your thoughts in an attempt to change your emotions is almost like trying to change your programming because emotions are harder to control than thoughts. In the movie Terminator 3, the evil terminator changed the programming of the good terminator to kill the hero of the movie. When it was time to kill the hero, the hero tried to convince the terminator that it didn't want to kill him. The terminator struggled with back and forth switching between programming commands until it finally was able to not kill.

In review, by exploring the importance of pleasure and pain on emotion in general we gained insight into emotions, and that gave us insight into how they can be manipulated with thoughts, or your thoughts be manipulated by your emotions. So pain and pleasure function with individual thoughts as well as with emotions, that is obvious if you remember how tied in emotions are with thought - and I already explained the importance of pain on emotion. Also, thoughts can be emotional, when you think something it can bring up pain. That pain could just be an enlarged version of the pain caused by the thoughts the rest of the time (the time you're not thinking consciously of them) unconsciously. You highlight the pain by thinking about what is causing it. That might help you to change the thought, however, and therefore the unconcsious thoughts and emotions making you feel at other times.

While my pain and pleasure instincts can be applied to almost every emotional situation, there are other principals which can be applied in many situations that are almost as important as those. For instance, the social aspect of the human experience is probably one of the most important generators of emotion. You could classify everything someone does as either social or non-social, and how important and emotional can be interacting with inanimate objects? The important aspect of the social aspect, however, is personality. That is so because no matter what someone says or does, their personality is going to have a large impact on the people around them because there is an unconscious emotional interaction going on between different personalities. Of course, what someone says and does is going to be reflective of their personality, but just by describing personality types it can be inferred what that type of person would do differently. Though it is important to note that basic interactions are almost all the same, the only thing that varies is how the people have different and individual personalities and this changes the emotional interchange.

There are several things that determine what someones personality is going to be. There are important factors and non-important ones. For the principals to be general and far-reaching, I am only going to talk about the important factors. Personality could be described and the things listed be important to what that person does, and what type of intellect they have, however this would not be looking at the important aspects of personality. The important aspects of someone's personality are the ones that going to affect how much emotion they experience, and those aspects are going to be ones that influence their social emotional interchanges. However, non-important personality traits may be related to important ones. For instance, although "Organized and hard working" is not an important factor, (how hard someone works is not going to play a large role in the emotional interchange when this person interacts) how serious that person is, which might be shown in how hard working they are, might play a role in a social interaction. For instance, there might be a violent clash between the personality of a serious person and a laid back person, generating a lot of emotion. So although two people might be equally hard working, maybe only one reflects this trait emotionally when they interact (or "radiates" it). There are only a few basic factors that generate large amounts of emotion when any two people interact:

- How serious (or mature) somone is could clash with how lazy (or immature) someone else is, causing either tension or an interesting interaction

- How cool or not people are or are perceived to be could cause a status conflict

- How physically appealing someone is could generate sexual interest or, if not sexual interest unconscious sexual interest that would be shown by how much someone likes someone else even though they might not be aware their interest is sexual in nature (that shows how this can function unconsciously)

- How old someone is could cause either identification and relation, or the opposite of that which might cause either tension or an interesting interaction

- How intelligent or dumb someone is could cause tension or relation (this also might vary depending on what the sitation is, becuase in certain situations different types of intellect are more valued)

- What someone's profession is would matter when interacting with that person in the context of their job (that shows how the context of the interaction (or what the interaction is even) also matters)

- How friendly or shy someone is could generate openness or seclusion in interaction

Table 123.0

Chapter 124

Physical Stimulus and its Role with Emotions {CP}

This topic is about the difference between physical feelings and mental feelings (feelings of emotions, of thoughts). It could be viewed that most stimulation is physical. More importantly, that physical feeling is mixed in with mental feelings. Also, that physical feeling is with you all the time and can even serve as a baseline for your emotions. Whenever you experience an emotion, or even in your general state, you are feeling physical feelings. If you look at this by the definition of stimulation then it makes sense that most stimulation is physical since stimulation is usually something strong, and physical feelings feel much more real and alive than mental ones. You know you are alive if you are experiencing pain. What happens when someone concentrates on physical feelings? Doing intense physical activity (like playing a sport), feeling pain, going to the bathroom, eating, and having sex are the five strongest physical feelings I can think of. However you also have physical feelings all the time because you are aware of yourself not only in a mental way but in a physical way. You are aware of the physical feelings your body produces all the time and how these feelings are mostly the same as time changes. You are also aware of what it feels like to be you, which is going to be mostly your mental feelings but also your physical ones. So intellectually your mental feelings are stronger if you are doing serious thinking, but if you are doing physical activity then your physical feelings are stronger. Also, your physical feelings interact with your mental feelings in a certain way, one might cause the other to increase, there might be a chain of cause and effect interaction.

This is related to the difference between emotion and thought because one distracts from the other, and physical feelings are more like emotions than thoughts. This is why pain isn't as much of an emotion than the other emotions because the other emotions are more mental and therefore intellectual. In fact, if you explore the feeling of pain it helps one to understand what a physical feeling is like because pain seems to be the strongest physical feeling. It is also a negative emotion similar to sadness, however, because it might make you feel sad very quickly or simultaneously. If it makes you feel sad simultaneously then it is like pain is an emotion because it is related to the feeling sad. So pain is a physical feeling that overlaps with the emotion sad. If someone is in pain it makes them sad, but that is much different from being sad in the normal way someone gets sad. It is like a physical sadness. Similarly if someone is having sex it might make them happy, but in a physical way much different from the normal emotion happy (that is pretty amusing). So saying pain is an emotion is like saying that sex is an emotion. Sex may provoke emotions but is it an emotion itself? The answer is really that physical feelings are so similar to emotions that the two are tied together. You get a small amount of real emotion from something physical whereby it seems like the emotion is part of the physical feeling because the physical feeling feels so much like a certain mental emotion.

People respond to emotions. They get a feeling or emotion, then they think about it. If a feeling is large enough to be felt consciously, then it is going to be thought about. "Thinking" is really processing in a larger context, thus all emotions are processed in the mind (even physical ones). In this way emotions become complicated, that is, life isn't just continuous sensory stimulation. All the sensory stimulation adds up and people have feelings about the total amount of sensory stimulation. Either that or there is a deeper feeling which people get simply from being alive, that isn't related to sensory stimulation. This feeling must come from something, however. The world (the physical world) is real and it exists, this is the only source of potential feeling (since that is the only thing to get feeling from). Pain feels extremely real, it might be that people are happy simply because it is an avoidance of pain, or that happy only exists relative to sad, so you understand how you are happy and can be happy because you know what happy is because you know it is at extreme pain. It seems like pain is too large to be compared to regular sensory stimulation, like visual stimulation. This means that most emotions (if you consider pain to be an emotion, here I just mean that people are more distracted by the physical than the mental emotions) people have are from just their immediate environment, feeling things and touching things. Feeling their own body and the physical feelings they get from it. Vision doesn't cause that much pleasure compared to physical.

When someone gets happy from emotions (non physical stimulus), however, they get very happy. This source of happiness must come at least partly from the physical, that is, they get happy because they feel better about their physical emotions (or when they get mentally happy, they can feel their body more because they are more alive and this experience is tied into being happy - the physical experience is also more real so it seems like your mental emotions derive from the physical). If someone is nice to them, then they feel like they are helping them, and this means helping them stay alive, which would prolong their life and the feelings get from their body. In a similar way, all emotions are tied into the physical. Part of what makes people happy is reward which they associate with prolonging their life. They feel deeply about prolonging their life because they get deep physical feelings from their body and from its existence. So emotions actually come partly from physical sensations, just not directly. That is if they were directly from physical sensations it would just be a physical sensation, but people feel deep emotions if it relates to protecting their physical sensations. In this way people are very animal-like. Seeing things and hearing things makes people feel good but this feeling is very mild. Most feeling comes just from a physical awareness of one's own body. This makes sense considering that physical pain at its height is much worse than any emotional pain.

In review, emotional pain has its source in physical feelings and pain. This also means that emotions are really physical things. Emotions cause physical feelings. Any "feeling" is really a physical feeling, even if it is from vision or hearing. The sensory feeling triggers a deeper physical feeling because the sensory feeling reminds you that you are alive and have a physical body. In this way all sensations are tied into your physical body.

This all just really means that the physical is much more "real" than emotions are. You could say that emotions are feelings by themselves, but whenever you experience an emotion, you are also experiencing physical sensations. The physical is always there and it is strong because it is real, it is who you are. It is like a baseline for your emotions, it is a reminder that you are alive. If there was no physical world, you couldn't experience emotions because emotions are in root all physical, since everything comes from sensory stimulation initially. Thinking of it that way, all emotions are physical themselves since they remind you of seeing and touching physical things, which brings up a sense of your physical presence in that environment. Also, if the emotion isn't physical, then how is it in any way real? How can someone feel something other than physically? Can you say, "I felt that intellectually?" How much sense does that make?

Table 124.0

How Emotion is Processed {CP}

Chapter 125

It can be inferred from my pleasure and pain principal instincts that people are motivated to process positive things, and discouraged from accepting negative ones. The idea that the mind processes positive things better than neutral and negative ones is not new. However, this idea is much more significant, and it applies in many more circumstances than you can probably guess. For instance, this idea could mean that people are simply more open to positive, happier emotions than negative ones. That things which cause pleasure are better and clearer understood than things that are painful. However, something painful may cause you to become more awake, and this in turn would lead you to process information better. This information itself might be pleasurable, even though the original stimulus was painful. Pain may also cause long term pleasure in a different way. If the stimulus is negative, you could still process it better because of the original negative stimulus which "woke" you up.

There are examples of negative things which cause people to pay attention, something like spanking, any loud noise (scratching a fingernail on a chalkboard for one), or even a painful emotional experience could cause you to take life more seriously temporarily, and this might cause you to be more awake, active, or intellectual. However, those negative things just make someone better able to receive or understand positive stimulus more so than negative, because someone is still probably going to ignore negative information more than positive information, even though they are in a more alert state. Negative things are ignored because, simply, people tend to believe what they want to believe. [The statement "people believe what they want to believe" shows how people can be delusional at times. It shows the people want positive things more than negative things, and since they want positive things more than negative ones, they are going to be more accepting of them.]

It is almost as if for every emotion someone says, "do I want that?" and if the answer is yes, they are much more responsive to it. [That sentence shows how for even emotions, which are a natural process, complicated thought patterns and selection processes occur with them] So someone might ignore someone they don't like, and pay attention to someone they do (what determines if they like someone could be based off of many factors). Or, if someone doesn't like someone, then that person doesn't cause as much pleasure because the other person has decided to ignore them. When someone sees an opportunity to enhance emotion they grab onto it, and similarly if they see something or someone is causing displeasure they instantly ignore it. It is pre-conceived notions and conceptions of the person, or even an understanding of who that person is (or an unconscious understanding determined by the emotional relationship), that determines what emotions that person causes. It is like real facts about that person are being stored unconsciously, and then those facts are brought up in the future to determine how much pleasure that person is going to cause.

That ties into the idea that positive things are processed better than negative ones because if something is positive, or if you "think" something is positive (which might mean having preconceived notions about someone) then that person is going to generate less pleasure for you because you think they are not positive. [So thinking someone is bad can be a conscious and/or unconscious experience, but even if you are thinking they are bad unconsciously, this is still going to be reflected in your conscious mind, so these "preconceived notions and facts" might determine what someone is thinking about the person and how open they are to them. Or (better phrased), you thinking that someone is bad is going to have a wider impact on your feelings about them then you might think because you might be shutting off that person because you think they are bad. This "wider impact" might happen because of all those negative unconscious things you might think about the person. At any one time you could be thinking (unconsciously) a thousand negative things about them, the effect of that might limit your emotional response].

What then is the difference between thinking if someone is positive and them actually being positive? The difference is at some level (unconsciously) you are thinking that they are positive, you just might not be consciously aware that you are thinking those things. You probably also don't have control over those thoughts. Conscious awareness of as much of what is going on unconsciously with those thoughts will enable someone to understand what is going on, and possibly change what those thoughts are. [So you could be ignoring someone and you might not know it because you haven't consciously recognized that you don't like them. It is clearly shown how a person can start to consciously recognize when they are ignoring someone by the example "Ah, I was ignoring you, I'm sorry" - that also shows how powerful your unconscious mind can be, and how you unconsciously can close off negative things.]

Table 125.0

Chapter 126

Life Is Tragic

126.1 Everything in Life Is Boring

Just add, "Well, all you're doing there" before something anyone can do, and you'll realize that what they are doing is actually boring, no matter what it happens to be. Say adding 1 to 1. "Well, all you're doing there" is adding 1 to 1 to get 2. See? You can go through everything in life and eliminate it this way as boring. It's a challenge; you won't be able to find something not boring. That's proof that life is boring, and it sucks. Or say you're walking, just add, well, all you're doing there is walking, and you realize how it's actually boring.

126.2 If You're Not Doing Something Intense You're Doing Something Boring

If you're not doing something intense, then you're doing something boring. Everything in this modern life is boring because there is no real intensity. Just ask about any activity you're doing, "is this intense"? And you'll realize that it isn't. The only real intense activities would happen if there was no human civilization, and you were just out in the wild. Typing at a computer is incredibly not interesting and not a very active activity. Watching a game involves you sitting there staring at a small field for an incredibly long period of time. Think harder, really everything you have ever done, no matter how small or how big, wasn't intense at all. To understand how intense something you're doing is, just compare it to how intense your life would be if you were in the wild trying to survive on your own. Everything really is boring now. Your mind really needs to be "woken up" naturally in order for it to have maximum stimulation. When you're out in the wild hunting all your senses are on the alert so you are very energized. When you have that energy you really feel it coursing through your body. You can't have any "relaxing" factors to relax your mind, you have to be trying your hardest, and the only way you are ever going to be trying your hardest is if you're going to die from starvation if you don't succeed. That's a really terrible, slow death that will motivate you to be at your most alert. Conditions like that simply don't exist in modern society anymore. In prehistoric times you'd be doing stuff like that all the time. Your entire life would be like that, all your memories and such, so it would all add up. Even if you could do it now for a short period somehow it wouldn't be the same because your mind would still be sedated by our modern society from its memories of it. You'd be more aware of your surroundings and your physical senses would be absorbing the world around you all the time, you'd feel fresh. People today are feel stale and not alert at all. It's like long term torture by not being in a healthy state, you're basically just sleeping. That causes inner mental pain and trauma in slight amounts that is there all the time. You can feel that that pain from your slowness would go away if you were in a more natural environment, and go away even more if you were there your entire life. That energy just doesn't exist anymore - "emotional intensity" will never equal physical alertness.

126.3 God Is Evil

Take all your dreams and aspirations and goals. Unless God gives them to you right away, then he is evil for denying them to you. Unless you are as happy as you could possibly be, then something is being held back. Don't "have faith" that God is doing the right thing if you want something and it is being denied. The only conclusion to come to there is that god is evil. Everything should be yours. Unless that is true, evil exists in the world. There isn't more modesty in a humble life, if you want something, that desire is real. Life sucks because no one will ever get everything they want, and they have a right to get it. There is no reason to deny a person happiness other than to be evil and cruel, and God must be playing the world like his own cosmic joke, with all the enjoyment going to him.

Being "content" all the time isn't enough. Life should be thrilling and adventurous. How exactly is that going to happen when literally nothing in life is thrilling or adventurous? How many things can you list that make you "glow". How many things in life really give you a thrill. I can bet that very very few things do. The only way to be "thrilled" all the time would be if you were under constant pressure to live like humans existed before civilization. Civilization just slowed everything down, took human's out of their natural state, and "domesticated" them. Domesticated animals are tame, not fierce. Without that ferocity there is nothing fun to live for, you're basically just walking around bored. The sad realization is that the only way to really have fun in life is if you are forced to have fun by being under threat. That wakes up your mind like it is supposed to be woken up. Otherwise you're not "awake", you're not "alive" and you're not living. No one in modern society today is alive. They're all dead walking. They're limited by their tame and sophisticated environment, appeased by gadgets and their domination of the natural world. That appeasement leads to complacency, it's a fact that whenever you get happy you are more relaxed, or even emotional in any way you let your guard down. In prehistoric times there wasn't time to be "emotional". If you weren't emotional all the time like we are today, you'd more awake and aware, more interested in things naturally because you wouldn't be content to stay in your own mind. Unless you are under constant threat, your life just isn't worth living. The only way to be happy is to go back to before humans became domesticated animals. It's hard to accept that because your mind is trained into being "content" and its hard to reintroduce domesticated animals into the wild. Imagine being slowly reintroduced into the wild and it is easier to understand then why that would be better. The rest of this article outlines conditions which exist only in modern society, for the domesticated human. And why those conditions are bad.

126.4 Life Sucks Big Time

There is nothing fun to do in life. This leaves a feeling of extreme depression. You just have to give in and be a robot/sheep and do something that you're not going to enjoy doing because it will keep you from being depressed. The expression, "busy hands are happy hands" is one out of desperation. If you're not busy then you are desperate. Therefore you get busy so you are no longer desperate, but just because you are busy doesn't mean that you are happy. In fact, no one gets happy in life because although there are some fun things to do, these fun things don't take up enough time to do them all the time. In fact, it's not possible to have too much fun or you'll get anxiety, so we're doomed to little fun. Pick your favorite activity in which you have the most fun, and imagine doing it all day, I find that it would get boring after a while, and I can't find anything else that exciting to replace it, I think this is true for other people as well. If you aren't doing something fun, then you're doing something boring or not fun, and your life sucks. Since you can't do something fun all the time because there just isn't that much fun to be had, life sucks.

126.5 Why Life Has No Meaning

Life has no meaning because there is no reason to do anything. No one has an ultimate "purpose" in life. Everything you do you do because you have to. Even when you are trying to have fun you do that only so you can have fun. Why do you even want to be happy? If you think about it you don't need to be happy, you just want to be happy. There is no ultimate purpose in you being happy. You're not going to achieve anything other than your own happiness. You're not going to be contributing anything to the world, or making yourself look better. The sad truth is no one really cares that you're happy. Why doesn't anyone care? Because the only reason someone else would want you to be happy is if it made them happy, and since all happiness is irrelevant you making someone else happy is irrelevant. Though I don't know why anyone would want anyone else to be happy unless it somehow fit their own ends. Everyone is fundamentally selfish so in the world each person is trying to beat everyone else. That is, if they are smart they are going to try to beat everyone else, and if they are stupid then they aren't going to be contributing anything to the world because they are dumb. So it's a lose lose situation. Why would someone smart only be looking after himself? Because that's the best way to get happy, and for some reason everyone wants to get happy. We're just robots that when we get sad, a chemical is sent to our brain to make us feel bad. None of us wants to feel bad when we get sad, it just happens because we happened to have been programmed that way. If we could program our self we would just make ourselves happy all the time. If we could design a human like robot that's what we'd do. God must be an evil person for creating sadness. It serves no ultimate purpose. It's just a reality of life. That's right, people get sad, and people get happy. In fact, you're never completely happy or completely sad, it's always some mixture of the two. So the sadness is always going to be there. Not only does it exist, but it's there all the time! There is no reason why humans couldn't be programmed to never have sadness. The only reason we get sad is because god (or evolution) designed us so that we would. It's just evolutions tool to get us to do stuff we don't want to do. If you think about if you're sad, it's either because you did some things you didn't want to do, or some things were done to you that you didn't want to happen to you. So it's a lose lose situation. Either way you lost out, and there is nothing you or I can do about it. The fact is everything in this world doesn't happen the way you want it to. You can't believe in a god because if there was a god he would work for you, and everything would happen the way you wanted it to. Therefore god can't exist. That is, a good god can't exist, an evil one surely does. That's just a fact, unless everything in the world happens the way you want it to, you are losing, and god doesn't work for you. It just means that god isn't working for you, but against you. That's not a big deal since it doesn't matter that you get sad anyway why? Because when you get sad you just get hurt emotionally, and no one cares that you get hurt emotionally because you weren't contributing anything to the world to begin with. Even you don't care that you get hurt emotionally really, you just get an automatic response when you feel bad to want to make yourself feel better, that isn't "caring". If you say that people don't really care about anything, including themselves, since their entire desire to want to care about themselves is based on a preprogrammed emotional response that they don't want, then they are really just trapped in their own minds. They don't care that they are trapped in their own minds, because they don't want to care about anything because then they wouldn't be sad. If you never got sad you'd never have any desire to do anything, because there would be no motivator, because one level of happy is only relevant relative to another level of happy. That is when you're "happier" you're only "happier" relative to a "sadder" state. Therefore you have to feel sad in order to feel happy. In fact by that logic, you'd have to be sad equally as much as you are happy, and that everything that happens in life is a part of that perfect balance. In order to make you happy just as much as you are sad the world would have to be designed so that events fall into place to make that occur, so that is proof that god exists. And that god supports having emotions, both sad and happy ones. God could have designed people to have no emotion, but then we wouldn't be doing anything or feeling anything. And we wouldn't be doing anything because we would never feel sad or happy so we'd never have anything to motivate our actions. Once again sad and happy are just emotions relative to each other, you can't feel sad without once having felt happy because sad is just relative to happy. Happy is something you feel when you are achieving victory over sadness, that is all happiness is. Happiness makes you feel good because it makes you not feel sad. That's the only reason to be happy, is to not be sad. Because being sad is your only motivator. That's the only thing that you HAVE to respond to, when you feel sad, you get the feeling that you have to do something about it, and that feeling is automatic and preprogrammed into your body/mind. When you get happy, the feeling is just that you are a farther away from sadness. Our bodies are entirely programmed. You can't be happy more than you're sad because happy exists only relative to sadness, so if you were happy most of the time you would really just be happy half the time, and sad the other half of the time, get it? And the only way that people would be happy half the time is if god made the world so that events would fall into place that made people happy half the time, otherwise the equation wouldn't work and the fabric of reality would fall apart. Also, what makes emotion real or meaningful? It is just emotion. Whoever said emotion had meaning? It is just a biological response that makes you feel good. Who really cares about feeling good anyway since they are just emotions? You are just an animal, and you only have emotions.

126.6 Bad Things Exist

There are lots of bad things in the world which exist that make life worse, and there is no reason that they need to be there. There are bad sights, bad tastes, bad smells, bad feelings, bad attitudes, bad noises, bad emotions, bad situations, bad things, bad objects, bad toys. All those bad things don't have to exist, but they do. That speaks for itself. It may seem like so far there is nothing insightful in this section, however bad things are really the source of all evil. If something is evil then it is bad and harmful. Those words contribute to sad feelings. There wouldn't be a good if there wasn't an evil however. If everything was good you wouldn't know what the word good meant. Everything has to exist on a gradient from bad to good. Nothing is exactly the same. So if everything was good I guess one good thing would be good relative to something else, which is also good, but it would be bad relative to the good thing. But I mean a person is more good than a tree doesn't make the tree bad. Only bad relative to the person. So if we eliminated all things that were actually bad by themselves and left only stuff that could be considered relatively bad, then the world would be good. So the expression, "there can't be good without evil" is actually false. Bad things exist. This refutes my previous happy sad argument and proves that god really is evil, because you can be happy and have sad stuff, the sad stuff would be relative to the happy stuff, but not have any real sad stuff. And it's the fact that real sad stuff exists which proves that god is evil.

126.7 No One Is Happy All the Time

No one is happy all the time. In fact, when you realize that you're not happy all the time, you get sad, worried, and stressed. If you're not happy all the time then during the times you aren't happy you're experiencing some negative emotion. The key thing is that being happy the rest of the time doesn't cancel out those periods of negative emotion, you're still going to be sad for certain periods, during those periods you are indeed sad, it doesn't "balance out". During those periods there is nothing you can do about your sadness or discontent. Whenever you have to do something you don't want to do or feel something you don't want to feel, there is nothing you can do to avoid that reality. It's there. You can't say to yourself, "overall I'm happy because I'm happy most of the time". That's not true, overall you're sad because the negatives in life overshadow all the positives. And you have to admit, there is always going to be a negative. Life is always going to be overshadowed and under the cover of evil. There is nothing any of us can do to eliminate that evil. It's there. Whenever you're sad or down, the statement, "it's ok because it is going to get better" is wrong, because its not ok, if you're suffering, then you're suffering, and no amount of hope you have is going to change that. The mere fact that evil exists in the world is indicative that life sucks. It's obvious that all evil is never going to be eliminated, and as long as a shred remains there is still going to be the probability that you are going to run into it, or think about it, or somehow it is going to invade your life. In fact, if there wasn't evil, you wouldn't even be able to comprehend what the word evil meant, because it wouldn't make sense without evidence. So the mere fact that you can comprehend the word is evidence that it exists. Sadness and unhappiness are evils. Pain, fear, rage, remorse, negativity, sorrow, shock, terror, worry, loneliness, hate, horror, guilt, frustration, embarrassment, disappointment, discontentment, depression, boredom, bitterness, agitation, apathy, alarm all exist in large amounts in our world. In fact, those emotions probably take up at least a significant amount of each person's life. And there is no way to justify their existence. They are there, they are going to stay, and there is nothing you can do about it. There is an evil which exists which will always remain.

126.8 Life Sucks because It's Just Feelings

Everything in life boils down to a feeling. Anything you do, anything you say, or anything you think it's just going to wind up making you feel some way about it. That's extremely pathetic, that means you have to worry about emotional/feeling attachments to every single object in the world, how they make you feel, and what they make you do. That's immensely complicated. Life sucks because it is way too complicated. There must be a million different types of feelings, even for the same piece of food you could probably eat it in 50 different ways. And each time the feeling you get when you eat it is going to be different, no single feeling is every exactly the same. That means you can never say, "ah I did that before, that was fun" instead each time something happens you have to spend time and figure out if you actually like it, and if it was actually fun. However, the work involved analyzing each feeling takes away any possible fun the actual feeling could cause, if you know what I mean. Humans are burdened because they have to think about everything. Humans are the only animals I have seen cry. It seems to me that the crying is much much worse than the happiness, and the happiness doesn't "balance it out". I mean when you see someone crying that's a much more intense emotion then any happy feeling they could get. You give someone crying or very sad a more attention then you'd give someone extremely happy. That's proof that the emotion is more intense. Have you ever seen a duck cry? Nope. Ducks are happy all the time, they don't have huge emotional swings like humans do. They don't have to deal with all the trauma and bull shit. I can tell you I would be much happier being a duck. It gets even worse when there are extremely complicated negative feelings, that makes you feel like you're being pressed in by a lot of evil.

126.9 Your Feelings Are At Best Robotic

Since most of your brain is neurons feelings don't really exist, and you're just a neurological robot, that thinks. You think you have feelings, but what's really going on is just what condition your physical body is in. If you've done something to make your physical brain happy and content its neurons, then you will think that you are happy. But really all you've done is achieved a healthier state of neurological stimulus. Or a different chemical balance in your brain. So you don't need to say "I'm happy" you can just say "the chemicals and neurons in my brain are in the state that I happen to call happy". I hope you don't seriously think you're happy when really you're just chemically altered. The happiest you ever were was really just a disgusting mess of guck in your brain acting differently than it ever had before. I mean why does one mental condition matter as being better than another? It's all biology. Your body is just a bunch of neurons in your brain which are now not moving around versus moving around. Your neurons don't care if they are "happy". All they do is send off chemical signals in your brain. In fact, your neurons are constantly rearranging themselves, you are never the same person you change all the time. One way you change is you forget most of what happens to you, if your eyes were a video camera they'd be a camera with a 5 second memory that's perfect. You forget 99% of what you see. What's the point of living if you are going to forget 99% of what happened in your environment in 5 seconds? What about 10 seconds? Can you remember everything that was in your vision exactly 10 seconds ago? I doubt it. You can't even process what everything you are seeing is at one time, you can only focus on one or a couple of things. You miss MOST of what is going on. You're just a very limited biological animal, that can't remember in detail anything that was going on near them after 10 seconds. How long does a "happy" feeling stay fresh in your mind? An hour or so, then it becomes just a memory, most of which you forget in a day. If you are happy at 12:00 today you are probably not going to remember you were happy then two days from now. 6 months from now you are going to forget most minor things that made you happy. 1 year from now you're probably going to forget everything but a few things that made you happy in this month, if you can even identify why you're happy in the first place. What's the point of living if you don't remember almost all of what you live through? And you were never really happy in the first place, just "neurologically satisfied". So most of the "feelings" that you are going to forget, didn't even really exist in the first place. Also, most of the "feelings" you have aren't even happy ones. If you look back to a long time ago you probably only remember good memories, but that's because that's all you remember. That's altering your perspective on how much you go through is actually "fun". Most of the feelings you have are not "happy" ones but mundane and ordinary. Most things in life aren't fun and you can check that by seeing how your "feelings" are doing. You will realize that you're not even "happy" a tiny portion of the time. What's the point of living if you only like living it 1% of the time? Are you even happy 1 minute out of every 100? Can you say that you're happy most of the time? When you typically say you're happy you are just looking at how happy you are relative to how happy you usually are, or to how happy other people are, not how happy you really are, which is determined by looking minute by minute how you feel. If you look at it that way, (in minutes), how many minutes of each day are you happy? Probably less than 60, that's a tiny portion of your time that you happy, that means that you were never actually happy in your entire life, since that one time you said you were happy it only actually lasted 60 minutes. When someone says they are happy they are just really looking at the little time they were happy when they said it, everyone is actually overly optimist about how happy they are. Assuming you're in the BEST mental state you can be in, then you'd be at best neither happy or sad most of the time, just "going through life mundanely, not really enjoying most of it, not really feeling anything". You're just unfeeling and cold most of the time, since most of the time you're neither happy and sad. Therefore all feeling is at best robotic. When someone says to you, "hi how are you doing" and you reply "good" by good you don't mean happy most of the time, you mean, most of the time you don't feel anything at all! Because that's your best, highest mental state, not feeling most of the time, rarely being happy, and at least being sad as much as you were happy, that's the highest state you can ever achieve. Sorry

126.10 Life Sucks because There Aren't Feelings, Just Neurological

Stimulus

You should realize that humans don't really feel anything - Any feeling you have is a chemical in your mind sending off "happy" or "sad". That beauty is just how pleasing the things you see are, there isn't a delusional idea that people really "feel" or "love" Love is just a chemical in your brain. Its not a "truly moving, fascinating, deep, wonderful experience". Sorry to break it to you, but there isn't anything magical going on. No need to be delusional. They're just neurons. You're just a practical person, trying to achieve practical goals. One of those practical goals might be happiness, and love might be a way to get there, but you're really just looking after your own neurons. This brings about the point that people are fundamentally selfish, if the only thing that matters is taking care of their own mind, the only thing they care about is themself. So how is the world exactly supposed to work out if each person only cares about themself? That's the only thing to care about, how happy your neurons are, love doesn't even exist. Sorry. Nothing is "meaningful" if everyone is entirely selfish, because the only meaning you'd be seeking is for yourself. So when you say, "ah, that was meaningful" add, "aha, that was meaningful to me, and to me only, and I only really care about myself". A delusional view of life might be that the most meaning you can find is from another person/people. The truth is the most meaning people find is from themselves. Since you're most similar to yourself, you are never going to connect with anyone else more than you connect with yourself. So you're always going to be your own best friend. It's easy to prove that people are selfish, because, unlike in movies, in real life no one would actually give their own life for someone else. There we go, proved. That was surprisingly easy to prove. Either I am the first to discover that proof, or everyone else was being delusional in thinking that the world is better and nicer then it actually is, blocking out the fact that people are actually fundamentally selfish, and that it was extremely easy to prove that they are. I mean when you are talking to someone else do you think they actually care more about you then they do about themself? Nope. Even if it's a loved one they are still going to care more about themself. Sorry. There just isn't any real connection. There's an imaginary connection, because everyone is in such denial of the reality of life, but there isn't a real one. Sorry again. This works for objects too. I mean, do you care more about yourself, or your computer. Yourself. I would think that my computer is better than I am because it is so efficent and sophisticated, but even though it doesn't make any sense, I am going to think that I am better than my computer. Thats because humans are in denial that life sucks and that they are inferior to computers and stuff like that. When you walk up to the typical person and say, hey does life suck, they are going to say no. It's not that they aren't capable of understanding that life sucks, it's just that they are permanently delusional because they want to think that the world is a better place than it actually is so they can be happy with the world and themselves. That's stupid. You can be wrong, but you are going to be stupid and wrong. Just don't leave out the stupid when admitting that you're wrong. (if you are wrong that is) If you respond "life is good" then you obviously don't care at all about the 155,000 people that die each day in the world. You know why you wouldn't care about them? Because a) people are fundamentally selfish and b) you only run into a few thousand or so people yourself in your lifetime, almost all of which you meet only briefly. You may think your life is exciting and you meet and get to know tons of new people all the time, but it's actually the opposite, by "a lot of people you run into" you do see a ton of people probably in your life, that adds some excitement, but you only talk to much less. However, since you want to think your life is exciting people are just going to delusionally think that they get to know Endless numbers of people in short periods of time, that they aren't worthless and, given the number of people that know them individually, are practically famous. That they have had the pleasure of getting to know a lot of people in their life time. See even if you were famous, you still only talk to about the same number of people a non famous person talks to. A lot fewer people actually "get to know" you. It takes years to really get to know someone else. That means you can only have anything resembling a real connection with a very, very, very tiny number of people, only a few or less. Everyone else is the world is really just blank unknowns to you. And you know what I have found, even the people that know me most, barely know me at all. So basically no one is ever going to know someone else. I find that only I know myself, and even there I only know myself a little. It's a cold, empty world. Maybe if I was super smart (way smarter than any existing human) I could know everyone perfectly, but people are extremely stupid (more on stupidity in the next paragraph). That fits in with what I said before, that a delusional view of life is that the most meaning you can find is from another person/people. The truth is you can't find any meaning from life, anywhere. Seriously how many things can you say you've "found meaning" in? Probably none. And I mean finding actual meaning, obviously not found in "little things".

If you can't decide if life sucks or not, that just means that you're not smart enough to ponder the nature of your own existence. Dogs can't decide if life sucks for them or not. Humans should be intelligent and be capable of pondering the nature of their world. But they're stupid. You can't come up with a definitive scale 1-10 of how much life sucks for who and for what reasons. Most people cannot definitively say that life is good, or that they feel good most of the time. I mean, you should be able to rate 1-10 how good you feel at any moment, but you can't. If people really understood life, they'd be able to say, "ah that day was a 9 for me" and you'd be hearing things like that all the time. But you don't, people are stupid. They are not capable of pondering their own existence, since they are not capable of deciding if life sucks or not. Let alone proving it. If they could prove it they'd say something like "oh I'd rate my life a 9 out of ten". They can't do a day by day rating or a lifetime rating, or monthly rating or whatever. They only have general opinions of some individual things or events, they can't rate everything exactly or see how everything works together. So as you can see I can easily prove that human's are too stupid to prove that life sucks or doesn't suck, but since they're that dumb, we'll just go with the life sucks argument :).

126.11 Clarification

We need to be clear. Since people have little feelings most of the time, and they aren't happy most of the time, and at best they are happy as much as they are sad, then people really are robots. That would explain why everyone doesn't kill themselves since all their lives suck, it's because they don't feel anything to begin with to want to kill themselves. That makes sense. People not feeling also fits in with people being selfish, if someone is selfish, they wouldn't have any feelings, because if they did, they would care about other people, which they don't. Love doesn't need to exist if no one is going to feel it anyway. How many times a day do you "get emotional" probably none. If you aren't being emotional then what are you being? The only thing left is logical. If you're logical then you're being selfish, so the right thing to do then would be best look after yourself. To be more clear, we've established now that the best thing to do is look after yourself, which you do because you're selfish and unfeeling, and experience little emotion. If you had emotion you might care about other people, but you don't. How many times a day do you feel a strong hate or anger or love? None times, that's how many. You might feel slight amounts of that emotion, but if you do it would be for only a very short period of time, during which you probably still have to deal with other people that aren't experiencing those emotions at the same time. Sorry. It could be that there's just so little to do that you can only find things to do which produce emotion a tiny amount of the time, and that in spirit you want to be emotional and happy all the time, but can't. That is just evidence that not only does life suck and people aren't emotional, but you want life to not suck, and are just dealing with being unemotional most of the time so you can live for the brief periods of life which exist in equal amounts of sadness and happiness. Hmmm. That means "life" is really just those brief periods in which you're actually "living". That explains why some people think they are happy, because they are just referring to those periods of time, not the null void of nothingness which exists in between (during which they are sad some of the time at best as least as much as they are happy). Or the sadness doesn't occur in the null void but occurs during the emotional periods, in which case they consider being sad a happy experience solely because it is an emotional one! It's ok because this makes sense, you want to have a balance in life, happy on one end and sad on the other, in the middle a large null void during which you are logical, unfeeling, and only looking after yourself. How can you be happy if you are only experiencing emotion a tiny portion of the time? Take a closer look at your life and when you say "I'm happy" or whatnot. You probably say you're happy because there isn't a word for "I'm unemotional". You're really "logical". So when someone asks you if you are happy just reply (if you're in your best condition that is) "I'm logical". So everyone's just logical, and all their feelings are really just neurons? Where is all the warmth and love? It doesn't exist. Sorry. How many "warm" feelings can you remember experiencing this past week? Not many. How many "cold" feelings did you have? Probably a lot more. This is the sad truth to reality.

Life is cold and uncaring, logical and cruel. God must be a mean, ruthless person. We should just go on praying with no hope of salvation. That's what Jehovah did. Even though life sucks, we should continue to hope that it will get better, even though it's never going to, because that's what Jehovah did. Perfect. Brilliant. Very smart thing to do. Life isn't going to get better, it is always going to suck. And if you hope that is going to get better, you're just being delusional.

126.12 Why School Sucks

All the subjects suck because they are boring. In math the problems are boring and take too much mental effort, or if they are simple then they are just boring. History is irrelevant because people only care what is going on in the world around them. On that topic the major issues seem to be crime and war, and I don't know why people would want to hear about those bloody subjects. Companies are boring, they are in the news. Politics is just all the boring school subjects wrapped into one, and as they apply in real life. You only have to learn a foreign language because everyone doesn't speak the same one language, so while it might be useful it still sucks that you have to learn it in the first place. I mean what exactly is the point of being able to say the same word two different ways? Studying your own language usually consists of reading endless boring books your teachers consider "intellectual" but you don't. Blowing things up is fun but knowing the chemistry and science behind it is boring. Things moving is also fun but understanding the physics behind it is boring and tedious. Biology is disgusting.

126.13 Why Work Sucks

Take any regular job, like working at a sandwich shop, that's just boring making sandwich after sandwich after sandwich, etc. Most jobs are like that, doing the same thing over and over and over, its usual boring and involves, well, work. That's why it's called work, its definition defeats it alone since the words "effort, exertion, labor, and toil" are in it. I don't need to go through each job, because every job if you think about it involves doing something tedious and boring. Unless your job was to do whatever you want, but no one would consider that work, by definition. Work involves a structure and that structure is usually something other than what you'd be doing by yourself. Being a doctor is bad because biology is gross and disgusting. Working at a cash register just involves taking people's money from them, and that too is boring and tedious, doing the same thing over and over. If a job a person has to do is mechanical, boring, machine-like (that is, the person doing the job acting like a machine), repetitious (doing simple things over and over) or doing hard things over and over. Intense intellectual activity is hard, intense physical labor is hard, simple physical labor is boring, and simple intellectual activity is boring. You can't do a medium amount of physical labor without starting and stopping. And you can only do a medium amount of intellectual activity for a short time before that too becomes boring. Hard or simple intellectual activity is boring right away, (pick some examples in your head to check all that). So too much or too little physical or mental activity sucks, and "right amount" gets boring after a short period of time. The only things that are actually fun involve almost no mental activity, like watching TV or just looking around you. (TV is limited itself because its only two dimensional). Just looking around is fun for a second but that gets boring quickly, so you have to find something else boring to do fast before just looking around gets extremely boring. So since we've decided that mental activity in amounts any more than a little sucks, you now realize that there is almost nothing to do that is fun which involves little mental activity. Intense physical activity can be fun but that only lasts a short time. Medium physical activity is boring. And a tiny amount of physical activity (like walking) is boring. So basically anything physical (unless its intense) is boring. So all we have left for fun things to do is mental stuff which requires little effort, but is still fun – good luck finding that. (sarcasm) Don't consider "walking around" fun either that is just really "looking around" which we already decided gets boring fast. Now how many fun, simple mental activities pop up in your head right now. None, that's how many. There is just nothing fun to do in life, it all sucks.

126.14 Rating Activity

In the last section we started to rate certain activities we did in order to find out if those activities were boring or hard or whatnot. In life you can either be doing something mental, something physical, or some combination of the two. A mental activity can be hard to a certain degree based on how much effort you're putting into it. You can rate any mental activity you do on a scale of 1-10 for mental hardness, something like putting a towel on a rack would be say a 1, and putting 5 towels on a rack in order of smallest to largest might be a 3. The purpose of rating everything you do is that you will realize that since nothing requires 0 work, everything there is to do in life sucks, because for all of it you have to work. Unless you do so much work that it overloads your body like if you got exhausted physically or mentally you might get some kind of ecstasy or high or something, in that case you've done well, but that feeling usually only lasts a short period of time, and you had to do a lot of work to get there (like exercise hard or something). You can also rate any physical activity or a combination of physical and mental activities. Once again everything in life involves work, or effort. The feelings resulting from the work and effort in life are rarely satisfying, because in order to get a feeling powerful enough to make you feel good you have to do a lot of work making the end result not worth it. Even something like watching TV involves work, just ask yourself (in order to figure out how much work you're doing) what are you thinking about while you're watching the television. Even having feelings counts as work, if you see something violent and get a bad or violent feeling, then how much does that feeling disrupt you and how much work do you have to do to get back to how you were before you had that feeling? For each activity that you do and rated their is a corresponding feeling for, when you do work, it makes you feel bad, so really everything in life makes you feel bad because its going to be a change from how you normally are, and you have to "work" to get back to feeling normal again. Your mind has to adjust to each new feeling and that feeling of adjustment you can identify in your own mind as work, or effort. If we look closer at putting the towel on the towel rack example, the reason just putting one towel up is easier is because it involves less mental and physical work, when you're only putting up one towel you just have to think "ok put this towel on the towel rack" but when you're organizing then by size you need to say "hmmm which towel is smallest, then you need to do more physical activities to get each towel up on the rack, which have corresponding mental thoughts, put this on the rack this way and that way, slide it right a little or whatnot". So just as everything thought has a corresponding feeling, every feeling has a corresponding thought, you can't really feel anything without being able to put words to it if you try hard enough, and everything you think causes you to feel something as well. Like doing anything physical causes physical feelings, and the words you'd put to those feelings would be to describe what you did physically to cause the feeling. You have to "think" each time you do a physical action even though you don't say the words in your head of what you are doing each time. This proves that all feelings actually take mental effort, and therefore are bad for you. Thankfully most of the time you're just breathing and not thinking or feeling, which requires little effort. It also means you're a robot, however (we've been over that a little). Whenever you get a new feeling your mind does work   to make room for that new feeling. Like with the watching violence on TV example, when you see that violence you get a huge feeling of repulsion or interest or whatnot, and you can tell that your body had to work to feel that. That's because you are thinking about the violence, in order to stop that work (of thinking about the violence, that takes work the thinking about the violence) just stop thinking about it. Your unconscious thoughts are what's causing the feelings about violence. You can use that tool to analyze any feeling you get and try to change how it is making you feel, just ask, "what am I thinking about when I get that feeling". Or you could ask "what other feelings does that feeling bring up". And figure out your entire structure of feelings and thoughts. Of course things happen in life that cause feelings that you can't change or do anything about - one more reason life sucks. But you don't want to shut down completely; I mean you could view everything as just work or you could ignore that.

126.15 There Are No Happy Feelings

I said before that you can look at any feeling and ask what other feelings it brings up. You can also break down any feeling into its parts. Let's take the feeling you get of giving someone money. You feel bad that you are losing money, that is one feeling. The other person feels bad for taking your money, which causes you to feel worse because now you made them feel bad. See any action in life actually has feelings and emotions attached to it, just look at anything from all its angles to get all the feelings involved. Maybe the other person isn't very nice and feels good that they are taking your money, maybe you have a lot of money and don't care that you are losing a little. Etc. The main point is, for anything that happens in life, you are going to feel someway about it. However, in order for you to process the action that is happening in life you have to do work to convert that action into a feeling. This work means that there are no happy feelings, because even if the end result is a happy feeling, it took work to get there, and the work outweighs the happy feeling. I found this to be true looking at all feelings, don't just look at the happy feeling, but when you look at the work involved you realize that you're actually sad. Let's look at computers, at first look you might say, sure a computer would cause good feelings, you have buttons you can press and little windows that pop up, that's awesome! But you aren't looking at the fact that you have to press the buttons and you have to think about the windows that pop up when they pop up, so both things which you perceived as happy are actually sad. Everything in life works like that, each and every feeling requires work. That brings about the point that everything is really physical, because when you think about the windows poping up the thinking that you are doing is work that your brain (which is physical) is doing. So everything requires physical work. So there aren't really any feelings anyway, just physical stuff going on. And physical stuff requires work. Since everything is physical, and you are constantly moving and alive, you are constantly doing work. You're never not doing work, you're always moving, unless you're dead. You're always doing mental work as well. What makes it worse is that you can't do "less work" mentally because then you start feeling bad, (if you just sat there and did nothing without thinking about anything) so you have to do work all the time. Life is work. Life is endless, nonstop work. That's all it is. This work comes in various shapes and sizes. Doing a math problem is just the work of you analyzing numbers. Doing a chemistry problem is you doing the work of analyzing chemicals. Doing a history problem is you doing the work of looking at a certain place in time. You can't do the same thing over and over either or you'll get bored. That's why a lot of jobs suck, because you have to do the same thing over and over, and it's boring. Look harder for repetitions in life and you'll find a lot. Take working at a cash register, although you may talk to people and although the variety of items you're scanning may change, you are still scanning all day and standing in the same spot. What happens to your feeling when you stand in the same place all day? It gets more and more boring as time passes. Similarly doing any type of work (even if its easy) gets more and more boring as time passes. In fact, you can get bored just reading the word more over and over – watch – more and more and more and more and more and more boring. When you think about it most of life is just repeating stuff you've already done, just in very slightly different ways. Nothing is completely new. And when something is new, you have to do work to figure out what it is exactly, which takes away the novelty of finding something new. So since all the time you are doing work, and that work involves feelings and thought, all the time you are feeling something and thinking about something!

126.16 Interaction Theory Shows That Although Life Seems Large, It's Actually Rather Small (below)

Life is how everything in your life interacts. Interaction theory is really everything in your life, which are interactions of things within everything. Confused? An example of an interaction of life would be a pot and its handle, each is a thing individually, but the two interact in life, and form a pot and a handle. On a more complicated level, a cave man might interact with a rock, and that interaction could produce a weapon, which could cause another interaction, fighting. (fighting being the interaction between the two people, and interaction between the rock and the man, you get the idea)

You can state how any multiple things in life interact (interaction theory). You can make a relationship between any multiple things in life (relationship theory). You can rate the strength of those relationships or interactions. Everything in life (including ideas) is made up of multiple parts, that sometimes can interact with themselves or other parts in other objects or ideas. Since everything in life interacts and forms relationships (including ideas - an example of a relationship between two ideas would be the idea, let's move to France, and the idea, let's not move to France, the relationship is that they are opposites), you can say that everything in life connects. You can categorize anything in life, including ideas. Words can interact with each other, sentences can interact with each other, paragraphs can interact with other. Any idea can be broken down or translated in words/sentences/paragraphs. Any sensation can interact or form relationships with any other sensation, or any object in the real world, or any idea. Anyone can have practically infinite ideas, about practically infinite objects (or ideas or theories or whatnot).

Surely that last paragraph can be potential for an enormous number of discussion topics. If it isn't then life really does suck. That paragraph should lead you to come up with endless numbers of interactions and relationships. There should be a lot to talk about in life. If I ask someone what are possible discussion topics they should be capable of eloquently responding to me and give a large list of things to talk about. Having things to talk about is very good entertainment if you can find those things. Since people can't find a lot of things to talk about, even after I give them a head start with a potential discussion topic, or say, any discussion topic it doesn't have to be mine, then life sucks. Again, how many topics can you think of to talk about? If you start listing in your head, you will realize that you can't come up with that many. That's miserable. That means any conversation can only be so long and life is really limited to you. Life sucks. If there are a very limited number of fun things to do in life, which there are, then life sucks. How many things can you list of things to do? We've already listed that conversation is very limited itself, and there is little else to do. Sure, you could come up with a list of a few hundred things, but that's IT. It is very limited. All of life can be easily quantified and defined, and you will find the list to be very short indeed. I mean seriously, what is there to do? Everyone one knows that school sucks. School is only the first 16 or MORE years of your life. Everyone knows that work sucks, which is the rest of your life. You can't play all the time, because, believe it or not, there are only so many things or you can only play for so long. Do a list or start one in your head now, you can only come up with a very limited number of fun things to do. VERY limited. You can't do nothing, if you just stand or sit or lie in place you can only do that for so long without thinking about anything or doing anything. At best you could sit there and think about something, but we've already been over how there are limited conversation topics, (if there are limited conversation topics, there then is limited things to think about). Go on list them in your head, how many fun things are there to think about? I gave one great example that would lead to all potential things to think about in the previous paragraph, and people can't come up with many things to think about from even that. If you can't come up with anything, then that's a lot worse then finding a very tiny limited number of fun things to do.

The conclusion reached thus far reveals that most advanced things in life suck, leaving the simple, natural ones natural and true, things like eating and sleeping, do in fact help people and are in fact the only truly enjoyable things there are to do (the simple things that is, like back before modern civilization. This paper argues that all activities humans do in a post hunter-gatherer culture they don't really enjoy doing, and are deceiving themselves that they like doing it do to societal pressure to conform.

In the cases where modern society brings peace, that peace is good and you like it, but you only like it more than the alternative, war in a modern society. These wars are enormous and involve systematic organized attacks, in a hunter gatherer society there weren't anything around the size of today's nations or even older tribes that formed for organization and cooperation in a war, so there were at most tiny "battles". That is much, much less scary then having to worry about dozens of people or hundreds forming together to kill you. You basically could be alone and have a chance to defend yourself against any band of humans; the packs they traveled in would be so small, deterring them from attacking any other band of humans, because they were all basically the same size. When a war is fought in large numbers the basic humanity and individuality is taken away, a leader can say, let's go to war, he says that because he can just hide behind his men in case things go wrong. If he was in say a 10 man pack, he wouldn't say attack unless it was a life and situation where he HAD to attack, because there wouldn't be any chance of getting away without horses or cars to escape with. One of the greatest fears of modern society is going to war (the dooms day clock, etc) in prehistoric times you wouldn't have to worry about that since there weren't any armies, and the shear brutality of a human to human fight would deter most individualistic competitions. We sometimes think everything sucks, because, sometimes, everything that is happening to you does!

People didn't evolve for this modern civilization they evolved to live in a hunter-gatherer society. It is very hard to entertain people and get their attention. If you were living under conditions where you had to do stuff, like you had to hunt or you won't get food and you had to do lots of work just in order to survive, you'd be under constant pressure, and your attention would always be there. You'd certainly always have stuff to do, and that stuff would be entertaining because you'd be giving it your full attention, so it would be fulfilling. Most of our lives is spent in buildings which are extremely boring, I mean what is in a building other than a line of sight of 5 feet or less in each direction! A building is also a hard and cold object but nature is much softer. For some reason I get the feeling that I would be happy just walking around outside without modern civilization to "comfort" me. Test it out, try to imagine how that would feel. It feels much better. The threat of your life being on edge gives you a healthy amount of threat that keeps you on edge and healthy. There is also a lot less to think about so your mind is clear. I don't think people were supposed to function having to think about 1000 things each day, it takes an emotional toll that people just weren't designed to handle. If you only dealt with simple things you wouldn't have a toll on your mind. Of course, it would suck to deal with the bugs and not having a bed, so that really isn't a good solution either, I was just pointing out that this is a lose lose situation. That's why life sucks. You have to deal with endless amounts of shit in modern society, and you would have to deal with endless amounts of life threatening shit in pre modern society! But at least the life threatening stuff would be fun and entertaining because your life would be on the line, giving you a healthy amount of anxiety. In today's world everyone is relaxed and not really interested in anything they do. I can prove that because you could see a glow in someone's eyes if their life is threatened, unless we are at that level (that glow) then we're not really entertained. We're not free at all but burdened by boredom. In pre modern society you'd be free to do what you want, any old time. Now we have the police, government, whatever structure your business or school imposes on you, your family or friends impose on you, etc. If you don't have commitments and attachments, then you don't have your emotions being played with and you don't have anything to lose. The problem with that is that you wouldn't have any commitments or attachments, so that's another lose lose situation. Yoda said, "train yourself to let go of anything you fear to lose" that's good advice, because it's eliminating emotional attachments and clearing your mind, like you would in pre modern society. But you can't do that in modern society, and in pre modern society you'd be worried about losing your life all the time! Life is just endless loss.

126.17 Modern Life Is Gay

Domesticated animals are a lot less tuff then non domesticated animals, therefore all domesticated animals are gay, especially relative to a non domesticated equivalent. This relates to life sucks because not only are humans domesticated, but most of the animals they deal with are domesticated by the fact that they interact with humans to some degree. Take wolves and dogs. A dog is a domesticated wolf, it is so domesticated that its entire species evolved from wolf into dog because of its interaction with humans. So in other words, before it was dependent on itself, and then it became dependent on humans. If you're not independent, you're gay. That means you have to rely on something or someone other than yourself for your survival. Modern life is entirely relying on massive amounts of other people and other stuff for your survival. So it's entirely gay. Encyclopedias are gay, they are just massive amounts of collections of information about nothing. Nothing could be more boring and uninteresting then an encyclopedia, except maybe a dictionary. It's gay because it isn't related to your survival, it's an accessory. Why is that gay? Because when you aren't thinking about your survival you're relaxed and doing something relaxing and boring. That's gay because its not intense and interesting. Humans should be dominant over their environment, not succumb to it. The typical view is that humans have dominated nature when the opposite is true, if you put a modern human out in nature they are much less likely to survive then a pre modern one. That makes all current humans gay. They are defeated by nature itself. Gay means non intense. Things that aren't gay are intense. Nothing is more gay than an encyclopedia, which is just massive amounts of the most boring things to think about you could imagine. Things that aren't directly in your environment, and things that you have to think deeply about, are gay because they aren't intense. Even sports are gay, mostly because you aren't trying to kill the other players. You're engaged in this huge battle based on a series of pre agreed upon rules. Rules don't exist in nature, only rules of life. Things that you have to think deeply about are gay because they don't grab your attention naturally, so it just isn't possible to put as much interest in them as you could in something in your immediate environment, say a rock or anything.

126.18 Humans are too Simple

The rest of a human can be easily understood and its entire mind figured out as well, as shown by how easily it can be reprogrammed into a robot. (below) The fact that the fundamentals of life can be broken down so easily shows just how simple and pathetic life really is.

Objective: to verbally explain how to create an artificial human. One way to do this is to show all the connections in the human mind and how they work. What is one connection to start. Your physical senses you have physical sense. You have mental senses. But everything begins with a type of physical sense/sensation. So what are all the physical sensations. There are the 5 senses taste, touch, sight, sound and smell. When you walk into a room you experience all of those senses. What if you think about something, that is just thinking about a physical sensation, anything you can think about is really just a physical sensation. Everything is neurological. Including logical thinking structures, which relate in the end to physical sensations as well. Now we need to verbally explain how the human mind works. So when you see things, you get sensations. You get sensations and you get thoughts. Those sensations and thoughts cause feelings. That's it. Why do you get those sensations and thoughts and feelings? Well a physical sensation is just neurological stimulation from a sense. If you touch something neurological signals are sent to your brain that you are having feeling at that touch, that is a feeling, just touching something causes a feeling. Similarly smelling something causes another feeling. As with the other senses. Thoughts can also cause feelings, you can think about something happy or something sad. Why would one thing cause happiness? Some things stimulate your neurons while other things don't stimulate them, so happiness would be the neurological stimulation.

"Meaning" is just neurological stimulation. How do some things stimulate your neurons and make you happy while others don't? A girl might have a pretty face that when you look at makes you happy. So visually you get pleased. When you think of the girl, you would get happy, and the reason would be it stimulates your visual center of the brain. Why do pretty things stimulate the visual center of your brain? Because they are easier to think about. Why are they easier to think about? Because they stimulate your neurons. Why do ugly things not stimulate your neurons? I think because something pretty puts you in a good mood. Why would something like a pretty lake calm someone down? Its obvious why seeing violence would not calm someone down, because it causes you to think about violence which is threatening to that person, causing them to shut down with worry. In that case the visual leads to thought. Maybe something like water or a large landscape leads to no thought because there is nothing to do in those environments, because they are so peaceful and have nothing in them. And something pretty has fun things to do in it and fun things to feel, like feelings jagged edges wouldn't be fun, but feeling smooth ones would be fun because it doesn't disrupt your senses. So smooth things are prettier and jagged things are usually uglier. So the entire visual sensation isn't really a sensation, it just causes you to think about more real sensations like touch and touching things. Something jagged feels bad when you touch it so it's ugly. Why else would you take pleasure from seeing something? Seriously… The pleasure has to derive from somewhere real. Smell is just stimulating different neurons in your brain. Same with taste. How would I verbally describe smell/taste? Maybe that's wrong and feeling is just what the physical object causes you to think about. Like if you had a mechanic arm it would feel… mechanical. When you have a human arm is feels real and mushy, which is what the arm causes you to think about, mushy stuff like blood and muscles interacting. And if you get shot you think about things getting destroyed, so you feel pain. So if you had a mechanical arm it would feel exactly like that, a mechanical arm, you'd feel like a robot. So we can give our robot a mechanical body and he'd feel it just by thinking about it. And a visual processor to process the lines and smoothness and patterns he sees. Then when sees a pattern that is harmonious, he will think of harmony and that will make him happy. We can tell him what to do "get up and walk around". How would he understand that. He can learn from his visual processor, getting up would just be his observation of other things and objects getting up, when he sees a human get up they move their legs and torso in a certain way, etc. So he just copies that with his body. Simple. So just give him lots of visual data to process. With descriptions of what everything that is going on is. Then when he hears someone say that, he will understand and respond.

126.19 Either Mental or Physical

Life is empty because it is filled with objects not emotions. When you look around you now you see cold, hard objects. When you touch those objects they are all cold and hard. How many soft warm things are there? Skin isn't really soft its more rough and callus. So that leaves out animals. Even if you can come up with a good conversation, then you're just stuck in your head thinking. You're not out and about, moving around. You're really alone in your little head. And you don't move very fast, you're looking at the world from the perspective of your head, and your body can only move so fast. Even if you're in a plane or a car or a bike, your body isn't moving that much. If you're running you're focusing on putting in all that effort moving and can't really look at the scenery. So you can never really feel like you're moving fast yourself.

Where is the fun in life if you can never move around without being jarred. If your body is being moved instead of you moving like running then you're not really feeling anything because all the sensations your body has aren't collecting sensations. Just visual isn't enough because the world is cold and hard like we went over before. And you can't get enough physical sensation to please yourself. Mental sensations (like thinking) are limited because they are just thinking. So all we have left to live in life is physical stuff. But you can only move around so fast. Visual can move quickly but when it does it just becomes too complicated. And admit it, most of the time you're not running around (which would be dizzying if you did) and exercising (which would involve a lot of sweat) so you're just being cold and unmoving yourself. Humans are just little pathetic creatures that think they are powerful when they are actually weak. All golf players can do with all their strength is put a little tiny ball in a hole. Hockey players can only shoot around a puck smaller than their hand. So clearly all physical activity sucks. And we eliminated mental activity as being bad because it's too boring. That's all there is to do in life, either something mental or something physical.

126.20 Rejoicing Too Much In Negativity

People like pain too much. They like watching violence, and they laugh at "funny" violent cartoons where the cartoon characters get hurt then spring right back up as if nothing happened. That is more evidence that people enjoy pain. People also like hurting other people, as that causes pain which they can experience. This all contributes the world being sick and life sucking. People enjoy pain as well as pleasure because both in the end boil down to stimulating your neurons, it's a stimulus, and since there is nothing to do in life, some stimulus is better than nothing, even if it happens to be pain. Pain might even be as fun as happy stuff because there is just as much happy stuff as sad stuff in the world, so for you to be happiest you'd have to get half your stimulation from pain and half from pleasure. If you're watching something and it involves pain and pleasure, and a person that enjoys both pain and pleasure is there he will enjoy it more then someone that just experiences pleasure, so that person wins. Evolutionarily we evolved so that we'd enjoy both for that reason. The reason you feel from both pain and pleasure is because of what the things cause you to think about. When you see someone in action that action is fun, but if they suddenly get shot that is fun too, I can prove it's fun because it happens in movies and stuff that people love to watch, so they must like seeing it. It's fun because it causes you to think more deeply about that person and their life, the fact that they had to get shot for you to think more deeply about them is a minor detail, it just means it causes you to think about that person, and how their life is ending. It's still a lot of stimulation so it's actually a lot of fun. Life is incredibly sick. You may not be smiling as it happens (unless you're sadistic or something) but it's still stimulation, which is a relief from boredom, which you are very happy to have.

126.21 Sad Vs Pain

When you're sad it's probably from a lack of stimulus, which would cause your neurons to fire less giving you less pleasure. Pain is fun because it causes you to have a reaction, so it's a stimulus. Too much pain might not be fun however but the right amount could "wake you up" or something, you know what I mean. Sad stuff causes your mind to shut down, and when your mind is shut down it doesn't really have pain from being shut down, so it's possible to be miserable and it not be a good thing like I said how right amounts of pain could be good sometimes, just like right amounts of pleasure can be good as well. This emphasizes the point that sometimes people do have depression, and are in fact actually sad, and their lives miserable. Boredom however isn't going to cause sadness it's going to cause pain, so if an activity is boring you can still do it because you'll still be getting stimulation from it. However that's sick because you are doing something is causing you to feel pain and you enjoy it, so that should be minimized. The more pain you have the more you hate other people and hate life because you're in pain. A healthy amount of pain is ok however because it gives you the right amount of stimulus to give you a healthy edge and keep you alert, but too much will cause you to be a hateful person. Most people are hateful people because of that, they do boring stuff a lot and it causes them to hate the world, and be in pain. In fact, since there isn't enough stuff to do not boring stuff all the time or even a small amount of the time (which we've already concluded) everyone hates the world and is bitter and mean. That makes sense, if most of the stuff you do is boring, it's going to cause you pain which is going to wake you up in terms of stimulus, which would make you not sad and appear to be normal. That is what a normal person is in fact. People aren't smiling all the time. They all have inner pain, which gives them strength. Of course there are some things people enjoy doing, but those things are very few compared to how much gives them pain. This all goes to show just how easily someone can tolerate the idea of pain, so they can give pain to other people very easily and not feel anything because they are driven by it. They even enjoy watching it like violent shows or movies. Fear causes pain as well, that would be the genre "horror". How do I know it causes pain? You can tell because it causes that sharp, fast reaction that wakes up your mind and gets your neurons firing. That's stimulus which comes from pain, and the sickening feeling you get when you see it is the pain itself. So I guess just intense fear like in horror causes pain, and small amounts of fear only cause small amounts of pain. So people actually like to terrify other people and cause them pain, because it will cause their mind to think about those things, waking them up neurologically and giving them stimulus causing them to be happy. Of course, if that kind of fear like in horror movies happened to you it would be too much fear (if you were the person in the movie) but it's the right amount of fear for you to watch a lot of fear in someone else. Because it causes you to think about what is going on, which causes the right about of pain and fear. Like I said before the right amount of pain and fear are good for people, but only in the right amount which usually isn't a lot of pain and fear. That small amount of pain and fear keep you on edge and happy and stimulated. So when you watch that violence and see someone else in pain or fear, you get happy because it causes you to have small amounts of pain or fear yourself (because you have to think about what is going on, causing similar neurons to fire in your mind as the person you are watching, aka empathy). So in other words, people like causing, or watching massive amounts of pain and fear in other people!

Table 126.0

Chapter 127

Dreams Are Fun Because They Are Emotional Not Logical

We need the escape of dreams from the logical, rational world in which we operate. There is a desire within humans to break everything down and tear everything apart. Why? Because breaking things is fun. No one wants to see everything continue as usual, why? Because things continuing as usual represents nothing out of the ordinary. Things that are out of the ordinary are going to be more emotional, and more stimulating. That's why humans intentionally engineer their dreams, to have something fun to escape into. Take this dream "We're in a hotel. We all have rooms, but we're in Steve's room. There are multiple beds that may be stacked. We are trying to make music. A boy starts playing guitar and it's fantastic. Steve holds up my cell phone, it's recording, he hands it to me. Steve asks me to play it back. There is a lot of music. One song my clarinet is so sharp. Steve says 'if you can't hear that...' condescending. Steve leaves the room. We are competing for his attention, girls and boys. I am on a bed that is high. I know I'm the favorite and they're asking me about it and I decide to leave. I slide off the bed, then reach up under the rail and grab a black candle (handmade) and a cigarette and something else." It should be obvious that that is a fun event.

If you take all dreams and think about them, you will realize that they are fun, even nightmares are fun because they are emotional. It is fun for a person to have a deeply emotional experience because it is stimulating, people will do anything for stimulation even if that stimulation is a negative emotion. All dreams represent some sort of significant or large emotional event. The event doesn't have to be real it just has to provoke a large emotional reaction in the person. As long as this emotional reaction doesn't incur damage, then all emotional reactions are good. It is the saying, what doesn't hurt you only makes you stronger, only it's more like, what doesn't hurt you only makes you stronger. So if it's emotion, and it doesn't hurt you, then it makes you stronger and you even like it.

People enjoy all their dreams while they are sleeping, because during sleep they are solely emotional beings. As solely an emotional being you aren't engaging the logical part of your brain. So even if you dream about something like the death of your parent, you are still going to enjoy the dream because it is emotional and you're not thinking about the consequences of that. That is why you dream, because dreaming is fun, even if it isn't fun to think about when you wake up. If you were awake and thinking clearly you'd realize that you don't want your parent to die, but during the dream you are solely and emotional being and just interested the thrill of the death of a loved one.

That is, you are interested in the emotional intensity of the death of a loved one because in dreams you are solely emotional. You are not thinking of the logical consequences, and therefore in dreams people are just emotional. There might be a little logic, but the emotional experience would tend to override it resulting in dreams like the death of relatives. The reason you might "enjoy" the death of a loved one is because the death causes you to think more about that person because you are emotionally involved in experiences such as deaths. While awake you are intellectually involved in experiences such as deaths and this intellectual involvement would lead to a realization that they are bad, but in dreams it would lead to no realization, just feeling for the person who is dying, which you might enjoy (not the fact that they are dying).

Why again would the death of a loved one be thrilling? Because it would be a huge emotional experience, and your system is interested in the shock of that experience, that is why you are likely to dream about it. In fact, any nightmare is just really a system shock that causes a healthy amount of anxiety. The person dreaming also "knows" that it is a dream when it is taking place. You know this because in dreams you don't really worry about consequences, since they are just emotional to begin with. Logic means worrying and such, you can tell that if you had a dream of a death of a loved one, you wouldn't worry about it in the dream, but you might worry about it while you are consciously awake. Let's go back to the playing music in the hotel, if you are playing music in the hotel room, you aren't going to worry about if there are other people near you in the dream that you might wake up (and you can tell that dreams are like that). But you are certainly going to think about it in reality. That's because in dreams the emotional content is emphasized, and the dreaming mind isn't aware that the logical one is going to be upset that the dream doesn't make any sense when it wakes up, or that the logical one is going to be upset you killed a relative for fun.

Just because something is emotional doesn't mean you worry about it while you are awake. Dreams try to eliminate thinking, the less thinking, the more emotional it is going to be. So dreams might have a lot of sexual content in them as well. You dream about things you want to experience, but only things you want to experience in the dreaming state. The dreaming state is a state in which you don't have control over your body, and you have a very childish control over your emotions. Your emotions run free in dreams, if you want it, it's yours (in the dream). So dreams are a reflection of your worse desires and worst fears, because those two things are most emotional. However, in the dream you aren't really afraid because you aren't clear thinking. It's like why people like scary movies, it is something scary that you aren't directly involved in, so you can safely experience it. You aren't directly involved with the dream because it is a dream, it is not reality, and your mind responds to that by making dreams that are entertaining to watch, not to experience, so it is very similar to watching a movie, you're equally distanced from the event.

It would be more real to watch something like a murder in real life then to watch a murder taking place in a dream, in the dream situation the murder might even seem fun. That is also how people can like watching violence in cartoons like Tom and Jerry, where all the characters do is beat each other up, people even find it amusing. Watching something like that of course in real life wouldn't be amusing however (unless you're sadistic). Dreams are just like cartoons, you're not involved in it, it isn't real, and if you are involved in the dream then it isn't very physical since you can't feel your limbs. You can even feel it, imagine a cartoon character in pain, is that fun or sad? It is fun because it is just the right amount of stimulation (it might be sad intellectually, but emotionally, like how dreams are emotional, it is fun). It's the right amount of stimulation because your mind recognizes it as not real, you recognize logically that it is just a cartoon, or just a movie, and you don't feel as bad as you would if it were real. That's why in dreams we need more to properly stimulate us, because simply it isn't real. That's why dreams need to be more emotional and entertaining. If you had that much entertainment in real life (like if the dreams you had were actually real), you'd have way too much stimulation and you wouldn't like it at all. Dreams just reflect the proper amount of stimulation you need to keep you stimulated. That's probably why people dream at all, for the same reason people think all the time while they are awake, because boredom causes an incredible amount of anxiety. People simply need to think about something all of the time, even while they are asleep. But since it is a dream, they can think about things that aren't realistic and don't make sense so they can have fun during those dreams. Doing something like moving some stuff around might be entertaining in real life because you are physically doing it, but in a dream it just wouldn't suffice, you would need something spicy taking place like death, sex, fear, desire, emotion, or strong emotion.

Table 127.0

Chapter 128

How Beauty Can Be Quantified

In order to quantify beauty we first need to come up with a scientific measure of attractiveness. Why are some things ugly and other things attractive? Attractive means appealing and why do some things cause pleasure visually while others don't. You can compare attractive objects to find the answer! Some pretty things have an organization to them, a structure to them like a messy room wouldn't be pretty because there isn't any structure. With structure it's easier to separate the objects in your head so it's not confusing and it's easy and pleasurable to "think" about (maybe you see confusion so the emotion is created in your mind, and you become confused). What about a star versus a circle? The star is more complicated than the circle. That is why it is more beautiful (a simple circle is clearly very plain compared to a star, so maybe because there is more think about with the star it is stimulating and therefore beautiful. Just think of your mind as a computer, the star would take more processing power to analyze. So what about a circle versus a square? The circle is one line but the square is 4 lines that's why the circle is more appealing, it isn't as jagged or rough so feel more cozy with the circle. A square looks flat and that's unattractive for similar reasons. Rough things might seem unattractive because when you touch them they feel bad (or you could say they are less wholesome in your mind causing them to generate more pain because people want to feel comforted). So your opinion is biased. A circle is easy to think about because you only have to think about one line. Since the star has more lines than the square and it's more beautiful, so maybe a triangle is prettier than a square (because a triangle looks like a star)? But a triangle is prettier than the circle because it is more complicated. So a square is too complicated, a star is just complicated enough, a triangle is a little less complicated than that, and the circle is too simple. So in order of prettiness there is star, triangle, circle, then square.

You can take that analysis of basic shapes and apply it to all other objects because all objects consist of some pattern of those basic shapes or shapes similar to them. Like the cushions of a couch might be pleasant because they are round and we described the circle as more pleasant than a square because it is round.

More Examples:

A dog would prettier (or cuter, more appealing) than a circle because it's more complicated than the circle, the circle is too easy to think about. A dog is much more interesting because it has many more lines that flow nicely and is cute. The star, however, is more pretty than the dog because it's more complicated, the dog might be cuter but since the triangle is structured it is more perfect and therefore more appealing in a pretty way, instead of a cute way like the dog. The dog is one wandering line but a triangle is more structured and structure is going to generally be considered to be more pretty and appealing. The star/ triangles however with its structure is harsher to look at with the sharp edges, a dog doesn't have any sharp edges. Like wrinkles might be considered to be uglier than a plain face because the plain straight face is cleaner and more structured.

There is more than just lines that makes something beautiful and ugly, however like color and brightness and texture. Crystal is usually more pretty than glass, it is because it is shinier and brighter so it catches your eye, you don't have to try hard to focus on it, so it's easier to think about and therefore more beautiful. If you could only see in black and white you would probably think the world is uglier than it is with color because with color you can more easily separate objects because they are more different from each other with all the colors. You could also compare it to seeing in just say green and blue. Black and white are also less bright than the rest of the colors, so it would be harder to see things because they wouldn't stand out as much and it would be harder to see. Therefore it would be harder to think about the objects causing less pleasure and cause you to name them as uglier. That's probably why the color gold is usually prettier because it is very shiny and attractive, it draws the eye and is easy to notice (hence think about). So there are different factors in beauty one is color/brightness the other is its structure and what shape the object takes and how big it is.

Start with what you have there (above) and try to come up with more examples to explore quantitatively figuring out beauty more.

Like when you look at a book, you see a flat plain on one side, and sharp edges. Looking at the edges doesn't cause pleasure because they are sharp, but because they are lines, it further causes pleasure because they are nice, straight, even lines. Looking at the face of the book, (the large flat area) causes a more peaceful type of pleasure that you get when looking at any wide open large flat area/plain, like a peaceful, calm lake. That's because there aren't any lines in the space to distract your mind, so it's peaceful.

Take that idea further, what feeling now do you get when you look at a line that curves? As your eye travels over it, you have to pause mentally to see it curve, your mind stops and pauses at the curve, which means you need to put more mental effort to see it, and since being active causes pleasure, this causes you more pleasure by causing more neurons to fire from the effort. You get that feeling when you look at a curving line too, not just one that curves suddenly, because your mind can't just go from one point to the next, it has to slow down and follow the curve.

Now put everything I said about lines and curves together, and try to get the larger picture of how it all works together, so you can sense the feeling of how beautiful each thing is.

Anything in life is made up of lines and curves. Since you know how much pleasure each line gives you, just add up the pleasure from all the lines in a certain object, (like a person, or a box) and subtract all the annoyance trying to look at that object causes you (sometimes an object has too many lines, unlike a lake, and it would cause head pain if you look at it too closely), so subtract the negative feelings from the positive ones to get the total pleasure looking at the object causes you. Just add up each line, each curve, each time your mind pauses (unconsciously and consciously) how each one of those unconscious pauses causes pleasure or pain and how much pleasure or pain. I showed you what an unconscious pause was when I showed a sharp curve or an angle with two lines meeting at a point, it would be a bigger pause to stop at the point, and a slower pause to see a curve, and slower and slower of a pause until that curve becomes a line, which has no mental pauses (conscious or unconscious) because you just look at the line, your mind doesn't have to consciously or unconsciously follow it around corners or up or down along the curve, it just goes from one point to the next. So when you're stopped and looking at something for a long time, your eye follows its lines, that's what happens when you look at it for a short time as well, only it happens mostly unconsciously and is what causes pleasure or pain to look at the object, and in differing amounts.

We need to relate this to our real experience of seeing things, and the real pleasure and real feelings we experience when we see them. Take looking at a lake. Isolate the pleasure and feelings you get when you look at the lake. If it's a large lake, you probably get a peaceful, calm feeling. Or even looking at nature scenes brings a sense peace and calmness to you, that's why they show pictures of prairies on a plane before it takes off, to calm down the passengers before the scary flight. What is beautiful about a lake or those nature scenes is that they are both large areas with all the lines connecting smoothly, moving about slowly and naturally in a way that is easy for your eye to follow. If something is easy for your eye to follow then it causes some mental stimulation, which is pleasurable, in fact, it causes the right amount of mental stimulation per minute, not too much too fast, (like how sharp edges cause you to pause over them suddenly, which hurts your mind because your eye has to stop (consciously or unconsciously) and go in another direction). That's why lake and nature scenes are pleasurable, because they give the right amount of stimulation per minute. Each line that is easy to look at is a smooth, flowing line that causes pleasure. So add up all the lines and you are just looking at a bunch of smooth, flowing lines that cause pleasure, yet fit in together so you don't have to repeat looking at each different one. Now analyze why you feel good when you look at a lake or a calming nature scene, it's for the reasons above. Those same principles of lines apply when you look at anything; just apply those principles to anything you look at.

To get the happy, peaceful feeling you get when you look at a lake, that feeling comes from all the lines in the lake. What are those lines? They are each wave or one wave, times one hundred, making up the entire lake, plus each blank space in between each wave. So just looking at one wave, or tiny wave that makes up lakes, I guess you could call them large ripples, won't cause pleasure by itself, but looking at all of them does. People are like lakes, they are made up lots of tiny lines added together. Try to add up all the lines and see what the feeling you get from all the lines added up is, not just one of the lines. To get the feeling a certain type of line causes, you can't just look at that one line to see what the feeling is, you have to take that one line and multiple it by a hundred or more, (like when looking at a lake) to see what the feeling the line causes. Then you can take each line and find out what its feeling is. Then when you have a bunch of different lines, you know the feeling for each little line, just add up the feelings of all the different little lines to get the feeling of the entire thing. People aren't just made up of curvy lines with blank spaces in between like lakes. To get the feeling of one curvy line with blank space around it (as in a lake) look at the entire lake and then divide by how much smaller one little wave is with blank area around it, and you then get the feeling for blank space with wave in it. You can look at that feeling (or feel that feeling) and then get the feeling for little, blank space, or little wave. You can then imagine what the feeling for large wave is (just multiply it by the little wave) or large blank space (just multiply it by the feeling of little small space). Since everything in life (including people) is made up of little wavy lines or little straight lines (straight lines from the book, wavy lines from the waves) or blank empty spaces in between (from looking at the spaces on the lake or the blank space in the center of the book cover). You can get the feeling for anything! Just add up all its individual lines, waves, and spaces. Make sure to cover each spot, until you get the entire space that you are looking at. And you can compare each spot to a wave, line, or space, as that is what everything is made up of.

Also when things form together it results in a different impression as well. Say if you were looking at something jagged, well that's lots of individual things which may look pretty by themselves, but together they look ugly because they don't match with the other thing. Or your eye has to pause from one thing to the next (so it's like pausing over an angle or a sharp curve, your mind has to slow down or your eye has to slow down when it hits the bend or angle because it has to stop). So your mind might have to stop a lot when looking at something jagged, but when looking at a lake it can process all the pretty waves and go smoothly from one wave to the next, instead of being interrupted. So the wave gives the right amount of stimulation, say if each wave was the same as each other wave, it would be boring looking at the entire lake, but since each wave is different it's fun to look at the entire lake, your mind and eye doesn't have to stop suddenly anywhere, and everything is different, new, and interesting. The large dynamic line structure of the lake is both pleasing and interesting and peaceful.

So it was easy to analyze how the lakes make you feel because it is just the combination of many similar lines or units of space. The way each line combines with the space around it is the same for each wave. A person has many different types of lines interacting with each other, so you have to look at how each line combines with the space around it. Say how a circle would interact with a square, instead of (with the lake) a wave interacting with a large blank space around it, than more waves and more blank spaces. We showed in the beginning that a circle was peaceful to look at because your eye never gets interrupted, but it causes pain to look too closely at a square because of the four sharp edges your eye has to stop at. So when you look at a circle that is in a square, or a square in a circle, you get the feeling of the square and the circle. Someone's face is made up of different angles as well, and things that look like squares and circles. Take each individual part, add them up, and you get the feeling for the entire face. Then do that to each arm, leg, major body part, and then see how each fits with each other, to get a look at the whole person, and how they appear. So individual parts of an object each add their own beauty to the whole, you can literally add up the parts to see what the feeling the entire thing causes is.

If you're projecting feelings for something but not actually looking at it, then you just aren't looking closely enough at the lines and angles. You can actually enhance the feeling of anything you look at by looking at it more closely. If you find that you can't look at something more closely, then unconsciously you don't want to look at it because you're projecting a false image of how that actually looks. So take the lake. If you just look at it for a second, you don't get a sense of peace and calmness, but if you pause and look at it thoughtfully, then you realize that it brings a sense of peace and happiness. If you're projecting that sense will never be there. You need to be in a normal, non-psychotic state of mind to properly appreciate beauty. It requires deep thought (and a calm mind) to appreciate true beauty. Like if you rush looking over the sharp angle (in the book) you wouldn't pause over it and you wouldn't really even see the book at all.

If you're just jumping from a sight to a feeling (you shouldn't get a strong feeling when you look at something because it is just something visual) then you don't have a clear state of mind. Make sure your mind is clear when you look at things in order to get a sense of its true beauty. You won't be able to take any pleasure looking at something if you are associating it with something else, because the fact is you can take pleasure from looking at anything in life, since it is all visual stimulation. You must have a preconceived notion about how someone that looks like what you are looking at should look to get that false feeling. That false feeling could come from anything, some inner fear you have of the world manifesting itself. A lack of self confidence leading you to believe you are a failure and worthless. That would lead to you think you are ugly,

if you think something, then when you look at it all you have to do is associate that thought with the object you are looking at.

So when you look at something and are appreciating it for its beauty, you should get a sensation, not a feeling. That's because everything visual is a sensation, not a feeling you get that would result from something psychological, or something deeply psychological. You know what a sensation is compared to a feeling because sensations are shallower things resulting from a different part of your brain. Sensations like touching, if you touch an object it might result in a feeling, like a feeling of a remembrance of a memory of when you were near that object before, but you can focus on the feeling from the physical sensation of touching it, or the physical sensation of seeing it, not thought or feelings that come up from deep inside your own mind which don't relate to how the thing actually appears or looks. And the feelings those looks or touching it or whatever causes you.

Only if you have an exceptionally strong feeling associated with the object would the feeling override the sensation of looking at it. It's logical to feel a sensation when looking at something because that is what you're doing, looking. You're not thinking about something that might cause a different feeling or any feeling at all, looking at things simply shouldn't result in feelings, just sensations. Looking and touching and smelling aren't deep emotions or feelings at all. Well the sensation of looking might cause a feeling of the sensation, but not a feeling of a thought in your head (say that you are ugly). There shouldn't be any thoughts when you look at something, just your natural, unhindered appreciation of how it looks. I say appreciation because it takes work to look at anything, and that work makes your mind contented by relieving it from boredom.

So it's clear that if the connection between an image and the sensation of that image is broken, you have a problem. Every image should have a sensation, because that's what seeing is, it's a sensation not an emotion. That sensation is just a sensation, and nothing more. The only reason it might be connected (the image) might be connected to an emotion is if the sensation you get when looking at something you have thoughts about, ah that sensation is an ugly sensation, or that sensation is a good sensation, therefore the object must be pretty. You just need to relate the image to a sensation, then the sensation to an emotion or feeling, not the image directly to an emotion. Your intellectual mind is overriding your natural feelings. It is very hard to explain why that is happening.

Why would someone's intellectual mind override their natural feelings about something? There must be some strong fear of the natural feeling. You would know if you have a fear about something if when you pause to think about it, you feel a slight (or large) sense of fear. Even a slight sense of fear about something might cause you to avoid the real feeling, because at a glance that slight fear is tiny, but if you paused over the fear it would become very large. So then it wouldn't be a tiny fear, but a large one. So that person simply isn't confronting their fear over the issue. To avoid the slight amount of fear they get over looking at something, they simply replace it with a larger emotion (something like, I'm ugly) which is worse then the actual sensation of just the feeling! They need to let that natural pause take place when the slight fear comes in, allowing them to experience the full fear. Then they can logically analyze it and see if that fear is actually rational.

So, basically, you need to confront your fear in order to figure out if you are blocking any sensations. In any event, at least don't associate a wrong sensation or emotion to what you are actually looking at.

We can further analyze how things look and therefore how they make us feel. So we figured out that flat surfaces make us feel good because they are peaceful, like the lake. If you pause and stare intently at any flat surface you get a sense of peace and happiness. The size of the flat surface changes the happy or sad emotions you are experiencing as well, if it was a very very large flat surface, like a plain outside in the wilderness, you would get a sense of awe because your eye can wander in any direction and you wouldn't have to stop your eye, and that would be even more peaceful in a way. Or something like a soda can has a small flat surface that is easy to look at because it is small so it isn't a lot to process, so it's fun to look at because it causes pleasure but doesn't overwhelm your eye by being too much to see. Something like the flat surface of a desk causes a little more pleasure (because of the larger flat surface) but it isn't as fun because your eye doesn't get to jump around as much due to the larger space, it would jump around more slowly. Now you are starting to get an idea of how you can take anything in your environment, or everything in your environment, put it all together, and get a general sense of how vision effects your emotions and how you are feeling at any given time.

So when you're in an office with mostly a desk you feel at peace because of the large flat surface of the desk which is separated by the floor by a large distance that makes the flat surface stand out so you notice it more and get more pleasure by looking at it. A flat surface on a wall causes some pleasure but not as much as the desk because it doesn't stand out as much. The floor of the room causes some pleasure, less than the desk and more than the walls, cause there is probably some pattern on it or it has a more appealing color/shininess than the walls. Like a stone, wood, or carpeted floor would have more shine to it than the ordinarily dull walls, that shine naturally draws in our eye which makes it easier to see, and, therefore, more pleasurable. Objects on the floor also stand out a lot because they are in three dimensions and very much unlike the walls and floor, and even the desk because the objects are small and stick out a lot like little towers. The desk your eye can't isolate because it is too big, and it doesn't have a pattern on it. The carpet on the floor would be more pleasing to look at than the desk because it has a pattern on it. The desk just isn't as much detail, but on the other hand the desk is probably more peaceful, the fact that it stands out more than the wall (because it is more 3d) makes you pay more attention to that flat, peaceful surface so it's a flat, peaceful surface that you are drawn into. The fact that you are drawn into it makes it more pleasing because you don't have to put as much effort into trying to analyze it as deeply. So now we have all the major aspects of the room analyzed and quantified for beauty.

Something like the sun causes peace and wonder because it is a large ball surrounded by a huge emptiness, the sky. The sky causes wonder and is a little daunting because it is so big and intimidating, it seems to even have a depth to it so your eye can wander through it at any level and you'd be wondering what is in there.

Looking at grass is like looking at a pincushion, there are multiple sharp points which your eye clearly focuses on, so it's like jumping around from one thing to another very fast, almost being traumatic to look at that takes so much effort to do. A mirror would be more pleasurable to look at because of its flat surface than a closed curtain, which is very wavy. That flat surface causes peace because your eye can stop and pause, but with the curvy surface you can't pause. It is interesting to see what happens to your feelings when you take your eye and go over objects slowly.

Table 128.0

Chapter 129

What Makes Humans Conscious?

Information processing can occur in computers and in life forms less advanced than humans (other animals), so therefore what makes humans conscious is advanced information processing. What consists of advanced information processing is primarily the ability to reflect and from this reflection, experience deep emotions. Dogs seem to experience deep emotions, they are known to be emotionally sensitive, and from that observation comes the conclusion that it takes more than emotion to be conscious. Simply experiencing deep emotions doesn't make someone conscious. If you understand the place each experience you have has relative to your life as a whole then you enrich the emotional and cognitive processing of each experience. A dog will also be able to reflect on each experience and its place in their life as a whole, but it doesn't seem like the dog really understands as well how important it is. The dog will not be able to describe with words different aspects of his experience, how it made the dog feel, why that experience was important to it. However, not all of experience can be defined by your ability to describe it with words, there can be very subtle levels of emotional learning involved, that even if you can't describe it with words can change who you are. When you process an experience, learning is going to be involved. You reflect on the experience on many levels, there is the actual experience, and then there is going to be what you think about it in your mind. You think about it in many ways, and how it relates to many aspects of your life. This reflection is a representation of the actual event in your mind. The nature of the experience becomes changed based on how it relates to your life. For example, you may say, "that event wasn't that serious because I have done that before and don't care", or you could say, "that experience was serious because I learned something new".

Those examples show how you can reflect on an experience on many levels. All those levels are processed unconsciously. If you think about them with words and describe them, it only makes them conscious and might change how you process them a little, but you still would process them and be changed by the experience if you don't reflect on it with words. The point is that high level thinking occurs by any simple experience. This is what makes humans conscious because it shows how we understand a situation and its place in our life. That type of higher level thinking shows that it is also possible that you learn from every situation in life. If you can process it on so many levels, and ask so many questions about it, then part of consciousness is learning. Sometimes people note how they are unconsciously pondering about something or worrying about something. Higher order thinking and conscious processing of events is similar. You unconsciously process events and they have a certain level of clarity and distinctiveness in your mind, or lack thereof. A micro level example of this would be that you might only process a certain event fully and gain a high quality understanding of it after a certain amount of time has passed. After certain periods of time the experience might be subject to different levels of thinking about it. So it might take time before you realize something in specific about an experience. The time processing it without words is a part of a higher order network of thinking and associations relating to each other in your mind that helps make us reflective and conscious.

After pointing out the importance of unconscious learning and knowledge, the next observation to make from that is how much unconscious knowledge influences our conscious understanding without our consciously understanding what it is that lead to your conscious understanding. For instance, real events are going to make you learn something, but you aren't going to necessarily know what exactly caused that learning, or even be aware that you learned something. Also, how is it so certain that people always learn from experiences? Just because you have more experiences does that necessarily mean that you are learning? Is it possible to have such a high order processing system without using words, that is independent and functions by itself and learns progressively?

Table 129.0

Chapter 130

What to Do About Negative Emotions

1. All emotions and feelings (positive and negative) arise from situations and stimuli in the physical world

2. Those emotions and feelings turn into thoughts in one's head that can either be (+) or (-) (negative emotions amplify probability of negative thoughts which are of the same nature as the corresponding emotion)

3. One can track the progression from stimuli to emotion/feeling to thought, and any other changes or developments that may arise from one specific emotion or feeling (i.e. other emotions or feelings, the changes in severity of emotional feeling, such as spikes etc.)

4. In abstracting and analyzing this progression one begins to remove oneself from the (+/-) emotions/thoughts themselves and brings themselves into a state of logical reasoning

5. In an abstracted state of logical reasoning the issues under analyzation become de-personalized, [as in they can even be viewed as emotions not belonging to you but to said subject person A who doesn't really exist].

6. As one attempts to logically analyze these thoughts, as if they belong to another person and not oneself, one becomes calm simply through the process of logical reasoning.

7. In addition to the calming process created through the logical reasoning and the gaining of distance from one's upsetting thoughts/emotions/feelings, one is now in a state from which one can start to understand the causes and reasons for one's negative feelings, emotions and thoughts

8. Once these causes have been identified, and the person is in a calmer state of mind through logical reasoning and abstraction, it becomes more possible to identify possible ways to prevent and/or alleviate the development of harmful negative feelings/emotions/thoughts in the future (as in, through asking oneself, was this stimuli worth the strong negative reaction I experienced from it? Etc).

The Eight-Fold Path; What you can do about it:

1. Recognize that all your emotions/feelings have a source

2. Identify source of negative feelings/emotions

3. Identify source of (a) positive feeling for comparison

4. Try and determine why source (stimuli) caused negative/positive emotion

5. Recognize that your negative emotion/feelings caused specific negative thoughts which may in turn cause further negative emotion

6. Identify the specific negative thought (if you can do this during the strongest part of your negative thought you will be most capable to combat it through creating the highest contrast- as in, become as clear thinking and logical as possible during the moment of high emotion to best remove yourself from the emotional moment) It is important to do this during the strongest parts of the negative thought/emotion/ feeling (this can be applied for long term depressions, or short anger tantrums, or short feelings of sadness, or short or long feelings of any negative emotion you don't want) In order to do that that means you have to closely follow your emotions so you can identify which parts are the worst, if you follow them even

more closely you will recognize that sometimes there are sharp spikes upwards of negative thought, and if you could use this method during those times it would be best.

(Through this pattern one stops and thinks about ones emotions/feelings in a logical/abstracted manner thereby removing oneself from the feelings themselves. Therefore logical reasoning becomes a therapeutic action by which the person starts to feel calm even in the action of analyzing his/her own emotions. This has the potential to combat depression in two ways:1) by first removing the person from their own emotional torment for the moment of analyzation 2) once in this state the person is in a better position to come to conclusions as to why they have developed negative thoughts/emotions 3) once certain conclusions have been discovered as to why the person has developed negative feelings/emotions/ thoughts, in combination with the greater state of calm induced by logical reasoning, the person then has a greater capacity to find ways to prevent and/or lessen current negative thoughts/emotions/feelings.)

7. Try and determine why the emotion caused a positive or negative thought

8. Ask yourself: (are you certain your depression is justified i.e. are you reacting appropriately to the outside world i.e. do you need to be depressed? i.e. can you be responding positively instead of negatively? Do the negative feelings/emotions/thoughts need to be negative? Are you giving too much attention to your negative emotions (or the stimuli that caused them); are they this important? Thinking about positive emotions enhances positive emotions...)

Table 130.0

Chapter 131

The Sum of Existence

131.1 Conscious Reality vs. Unconscious Reality

The world is processed consciously and unconsciously, so reality exists in conscious and unconscious forms. The world is processed unconsciously first, since the unconscious is much faster and more powerful than the conscious mind. This means that all consciousness is is an understanding of what it is your unconscious is processing. So there is a reality which is unconscious, however, consciousness is the only reality that really matters because although you can feel things which are unconscious, and although you are currently feeling things which are unconscious all the time you only truly feel things until they come into your conscious understanding. This conscious understanding usually is slower and occurs after the unconscious experience. If you swim in a lake you feel the water and such, however you only actually feel the water when it occurs to you that you were feeling the water. The conscious experience occurs just slightly after you touch the water. The immediate feelings you get from the water are physical ones, when you touch the water with your hand you are going to feel something, but then you think about what you just did, and you feel it deeper. The longer you process what you just did (touch the water) the more the experience sinks into consciousness. Consciousness then is really just awareness that you can identify and play with in your mind. Conscious feelings are feelings that are tangible enough for you to understand. You can have a reality that is solely unconscious, but it is going to be harder to remember this unconscious reality unless you can "grasp" onto it consciously. You feel the water when you touch it, but it only really matters that you touched it until a few split seconds after you touched the water when you realize consciously, almost in a verbal manner (you almost saying to yourself unconsciously "I touched the water").

131.2 Who Am I?

When someone thinks, "who am I, what is the essence of me" they would then think about their feelings, because who someone is is a compilation of what they feel. People are the sum of their emotions. Emotions are longer than thoughts and there are much fewer of them, so when someone thinks "who am I" they think about their consistent emotional response to the world. They might respond to the world in a similar manner throughout life, and the things which are the same about why they originally responded to the world (their earliest memory of how they responded to the world emotionally) and the way they respond to the world now, are going to be the things which composite the core of their being, because there is something about humans that stays the same since birth till their death, and this thing is going to be the core of their being. People obviously change over time, but their original response to the world is going to be the simplest way to understand what emotions that person is trying to evoke from the world. It is also going to be the response they are ultimately trying to achieve throughout their life, only more and more complicated versions of it as they get older. Say someone was trying to get the world to invoke in them a feeling of slight delight. When they are first born they are going to experience this feeling immediately as their primary emotion, there may be other feelings that person is feeling, but this feeling is going to be clearly dominant. As that person gets older more and more feelings are going to appear but the goal of all of these new feelings is going to be to try to understand why their original, primary feeling felt the way it did. It feels like the goal of all those feelings is that your primary intent in the world is to understand your true nature.

How a person responds to the world originally is the core of their nature. This core never changes because you forever remember that response (consciously or unconsciously) who you are is just a building up of more and more responses over that one. You are still the same person you were when you were born, however, because you remember how it was that you first responded to the world and all your new responses are primarily based off of your old ones. This means that you are going to be trying to invoke the same feelings in yourself forever. How you originally felt when you came into the world is how you originally thought about yourself, your original understanding of who you are. This makes it not necessary for understanding of oneself to be completely conscious, because you understand yourself to be who you want to be otherwise you wouldn't have any feelings because you wouldn't agree with who it is you are. Someone can dislike something they did, but when they did that action they purposefully did that action weather or not they did it consciously or unconsciously, because if you do something it is coming from yourself, and you are pleased with who it is you are and who you are is going to determine how you respond to the world. If someone wished they were better at football then it might be a future goal to get better in the future, but they are still pleased with how good they are at football at that moment, because they are pleased with who they are as a person. If someone is not pleased with who they are then they are not in agreement with their existence. That is not possible because then you would cease to exist. Conceptually one has to exist as well as physically, and someone wouldn't exist on a conceptual level unless they were capable of thinking and feeling. If you are capable of doing those things then you would simply (conceptually) feel and think what you wanted to feel and think. You exist, and your existence is a singular point. This point is so simple that it can feel and think what it wants. If reality doesn't correspond with those thoughts and feelings then that fragile point would cease to exist. Therefore for anything to exist in reality all of reality must correspond with the thoughts and feelings of this tiny, tiny singular point.

Someone fundamentally feels what they want to feel and thinks what they want to think. People have control over their own actions and can direct what they do and think, those things then direct what they are going to feel. If someone does things and they don't understand what feelings their action is going to cause then they are not a conscious being. They need to understand the full impact of what their actions are going to do to themselves otherwise they don't fully understand their existence. If someone doesn't fully understand their own existence then it would be possible for things to happen which should cause them to be fundamentally upset with themselves because those things are not in concordance with who it is they really are. Who it is they are is someone that wants to think what they want to think and feel what they want to feel. Reality may not correspond with those desires, however, if you don't understand that reality is not corresponding with those desires. You will not be at odds with your existence if you don't understand that you are actually, truly sad. If someone is at odds with their existence then they would cease to exist because conceptually their existence would no longer make any sense. So therefore the degree to which you understand yourself is also the degree to which you can control reality. If someone is fundamentally upset with something then they aren't going to be getting what they want. This would not work because then there would be no meaning to their existence, and if there is no meaning to their existence then conceptually reality would no longer exist because otherwise they wouldn't have been born in the first place. They wouldn't have if they are capable of thought, which means then that they would conceptually view their existence as positive, and people tend to view themselves as good people otherwise they would have no meaning to their existence.

If someone is capable of clear thought then the conclusion they are going to reach (consciously or unconsciously) about their existence is that it should be positive. If someone actually has a soul (or a clear thinking unconscious) then that would be displeased with the idea of reality not being positive and therefore would get so upset that reality wasn't positive that it would no longer exist. If things don't agree on the conceptual, perfectly clear level of thinking arena then there isn't an emotional battle or struggle like their might be in real life, either it works or it doesn't work, like how you can't get a partially right answer in math because it is so concrete, there is only one way for things to work because conceptually everything is perfect because it is so real or solid (concrete).

What if someone doesn't know everything that they want? Someone can want things consciously and unconsciously. The ideal would be to get everything that you want unconsciously because the unconscious determines how you feel much better than the conscious. You can think that you want something but you might be consciously wrong. You cannot be unconsciously wrong because the unconscious is just feelings, and if something is going to make you feel better then your unconscious would feel that and "understand". On the other hand you and your unconscious might not know everything that would make it feel better, it might not understand that if it was in a more complicated state (more developed) that it would then want that. The only thing to happen then is that it would have to be developed. But conceptually you might also want this development and that could occur as well as getting what it is that you want currently. Conceptually you are going to want what you want and it wouldn't seem right if reality then didn't take the next step and give you what you really wanted, which is a more complicated existence that would need to be developed. However that means that currently you aren't at your highest point, and therefore aren't getting what you really want. Except you also want development so it would it might be a trade off since you are only capable of wanting so much at one time, so you might sacrifice current pleasure to focus on wanting development. The natural tendency would be to want everything in the world at once, but that is simply not possible because it would overload you. Therefore not getting what you want is part of the human condition. You cannot simply take the "pleasure" factor of human existence and increase it infinitely. There are multiple components to life.

To achieve ultimate pleasure humans don't just experience "pleasure" but there are other factors such as physical pleasure, emotional pleasure, physical stimulus, emotional stimulus, being at peace, being excited, there are other emotions aside from pleasure which all combine to make life (also thoughts). So reality and what you "want" is going to be very complicated. You achieving current satisfaction might not be satisfaction on the conceptual, intellectual level. You might be more satisfied that you are developing, or that some long term goal is going to be achieved then the current pleasure. An example of that would be not overeating and enjoying yourself because you know that in the long term you are going to get fat. Although currently you are going to be experiencing less pleasure by not overeating, you would also feel bad that you are sacrificing your long term health. There thought takes over from pleasure. Thought is one of the other components of life that seemingly defies pleasure because it can override it and leave you feeling less satisfied in the animal, pleasure like way but more satisfied on the conceptual, thought level. It also feels like this long term "problem" of doing things that reality requires is getting the way of current pleasure and that might make someone feel bad that they aren't getting everything that they want right then.

Therefore what someone unconsciously wants fully might not be what it seems you might unconsciously want fully. There might be more advanced concepts involved in what you unconsciously fully want because of the long-term reality factor discussed in the previous paragraph. However if you understand that some things clearly are not going to be good for you then those things aren't going to exist if they really aren't good for you. You might be wrong, but if you conviction of belief that you understand something to be really bad for you and therefore shouldn't exist is strong enough then it probably isn't going to exist because you would be at odds with your existence. You cannot be at odds with your existence because who you are is someone that fundamentally is what they want (conceptually). As someone develops their convictions in what they want might become stronger, thereby causing reality to change to reflect this. But what about the unconscious? What if your fundamental existence, your singular point or even soul isn't advanced enough to want more grand things. Like a rock doesn't seem likes its existence is that meaning full. But the soul of the rock might only be capable of comprehending that it wants a sturdy, stable life. And that is what it is then going to receive. If someone's soul was infinite conceptually then they might receive everything that they conceptually want, but what about what they physically want? Or are there even other factors in life other than conceptual or physical? Also what is really conceptual since all of life appears to actually be physical and therefore all concepts are based off of reality. The conceptual then is just a way of intellectualizing things. If someone was infinitely intelligent then would that mean that they don't exist physically because they are so conceptual? It seems as if conceptual removes one from the physical because when one thinks their thoughts drift away from one singular physical thing that might be in front of them to more complex events in life, involving many more physical things which might be moving and therefore make them more intellectual and complex. Like the idea "I went to the store", involves many physical and even emotional factors (like if you want to go to the store) but the idea of just some object in front of you is just physical and it is there and you can feel it more directly and therefore more intently. It is the same concept as if you were to do or experience the actions in a book it would be more intense then just reading the book. Just reading the book, however would probably be more intellectually intense because you are being less physical and can therefore focus more on the ideas and concepts in the book.

All those ideas and concepts that someone unconsciously wants then ties back into the "reality" factor where some things in the long term might be bad for you that would cause pleasure in the short term. That also ties into the idea that there are many components to life, many ways in which someone can feel that doesn't really reflect what it might be that it seems like what they want. So going to back to the statement "someone fundamentally is just feelings and thoughts that want things and therefore your existence is going to reflect those feelings and thoughts" is actually much more complicated than it seems. You want things unconsciously and consciously. It seems though that if you don't consciously understand everything that you want then your existence is simply going to be less because you cannot comprehend what it would be like to receive that reward (of what you want). If you cannot comprehend what it is that you want (consciously and unconsciously) then you probably aren't going to be able to experience pleasure from it.

Table 131.0

Table 132.0

Chapter 132

The Relationship Between Sadness And Depression

What is the relationship between sadness and depression? How long does a sad feeling last in your mind? Is sadness a feeling or an emotion? I guess it doesn't matter what if we call sadness a feeling or an emotion, it only matters how sadness makes us feel. Depression can be viewed as simply a worse form of sadness, one that affects your entire system, whereas sadness is more like an individual emotion or feeling. Depression is usually described as an aspect of mood.

Mood is something noticeable to everyone around you (not always, but it is a lot more noticeable than individual feelings), while an individual feeling like jealousy or hate that people regularly have isn't going to be as much noticed. You can say, oh that person looks happy, or that person looks sad, but you rarely say, that person looks jealous or that person looks angry (only for brief periods of time that is). You can't tell when someone is angry for a long time, you usually can only tell temporary feelings or emotions of anger someone can look angry but the expression on their face is only going to be there for a few seconds. That would mean you can only tell extreme feelings but something like sadness or happiness people often comment on (oh you look happy, or are you ok?) and they don't just last a few seconds.

So sad feelings only last a few seconds, and sad emotions also only last a few seconds. If someone looks sad and it is isn't for a few seconds, then it is a part of their mood, and could be either a temporary depression or a long term depression (temporary being anywhere from a few minutes to a few hours to a few days or whatever). Depression is a system wide thing, it affects someone's mood, and it takes a while to kick in. Sadness (sad feelings or emotions) only last a few seconds, because they are individual and by themselves. If those feelings continue to linger, then it becomes a depression, which affects all the emotions and feelings in your brain. So the process goes, you are upset about thing A (for a few seconds on minutes) then if you are going to continue to be upset about thing A it is going to start affecting your mood, and the rest of your emotions and feelings, and be visible to everyone that you are sad or depressed. The first period of the sad feeling or emotion (which only lasted a few seconds) the person would look thoughtful because the event which caused that sadness had just happened, and that person is going to be thinking about it consciously or unconsciously for the brief period after it occurred. The sadness and depression hasn't sunk in yet, and upset feelings and thoughtful feelings are likely to be mixed in with the sad one. (this is during the first seconds or minutes after the initiating event). The initiating event could be something sad that happens in real life, or it could be just a sad thought that occurs to you which made you upset.

The point is, for the time immediately after the sadness initiates, you are going to have elements of upset/ thoughtful in there because that is the natural human (or animal) response to think about what occurred, and to be upset that you are sad. If that sadness continues you aren't going to be as upset about it and thoughtful about it, but it would have invaded your system and made you generally sad (which is what is called a depression) it is not an individual emotion whose source can be identified easily. During the time of the initial sadness the person would be able to recognize what they are feeling because it is obvious at that point what they are thinking or what they just thought, so it is an individual emotion/feeling. After it sinks into their system that sadness might have triggered another sadness they were feeling which resulted from something else initially, so you can't say it is clearly an individual emotion anymore. The new source of the depression may be an individual emotion, but it is your entire system which is suffering from its effects.

Table 132.0

Table 133.0

Chapter 133

Sherlock Holmes: a series devoid of emotional content

Sherlock Holmes is a warm and friendly character trying to solve murders and robberies. There is a high contrast between someone warm and friendly trying to solve crimes. If you have a warm and friendly main character in a crime investigation, you can't have a strongly evil villain because there would be too high a contrast and it wouldn't work. Furthermore there was little character development in Sherlock Holmes; it was all investigation and logic. With no character development at all of the person committing the crime, you can't have a strongly evil character. Then again each episode was too short to develop the characters that much, so it was basically a short thriller, a quick in and out of a highly intense crime, no character development, just the facts of the murder. Furthermore the crimes were usually economically motivated not personal, that is because for them to be personal you'd have to back that up with character development which didn't exist. You have to have two opposing personalities for a personal crime, and there weren't really any personalities in Sherlock. The crimes being economically, not personally motivated adds to the logical, non emotional tone of the series. Furthermore, when crimes are committed, the person committing them is less emotional during the action of the crime in order to do the deed. That is because one needs to isolate oneself from the drama of doing something bad. With personal crimes someone has an emotional relationship to the person, and therefore it is harder to be remote from the crime, and therefore that person appears softer. That softer appearance would lessen the intensity of the crime because it is a situation where the two people have an emotional relationship. The emotion makes the crime more emotional and less logical. Something emotional isn't as scary as something logical because you add those fuzzy emotions in. Even if the emotion is hate, it still intensifies the interpersonal relationship. That is because with humans a hate on hate interaction is actually more amusing than scary. That is because humans aren't aggressive, lions hating each other would be scary, but humans hating each other isn't. Sherlock Holmes crimes were of cold calculation, not emotional interest. Take two monkeys that hate each other, it is amusing, that is what a human hating another human is like, funny. That is why there weren't personal hatreds in Sherlock Holmes, it would have appeared amusing. In other crime stories the villain is usually at least looking for a goal of some sort, some greater aspiration of evil like to do more crime (a repeated criminal). But in Sherlock Holmes the criminals were mostly one time committers, not serial criminals. That is because a serial criminal would be too emotionally involved in committing crimes. A serial criminal is something to be emotional about, it is much more intense then someone just doing one crime. The lack of serial criminals also takes away from the emotional content in the series, and adds to the lack of character development of the potential criminals. Furthermore if someone was a serial murderer they would have been more suspected than the other potential criminals, throwing off the intensity of wondering "who done it?". As a TV series, Sherlock Holmes was just something you sat down, watched for a short period of time, and finished, it wasn't something you would get deeply or emotionally involved in, there were only two characters that repeated from each show to the next, most shows have a few more than that. Furthermore the details of Sherlock Holmes life were minimal, we weren't even aware of where the main characters lived. The logical tone to the series, however, added to its suspense. If you made the series emotional then it wouldn't be as scary, there needs to be that emptiness in your head that comes from logic and a lack of emotion, in order to add to the scary feeling. Emotion is comforting and safe, logic and clear thinking is potentially very scary if you put it in the hands of a criminal. So people sit down to watch a short, intense logical, scary, emotionless experience of Sherlock Holmes.

Table 133.0

Table 133.0

Chapter 134

Lauren Caitlin Upton Answered Question Intelligently

This was her question:

Q: Recent polls have shown a fifth of Americans can't locate the U.S. on a world map. Why do you think this is?

Her answer:

During the 2007 pageant: "I personally believe that U.S. Americans are unable to do so because, um, some people out there in our nation don't have maps and, uh, I believe that our, uh, education like such as, uh, South Africa and, uh, the Iraq and everywhere like such as, and I believe that they should, uh, our education over here in the U.S. should help the U.S., uh, should help South Africa and should help Iraq and the Asian countries, so we will be able to build up our future."

She meant that we should raise our priorities on education and foreign awareness, she just said this indirectly. She said in a more complicated and intelligent way that the united states should promote education in other countries. If we did that then our awareness of world countries would rise, which would cause us to place a higher priority on understanding our place in the world, which would then cause people to want to understand where the united states is in the world better. Promoting education itself would raise our awareness of education as well, instead of just promoting something else in another country or going to war with them. That is why she mentioned Iraq specifically because she was saying instead of placing our priorities on war, we should place them on education. It is a matter of priorities. We don't really promote education in other countries now, so if we did then our awareness of education and the world would rise dramatically because it would be showing a lot about the United States if it did such a generous act. It would be so generous it would cause people to become more motivated to learn themselves because it would raise their awareness that learning and education is important. It becomes especially clear that it is important when you see that other foreign countries which are doing very poorly are that way because of their lack of education. So Miss Teen South Carolina answered her question in a philanthropic way not only a brilliant one.

Table 134.0

Chapter 135

Definition of Spirituality

What is the definition of spirituality? I like this definition: predominantly spiritual character as shown in thought, life, etc.; spiritual tendency or tone. Something needs to be added to that what this "spiritual" character is, however. I would say that it is the same attitude that a religious person would have about being religious, that is, by "spiritual character" they mean someone who is likely to be religious. Spirit is someone's soul, so spirituality would be focused on the self, but focused on the self in a manner in which they can understand it more deeply than just standard cognitive thinking about it, so religion might help you understand yourself in that "higher" manner. That is, it is almost like faith to believe in yourself like that, so it is like religion. The relationship between faith/religion and spirituality then is that both are "higher" methods of understanding the world. Spirituality is just focused on the self, while religion is focused on god. So there is an inner peace that spirituality brings because spirituality is about yourself. You can also say it is about your soul, not just your state of being, because soul is who you really are, the core of yourself, and if you are more connected to the core of yourself you are going to be more at peace, and therefore have more of that spiritual connection, which is one that is a "higher" connection to yourself, like how religion is a "high" connection to god. This "high" connection is higher because it is connected to who you really are, which is the spirit part of spirituality which implies a soul, because when you imagine someone as being a spirit or a ghost you take away their physical form and focus more on who they are mentally, or the core of their being or soul. Also use of the word soul, like that is using energy from your soul, appeals more to your higher morals which you would consider to be more consistent with who you are at the core.

Table 135.0

Chapter 136

Consciousness is Thoughts and Emotions: A Whole Brain Approach

When someone thinks, "What is consciousness?" they might at first associate just thinking to consciousness, or, as Descarte said, "I think, therefore I am". This, however, is not completely true because people also have emotions and feelings which also contribute to who they are. The statement should really be, "I think and feel therefore I am". Is consciousness just thoughts and feelings that you can identify, so when you have a thought or when you feel you have a feeling are you then conscious – but not conscious when you don't have as tangible thoughts and feelings? It certainly seems like one is conscious when they are feeling something they can really feel and think, and by that logic consciousness then is really just you feeling alive. But Descarte said "I think, therefore I am", so maybe consciousness is more a function of thought and therefore related more to logic and understanding your place in the world then just "feeling alive". But when you feel alive, or are more energetic, you are also going to be more aware of your place in the world because you are more alert. So it is really, "I think, and therefore I can understand who I am, but this understanding also becomes enhanced when I am feeling a lot too". That means that your long term consciousness is determined by your understanding of who you are, which comes from your ability to think, and your short term consciousness comes from your ability to feel and think.

Table 136.0

Chapter 137

Commentary on Descartes' Discourse on Method and

Meditations on First Philosophy

Descartes thought that learning for yourself would be better then learning from someone else, since people tend to have emotional influences. It is probably true that learning from the source when studying human behavior is going to be more efficient than learning from someone's interpretation of the source if you use good judgment yourself. In the case of emotional observations (or observing human behavior) this is especially obvious because the people who preach have a tendency to pretend they know more than they actually do, or try to appear to be better than they are. In this emotional prejudice the truth can be altered from reality, or the source. As Descartes said, "Those who set about giving precepts must esteem themselves more skilful than those to whom they advance them" (pg 7). In other words, someone might alter the truth solely so they could come up with something to say, while the real truth might not be capable of being expressed so easily, it can only be observed. Some things in life are too complicated to express, but however there are going to be people who believe they can express those things, even though they cannot accurately do so. Even knowing your own understanding of the truth might not be completely certain, as you might distort reality or truth so it can be easier to understand, yet possibly not understood at the same time. However, someone's version of the truth might help you to think about the things you have observed and make you better able to interpret reality for yourself – you just should remember that what they say might be wrong and that you need to rely on your own observations and empirical evidence to make certain of its truth. That shows how even something you label false might have elements of truth.

It is hard to assess the truth of many emotional circumstances, however, because emotions are not easily measured. For instance, if you are going to assess how much one person likes someone else, you cannot say, "this person likes that person with 60% passion". You could take various factors of the relationship and analyze them, however for each one of those factors you are going to have an emotional (possibly wrong) opinion as to how much each of those factors weigh in. Dealing with emotional intelligence is basically dealing with an endless number of unknowns, only leading to more unknowns. The only thing to do would be to keep exploring unknowns until you find some minor degree of things you know to a reasonable degree are true. In that manner anyone's idea of what is real could be very uncertain, and that is why it is best to explore reality for yourself. Everyone obviously takes information from reality for themselves, and they are living in the real world just like everyone else, however there can be degrees of separation from an actual experience. A clear example of that would be that you could possibly learn more about the truth better from someone directly then indirectly.

Another question entirely is - are the emotions which are based off of your opinions even real, since they are based off of opinions? For instance, when you judge how cool or interesting something is, that judgment is going to influence how much enjoyment you get from that thing, since your enjoyment of it comes from both how cool it actually is, and how cool you think it is. For instance, if you think that a person is not interesting, you are going to not be as interested in them and therefore not feel good things from them like you would from a person you are interested in. The questions are, how much does your opinion of them differ from the truth, and how much does your opinion of them influence how you feel about them? Those questions can be applied to anything in life. If you think something is interesting, you are going to be more interested in it. It is almost as if your opinions trigger and direct your emotions. If you think something is more valuable then you might be better able to recognize value that is actually there.

How much does your perception of what is going on impact how what you feel is going on? Your perception is going to determine what it is that you feel, that is, your conscious and unconscious perception of what is going on is. If you have a strong false conscious perception of what is going on you are going to feel differently, or think different things from the reality. Your unconscious mind, however, probably isn't going to have a false perception of what is going on by itself since your unconscious mind is your natural mind and many other factors could be being influenced there that trigger real emotions which you don't have conscious control over. For instance, a situation may be very complicated, so your conscious perception can only be so complicated because you can only have so advanced a perception of the situation that you are aware of, so thankfully you can only alter reality so much. The rest of how you feel is going to be determined by lots of complicated unconscious factors, or every factor that is a factor, technically so because that is all going to be processed at least unconsciously. That is also why learning from the source is going to be better than someone's interpretation of it, because the source is going to be much more complicated than a simple verbal explanation. So the statement, "nothing is real, only your perception of it is" is not true because your perception is going to be limited by how much you are capable of consciously perceiving.

That previous quote from Descartes also explains another passage he used:

For it seemed to me that I might meet with much more truth in the reasonings that each man makes on the matters that specially concern him, and the issue of which would very soon punish him if he made a wrong judgment, than in the case of those made by a man of letters in his study touching speculations that lead to no result, and that bring about no other consequences to himself excepting that he will be all the more vain the more they are removed from common sense, since in this case proves to him to have employed so much more ingenuity and skill trying to make them seem probable. (pg 10 the European philosophers)

That passage shows well how everything that someone thinks is going to be true to a certain degree. It is going to be absorbed a certain amount; however your understanding of how much it is absorbed is also going to vary by degree, not necessarily related to the reality. There are also going to be different types of truths, and different ways in which knowledge can be absorbed. It can be understood emotionally. It can be understood emotionally in different ways and in each different way, it could affect a different other sort of knowledge already in your mind. For instance, one piece of knowledge could change your viewpoint on another piece of knowledge or opinion in your mind. This shows how all knowledge is really just opinion, or belief, since it can vary so much based off of new material, or, since we just defined knowledge as belief, new beliefs. By stating "knowledge" or "belief" here, you should understand that both are clearly emotional intelligence. As an example you could use the idea of how much you enjoy going to playgrounds and parks. The idea of that and what you understand about it could be influenced by your understanding of how much you like going to other events. A whole set of experiences could be used and that could be one way your mind compares or processes things. One certain experience, or a few ideas however might be much more significant and relevant to other ideas then all the ideas you have in your mind, however. So it is not as if everything is infinitely complicated, with everything tying into everything else in some infinitely complicated way.

The previous passage is in turn explained by the quote:

More especially did I reflect in each matter that came before me as to anything that could make it subject to suspicion of doubt, and give occasion for mistake, and I rooted out of my mind all the errors that might have formerly crept in. Not that indeed I imitated the skeptics, who only doubt for the sake of doubting, and pretend to by always uncertain; for, on the contrary, my design was only to provide myself with good ground for assurance, and to reject the quicksand and mud in order to find the rock or clay." (pg 22 the European philosophers)

Using experiences in life, or anything that is complicated beyond a practical reality is going to involve emotional intelligence. When I talked about how a lot of reality is going to be knowledge of belief I was referring to understanding things that can be manipulated in your mind as to your viewpoint, versus thinking about things that don't have an emotional impact on you and is more like you are just manipulating a certain real reality in different numbers or amounts (like doing math) but not your personal viewpoint. When your viewpoint for a specific thing, or even your overall viewpoint is being manipulated by yourself you are using emotional intelligence. That manipulation might occur when you are thinking about anything that can have various different perspectives, which could be a lot of things. In fact, even something mathematical is going to have different perspectives, for instance, if you get the wrong answer you have a wrong perspective of what you think is the truth. That shows how emotions are going to play a role in even simple things in life, like calculating how many objects there are in a room, or doing other mathematical like calculations. They play a role because for each different perspective you have on the answer, there is going to be a different emotional outlook. For instance, you might be happy if there are a large number of objects in a room, but sad if there are very few. A lot of life is going to consist of observations and behaviors that can be described simply. In that way it is easy to see how a lot of life can be "true", because when you describe what happens in life in a simple way you also see a certain emotional truth, which would seem to be a more significant aspect of how reality functions.

However, since emotional intelligence is not completely concrete, it can be subject to skeptics, or however as Descartes puts it you should try "to reject the quicksand and mud in order to find the rock or clay". It is also shown here that since emotional intelligence consists of calculating real things which exist in certain numbers, and can be manipulated in a mathematical like way, that emotional intelligence and non-emotional intelligence - where you manipulate real things in certain numbers – are the same. So you can do math for emotional things and you would be using your emotional intelligence, or you could manipulate non emotional things in your mind (say just calculating different probabilities of something simple) and it wouldn't be using your emotional intelligence as much. Emotional intelligence and non- emotional intelligence are similar in nature because you are manipulating things in both instances; one just affects you to a greater degree.

There is another question Descartes asked that relates to the previous quote of those, and it is basically "how do I know that anything is even real"? He states the following showing how someone could doubt the existence of everything:

Accordingly I shall now suppose, not that a true God, who as such must be supremely good and the fountain of truth, but that some malignant genius exceedingly powerful and cunning has devoted all his powers in the deceiving of me; I shall suppose that the sky, the earth, colors, shapes, sounds and all external things are illusions and impostures of which this evil genius has availed himself for the abuse of my credulity..." (pg 32 the European philosophers)

Asking that question is like asking how certain and true anything is, only it is suggesting that there could be a large degree of uncertainly present. It also might mean that the world is either false and simply not there at all. If the latter two things can be identified then the degree of uncertainty involved will also be somewhat resolved.

Saying that the world is false is implying that it is generating emotions in you that are not accurate. The ultimate objective of anything real is to generate emotion, so if something is real but "false" then it must be generating emotions that it shouldn't be generating. It would still have to be real, however, since it is generating emotions (unless you are imagining it, but then in that case what your imagination is creating can be considered real, and that thing is itself based off of something else that was real – or had some real characteristics – at one point). So if everything was false someone wouldn't have any basis to know what truth is at all. If something generates an emotion, then that emotion is real. Your mind might have an emotional bias, however, and be distorting that emotion. For instance, if you have a prejudice against someone they are going to cause you to feel things about them which are false. So how does anyone know that anything they feel is unbiased? The physical world must be real because we can be certain that something physical is there, however it could be shaped in a way that deceives our emotions. A way to figure out how true something is is to take that thing and compare it in all ways it presents itself in various situations, that way you can take data from where you see it more true in one instance and apply that to see how it might be false in another.

Saying that the world is not there entirely is like saying that the world is false, only it suggests that instead of generating a false or biased feeling, it is not generating any feeling at all. If a feeling is being generated, something must be there, but you might not know how deceiving that thing is. So ultimately it is best to know a combination of all three things, or the certainty of how true and false something is (and those things related to everything else).

Another question altogether is not whether the world exists, but if the person contemplating if the world exists, exists. Descartes seemed to believe that since he was capable of thought, he existed:

I am, I exist. This is certain. How often? As often as I think. For it might indeed be that if I entirely ceased to think, I should thereupon altogether cease to exist. I am not at present admitting anything which is not necessarily true; and, accurately speaking, I am therefore [taking myself to be] only a thinking thing, that is to say, a mind, an understanding or reason-terms the significance of which has hitherto been unknown to me. I am, then a real thing, and really existent. What thing? I have said it, a thinking thing. (pg 35 the European philosophers)

He says he is "a mind, an understanding or reason" which means that all his thoughts together form this understanding and complete mind. He is not just one understanding, people understand lots of things, but all of them would form who he is. Maybe the understanding of who he is occurs in an instant, and in this instant he is only one understanding, reason or mind. He can spend a lot of time contemplating his existence, or glimpse it in an instant. However, this understanding of who he is he carries with him all of the time, only more in the background then when he is thinking about his existence. So it really is thought that makes him who he is, since he is thinking about himself all of the time, in addition to thinking about and in regular life.

Thought determines who someone is because your thoughts are controlled, and all your thoughts over your lifetime caused your emotional development, which causes you to be who you are. There are also feelings, but since someone cannot control their feelings their feelings aren't a part of who they really are. Who you really are is someone that is what they want to be, and what they want to be is going to be something they can think about. If you are emotionally damaged you might act in a way you don't want to, and be presenting yourself to be different from who you really are. That would only cause other people to view you as different from who you are, your thoughts are still intact and you are still who you really are inside (for the most part). Thoughts are controlled and directed; feelings mostly cannot be directed or controlled. Your consciousness is therefore going to be more determined by your thoughts, not your emotions. So it is easy to say that your thoughts understand and/or control who you are, but it is much harder to say that your emotions understand and/or control who you are.

That question, of who someone is, is so large and complicated that it brings up another question that maybe God Himself is deceiving us in this world, for this world (and understand who we are) is so complicated that maybe we are being deceived. Descartes also had his own ideas about the existence of God and his capability of deception:

I recognize it is impossible that He should ever deceive me, since in all fraud and deception there is some element of imperfection. The power of deception may indeed seem to be evidence of subtlety or power; yet unquestionably the will to deceive testifies to malice and feebleness, and accordingly cannot be found in God. (pg 54 the European philosophers)

If a human or a God created infinite pain in people, or was infinitely evil and deceptive, then this being would not be considered to be perfect because he or she would irritate everyone. The idea of a successful human is one that achieves personal fulfillment, and it is hard to imagine someone achieving a lot of satisfaction if they alienate everyone extremely. This doesn't mean, however that if someone pleases everyone infinitely their life is going to be infinitely good as well. Also, since a perfect God would do everything perfectly, if He irritated people, He would do it perfectly, and that would mean irritating them infinitely, which doesn't seem like a perfect thing to do. Although it isn't conclusive as to whether or not pleasing other people infinitely is going to be self-beneficial, it could be considered a perfect thing to do since it is positively contributing to life. Even if someone is cruel to someone else, there is still a human connection that exists between them. This connection would become evident if the cruel person tried to be perfectly cruel, or cruel in such a way that the feelings of the other person became too evident, at which point the cruel person wouldn't be capable of doing harm. For instance, a person couldn't spend all day shooting people lined up, one after another, without it causing them distress. Since God is perfect, he would either do perfect harm or perfect good, but perfect harm isn't possible because it would intensify negative feelings so much that they would become destructive to even the person doing the damage. Perfectly good feelings, however, don't have to be intense - they could just be ordinary feelings and still be considered perfectly good. It is as if the true nature of evil is too vile to even exist. This philosophy is portrayed in a quote by Ralph Emerson - "To laugh often and much; To win the respect of intelligent people and the affection of children; To earn the appreciation of honest critics and endure the betrayal of false friends; To appreciate beauty, to find the best in others; To leave the world a bit better, whether by a healthy child, a garden patch, or a redeemed social condition; To know even one life has breathed easier because you have lived. This is to have succeeded" The quote is a reflection of the ideas behind a good person and that this person is so good that any hint of cruelty wouldn't be tolerated (especially perfect cruelty), and therefore perfect cruelty couldn't exist. So when someone contemplates if they want to be cruel or good, when they realize they can only be so cruel so they also realize how they are good, and this sympathy can be conveyed in grand kind statements (like the Emerson quote).

Bibliography

Beardsley, M. C. (ED.) [1992 Modern library Edition Copyright 1960 Random House, Inc Copyright renewed 1988 by Random House, Inc.]. The European Philosophers from Descartes to Nietzsche. New York, USA and Toronto, Canada.

Table 137.0

www.ingramcontent.com/pod-product-compliance
Lightning Source LLC
Chambersburg PA
CBHW061759260326

41914CB00006B/1164